HOLT ALGEBRA 1

Eugene D. Nichols

Mervine L. Edwards

E. Henry Garland

Sylvia A. Hoffman

Albert Mamary

William F. Palmer

HOLT ALGEBRA 1

Holt, Rinehart and Winston
New York, Toronto, London, Sydney

About the Authors

Eugene D. Nichols is Professor and Head of the Department of Mathematics Education, and Lecturer of the Department of Mathematics, The Florida State University, Tallahassee, Florida.

Mervine L. Edwards is Chairman of the Mathematics Department, Shore Regional High School, West Long Branch, New Jersey.

E. Henry Garland is Head of the Mathematics Department at the Developmental Research School, and Associate Professor of Mathematics Education, The Florida State University, Tallahassee, Florida.

Sylvia A. Hoffman is Curriculum Development Specialist for the Office of the Superintendent of Public Instruction, State of Illinois.

Albert Mamary is Assistant Superintendent of Schools for Instruction, Johnson City Central School District, Johnson City, New York.

William F. Palmer is Professor and Chairman of the Department of Education, Catawba College, Salisbury, North Carolina.

Photo credits are on page viii.

Copyright © 1974 by Holt, Rinehart and Winston
All Rights Reserved
Printed in the United States of America

ISBN: 0-03-091319-5

6789012 032 9876

CONTENTS

1 BASIC OPERATIONS

Order of Operations 1 . Variables 4 . Commutative and Associative Properties 6 . Distributive Property 9 . Distributive Property and Variables 14 . Applying the Distributive Property 16

2 INTEGERS

Adding Integers 21 . Properties of Addition of Integers 24 . Multiplying Integers 28 . Dividing Integers 31 . A New Look at Addition 36 . Evaluating Expressions 40 . Combining Like Terms 42 . $(1)(a) = a$ and $(-1)(a) = -a$ 44 . Removing Parentheses 46 . Applying the Property $-a = -1(a)$ 48 . Subtracting Integers 50

3 LINEAR EQUATIONS

Open Sentences 56 . Solving Equations 59 . Equations: The Variable on Both Sides 64 . Equations with Parentheses 68 . English Phrases to Algebra 70 . Number Problems 72 . More Number Problems 76 . Coin Problems 80 . Perimeter Problems 84

4 LINEAR INEQUALITIES

Sets 91 . Inequalities 94 . Properties for Inequalities 98 . Solving Inequalities 102 . Intersection and Union of Sets 105 . Graphing Intersections and Unions 112

5 FACTORING

Exponents 119 . Properties of Exponents 121 . Polynomials 124 . Simplifying Polynomials 128 . Concept of Factoring 132 . Factoring Out a Common Monomial 135

6 FACTORING TRINOMIALS

Multiplying Polynomials 141 • Factoring Trinomials 145 • The Difference of Two Squares 150 • Combined Types of Factoring 153 • Factoring Polynomials in Two Variables 156 • Quadratic Equations 158 • Quadratic Equations: Standard Form 162 • Consecutive Integers 165 • Consecutive Integer Problems 168

7 SIMPLIFYING FRACTIONS

Fractions 175 • Multiplying Fractions 180 • Rewriting Fractions in Simplest Form 184 • Using The -1 Technique 188 • Fractions with Common Monomial Factors 191 • Simplifying Products of Fractions 194 • Dividing Fractions 198

8 COMBINING FRACTIONS

Adding Fractions: Same Denominator 203 • Adding: Different Denominators 210 • Adding: Polynomial Denominators 214 • More on Adding Fractions 218 • Subtracting Fractions 221 • Simplifying Fractions: -1 Technique 224

9 ALGEBRA IN A PLANE

Absolute Value 231 • Equations with Absolute Value 234 • Directed Distance on a Number Line 236 • Locating Points in a Plane 240 • Plotting Points in a Plane 242 • Lines Parallel to the Axes 246 • Directed Distances 248 • Slopes of Line Segments 251 • Slope of Lines 255

10 LINEAR SENTENCES

Ratio and Proportion 261 • Equation of a Line 265 • More Difficult Equations 268 • $y = mx + b$ 272 • Graphing a Line 276 • Vertical Lines 279

11 LINEAR SYSTEMS

Systems of Equations: Graphing 285 • Systems of Equations: Substitution 290 • Systems of Equations: $\begin{matrix} ax + by = c \\ dx - by = e \end{matrix}$ 293 • Systems of Equations: $\begin{matrix} ax + by = c \\ dx + ey = f \end{matrix}$ 296 • Dry Mixtures: Representing Costs 300 • Solving Dry Mixture Problems 302 • Solving Number Relation Problems 310

$-1 > \frac{2}{3}(3) - 2$

32)

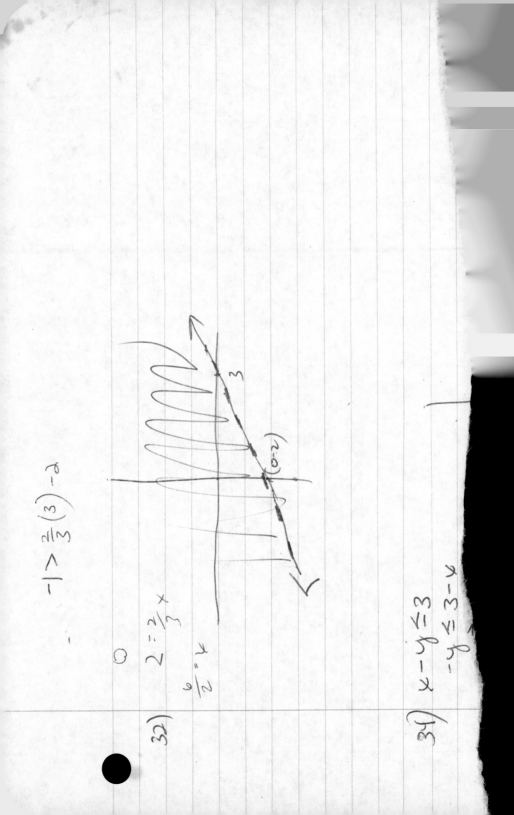

$2 = \frac{2}{3}x$

$y = \frac{2}{3}x$

(0,-2)

3

31) $x - y \leq 3$

$-y \leq 3 - x$

344 2-10 cm

344 2-12

360÷2-10

12 FUNCTIONS

Relations and Functions 317 • Types of Functions 320 • $f(x)$ Notation 323 • Graphing Inequalities in Two Variables 326 • Direct Variation 330 • Inverse Variation 334

13 FRACTIONAL EQUATIONS

Solving Fractional Equations 341 • More Fractional Equations 346 • Representing Amounts of Work 350 • Work Problems 353 • Equations with Decimals 358 • Rational Numbers 361 • Complex Fractions 368 • More Complex Fractions 371 • Formulas 374

14 REAL NUMBERS

The Set of Real Numbers 382 • Square Roots 384 • Approximating Square Roots 388 • Simplifying Radicals 391 • Even Exponents 394 • Odd Exponents 396 • The Pythagorean Theorem 399 • Combining Radicals 402 • Products of Radicals 404 • Rationalizing Denominators 408 • Fractional Radicands 411

15 EQUATIONS WITH REAL SOLUTIONS

Radical Equations 417 • The Solution Set of $x^2 = a$ 420 • Completing the Square 423 • The Quadratic Formula 427 • Applying the Quadratic Formula 434 • Area Problems 437

16 PLANE TRIGONOMETRY

Angles and Triangles 445 • Similar Triangles 448 • Trigonometric Ratios 451 • Tables of Trigonometric Ratios 456 • Solving Right Triangles 458 • Applications of Trigonometry 461

GLOSSARY   467
TABLES   477
INDEX   481
SELECTED ANSWERS   489

SPECIAL TOPICS

Lattice Multiplication	x	Rings	217
Mathematics in Aviation	3	Fields	227
Vigenère Code	12	The Great Swami	230
Operations	20	Fun for Philatelists	239
Probability	27	Equivalence Relations	245
Clock Arithmetic	34	Mathematics in Construction	260
Magic Squares	39	Pascal's Triangle	271
Computer Programs: Flow Charts	54	Diophantus	281
Slide Ruler for Adding and Subtracting	63	Linear Programming	284
Groups	67	Flow Chart: Ordering Numbers	288
Number Mysteries	83	Men of Mathematics	299
Mathematics in the Hospital	87	Digit Problems	306
Sequences	90	Galileo and Free Fall	316
Input and Output	97	The Greatest Integer Function	325
Motion Problems	108	Continued Fractions	340
More Clock Arithmetic	115	A Step Function	345
Women of Mathematics	118	Zeller's Congruence	356
Venn Diagrams	126	Investment Problems	364
Perfect Numbers	131	Mathematics in Pharmacy	377
Using Exponents	140	The Normal Curve	380
Rectangle Products	144	The Galton Board	387
Flow Chart: Solving a Simple		Flow Chart: Finding Square Roots	398
Equation	149	Points for Irrational Numbers	407
Computing Mentally	161	Venn Diagram of the	
Complement of a Set	171	Real Number System	413
Mathematics in Music	174	Pythagorean Triples	416
Zero and Negative Exponents	179	Wet Mixture Problems	430
What is the Navigator's Name?	187	Flow Chart: Quadratic Formula	440
Puzzlers	197	Flow Chart: Cube Roots	444
Two Games	202	Graphing Points in Space	454
Age Problems	206	Distance Formula	466

ACKNOWLEDGEMENTS FOR PHOTOGRAPHS

Page   3   Top & Bottom: SAS Photo
Page   87   Top & Bottom: Irene Fertik
Page 260   Top & Bottom: Irene Fertik
Page 377   Courtesy of Pfizer, Inc.

SYMBOL LIST

$=$	is equal to	1
. . .	goes on forever	21
$-a$	the opposite of a	24
{ }	set	57
ϕ	empty set	92
$\neq$	is not equal to	94
$<$	is less than	94
$>$	is greater than	94
$\leq$	is less than or equal to	95
$\geq$	is greater than or equal to	95
$\{x \mid x < 4\}$	the set of all numbers x such that $x < 4$	95
$\subseteq$	is a subset of	105
$\nsubseteq$	is not a subset of	105
$\cap$	intersection of sets	106
$\cup$	union of sets	106
3^4	the fourth power of 3	119
x^3	the third power of x, or x cubed	119
GCF	greatest common factor	135
LCD	least common denominator	211
$\lvert x \rvert$	the absolute value of x	232
$\vec{d}(PQ)$	the directed distance from P to Q	236
$\perp$	is perpendicular to	240
$P(x, y)$	point P with coordinates x, y	242
$\overleftrightarrow{MN}$	line MN	247
$\overline{AB}$	line segment AB	251
$5:7$	the ratio 5 to 7	261
$f(x)$	the value of f at x	323
$.3\overline{3}$	the 3 repeats forever	362
$\sqrt{x}$	the principal square root of x	384
$\doteq$	is approximately equal to	385
$\triangle ABC$	triangle ABC	399
$\pm$	plus or minus	428
$m \angle A$	degree measure of angle A	445
$\cong$	is congruent to	448
$\sim$	is similar to	448
$\tan A$	tangent of $m \angle A$	451
$\sin A$	sine of $m \angle A$	451
$\cos A$	cosine of $m \angle A$	451

Lattice Multiplication

The lattice method of multiplication was named because the lattice resembles a grating used on Venetian windows.

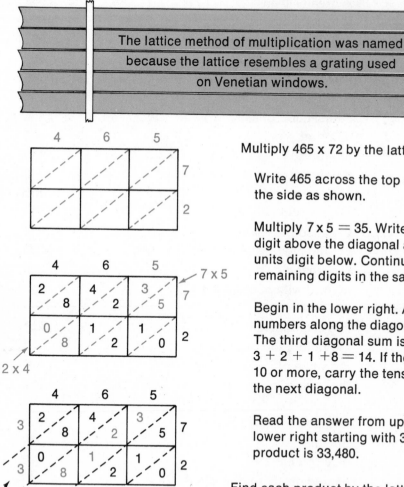

Multiply 465 x 72 by the lattice method.

Write 465 across the top and 72 on the side as shown.

Multiply 7 x 5 = 35. Write the tens digit above the diagonal and the units digit below. Continue with the remaining digits in the same way.

Begin in the lower right. Add the numbers along the diagonals. The third diagonal sum is 3 + 2 + 1 + 8 = 14. If the sum is 10 or more, carry the tens digit to the next diagonal.

Read the answer from upper left to lower right starting with 3. The product is 33,480.

carry
1   33,480
Thus, 465 x 72 = 33,480.

Find each product by the lattice method.

1. 345 x 47   2. 564 x 425
3. 38 x 1,257   4. 24 x 3,421
5. 256 x 372   6. 524 x 626

Order of Operations

OBJECTIVE

■ To compute expressions like (5)(2) + (3)(6) and 2 + 4 · 5 + 3 + 7 · 10

 REVIEW CAPSULE

Ways to show multiplication:

times sign	raised dot	parentheses
↓	↓	↙ ↘
2 × 5	2 · 5	(2)(5), or 2(5)

Read each as 2 times 5.

EXAMPLE 1 What does this mean? (2)(5) + 3

There are two possibilities.

	(2)(5) + 3			(2)(5) + 3	
Multiply first. →	10 + 3			(2)(8)	← Add first.
Then add. →	13			16	← Then multiply.

Two different answers → 13 or 16?

> ### Order of Operations
> When both multiplications and additions occur, we multiply first and then add.

We make this agreement to avoid confusion. →

Thus, in Example 1, (2)(5) + 3

Multiply first. → 10 + 3

Then add. → 13

EXAMPLE 2 Compute 6 + (3)(4).

6 + (3)(4)

Multiply first. → 6 + 12

Then add. → 18

Thus, 6 + 3(4) = 18.

EXAMPLE 3 Compute $(4)(2) + (3)(1)$.

$$(4)(2) + (3)(1)$$
$$8 \quad + \quad 3$$
$$11$$

EXAMPLE 4 Compute $7 + 4 \cdot 2 + 1 + 6 \cdot 5$.

Remember the order of operations. $\longrightarrow$

$$7 + \underbrace{4 \cdot 2} + 1 + \underbrace{6 \cdot 5}$$
$$7 + \quad 8 \quad + 1 + \quad 30$$
$$46$$

EXERCISES

PART A

Compute.

1. $(4)(6) + 1$
2. $(7)(5) + 8$
3. $6 \cdot 3 + 12$
4. $7 + 5 \cdot 8$
5. $8(3) + 5$
6. $6 + (4)(11)$
7. $8 + (3)(9)$
8. $(9)(1) + 12$
9. $10 + (8)(1)$
10. $(4)(0) + 6$
11. $0 + (8)(7)$
12. $7(9) + 8$
13. $(3)(9) + 13$
14. $6 \cdot 11 + 2$
15. $8 + (3)(9)$
16. $14 + (1)(10)$
17. $(8)(8) + 8$
18. $9 + 6(3)$
19. $14 + 12 \cdot 1$
20. $5(0) + 0$
21. $3(2) + 4(1)$
22. $(6)(5) + (8)(3)$
23. $(7)(9) + (10)(1)$
24. $(6)(2) + (5)(0)$
25. $(0)(3) + (12)(0)$
26. $1 \cdot 9 + 8 \cdot 1$
27. $(6)(11) + (2)(9)$
28. $(4)(8) + (0)(7)$
29. $(6)(3) + (17)(2)$
30. $5 \cdot 8 + 4 \cdot 9$
31. $(6)(9) + 1 + (8)(2)$
32. $(7)(5) + (4)(8) + 2$
33. $0 \cdot 8 + 5 + 0 \cdot 9$

PART B

Compute.

34. $1 + (0)(18) + (2)(9)$
35. $6 + (4)(13) + 12$
36. $7(9) + 8 + 4(2)$
37. $(3)(9) + (2)(12) + 8$
38. $6 + (3)(9) + 5 + (1)(8)$
39. $5(8) + 2 + 3(6) + 9$
40. $(7)(4) + 8 + 10 + (9)(3)$
41. $2 + (6)(7) + (3)(5) + 4$
42. $6 + 2 \cdot 9 + 4 \cdot 6 + 5$
43. $(1)(8) + 7 + (0)(3) + (2)(4)$
44. $3 + (4)(8) + 7 + (2)(9) + 1$
45. $(6)(0) + 8 + (4)(9) + 7 + (8)(3)$
46. $(0)(8) + 2 + (9)(4) + (3)(5) + 4$
47. $7 + (2)(13) + (5)(7) + 1 + (4)(5)$
48. $(2)(36) + 15 + (9)(14) + 7$
49. $28 \cdot 5 + 4 \cdot 16 + 17 + 8 \cdot 3$
50. $38 + 12 \cdot 5 + 27 \cdot 4 + 56$
51. $1 + 0 \cdot 15 + 8 \cdot 40 + 29 + 1 \cdot 5$

Mathematics in Aviation

Airplane pilots make careful checks of the instrument panel before and during flights.

Air traffic is monitored by traffic controllers in control towers of airports. They carefully calculate the flight patterns of arriving and departing planes.

Variables

 REVIEW CAPSULE

Order of Operations
Multiply first. Then add.

$$7 + 5(8)$$
$$7 + 40 \quad \leftarrow \text{Multiply } 5(8) \text{ first.}$$
$$47 \quad\quad \leftarrow \text{Then add.}$$

Think of a number.   Multiply 5 by the number.   Then add 2 to the result.

$$5(\text{number}) + 2$$
$$5n \quad\quad + 2$$
$$\uparrow$$
$$\text{variable}$$

$5n$ means $5(n)$. ⟶

A *variable* takes the place of a number. ⟶

EXAMPLE 1   Evaluate $5n + 2$ for the values of n shown.

To evaluate means to find the value.
Substitute the values
for the variable. ⟶

Let n be 3.	Let n be 8.	Let n be 20.
$5n + 2$	$5n + 2$	$5n + 2$
$5(3) + 2$	$5(8) + 2$	$5(20) + 2$
$15 + 2$	$40 + 2$	$100 + 2$
17	42	102

EXAMPLE 2   Evaluate $5 + 8a + 2b$ if $a = 7$ and $b = 4$.

Order of operations:
Multiply first.
Then add.

$$5 + 8(7) + 2(4)$$
$$5 + 56 + 8$$
$$69$$

Terms

Terms are added.

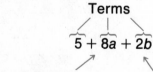

$$5 + 8a + 2b$$

A coefficient is the multiplier of a variable.

8 is the coefficient of a.   2 is the coefficient of b.

EXAMPLE 3   Name the terms and the variables in $3w + 8z + 2$.
Then name the coefficient of each variable.

Terms are added.
Variables are letters which take the
place of numbers.

The terms are $3w$, $8z$, and 2.
The variables are w and z.

$$3w + 8z + 2$$

3 is the
coefficient of w.

8 is the
coefficient of z.

ORAL EXERCISES

Name the terms and the variables. Then name the coefficient of each variable.

1. $6x + 1$ **2.** $4 + 3c$ **3.** $2y + 5$
4. $5a + 6 + 4b$ **5.** $7 + 3x + 8y$ **6.** $9m + 1 + 2n$
7. $3c + 2d + 6$ **8.** $7g + 3h + 12k$ **9.** $4y + 12z + 5w$

EXERCISES

PART A

Evaluate.

1. $2x + 3$ if $x = 5$ **2.** $5 + 3y$ if $y = 4$ **3.** $7 + 6a$ if $a = 7$
4. $7y + 3$ if $y = 2$ **5.** $9a + 1$ if $a = 6$ **6.** $5 + 6z$ if $z = 1$
7. $3x + 9$ if $x = 3$ **8.** $7 + 4c$ if $c = 8$ **9.** $2m + 6$ if $m = 4$
10. $5x + 4 + 2y$ if $x = 2$, $y = 4$ **11.** $3a + 6b + 1$ if $a = 3$, $b = 6$
12. $4m + 8 + 7n$ if $m = 6$, $n = 1$ **13.** $2k + 8 + 5t$ if $k = 9$, $t = 1$
14. $2 + 4y + 5z$ if $y = 7$, $z = 8$ **15.** $8g + 5 + 3e$ if $g = 8$, $e = 3$
16. $4p + 9 + 3q$ if $p = 9$, $q = 2$ **17.** $6r + 7s + 2$ if $r = 6$, $s = 5$

PART B

EXAMPLE   Evaluate $xz + 7y$ if $x = 3$, $y = 5$, and $z = 2$.

$$3(2) + 7(5)$$
$$6 \ + \ 35, \text{ or } 41$$

Evaluate if $x = 3$, $y = 8$, and $z = 5$.

18. $3x + 2y + 4z$ **19.** $5z + 4x + 7y$ **20.** $8y + 3z + 7x$
21. $2yz + xz$ **22.** $yz + 5xy$ **23.** $4xy + 8zy$
24. $6xy + 3yz + 1$ **25.** $9y + 5xy + 2zx$ **26.** $2xy + 6xz + 4yz$

Commutative and Associative Properties

OBJECTIVES

■ To compute expressions like (56 + 9) + 4 and (50 · 7) · 2

■ To identify the commutative and associative properties

 REVIEW CAPSULE

$4 + 7 = 11$ and $7 + 4 = 11$

Thus, $4 + 7 = 7 + 4.$

$5 \cdot 6 = 30$ and $6 \cdot 5 = 30$

Thus, $5 \cdot 6 = 6 \cdot 5.$

When adding or multiplying two numbers, we can change the order.

The Review suggests this. ⟶

Commutative Property

Addition: $a + b = b + a$, for all numbers a and b.

Multiplication: $a \cdot b = b \cdot a$, for all numbers a and b.

EXAMPLE 1   Is this statement true? $(3 + 1) + 9 = 3 + (1 + 9)$

$(3 + 1) + 9$	$3 + (1 + 9)$
4 + 9	3 + 10
13	13

Add inside the parentheses first. ⟶
Answers are the same. ⟶

Yes, $(3 + 1) + 9 = 3 + (1 + 9)$ is a true statement.

EXAMPLE 2   Is this statement true? $(5 \cdot 2) \cdot 4 = 5 \cdot (2 \cdot 4)$

$(5 \cdot 2) \cdot 4$	$5 \cdot (2 \cdot 4)$
10 · 4	5 · 8
40	40

Multiply inside the parentheses first. ⟶
Answers are the same. ⟶

Yes, $(5 \cdot 2) \cdot 4 = 5 \cdot (2 \cdot 4)$ is a true statement.

Examples 1 and 2 suggest this. ───────→

When adding or multiplying, we can change the grouping.

Associative Property

Addition: $(a + b) + c = a + (b + c)$, for all numbers a, b, and c.

Multiplication: $(a \cdot b) \cdot c = a \cdot (b \cdot c)$, for all numbers a, b, and c.

EXAMPLE 3   Rewrite $295 + 42 + 5$ by using the commutative and associative properties. Then compute.

Associative property of addition

$$
\begin{aligned}
295 + 42 + 5 &= (295 + 42) + 5 \\
&= 295 + (42 + 5)
\end{aligned}
$$

Commutative property of addition ─────→
Associative property of addition ─────→

$$
\begin{aligned}
&= 295 + (5 + 42) \\
&= (295 + 5) + 42 \\
&= 300 + 42 \\
&= 342
\end{aligned}
$$

Thus, $295 + 42 + 5 = 342$.

EXAMPLE 4   Rewrite $25 \cdot 7 \cdot 4$ by using the commutative and associative properties. Then compute.

Associative property of multiplication

$$
\begin{aligned}
25 \cdot 7 \cdot 4 &= (25 \cdot 7) \cdot 4 \\
&= 25 \cdot (7 \cdot 4)
\end{aligned}
$$

Commutative property of multiplication ─────→
Associative property ─────→

$$
\begin{aligned}
&= 25 \cdot (4 \cdot 7) \\
&= (25 \cdot 4) \cdot 7 \\
&= 100 \cdot 7 \\
&= 700
\end{aligned}
$$

Thus, $25 \cdot 7 \cdot 4 = 700$.

SUMMARY   **Addition can be done in any order. Multiplication can be done in any order. The commutative and associative properties make this possible.**

EXAMPLE 5 Which property is illustrated by each equation?

Comm. is short for commutative.
Assoc. is short for associative.

$6x + 8y = 8y + 6x$
$(4 \cdot r)s = 4(rs)$
$3x(8) = 8(3x)$

Answers
Comm. Prop. Add.
Assoc. Prop. Mult.
Comm. Prop. Mult.

EXERCISES

PART A

Rewrite by using the commutative and associative properties. Then compute.

1. $17 + 4 + 56$
2. $49 + 16 + 1$
3. $2 + 56 + 38$
4. $27 + 2 + 98$
5. $67 + 35 + 3$
6. $25 + 47 + 5$
7. $29 + 44 + 6 + 1$
8. $2 + 167 + 38 + 3$
9. $121 + 136 + 4 + 9$
10. $522 + 7 + 28 + 43$
11. $632 + 271 + 29 + 68$
12. $285 + 24 + 15 + 66$
13. $4 \cdot 17 \cdot 25$
14. $50 \cdot 23 \cdot 2$
15. $5 \cdot 164 \cdot 2$
16. $20 \cdot 39 \cdot 5$
17. $250 \cdot 49 \cdot 4$
18. $2 \cdot 78 \cdot 50$
19. $8 \cdot 56 \cdot 125$
20. $2 \cdot 187 \cdot 25 \cdot 2$
21. $20 \cdot 36 \cdot 2 \cdot 5$

Which property is illustrated?

22. $8 + 2 = 2 + 8$
23. $(4 \cdot 5) \cdot 7 = 4 \cdot (5 \cdot 7)$
24. $(2 + 8) + 1 = 2 + (8 + 1)$
25. $9 \cdot 4 = 4 \cdot 9$
26. $(xy)z = x(yz)$
27. $5 + (8 + x) = (5 + 8) + x$
28. $4c + 8d = 8d + 4c$
29. $7(5b) = (7 \cdot 5)b$
30. $4y(9) = 9(4y)$
31. $(5p)q = 5(pq)$
32. $6 + (8 + 3x) = (6 + 8) + 3x$
33. $3(a + b) = (a + b)3$

PART B

EXAMPLE Is division commutative?
(Is $a \div b = b \div a$ always true?)

Let's try $6 \div 2$ and $2 \div 6$.

$6 \div 2 = 3$ and $2 \div 6 = \dfrac{2}{6}$, or $\dfrac{1}{3}$. So, $6 \div 2 \neq 2 \div 6$.

Thus, division is not commutative.

34. Is subtraction commutative?
(Is $a - b = b - a$ always true?)

35. Explain why division is not commutative.

36. Is subtraction associative?
[Is $(a - b) - c = a - (b - c)$ always true?]

37. Is division associative?
[Is $(a \div b) \div c = a \div (b \div c)$ always true?]

Distributive Property

OBJECTIVE

■ To rewrite expressions by using the distributive property

 REVIEW CAPSULE

Rewrite $5(6)$ and $4(3 + 8)$ by using the commutative property of multiplication.

$$5(6) \qquad\qquad 4(3 + 8)$$
$$6(5) \qquad\qquad (3 + 8)4$$

EXAMPLE 1   Show that $5(6 + 3) = 5 \cdot 6 + 5 \cdot 3$.

Compute $5(6 + 3)$ and $5 \cdot 6 + 5 \cdot 3$.

Answers are the same. ⟶

$5(6 + 3)$	$5 \cdot 6 + 5 \cdot 3$
$5(9)$	$30 \; + \; 15$
45	45

Thus, $5(6 + 3) = 5 \cdot 6 + 5 \cdot 3$.

EXAMPLE 2   Show that $(5 + 3)4 = 5 \cdot 4 + 3 \cdot 4$.

$(5 + 3)4$	$5 \cdot 4 + 3 \cdot 4$
$8(4)$	$20 \; + \; 12$
32	32

Answers are the same. ⟶

Thus, $(5 + 3)4 = 5 \cdot 4 + 3 \cdot 4$.

Examples 1 and 2 suggest this. ⟶

Distributive Property of Multiplication over Addition

$a(b + c) = a \cdot b + a \cdot c$ and $(b + c)a = b \cdot a + c \cdot a$, for all numbers a, b, and c.

EXAMPLE 3   Rewrite $5(4 + 7)$ by using the distributive property. Then compute both expressions.

Distribute 5. ⟶

$$5(4 + 7) = 5 \cdot 4 + 5 \cdot 7$$

Compute $5(4 + 7)$ and $5 \cdot 4 + 5 \cdot 7$.

$5(4 + 7)$	$5 \cdot 4 + 5 \cdot 7$
$5(11)$	$20 \; + \; 35$
55	55

Answers are the same. ⟶

EXAMPLE 4   Rewrite $(8 + 3)5$ by using the distributive property.

$$(8 + 3)5 = 8 \cdot 5 + 3 \cdot 5$$

EXAMPLE 5   Show that $3(7 + 4 + 2) = 3 \cdot 7 + 3 \cdot 4 + 3 \cdot 2$.

$3(7 + 4 + 2)$	$3 \cdot 7 + 3 \cdot 4 + 3 \cdot 2$
$3(13)$	$21 + 12 + 6$
39	39

Answers are the same. ⟶

The distributive property may be used with three or more terms.

Thus, $3(7 + 4 + 2) = 3 \cdot 7 + 3 \cdot 4 + 3 \cdot 2$.

EXAMPLE 6   Rewrite $3(8) + 3(1)$ by using the distributive property.

3 is distributed.
Use the property "in reverse."

$$3(8) + 3(1) = 3(8 + 1)$$

EXAMPLE 7   Rewrite $5 \cdot 10 + 5 \cdot 2 + 5 \cdot 3 + 5 \cdot 5$ by using the distributive property.

$$5 \cdot 10 + 5 \cdot 2 + 5 \cdot 3 + 5 \cdot 5 = 5(10 + 2 + 3 + 5)$$

EXAMPLE 8   Rewrite $6(2) + 9(2)$ by using the distributive property.

2 is distributed. ⟶

$$6(2) + 9(2) = (6 + 9)2$$

EXAMPLE 9   Rewrite $6(3) + 1(3) + 8(3)$ by using the distributive property.

$$6(3) + 1(3) + 8(3) = (6 + 1 + 8)3$$

EXAMPLE 10   Rewrite $(6)(5) + (4)(6) + (6)(8)$ by using the distributive property.

$$(6)(5) + (4)(6) + (6)(8)$$

$$(6)(5) + (6)(4) + (6)(8)$$
$$6(5 + 4 + 8)$$

Thus, $(6)(5) + (4)(6) + (6)(8) = 6(5 + 4 + 8)$.

EXERCISES

Rewrite by using the distributive property. Then compute both expressions.

1. $4(6 + 2)$ **2.** $5(3 + 8)$ **3.** $2(9 + 4)$
4. $(9 + 7)1$ **5.** $(2 + 9)6$ **6.** $(3 + 7)5$
7. $7(4 + 8 + 2)$ **8.** $(9 + 4 + 1)6$ **9.** $2(7 + 6 + 5)$

Rewrite by using the distributive property.

10. $6(3 + 5)$ **11.** $8(4 + 9)$ **12.** $3(8 + 1)$
13. $(8 + 1 + 9)5$ **14.** $4(2 + 7 + 6)$ **15.** $(5 + 4 + 9)3$
16. $7(5 + 1 + 9 + 2)$ **17.** $(6 + 8 + 4 + 3)5$ **18.** $(1 + 9 + 7 + 2)4$
19. $3(2 + 6 + 4 + 8)$ **20.** $7(8 + 4 + 3 + 5)$ **21.** $(5 + 2 + 6 + 5)5$
22. $4(8 + 1 + 3 + 5 + 9)$ **23.** $(2 + 7 + 1 + 6 + 3)7$ **24.** $(8 + 9 + 1 + 4 + 6)3$
25. $4(6) + 4(2)$ **26.** $7(3) + 7(9)$
27. $(5)(6) + (9)(6)$ **28.** $(1)(5) + (9)(5)$
29. $3 \cdot 8 + 8 \cdot 7$ **30.** $9 \cdot 2 + 4 \cdot 9$
31. $5 \cdot 4 + 5 \cdot 2 + 5 \cdot 7$ **32.** $1 \cdot 3 + 2 \cdot 3 + 8 \cdot 3$
33. $(6)(8) + (4)(8) + (7)(8)$ **34.** $2(9) + 2(4) + 2(6)$
35. $(4)(3) + (7)(4) + (4)(1)$ **36.** $(6)(5) + (4)(6) + (9)(6)$
37. $8 \cdot 7 + 7 \cdot 4 + 7 \cdot 2$ **38.** $1(9) + 5(9) + 9(3)$
39. $6(3) + 4(6) + 6(1) + 2(6)$ **40.** $(7)(4) + (4)(7) + (2)(4) + (7)(4)$

PART B

EXAMPLE   Is subtraction distributive over multiplication? [Is it always true that $a - (b \cdot c) = (a - b) \cdot (a - c)$?]

Let's try $12 - (2 \cdot 4)$ and $(12 - 2)(12 - 4)$.

$12 - (2 \cdot 4)$	$(12 - 2)(12 - 4)$
$12 - 8$	$10(8)$
4	80

Two different answers ⟶

Subtraction is not distributive over multiplication.

41. Is multiplication distributive over subtraction? [Is it always true that $a(b - c) = ab - ac$?] If not, give an example.

42. Is addition distributive over multiplication? [Is it always true that $a + (b \cdot c) = (a + b) \cdot (a + c)$?] If not, give an example.

43. Is division distributive over addition? [Is it always true that $a \div (b + c) = (a \div b) + (a \div c)$?]

44. Is division distributive over addition from the right? [Is it always true that $(a + b) \div c = (a \div c) + (b \div c)$?]

The Vigenère Code

The Vigenère Code was invented by the French nobleman,
Blaise de Vigenère. Secret messages written in this code are very
difficult to decode.

CODING AND DECODING CHART

	A	B	C	D	E	F	G	H	I	•	•	•	X	Y	Z
A	a	b	c	d	e	f	g	h	i	•	•	•	x	y	z
B	b	c	d	e	f	g	h	i	j	•	•	•	y	z	a
C	c	d	e	f	g	h	i	j	k	•	•	•	z	a	b
D	d	e	f	g	h	i	j	k	l	•	•	•	a	b	c
•						•								•	
•						•								•	
•						•								•	
X	x	y	z	a	b	c	d	e	f	•	•	•	u	v	w
Y	y	z	a	b	c	d	e	f	g	•	•	•	v	w	x
Z	z	a	b	c	d	e	f	g	h	•	•	•	w	x	y

Do you see the pattern? Complete the chart.

To code a message, choose any key word.

Sample keyword: **BRAIN**

Write the keyword underneath the message.

Message: GO   TO   THE   BRIDGE   AT   MIDNIGHT
Keyword: **BR**   **AI**   **NBR**   **AINBRA**   **IN**   **BRAINBRA**

For each letter, look in the coding chart
under the message letter and across
from the keyword letter.

Message: GO   TO   THE   BRIDGE   AT   MIDNIGHT

Keyword: **BR**   **AI**   **NBR**   **AINBRA**   **IN**   **BRAINBRA**

CODE: hf   tw   giv   bzvexe   ig   nzdvvhyt

The coded message would appear as

hftwgivbzvexeignzdvvhyt

To decode a message easily the receiver must have the keyword.

CODE: j c l j r u v n u v m l t m f m r t m

Keyword: **B R A I N B R A I N B R A I N B R A I**

For each letter, look in the coding
chart across from the keyword letter
for the code letter. Then look up to the
top of the column for the message
letter.

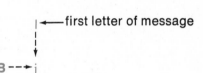

CODE: j c l j r u v n u v m l t m f m r t m

Keyword: **B R A I N B R A I N B R A I N B R A I**

Message: I L L B E

Finish decoding the message.

Decoding is extremely difficult when you do not know the keyword.
Cryptologists decode messages without the keyword. One of their chief
tools is the computer.

Write some messages of your own using the Vigenère Code. Use a keyword
other than **BRAIN.**

Distributive Property and Variables

OBJECTIVE
■ To simplify and to evaluate expressions like $7x + 3 + 9y + 4x$ if $x = 4$ and $y = 7$

 REVIEW CAPSULE

Rewrite $7(4) + 2(4)$ by using the distributive property.

$$7(4) + 2(4) = (7 + 2)4$$

EXAMPLE 1

Rewrite $6y + 7y$ by using the distributive property. Simplify the result.

y is distributed. ⟶

$$6y + 7y = (6 + 7)y$$
$$= (13)y$$
$$= 13y$$

Thus, $6y + 7y = 13y$.

$$6y + 7y \qquad\qquad x + 9y + 4$$

like terms　　　　　unlike terms

To *simplify* an expression, we combine like terms.

EXAMPLE 2

Simplify $5x + 7x$.

Combine like terms. ⟶

$$5x + 7x = 12x$$

EXAMPLE 3

Simplify $4a + 5b + 2$, if possible.

$4a$, $5b$, and 2 are unlike terms. ⟶ $4a + 5b + 2$ cannot be simplified.

EXAMPLE 4

Simplify $9x + 8y + 5x + 1 + 9$, if possible.

$9x$ and $5x$ are like terms.
Rearrange terms to group
$9x$ and $5x$ together.

$$9x + 8y + 5x + 1 + 9$$
$$9x + 5x + 8y + 1 + 9$$

$$14x \quad + 8y + \quad 10$$

ORAL EXERCISES

Simplify, if possible.

1. $2x + 3x$
2. $4p + 7p$
3. $2a + 3$
4. $6b + 7b$
5. $5y + 6y$
6. $5a + 8b$
7. $6r + 9r$
8. $8 + 3y$
9. $2m + 8m$
10. $7x + 9x$
11. $4y + 8z$
12. $5c + 8c$
13. $4 + 9y$
14. $2x + 5x$
15. $9w + 4w$
16. $7e + 8f$
17. $2z + 6z$
18. $8x + 9y$
19. $3g + 7g$
20. $5 + 5e$

EXERCISES

PART A

Simplify, if possible.

1. $6x + 3 + 4x$
2. $6 + 8x + 7$
3. $5y + 9 + 2y$
4. $3m + 2 + 5m$
5. $3a + 8a + 9$
6. $2r + 8 + 6r$
7. $7 + 6z + 5$
8. $9 + 5z + 8z$
9. $4b + 7 + 5b$
10. $8 + 6x + 3$
11. $5k + 7 + 4k$
12. $9 + 6x + 8$
13. $2y + 1 + 3y$
14. $2a + 7 + 5$
15. $3z + 8z + 4$
16. $2m + 3m + 8 + 1$
17. $6t + 7 + 4t + 9$
18. $7y + 3 + 7 + 3y$
19. $9 + 5z + 4 + 3z$
20. $5 + 4x + 3 + 8x$
21. $5x + 2y + 4x + 7y$
22. $6a + 7b + 8b + 2a$
23. $4m + 2q + 3m + 7q$
24. $3c + 5d + 9c + 4d$
25. $7x + 8y + 4x + 1$
26. $2 + 3z + 5 + 4y$
27. $7a + 8b + 9a + 6$
28. $5a + 4b + 9c + 5a$
29. $7x + 2y + 5z + 1$
30. $6g + 4 + 5h + 9g$

PART B

EXAMPLE Simplify $5x + 9y + 3x + 2y$. Then evaluate if $x = 6$ and $y = 1$.

Group x terms together and y terms together. ⟶

$$5x + 9y + 3x + 2y$$
$$5x + 3x + 9y + 2y$$
$$8x \ + \ 11y$$

$$\downarrow \qquad \downarrow$$

Substitute 6 for x, 1 for y. ⟶

$$8(6) + 11(1)$$
$$48 \ + \ 11, \text{ or } 59$$

Simplify. Then evaluate for the given values of the variables.

31. $4a + 6a + 5$ if $a = 2$
32. $9 + 5r + 7r$ if $r = 3$
33. $2y + 8 + 5y$ if $y = 8$
34. $8 + 4k + 7$ if $k = 9$
35. $9 + 4y + 3 + 2y$ if $y = 7$
36. $6x + 4 + 9 + 3x$ if $x = 3$.
37. $4z + 2 + 3w + 8z$ if $z = 6$, $w = 4$
38. $5a + 6b + 4 + 3b + 7a$ if $a = 4$, $b = 5$

Applying the Distributive Property

 REVIEW CAPSULE

Simplify $4x + 3 + 2x + 9$.

Group like terms. $\rightarrow$ $(4x + 2x) + (3 + 9)$
Combine like terms. $\rightarrow$ $6x$ $+$ 12

EXAMPLE 1 Simplify $7(5x)$.

Associative property ————————→
$$7(5x) = (7 \cdot 5)x$$
$$= \ 35x$$

EXAMPLE 2 Simplify $(9y)3$.

Rearrange and regroup. ————————→
$$(9y)3 = (9 \cdot 3)y$$
$$= \ 27y$$

EXAMPLE 3 Simplify $7(4x + 5)$.

Distribute 7. ————————————→
$7(4x) = (7 \cdot 4)x = 28x$ ————————→
$$7(4x + 5) = 7(4x) + 7(5)$$
$$= \ 28x \ + \ 35$$

EXAMPLE 4 Simplify $6 + 7(3c + 2) + 4c$.

$$6 + 7(3c + 2) + 4c = 6 + 7(3c) + 7(2) + 4c$$
$$= 6 + \ 21c \ + \ 14 \ + 4c$$
$$= (21c + 4c) + (6 + 14)$$
$$= 25c + 20$$

EXAMPLE 5 Simplify $8 + (2y + 5)3 + 7y$.

$$8 + (2y + 5)3 + 7y$$
$$8 + (2y)3 + (5)3 + 7y$$
$$8 + 6y + 15 + 7y$$
$$(6y + 7y) + (8 + 15)$$
$$13y + 23$$

Thus, $8 + (2y + 5)3 + 7y = 13y + 23$.

ORAL EXERCISES

Simplify.

1. $8(3x)$
2. $7(9r)$
3. $5(4y)$
4. $3(9z)$
5. $7(4a)$
6. $8(7x)$
7. $3(2a + 5)$
8. $4(3x + 2)$
9. $7(5c + 4)$
10. $(1 + 9a)5$

EXERCISES

PART A

Simplify.

1. $7(1 + 5y) + 8y$
2. $4z + (2z + 5)3$
3. $(6m + 9)4 + 5m$
4. $9 + 3(2m + 8)$
5. $8c + 7(2 + 4c)$
6. $7b + (1 + 8b)6$
7. $3(9x + 4) + 2x$
8. $(5 + 2d)4 + 9$
9. $2r + 8(7 + 5r)$
10. $4 + (7n + 8)2$
11. $5(6 + 4y) + 7y$
12. $(2d + 8)7 + 9d$
13. $(1 + 7c)5 + 4c$
14. $3z + 6(4 + 8z)$
15. $9 + 2(4x + 1)$
16. $6(7a + 2) + 5a$
17. $2x + 4(6 + 2x) + 3x$
18. $5 + 7(4y + 3) + 5y$
19. $5 + (4c + 2)3 + 6c$
20. $3g + 5(7 + 4g) + 8$
21. $2x + 6 + (5 + 3x)4$
22. $4z + 8(7 + 3z) + 5$

PART B

Simplify.

23. $(5 + 6r)3 + (7 + 2r)2$
24. $5(7y + 3) + 9(1 + 2y)$
25. $4(6e + 5) + 2(7e + 9)$
26. $(8a + 9)3 + (4a + 2)7$

PART C

EXAMPLE   Simplify $2[5x + 4(2x + 3)]$.

Remove inner parentheses first by distributing 4. $\longrightarrow$

$$
\begin{aligned}
2[5x + 4(2x + 3)] &= 2[5x + 4(2x) + 4(3)] \\
&= 2(5x + 8x + 12) \\
&= 2(13x + 12) \\
\end{aligned}
$$

Now distribute 2. $\longrightarrow$

$$
\begin{aligned}
&= 2(13x) + 2(12) \\
&= 26x + 24
\end{aligned}
$$

Simplify.

27. $5[6c + 7(4c + 2)]$
28. $2a + 5[(6a + 8)2 + 3a]$
29. $7x + 4[2x + (5 + 3x)6]$
30. $6[2y + 3(2y + 4) + 1] + 3(5 + 8y)$

Chapter One Review

Compute. $[p.\ 1]$

1. $(7)(2)+8$

2. $9+(3)(4)$

3. $4+(9)(0)$

4. $6(7)+5(9)$

5. $0\cdot4+6+8\cdot1$

6. $3\cdot9+2\cdot7+4$

7. $6+2(1)+5+4(3)$

8. $5+2\cdot8+3\cdot2+6+5\cdot2$

Evaluate for the given values of the variables. $[p.\ 4]$

9. $4a+5$ if $a=2$

10. $7+5x$ if $x=4$

11. $9+7r$ if $r=8$

12. $2d+9$ if $d=9$

13. $6+5x+3y$ if $x=4$, $y=6$

14. $7a+8+5b$ if $a=1$, $b=9$

15. $4g+9h+2$ if $g=5$, $h=7$

16. $8+4x+7y$ if $x=2$, $y=8$

Name the terms and the variables. Then name the coefficient of each variable. $[p.\ 4]$

17. $5+9x$

18. $5y+1+4z$

19. $8a+7b+2c$

Rewrite by using the commutative and associative properties. Then compute. $[p.\ 6]$

20. $2+57+28$

21. $23+9+7+41$

22. $422+36+24+38$

23. $(50)(47)(2)$

24. $97\cdot125\cdot8$

25. $(25)(41)(4)(2)$

Which property is illustrated? $[p.\ 6]$

26. $6+5=5+6$

27. $(7\cdot2)\cdot6=7\cdot(2\cdot6)$

28. $9+(4+x)=(9+4)+x$

29. $3(x+y)=(x+y)3$

Rewrite by using the distributive property. $[p.\ 9]$

30. $7(4+9)$

31. $(6+8)3$

32. $(5+2+6)9$

33. $8(3+7+5)$

34. $5(6)+5(3)$

35. $(8)(9)+(9)(2)$

36. $(6)(7)+(7)(1)+(7)(6)$

37. $(4)(5)+(8)(4)+(3)(4)+(1)(4)$

Simplify. $[p.\ 14,\ 16]$

38. $3x+8+7x$

39. $9+4y+8y$

40. $3t+7+5t+9$

41. $4p+6q+7p+8q+3$

42. $5r+6(1+3r)$

43. $(6y+8)3+2y$

44. $9(5p+2)+4p$

45. $8+2(7z+3)$

46. $7+(3x+5)4+8x$

47. $6y+(9+3y)5+8$

48. $(3x+5)4+(8x+7)6$

49. $5(9+3y)+7(8+6y)$

Simplify. Then evaluate for the given values of the variables. $[p.\ 14]$

50. $7x+9+3x$ if $x=8$

51. $5+3y+8+6y$ if $y=2$

52. $4a+3b+6a+7b$ if $a=2$, $b=1$

53. $4+3x+7y+9x+4y$ if $x=8$, $y=6$

Chapter One Test

Compute.

1. $8 + (5)(6)$

2. $0 \cdot 4 + 7 + 5 \cdot 6$

3. $7(1) + 8 + 4(6)$

4. $7 + 3 \cdot 9 + 5 + 4 \cdot 6$

Evaluate for the given values of the variables.

5. $4 + 9y$ if $y = 7$

6. $2d + 12$ if $d = 7$

7. $6a + 2b + 4$ if $a = 3$, $b = 8$

Name the terms and the variables. Then name the coefficient of each variable.

8. $4 + 7x + 9y$

Rewrite by using the commutative and associative properties. Then compute.

9. $5 + 67 + 15$

10. $25 \cdot 58 \cdot 4$

11. $47 + 21 + 3 + 39$

12. $(50)(31)(2)(6)$

Which property is illustrated?

13. $(x + y) + z = x + (y + z)$

14. $12 + y = y + 12$

15. $b(5a) = (5a)b$

16. $(4 \cdot c) \cdot d = 4 \cdot (c \cdot d)$

Rewrite by using the distributive property.

17. $6(4 + 9)$

18. $(8 + 1 + 7)3$

19. $9(7) + 9(2)$

20. $(4)(5) + (5)(6) + (7)(5)$

Simplify.

21. $6x + 7 + 3x$

22. $5y + 8 + 4z + 7y + 3z$

23. $2a + 4(7 + 5a)$

24. $7r + (6 + 2r)3 + 9$

25. $4(3x + 2) + 5(7x + 5)$

26. $(8y + 4)5 + (2y + 9)3$

Simplify. Then evaluate for the given values of the variables.

27. $3x + 7 + 9x$ if $x = 4$

28. $5a + 9 + 6b + 4a + 8b$ if $a = 5$, $b = 2$

Operations

Binary Operations on
(a, b)

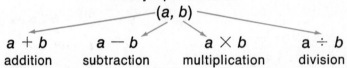

$a + b$	$a - b$	$a \times b$	$a \div b$
addition	subtraction	multiplication	division

A binary operation is a rule which assigns one element to an ordered pair (a, b).

$(a, b) \rightarrow a + b + 2$ is a binary operation.
↑
Read: maps into.

$(2, 5) \rightarrow 2 + 5 + 2$ $\qquad$ $(3, 1) \rightarrow 3 + 1 + 2$
$\qquad = 9$ $\qquad\qquad\qquad = 6$

Does this operation on (4, 5) give the same number as on (5, 4)?

$(4, 5) \rightarrow 4 + 5 + 2$ $\qquad$ $(5, 4) \rightarrow 5 + 4 + 2$
$\qquad = 11$ $\qquad\qquad\qquad = 11$
$\qquad\qquad\qquad$ Yes

Thus, the operation $(a, b) \rightarrow a + b + 2$ is commutative in these cases. Find the values of (3, 2) and (1, 4) assigned by the following operations.

1. $(a, b) \rightarrow ab + 3$ $\qquad$ 2. $(a, b) \rightarrow 2a + 3b$ $\qquad$ 3. $(a, b) \rightarrow (a + b)^2$

4. Do you think that $(a, b) \rightarrow a + b + 2$ is associative?
$\left[\begin{array}{l} \text{Hint: Use 4, 3, 5 to check your guess.} \\[2mm] [(4 + 3) + 2] + 5 + 2 \overset{?}{=} 4 + [(3 + 5) + 2] + 2 \end{array} \right]$

5. For the operations described in 1-3, which might be commutative? associative?

Adding Integers

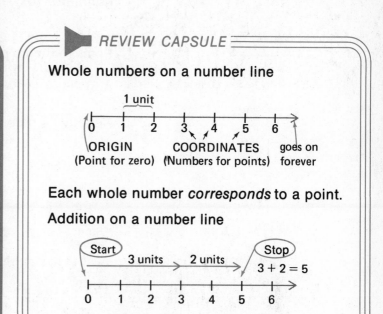

▶ *REVIEW CAPSULE*

Whole numbers on a number line

Each whole number *corresponds* to a point.

Addition on a number line

We can extend a number line to the left of 0.

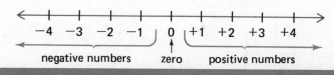

Integers on a number line ───────→

. . . means the numbers go on forever.

The numbers, . . . , −3, −2, −1, 0, +1, +2, + · · · are *integers*.

Positive integers ───────────→   +1,   +2,   +3, . . .
Read. ──────────────────────→ positive 1,   positive 2,   positive 3, and so on

Zero ───────────────────────→ 0 Zero is neither positive nor negative.

Negative integers ──────────→   −1,   −2,   −3, . . .
Read. ──────────────────────→ negative 1,   negative 2,   negative 3, and so on

The regular sign + will be used for positive integers.

To avoid confusion, we will use a heavy plus sign + to show addition.

Adding positive integers is like adding whole numbers. For example,

Positive plus positive
Read. ————————————————→

$+8 + +3 = +11$
Positive 8 plus positive 3 equals positive 11.

EXAMPLE 1 Add $-4 + -2$.

Negative plus negative
Read. ————————————————→

Negative 4 plus negative 2

Start at 0. Move 4 units to the *left* to -4.
Then move 2 more units to the *left.*
The sum is -6.

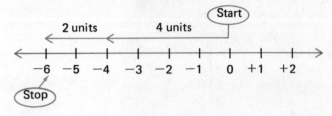

$$-4 + -2 = -6$$

EXAMPLE 2 Add $+4 + -5$.

Positive plus negative
Start at 0. Move 4 units to the *right* to $+4$.
Then move 5 units to the *left.*
The sum is -1.

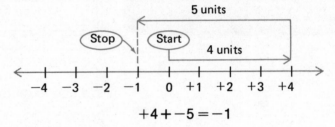

$$+4 + -5 = -1$$

EXAMPLE 3 Add $+5 + -3$.

Positive plus negative
Start at 0.
Move 5 right to $+5$.
Move 3 left.
The sum is $+2$.

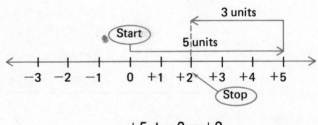

$$+5 + -3 = +2$$

EXAMPLE 4 Add $-3 + +7$.

Negative plus positive
Start at 0.
Move 3 left to -3.
Move 7 right.
The sum is $+4$.

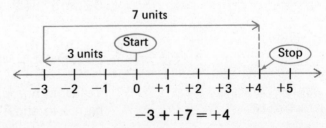

$$-3 + +7 = +4$$

EXERCISES

Add.

1. $+3 + +7$ 2. $+8 + +5$ 3. $-6 + -8$ 4. $+4 + -2$
5. $-6 + -4$ 6. $-1 + +7$ 7. $+9 + -2$ 8. $-5 + -3$
9. $+7 + -2$ 10. $+4 + +4$ 11. $+6 + -9$ 12. $-3 + -7$
13. $+8 + -9$ 14. $+6 + -2$ 15. $-4 + -5$ 16. $+6 + +1$
17. $-9 + -7$ 18. $+3 + -8$ 19. $+1 + +2$ 20. $-8 + +9$
21. $-4 + -6$ 22. $-6 + +2$ 23. $+5 + -9$ 24. $+3 + +6$
25. $-8 + +5$ 26. $+2 + -3$ 27. $-9 + -4$ 28. $+7 + -7$
29. $-10 + -3$ 30. $+11 + +5$ 31. $+12 + -9$ 32. $-3 + +15$
33. $+13 + -8$ 34. $-17 + -2$ 35. $-16 + +5$ 36. $+8 + -19$
37. $-14 + -9$ 38. $-6 + +17$ 39. $+13 + +7$ 40. $-18 + -8$

Add.

41. $+4 + +5$ 42. $+5 + +4$ 43. $-6 + -1$ 44. $-1 + -6$
45. $-3 + +8$ 46. $+8 + -3$ 47. $+2 + -6$ 48. $-6 + +2$
49. $+9 + -3$ 50. $-3 + +9$ 51. $-8 + -2$ 52. $-2 + -8$
53. $-6 + +2$ 54. $+2 + -6$ 55. $+5 + +3$ 56. $+3 + +5$
57. $-2 + 0$ 58. $0 + -2$ 59. $+8 + 0$ 60. $0 + +8$

Add.

61. $+6 + -6$ 62. $-3 + +3$ 63. $+8 + -8$ 64. $-6 + +6$
65. $-5 + +5$ 66. $+8 + -8$ 67. $+3 + -3$ 68. $-9 + +9$

Add.

69. $+10 + -32$ 70. $-27 + -31$ 71. $+46 + -22$ 72. $-38 + +28$
73. $+46 + +21$ 74. $-37 + +56$ 75. $-62 + -19$ 76. $+45 + -45$
77. $-28 + +36$ 78. $+59 + -63$ 79. $+12 + -87$ 80. $-56 + -23$
81. $-96 + -35$ 82. $+48 + -37$ 83. $-56 + +56$ 84. $+43 + -39$
85. $+87 + +102$ 86. $-179 + +58$ 87. $-105 + -93$ 88. $+59 + -192$
89. $+158 + -136$ 90. $+279 + +346$ 91. $-458 + -329$ 92. $+728 + -958$
93. $-379 + +247$ 94. $-586 + -431$ 95. $+372 + +622$ 96. $-489 + +262$

For each case below, state a rule for addition of integers.

97. positive plus positive   98. negative plus negative
99. positive plus negative   100. negative plus positive

Properties of Addition of Integers

REVIEW CAPSULE

Adding Integers

Signs the same	Signs different
$+5 + +9 = +14$	$+8 + -3 = +5$
$-8 + -9 = -17$	$-6 + +4 = -2$

Commutative Property of Addition

$8 + 3 = 3 + 8$ ← Whole numbers
$-8 + +3 = +3 + -8$ ← Integers

EXAMPLE 1

Use the associative property to group negative numbers. ⟶

Add $(+4 + -6) + -3$.

$$(+4 + -6) + -3 = +4 + (-6 + -3)$$
$$= +4 + -9$$
$$= -5$$

EXAMPLE 2

Draw a conclusion from these additions.

$+6 + 0 = +6$ ┊ $-4 + 0 = -4$ ┊ $0 + -6 = -6$

Adding zero gives the same number.

The sum of any integer and zero is that integer.

Example 2 suggests this. ⟶
Zero is the additive identity.

Property of Additive Identity
$a + 0 = a$ and $0 + a = a$, for each number a.

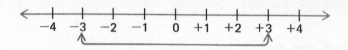

Opposites are the same distance from 0 on a number line.

-3 and $+3$ are opposites. 0 is its own opposite.

Read $-a$ as the opposite of a, or as the additive inverse of a.

The symbol $-a$ means the opposite of a, or the additive inverse of a.

EXAMPLE 3 For each value of a, give the value of $-a$.

-a (the opposite of a) can be positive, negative, or zero, depending upon the value of a.

a	Answers	$-a$
+6		-6
-2		+2
0		0

EXAMPLE 4 Draw a conclusion from these additions.

$$+4 + -4 = 0 \qquad -2 + +2 = 0$$

The sum of any integer and its opposite is zero.

Property of Additive Inverses

$a + -a = 0$, for each number a.

SUMMARY

Commutative Property: $a + b = b + a$

Associative Property: $(a + b) + c = a + (b + c)$

Property of Additive Identity: $a + 0 = a$ and $0 + a = a$

Property of Additive Inverses: $a + -a = 0$

EXAMPLE 5 Which property of addition of integers is illustrated?

	Answers
$-6 + +6 = 0$	Additive Inverses
$0 + +8 = +8$	Additive Identity
$-7 + +2 = +2 + -7$	Commutative
$(-8 + -3) + +3$	
$\quad = -8 + (-3 + +3)$	Associative

ORAL EXERCISES

Give the opposite of each.

1. +2   **2.** -6   **3.** +10   **4.** 0   **5.** -1   **6.** -9

7. +7   **8.** -5   **9.** +18   **10.** -93   **11.** +87   **12.** -125

13. -50   **14.** +233   **15.** -424   **16.** a **17.** $-x$ **18.** $-n$

19. Tell how to read the symbol $-x$.

20. Explain why the symbol $-a$ should not be read as negative a.

EXERCISES

PART A

Add.

1. $(+6 + -2) + -3$
2. $(+8 + -9) + -5$
3. $(-7 + +4) + +8$
4. $(-5 + +6) + +9$
5. $-10 + (-8 + +5)$
6. $+15 + (+7 + -25)$
7. $(-8 + +16) + -16$
8. $+37 + (-37 + +52)$

Which property of addition of integers is illustrated?

9. $+5 + -2 = -2 + +5$
10. $-6 + +6 = 0$
11. $0 + +8 = +8$
12. $(+2 + -5) + +7 = +2 + (-5 + +7)$
13. $-9 + 0 = -9$
14. $+4 + -4 = 0$
15. $-7 + -4 = -4 + -7$
16. $-8 + +3 = +3 + -8$
17. $(-8 + +6) + +3 = -8 + (+6 + +3)$
18. $+15 + -15 = 0$
19. $x + -x = 0$
20. $y + 0 = y$
21. $c + d = d + c$
22. $(x + y) + z = x + (y + z)$

PART B

Find the value of each.

23. $-x$ if $x = 3$
24. $-b$ if $b = -5$
25. a if $-a = -2$
26. y if $-y = 8$
27. z if $z = -7$
28. n if $-n = 0$

Explain why each statement is true.

29. If x is negative, then $-x$ is positive.
30. If $-x$ is negative, then $-(-x)$ is positive.

PART C

EXAMPLE   Prove $(-3 + +5) + -7 = (-7 + +5) + -3$.

Expression	Reason
$(-3 + +5) + -7$	Given
$-7 + (-3 + +5)$	Commutative Property
$-7 + (+5 + -3)$	Commutative Property
$(-7 + +5) + -3$	Associative Property

Prove.

31. $(-9 + +4) + -8 = (-8 + +4) + -9$
32. $(-6 + +7) + -5 = (-5 + +7) + -6$
33. $(-3 + +5) + +3 = +5$
34. $(-8 + -3) + +8 = -3$
35. $(x + y) + z = (z + y) + x$
36. $(-x + -y) + x = -y$

Probability

How can the coin land?

$$S = \{H, T\}$$

H: heads   T: tails

> The set, S, of all possibilities for
> an experiment is called the SAMPLE SPACE.

What is the sample space for tossing 3 coins?

$$S = \{HHH, HHT, HTH, HTT, THH, THT, TTH, TTT\}$$

In tossing 3 coins, what is the probability of 2 H?

$P(2H) = \dfrac{3}{8}$ ← Appears three times in S: HHT, HTH, THH

← Total elements in S.

> $P(A)$ $=$ $\dfrac{\text{Number of times } A \text{ appears in Sample Space}}{\text{Total number of elements in Sample Space}}$
>
> Read: the probability
> of A

In tossing 2 dice, what is the probability that the sum is 7?

$$P(7) = \frac{6}{36}, \text{ or } \frac{1}{6}$$

Sample Space for 2 dice
FIRST DIE

	1	2	3	4	5	6
1	2	3	4	5	6	⑦
2	3	4	5	6	⑦	8
3	4	5	6	⑦	8	9
4	5	6	⑦	8	9	10
5	6	⑦	8	9	10	11
6	⑦	8	9	10	11	12

SECOND DIE

Sum of dice

1. A coin and a die are tossed. Find the sample space.
2. A die is rolled once. Find the sample space. What is P (even)?
3. In tossing two dice what is P (8)? P (even)?
4. In tossing 2 dice, what is P (both dice are same)? P (0)?

Multiplying Integers

 REVIEW CAPSULE

Multiplying positive integers is like multiplying whole numbers.

Whole numbers	Positive integers
$(3) (4) = 12$	$(+3) (+4) = +12$
$(1) (7) = 7$	$(+1) (+7) = +7$
$(8) (2) = 16$	$(+8) (+2) = +16$

The Review Capsule suggests this rule. →
$(+) (+) = +$ ────────────────→

The product of two positive numbers is a positive number.
$$\text{positive} \times \text{positive} = \text{positive}$$

EXAMPLE 1　Draw a conclusion from these multiplications.

$$(+3) (0) = 0 \qquad (0) (-4) = 0 \qquad (0) (0) = 0$$
The product of any number and 0 is 0.

Example 1 suggests this. ────────→

Property of Zero for Multiplication
$a \cdot 0 = 0$ and $0 \cdot a = 0$, for each number a.

EXAMPLE 2　Determine a logical answer for the product $(+5) (-3)$.

Start with this expression: $(+5) (-3 + +3)$.
Simplify it.

$$+5 \ (-3 + +3)$$
$$+5 \ (0)$$
$$0$$

$-3 + +3 = 0$ ────────────────→

So, 　　　　$+5 \ (-3 + +3) = 0.$
$$(+5) (-3) + (+5) (+3) = 0$$

Distribute $+5$. ────────────→
The result is still 0.
What number plus $+15$ equals 0?

$$\boxed{} + +15 = 0$$
$$\boxed{-15} + +15 = 0$$

Answer: -15 ────────────→

Thus, $(+5) (-3) = -15.$

EXAMPLE 3 Determine a logical answer for the product $(-3)(+5)$.

Use the commutative property.

$$(-3)(+5) = (+5)(-3)$$
$$= -15 \qquad \textbf{Thus,} \ (-3)(+5) = -15$$

Examples 2 and 3 suggest this rule. ⟶
$(+)(-) = -$ ————————————
$(-)(+) = -$ ————————————

The product of a positive number and a negative number is a negative number.
positive × negative = negative
negative × positive = negative

EXAMPLE 4 Multiply $(+8)(-4)$.   Multiply $(-5)(+7)$.

$(+)(-) = - \quad (-)(+) = -$

$$(+8)(-4) = -32 \qquad\qquad (-5)(+7) = -35$$

EXAMPLE 5 Determine a logical answer for the product $(-4)(-9)$.

Start with this expression: $-4(-9 + {}^+9)$. Simplify it.

$$-4(-9 + {}^+9)$$
$$-4(0)$$
$$0$$

So, $\qquad -4(-9 + {}^+9) = 0.$

Distribute -4. ⟶
$$(-4)(-9) + (-4)(+9) = 0$$

What number plus -36 equals 0? ⟶
Answer: $+36$

$$\boxed{} + -36 = 0$$
$$\boxed{+36} + -36 = 0$$

Thus, $(-4)(-9) = +36.$

Example 5 suggests this rule. ⟶

$(-)(-) = +$ ————————————

The product of two negative numbers is a positive number.
negative × negative = positive

EXAMPLE 6 Multiply $(-8)(-7)$.

$(-)(-) = +$ ⟶

$$(-8)(-7) = +56$$

SUMMARY   **Like signs give a**   **Unlike signs give a**
                   positive product.   **negative product.**
      $(+)(+) = + \quad (-)(-) = + \quad\quad (+)(-) = - \quad (-)(+) = -$

ORAL EXERCISES

Is the product positive or negative?

1. (+100) (−25)　　　**2.** (−80) (−90)　　　**3.** (+15) (+15)　　　**4.** (−37) (+83)

EXERCISES

PART A

Multiply.

1. (+3) (+7)	**2.** (−2) (+4)	**3.** (+6) (−8)	**4.** (−3) (−1)
5. (−5) (+9)	**6.** (−1) (0)	**7.** (+7) (−4)	**8.** (0) (+6)
9. (+7) (−1)	**10.** (−5) (−6)	**11.** (−8) (+2)	**12.** (−9) (0)
13. (+3) (+9)	**14.** (−7) (+6)	**15.** (0) (−4)	**16.** (−6) (−1)
17. (+1) (−8)	**18.** (−3) (−9)	**19.** (+6) (+10)	**20.** (+5) (−12)
21. (−9) (−8)	**22.** (0) (−12)	**23.** (+3) (−6)	**24.** (+10) (+13)
25. (−20) (0)	**26.** (−5) (+14)	**27.** (−25) (−4)	**28.** (−7) (−11)
29. (0) (+36)	**30.** (−6) (+6)	**31.** (+10) (−10)	**32.** (−8) (+12)
33. (+13) (−3)	**34.** (−12) (+4)	**35.** (+15) (−8)	**36.** (−26) (0)
37. (+16) (−2)	**38.** (−15) (+5)	**39.** (−36) (−2)	**40.** (0) (−40)
41. (+5) (+50)	**42.** (−30) (−4)	**43.** (+60) (−8)	**44.** (−65) (−2)
45. (+80) (−9)	**46.** (+41) (+1)	**47.** (−40) (+40)	**48.** (−1) (−89)
49. (−18) (−50)	**50.** (+42) (−13)	**51.** (0) (+72)	**52.** (+63) (−63)

PART B

EXAMPLE Multiply (−2) (+8) (−5) (+6).

Multiplication can be done in any order. ───────────→

$$(-2) (+8) (-5) (+6) = \underbrace{(-2) (-5)}\ \underbrace{(+8) (+6)}$$
$$= \quad (+10) \qquad (+48)$$
$$= \quad +480$$

Multiply.

53. (−6) (+3) (−5)	**54.** (+8) (−2) (−3)
55. (−6) (+8) (+3) (−1)	**56.** (+9) (−7) (−3) (+5)
57. (+3) (−7) (+8) (−9)	**58.** (+6) (0) (−7) (−9)
59. (−3) (+8) (−5) (+6) (−7)	**60.** (+8) (+3) (−9) (−1) (+5)

PART C

Give two examples to illustrate each property for integers.

61. Commutative property of multiplication　　**62.** Associative property of multiplication　　**63.** Distributive property of multiplication over addition

Dividing Integers

 REVIEW CAPSULE

Multiplication and division are related operations.

Multiplication	Division
(3) (2) = 6	$6 \div 2 = 3$, or $\frac{6}{2} = 3$
(5) (9) = 45	$45 \div 9 = 5$, or $\frac{45}{9} = 5$
(6) (8) = 48	$48 \div 8 = 6$, or $\frac{48}{8} = 6$
The product 3 times 2 is 6.	The quotient 6 divided by 2 is 3.

EXAMPLE 1 Divide $+8 \div +2$.   Divide $-10 \div -5$.

Start with this division sentence.
Write a related multiplication. ———→
Replace the □ to make the sentence true. ———→

$+8 \div +2 = \square$	$-10 \div -5 = \square$
$(\square)(+2) = +8$	$(\square)(-5) = -10$
↓	↓
$(+4)(+2) = +8$	$(+2)(-5) = -10$
Thus, $+8 \div +2 = +4$,	**Thus,** $-10 \div -5 = +2$,
or $\frac{+8}{+2} = +4$.	or $\frac{-10}{-5} = +2$.

Example 1 suggests this rule. ———→

$\frac{(+)}{(+)} = +$; $\frac{(-)}{(-)} = +$ ———

The quotient of two numbers with like signs is a positive number.

$\frac{positive}{positive} = positive \qquad \frac{negative}{negative} = positive$

EXAMPLE 2 Divide $\frac{+15}{+3}$.   Divide $-16 \div -2$.

$\frac{+15}{+3} = +5$ $-16 \div -2 = +8$

EXAMPLE 3   Divide $-18 \div +3$.   Divide $+24 \div -6$.

Start with this division sentence.

Write a related multiplication. ⟶

$$-18 \div +3 = \square$$
$$(\square)\,(+3) = -18$$
$$\downarrow$$

$$+24 \div -6 = \square$$
$$(\square)\,(-6) = +24$$
$$\downarrow$$

Replace the $\square$. ⟶

$$(-6)\,(+3) = -18$$
Thus, $-18 \div +3 = -6$,

or $\dfrac{-18}{+3} = -6$.

$$(-4)\,(-6) = +24$$
Thus, $+24 \div -6 = -4$,

or $\dfrac{+24}{-6} = -4$.

Example 3 suggests this rule. ⟶

The quotient of two numbers with unlike signs is a negative number.

$\dfrac{(-)}{(+)} = -$; $\dfrac{(+)}{(-)} = -$ ⟶

$$\dfrac{\text{negative}}{\text{positive}} = \text{negative} \qquad \dfrac{\text{positive}}{\text{negative}} = \text{negative}$$

EXAMPLE 4   Divide $\dfrac{-20}{+4}$.   Divide $+21 \div -7$.

$$\dfrac{-20}{+4} = -5$$ $$+21 \div -7 = -3$$

SUMMARY

Like signs give a positive quotient.

$$\dfrac{(+)}{(+)} = + \qquad \dfrac{(-)}{(-)} = +$$

Unlike signs give a negative quotient.

$$\dfrac{(+)}{(-)} = - \qquad \dfrac{(-)}{(+)} = -$$

The rules for division of integers are the same as for multiplication.

ORAL EXERCISES

Is the quotient positive or negative?

1. $+76 \div +19$ **2.** $-84 \div -21$ **3.** $-75 \div +25$ **4.** $+100 \div -20$ **5.** $-800 \div -400$

6. $\dfrac{+125}{-25}$ **7.** $\dfrac{-216}{-24}$ **8.** $\dfrac{-527}{+527}$ **9.** $\dfrac{+800}{+200}$ **10.** $\dfrac{-1,926}{-18}$

EXERCISES

Divide.

1. $\dfrac{+8}{+4}$ 2. $\dfrac{-12}{+3}$ 3. $\dfrac{+35}{-7}$ 4. $\dfrac{-72}{-9}$ 5. $\dfrac{+28}{+4}$ 6. $\dfrac{-46}{+2}$

7. $\dfrac{-45}{-5}$ 8. $\dfrac{+8}{-8}$ 9. $\dfrac{-81}{+9}$ 10. $\dfrac{+100}{-25}$ 11. $\dfrac{0}{+9}$ 12. $\dfrac{+85}{+5}$

13. $\dfrac{-60}{-10}$ 14. $\dfrac{-56}{+8}$ 15. $\dfrac{+21}{+7}$ 16. $\dfrac{-25}{-5}$ 17. $\dfrac{+44}{+11}$ 18. $\dfrac{-80}{+16}$

19. $\dfrac{-72}{+24}$ 20. $\dfrac{+45}{-9}$ 21. $\dfrac{-30}{-30}$ 22. $\dfrac{-42}{+7}$ 23. $\dfrac{+60}{+12}$ 24. $\dfrac{-32}{-8}$

25. $\dfrac{+42}{-1}$ 26. $\dfrac{-36}{+6}$ 27. $\dfrac{-52}{+13}$ 28. $\dfrac{-48}{-6}$ 29. $\dfrac{+49}{+7}$ 30. $\dfrac{+38}{-19}$

Divide.

31. $-63 \div +7$ 32. $+48 \div -12$ 33. $-72 \div +9$ 34. $-64 \div -8$

35. $+45 \div +3$ 36. $-50 \div +5$ 37. $-65 \div -13$ 38. $-49 \div +7$

39. $+100 \div -5$ 40. $-81 \div -9$ 41. $-63 \div +3$ 42. $+34 \div +17$

Divide.

43. $+6 \div +1$ 44. $-8 \div +1$ 45. $-32 \div +1$ 46. $+46 \div +1$

47. What conclusion can you draw from Exercises **43–46**?

Divide.

48. $+9 \div +9$ 49. $-7 \div -7$ 50. $+12 \div +12$ 51. $-38 \div -38$

52. What conclusion can you draw from Exercises **48–51**?

EXAMPLE   Compute $-72 \div (+24 \div -3)$.

Divide within the parentheses first. $\longrightarrow$
$$-72 \div (+24 \div -3)$$
$$-72 \div -8$$
$$+9$$

Compute.

53. $-27 \div (-18 \div +6)$ 54. $-32 \div (-28 \div +7)$

55. $(+10 \div -2) \div -5$ 56. $-60 \div (+48 \div -4)$

57. $(-36 \div -4) \div -3$ 58. $+72 \div (-12 \div +3)$

59. $(+100 \div -5) \div +4$ 60. $(+90 \div +3) \div -10$

61. $-16 \div (-32 \div -4)$ 62. $+56 \div (+35 \div -5)$

Clock Arithmetic

An arithmetic using only the numbers
0, 1, 2 is based on a three-minute clock.

| To add 1 ⊕ 1. Start at 0. Move the hand 1 place forward to 1. | Then move 1 place forward to 2. Thus, 1 ⊕ 1 = 2. | To add 2 ⊕ 2. Start at 0. Move 2 places forward to 2. | Then move 2 places forward to 1. Thus, 2 ⊕ 2 = 1. |

 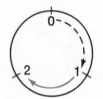 

We can fill in the entire addition table by using the clock.

Because the sum of every pair of numbers is always 0, 1, or 2, we say that three-minute clock arithmetic is closed under addition.

Second Addend

⊕	0	1	2
0	0	1	2
1	1	2	0
2	2	0	1

First Addend

1. Which properties of addition does three-minute clock arithmetic have?
   The commutative poperty?
   The associative property?

2. Give the addive inverse for each number in three-minute clock arithmetic.

3. Construct an addition table for four-minute clock arithmetic. What addition properties does this arithmetic have?

We can use the three-minute clock for multiplication as well.

To multiply 2 ⊗ 1,
move the hand 1 place
forward 2 times. Thus
2 ⊗ 1 = 2.

To multiply 2 ⊗ 2,
move the hand 2
places forward 2 times.
Thus, 2 ⊗ 2 = 1.

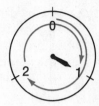

We can make a multiplication table
by using the clock.

⊗	0	1	2
0	0	0	0
1	0	1	2
2	0	2	1

4. Is the three-minute clock arithmetic closed under multiplication?

5. What properties of multiplication does the three-minute clock have?
    The commutative property?
    The associative property?

Use both the addition and multiplication tables. Calculate each
expression

6. 2 ⊗ (2 ⊕ 1)

7. 1 ⊗ (2 ⊕ 2)

8. 1 ⊗ (2 ⊕ 0)

9. (2 ⊗ 2) ⊕ (2 ⊗ 1)

10. (1 ⊗ 2) ⊕ (1 ⊗ 2)

11. (1 ⊗ 2) ⊕ (1 ⊗ 0)

12. Does the three-minute clock arithmetic have the distributive
    property of multiplication over addition?

13. Construct a multiplication table for a four-minute clock.
    What multiplication properties does this clock have?

A New Look at Addition

REVIEW CAPSULE

Commutative Property of Addition
$$+6 + -2 = -2 + +6$$

Associative Property of Addition
$$(-4 + -8) + +3 = -4 + (-8 + +3)$$

EXAMPLE 1   Add $6 + -13$.

6 is like $+6$. ← (positive 6)
Read $6 + -13$ as

positive 6 plus negative 13.

Thus, $6 + -13 = -7$.

EXAMPLE 2   Add $-9 + 12$.

12 is like $+12$. ← (positive 12)

Thus, $-9 + 12 = 3$. ← (positive 3)

EXAMPLE 3   Add $(-18 + +25) + -2$.

Associative property ⟶
Commutative property ⟶
Associative property ⟶

$$(-18 + +25) + -2 = -18 + (+25 + -2)$$
$$= -18 + (-2 + +25)$$
$$= (-18 + -2) + +25$$
$$= \quad -20 \quad + +25$$
$$= +5, \text{ or } 5$$

We can shorten our work in Example 3.

$$(-18 + +25) + -2$$

Associative and commutative properties ⟶
$$(-18 + -2) \quad + +25$$
$$-20 \quad + +25$$
$$+5, \text{ or } 5$$

EXAMPLE 4   Add $-3 + +8 + -7$.

$$-3 + +8 + -7$$

Group negatives together. ──────────→

$$(-3 + -7) + +8$$
$$-10 \quad + +8$$
$$-2$$

Thus, $-3 + +8 + -7 = -2$.

In Example 4 we added these three numbers.

$$-3 \qquad +8 \qquad -7$$

To simplify our writing, we will agree that we can omit the + signs when adding. That is,

The heavy plus signs are not written but are understood. ──────────→

$$-3 +8 -7 \qquad \text{will mean}$$

Read. ──────────→   negative 3 *plus* positive 8 *plus* negative 7

EXAMPLE 5   Read $-5 +6 -4$.

$$-5 +6 -4$$

Read. ──────────→   negative 5 *plus* positive 6 *plus* negative 4

EXAMPLE 6   Read $8 - 3x$.

8 means +8. + is understood. ──────────→

$$8 -3x \text{ means } +8 + (-3)x$$

Thus, $8 -3x$ is read as
positive 8 *plus* negative 3 times *x*.

EXAMPLE 7   Compute $8 -7 +9$.

$$8 -7 +9 \text{ means } +8 + -7 + +9.$$

Group positives together. ──────────→

$$+8 + -7 + +9 = (+8 + +9) + -7$$
$$= \quad +17 \quad + -7$$
$$= \quad +10, \text{ or } 10$$

We can shorten our work in Example 7.

$$8 - 7 + 9 = (8 + 9) - 7$$
$$= \quad 17 \quad - 7$$
$$= \quad 10$$

EXAMPLE 8   Compute $-5 + 8 - 6 + 4$.

Addition can be done in any order.

$$-5 + 8 - 6 + 4 = \underbrace{-5 - 6}\ +\ \underbrace{8 + 4}$$
$$= \quad -11 \ + \ 12$$
$$= \quad +1, \text{ or } 1$$

We have seen that problems like $7 - 5$ may be interpreted as addition problems.

$$7 - 5 \text{ means } +7 + -5$$

These problems look like subtraction problems, but we can think of them as addition of positive and negative numbers. We will study the operation of subtraction on pages 50 and 51.

ORAL EXERCISES

Read.

1. $3 - 8$
2. $-7 + 6$
3. $-5 - 9$
4. $2 + 8$
5. $4 - 3 + 10$
6. $-8 + 12 - 7$
7. $-3 - 1 - 6$
8. $3 - 7 + 9$
9. $-8 + 3z - 1$
10. $-4x - 3$
11. $6x - 5y + 1$
12. $7x - 5y - 3$

EXERCISES

PART A

Compute.

1. $4 - 10$
2. $-9 + 3$
3. $5 + 8$
4. $-3 - 9$
5. $-6 - 9 + 15$
6. $5 + 6 - 17$
7. $-16 - 31 + 3$
8. $-28 + 3 + 42$
9. $-15 - 9 + 36$
10. $-12 + 5 - 2$
11. $18 - 13 + 2$
12. $-42 + 7 + 16$
13. $-5 + 3 + 21$
14. $-36 - 8 + 14$
15. $16 + 8 - 14$
16. $21 - 7 - 23$
17. $58 - 39 - 2$
18. $18 - 47 - 12$
19. $-36 + 17 - 2$
20. $42 - 17 - 36$
21. $-22 + 12 + 15$
22. $63 - 47 + 17$
23. $65 - 2 - 29$
24. $-38 - 9 + 46$

PART B

Compute.

25. $-28 + 36 - 43 - 91$
26. $-81 + 49 - 38 + 16$
27. $76 - 85 - 79 + 5$
28. $47 - 13 - 68 + 17$
29. $31 - 57 + 14 + 28$
30. $68 - 79 - 85 - 31$
31. $-56 + 14 - 72 + 12$
32. $72 - 36 + 41 + 13$
33. $-62 - 58 + 43 - 17$
34. $29 - 45 - 62 + 73$
35. $58 - 46 + 71 - 83$
36. $-105 + 56 + 63 - 21$

Magic Squares

In ancient China and India the people often wore jewelry which was assumed to contain mystical powers. One such ornament was the magic square.

8	1	6
3	5	7
4	9	2

The sum of the numbers along any row, column, or diagonal is 15.

Arrange the numbers 1 to 16 in each of these 4 x 4 squares to make magic squares.

1		7	
	13		11
10		16	
	6		4

16			
			8
		7	
4			1

Evaluating Expressions

OBJECTIVE

■ To evaluate expressions like $-6x + 5y - 3z$ if $x = -2$, $y = -4$, $z = -3$

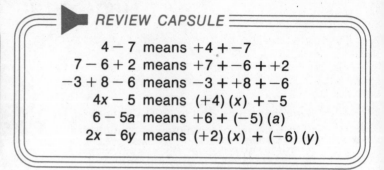

▶ REVIEW CAPSULE

$4 - 7$ means $+4 + -7$
$7 - 6 + 2$ means $+7 + -6 + +2$
$-3 + 8 - 6$ means $-3 + +8 + -6$
$4x - 5$ means $(+4)(x) + -5$
$6 - 5a$ means $+6 + (-5)(a)$
$2x - 6y$ means $(+2)(x) + (-6)(y)$

EXAMPLE 1 Evaluate $4x - 3$ if $x = 7$.

Read: positive 4 times x
    plus negative 3. ⟶

Substitute $+7$ for x. ⟶

Multiply first. Then add. ⟶

We can omit the $+$. ⟶

$$
\begin{aligned}
4x - 3 &= (+4)(x) \quad + -3 \\
&= (+4)(+7) + -3 \\
&= \quad +28 \quad + -3 \\
&= \quad\quad +28 - 3 \\
&= \quad\quad\quad +25
\end{aligned}
$$

EXAMPLE 2 Evaluate $-6 + 5a$ if $a = 3$.

$5a$ means $(+5)(a)$. ⟶

$(+)(+) = (+)$ ⟶

$-6 + 15 = +9$, or 9 ⟶

$$
\begin{aligned}
-6 + 5a &= -6 + (5)(a) \\
&= -6 + (5)(3) \\
&= -6 \quad + 15 \\
&= \quad\quad 9
\end{aligned}
$$

EXAMPLE 3 Evaluate $2x - 6y$ if $x = -3$ and $y = -1$.

$2x$ means $(+2)(x)$. ⟶

$(+)(-) = (-)$ $(-)(-) = (+)$ ⟶

$$
\begin{aligned}
2x - 6y &= (2)(x) \quad + (-6)(y) \\
&= (2)(-3) + (-6)(-1) \\
&= \quad -6 \quad\quad\quad +6 \\
&= \quad 0
\end{aligned}
$$

EXAMPLE 4 Evaluate $-5a - 8b + 7c$ if $a = -1$, $b = -3$, $c = -4$.

$$
\begin{aligned}
-5a - 8b + 7c &= (-5)(a) \quad + (-8)(b) \quad + (7)(c) \\
&= (-5)(-1) + (-8)(-3) + (7)(-4) \\
&= \quad 5 \quad\quad\quad +24 \quad\quad\quad -28 \\
&= \quad 1
\end{aligned}
$$

Add 5 and 24 first, then add -28.

EXERCISES

PART A

Evaluate for the given values of the variables.

1. $6x + 2$ if $x = 2$
2. $7g + 9$ if $g = 5$
3. $5a + 3$ if $a = -1$
4. $-3x - 5$ if $x = -2$
5. $7c - 2d$ if $c = 3, d = 5$
6. $8r - 7s$ if $r = 7, s = 7$
7. $-5y + 4z$ if $y = -4, z = -2$
8. $-2k - 5t$ if $k = -4, t = -6$
9. $7e - 3f$ if $e = 6, f = -7$
10. $-5m + 3n$ if $m = -5, n = 1$
11. $4x + 5y + 3z$ if $x = 1, y = -2, z = 3$
12. $2a - 3b + 6c$ if $a = -5, b = 7, c = -9$
13. $6r - 9s - 5t$ if $r = 6, s = -2, t = -8$
14. $-8e + 7f - 4g$ if $e = 3, f = -4, g = -5$
15. $-2p - 8q + 6r$ if $p = -2, q = -9, r = -6$
16. $-5x - 2y - 9z$ if $x = 8, y = -1, z = -7$
17. $4f + 7g - 2h$ if $f = -5, g = -8, h = -4$
18. $-7d + 8e - 3f$ if $d = -3, e = 7, f = -6$
19. $7a - 2b + 9c$ if $a = -1, b = -7, c = -9$
20. $-4p - 3q - 7r$ if $p = -3, q = -4, r = -8$

PART B

EXAMPLE Simplify $(6x + 3y)2 + 7x + 4$. Then evaluate if $x = -3, y = -7$.

$$(6x + 3y)2 + 7x + 4$$

Distribute 2. $\longrightarrow$
$$(6x)(2) + (3y)(2) + 7x + 4$$
$$12x + 6y + 7x + 4$$

Combine like terms. $\longrightarrow$
$$19x + 6y + 4$$

Substitute -3 for x, -7 for y. $\longrightarrow$
$$(19)(-3) + 6(-7) + 4$$
$$-57 - 42 + 4$$
$$-99 + 4$$
$$-95$$

Simplify. Then evaluate if $x = -5$, $y = 3$, and $z = -1$.

21. $4(7x + 3y) + 6x + 2$
22. $9 + 3(5x + 2y) + 7$
23. $7y + 3(2x + 5y) + 8$
24. $6x + (3z - 2x)5 + 3$
25. $8 + 4z + 2(3x + 5z)$
26. $(4y + 3z)8 + 7y + 1$
27. $(7x + 3y)4 + 8x + 9y$
28. $6z + 2(9y + 3z) + 8y + 5$
29. $2(6x + 3y + 2z) + 8y + 4z$
30. $(6x + 9z)4 + 5(7x + 8y)$
31. $(4y + 2x + 9z)3 + 7z + 2x$
32. $2z + 5(7y + 4z) + 3x + 5y$

Combining Like Terms

REVIEW CAPSULE

Combine like terms.

$$3x + 5x = 8x$$
$$6a + 3a = 9a$$
$$5c + 2 + 8c = 13c + 2$$

EXAMPLE 1   Simplify $-2x + 5x$.

$-2x$ and $+5x$ are like terms.
Use the distributive property. ⟶

$$-2x + 5x = (-2 + 5)x$$
$$= 3x$$

Thus, $-2x + 5x = 3x$.

EXAMPLE 2   Simplify $8a - 3a$.

To combine like terms,
add the coefficients. ⟶

$$8a - 3a = (8 - 3)a$$
$$= 5a$$

EXAMPLE 3   Simplify $-5b - 9b$.

$$-5b - 9b = -14b$$

EXAMPLE 4   Simplify $4y - 9 - 7y + 14$.

Group like terms. ⟶

$$4y - 9 - 7y + 14 = \underbrace{4y - 7y}\ \underbrace{-9 + 14}$$
$$= -3y + 5$$

EXAMPLE 5   Simplify $6x - 4 - 2y - 9x + 7y - 8$.

$$6x - 4 - 2y - 9x + 7y - 8$$
$$\underbrace{6x - 9x}\ \underbrace{-2y + 7y}\ \underbrace{-4 - 8}$$
$$-3x + 5y - 12$$

EXERCISES

PART A

Simplify.

1. $-3y + 8y$
2. $4a - 7a$
3. $-6b + 8b$
4. $-9x - 2x$
5. $-7z + 5z$
6. $-4c - 7c$
7. $-8r + 3r$
8. $-5y - 5y$
9. $2r - 9r$
10. $4x - 5 - 2x$
11. $5z - 8 - 9z$
12. $-7c - 8 - 5c$
13. $6 + 3y - 8y$
14. $3d - 6d - 4$
15. $5r - 6 - 8r$
16. $-5q - 9 + 3q$
17. $8x - 4 - 3x$
18. $-6y - 4 - 3y$
19. $4a - 5 + 3a - 2$
20. $-6b + 6 - 2b - 4$
21. $8z - 4 - 7 + 5z$
22. $7 - 5t + 9 + 7t$
23. $-4x + 3 - 8x - 2$
24. $-6y + 3 + 8 - 7y$

Simplify.

25. $6x - 2y - 4x + 3 + 8y$
26. $5a + 3b - 4 - 7a - 6b$
27. $-5r - 9s + 9r + 3s - 6$
28. $3p - 7q - 5 + 9q - 7p$
29. $-9x + 8 - 3y - 5x + 7y$
30. $4d - 5 - 8d + 3e - 6$
31. $3r - 9s + 6 - 8r - 5s$
32. $-7 - 5g + 8h - 5g + 4$
33. $-6x + 9y - 4 - 4x - 6y$
34. $4j - 7k + 2 - 9j - 8$
35. $-9 + 8a - 4c - 7 + 5a$
36. $-8q + 9s - 2 + 6q - 4s$
37. $-4 + 3r + 6t - 8t + 1 - 7r$
38. $6x - 5 - 3y - 8x + 7y - 9$
39. $6b - 7 - 4a + 8 - 3b - 2a$
40. $-7a + 4 - 5a + 6b + 4a - 2b$

PART B

EXAMPLE Simplify $-3x - 5 + 8y - 4x - 4y$. Then evaluate if $x = -4$ and $y = -9$.

Regroup. $\longrightarrow$

Combine like terms. $\longrightarrow$

Substitute -4 for x, -9 for y. $\longrightarrow$

$$-3x - 5 + 8y - 4x - 4y$$
$$\underbrace{-3x - 4x} + \underbrace{8y - 4y} - 5$$
$$-7x \qquad +4y \quad -5$$
$$-7(-4) + 4(-9) - 5$$
$$28 \qquad -36 \quad -5$$
$$28 - 41$$
$$-13$$

Simplify. Then evaluate for $x = -2$, $y = -3$, and $z = 8$.

41. $5x - 3 + 8y - 2y - 3x$
42. $-4z + 8 - 2x - 9z + 8x$
43. $-3x + 7y - 4z + 9x - 3y$
44. $-7z - 8y - 3x - 4y + 5z$
45. $-6x + 3 + 2y - 9 - 5x + 4y$
46. $-8y + 4z + 2y - 7 - 9z - 2y$
47. $5z + 4x - 3y - 8z - 2 - 7x$
48. $5 - 8x + 2y - 1 + 3z - 7x - 4y$

$(1)(a) = a$ and $(-1)(a) = -a$

▶ REVIEW CAPSULE

Simplify $4x - 7 + 5x$.

$$4x - 7 + 5x = 4x + 5x - 7$$
$$= 9x - 7$$

EXAMPLE 1 Draw a conclusion from these multiplications.

$(1)(6) = 6$ ┆ $(1)(-2) = -2$ ┆ $(8)(1) = 8$
The product of one and any number is that number.

Example 1 suggests this. ──────→
One is the multiplicative identity.

Property of Multiplicative Identity
$(1)(a) = a$ and $(a)(1) = a$, for each number a.

EXAMPLE 2 Draw a conclusion from these multiplications.

−5 is the opposite of 5. ──────→ $(-1)(5) = -5$ ┆ $(-1)(-4) = 4$ ┆ $(7)(-1) = -7$
The product of negative one and any number is the opposite (additive inverse) of the number.

Example 2 suggests this. ──────→

Multiplication Property of −1
$(-1)(a) = -a$ and $(a)(-1) = -a$,
for each number a.

EXAMPLE 3 Simplify $6a + 2a + a$.

Replace a with $1a$. ──────→ $6a + 2a + 1a = 9a$

EXAMPLE 4 Simplify $-9 + 3b + 4 - b$.

Replace $-b$ with $-1b$. ──────→ $-9 + 3b + 4 - 1b$
Rearrange terms. ──────→ $3b - 1b - 9 + 4$
Combine like terms. ──────→ $2b - 5$

EXAMPLE 5   Simplify $3m - 9 + 4m + 7 - 8m$.

Rearrange terms. $\longrightarrow$

$$\underbrace{3m + 4m - 8m}_{-1m} \underbrace{- 9 + 7}_{-2}$$

Replace $-1m$ with $-m$. $\longrightarrow$ $- m - 2$

ORAL EXERCISES

Which property is illustrated?

1. $(-1)(-8) = 8$ **2.** $(x)(1) = x$ **3.** $(-y)(1) = -y$ **4.** $-c = (-1)(c)$

EXERCISES

PART A

Simplify.

1. $4x - 5x + x$ **2.** $a + 4a - 7a$
3. $6b - 4b + b$ **4.** $-c + 8c - 2c$
5. $5r - r + 8r$ **6.** $6y - y - 6y$
7. $a - 4 - 2a + 6$ **8.** $7 - z - 3z + 4$
9. $7c + 8 - 6c - 9$ **10.** $9d - 4 - d + 8$
11. $4e - 9 - 5e + 6$ **12.** $2 + 3x - 7 - 2x$
13. $9 - q + 6 - 8q$ **14.** $2s - 9 - s + 5$
15. $3p - 2 - 5 - p$ **16.** $7a - 5 - a + 6$
17. $6x - 5 - x + 4 + 8x$ **18.** $y + 2 - 7y + 4y - 8$
19. $-7 + d - 8 - 6d + 5$ **20.** $4z - 8 + z - 6 - 5z$
21. $-5a + 9 - a - 7 + 3a$ **22.** $3r - 5 - 7r - 8 + r$
23. $2x - x + 7 - 3 + 8x$ **24.** $-h + 3 + 5h - 1 + 9$
25. $5 - 4z + 7 - 2z + 4 - z$ **26.** $4y - 5 - 6y + 8 - y + 7$
27. $-1 - 7g - 5 - g + 9 + 7g$ **28.** $3m - 8 - 2m - 9 + 8 - 2m$
29. $8b - 9 - b + 7b + 4 - 9$ **30.** $-f + 4 - 7f - 8 + 2f + 6$

PART B

Simplify. Then evaluate if $x = -2$, $y = 6$, and $z = -3$.

31. $3x - 4y - x - 8$ **32.** $6y + z - 7y - 5$
33. $6 + 5x - 2y - 6x$ **34.** $-x + 3z + 9 - 7z$
35. $7x - y + 8z - 8x$ **36.** $5x + z - 6x + 3y$
37. $6z - 8y + x - 7z$ **38.** $-y + 8x - z - 2x$
39. $-2x - z + 8y - 7y + 3$ **40.** $-4z - 7 + 8x - y + 3z$
41. $-8y - 4z + x - y - 2z + 1$ **42.** $4z - y - 7x - 2z - 8x + 3 + y$

Removing Parentheses

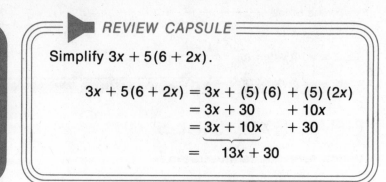

► *REVIEW CAPSULE*

Simplify $3x + 5(6 + 2x)$.

$$3x + 5(6 + 2x) = 3x + (5)(6) + (5)(2x)$$
$$= 3x + 30 \qquad + 10x$$
$$= \underbrace{3x + 10x} \qquad + 30$$
$$= \qquad 13x + 30$$

EXAMPLE 1 Simplify $4a - 5(7 + 3a)$.

Read: $4a$ plus -5 times the quantity 7 plus $3a$. ────→
Distribute -5. ────────────→
Omit the $+$ signs. ──────────→
Rearrange terms. ──────────→

$$4a - 5(7 + 3a) = 4a + {-5}(7 + 3a)$$
$$= 4a + (-5)(7) + (-5)(3a)$$
$$= 4a - 35 - 15a$$
$$= \underbrace{4a - 15a} - 35$$
$$= \quad -11a - 35$$

EXAMPLE 2 Simplify $3n - 6(4 - 5n)$.

$$3n - 6(4 - 5n)$$

Distribute -6. Omit the $+$ signs. ───→
Combine like terms. ──────────→

$$3n - 24 + 30n$$
$$33n - 24$$

EXAMPLE 3 Simplify $-2(7x + 3) - 8x$. Then evaluate the result if $x = -3$.

$$-2(7x + 3) - 8x$$

$$-14x - 6 - 8x$$
$$-22x - 6$$
$$\downarrow$$

Substitute -3 for x. ──────────→
Multiply first. ──────────────→
Then add. ────────────────→

$$-22(-3) - 6$$
$$66 - 6$$
$$60$$

EXERCISES

Simplify.

1. $5x - 8(2 - 3x)$
2. $4 - 3(7 - 9z)$
3. $4y - 2(7 - 5y)$
4. $6b - 8(3b + 7)$
5. $6 - 4(2a - 8)$
6. $5c - 6(8 - 4c)$
7. $3(2x - 9) - 4x$
8. $-7(3 - 2x) + 8x$
9. $-9(4a + 7) - 3a$
10. $-6(-5d - 8) + 2d$
11. $5y - 9(3y - 7)$
12. $-4x - 7(3 + 5x)$
13. $-7(5a + 3) + 6a$
14. $7c - 2(3c - 5)$
15. $2x - 2(4x + 3) - 5$
16. $6y - 8(4 + 7y) - 3y$
17. $8 - 7(5 - 3c) + 4c$
18. $-7r + 6 - 3(4r - 2)$
19. $5x - 2(4 - 6x) + 8$
20. $-3(8 - 5z) + 2 - 6z$
21. $7c - 5(4 - 2c) - 9 + 4c$
22. $-2x + 8 - 4(7x - 3) + 6x$
23. $-5 - 9(4y + 8) - 2y + 3$
24. $7x - 8 - 5(4x - 9) + 2x$

Simplify. Then evaluate the result for the given value of the variable.

25. $4(5y - 8) - 3y$ if $y = 8$
26. $8 - 5(4 - 3c)$ if $c = -5$
27. $-6(7x + 1) + 5x$ if $x = -4$
28. $7x - 2(4x - 6)$ if $x = 6$
29. $9 - 2(-5x + 8)$ if $x = -9$
30. $-5y - 4(8 - 9y)$ if $y = -6$
31. $7d - 8(4 - 3d) + 6$ if $d = 3$
32. $-6r + 5 - 3(2r - 1)$ if $r = -7$
33. $-2(4e - 3) + 6e - 9$ if $e = -8$
34. $-7(6 - 4z) + 8 - 3z$ if $z = 5$
35. $4(-3x + 2) - 5x - 9$ if $x = -1$
36. $9 - 2(8g + 7) + 2g$ if $g = -3$

EXAMPLE   Simplify $-3(5x - 7) - 6(4 + 2x)$.

$$-3(5x - 7) - 6(4 + 2x)$$

Distribute -3. Then distribute -6.

$$-15x + 21 - 24 - 12x$$
$$-15x - 12x + 21 - 24$$
$$-27x - 3$$

Simplify.

37. $-4(3x - 5) - 3(2 + 7x)$
38. $-5(3y - 7) - 2(6 + 4y)$
39. $-5(6 + 3y) - 7(2y - 9)$
40. $-3(5x - 4) + 8(-3x + 2)$
41. $5(3z - 7) - 9(-8z - 6)$
42. $-4(7 - 8d) - 2(-6d + 5)$
43. $4(-8a + 2) - 6(5 - 2a)$
44. $8 - 5(-4x + 3) + 6(9x - 2)$
45. $7x - 3(5x + 2) - 6(7 + 2x)$
46. $-3(8 - 7z) + 6z - 9(4 - 3z)$
47. $3y - 7(5y + 2) - 2(6 + 7y)$
48. $-4(7e - 9) + 3e - 5(9 - 4e)$

Applying the Property $-a = -1(a)$

OBJECTIVE

■ To simplify expressions like $8y - (3 - 2y)$ and to evaluate the result if $y = -6$

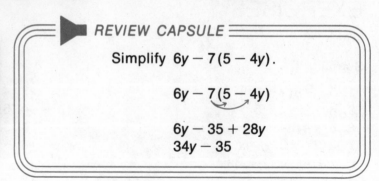

▶ REVIEW CAPSULE

Simplify $6y - 7(5 - 4y)$.

$$6y - 7(5 - 4y)$$

$$6y - 35 + 28y$$
$$34y - 35$$

EXAMPLE 1   Simplify $5x - (4 + 3x)$.

$-(a) = -1a$, so
$-(4 + 3x) = -1(4 + 3x)$

$$5x - (4 + 3x) = 5x - 1(4 + 3x)$$

Distribute -1. ⟶

$$= 5x - 4 - 3x$$

Combine like terms. ⟶

$$= 2x - 4$$

EXAMPLE 2   Simplify $-6b - (8 - 7b)$.

Replace $-(8 - 7b)$ with $-1(8 - 7b)$. ⟶ $-6b - (8 - 7b) = -6b - 1(8 - 7b)$

$$= -6b - 8 + 7b$$
$$= 1b - 8$$

Replace $1b$ with b. ⟶

$$= b - 8$$

EXAMPLE 3   Simplify $2 - (9 - c) + 5c$. Then evaluate the result if $c = -4$.

$-a = -1a$ ⟶

$$2 - (9 - c) + 5c = 2 - 1(9 - 1c) + 5c$$

$$= 2 - 9 + 1c + 5c$$
$$= -7 + 6c$$

$$\downarrow$$

Replace c with -4. ⟶

$$-7 + 6(-4)$$

Multiply first. ⟶

$$= -7 - 24$$

Then add. ⟶

$$= -31$$

EXERCISES

PART A
Simplify.

1. $-5y - (6y + 2)$
2. $3 - (6x - 9)$
3. $-8 - (5z + 4)$
4. $-6x - (3 + 5x)$
5. $7c + (8 - 9c)$
6. $-(4x - 3) + 2x$
7. $-(8 - 6f) - 3f$
8. $-(7z + 8) - 9z$
9. $6y - (7 - 3y) - 2$
10. $-8 + (-4p + 7) - 9p$
11. $y - (9 - 7y) - 8$
12. $6r - 3(r - 7) + 8r$
13. $-(e + 7) - 5e - 6$
14. $4c - (3c + 2) - 10c$
15. $-5d + (8 - d) - 9$
16. $7x - 8 - (5x + 6)$
17. $-(3y - 8) + 7y - 12$
18. $9q + (8 - 3q) + 16$
19. $3z + 8 - (5z + 2) - 9z$
20. $5x - (2 - 4x) + 8x - 7$
21. $-9b - 4 - (7b + 6) - 3b$
22. $-(-5c - 8) + 6 - 9c - c$

Simplify. Then evaluate the result for the given value of the variable.

23. $-4x - (6 - 3x)$ if $x = 6$
24. $-9z - (8 + z)$ if $z = -7$
25. $-(c + 8) + 6c$ if $c = -3$
26. $-(4y - 6) + 3y$ if $y = 9$
27. $5r - (-7 + 2r) + 8$ if $r = 8$
28. $-6 - (3b - 2) + 5b$ if $b = -4$
29. $-(-7x + 2) - 8x + 1$ if $x = 6$
30. $-8z - (5z + 6) + 3z$ if $z = -9$
31. $5y - 9 - (7y - 6)$ if $y = 2$
32. $7r - (8 - r) + 12$ if $r = -8$

PART B

EXAMPLE Simplify $-4(7 - x) - (5x + 3)$.

$-a = -1a$ $\longrightarrow$ $\qquad -4(7 - x) - (5x + 3) = -4(7 - x) - 1(5x + 3)$

Distribute -4. Then distribute -1. $\longrightarrow$ $\qquad = -28 + 4x - 5x - 3$

$\qquad\qquad\qquad\qquad\qquad\qquad\qquad\qquad = -1x - 31$

Replace $-1x$ with $-x$. $\longrightarrow$ $\qquad\qquad = -x - 31$

Simplify.

33. $-(7 + 3y) - 5(4y - 8)$
34. $-6(7x - 5) - (4 - x)$
35. $-(5z - 7) - (9 - z)$
36. $-(a + 4) - 3(7 - a)$
37. $-(-6r + 9) - (-7 - 3r)$
38. $-(-5 + c) - (-8 - c)$

PART C

Simplify. [Hint: Work within the brackets first.]

39. $-[3(x - 2) - (4 - 5x)]$
40. $-2a - [-2(1 - 7a) - (5 - 3a)]$

Subtracting Integers

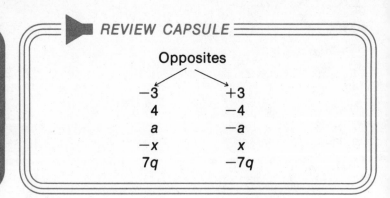

REVIEW CAPSULE

Opposites

-3	$+3$
4	-4
a	$-a$
$-x$	x
$7q$	$-7q$

EXAMPLE 1   Subtract 3 from 8.

8 subtract 3

8 subtract 3 is
8 plus the opposite of 3. ⟶

$$8 \quad - \quad 3$$
$$8 \quad + \quad -3$$
$$5$$

> a subtract b means
> a plus the opposite of b.
> $a - b = a + -b$, for all numbers a and b.

EXAMPLE 2   Subtract 6 from 4.

4 subtract 6

4 subtract 6 is
4 plus the opposite of 6. ⟶

$$4 \quad - \quad 6$$
$$4 \quad + \quad -6$$
$$-2$$

EXAMPLE 3   Subtract -9 from 7.

7 subtract -9

7 subtract -9 is
7 plus the opposite of -9. ⟶

$$7 \quad - \quad (-9)$$
$$7 \quad + \quad +9$$
$$16$$

Recall the Property of -1. ───────→ The opposite of a is equal to -1 times a.
$$-a = (-1)(a)$$

EXAMPLE 4   Subtract $-7a + 5$ from $3a - 2$.

$$3a - 2 \text{ subtract} \quad -7a + 5$$
$$3a - 2 \quad - \quad (-7a + 5)$$

Add the opposite of $(-7a + 5)$. ───────→ $3a - 2 \quad + \quad -(-7a + 5)$
$-(-7a + 5) = (-1)(-7a + 5)$ ───────→ $3a - 2 \quad + \quad -1(-7a + 5)$
Distribute -1. ───────→ $3a - 2 + 7a - 5$
$$10a - 7$$

EXAMPLE 5   Subtract $-5a + 2$ from $3a - 4$.

$$3a - 4 \text{ subtract} \quad -5a + 2$$
$$3a - 4 \quad - \quad (-5a + 2)$$

Add the opposite of
$(-5a + 2)$, which is $(-1)(-5a + 2)$. ───────→ $3a - 4 \quad + \quad (-1)(-5a + 2)$
Distribute -1. ───────→ $3a - 4 + 5a - 2$
$$8a - 6$$

EXERCISES

PART A

1. Subtract 2 from 5.
2. Subtract -1 from 6.
3. Subtract -5 from -7.
4. Subtract 5 from -8.
5. Subtract 4 from -10.
6. Subtract 7 from 1.
7. Subtract -12 from -3.
8. Subtract -10 from 6.
9. Subtract 17 from -1.
10. Subtract 16 from 5.
11. Subtract -8 from -8.
12. Subtract 7 from -7.
13. Subtract -9 from 9.
14. Subtract 12 from 0.
15. Subtract -19 from 0.
16. Subtract -18 from 15.
17. Subtract -43 from -43.
18. Subtract -58 from 0.

19. Subtract $4x - 3$ from $6x - 4$.
20. Subtract $b - 7$ from $4b + 1$.
21. Subtract -5 from $5y + 3$.
22. Subtract $3x + 7$ from $2x - 5$.
23. Subtract $-2x - 5$ from $x + 4$.
24. Subtract $-4y - 9$ from $-2y + 8$.
25. Subtract $-x - 8$ from $7x + 9$.
26. Subtract $3x - 4$ from $-2x - 1$.
27. Subtract $5a + 3$ from $-7a + 6$.
28. Subtract $-5c - 8$ from $-c - 6$.
29. Subtract $-12y - 1$ from $8y + 2$.
30. Subtract $16z + 3$ from $-7 - 4z$.
31. Subtract $-5x + 3$ from $-1 - x$.
32. Subtract $2y - 9$ from $-y + 18$.
33. Subtract $-7a - 8$ from $-4a - 5$.
34. Subtract $-2y + 9$ from $y - 18$.

PART B

35. Show that $a - b = a + (-1)b$. Justify each step.

Chapter Two Review

Add. [p. 21]

1. $+3 + +7$
2. $+6 + -2$
3. $-5 + +8$
4. $+4 + -9$
5. $-6 + +9$
6. $-7 + 0$
7. $+19 + -3$
8. $+7 + +11$
9. $-3 + -15$

Compute. [p. 36]

10. $-9 + 7 - 3$
11. $6 + 7 - 4$
12. $-8 - 3 + 2$
13. $-16 + 8 - 15$
14. $-5 - 9 + 22$
15. $36 - 21 - 4$

Multiply. [p. 28]

16. $(-9)(+7)$
17. $(+8)(-2)$
18. $(+6)(+4)$
19. $(-21)(-5)$
20. $(0)(-7)$
21. $(-5)(-3)(-5)$

Divide. [p. 31]

22. $\dfrac{+14}{+2}$
23. $\dfrac{-47}{+7}$
24. $\dfrac{+36}{-6}$
25. $-52 \div -4$
26. $+45 \div -9$
27. $(-63 \div +7) \div -3$

Evaluate for the given values of the variables. [p. 40]

28. $5r + 7s$ if $r = 3$, $s = 6$
29. $-2x + 7y$ if $x = 4$, $y = 9$
30. $6x + 7y - 9z$ if $x = 3$, $y = -2$, $z = -5$

Simplify. [p. 42, 44, 48]

31. $3y + 8y + 6y$
32. $x + 5x - 9x$
33. $5d - 8 - d + 6$
34. $-4p + 7 + 13 - p$
35. $c - 9 - 8c + 6 - 3c$
36. $-a + 4 - 6a - 2a - 7 + 9$
37. $6y - 2(3 - 5y)$
38. $-6 + (-3y + 2) - 8y$
39. $-4(6x - 2) - 3x$
40. $-(z - 2) - 8z - 7$

Simplify. Then evaluate the result for the given value of the variable. [p. 44, 48]

41. $5(6x - 7) - 3x$ if $x = 4$
42. $-6k - 8(3k - 2)$ if $k = -5$
43. $-4(3 + 8z) - 5$ if $z = 2$
44. $8x - (1 - 3x)$ if $x = 4$

[p. 50]

45. Subtract 5 from -8.
46. Subtract -9 from 6.
47. Subtract -4 from -1.
48. Subtract $3x - 10$ from $7x + 2$.
49. Subtract $-7a + 8$ from $4a - 2$.

Which property of addition of integers is illustrated? [p. 24]

50. $-2 + -7 = -7 + -2$
51. $0 + x = x$

Chapter Two Test

Add.

1. $+9 + -4$

2. $-6 + -7$

3. $-12 + +7$

Compute.

4. $8 - 3 - 19$

5. $-5 + 12 - 81$

6. $16 - 14 + 5$

Multiply.

7. $(-8)(-2)$

8. $(+7)(-3)$

9. $(-9)(+6)$

10. $(-7)(0)$

11. $(-5)(-9)$

12. $(+8)(+7)(-2)$

Divide.

13. $\dfrac{-24}{+6}$

14. $\dfrac{-18}{-3}$

15. $\dfrac{+42}{-3}$

16. $-9 \div -1$

17. $+56 \div +14$

18. $-72 \div (-8 \div +4)$

Evaluate for the given values of the variables.

19. $6x + 8y$ if $x = 3$, $y = -5$

20. $-7a - 9 + 8b$ if $a = -2$, $b = -8$

Simplify.

21. $-4x - 2x$

22. $6 + 8c - 2c$

23. $5a + 2b - 9 - 3a - 7b$

24. $4z + 8 - z - 3$

25. $-y + 7 - 9y - 8 + 2y$

26. $-5(3x - 2) - 5x$

27. $-4a - 8(2 - 3a) - 9$

28. $4y - (7 - 2y)$

29. $-(7b + 8) - 6b - 2$

30. $4p - (8 - p) + 5 - p$

Simplify. Then evaluate for the given value of the variable.

31. $-5r - 2(6 + 3r)$ if $r = -3$

32. $-(5y - 3) - 7y + 8$ if $y = -9$

33. Subtract -12 from -7.

34. Subtract 4 from -9.

35. Subtract $-8y + 6$ from $5y - 2$.

Which property of addition of integers is illustrated?

36. $(-7 + +3) + -5 = -7 + (+3 + -5)$

37. $+8 + -3 = -3 + +8$

Computer Programs: Flow Charts

An electronic computer has amazing capabilities. We give instructions to a computer by means of a *program.* The program is outlined with a flow chart.

Problem: Write a flow chart to cross from corner *A* to corner *B.*

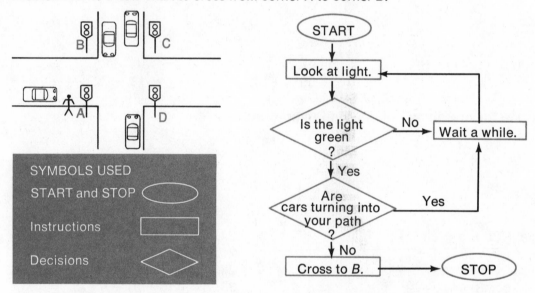

There are two loops in the flow chart. Loops call for instructions to be repeated.

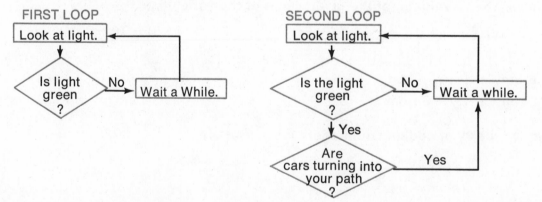

Below is a flow chart to cross from corner *A* to corner *C*. The traffic is eliminated to simplify matters.

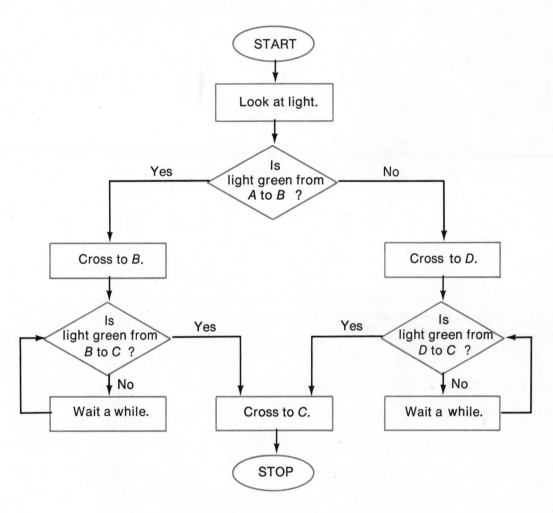

How many loops can you identify in the flow chart above?

Draw a flow chart showing all of the steps for each process.

1. Unlocking a certain door with a choice of three keys.

2. Changing a burnt-out light bulb. (Begin by selecting an unused bulb.)

Open Sentences

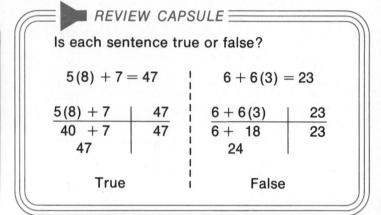

▶ *REVIEW CAPSULE*

Is each sentence true or false?

$$5(8) + 7 = 47 \qquad\qquad 6 + 6(3) = 23$$

$5(8) + 7$	47
$40 + 7$	47
47	

$6 + 6(3)$	23
$6 + 18$	23
24	

True | False

A sentence like $8x + 3 = 35$ is an open sentence.
It contains a variable, x.

EXAMPLE 1 In the sentence $8x + 3 = 35$, replace x with 3.
Is the resulting sentence true or false? Then
replace x with 4. True or false?

Replace x with 3.

$8x + 3$	35
$8(3) + 3$	35
$24 + 3$	
27	

Replace x with 4.

$8x + 3$	35
$8(4) + 3$	35
$32 + 3$	
35	

False | True

EXAMPLE 2 The sentence below is an open English sentence.

Neither true nor false ⟶ It is the shortest month of the year.

Replace "It" with the name of a month to make a
true sentence. Then replace "It" to make a
false sentence.

Replace "It" with any month
except February. ⟶ February is the shortest month of the year. — True
May is the shortest month of the year. — False

A solution of an open sentence is a replacement which makes it true.

EXAMPLE 3

Which members of the replacement set $\{1, 2, 3\}$ are solutions of $4x + 3 = x + 9$?

Replace x with each member of the set $\{1, 2, 3\}$.

Replace x with 1.

$4x + 3$	$x + 9$
$4(1) + 3$	$1 + 9$
$4\ + 3$	10
7	

False

Replace x with 2.

$4x + 3$	$x + 9$
$4(2) + 3$	$2 + 9$
$8\ + 3$	11
11	

True

Replace x with 3.

$4x + 3$	$x + 9$
$4(3) + 3$	$3 + 9$
$12\ + 3$	12
15	

False

2 is the only member of the replacement set which makes the sentence true. ⟶ **Thus,** 2 is the solution of $4x + 3 = x + 9$.

EXAMPLE 4

Which members of the replacement set $\{2, 0, -1, -2\}$ are solutions of $23 - 6c = 15 - 10c$?

Replace c with each member of $\{2, 0, -1, -2\}$

Replace c with 2.

$23 - 6c$	$15 - 10c$
$23 - 6(2)$	$15 - 10(2)$
$23 - \ 12$	$15 - \ 20$
11	-5

False

Replace c with 0.

$23 - 6c$	$15 - 10c$
$23 - 6(0)$	$15 - 10(0)$
$23 - \ 0$	$15 - \ 0$
23	15

False

$(-)(-) = (+)$

Replace c with -1.

$23 - 6c$	$15 - 10c$
$23 - 6(-1)$	$15 - 10(-1)$
$23 + \ 6$	$15 + \ 10$
29	25

False

Replace c with -2.

$23 - 6c$	$15 - 10c$
$23 - 6(-2)$	$15 - 10(-2)$
$23 + \ 12$	$15 + \ 20$
35	35

True

-2 is the only member which makes the sentence true. ⟶ **Thus,** -2 is the solution of $23 - 6c = 15 - 10c$.

ORAL EXERCISES

Which are open sentences?

1. $5x + 6 = 22$

2. $13 = (6)(2) + 1$

3. $14 - 2y = 8$

4. $7(5) + 8 = c$

5. $6x = 9 + 2y$

6. $4 + 9 = 2 + 11$

7. $5(9) - 12 = 17$

8. $8 + 9x = 36$

9. $2(4 + 5) = 20$

10. $3(7 + 2a) = 4$

11. $23 = 3(5) + 8$

12. $8 + 3(7) = 9d$

13. He is president of his class.

14. Texas is the smallest state in the U.S.A.

15. It is the largest planet in the solar system.

For each sentence above which is *not* an open sentence, tell whether it is true or false.

EXERCISES

Part A

Which members of the given replacement set are solutions of the sentence?

1. $6x + 5 = 35$ $\{1, 5\}$

2. $47 = 5y + 7$ $\{4, 8, 12\}$

3. $9 + 4z = 45$ $\{4, 2, 9\}$

4. $22 = 8 + 2d$ $\{7, 8\}$

5. $5r - 1 = 24$ $\{1, 3, 5\}$

6. $29 - 4g = 21$ $\{2, 5, 8\}$

7. $58 - 5x = 13$ $\{3, 4, 9\}$

8. $56 = 29 + 9b$ $\{1, 3, 5, 7\}$

9. $39 = 7y - 10$ $\{4, 7, 10\}$

10. $8r - 38 = 26$ $\{4, 6, 8\}$

11. $12x + 8 = 56$ $\{2, 4, 6, 8\}$

12. $7m - 32 = 31$ $\{1, 5, 9, 10, 12\}$

13. $5 + 6z = 35$ $\{5, 6, 7\}$

14. $68 = 9x - 85$ $\{17, 19, 21\}$

15. $10r = 7r + 21$ $\{3, 7\}$

16. $6a - 48 = 6$ $\{9, 10, 11\}$

17. $8d - 32 = 0$ $\{1, 4, 9\}$

18. $70 = 2y + 56$ $\{5, 7, 9\}$

19. $15 + y = 5y + 3$ $\{3, 4, 5, 6, 7\}$

20. $4x - 3 = 3x - 1$ $\{1, 2, 3, 4, 5\}$

21. $9c - 5 = 7c + 3$ $\{2, 4, 6\}$

22. $2r - 6 = r + 3$ $\{2, 5, 9\}$

23. $18 - 5r = 2r + 4$ $\{1, 2, 3, 4\}$

24. $40 - 9a = 13a - 26$ $\{3, 4, 5\}$

25. $10y - 22 = 8y - 10$ $\{12, 14, 6\}$

26. $4z + 2 = -z + 27$ $\{5, 8, 9\}$

27. $8x - 13 = 21x - 52$ $\{3, 8, 11\}$

28. $5y + 2 = 8y - 10$ $\{1, 2, 4, 8\}$

PART B

Which members of the given replacement set are solutions of the sentence?

29. $7y + 6 = 6 - y$ $\{0, 1, 2\}$

30. $24 - 5t = 19 - 10t$ $\{-3, -2, -1\}$

31. $6d + 7 = 2d + 8$ $\{\frac{1}{2}, \frac{1}{3}, \frac{1}{4}\}$

32. $1 + 5x = 9 - x$ $\{\frac{3}{2}, \frac{4}{3}, \frac{3}{4}\}$

33. $9a - 2 = 3a - 20$ $\{-1, -3, -5\}$

34. $2x + 2 = 4x + 2$ $\{-1, 0, 1, 2\}$

35. $5y + 12 = 3 + y$ $\{1, 2, 3, 4\}$

36. $-8z - 46 = 7z - 1$ $\{-3, -2, -1\}$

37. $8r + 4 = 7 + 2r$ $\{\frac{1}{2}, \frac{1}{3}, \frac{1}{4}\}$

38. $5x + 8 = x - 6$ $\{2, 3, 4, 5, 6\}$

Solving Equations

REVIEW CAPSULE

Additive Inverses, or Opposites

6	−6	$6 + -6 = 0$
−3	3	$-3 + 3 = 0$
x	$-x$	$x + -x = 0$

A sentence with = is an equation. To solve
an equation means to find all of its solutions.
We will assume that the replacement set is the
set of all numbers.

EXAMPLE 1 Add 8 to each side of the equation $n = 3$.
Then find the solution.

The solution of $n = 3$ is 3.

$$\begin{aligned} n &= 3 \\ n + 8 &= 3 + 8 \\ \text{or} \quad n + 8 &= 11 \end{aligned}$$

3 is the solution of both equations.

The solution of $n + 8 = 11$ is 3, since $3 + 8 = 11$.

Example 1 suggests this. ⟶
We can add the same number to each
side of an equation.

Addition Property for Equations

If $a = b$ is true, then $a + c = b + c$ is also true,
for all numbers a, b, and c.

EXAMPLE 2 Multiply each side of the equation $x = 5$
by 2. Then find the solution.

The solution of $x = 5$ is 5.

$$\begin{aligned} x &= 5 \\ 2(x) &= 2(5) \\ 2x &= 10 \end{aligned}$$

5 is the solution of both equations.

The solution of $2x = 10$ is 5, since $2(5) = 10$.

Example 2 suggests this. ⟶
We can multiply each side of an equation by the same number.

Multiplication Property for Equations

If $a = b$ is true, then $a(c) = b(c)$ is also true, for all numbers a, b, and c.

EXAMPLE 3 Divide each side of the equation $7x = 42$ by 7. Is the solution of the resulting equation the same as the solution of $7x = 42$?

$7x = 42$

$\dfrac{7x}{7} = \dfrac{42}{7}$

$\dfrac{7}{7} = 1$ ⟶ $1x = 6$

The solution of $x = 6$ is 6.

$x = 6$

$7x = 42$

The solution of $7x = 42$ is 6, since $7(6) = 42$.

Yes, 6 is the solution of both equations.

Example 3 suggests this. ⟶
We can divide each side of an equation by the same nonzero number.

Division Property for Equations

If $a = b$ is true, then $\dfrac{a}{c} = \dfrac{b}{c}$ is also true, for all numbers, a, b, and c $[c \neq 0]$.

EXAMPLE 4 Solve $3c + 5 = 17$. Then check your solution.

-5 is the additive inverse of 5.

Add -5 to each side. ⟶

$\begin{aligned} 3c + 5 &= 17 \\ -5 \quad &-5 \\ \hline 3c + 0 &= 12 \end{aligned}$ $\left\{\begin{array}{l}\text{Addition Property} \\ \text{for Equations}\end{array}\right.$

Now $3c$ is alone. ⟶

$3c = 12$

Divide each side by 3. ⟶

$\dfrac{3c}{3} = \dfrac{12}{3}$ $\left\{\begin{array}{l}\text{Division Property} \\ \text{for Equations}\end{array}\right.$

$\dfrac{3}{3} = 1$ ⟶

$1c = 4$

Now c is alone. ⟶

$c = 4$

Check. ⟶

Replace c with 4. ⟶

$\begin{array}{c|c} 3c + 5 & 17 \\ 3(4) + 5 & 17 \\ 12 + 5 & \\ 17 & \end{array}$

True

Thus, 4 is the solution of $3c + 5 = 17$.

EXAMPLE 5   Solve $6x - 7 = 11$. Then check your solution.

7 is the additive inverse of -7.
Add 7 to each side. $\longrightarrow$

$$\begin{array}{rl} 6x - 7 = & 11 \\ \underline{+7 \quad +7} & \\ 6x + 0 = & 18 \end{array}$$ $\Big\{$ Addition Property for Equations

Now $6x$ is alone. $\longrightarrow$
Divide each side by 6. $\longrightarrow$

$$\begin{array}{l} 6x = 18 \\ \dfrac{6x}{6} = \dfrac{18}{6} \end{array}$$ $\Big\{$ Division Property for Equations

$$1x = 3$$

Now x is alone. $\longrightarrow$

$$x = 3$$

Check. $\longrightarrow$
Replace x with 3. $\longrightarrow$

$6x - 7$	11
$6(3) - 7$	11
$18 - 7$	
11	

True

Thus, 3 is the solution of $6x - 7 = 11$.

EXAMPLE 6   Solve $8 = -12 - 4a$.

$$8 = -12 - 4a$$

Add 12 to each side. $\longrightarrow$

$$\begin{array}{rl} \underline{+12 \quad +12} & \\ 20 = \quad 0 - 4a \end{array}$$ $\Big\{$ Addition Property for Equations

Now $-4a$ is alone. $\longrightarrow$

$$20 = -4a$$

Divide each side by -4. $\longrightarrow$

$$\dfrac{20}{-4} = \dfrac{-4a}{-4}$$ $\Big\{$ Division Property for Equations

$\dfrac{20}{-4} = -5 \qquad \dfrac{-4}{-4} = 1$

$$-5 = 1a$$

Now a is alone. $\longrightarrow$

$$-5 = a$$

Check -5 in $8 = -12 - 4a$. $\longrightarrow$ **Thus,** -5 is the solution of $8 = -12 - 4a$.

SUMMARY

To solve $ax + b = c$ for x:

$$ax + b = c$$

Add the additive inverse of b to each side. $\longrightarrow$

$$\begin{array}{rl} \underline{-b \quad -b} & \\ ax + 0 = c - b \end{array}$$

Divide each side by a. $\longrightarrow$

$$\dfrac{ax}{a} = \dfrac{c - b}{a}$$

$$x = \dfrac{c - b}{a}$$

ORAL EXERCISES

To solve each equation, what number would you add to each side?
By what number would you divide each side?

1. $2x + 9 = 17$
2. $-8 = 2 + 5z$
3. $-6c + 30 = -6$
4. $14 - 3y = -13$
5. $4d - 7 = -11$
6. $40 - 8x = -16$
7. $7 = 19 + 4c$
8. $3z - 7 = 8$
9. $7y + 20 = 6$
10. $8 = 10d - 32$
11. $-58 - 9r = 14$
12. $62 = 20 + 7x$
13. $4z - 5 = -9$
14. $8p - 42 = 38$
15. $-36 = 10y + 14$
16. $24 = 2 + 11q$
17. $-41 = 12z - 5$
18. $9c + 8 = 8$
19. $10x - 17 = -7$
20. $-16 = 62 + 13y$
21. $15g - 7 = -37$
22. $73 - 20r = -27$
23. $10c - 9 = -9$
24. $87 = 51 - 9b$
25. $5a - 21 = 29$
26. $-32 = 3x - 8$
27. $6 - 2d = -8$
28. $4 + 4p = 48$
29. $-17 = 9r - 8$
30. $8b - 9 = 7$

EXERCISES

PART A

Solve each equation in Exercises 1–30 above.

PART B

EXAMPLE Solve $2x - 8 = -7$.

Add 8 to each side. ⟶

$$2x - 8 = -7$$
$$\underline{+8 \quad +8}$$
$$2x \quad = 1$$

Divide each side by 2. ⟶

$$\frac{2x}{2} = \frac{1}{2}$$

The solution is a fraction. ⟶

$$x = \frac{1}{2}$$

Check on your own. ⟶ **Thus,** $\frac{1}{2}$ is the solution of $2x - 8 = -7$.

Solve.

31. $5r + 8 = 9$
32. $12 = 4y + 9$
33. $8 = 6r + 7$
34. $9 + 3x = 10$
35. $18 = 19 - 8d$
36. $17 = 20 - 4x$
37. $13 - 5z = 11$
38. $17 - 3a = 15$
39. $4x + 19 = 20$
40. $14 - 6y = 9$
41. $8x = 22 - 19$
42. $5 = 9 - 7x$
43. $3x + 9 = 17$
44. $18 - 4x = 9$
45. $12 + 6y = 19$
46. $17 - 8z = 4 + 8$
47. $7x + 9 = 23 - 4$
48. $38 - 25 = 3d + 8$

Slide Ruler for Adding and Subtracting

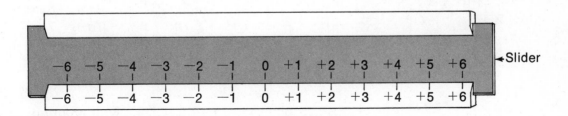

←Slider

Make your own cardboard model of the slide ruler. Use it to add integers.

Place the 0 on the slide over the first number. Read the sum below the second number.

Add 4 + (−3)

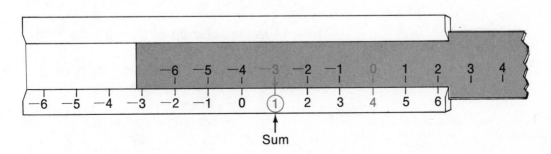

Sum

Subtraction may be done by rewriting the problem as an addition.
2 − 4 means 2 + (− 4).

Use your slide ruler to do the following problems.

1. − 3 + 4	2. 2 + (− 5)	3. − 3 + (− 4)
4. 5 + 2	5. − 6 + 4	6. 6 + (− 4)
7. 5 − 2	8. − 3 − (− 3)	9. 4 − (− 2)
10. − 3 − (− 2)	11. − 6 − 1	12. − 7 − (−3)

Equations: The Variable on Both Sides

<table>
<tr><td>

OBJECTIVE

■ To solve an equation like
$5x - 8 = 3x + 12$

</td><td>

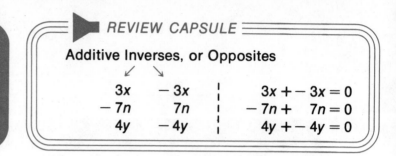

▶ REVIEW CAPSULE

Additive Inverses, or Opposites

$3x$	$-3x$		$3x + -3x = 0$
$-7n$	$7n$		$-7n + 7n = 0$
$4y$	$-4y$		$4y + -4y = 0$

</td></tr>
</table>

EXAMPLE 1 Solve $5n - 4 = 3n + 18$. Check your solution.

$-3n$ is the additive inverse of $3n$.
Add $-3n$ to each side. ────────────▶

Now the variable term is on one
side only. ────────────────────▶

Add 4 to each side. ───────────▶

Divide each side by 2. ─────────────▶

$$
\begin{array}{rl}
5n - 4 = & 3n + 18 \\
-3n & -3n \\
\hline
2n - 4 = & 0 + 18 \\
2n - 4 = & 18 \\
+4 & +4 \\
\hline
2n + 0 = & 22 \\
2n = & 22 \\
\dfrac{2n}{2} = & \dfrac{22}{2} \\
n = & 11
\end{array}
$$

Check.

$5n$ -4	$3n$ $+18$
$5(11) - 4$	$3(11) + 18$
$55 - 4$	$33 + 18$
51	51

Thus, 11 is the solution of $5n - 4 = 3n + 18$.

EXAMPLE 2 Solve the equation in Example 1 by adding
$-5n$, rather than $-3n$, to each side.

$-5n$ is the additive inverse of $5n$.
Add $-5n$ to each side. ───────────▶

Add -18 to each side. ──────────▶

Divide each side by -2. ──────────▶

$$
\begin{array}{rl}
5n - 4 = & 3n + 18 \\
-5n & -5n \\
\hline
-4 = & -2n + 18 \\
-18 & -18 \\
\hline
-22 = & -2n + 0 \\
-22 = & -2n \\
\dfrac{-22}{-2} = & \dfrac{-2n}{-2} \\
11 = & n
\end{array}
$$

Thus, 11 is the solution of $5n - 4 = 3n + 18$.

EXAMPLE 3 Solve $4y - 21 = 9y - 16$.

Add $-9y$ to each side. ⟶

$$
\begin{array}{rcl}
4y - 21 &=& 9y - 16 \\
-9y && -9y \\
\hline
-5y - 21 &=& 0 - 16 \\
-5y - 21 &=& -16
\end{array}
$$

Add 21 to each side. ⟶

$$
\begin{array}{rcl}
& +21 & +21 \\
\hline
-5y + 0 &=& 5 \\
-5y &=& 5
\end{array}
$$

Divide each side by -5. ⟶

$$
\frac{-5y}{-5} = \frac{5}{-5}
$$

$$
y = -1
$$

Check on your own. ⟶ **Thus,** -1 is the solution of $4y - 21 = 9y - 16$.

EXAMPLE 4   Solve $5x - 7 = x + 9$.

x means $1x$. ⟶
Add $-1x$ to each side. ⟶

$$
\begin{array}{rcl}
5x - 7 &=& 1x + 9 \\
-1x && -1x \\
\hline
4x - 7 &=& 0 + 9 \\
4x - 7 &=& 9
\end{array}
$$

Add 7 to each side. ⟶

$$
\begin{array}{rcl}
& +7 & +7 \\
\hline
4x + 0 &=& 16 \\
4x &=& 16
\end{array}
$$

Divide each side by 4. ⟶

$$
\frac{4x}{4} = \frac{16}{4}
$$

$$
x = 4
$$

Check on your own. ⟶ **Thus,** 4 is the solution of $5x - 7 = x + 9$.

EXAMPLE 5   Solve $8x - 12 = 15x - 4x$.

$$
\begin{array}{rcl}
8x - 12 &=& 15x - 4x
\end{array}
$$

$15x - 4x = 11x$ ⟶
Add $-11x$ to each side. ⟶

$$
\begin{array}{rcl}
8x - 12 &=& 11x \\
-11x && -11x \\
\hline
-3x - 12 &=& 0
\end{array}
$$

Add 12 to each side. ⟶

$$
\begin{array}{rcl}
& +12 & +12 \\
\hline
-3x + 0 &=& 12 \\
-3x &=& 12
\end{array}
$$

Divide each side by -3. ⟶

$$
\frac{-3x}{-3} = \frac{12}{-3}
$$

$$
x = -4
$$

Check on your own. ⟶ **Thus,** -4 is the solution of $8x - 12 = 15x - 4x$.

EXERCISES

Solve.

1. $5x + 6 = 2x + 15$
2. $6y - 8 = 20 + 2y$
3. $5 + 9x = 7x + 11$
4. $3z + 10 = 2 + 5z$
5. $4a - 9 = 3a - 1$
6. $21r - 26 = 8r - 13$
7. $2x - 12 = x + 3$
8. $5d + 11 = 8d - 7$
9. $-x + 22 = 4x + 2$
10. $6c - 20 = 2c$
11. $9e + 14 = 11e$
12. $7c = -24 + c$
13. $8y + 11 = 7y$
14. $17x - 8 = 5x + 4$
15. $3y = 15y - 72$
16. $7 + 11z = 97 - 7z$
17. $18 - 9x = 2x + 7$
18. $3r - 2 = -9 + 2r$
19. $10g - 22 = 8g - 14$
20. $7z + 8 = -16 + 3z$
21. $x - 3 = 22 - 4x$
22. $20x - 16x = 6x - 8$
23. $5x - 2x = 24 - 9x$
24. $13x - 4x = 10x - 21$
25. $-x + 3x = 6 + x$
26. $4y - 3y = 18 - 2y$
27. $4z - 5z = -28 + 3z$
28. $27 - 6y = 4y - 7y$
29. $3x + 8 = 2x - x$
30. $x + x + 18 = 30$
31. $2y + 5y + 3 = 10y$
32. $8 + 2x = 5x - 13$
33. $25 - 4y = 1 + 4y$
34. $13x + 11 = 10x - 7$
35. $7x - 8x = 4 - 2x$
36. $13y - 4y = -14 + 2y$

PART B

EXAMPLE   Solve $7x + 8 = 5 + 3x$.

$$7x + 8 = 5 + 3x$$

Add $-3x$ to each side. $\longrightarrow$ $4x + 8 = 5$

Add -8 to each side. $\longrightarrow$ $4x = -3$

Divide each side by 4. $\longrightarrow$ $x = \frac{-3}{4}$

Thus, $\frac{-3}{4}$ is the solution.

Solve.

37. $7x + 6 = 9 + 8x$
38. $3y + 9 = -2y + 7$
39. $y + 6 = 7 - 3y$
40. $-6a - 15 = -17 - 9a$
41. $2 + 6c = -1 + 11c$
42. $10x - 5 = -9 + 3x$
43. $2x + 13 = -4x + 18$
44. $-11 + 4x = -13 - 3x$
45. $12 - 5y = 7 - y$
46. $13z - 3 = 8z + 6$
47. $2y - 15 = -3y - 22$
48. $a + 11 = -2a + 7$

PART C

Solve.

49. $3x + x - 2 = 7 - 2x$
50. $7c + 4 - c = 2c - 3$
51. $6a + 8 = 19 + 9a + 7 - 15a$
52. $-4 - d + 2d = 3 + 4d$
53. $8y + 7 = 22 - y + 3y$
54. $3x + 6x + 2 = 4x - 3 - 2x$

Groups

Test Case: Let the **integers** be the set and **addition** the operation.

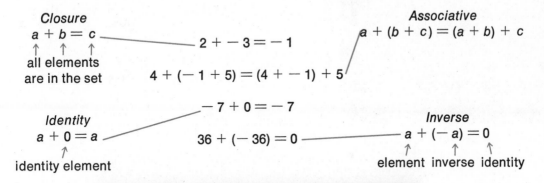

Closure	*Associative*
$a + b = c$	$a + (b + c) = (a + b) + c$

all elements
are in the set

$2 + -3 = -1$

$4 + (-1 + 5) = (4 + -1) + 5$

$-7 + 0 = -7$

Identity
$a + 0 = a$

identity element

$36 + (-36) = 0$

Inverse
$a + (-a) = 0$

element inverse identity

An operation on a set forms a group if
• the set is closed under the operation
• the operation is associative
• there is an identity element
• every element has an inverse

We have not proved that the integers form a group under addition,
but we can think of no case where the four conditions do not hold.

A group is a COMMUTATIVE GROUP if the operation is commutative.

Which do you think form groups? Commutative groups?

1. The odd numbers under addition

2. The odd numbers under
   multiplication *

3. The even numbers under addition

4. The even numbers under
   multiplication *

5. Three-minute clock arithmetic
   under addition

6. Three-minute clock arithmetic
   under multiplication *

Note: for multiplication, the zero element does not have to have an
inverse to form a group.

Equations with Parentheses

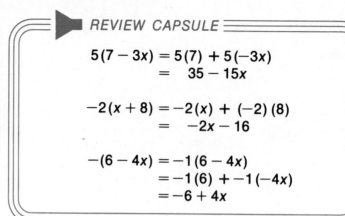

▶ *REVIEW CAPSULE*

$$5(7 - 3x) = 5(7) + 5(-3x)$$
$$= 35 - 15x$$

$$-2(x + 8) = -2(x) + (-2)(8)$$
$$= -2x - 16$$

$$-(6 - 4x) = -1(6 - 4x)$$
$$= -1(6) + -1(-4x)$$
$$= -6 + 4x$$

EXAMPLE 1   Solve $10x - 3(5 - 3x) = 23$. Then check your solution.

Check.

			$10x - 3(5 - 3x)$	23

Remove parentheses first. ⟶

$10x + 9x = 19x$ ⟶

Add 15 to each side. ⟶

Divide each side by 19. ⟶

$$10x - 3(5 - 3x) = 23$$
$$10x - 15 + 9x = 23$$
$$19x - 15 = 23$$
$$\underline{+15 \quad +15}$$
$$19x \qquad = 38$$
$$x = 2$$

$$10(2) - 3[5 - 3(2)] \quad | \quad 23$$
$$20 - 3(5 - 6)$$
$$20 - 3(-1)$$
$$20 + 3$$
$$23$$

Thus, 2 is the solution.

EXAMPLE 2   Solve $7x - (9 - 4x) = 3(x - 11)$.

Remove parentheses. ⟶

$7x + 4x = 11x$ ⟶

Add $-3x$ to each side. ⟶

Add 9 to each side. ⟶

Divide each side by 8. ⟶

$$7x - (9 - 4x) = 3(x - 11)$$
$$7x - 1(9 - 4x) = 3(x - 11)$$
$$7x - 9 + 4x = 3x - 33$$
$$11x - 9 = 3x - 33$$
$$\underline{-3x \qquad -3x}$$
$$8x - 9 = -33$$
$$\underline{+9 \qquad +9}$$
$$8x \quad = -24$$
$$x = -3$$

Check on your own. ⟶ **Thus,** −3 is the solution.

EXERCISES

PART A

Solve.

1. $4(x - 2) = 20$
3. $-5(x + 4) = 15$
5. $5(z - 6) = 10$
7. $2(2s + 3) = -18$
9. $y - (8 - y) = 32$ *20*
11. $20 - (8 + x) = -(1 - x) + 29$
13. $5z + 10(-z + 14) = 95$
15. $2(c + 3) + 5c = 15 - (2c + 18)$
17. $(x + 4) - (x - 6) = 5(x - 8)$
19. $3y - (4 - 2y) = 3(y + 2)$
21. $2(2 - 3z) = 8 - 2(4z + 5)$
23. $5 - 3(4 - 2x) = 4(x - 3) - 3$
25. $7y - 2(3 - y) = 4(y + 1)$
27. $2(3 - z) = 16 - 2(3 + 2z)$
29. $3 + 7(x + 1) = 6 - (5 + 2x)$
31. $-2(3 - 4z) + 7z = 13z - 4$
33. $5 - (x + 8) + 6x = 4(x + 2)$
35. $-(2x + 6) + 3x = 1 + 2(4 - 2x)$
37. $6y + 3(4 - y) = 8 - 2(y + 3)$
39. $16 - 4(2a + 1) = 6a + (1 - 3a)$

2. $2(5 + x) = 22$
4. $8 - 4(y - 1) = -36$
6. $3(c - 1) + 8 = -10$
8. $-4(2x + 6) = 16$
10. $(50 - x) - (3x + 2) = 0$
12. $3c + 2(c + 2) = 13 - (2c - 5)$
14. $x + (x + 1) + (x + 2) = 15$
16. $5d - (d + 3) = (d + 2) + 7$
18. $4 + 7x = -(3 - 2x) - 3x$
20. $6(x + 2) = 4 - (3 - 2x) - 1$
22. $7y - (4 - 2y) = 3(y + 3) - 1$
24. $2(x + 1) + 15x = -(3x - 17) + 5x$
26. $7(x - 1) + 5 = -2(3 - 4x) + 5$
28. $8y - 3(4 - 2y) = 6(y + 1) - 2$
30. $7(a - 1) + 4 = -(2a - 4) + 6a + 2$
32. $-4(2x - 5) + 3x = x - 28$
34. $7 - 3(y + 1) + 8 = 4 - 5(y - 2)$
36. $5 - 3(x + 1) = -(x - 9) + 5x$
38. $-(6 - 4c) + 3c = 10 - 2(c - 1)$
40. $7 - 2(4 - 3x) + 8x = -(x + 31)$

PART B

Solve.

41. $7(2x - 2) - 5x = 4x + 2$
43. $-5y - 2(y + 4) = 6y - 9$
45. $3(-2x + 1) = 4(1 + 3x) + 2$
47. $7(1 - 3a) + a = 6 - (a - 4)$
49. $9 - 4(2 - y) = 7y - (3 + y)$
51. $5z + 3(z - 2) - 6z = 12$

42. $4z - 3 - 7(z + 1) = 6z$
44. $8y + 5(1 - y) = 4y - 6$
46. $5r + 3(r - 7) = -(r + 8)$
48. $2z - 8(z + 1) = 6z + (3z - 4)$
50. $6(r - 2) - 3r - 1 = 8(5r + 1) - 10r$
52. $-3(6 - 2x) + 4x = -(2x - 8)$

PART C

Solve.

53. $6[5 - 3(x - 4)] = 4x + 18$
55. $-7x - [2(3x + 1) + 4] = 3x$
57. $-[-7 + 2(1 - 2x)] = 1 - 5x$

54. $3 - 2x = -[4 + 5(2x - 1)]$
56. $-2[4 - (2 + 3x)] = 4x + 5$
58. $4x - 2[5(x + 1) + 3] = 8x$

English Phrases to Algebra

REVIEW CAPSULE

English phrase: 6 decreased by 2

Mathematical terms: 6   −   2
6 decreased by 2 means 6 made
smaller by 2, or 6 − 2

English phrase: 8 increased by 3

Mathematical terms: 8   +   3
8 increased by 3 means 8 made
greater by 3, or 8 + 3

EXAMPLE 1   Write in mathematical terms.

Diminished by means decreased by.
Use −.

7 diminished by 5   9 increased by 4

7   −   5   9   +   4

EXAMPLE 2   Write in mathematical terms.

3 decreased by x

The value of *x* is not known.

3   −   x

EXAMPLE 3   Write in mathematical terms.

Let a variable represent the number.

12 increased by 4 times a number

12   +   (4) (*y*), or 12 + 4*y*

EXAMPLE 4   Write in mathematical terms.

7 less than 10

7 less than 10 does not mean 7 − 10.
It means 10 − 7.

10   −   7

EXAMPLE 5   Write in mathematical terms.

9 more than 5 means 5 made greater by 9.

9 more than 5

5   +   9

EXAMPLE 6

Write in mathematical terms.

5 less than 3 times a number

Let *n* represent the number.

(3) (*n*)   −   5, or $3n - 5$

EXAMPLE 7   Write in mathematical terms.

8 more than twice *x*

Twice *x* means 2 times *x*.

(2) (*x*)   +   8, or $2x + 8$

EXERCISES

PART A

Write in mathematical terms.

1. 8 decreased by 5
2. 9 increased by 7
3. 12 diminished by 6
4. 8 less than 15
5. 2 more than 23
6. 15 decreased by *x*
7. *y* increased by 4
8. 7 more than *x*
9. 8 less than *n*
10. 8 diminished by twice *x*
11. 3 more than 5 times *y*
12. 7 times a number, decreased by 2
13. 6 less than 3 times a number
14. 5 diminished by twice *n*
15. 25 decreased by 4 times a number
16. 8 more than 7 times a number
17. 4 times *x*, increased by 8
18. 12 less than 3 times a number
19. 14 increased by twice a number
20. 2 times *n*, decreased by 4
21. 9 times a number, diminished by 7
22. twice a number, increased by 1

PART B

Write in mathematical terms.

23. *x* increased by *y*
24. *x* more than *y*
25. 7 times *x*, decreased by twice *y*
26. *m* less than 3 times *n*
27. 9 more than *x* times *y*
28. *m* times *n* less than 20
29. *y* diminished by 5 times *x*
30. 6 times *x*, increased by 5 times *y*
31. 5 increased by 8 more than 7 times *y*
32. 7 more than twice a number, increased by 6
33. 2 less than 5 times a number, increased by 9
34. *x* more than 8 times *y*, decreased by twice *x*

Number Problems

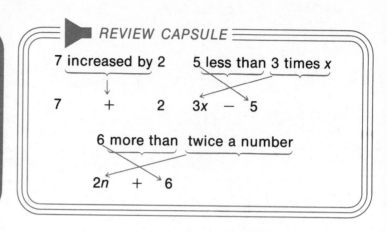

▶ *REVIEW CAPSULE*

7 increased by 2   5 less than 3 times x

7   +   2 $3x$ − 5

6 more than twice a number

$2n$ +   6

EXAMPLE 1   Write an equation for each sentence.

Three more than a number is 9.

$$n + 3 = 9$$

A number decreased by 7 is 8 times the number.

$$n - 7 = 8n$$

EXAMPLE 2   Seven more than 4 times a number is 31. Find the number.

Let n = the number

7 more than 4 times n is 31.

Write an equation. ⟶
Add −7 to each side. ⟶

Divide each side by 4. ⟶

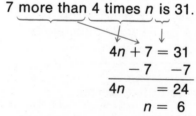

$$4n + 7 = 31$$
$$\underline{\quad -7 \quad -7}$$
$$4n \quad\;\; = 24$$
$$n = 6$$

Check 6 in the problem. ⟶

7 more than 4 times 6 is 31.

4 (6) + 7	31
24 + 7	
31	

Thus, the number is 6.

EXAMPLE 3   A number decreased by 14 is the same as 8 times the number. Find the number.

Let n = the number

n decreased by 14 is the same as 8 times n.

Write an equation. $\longrightarrow$

$n = 1n$ $\longrightarrow$

Add $-1n$ to each side. $\longrightarrow$

Divide each side by 7. $\longrightarrow$

$$
\begin{array}{rcl}
n - 14 &=& 8n \\
1n - 14 &=& 8n \\
-1n & & -1n \\
\hline
-14 &=& 7n \\
-2 &=& n
\end{array}
$$

Check -2 in the problem. $\longrightarrow$

n decreased by 14 is 8 times n.

$-2 - 14$	$8\,(-2)$
-16	-16

Thus, the number is -2.

EXAMPLE 4   Three less than twice a number is the same as the number increased by 8. Find the number.

Let x = the number

Twice x is $2x$.

3 less than $2x$ is the same as x increased by 8.

$$
\begin{array}{rcl}
2x - 3 &=& x + 8 \\
2x - 3 &=& 1x + 8 \\
-1x & & -1x \\
\hline
1x - 3 &=& 8 \\
+3 & & +3 \\
\hline
x &=& 11
\end{array}
$$

$1x = x$ $\longrightarrow$

Check 11 in the problem. $\longrightarrow$ **Thus,** the number is 11.

EXAMPLE 5   A number increased by 6 times the number is -63. Find the number.

Let n = the number

$$
\begin{array}{rcl}
n + 6n &=& -63 \\
7n &=& -63 \\
n &=& -9
\end{array}
$$

$n + 6n = 1n + 6n = 7n$ $\longrightarrow$

Check -9 in the problem. $\longrightarrow$ **Thus,** the number is -9.

ORAL EXERCISES

Give an equation for each sentence.

1. Five more than twice *x* is 14.
2. Six decreased by 4 times *n* is 18.
3. Seven times *n* is 3 more than *n*.
4. Two less than a number is 20.
5. Eight more than twice a number is 2.
6. The sum of *x* and 6 is 8 times *x*.
7. Two diminished by 4 times *x* is 15.
8. Twelve is 5 more than 6 times *x*.
9. Sixteen less than twice *x* is 32.
10. Nine increased by 5 times *n* is 18.

EXERCISES

PART A

1. Nine more than a number is 13. Find the number.
2. A number decreased by 10 is 16. Find the number.
3. Eleven increased by twice a number is 17. Find the number.
4. Eight less than 5 times a number is 22. Find the number.
5. Twelve diminished by 3 times a number is 9. Find the number.
6. Three more than 8 times a number is -29. Find the number.
7. Sixteen is 5 less than 7 times a number. Find the number.
8. Thirteen increased by 9 times a number is 4. Find the number.
9. Ten less than twice a number is the same as 7 times the number. Find the number.
10. A number increased by 30 is 14 decreased by 3 times the number. Find the number.
11. Nine more than 5 times a number is the same as 2 times the number. Find the number.
12. Twice a number is the same as 6 more than 8 times the number. Find the number.
13. Seven less than 6 times a number is the same as the number decreased by 2. Find the number.
14. Five times a number is the same as 30 more than 8 times the number. Find the number.
15. Two less than 2 times a number is the same as the number decreased by 38. Find the number.
16. A number increased by 5 is the same as 37 decreased by 7 times the number. Find the numbers.
17. Eight times a number decreased by the number is 35. Find the number.
18. Twice a number plus 4 times the number is -54. Find the number.
19. A number plus 3 more than the number is 17. Find the number.
20. Six more than a number increased by the number is 40. Find the number.
21. Seven times a number decreased by the number is -48. Find the number.
22. Five less than 3 times a number is -20. Find the number.
23. Eight times a number is the same as 30 less than 5 times the number. Find the number.
24. Three less than 3 times a number is the same as 5 less than twice the number. Find the number.

PART B

EXAMPLE   Three times the sum of a number and 2 is the same as 8 increased by the number. Find the number.

Let x = the number

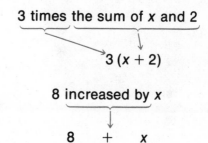

3 times the sum of x and 2

$3(x + 2)$

8 increased by x

8   + x

$3(x + 2)$ is the same as $8 + x$

$$3(x + 2) = 8 + x$$

Remove parentheses. ⟶ $3x + 6 = 8 + x$
Add $-1x$ to each side. ⟶ $2x + 6 = 8$
Add -6 to each side. ⟶ $2x = 2$
Divide each side by 2. $x = 1$

Check 1 in the problem. ⟶ **Thus,** the number is 1.

---

25. Five times the sum of a number and 2 is 45. Find the number.

26. Six times the sum of a number and -4 is 30. Find the number.

27. Five more than a number is 4 times the sum of the number and 8. Find the number.

28. Three times the sum of 4 and a number is the same as 18 increased by the number. Find the number.

29. Twice the sum of 6 and a number is the same as 15 decreased by the number. Find the number.

30. Eight more than three times a number is the same as twice the number decreased by 6. Find the number.

PART C

31. If 6 times the sum of twice a number and 8 is decreased by 4, the result is 1 less than 3 times the sum of the number and 6. Find the number.

32. If 15 is decreased by 7 times the sum of 5 and 3 times a number, the result is 12 more than twice the sum of the number and 7. Find the number.

More Number Problems

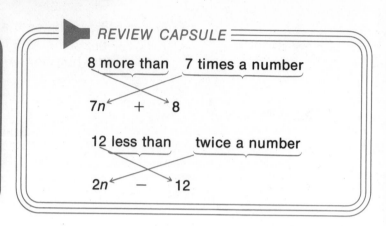

REVIEW CAPSULE

8 more than   7 times a number

$7n$ $+$ 8

12 less than   twice a number

$2n$ $-$ 12

EXAMPLE 1   Clyde is thinking of two numbers. The second number is 5 more than twice the first. Repesent the two numbers.

5 more than twice the first ⟶

Let f = first number
$2f + 5$ = second number

Thus, f and $2f + 5$ represent the two numbers.

EXAMPLE 2   The greater of two numbers is 8 less than 4 times the smaller. Represent the two numbers.

Let s = smaller number
$4s - 8$ = greater number

Thus, s and $4s - 8$ represent the two numbers.

EXAMPLE 3   The second of three numbers is 6 times the first. The third is 1 more than the second. Represent the three numbers.

6 times the first ⟶
1 more than the second ⟶

Let f = first number
$6f$ = second number
$6f + 1$ = third number

Thus, f, $6f$, and $6f + 1$ represent the three numbers.

EXAMPLE 4　The greater of two numbers is 12 more than 8 times the smaller. Their sum is 21. Find the numbers.

Represent the two numbers.

Let s = smaller number
$8s + 12$ = greater number

Smaller + greater = 21. ————————→
Write an equation and solve it.

$$s + (8s + 12) = 21$$
$$9s + 12 = 21$$
$$9s = 9$$
$$s = 1$$

Find both numbers.

Smaller number, s is 1.
Greater number, $8s + 12$ is $8(1) + 12$, or 20.

Check 1 and 20 in the first part of the problem.

Greater is 12 more than 8 times smaller.	
20	$8(1) + 12$
20	20

Check 1 and 20 in the second part of the problem. }

Their sum is 21.	
$1 + 20$	21
21	

Thus, 1 and 20 are the two numbers.

EXAMPLE 5　Find two numbers whose sum is 24 if the second is 16 less than 3 times the first.

Let f = first number
$3f - 16$ = second number

First + second = 24. ————————→

$$f + (3f - 16) = 24$$
$$4f - 16 = 24$$
$$4f = 40$$
$$f = 10$$

Find both numbers. $3(10) - 16 = 30 - 16$, } or 14

First number, f is 10.
Second number, $3f - 16$ is $3(10) - 16$, or 14.

Check. ————————————→

The sum is 24.	
$10 + 14$	24
24	

Second is 16 less than 3 times first.	
14	$3(10) - 16$
	14

Thus, 10 and 14 are the two numbers.

EXAMPLE 6 Separate $90 into two parts so that the first part is $30 less than twice the second part.

First is 30 less than twice second.
Their sum is 90. ──────────→

Let s = second part
$2s - 30$ = first part

$$s + (2s - 30) = 90$$
$$3s - 30 = 90$$
$$3s = 120$$
$$s = 40$$

Find both parts.
$2(40) - 30 = 80 - 30$, or 50

Second part, s is 40.
First part, $2s - 30$ is $2(40) - 30$, or 50

Thus, $50 and $40 are the two parts.

ORAL EXERCISES

Represent the two numbers in mathematical terms.

1. The second of two numbers is 7 more than 4 times the first.
2. The greater of two numbers is 6 less than 3 times the smaller.
3. The second of two numbers is 8 less than twice the first.
4. The smaller of two numbers is 21 less than twice the greater.
5. The second of two numbers is 6 more than 5 times the first.
6. The second of two numbers is 8 more than twice the first.
7. The greater of two numbers exceeds 3 times the smaller by 9.
8. The first of two numbers exceeds 4 times the second by 1.

EXERCISES

PART A

1. The second of two numbers is 5 times the first. Their sum is 42. Find the numbers.
2. The greater of two numbers is 3 more than twice the smaller. Their sum is 24. Find the numbers.
3. The sum of two numbers is 50. The first is 5 less than 4 times the second. Find the numbers.
4. Find two numbers whose sum is 55 if the second is 7 more than 5 times the first.
5. The greater of two numbers is 9 more than the smaller. Their sum is 83. Find the numbers.
6. The sum of two numbers is 19. The second is 8 less than twice the first. Find the numbers.
7. The greater of two numbers is 12 less than 4 times the smaller. Their sum is 23. Find the numbers.
8. Find two numbers whose sum is 62 if the greater is 10 more than 3 times the smaller.

9. Sixty-eight students are separated into two groups. The first group is 3 times as large as the second. How many students are in each group?

10. Separate $115 into two parts so that the greater part is $12 more than the smaller part.

11. Separate $89 into two parts so that the second part is $4 less than twice the first part.

12. Separate 43 people into two groups so that the first group is 5 less than 3 times the second.

13. The sum of three numbers is 34. The first is 3 less than the second, while the third is 4 more than the second. Find the numbers.

14. The sum of three numbers is 26. The second number is twice the first, and the third is 6 more than the second. Find the numbers.

PART B

EXAMPLE   The smaller of two numbers is 3 less than the greater. If the greater is decreased by twice the smaller, the result is -5. Find the numbers.

Let g = greater number
$g - 3$ = smaller number
greater decreased by twice smaller is -5

$$g \qquad - \qquad 2(g - 3) \quad = -5$$

$-2(g - 3) = -2g + 6 \longrightarrow$

$$g - 2g + 6 = -5$$
$$1g - 2g + 6 = -5$$
$$-1g + 6 = -5$$
$$-1g = -11$$
$$g = 11$$

Greater number, g is 11.
Smaller number, $g - 3$ is $11 - 3$, or 8.
Thus, the numbers are 11 and 8.

15. The greater of two numbers is 3 more than the smaller. If twice the smaller is added to the greater, the result is 30. Find the numbers.

16. The second of two numbers is 4 more than the first. If the second is increased by 1, the result is twice the first. Find the numbers.

17. The first of two numbers is twice the second. Seven more than the second number is equal to the first number decreased by 6. Find the numbers.

18. The greater of two numbers is 7 more than the smaller. Twice the smaller plus 3 times the larger is 46. Find the numbers.

19. The second of two numbers is 3 more than the first. If 4 times the first is increased by the second, the result is 73. Find the numbers.

20. The greater of two numbers is 6 more than the smaller. Three times the smaller plus 5 more than the larger is 95. Find the numbers.

Coin Problems

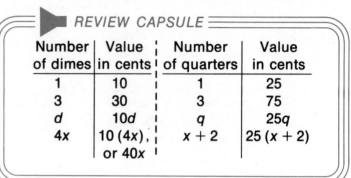

REVIEW CAPSULE

Number of dimes	Value in cents	Number of quarters	Value in cents
1	10	1	25
3	30	3	75
d	$10d$	q	$25q$
$4x$	$10(4x)$, or $40x$	$x + 2$	$25(x + 2)$

EXAMPLE 1   Find the total value in cents.
3 nickels and 7 dimes

$$\text{Total value} = 3(5) + 7(10)$$
$$= 15 \quad + 70, \quad \text{or } 85 \text{ cents}$$

EXAMPLE 2   Represent the total value in cents.
d dimes and q quarters

Number of coins ————————→

Value in cents ————————→

	Dimes	Quarters
Number	d	q
Value	$10d$	$25q$

Thus, the total value in cents is $10d + 25q$.

EXAMPLE 3   Represent the total value in cents.
x quarters and $15 - x$ nickels

	Quarters	Nickels
Number	x	$15 - x$
Value	$25x$	$5(15 - x)$

$$\text{Total value} = 25x + 5(15 - x)$$
$$= 25x + 75 - 5x$$
$$= 20x + 75$$

Thus, the total value in cents is $20x + 75$.

EXAMPLE 4 Eleanor had three times as many quarters as nickels. She had $1.60 in all. How many nickels and how many quarters did she have?

	Nickels	Quarters
Number	n	$3n$
Value	$5n$	$25(3n)$

Let n = number of nickels
$3n$ = number of quarters

$1.60 = 160 cents
total value = 160 cents

$$5n + 25(3n) = 160$$
$$5n + \quad 75n = 160$$
$$80n = 160$$
$$n = 2$$

Find both numbers.

Number of nickels, n is 2.
Number of quarters, $3n$ is 3(2), or 6.

Check 2 and 6 in the first part of the problem.

Number of quarters is 3 times number of dimes.

6	3(2)
	6

Check 2 and 6 in the second part of the problem.

Total value	is 160 cents.
5(2) + 25(6)	160
10 + 150	
160	

Thus, she had 2 nickels and 6 quarters.

EXAMPLE 5 Paul had 23 coins in nickels and dimes. Their total value was $1.55. How many were nickels and how many were dimes?

	Nickels	Dimes
Number	n	$23 - n$
Value	$5n$	$10(23 - n)$

23 coins in all.
Let n = number of nickels
$23 - n$ = number of dimes

$1.55 = 155 cents
total value = 155 cents

$$5n + 10(23 - n) \quad = 155$$
$$5n + \quad 230 - 10n = 155$$
$$230 - 5n \quad = 155$$
$$-5n \quad = -75$$
$$n = 15$$

Find both numbers.

Number of nickels, n is 15.
Number of dimes, $23 - n$ is $23 - 15$, or 8.

Check 15 and 8 in the problem.

Thus, he had 15 nickels and 8 dimes.

EXERCISES

1. A coin collection of nickels and dimes amounts to $.90. There are 4 times as many nickels as dimes. How many coins of each kind are there?

2. The value of the half dollars and quarters in a cash box is $5.75. There are 16 coins in all. How many of each kind of coin are in the box?

3. In changing a $1 bill, Ted received 3 more dimes than quarters. How many quarters did he receive?

4. Chris had 5 times as many nickels as quarters. Their value was $1.50. How many nickels did she have?

5. A cash drawer contains $138 in $1 and $5 bills. There are 6 more $5 bills than $1 bills. How many of each are there?

6. Bill had $1.19 in pennies and nickels. He had 7 more nickels than pennies. How many of each did he have?

7. Jim had 11 coins in dimes and quarters. Their value was $1.70. How many of each did he have?

8. A collection of 24 dimes and half dollars amounts to $3.60. How many dimes are there?

9. Maria has only quarters and nickels in her coin collection. She has 39 coins which total $5.15. How many are quarters and how many are nickels?

10. A cash drawer contains $187 in $1 and $5 bills. There are 7 more $1 bills than $5 bills. How many of each are there?

PART B

11. For a school play, 738 tickets values at $856 were sold. Some cost $1 and some cost $1.50. How many $1 tickets were sold?

12. A parking meter which takes only dimes and quarters contains $6.25. The number of dimes is 2 more than 3 times the number of quarters. How many of each are there?

13. John had 6 times as many dimes as nickels, and 2 more pennies than dimes. He had $2.15 in all. How many of each kind of coin did he have?

14. Mary had $3.41. She had 2 more dimes than half dollars and 3 times as many pennies as dimes. How many pennies did she have?

PART C

15. A coin box contains $17.17 in pennies, nickels, dimes, and quarters. There are 5 more nickels than pennies, twice as many dimes as nickels, and 2 more quarters than dimes. How many of each coin are in the box?

16. In changing a $5 bill, Marge received 9 more dimes than nickels and 7 fewer quarters than dimes. How many of each coin did she receive?

Number Mysteries

Ask a friend to do the following.

1. Choose a number.
2. Add 2.
3. Multiply by 8.
4. Subtract 10.
5. Divide by 2.
6. Add 9.
7. Divide by 4.
8. Give the result.

Can you tell your friend what number he started with?

1. Let x be the number.
2. Add 2. $x + 2$
3. Multiply by 8. $8x + 16$
4. Subtract 10. $8x + 6$
5. Divide by 2. $4x + 3$
6. Add 9. $4x + 12$
7. Divide by 4. $x + 3$
8. Give the result. $x + 3$

The result will always be 3 more than the starting number.

Now try this. Explain how to find the mystery number.

1. Choose a mystery number.
2. Double it.
3. Add 6.
4. Add the mystery number.
5. Divide by 3.
6. Give the result.

Make up your own number mysteries.

Perimeter Problems

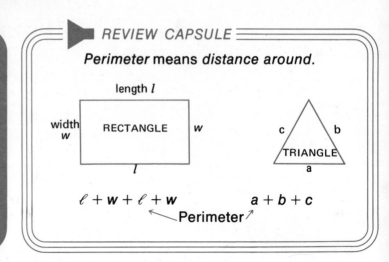

REVIEW CAPSULE

Perimeter means *distance around.*

$$\ell + w + \ell + w \qquad a + b + c$$

← Perimeter ↗

EXAMPLE 1 The length of a rectangle is 5 feet greater than the width. The perimeter is 38 feet. Find the length and the width.

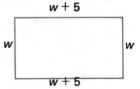

Let w = width

Length is 5 greater than width. ⟶ $w + 5$ = length

Formula for perimeter ⟶
Substitute $w + 5$ for ℓ. ⟶

$$2\ell + 2w = \text{perimeter}$$
$$2(w + 5) + 2w = 38$$
$$2w + 10 + 2w = 38$$
$$4w + 10 = 38$$
$$4w = 28$$
$$w = 7$$

Width, w is 7.
Length, $w + 5$ is $7 + 5$, or 12.

● Check 7 and 12 in the problem.

Length is 5 greater than width.

12	7 + 5
12	12

Perimeter   is 38.

2(12) + 2(7)	38
38	

Thus, the length is 12 feet and the width is 7 feet.

EXAMPLE 2 The length of a rectangle is 8 yards more than 6 times the width. The perimeter is 156 yards. Find the length and the width.

$$6w + 8$$

$$\text{Let } w = \text{width}$$
$$6w + 8 = \text{length}$$

w [rectangle] w

$$6w + 8$$

$$2\ell + 2w = \text{perimeter}$$

Substitute $6w + 8$ for ℓ. ⟶

$$2(6w + 8) + 2w = 156$$
$$12w + 16 + 2w = 156$$
$$14w + 16 = 156$$
$$14w = 140$$
$$w = 10$$

Check.
Perimeter $= 2\ell + 2w$
$= 2(68) + 2(10)$
$= 136 + 20$
$= 156$ yards

Width, w is 10.
Length, $6w + 8$ is $6(10) + 8$, or 68.

Thus, the length is 68 yd and the width is 10 yd.

EXAMPLE 3 Side b of a triangle is twice as long as side c. Side a is 3 meters longer than side b. The perimeter is 48 meters. Find the length of each side.

$$\text{Let } c = \text{side } c$$
$$2c = \text{side } b$$
$$2c + 3 = \text{side } a$$

It is easy to represent a and b in terms of c.

c ... b $(2c)$

a
$(2c + 3)$

$$a + b + c = \text{perimeter}$$

$$(2c + 3) + 2c + c = 48$$
$$5c + 3 = 48$$
$$5c = 45$$
$$c = 9$$

Side c is 9.
Side b, $2c$ is $2(9)$, or 18.
Side a, $2c + 3$ is $2(9) + 3$, or 21.

Check.
Perimeter $= a + b + c$
$= 21 + 18 + 9$
$= 48$ meters

Thus, the lengths of the sides are 21 meters, 18 meters, and 9 meters.

EXERCISES

1. The length of a rectangle is 6 ft greater than the width. The perimeter is 40 ft. Find the length and the width.

2. The length of a rectangle is twice the width. The perimeter is 42 cm. Find the length and the width.

3. The length of a rectangle is 3 ft more than twice the width. The perimeter is 54 ft. Find the length and the width.

4. The length of a rectangle is 2 ft less than 3 times the width. The perimeter is 68 yd. Find the length and the width.

5. Side x of a triangle is 2 ft longer than side y. Side z is 5 ft shorter than twice side y. The perimeter is 49 ft. Find the length of each side.

6. The perimeter of a triangle is 40 ft. The first side is twice the second. The third side is 5 more than the first. Find the length of each side.

7. The perimeter of a triangle is 38 in. The first side is 3 in. less than the second, and the third is 5 in. more than the second. Find the lengths of the three sides.

8. The perimeter of a triangle is 47 in. The first side is 5 in. less than twice the second, and the third is 2 in. more than the first. Find the lengths of the sides.

9. The base of an isosceles triangle is 8 in. The perimeter is 30 in. Find the lengths of the two congruent sides.

10. One of the two congruent sides of an isosceles triangle is 7 ft. The perimeter is 24 ft. Find the base.

PART B

11. A square and an equilateral triangle have the same perimeter. Each side of the square is 12 ft. Find the length of each side of the triangle.

12. A square and an equilateral triangle have the same perimeter. Each side of the triangle is 20 cm. Find the length of each side of the square.

13. A rectangle and an equilateral triangle have the same perimeter. The length of the rectangle is twice the width. Each side of the triangle is 18 cm. Find the length and width of the rectangle.

14. Each side of an equilateral triangle is 2 ft more than each side of a square. Their perimeters are the same. Find the length of each side of the triangle.

PART C

15. The length of a rectangle is 3 in. less than twice the width. If the length is decreased by 2 in. and the width by 1 in., the perimeter will be 24 in. Find the dimensions of the original rectangle.

16. A rectangular field is 4 times as long as it is wide. If the length is decreased by 10 m and the width is increased by 2 m, the perimeter will be 64 m. Find the dimensions of the original field.

Mathematics in the Hospital

Many important jobs are done in hospitals by technicians and lab specialists. Pictured above is a technician setting up one of the many machines used to monitor a patient's health. Below a lab specialist analyses blood samples.

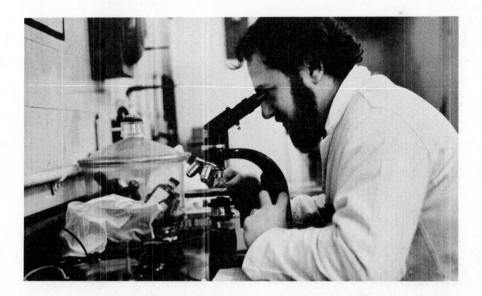

Chapter Three Review

Which members of the given replacement set are solutions of the sentence? [p. 56]

1. $20 = 2x + 6$ {7, 8, 9}
2. $13 + 2x = 3 + 6x$ {1, 2, 3, 4, 5}
3. $23 + 9y = 50$ {1, 3, 5, 7}
4. $7x - 21 = 5x - 9$ {5, 6}
5. $8y - 36 = 24$ {4, 6, 8}
6. $6y - 13 = -52 + 19y$ {3, 8, 11}
7. $-4c - 46 = -2$ {−9, −10, −11}
8. $4x - 4 = 3x - 2$ {1, 2, 3, 4}

Solve. [p. 59, 64, 68]

9. $-7 = 5x + 1$
10. $8r - 22 = 58$
11. $3y - 6 = 9$
12. $-39 = -3 + 12y$
13. $10c - 15 = -5$
14. $5x - 8 = -8$
15. $1 + 4x = 55 - 8$
16. $-42 + 39 = 11 - 2z$
17. $5 + 8x = 6x + 11$
18. $3c + 2 = -70 + 15c$
19. $9x - 20 = 8x + 2$
20. $27 - 5y = 4y - 6y$
21. $3z - 2z = -8 - z$
22. $33 - 4x = 1 + 4x$
23. $x + 12 + x = -14$
24. $16 - 9 = 5x - 8$
25. $-4(2x + 6) = -3x + 1$
26. $5 - 10x = -(3 - 2x)$
27. $6(y + 3) = 9 - (3 - 2y)$
28. $7(x - 1) = -2(-4x + 3)$
29. $5x - 4(2x - 6) = 3x - 24$
30. $-3(2x + 1) + 5 = -(4x - 9) + 5x$
31. $8y - 2(-3y + 4) = -(y + 38)$
32. $12 - 3(y + 1) = 1 - 5(y - 2)$

Write in mathematical terms. [p. 70]

33. 6 increased by x
34. 12 less than y.
35. n diminished by 3
36. 6 more than 3 times x
37. 5 less than twice y
38. 7 less than 9 times a number

Solve each problem. [p. 72, 76, 80, 84]

39. A number increased by 8 is the same as 3 times the number. Find the number.

40. The sum of two numbers is 26. The second is 2 less than 3 times the first. Find the two numbers.

41. One number is 17 more than another. If the greater number is increased by 3, the result is 5 times the smaller. Find the two numbers.

42. Paula had 7 times as many nickels as quarters. Their value was $1.80. How many quarters did she have?

43. The perimeter of a rectangle is 68 ft. The length exceeds 3 times the width by 2 ft. Find the length and the width.

44. Side x of a triangle is 3 yd longer than side y. Side z is 2 yd shorter than twice side y. The perimeter is 17 yd. Find the lengths of the three sides.

Chapter Three Test

Which members of the given replacement set are solutions of the sentence?

1. $13 + x = 5x + 1$ $\{3, 4\}$

2. $9y - 7 = 11 + 7y$ $\{7, 8, 9\}$

3. $5x + 2 = 8x - 10$ $\{1, 2, 4, 5\}$

4. $-6 + 8z = 21z - 45$ $\{3, 8, 11\}$

5. $5x - 7 = 4x - 12$ $\{-4, -5, -6\}$

6. $8y - 9 = 5y + 3$ $\{1, 2, 4, 5\}$

Solve.

7. $38 - 8x = -18$

8. $6y + 7 = 7$

9. $15r - 5 = -35$

10. $8c - 9 = -2c - 9$

11. $9 + 15 = 10z - 7$

12. $-2 + 5x = 38 - 10$

13. $3(x + 5) = x + 21$

14. $-(3x + 2) = x - 50$

15. $6y + (1 - 3y) = 16 - 4(2y + 1)$

16. $7(x + 1) - 1 = 2 - (5 + 2x)$

17. $2(3 - x) - 7 = 9 - 2(3 + 2x)$

18. $(x + 2) + (x + 4) = 42 - (x + 6)$

Write in mathematical terms.

19. 7 diminished by 2

20. 5 increased by x

21. x less than twice y

22. 8 more than 3 times a number

Solve each problem.

23. Seven less than 4 times a number is the same as the number increased by 8. Find the number.

24. The greater of two numbers is 8 less than 3 times the smaller. Their sum is 36. Find the two numbers.

25. A collection of 25 dimes and quarters amounts to $5.05. How many of each kind of coin are there?

26. The length of a rectangle is 3 ft less than 3 times the width. The perimeter is 66 ft. Find the length and the width.

Sequences

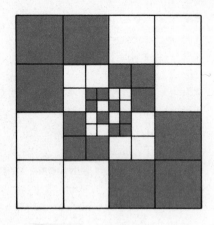

Mathematics is concerned with patterns formed by numbers. There is a pattern displayed in each sequence of numbers below. See if you can give the next three numbers of each sequence.

1. −6, −7, −8, −9, −10, • • •

2. 3, 9, 27, 81, • • •

3. −3, −3, −3, −3, • • •

4. 2, −2, 2, −2, 2, • • •

5. .1, .01, .001, .0001, • • •

6. 3, −6, 12, −24, • • •

7. 1, 2, 4, 5, 7, 8, 10, 11, • • •

8. 1, 4, 9, 16, 25, • • •

9. 1, 8, 27, 64, • • •

10. −6, −2, 2, 6, 10, • • •

11. $\frac{1}{2}, \frac{2}{3}, \frac{3}{4}, \frac{4}{5},$ • • •

12. $\frac{1}{2}$, 2, 8, 32, • • •

13. 0, 3, 8, 15, • • •

14. $\frac{1}{2}, \frac{4}{3}, \frac{9}{4}, \frac{16}{5},$ • • •

15. 0, 7, 26, 63, • • •

16. 0, 1, 1, 2, 3, 5, 8, 13, • • •

Sets

OBJECTIVES

■ To identify equal sets
■ To identify and describe finite and infinite sets
■ To find and graph solution sets of equations like $3x - 14 = 5x - 16$

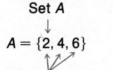
► *REVIEW CAPSULE*

A *set* is a collection of objects. The objects are *members,* or *elements* of the set. Braces are used to enclose the names of the elements of a set.

Set A   Set B
↓   ↓
$A = \{2, 4, 6\}$ $B = \{-2, -1, 0, 1, 2\}$

elements of A   elements of B

Definition of equal sets ——————→

Two sets are *equal* if they have the same elements.

Examples of equal sets

The order of listing the elements does not matter. ——————→ $\{-1, 3, 8\} = \{3, 8, -1\}$ $\{1, 2, 3\} = \{1, 1+1, 1+2\}$

Finite sets   Infinite sets
↙   ↘   ↙   ↘
$\{1, 2, 3\}$ $\{-1, 0, 1, 2\}$ $\{1, 2, 3, 4, \ldots\}$ $\{integers\}$

A definite number   No definite number
of elements   of elements

EXAMPLE 1 Tell whether each set is finite or infinite. Then describe each set in words.

$\{5, 6, 7\}$ finite
$\{2, 4, 6, 8, \ldots\}$ infinite

Between 4 and 8 means *not* including 4 and 8. Other descriptions are possible.

$\{5, 6, 7\}$ is the set of whole numbers between 4 and 8.
$\{2, 4, 6, 8, \ldots\}$ is the set of positive even integers.

EXAMPLE 2 $C = \{$integers between -3 and $2\}$. Describe set C by listing its elements.

Examine the integers on a number line.

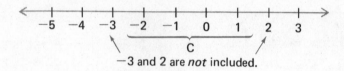
-3 and 2 are *not* included.

Thus, $C = \{-2, -1, 0, 1\}$.

EXAMPLE 3 $A = \{$integers between 5 and $6\}$. Describe set A by listing its elements.

There are no integers between 5 and 6. ————————→ Thus, $A = \phi$ (the set with no elements).

Definition of empty set ————————→

> The set with no elements is the empty set.
>
> Symbol for the empty set: ϕ

EXAMPLE 4   Find the set of all solutions of $6x - 9 = 2x + 19$. Then graph the set.

The replacement set is {all numbers}.

$$6x - 9 = 2x + 19$$
$$4x - 9 = 19$$
$$4x = 28$$

7 is the solution. ————————→ $x = 7$

Thus, $\{7\}$ is the set of all solutions.

To graph $\{7\}$, place a dot at 7 on a number line.

Definition of solution set ————————→
For Example 4, the solution set is $\{7\}$.

> The *solution set* of an open sentence is the set of all members of the replacement set which are solutions of the sentence.

EXAMPLE 5   Find the solution set of $x + 5 = x + 2$.

$$\begin{array}{r} x + 5 = \quad x + 2 \\ \underline{-x \qquad\qquad -x} \\ 5 = \quad 2 \quad \leftarrow \text{ False sentence} \end{array}$$

Add $-x$ to each side. ————————→

There is no number which makes $x + 5 = x + 2$ true. ————————→ Thus, the solution set of $x + 5 = x + 2$ is ϕ.

EXERCISES

PART A

Which sets are equal to $\{1, 3, 5, 6\}$?

1. $\{1, 6, 3, 5\}$ **2.** $\{1, 3, 7, 6\}$ **3.** $\{5, 2, 1, 6\}$
4. $\{6, 3, 1, 5\}$ **5.** $\{1, 1 + 2, 1 + 4, 1 + 5\}$ **6.** $\{3, 8 - 1, 7 - 1, 1\}$

For each set, tell whether it is finite or infinite. Then describe the set in words.

7. $\{0, 1, 2, 3, 4\}$ **8.** $\{0, 1, 2, 3, 4, \ldots\}$ **9.** $\{1, 3, 5, 7, \ldots\}$
10. $\{-1, -2, -3, -4\}$ **11.** $\{-1, -2, -3, -4, \ldots\}$ **12.** $\{\ldots -2, -1, 0, 1, 2, \ldots\}$
13. $\{-2, -1, 0, 1, 2\}$ **14.** ϕ **15.** $\{4, 6, 8, 10\}$

Describe each set by listing its elements.

16. $A = \{$positive integers less than 6$\}$ **17.** $B = \{$positive integers greater than 8$\}$
18. $C = \{$negative integers between -4 **19.** $D = \{$negative integers between -5
        and $-1\}$ and $-4\}$
20. $E = \{$integers between 8 and 9$\}$ **21.** $F = \{$integers between -2 and 4$\}$

Find the solution set of each sentence. Then graph it.

22. $5y - 8 = 20 + y$ **23.** $3x - 5 = 7 + 3x$ **24.** $9z + 17 = 11z + 3$
25. $-16 - 5x = 2x + 5$ **26.** $9 + 11x = 99 - 7x$ **27.** $2d + 18 = 23 + 2d$
28. $9 + 4y = 4y - 12$ **29.** $8y - 22 = -14 + 6y$ **30.** $3x + 4 = -68 + 15x$
31. $2r + 8 = -16 - 2r$ **32.** $14 - 6y = -10 + 6y$ **33.** $15 - 4z = 11 + 4z$
34. $-8y + 7y = 4 - 2y$ **35.** $13 + 20 = 10x - 7$ **36.** $27 - 6y = -8y + 5y$
37. $-3x + 2 = x - 8 - 4x$ **38.** $x + x + 5x = -7$ **39.** $6x + 8 + x = -4 + 7x$

PART B

EXAMPLE   Find the solution set of $7x + 2 = 2 + 3x + 4x$.
Then graph it.

$$7x + 2 = 2 + \underbrace{3x + 4x}$$
$$7x + 2 = 2 + \quad 7x$$

Add -2 to each side. ⟶ $7x = 7x$
Divide each side by 7. ⟶ $x = x$

Every number also makes   Every number makes $x = x$ true.
$7x + 2 = 2 + 3x + 4x$ true.   **Thus,** the solution set is $\{$all numbers$\}$.

Graph of $\{$all numbers$\}$ ⟶

$$\xleftarrow{\hspace{1cm}} \overset{\;-4\;\;-3\;\;-2\;\;-1\;\;\;\;0\;\;\;\;1\;\;\;\;2\;\;\;\;3\;\;\;\;4}{+\!\!+\!\!+\!\!+\!\!+\!\!+\!\!+\!\!+\!\!+} \xrightarrow{\hspace{1cm}}$$

Find the solution set of each sentence. Then graph it.

40. $3x - 6 = -6 + 3x$ **41.** $x + x - 2x = -12$ **42.** $4x + 7 + 5x = 7 + 9x$

Inequalities

OBJECTIVE

■ To graph the solution sets
of inequalities like
$x > 3$ and $-4 \leq x$

▶ *REVIEW CAPSULE*

SENTENCES

Types & Symbols		Examples	
EQUATIONS	True	False	Open
= is equal to	$2+3=5$	$4+6=9$	$x+3=8$
INEQUALITIES	True	False	Open
≠ is not equal to	$5 \neq 7$	$1+2 \neq 3$	$y \neq 6$
< is less than	$4 < 8$	$10 < 7$	$x < 2$
> is greater than	$7 > 2$	$3 > 9$	$c+2 > 4$

$a < b$ means $b > a$.

EXAMPLE 1   Graph the solution set of $x < 4$.

Read: x is less than 4. ────────────→
Many numbers make $x < 4$ true.

$$
\begin{array}{r}
x < 4 \\
\hline
3\tfrac{1}{2} < 4 \\
3 < 4 \\
1 < 4 \\
0 < 4 \\
-2 < 4 \\
-4\tfrac{1}{3} < 4 \\
-5 < 4
\end{array}
$$

We could go on forever. ────────────→

Mark the points with the ────────────→
coordinates listed above.

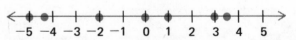

Any point to the left of the point with coordinate
4 has a coordinate less than 4. We draw an
arrow to show all such points.

Graph of solution set of $x < 4$:

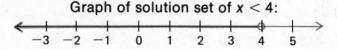

Note the circle around 4.
4 is not in the solution set.

Read: the set of all numbers x, such that x is less than 4. ─────→

The solution set of $x < 4$ is an infinite set.
$$\{x \mid x < 4\}$$

EXAMPLE 2   Graph the solution set of $x > -2$.

Read: x is greater than -2. ─────→
Substitute numbers for x. ─────→

We could go on forever. ─────→

x	$>$	-2
-1	$>$	-2
$-\dfrac{1}{2}$	$>$	-2
0	$>$	-2
3	$>$	-2
20	$>$	-2

Graph of $\{x \mid x > -2\}$ ─────→
-2 is not in the solution set.

Any point to the right of the point with coordinate -2 has a coordinate greater than -2.

EXAMPLE 3   Graph the solution set of $x \leq 1$.
  $x \leq 1$ means x is less than or equal to 1.

Graph of $\{x \mid x \leq 1\}$ ─────→

The dot shows that 1 is in the solution set.

Any number which is less than or equal to 1 makes $x \leq 1$ true. **Thus,** the graph includes 1 and all points to the left.

EXAMPLE 4   Graph the solution set of $-3 \leq x$.

$$-3 \leq x \text{ means } \underbrace{x \geq -3}$$

  x is greater than or equal to -3

Graph of $\{x \mid x \geq -3\}$ ─────→
-3 is in the solution set.

Any number which is greater than or equal to -3 makes $x \geq -3$ true. **Thus,** the graph includes -3 and all points to the right.

ORAL EXERCISES

Tell whether each sentence is an equation or an inequality. Then tell whether it is true, false, or open.

1. $6 + 9 = 15$	**2.** $24 = 6x$	**3.** $5 + y \leq 7$	**4.** $(3)(5) > 14$
5. $x + 8 = 5$	**6.** $4 \geq 4$	**7.** $5 + 2 < 7$	**8.** $6n \neq 18$
9. $(4)(1) < 3$	**10.** $18 \div 3 > 0$	**11.** $6 = 10 + x$	**12.** $7y - 3 > 19$
13. $y - 2 > 7$	**14.** $6x + 2 = 20$	**15.** $7 + 1 \geq 8$	**16.** $2 + 6 \geq 3 + 4$
17. $6 + 3 \neq 9$	**18.** $5 + 8 \neq 14$	**19.** $4 + 9 = 12$	**20.** $y \leq 4 + 6$
21. $7y = 8$	**22.** $5 < 3 + 2$	**23.** $4x + 8 = 2 + x$	**24.** $9 = 5 + 5$
25. $6 + 9 \leq c$	**26.** $7 + z \neq 2$	**27.** $2 \geq 3$	**28.** $0 \leq 1 + 2$

EXERCISES

PART A

Graph the solution set of each sentence.

1. $b < 3$	**2.** $y > 1$	**3.** $x = 5$	**4.** $d \geq -5$
5. $x \leq -2$	**6.** $y > -4$	**7.** $2 < c$	**8.** $r < 4$
9. $z \geq 0$	**10.** $z \leq -1$	**11.** $y > 3$	**12.** $x = 0$
13. $a = -1$	**14.** $x > -5$	**15.** $2 > g$	**16.** $x \leq 0$
17. $4 < y$	**18.** $z \geq 4$	**19.** $r = 4$	**20.** $y < -1$
21. $y \leq 1$	**22.** $x = 2$	**23.** $0 < z$	**24.** $4 \geq x$
25. $a < -3$	**26.** $r > 0$	**27.** $x \geq 1$	**28.** $a \leq 3$
29. $b = -3$	**30.** $1 > z$	**31.** $y < -2$	**32.** $3 \leq c$
33. $c \geq -1$	**34.** $-2 = x$	**35.** $r \leq -4$	**36.** $x < -5$
37. $x > -2$	**38.** $x > -1$	**39.** $a \geq 2$	**40.** $y \leq 2$
41. $1 = b$	**42.** $y < -3$	**43.** $5 \geq g$	**44.** $r < -4$
45. $y > -3$	**46.** $6 = x$	**47.** $c \geq -2$	**48.** $z \leq -3$

PART B

EXAMPLE Graph the solution set of $y \neq -\frac{1}{3}$.

Every number except $-\frac{1}{3}$ is in the solution set.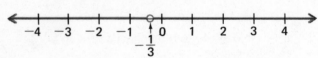

Graph the solution set of each sentence.

49. $x \neq 2\frac{1}{2}$	**50.** $-\frac{1}{4} > y$	**51.** $x < \frac{5}{4}$	**52.** $-\frac{3}{2} \leq x$
53. $\frac{1}{2} \geq y$	**54.** $0 \neq x$	**55.** $x \geq -\frac{2}{3}$	**56.** $0 \geq y$
57. $\frac{5}{2} < x$	**58.** $-\frac{5}{3} > y$	**59.** $-\frac{8}{5} \leq x$	**60.** $x \neq -\frac{7}{4}$

Computer Programs: Input and Output

Some computer programs call for information to be entered into the machine before calculations can be done, and the answer printed out.
Problem. Write a flow chart to evaluate
$4x + 3y - 5$ for given values of x and y.

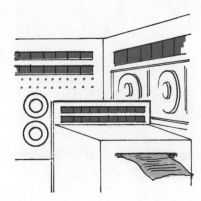

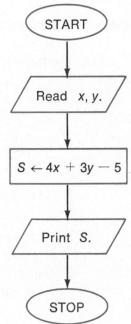

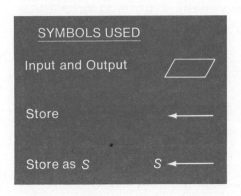

START

Read x, y.

Input: Feed the values of x and y into the machine.

$S \leftarrow 4x + 3y - 5$

Replace x and y with input values. Compute. Store as S.

Print S.

Output: Print the result.

STOP

SYMBOLS USED

Input and Output

Store

Store as S $S \leftarrow$

Use of the flow chart above to evaluate $4x + 3y - 5$ for these given values of x and y.

1. $x = 2, y = -3$ 2. $x = 5, y = 4$ 3. $x = -1, y = 5$

4. Write a flow chart for averaging three numbers.

Properties for Inequalities

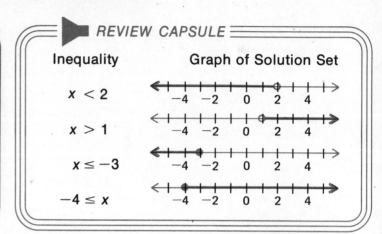

▶ REVIEW CAPSULE

Inequality	Graph of Solution Set
$x < 2$	
$x > 1$	
$x \leq -3$	
$-4 \leq x$	

EXAMPLE 1 Consider the inequality $4 < 7$. Add 2 to each side. Use the symbol, $<$ or $>$, to write a true inequality.

Different numbers ⟶
Same number ⟶
Different numbers ⟶

$$\begin{array}{rr} 4 < & 7 \\ +2 & +2 \\ \hline 6 < & 9 \end{array}$$ same order

EXAMPLE 2 Consider $-6 < -1$. Add -3 to each side. Write a true inequality.

$$\begin{array}{rr} -6 < & -1 \\ -3 & -3 \\ \hline -9 < & -4 \end{array}$$ same order

EXAMPLE 3 Consider $4 \geq -2$. Add 7 to each side. Write a true inequality.

$$\begin{array}{rr} 4 \geq & -2 \\ +7 & +7 \\ \hline 11 \geq & 5 \end{array}$$ same order

EXAMPLE 4 Consider $8 > -1$. Add -10 to each side. Write a true inequality.

$$\begin{array}{rr} 8 > & -1 \\ -10 & -10 \\ \hline -2 > & -11 \end{array}$$ same order

Examples 1–4 suggest this property.

Inequalities of the same order: Both are < or both are >.

EXAMPLE 5 Consider $2 < 7$. Multiply each side by 3 and write a true inequality. Then multiply each side by -3 and write a true inequality.

Multiplying by a negative number reverses the order.

$$
\begin{array}{l}
2 < 7 \\
2(3) \ ? \ 7(3) \\
6 < 21
\end{array}
\bigg\} \ \text{same order}
\qquad
\begin{array}{l}
2 < 7 \\
2(-3) \ ? \ 7(-3) \\
-6 > -21
\end{array}
\bigg\} \ \text{reverse order}
$$

EXAMPLE 6 Consider $3 \geq -5$. Multiply each side by 2 and write a true inequality. Then multiply each side by -2 and write a true inequality.

Multiplying by a negative number reverses the order.

$$
\begin{array}{l}
3 \geq -5 \\
3(2) \ ? \ -5(2) \\
6 \geq -10
\end{array}
\bigg\} \ \text{same order}
\qquad
\begin{array}{l}
3 \geq -5 \\
3(-2) \ ? \ -5(-2) \\
-6 \leq 10
\end{array}
\bigg\} \ \text{reverse order}
$$

Examples 5 and 6 suggest this property.

Inequalities of reverse order: One is < and the other is >.

EXAMPLE 7   Consider $9 > 6$. Divide each side by 3 and write a true inequality. Then divide each side by -3 and write a true inequality.

$$9 > 6$$
$$\frac{9}{3} \; ? \; \frac{6}{3} \quad \text{same order}$$
$$3 > 2$$

$$9 > 6$$
$$\frac{9}{-3} \; ? \; \frac{6}{-3} \quad \text{reverse order}$$
$$-3 < -2$$

EXAMPLE 8   Consider $-4 \leq 12$. Divide each side by 4 and write a true inequality. Then divide each side by -4 and write a true inequality.

$$-4 \leq 12$$
$$\frac{-4}{4} \; ? \; \frac{12}{4} \quad \text{same order}$$
$$-1 \leq 3$$

$$-4 \leq 12$$
$$\frac{-4}{-4} \; ? \; \frac{12}{-4} \quad \text{reverse order}$$
$$1 \geq -3$$

Examples 7 and 8 suggest this property.

> **Division Property for Inequalities**
>
> If we divide each side of a true inequality by the same *positive* number, the result is another true inequality of the *same* order.
>
> If $a > b$ and $c > 0$, then $\dfrac{a}{c} > \dfrac{b}{c}$.
>
> If we divide each side of a true inequality by the same *negative* number, the result is another true inequality of the *reverse* order.
>
> If $a > b$ and $c < 0$, then $\dfrac{a}{c} < \dfrac{b}{c}$.

EXAMPLE 9   Tell what operation was performed on each side of the first inequality to give the second inequality.

$$-21 < 14 \qquad 3 > -2$$

$$\left. \begin{array}{cc} \dfrac{-21}{-7}; & \dfrac{14}{-7} \\ \downarrow & \downarrow \\ 3 & -2 \end{array} \right\}$$

Thus, each side of $-21 < 14$ was divided by -7 to give $3 > -2$.

Properties for Inequalities

Operation	Addition		Multiplication		Division	
Sign of operator	pos.	neg.	pos.	neg.	pos.	neg.
Order of resulting inequality	same	same	same	reverse	same	reverse

ORAL EXERCISES

If the indicated operation is performed, will the order of the inequality change?

1. $4 > 3$ Add 6.
2. $-6 < -2$ Divide by -2.
3. $6 > -1$ Multiply by -4.
4. $8 > -4$ Divide by 4.
5. $-8 < -2$ Divide by 2.
6. $9 > -2$ Add -5.
7. $-3 < 2$ Multiply by 7.
8. $4 > 0$ Multiply by 5.
9. $0 < 5$ Multiply by -3.
10. $-9 \leq -3$ Divide by -3.
11. $-24 < 12$ Divide by 3.
12. $-8 < 1$ Add 7.
13. $7 > -1$ Multiply by -6.
14. $-6 \leq 2$ Divide by -2.
15. $2 \leq 3$ Divide by 1.
16. $-5 \leq 0$ Add -4.
17. $0 > -4$ Add 2.
18. $6 \geq 3$ Divide by -3.
19. $9 \geq -4$ Add -6.
20. $0 < 8$ Multiply by 6.
21. $0 \leq 5$ Multiply by 3.
22. $-4 < 0$ Multiply by -5.
23. $3 \leq 7$ Add 4.
24. $-8 < 6$ Multiply by -1.
25. $-2 > -3$ Add 8.
26. $-6 > -7$ Multiply by 4.

EXERCISES

PART A

For each inequality in Exercises 1–26 above, write a true inequality by performing the indicated operation on each side.

PART B

Tell what operation was performed on each side of the first inequality to give the second inequality.

27. $5 > 3$ $2 > 0$
28. $4 \leq 7$ $8 \leq 14$
29. $-6 < 2$ $18 > -6$
30. $8 > 4$ $2 > 1$
31. $-2 \geq -3$ $3 \geq 2$
32. $3 \geq -1$ $12 \geq -4$
33. $-9 < -6$ $3 > 2$
34. $-8 < 2$ $-5 < 5$
35. $2 > 0$ $-6 < 0$
36. $-7 < 14$ $1 > -2$

Solving Inequalities

 REVIEW CAPSULE

Find the solution set of $6x + 7 = -2x + 31$.

$$6x + 7 = -2x + 31$$
$$\underline{+2x \qquad\qquad +2x}$$
$$8x + 7 = \qquad\quad 31$$
$$\underline{\quad -7 \qquad\qquad -7}$$
$$8x \quad = \qquad\quad 24$$
$$\frac{8x}{8} = \frac{24}{8}$$
$$x = 3$$

Thus, the solution set is {3}.

EXAMPLE 1

Find and graph the solution set of $4x + 7 > 3x + 10$.

Add $-3x$ to each side. ⟶

The order is the same. ⟶

Add -7 to each side. ⟶

Same order ⟶

$$4x + 7 > \quad 3x + 10$$
$$\underline{-3x \qquad\quad -3x}$$
$$1x + 7 > \qquad\quad 10$$
$$\underline{\quad -7 \qquad\qquad -7}$$
$$1x \quad > \qquad\quad 3,\ \text{or}\ x > 3$$

Any number greater than 3 should make $4x + 7 > 3x + 10$ true.

Check two numbers greater than 3.

Try 4.

$4x + 7 > 3x + 10$	
$4(4) + 7$	$3(4) + 10$
$16 + 7$	$12 + 10$
23	22
	$23 > 22$ True

Try 7.

$4x + 7 > 3x + 10$	
$4(7) + 7$	$3(7) + 10$
$28 + 7$	$21 + 10$
35	31
	$35 > 31$ True

Check two numbers *not* greater than 3.

Try 3.

$4x + 7 > 3x + 10$	
$4(3) + 7$	$3(3) + 10$
$12 + 7$	$9 + 10$
19	19
	$19 > 19$
	False

Try -2.

$4x + 7 > 3x + 10$	
$4(-2) + 7$	$3(-2) + 10$
$-8 + 7$	$-6 + 10$
-1	4
	$-1 > 4$
	False

We could check numbers forever!

It appears that any number greater than 3 makes the sentence true. Any number less than or equal to 3 makes the sentence false.

Thus, the solution set of $4x + 7 > 3x + 10$ is
$$\{x \mid x > 3\}.$$

Graph of $\{x \mid x > 3\}$ ⟶
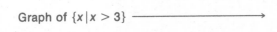

3 is not a solution.

EXAMPLE 2   Find and graph the solution set of $5x - 10 \le 6x - 8$.

$$
\begin{array}{r}
5x - 10 \le 6x - 8 \\
-5x -5x \\
\hline
-10 \le 1x - 8 \\
+8 +8 \\
\hline
-2 \le x \\
x \ge -2
\end{array}
$$

$-2 \le x$ means $x \ge -2$. ⟶
Check -2 and several numbers greater than -2.

Thus, the solution set is $\{x \mid x \ge -2\}$.

-2 is a solution.

Graph of $\{x \mid x \ge -2\}$ ⟶
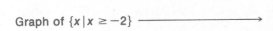

EXAMPLE 3   Find and graph the solution set of $10x + 3 < 7x - 9$.

$$
\begin{array}{r}
10x + 3 < 7x - 9 \\
-7x \phantom{+3 <} -7x \\
\hline
3x + 3 < -9 \\
-3 -3 \\
\hline
3x < -12 \\
\dfrac{3x}{3} < \dfrac{-12}{3} \\
x < -4
\end{array}
$$

Divide each side by 3. ⟶
The order is the same since 3 is positive.

Thus, the solution set is $\{x \mid x < -4\}$.

Graph of $\{x \mid x < -4\}$ ⟶
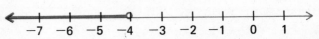

SOLVING INEQUALITIES   **103**

EXAMPLE 4 Solve $10x + 3 < 7x - 9$ again. This time add $-10x$ to each side rather than $-7x$. Is the result the same?

Add $-10x$ to each side. ⟶

$$
\begin{array}{r}
10x + 3 < \quad 7x - 9 \\
-10x \qquad\quad -10x \\
\hline
3 < -3x - 9
\end{array}
$$

Add 9 to each side. ⟶

$$
\begin{array}{r}
+9 \qquad\qquad +9 \\
\hline
12 < -3x
\end{array}
$$

Divide each side by -3.

Reverse the order, since -3 is ⟶
negative.

$$\frac{12}{-3} > \frac{-3x}{-3}$$

$$-4 > x$$

$-4 > x$ means $x < -4$. ⟶

$$x < -4$$

Yes, the result is the same.

EXERCISES

PART A

Find and graph the solution set.

1. $2 + 5x > -8$

2. $10x + 14 \geq -36$

3. $-17 < 9y - 8$

4. $7 > 3x - 8$

5. $-2x - 28 > -5x - 7$

6. $5y + 8 < -4 + 17y$

7. $4a + 1 \leq 3a + 9$

8. $8x - 11 \geq 5x + 7$

9. $3 - 6x \geq 8 - 7x$

10. $7y + 8 \leq -16 + 3y$

11. $7d - 6 < -24 + d$

12. $7y + 3 > 10y - 12$

13. $-3r + 13 \leq 2r - 7$

14. $-22 + 10x > -14 + 8x$

15. $25 - 4x \geq 4x + 1$

16. $8 - 7y < y + 8$

17. $-x + 12 > 3x - 4$

18. $8 - 3x < -4x + 7$

19. $-2y + 9 \geq 2y - 3$

20. $7x - 8x \geq 12 + 3x$

21. $9x - 5 \leq 25 + 4x$

22. $9y + 7 \geq 13 + 11y$

23. $10y - 24 > 3y - 3$

24. $6x - 18 \leq 3x - 6$

25. $6x + 3 \geq 91 - 5x$

26. $4y + 3 > 9y - 17$

27. $17x + 28 \leq 9x - 4$

28. $5x - 38 < 2 + x$

29. $12y - 8 > 55 + 5y$

30. $4x + 8 > -9 + 5x$

31. $8d - 88 < 8 + 2d$

32. $2r - r \geq -8r - 27$

PART B

Find and graph the solution set. [Hint: Remove parentheses first.]

33. $2(x + 5) > x + 15$

34. $2(3 + 2x) < -3x - 8$

35. $4(y + 1) < 7y - 2(3 - y)$

36. $5a + 3(a - 7) > -(a + 8)$

Intersection and Union of Sets

▶ *REVIEW CAPSULE*

$A = \{1, 2, 3\}$ $\qquad$ $B = \{1, 2, 3, 4, 5\}$

A is a subset of *B*
means
every element of *A* is also in *B*.

Write $A \subseteq B$ to mean *A* is a subset of *B*.

EXAMPLE 1

Consider sets *A* and *B* above. Is *B* a subset of *A*?

Think: Is every element of *B* also an element of *A*? $B \not\subseteq A$ means *B* is not a subset of *A*. $\longrightarrow$

B contains the elements 4 and 5, which are not in *A*. **Thus, $B \not\subseteq A$.**

We make these agreements about subsets.

> Every set is a subset of itself.
> The empty set is a subset of every set.

EXAMPLE 2

List all the subsets of *C*. How many are there?
$C = \{5, 7, 9\}$

Subsets of *C*:

Every set is a subset of itself. $\longrightarrow$

$\{5, 7, 9\}$
$\{5, 7\}$
$\{5, 9\}$
$\{7, 9\}$
$\{5\}$
$\{7\}$
$\{9\}$

The empty set is a subset of every set. $\longrightarrow$

ϕ

Thus, *C* has 8 subsets.

Consider sets R and S.

$$R = \{2, 4, 6, 8\} \quad S = \{2, 6, 10\}$$

The *intersection* of two sets contains all the elements common to *both* sets.

$$\{2, 6\}$$

The *intersection* of sets R and S is $\{2, 6\}$.

$\cap$ is the symbol for intersection.

We write $\{2, 4, 6, 8\} \cap \{2, 6, 10\} = \{2, 6\}$,
or $\quad R \quad \cap \quad S \quad = \{2, 6\}$.

EXAMPLE 3 $\quad X = \{-3, -2, 0, 1, 2\}$ and $Y = \{-2, 1, 2, 3\}$.
Find $X \cap Y$.

−2, 1, and 2 are common to sets X and Y. ⟶

$$X \cap Y = \{-2, 1, 2\}.$$

Consider sets P and Q.

$$P = \{1, 2, 3, 7\} \quad Q = \{2, 3, 4\}$$

The *union* of two sets contains the elements which are in the 1st set, or 2nd set, or in both sets.

$$\{1, 2, 3, 4, 7\}$$

The *union* of sets P and Q is $\{1, 2, 3, 4, 7\}$.

$\cup$ is the symbol for union.

We write $\{1, 2, 3, 7\} \cup \{2, 3, 4\} = \{1, 2, 3, 4, 7\}$
or $\quad P \quad \cup \quad Q \quad = \{1, 2, 3, 4, 7\}$

EXAMPLE 4 $\quad C = \{0, 2, 4, 6\}$ and $D = \{0, 1, 2\}$.
Find $C \cup D$.

Each element in $C \cup D$ is in C, or in D, or in both. ⟶

$$C \cup D = \{0, 1, 2, 4, 6\}.$$

SUMMARY

Intersection
$A \cap B$ **is the set of all elements common to both set** A **and set** B**.**

Union
$A \cup B$ **is the set of elements belonging to set** A **or set** B **or both set** A **and set** B**.**

EXERCISES

PART A

For each pair of sets, determine if $A \subseteq B$. Then determine if $B \subseteq A$.

1. $A = \{0, 2, 4\}$ $B = \{0, 4\}$
2. $A = \{1, 2, 3\}$ $B = \{2, 3, 4\}$
3. $A = \{-1, -2\}$ $B = \{-3, -2, -1\}$
4. $A = \{4, 5, 6\}$ $B = \{6, 4, 5\}$
5. $A = \{2, 4, 6\}$ $B = \{2, 4, 6, 8, 10\}$
6. $A = \{-6, 0, 6\}$ $B = \{-7, 0, 7\}$
7. $A = \phi$ $B = \{2, 3, 6\}$
8. $A = \{1, 2, 3, 4\}$ $B = \{1, 3\}$
9. $A = \{1, 2, 3\}$ $B = \{1, 1 + 1, 1 + 2\}$
10. $A = \{-1, 0, 1\}$ $B = \{-2, -1, 0, 1, 2\}$
11. $A = \{5\}$ $B = \{6, 7, 8\}$
12. $A = \{0\}$ $B = \phi$
13. $A = \{\text{integers}\}$ $B = \{\text{negative integers}\}$
14. $A = \{0\}$ $B = \{\text{integers}\}$
15. $A = \{\text{positive integers}\}$
    $B = \{\text{whole numbers}\}$
16. $A = \{\text{negative integers}\}$
    $B = \{\text{positive integers}\}$

List all the subsets of each set. Then give the number of subsets.

17. $\{1, 2\}$
18. $\{2, 4, 6\}$
19. $\{8\}$
20. ϕ
21. $\{-1, 0\}$
22. $\{1, 3, 5, 7\}$

For each pair of sets, find the intersection. Then find the union.

23. $\{1, 3, 5\}$ $\{3, 5\}$
24. $\{2, 4, 6\}$ $\{6, 4, 2\}$
25. $\{4, 5, 6\}$ $\{7\}$
26. $\{1, 4, 5, 9\}$ $\{1, 2, 5\}$
27. ϕ $\{0, 2, 4\}$
28. $\{-4, 0, 4\}$ $\{-8, 0, 8\}$
29. $\{-1, -2, -3\}$ $\{1, 2, 3\}$
30. $\{1, 2, -1, -2\}$ $\{0, -1, -2\}$
31. $\{1, 4, 5\}$ $\{1, 2, 3, 4, 5\}$
32. $\{0\}$ ϕ
33. $\{2, 4, 6\}$ $\{6, 8, 10\}$
34. $\{1, 3, 5, 7\}$ $\{2, 4, 6, 8\}$
35. $\{5, 8, 9, 2\}$ $\{2, 5, 8, 9\}$
36. $\{0, 2, 4, 6\}$ $\{0, 3, 6, 9\}$

PART B

For each pair of sets, find the intersection. Then find the union.

37. $\{0, 2, 4, 6, 8, \ldots\}$ $\{1, 3, 5, 7, 9, \ldots\}$
38. $\{0, -1, -2, -3, \ldots\}$ $\{0, 1, 2, 3, \ldots\}$
39. $\{0, 2, 4, 6, 8, \ldots\}$ $\{0, 3, 6, 9, 12, \ldots\}$
40. $\{0, -2, -4, -6, -8, \ldots\}$
    $\{0, -4, -8, -12, -16, \ldots\}$
41. $\{0\}$ $\{\text{integers}\}$
42. $\{\text{negative integers}\}$ $\{\text{positive integers}\}$
43. $\{\text{positive integers}\}$ $\{\text{whole numbers}\}$
44. $\{\text{integers}\}$ $\{\text{negative integers}\}$

PART C

$A = \{0, 1, 2, 3, 4\}$ $B = \{1, 3, 5\}$, and $C = \{0, 2, 4, 6\}$. **List each set.**

45. $(A \cup B) \cup C$
46. $A \cup (B \cup C)$
47. $(A \cap B) \cap C$
48. $A \cap (B \cap C)$
49. $(A \cup B) \cap C$
50. $(A \cap B) \cup C$

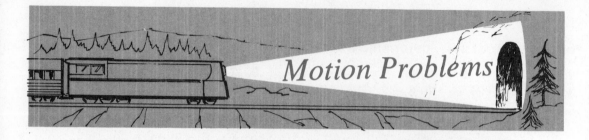

Motion Problems

DISTANCE = RATE • TIME $(d = r\,t)$

If Bill travels 60 mph for 3 hours, how far does he go?

⊢—60—⊢—60—⊢—60—⊣ $d = r\,t$

⊢————180————⊣ $d = (60)\,(3)$, or 180 miles

Practice Problem 1

Write an equation for this problem. Two cars travel in opposite directions from the same point. The rate of one car is 10 mph less than the rate of the other car. After 8 hours, the cars are 560 miles apart. Find the rate of each car.

Draw a diagram. ⟶

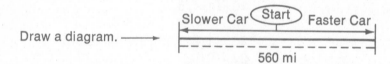

Represent the rates algebraically. } Let x = rate of faster car in mph

x-10 = rate of slower car in mph

Make a chart ⟶

	Rate	Time	Distance ($d = r\,t$)
Faster car	x	8	8 x
Slower car	x-10	8	8·(x-10)

Write an equation. → $\begin{pmatrix}\text{Distance of}\\\text{faster car}\end{pmatrix} + \begin{pmatrix}\text{Distance of}\\\text{slower car}\end{pmatrix} = \begin{pmatrix}\text{Total}\\\text{distance}\end{pmatrix}$

Substitute →   8 x +   8 (x-10)   =   560

Solve → x =   40

$\begin{pmatrix}8\,x + 8\,x - 80 = 560\\16\,x = 640\\x = \;\;40\end{pmatrix}$ x-10   =   30

Thus, the rates are 40 mph and 30 mph.

| Practice Problem 2 | Two trains leave the same station at the same time and travel in opposite directions. The E train travels at an average rate of 72 mph. The A train at 75 mph. In how many hours will they be 441 miles apart? |

Draw a diagram. →

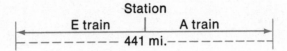

Represent the time algebraically. }

Let x = number of hours until they are 441 miles apart.

Make a chart. →

	Rate	Time	Distance ($d = rt$)
E train	72	x	$72x$
A train	75	x	$75x$

Write an equation. →

(Distance of E train) + (Distance of A train) = (Total distance)

Substitute. →
Solve. →

$$72x \quad + \quad 75x \quad = \quad 441$$
$$x \quad = \quad 3$$

Thus, in 3 hours the trains will be 441 miles apart.

Practice Problem 3

Dawn drove to her office at 32 mph. On her return trip she averaged 24 mph. Her total trip took 7 hours. How far is it to her office.

Draw a diagram. →

Home ⌂ ——————— To ——————→ ▢ Office
←— From ———————————

Represent the times algebraically. }

Let x = time of the trip to office in hours
$7 - x$ = time of the return trip in hours

Make a chart. →

	Rate	Time	Distance ($d = rt$)
To office	32	x	$32x$
Return trip	24	$7 - x$	$24(7 - x)$

Write an equation. →

(Distance of trip of office) = (Distance of return trip)

Substitute. →
Solve. $\left(\begin{array}{l}32x = 168 - 24x \\ 56x = 168\end{array}\right)$

$$32x \quad = \quad 24(7 - x)$$
$$x \quad = \quad 3$$

Thus, 32 (3), or 96, miles is the distance to her office.

Practice Problem 4   Ray starts out on his bicycle at a rate of 10 mph. Two hours later, Carol drives her car from the same point along the same road at 30 mph. Write an equation to determine how many hours Carol will have driven when she catches up with Ray?

Draw a diagram. → Start |————— Ray —————→| Point where
                         |————— Carol ————→| Carol catches up

Represent the time algebraically. }

Let x = time Carol travels
$x + 2$ = time Ray travels

Make a chart. →

	Rate	Time	Distance ($d = rt$)
Ray	10	$x + 2$	$10(x + 2)$
Carol	30	x	$30x$

Write an equation. →
Substitute. →

(Ray's distance) = (Carol's distance)
$$10(x + 2) = 30x$$

Practice Problem 5   A train leaves the station at 3:00 p.m. and travels east at 65 mph. Another train leaves the station at 4:00 p.m. and travels in the same direction at 75 mph. At what time will the second train overtake the first?

Draw a diagram. → Start |————— first train ————→| Point where second
                         |————— second train ———→| train overtakes first

Represent the time algebraically. }

Let x = time second train travels
$x + 1$ = time first train travels

Make a chart. →

	Rate	Time	Distance ($d = rt$)
First train	65	x	$65x$
Second train	75	$x - 1$	$75(x - 1)$

Write an equation. →
Substitute. →
Solve. →

(First train's distance) = (Second train's distance)
$$65x = 75(x - 1)$$
$$65x = 75x - 75$$
$$-10x = -75$$

First train travels
$7\frac{1}{2}$ hr. →

3:00 + 7 hr. 30 min. = 10:30 →

$$x = 7\frac{1}{2}$$

Thus, at 10:30 p.m. the second train will overtake the first.

EXERCISES

1. Two trucks start toward each other at the same time from towns 300 miles apart. One truck travels at a rate of 40 mph, the other at 35 mph. After how many hours will they meet?

2. Marita drives her car at 25 mph to the bus stop where she takes a bus that goes 50 mph. If her total trip was 175 miles and took 4 hours, how long was she on the bus?

3. Jan and Joel start from the same point at the same time and travel in opposite directions on their bicycles. If Jan travels at 8 mph and Jim at 7 mph, in how many hours will they be 45 miles apart?

4. A car and a truck, traveling in opposite directions pass each other at a cross roads in the country. If the car is traveling at 50 mph and the truck at 30 mph, in how many hours will they be 440 miles apart?

5. A train leaves the station and travels north at 70 mph. Two hours later, another train leaves the same station and travels south at 65 mph. How many hours will the first train have traveled when they are 275 miles apart?

6. A train leaves the station and travels south at 60 mph. Two hours later, another train leaves and travels in the same direction at 65 mph. How many hours will the first train have traveled when the second overtakes it?

7. Tom drove his car to the service station at 30 mph and returned home by bicycle at 10 mph. If the entire trip took 4 hours, how far is it from Tom's home to the service station?

8. Carol walks toward town at 3 mph. Half an hour later, Theresa leaves for town and walks at 4 mph. For how many hours will Carol have walked when Theresa catches up with her?

9. Dick left home for a fishing trip at 8:30 am, driving at a rate of 30 mph. Part of the way there, his car broke down and he walked back home at a rate of 4 mph. If he returned at 10:30 am, how far from home was he when his car broke down?

10. An airplane left Newark Airport and traveled due north at 650 mph. Two hours later, another plane left Newark and traveled due south at 600 mph. How many hours will the first plane have flown when they are 1,800 miles apart?

Graphing Intersections and Unions

OBJECTIVE

■ To graph and describe the intersection and the union of two sets like $\{x\,|\,x < 3\}$ and $\{x\,|\,x \geq 3\}$

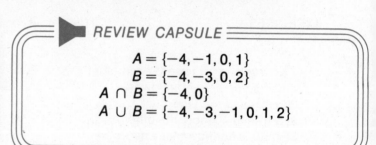

▶ REVIEW CAPSULE

$$A = \{-4, -1, 0, 1\}$$
$$B = \{-4, -3, 0, 2\}$$
$$A \cap B = \{-4, 0\}$$
$$A \cup B = \{-4, -3, -1, 0, 1, 2\}$$

EXAMPLE 1 $P = \{x\,|\,x \geq -2\}$ and $Q = \{x\,|\,x < 3\}$. Graph P, Q, and $P \cap Q$. Then describe the intersection.

Graph of $P = \{x\,|\,x \geq -2\}$ ————————→

Graph of $Q = \{x\,|\,x < 3\}$ ————————→

Graph of $P \cap Q$ ————————→

$P \cap Q$ contains all numbers common to sets P and Q.

Description of $P \cap Q$ ————————→ **Thus,** $P \cap Q = \{x\,|\, \geq -2$ *and* $x < 3\}$.

x is between -2 and 3. ————————→ We may also write $P \cap Q = \{x\,|\,-2 \leq x < 3\}$.

EXAMPLE 2 $P = \{x\,|\,x \geq -2\}$ and $Q = \{x\,|\,x < 3\}$. Graph P, Q, and $P \cup Q$. Then describe the union.

Graph of $P = \{x\,|\,x \geq -2\}$ ————————→

Graph of $Q = \{x\,|\,x < 3\}$ ————————→

Graph of $P \cup Q$ ————————→

$P \cup Q$ contains all numbers belonging to P, or Q, or both P and Q.

We may also write
$P \cup Q = \{x\,|\,x \geq -2 \text{ or } x < 3\}$. ————————→ **Thus,** $P \cup Q = \{\text{all numbers}\}$.

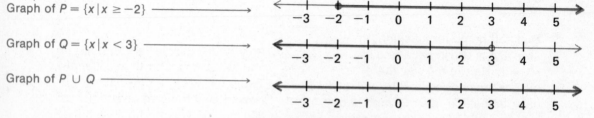

EXAMPLE 3 $R = \{x \mid x < -1\}$ and $S = \{x \mid x \geq 2\}$. Graph
R, S, and $R \cap S$. Then describe the intersection.

Graph of $R = \{x \mid x < -1\}$ ⟶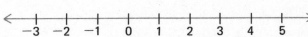

Graph of $S = \{x \mid x \geq 2\}$ ⟶

Graph of $R \cap S$ ⟶

There are no numbers common to sets R and S.

Description of $R \cap S$ ⟶ **Thus, $R \cap S = \phi$, or**
$$R \cap S = \{x \mid x < -1 \text{ and } x \geq 2\}.$$

EXAMPLE 4   Consider sets R and S graphed in Example 3.
Graph $R \cup S$. Then describe the union.

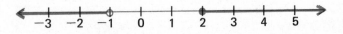

Graph of $R \cup S$ ⟶

$R \cup S$ contains all numbers belonging to R, or S,
or both R and S.

Description of $R \cup S$ ⟶ **Thus, $R \cup S = \{x \mid x < -1 \text{ or } x \geq 2\}$.**

EXAMPLE 5 $C = \{x \mid x < 4\}$ and $D = \{x \mid x \leq -1\}$. Graph
C, D, $C \cap D$, and $C \cup D$. Then describe the
intersection and the union.

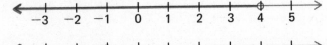

Graph of $C = \{x \mid x < 4\}$ ⟶

Graph of $D = \{x \mid x \leq -1\}$ ⟶

Graph of $C \cap D = \{x \mid x \leq -1\}$ ⟶

Graph of $C \cup D = \{x \mid x < 4\}$ ⟶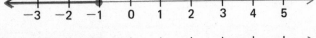

Description of $C \cap D$;
actually, $C \cap D = D$. ⟶ **Thus, $C \cap D = \{x \mid x \leq -1\}$**

Description of $C \cup D$;
actually, $C \cup D = C$. ⟶ and $C \cup D = \{x \mid x < 4\}$.

EXERCISES

PART A

Graph A, B, $A \cap B$, and $A \cup B$ on four separate number lines. Then describe the intersection and the union.

1. $A = \{x \,|\, x > -2\}$ $B = \{x \,|\, x < 5\}$
2. $A = \{x \,|\, x > 3\}$ $B = \{x \,|\, x < -1\}$
3. $A = \{x \,|\, x \geq -4\}$ $B = \{x \,|\, x < 2\}$
4. $A = \{x \,|\, x > 4\}$ $B = \{x \,|\, x \leq 0\}$
5. $A = \{x \,|\, x > -3\}$ $B = \{x \,|\, x \geq -1\}$
6. $A = \{x \,|\, x \leq 5\}$ $B = \{x \,|\, x < 3\}$
7. $A = \{x \,|\, x \geq -1\}$ $B = \{x \,|\, x \leq 3\}$
8. $A = \{x \,|\, x \leq 1\}$ $B = \{x \,|\, x \geq 4\}$
9. $A = \{x \,|\, x < 4\}$ $B = \{x \,|\, x < 0\}$
10. $A = \{x \,|\, x > -1\}$ $B = \{x \,|\, x > -7\}$
11. $A = \{x \,|\, x \geq 1\}$ $B = \{x \,|\, x \leq 1\}$
12. $A = \{x \,|\, x > 3\}$ $B = \{x \,|\, x \leq 3\}$
13. $A = \{x \,|\, x > -5\}$ $B = \{x \,|\, x > -4\}$
14. $A = \{x \,|\, x > -1\}$ $B = \{x \,|\, x \leq 0\}$
15. $A = \{x \,|\, x \leq 2\}$ $B = \{x \,|\, x > -1\}$
16. $A = \{x \,|\, x < -3\}$ $B = \{x \,|\, x > -3\}$
17. $A = \{x \,|\, x > 3\}$ $B = \{x \,|\, x \geq 3\}$
18. $A = \{x \,|\, x > 2\}$ $B = \{x \,|\, x < -2\}$
19. $A = \{x \,|\, x \geq 0\}$ $B = \{x \,|\, x < 0\}$
20. $A = \{x \,|\, x < -2\}$ $B = \{x \,|\, x \leq -2\}$
21. $A = \{x \,|\, x = 5\}$ $B = \{x \,|\, x > 5\}$
22. $A = \{x \,|\, x \geq 3\}$ $B = \{x \,|\, x \leq -3\}$
23. $A = \{x \,|\, x \geq -3\}$ $B = \{x \,|\, x \leq 3\}$
24. $A = \{x \,|\, x = 0\}$ $B = \{x \,|\, x \geq 0\}$
25. $A = \{x \,|\, x = -3\}$ $B = \{x \,|\, x \leq -3\}$
26. $A = \{x \,|\, x > 0\}$ $B = \{x \,|\, x = 0\}$
27. $A = \{x \,|\, x > 3\}$ $B = \{x \,|\, x \leq 4\}$
28. $A = \{x \,|\, x \leq 1\}$ $B = \{x \,|\, x > 2\}$
29. $A = \{$all numbers$\}$ $B = \{x \,|\, x > 2\}$
30. $A = \{$all numbers$\}$ $B = \{x \,|\, x = -1\}$

PART B

EXAMPLE   Describe the set graphed.   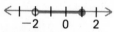

Also written $\{x \,|\, -2 < x \leq 1\}$ ⟶ The set graphed is $\{x \,|\, x > -2$ *and* $x \leq 1\}$.

Describe the set graphed.

31.
32.
33.
34.
35.
36.
37.
38.

PART C

If $A = \{x \,|\, x > -4\}$, $B = \{x \,|\, x \leq 5\}$, and $C = \{x \,|\, x \geq 0\}$, graph the following.

39. $(A \cap B) \cap C$ 40. $(A \cup B) \cup C$ 41. $(A \cap B) \cup C$ 42. $(A \cup B) \cap C$

More Clock Arithmetic

Here is a
five-minute clock.

Addition

$2 \oplus 1 = 3$ $2 \oplus 3 = 0$

Complete the addition table.

⊕	0	1	2	3	4
0	0	1	2	3	4
1	1	2			
2	2		4		
3	3			1	2
4					

Multiplication

$2 \otimes 1 = 2$ $2 \otimes 3 = 1$

Complete the multiplication table

⊗	0	1	2	3	4
0	0	0	0	0	0
1	0	1			
2	0		4		
3	0			4	
4	0				1

Here is a
seven-minute clock.

Addition

Complete the addition table.

⊕	0	1	2	3	4	5	6
0	0	1	2	3	4	5	6
1	1	2					
2	2	3		5		0	1
3	3						
4	4		6	0			
5	5	6					
6	6	0				4	5

Multiplication

Complete the multiplication table.

⊗	0	1	2	3	4	5	6
0	0	0	0	0	0	0	0
1	0	1	2	3	4	5	6
2	0	2					
3	0		6		5	1	
4	0		1			6	
5	0			1			
6	0	6					

Construct an addition table and a multiplication table for a six-minute clock.

Chapter Four Review

Which sets are equal to $\{2, 5, 8, 9\}$? [p. 91]

1. $\{8, 9, 5, 2\}$ **2.** $\{2, 9, 6, 5\}$ **3.** $\{5, 8, 3, 9\}$ **4.** $\{2, 2 + 3, 2 + 6, 2 + 7\}$

For each set tell whether it is finite or infinite. Then describe the set in words. [p. 91]

5. $\{1, 3, 5, 7, \ldots\}$ **6.** $\{2, 4, 6, 8\}$ **7.** $\{-1, -2, -3, -4, \ldots\}$

Describe each set by listing its elements. [p. 91]

8. {negative integers greater than -5}   **9.** {positive integers less than 1}

Find the solution set of each sentence. Then graph it. [p. 91]

10. $6x - 3 = 8 + 6x$ **11.** $10z + 17 = -9 + 8z$ **12.** $5c + 8 = -5c - 22$
13. $4 - 7y = -8y + 4$ **14.** $-2 + 10x = 28$ **15.** $3x - 8 + 4x = -12 + 7x$

Graph the solution set of each sentence. [p. 94]

16. $x > -2$ **17.** $y \le 5$ **18.** $z \ge 0$ **19.** $y = -4$
20. $-1 > c$ **21.** $y > 2$ **22.** $-2 \ge x$ **23.** $-3 = z$

For each inequality, write a *true* inequality by performing the indicated operation on each side. [p. 98]

24. $-3 \le 9$ Divide by -3.   **25.** $-7 \ge -8$ Multiply by -1.
26. $6 > -1$ Add -5.   **27.** $-8 < -4$ Divide by 2.

Find and graph the solution set. [p. 102]

28. $11x + 8 \le -14$ **29.** $8 > 5y - 7$
30. $4z + 12 < -3 + 7z$ **31.** $24 - 4x \ge -16 + 4x$
32. $18x - 18 > -6 + 5x$ **33.** $5y - 6y \le 3(4 + y)$

For each pair of sets, determine if $A \subseteq B$. Then determine if $B \subseteq A$. [p. 105]

34. $A = \{2, 4\}$ $B = \{6, 4, 2\}$ **35.** $A = \phi$ $B = \{0, 1\}$ **36.** $A = \{6, 10, 12\}$ $B = \{10, 6, 12\}$

List all the subsets of each set. Then give the number of subsets. [p. 105]

37. $\{3\}$ **38.** $\{4, 1\}$ **39.** $\{9, 8, 7\}$

For each pair of sets, find the intersection. Then find the union. [p. 105]

40. $\{4, 5, 9\}$ $\{9, 5\}$ **41.** $\{1, 3, 5\}$ $\{2, 4, 6\}$ **42.** $\{-2, 0, 2\}$ $\{-1, 0, 1\}$

Graph A, B, $A \cap B$, and $A \cup B$ on four separate number lines. Then describe the intersection and the union. [p. 112]

43. $A = \{x \mid x > 3\}$ $B = \{x \mid x \le 4\}$ **44.** $A = \{x \mid x \ge -4\}$ $B = \{x \mid x < 1\}$
45. $A = \{x \mid x \le 5\}$ $B = \{x \mid x < 1\}$ **46.** $A = \{x \mid x < -1\}$ $B = \{x \mid x > -1\}$

Chapter Four Test

Which sets are equal to $\{3, 6, 8, 9\}$?

1. $\{6, 3, 9, 8\}$

2. $\{9, 8, 3, 7\}$

3. $\{1+2, 7+1, 7-1, 8+1\}$

For each set tell whether it is finite or infinite. Then describe the set in words.

4. $\{5, 6, 7, 8, \ldots\}$

5. $\{1, 3, 5, 7\}$

6. $\{-2, -4, -6, -8, \ldots\}$

Describe each set by listing its elements.

7. {integers between -3 and 2}

8. {positive integers less than 4}

Find the solution set of each sentence. Then graph it.

9. $4y + 9 = -17 + 4y$

10. $3x + 8 = -3x - 16$

11. $-2p + 7 = 2p - 9$

12. $8r + 12 = 15r - 9 - 7r$

Graph the solution set of each sentence.

13. $x > -3$

14. $y \leq 0$

For each inequality, write a *true* inequality by performing the indicated operation on each side.

15. $6 > -5$ Add -8.

16. $-12 \leq -8$ Divide by -4.

Find and graph the solution set.

17. $6 - 9x < -21$

18. $7z - 9 \geq -14 + 6z$

19. $5y + 9 > -5 - 2y$

20. $x - 2x \leq -18 + 2x$

For each pair of sets, determine if $A \subseteq B$. Then determine if $B \subseteq A$.

21. $A = \{3, 5, 7, 9\}$ $B = \{9, 5\}$

22. $A = \{1, 6, 8\}$ $B = \{8, 1, 6\}$

List all the subsets of each set. Then give the number of subsets.

23. $\{7\}$

24. $\{1, 3, 5\}$

For each pair of sets, find the intersection. Then find the union.

25. $\{-5, 0, 5\}$ $\{-4, 0, 4\}$

26. $\{0, 2, 4\}$ $\{1, 3, 5\}$

Graph A, B, $A \cap B$, and $A \cup B$ on four separate number lines. Then describe the intersection and the union.

27. $A = \{x \mid x \geq -3\}$ $B = \{x \mid x < 1\}$

28. $A = \{x \mid x < -4\}$ $B = \{x \mid x \geq -1\}$

Women of Mathematics

Sophie Germain was born in Paris on the brink of the French Revolution. Confined to her house, Sophie amused herself by spending long hours in her father's library. Here she read of the violent death of Archimedes as he contemplated a mathematical figure in the sand. Impressed with his absorption in the subject, Sophie decided to study mathematics, much against the wishes of her parents.

Sophie Germain
(1776-1831)

Germain would get up at night and study the language of analysis until dawn. During the reign of terror, she studied differential calculus. She was able to get the lecture notes of various professors from the École Polytechnique, even though the school did not accept women. She began a correspondence with the famous mathematician Lagrange but signed herself M. Leblanc. Lagrange was very impressed with this young mathematician. He eventually learned of her identity and openly praised her work. Germain began to think of herself as a mathematician.

Most of her work was in the fields of number theory and mathematical analysis. In 1815, she was awarded a prize by the Institut de France. Germain was highly regarded by other mathematicians of her time and was recommended for an honorary degree from the University of Gottingen. Unfortunately, she died before the degree could be awarded.

Exponents

REVIEW CAPSULE

$(6)(2) = 12.$

6 is a factor of 12;   2 is a factor of 12.

Numbers which are multiplied are factors.

$(3)(3)(3)(3)$

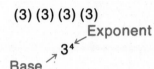

Base 3^4 Exponent

3^4

Fourth power of 3

A positive integer exponent tells the number of times the base is used as a factor.

x^1 means x, for each number x.

EXAMPLE 1   Find the value of 2^5.

Use 2 as a factor 5 times. $\longrightarrow$
2^5 does not mean $2(5)$.

$$2^5 = \underline{(2)(2)(2)(2)(2)}$$
$$= 32$$

EXAMPLE 2   Rewrite x^3 without an exponent.

Write x as a factor 3 times. $\longrightarrow$

Base x^3 Exponent $= (x)(x)(x)$

EXAMPLE 3   Evaluate a^5 if $a = -2$.

Write a as a factor 5 times. $\longrightarrow$

$(a)\quad(a)\quad(a)\quad(a)\quad(a)$

Substitute -2 for 1. $\longrightarrow$

$(-2)(-2)(-2)(-2)(-2)$

$(4)\qquad(4)\qquad(-2)$

Multiply. $\longrightarrow$

$(16)(-2)$
-32

EXAMPLE 4   Evaluate $-2a^3$ if $a = -3$.

Use a as a factor 3 times. ──────→
Substitute -3 for a. ──────→

$$-2a^3 = (-2)(a)(a)(a)$$
$$(-2)\underbrace{(-3)(-3)(-3)}$$
$$= (-2)\quad(-27)$$
$$= 54$$

EXAMPLE 5   Evaluate $-m^2b^3$ if $m = -2$, $b = 3$.

Replace $-m^2b^3$ with $-1m^2b^3$. ──────→
$m^2 = (m)(m)$; $b^3 = (b)(b)(b)$ ──────→
Substitute -2 for m, 3 for b. ──────→

$$-m^2b^3 = -1m^2b^3$$
$$= -1(m)(m)(b)(b)(b)$$
$$= -1(-2)(-2)(3)(3)(3)$$
$$= -1\quad(4)\quad\quad(27)$$
$$= -1\quad(108)$$
$$= -108$$

ORAL EXERCISES

Give without exponents.

1. x^5 **2.** x^3 **3.** a^4 **4.** a^2 **5.** $4n^3$ **6.** m^6 **7.** $-3a^2$ **8.** a^3b^2

EXERCISES

PART A

Evaluate for the given values of the variables.

1. a^3 if $a = -3$ **2.** b^5 if $b = -2$ **3.** m^4 if $m = 2$
4. $-2m^2$ if $m = -3$ **5.** $-3x^3$ if $x = 2$ **6.** $2a^5$ if $a = -2$
7. $-x^3$ if $x = -4$ **8.** $-a^2$ if $a = 5$ **9.** $-x^5$ if $x = -3$
10. $2ab^4$ if $a = -1$, $b = 2$ **11.** $-3x^3y^2$ if $x = -2$, $y = -1$ **12.** $-xy^5$ if $x = -2$, $y = -2$
13. $-x^3y^3$ if $x = -1$, $y = -3$ **14.** $-a^3b^2c$ if $a = -4$, $b = 2$,   **15.** $-2x^3yz$ if $x = 1$, $y = 1$,
                                          $c = -1$ $z = 2$

PART B

EXAMPLE   Evaluate $(5b)^2$ if $b = 4$.

$$[(5)(4)]^2 = (20)^2$$
$$= (20)(20),\text{ or }400$$

Evaluate for the given values of the variables.

16. $(4a)^3$ if $a = -1$ **17.** $(-2m)^3$ if $m = -2$ **18.** $(-x^2y^3)^2$ if $x = -2$,
                                                                             $y = 3$

Properties of Exponents

▶ REVIEW CAPSULE

Evaluate $-4a^3$ if $a = -2$.

$$-4a^3 = (-4)(a)(a)(a)$$
$$= (-4)(-2)(-2)(-2)$$
$$= 32$$

EXAMPLE 1   Simplify $a^3 \cdot a^4$.

Same base

$\underbrace{\text{(3 factors, } a) \text{ (4 factors, } a)}}$

7 factors, a

$$\underbrace{a \cdot a \cdot a \cdot a \cdot a \cdot a \cdot a}$$
$$a^7$$

Example 1 suggests this. ⟶
Add exponents.

Product of Powers
$$x^m \cdot x^n = x^{m+n}$$

EXAMPLE 2   Simplify $y^2 \cdot y^7$.   Simplify $x^5 \cdot x^4$.

$x^m \cdot x^n = x^{m+n}$ ⟶

$$y^{2+7} \qquad\qquad x^{5+4}$$
$$y^9 \qquad\qquad x^9$$

EXAMPLE 3   Simplify $(-5t^3)(-3t)$.   Simplify $(4a^3)(-6a^4)$.

t means t^1. ⟶
Group like factors. ⟶

$$(-5t^3)(-3t^1) \qquad 4 \cdot -6 \cdot a^3 \cdot a^4$$
$$-5 \cdot -3 \cdot t^3 \cdot t^1 \qquad -24 \cdot a^{3+4}$$
$$15 \quad \cdot t^{3+1} \qquad -24a^7$$
$$15t^4$$

EXAMPLE 4   Simplify $x^2 \cdot y^3$.

Different bases ⟶

$$x^2 \cdot y^3 = x \cdot x \cdot y \cdot y \cdot y$$
$$x^2 \quad \cdot \quad y^3$$

Thus, $x^2 \cdot y^3$ cannot be simplified.

EXAMPLE 5   Show that $(3^2)^3 = 3^{2 \cdot 3}$.

$(3^2)^3$	$3^{2 \cdot 3}$

Use 3^2 as a factor three times. ⟶ $3^2 \cdot 3^2 \cdot 3^2$ | 3^6
3^{2+2+2}

Same answers ⟶ 3^6 | **Thus,** $(3^2)^3 = 3^{2 \cdot 3}$.

Example 5 suggests this. ⟶
Multiply exponents.

Power of a Power
$$(x^m)^n = x^{m \cdot n}$$

EXAMPLE 6   Simplify $(x^3)^2$.   Simplify $(a^8)^3$.

$(x^m)^n = x^{m \cdot n}$ ⟶
$$(x^3)^2 = x^{3 \cdot 2} \qquad (a^8)^3 = a^{8 \cdot 3}$$
$$= x^6 \qquad\qquad = a^{24}$$

EXAMPLE 7   Show that $(a^3 b^2)^4 = (a^3)^4 \cdot (b^2)^4$.

$(a^3 b^2)^4$	$(a^3)^4 \cdot (b^2)^4$

Use $a^3 b^2$ as a factor 4 times. | $a^3 b^2 \cdot a^3 b^2 \cdot a^3 b^2 \cdot a^3 b^2$ | $a^{3 \cdot 4} \cdot b^{2 \cdot 4}$
$a^3 \cdot a^3 \cdot a^3 \cdot a^3 \cdot b^2 \cdot b^2 \cdot b^2 \cdot b^2$ | $a^{12} \cdot b^8$
$a^{3+3+3+3} \cdot b^{2+2+2+2}$

Same answers ⟶ $a^{12} \cdot b^8$

Thus, $(a^3 b^2)^4 = (a^3)^4 \cdot (b^2)^4$.

Example 7 suggests this. ⟶

Power of a Product
$$(x^m \cdot y^n)^p = x^{m \cdot p} \cdot y^{n \cdot p}$$

EXAMPLE 8   Simplify $(2a^2 b^4)^3$.

$(x^m \cdot y^n)^p = x^{m \cdot p} \cdot y^{n \cdot p}$ ⟶
Multiply exponents. ⟶
$$(2a^2 b^4)^3 = (2^1)^3 \cdot (a^2)^3 \cdot (b^4)^3$$
$$= 2^{1 \cdot 3} \cdot a^{2 \cdot 3} \cdot b^{4 \cdot 3}$$
$$= 2^3 \cdot \quad a^6 \cdot \quad b^{12}$$
2^3 is $2 \cdot 2 \cdot 2$, or 8. ⟶ $= 8a^6 b^{12}$

EXAMPLE 9   Simplify $(-3x^3 y^5)^3$.

$(x^m \cdot y^n)^p = x^{m \cdot p} \cdot y^{n \cdot p}$ ⟶
Multiply exponents. ⟶
$$(-3x^3 y^5)^3 = (-3^1)^3 \cdot (x^3)^3 \cdot (y^5)^3$$
$$= (-3)^{1 \cdot 3} \cdot x^{3 \cdot 3} \cdot y^{5 \cdot 3}$$
$$= (-3)^3 \cdot \quad x^9 \quad \cdot \quad y^{15}$$
$(-3)^3$ is $(-3)(-3)(-3)$, or -27. ⟶ $= -27x^9 y^{15}$

ORAL EXERCISES

Simplify.

1. $(m^3)(m^2)$ 2. $(b^3)(b^7)$ 3. $(b^2)(b^5)$ 4. $(c^6)(c^5)$ 5. $(b^5)(b)$
6. $(m^4)(m)$ 7. $(b)(b)$ 8. $(a)(a^6)$ 9. $(x)(x^3)$ 10. $(m)(m^9)$
11. $(c^2)^3$ 12. $(a^4)^5$ 13. $(x^8)^2$ 14. $(y^3)^4$ 15. $(x^6)^3$

EXERCISES

PART A

Simplify.

1. $(3a^2)(4a^6)$ 2. $(5a^4)(3a^7)$ 3. $(2m^5)(3m^6)$ 4. $(2b^3)(3b^4)$
5. $(4x^2)(7x^{10})$ 6. $(2n^5)(4n^2)$ 7. $(5a^4)(3a^5)$ 8. $(2y^3)(5y^4)$
9. $(a^2)(4a^3)$ 10. $(3b^5)(b^2)$ 11. $(6a^5)(a^6)$ 12. $(m^5)(3m^5)$
13. $(-4a^3)(2a^5)$ 14. $(-6b^5)(-2b^7)$ 15. $(4m^3)(-2m^5)$ 16. $(a^7)(-3a^8)$
17. $(4a^3)(2a)$ 18. $(5b^2)(-4b)$ 19. $(-3b)(5b^7)$ 20. $(4b^4)(-3b)$
21. $(3a^3b^2)(4a^2b^4)$ 22. $(4x^2y^3)(2x^3y^4)$ 23. $(5m^2n^3)(-4m^2n^4)$
24. $(-2a^2b^3)(4ab^5)$ 25. $(-2ab^3)(-3a^4b)$ 26. $(ab)(ab)$
27. $(a^2)^3$ 28. $(b^3)^4$ 29. $(x^2)^6$ 30. $(y^5)^3$ 31. $(z^6)^5$ 32. $(c^9)^3$
33. $(r^3)^{10}$ 34. $(f^7)^7$ 35. $(g^{15})^3$ 36. $(d^{25})^4$ 37. $(c^4)^7$ 38. $(h^{10})^{20}$
39. $(2x^2)^4$ 40. $(-3y^3)^2$ 41. $(-2z^4)^3$ 42. $(5a^5)^3$ 43. $(4x^3)^4$

PART B

Simplify.

44. $(4a^3m^2)^2$ 45. $(3a^2x^3)^2$ 46. $(2x^2y^3)^2$ 47. $(2m^3n^4)^3$ 48. $(5a^2b^3)^3$
49. $(-4a^3m^4)^3$ 50. $(3x^2y^4)^4$ 51. $(2xa^2)^3$ 52. $(-3a^2b^3)^3$ 53. $(-3xy^2m)^5$
54. $(x^3y^2z^4)^3$ 55. $(a^2b^4c^3)^5$ 56. $(x^2y^3z^4)^7$
57. $(3a^3b^2)^3$ 58. $(2x^6y^4)^3$ 59. $(-3x^3y^4z^2)^3$

PART C

EXAMPLE   Simplify $(x^3)^{2a} \cdot (x^a)^3$.

$(x^m)^n = x^{m \cdot n}$ ⟶ $x^{3 \cdot 2a} \cdot x^{a \cdot 3}$
                    $x^{6a} \cdot x^{3a}$

$x^{6a} \cdot x^{3a} = x^{6a+3a}$, or x^{9a} ⟶ x^{9a}

Simplify.

60. $(x^{2a})(x^{2a})$ 61. $(y^b)(y^{3b})$ 62. $(2x^3)(3x^a)$
63. $(x^{3a})^2$ 64. $(y^{5b})^3$ 65. $(2x^{5a})^a$

Polynomials

OBJECTIVES
- To classify polynomials
- To simplify polynomials by combining like terms

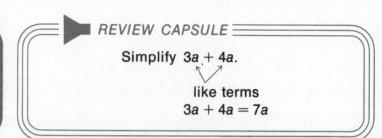

REVIEW CAPSULE

Simplify $3a + 4a$.

like terms

$3a + 4a = 7a$

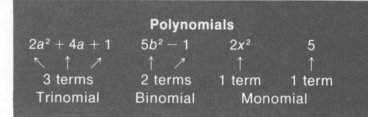

Polynomials

$2a^2 + 4a + 1$	$5b^2 - 1$	$2x^2$	5
3 terms	2 terms	1 term	1 term
Trinomial	Binomial	Monomial	

EXAMPLE 1

Classify each polynomial.

Tri means three; bi means two; mono means one.

$2a^2 + 7a + 9$	$4m^2 - 6$	$12x^2$
3 terms	2 terms	1 term
Trinomial	Binomial	Monomial

EXAMPLE 2

Simplify $9 + 7x^3 + 2x^2 - 5x^2 + 4x^3 - 8$

Group like terms together.
$(7x^3 + 4x^3) = (7 + 4)x^3$

$(7x^3 + 4x^3) + (2x^2 - 5x^2) + (9 - 8)$
$\quad 11x^3 \qquad\quad -3x^2 \qquad\quad +1$, or $11x^3 - 3x^2 + 1$

EXAMPLE 3

Simplify $8x^3 - 7x^5 + 5x - 4x^2 + 3x^3 - 2x + 6$.
Then write the result in descending order of exponents.

Group like terms.
Combine like terms.

$$8x^3 + 3x^3 - 7x^5 + 5x - 2x - 4x^2 + 6$$
$$11x^3 \quad - 7x^5 \quad +3x \quad - 4x^2 + 6$$

Arrange terms in order of exponents with highest exponent first.

Now write the result in descending order of exponents.

$$-7x^5 + 11x^3 - 4x^2 + 3x + 6$$

EXAMPLE 4

Simplify $7x^3 + 4x^2$.

$7x^3$ and $4x^2$ are not like terms.
Thus, $7x^3 + 4x^2$ cannot be simplified.

EXAMPLE 5   Simplify $x^2 - 8 + 5x^4 - 7x + 3x^3 - 2x^4 + 5x^2 + 6x + 3$.

Group like terms.⟶ $1x^2 + 5x^2 - 8 + 3 + 5x^4 - 2x^4 - 7x + 6x + 3x^3$

Combine like terms. ⟶ $\quad 6x^2 \qquad -5 \qquad + 3x^4 \qquad -1x \quad + 3x^3$

Descending order ⟶ $\qquad 3x^4 + 3x^3 + 6x^2 - x - 5$

ORAL EXERCISES

Classify each polynomial.

1. $3x^3 - 5x$
2. $-4x^2$
3. $5x^3 - 4x^2 + 7x$
4. 3

Arrange each polynomial in descending order of exponents.

5. $3x^2 - 5x^3 + 7x - 4$
6. $5x - 4x^2 - 3$
7. $4a^2 - 5a^3 + 2a + 1$
8. $-4x^2 - 7x^3 + x^4 + 5x + 1$
9. $5x - 4x^3 + 7x^2 + 2$
10. $6 - 5x^3 + 2x + 3x^2 + x^4$
11. $6x^4 - 3x^2 + 2x^3 - 5 + x$

EXERCISES

PART A

Simplify. Then write the result in descending order of exponents.

1. $3x^2 - 5x + 2x - 8$
2. $5x^2 - 8x + 3x + 4$
3. $5x^2 - 3x + 2 + 4x^2 + 7x + 3$
4. $4 + 8x^2 - 2x + 6x^2 - 4x - 6$
5. $-7x + 2x^2 - 5 + 3x^2 + 8 - 4x$
6. $8x - 2x^2 + 5x - 4 + 5x^2 - 3$
7. $-4 + 3m^2 - 5 - 2m^2$
8. $5m^2 - 4 - 7m^2 + 8$
9. $4x - 6x^2 + 5x^3 - 3x^2 + 2x^3 + 5x$
10. $4x^3 - 5x + 2x^2 + 7x - 3x^3 + 5x^2$
11. $4m^3 - 5m^3 + 4m^2 - 4m^2 - 3m + 8m$
12. $m^3 - 9m - 5m^2 + 9m + 4m^2 + 5m^3$
13. $6a^4 - 3a^2 + 2a^4 + 4a^2$
14. $5a - 3a^4 + 7a + 2a^4$
15. $3 + 6a - 2a^2 - 5a + 4a^2 - 4$
16. $7a - 3 - a^2 + 5a - 4 - 2a^2$
17. $7b^3 - 4b - 2b^2 + 3b + 8$
18. $4b - 3 - 9b^3 + 5b + 2b^2 - 8$

Simplify.

19. $1 + 3a^3 - 4a - 2a^2 + 7a^3 - 8a + 4a^2 - 5$
20. $6a^2 - 5a - 3 + a^2 - 4a^2 + 3a^3 + 8a + 5$
21. $a^2 + a^4 - 2a^3 - 7a - 2 + 2a^4 - 5a^3 + 8a - 4 + a^2$
22. $7b^2 - 5b^4 + 2b^3 + 2b - 1 - 4b^4 - 3b^3 + 2b^2 - 8b - 2$
23. $1 - 3m^9 - 7m^6 - 19m^9 + 6m^6 - 4$
24. $3b^5 - 6b^7 + b^5 - b^7 - b^4 - 2b^2 + 5b^4$
25. $-3a^2 + 7a - 2a^2 + 4a^3 + 6a - 9 + 8a^3 - 10 + a^4 - 5a^2$

Venn Diagrams

Venn diagrams show unions and intersections of sets.

$U = \{1, 2, 3, 4, 5, 6, 7, 8, 9\}$
$A = \{1, 2, 6\}$
$B = \{1, 5, 6, 8\}$
$C = \{3, 7\}$

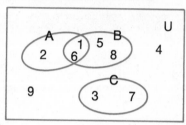

$A \cup B = \{1, 2, 5, 6, 8\}$
$A \cap B = \{1, 6\}$
$B \cup C = \{1, 3, 5, 6, 7, 8\}$
$B \cap C = \phi$
$A \cup C = \{1, 2, 3, 6, 7\}$
$A \cap C = \phi$

B and C are disjoint sets and A and C are disjoint sets
Since $B \cap C = \phi$ and $A \cap C = \phi$.

U = universe
$R = ///$
$S = \backslash\backslash\backslash$

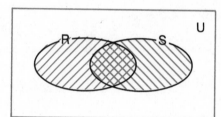

$R \cup S$ = entire hatched region, the set of all elements in R or S or both

$R \cap S = $ ☒☒☒
the set of all elements common to R and S

$U = \{0, 2, 4, 6, 8, 10\}, \quad A = \{0, 4, 8\}, \quad B = \{4, 6\}, \quad C = \{2, 10\}.$

$A \cap B = \{4\}$

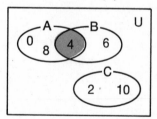

$A \cup B = \{0, 4, 6, 8\}$

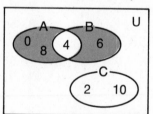

$B \cup C = \{2, 4, 6, 10\}$

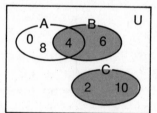

Draw a Venn diagram for each. Show $A \cap B$, $B \cap C$, and $A \cup B$.

1. $U = \{1, 3, 5, 7, 9, 11\}, A = \{3, 5\}, B = \{5, 9, 11\}, C = \{7\}$
2. $U = \{1, 2, 3, 4, 5, 6, 7\}, A = \{3, 5, 6\}, B = \{2, 4, 7\}, C = \{1, 4, 7\}$
3. $U = \{0, 1, 2, 3, 8, 9, 10\}, A = \{1, 2\}, B = \{8, 9\}, C = \{3, 10\}$
4. $U = \{10, 20, 30, 40, 50, 60, 80\}, A = \{10, 20, 30\}, B = \{30, 40\ 50\}, C = \{30, 80\}$

100 students participated in a sports survey at Hill Regional High School. The results are given below.

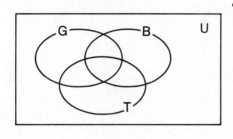

"Out for"	Sport	Symbol
38	Golf	G
29	Basketball	B
41	Tennis	T
17	Golf and Basketball	$G \cap B$
20	Golf and Tennis	$G \cap T$
15	Basketball and Tennis	$B \cap T$
12	All three sports	$G \cap B \cap T$

5. How many play golf and basketball but not tennis?
6. How many play only golf?
7. How many play none of these sports?

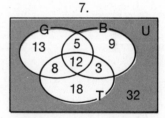

5.

$G \cap B = 17$
$G \cap B \cap T = 12$
golf and basketball, but not tennis: 5

6.

$G = 38$
$G \cap B = 17$
$G \cap T = 20$
$G \cap B \cap T = 12$
only golf: $38 - (8 + 12 + 5)$
$= 13$

7.

none of these sports:
$100 - (13 + 5 + 12 + 8 + 18 + 3 + 9)$
$= 100 - 68$
$= 32$

30 students in Mr. Jones' science class participated in a pet survey. The results are given below. Draw a Venn diagram, then answer the questions.

Pet	Number of students with pets
Dog	19
Cat	11
Other	17
Dog and Cat	7
Dog and Other	12
Cat and Other	5
All Three	3

8. How many had a dog and a cat, but no other pet?
9. How many had only a cat?
10. How many did not have a pet?

Simplifying Polynomials

OBJECTIVES
- To simplify polynomials
- To add and subtract polynomials

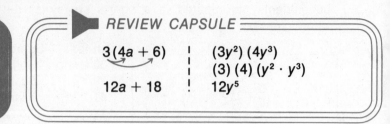

REVIEW CAPSULE

$3(4a + 6)$

$12a + 18$

$(3y^2)(4y^3)$
$(3)(4)(y^2 \cdot y^3)$
$12y^5$

EXAMPLE 1 Multiply $a^2(3a^3 + 2a^2)$.

Distribute a^2. →
Regroup factors. →
$x^m \cdot x^n = x^{m+n}$ →

$$a^2(3a^3) + a^2(2a^2)$$
$$3 \cdot a^2 \cdot a^3 + 2 \cdot a^2 \cdot a^2$$
$$3a^5 + 2a^4$$

EXAMPLE 2 Multiply $4m^5(2m^6 - 3m^3 + 4m)$.

m means m^1. →
Distribute $4m^5$. →

$$4m^5(2m^6 - 3m^3 + 4m^1)$$
$$4m^5(2m^6) + 4m^5(-3m^3) + 4m^5(4m^1)$$
$$4 \cdot 2 \cdot m^5 \cdot m^6 + 4 \cdot -3 \cdot m^5 \cdot m^3 + 4 \cdot 4 \cdot m^5 \cdot m^1$$
$$8m^{11} - 12m^8 + 16m^6$$

EXAMPLE 3 Simplify $-(p^2 + 2p - 4)$.

$-a = -1 \cdot a$ →

$-1p^2 = -p^2$ →

$$-1(1p^2 + 2p - 4)$$
$$(-1)(1p^2) + (-1)(2p) + (-1)(-4)$$
$$-1p^2 \qquad -2p \qquad +4$$
$$-p^2 - 2p + 4$$

EXAMPLE 4 Simplify $x^3 + 2x^2 - 8x - (-2x^2 + 7x - 5)$.

$a = 1a, -a = -1a$ →

Distribute -1. →
Group like terms. →
Combine like terms. →
$1x^3 = x^3$ →

$$1x^3 + 2x^2 - 8x - 1(-2x^2 + 7x - 5)$$
$$1x^3 + 2x^2 - 8x + 2x^2 - 7x + 5$$
$$1x^3 + 2x^2 + 2x^2 - 8x - 7x + 5$$
$$1x^3 + 4x^2 - 15x + 5$$
$$x^3 + 4x^2 - 15x + 5$$

EXAMPLE 5   Add $(c^4 - 5c + 8) + (c^5 - c^4 + c^3)$.

$$(1c^4 - 5c + 8) + (1c^5 - 1c^4 + 1c^3)$$

Group like terms. ⟶ $1c^4 - 1c^4 - 5c + 8 + 1c^5 + 1c^3$

Combine like terms. ⟶ $0 - 5c + 8 + 1c^5 + 1c^3$

Descending order of exponents ⟶ $1c^5 + 1c^3 - 5c + 8$

$1c^5 = c^5; \ 1c^3 = c^3$ ⟶ $c^5 + c^3 - 5c + 8$

EXAMPLE 6   Simplify $m^2 + 3m + 7 + 2(m^2 - 5m + 7)$

m^2 means $1m^2$. ⟶ $1m^2 + 3m + 7 + 2(1m^2 - 5m + 7)$

Distribute 2. ⟶ $1m^2 + 3m + 7 + 2m^2 - 10m + 14$

$1m^2 + 2m^2 + 3m - 10m + 7 + 14$

Combine like terms. ⟶ $3m^2 - 7m + 21$

EXAMPLE 7   Subtract $y^3 - 3y^2$ from $6y^4 - 5y^3 + 7y^2 - 8$.

$$(6y^4 - 5y^3 + 7y^2 - 8) - (y^3 - 3y^2)$$

$-a = -1a; \ a = 1a$ ⟶ $(6y^4 - 5y^3 + 7y^2 - 8) - 1(1y^3 - 3y^2)$

$6y^4 - 5y^3 + 7y^2 - 8 - 1y^3 + 3y^2$

$6y^4 - 5y^3 - 1y^3 + 7y^2 + 3y^2 - 8$

$6y^4 - 6y^3 + 10y^2 - 8$

ORAL EXERCISES

Multiply.

1. $3(2a^2 - 6a - 4)$
2. $5(2a^2 - 4a + 3)$
3. $2(3a^2 - 5a + 6)$
4. $5(4a^3 - 2a^2 + 5a - 2)$
5. $2(3a^3 - 2a^2 + 5a - 2)$
6. $4(4a^3 - 2a^2 + 7a - 3)$
7. $a^2(a^3 + a^2)$
8. $b^3(b^4 + b^2)$
9. $b^5(b^3 + b^2)$
10. $m^2(m^2 + m)$
11. $m^3(m^4 + m)$
12. $a^2(a^2 + a)$
13. $a^4(a^2 + a)$
14. $a^2(a^2 + a + 5)$
15. $a^3(a^2 + a + 1)$

EXERCISES

PART A

Multiply.

1. $2f^2(3f^2 - 5f + 4)$
2. $2t^2(3t^2 - 5t + 6)$
3. $3a(2a^2 - 5a + 4)$
4. $5b(3b^2 - 4b + 3)$
5. $2x^3(3x^2 - 7x)$
6. $5a^3(3a^2 - 7a)$

Simplify.

7. $6b(4b^2 - 5b)$
8. $3m(2m^2 - 5m)$
9. $5c(4c^3 - 5c^2)$
10. $-(2b^2 - 5b)$
11. $-(4x^2 - 5x)$
12. $-(3x^2 - 4x + 2)$
13. $-(2x^2 + 5x - 7)$
14. $-(-b^2 - 5b)$
15. $-(-b^2 + 2b)$
16. $-(-x^2 - x - 2)$
17. $-(a^2 - a - 4)$
18. $-(-c^3 + c - 5)$
19. $-3a(-3a^2 - 5a + 2)$
20. $-5b(-2b^2 - 3b - 4)$
21. $-2a^2(2a^2 - 6a - 8)$
22. $-a(2a^2 - a - 3)$
23. $-m(-m^2 - m - 5)$
24. $-g(-g^2 - 2g + 5)$
25. $x^3 + 5x^2 - 7x - (-3x^2 + 5x - 9)$
26. $x^3 + 4x^2 - 5x - (+2x^2 \mp 3x + 8)$
27. $2x^3 - x^2 - x - 4 - (-x^2 - 2x + 5)$
28. $-3c^2 - 5c + 2 - (+2c^2 + 3c + 4)$

Add.

29. $(x^4 - 8x + 7) + (x^5 - x^4 + x^3)$
30. $(a^3 - 3a + 5) + (a^4 - a^3 + a^2)$
31. $(a^2 - a - 4) + (2a^2 - a - 3)$
32. $(-3b^2 - 5b + 2) + (-2b^2 - 3b - 4)$

Simplify.

33. $x^2 + 3x + 2 + 3(x^2 - 4x + 5)$
34. $y^2 - 4y + 3 + 4(y^2 + y - 5)$
35. $2a^2 - 5a - 10 + 2(2a^2 - 3a + 5)$
36. $3c^2 - c + 6 + 3(c^2 - 3c - 5)$

37. Subtract $x^3 - 2x^2$ from $5x^4 - x^3 + 2x^2 - 3$.
38. Subtract $a^2 - 2a$ from $5a^3 - 7a^2 + 8a - 3$.
39. Subtract $-x^3 - 2x$ from $x^4 + 3x^2 - 5x + 3$.
40. Subtract $-c^2 + 5$ from $3c^3 - 2c^2 + c - 5$.

PART B

| | **EXAMPLE** | Simplify $a^2b^3(2a^2 - 3ab + b^2)$. |

Distribute a^2b^3. $\longrightarrow a^2b^3(2a^2) + a^2b^3(-3ab) + a^2b^3(b^2)$

Regroup factors. $\longrightarrow 2(a^2)(a^2)(b^3) + (-3)(a^2)(a^1)(b^3)(b^1)$
$$+ (a^2)(b^3)(b^2)$$

$x^m \cdot x^n = x^{m+n} \longrightarrow 2(a^4)(b^3) \qquad -3 \quad (a^3) \quad (b^4) + 1(a^2)(b^5)$
$$2a^4b^3 - 3a^3b^4 + a^2b^5$$

Simplify.

41. $m^3n^2(2m^2 - 3mn + n^2)$
42. $ab(a^2 - 5ab + 7b^2)$
43. $2ab(a^2 - 3ab + 5b^2)$
44. $3m^2n^2(m^3 - 3m^2n + mn^2 + n^3)$
45. $-xy^2(2x^2 - xy + y^2)$
46. $-pq(p^2 - pq + q^2)$
47. $-2ac(a^3 - a^2c + ac^2 - c^3)$
48. $-3x^2y(-x^2 - 2xy - y^2)$

PART C

Simplify.

49. $m^3n^2(2m^2 - 3mn + n^2) + m^3n^2(m^2 - 2mn + 3n^2)$
50. $2ab(a^2 - 3ab + 5b^2) - 3ab(3a^2 - 7ab - 9b^2)$
51. $-xy^2(3x^2 - 2xy + 5y^2) + xy^2(x^2 - xy - y^2)$
52. $-3ab^2(-a^3 - 2a^2b + ab^2 - b^3) - 2ab^2(a^3 + 3a^2b - ab^2 + 2b^3)$

Perfect Numbers

28 is a perfect number

Factors of 28 less than 28.
{1, 2, 4, 7, 14}

28

$$1 + 2 + 4 + 7 + 14 = 28$$

A whole number is perfect if it is the sum
of all of its factors less than itself.

1. There is one perfect number less
   than 28. Can you find it?

2. Is 18 a perfect number?

3. Is 36 a perfect number?

4. The third perfect number is between
   490 and 500. Can you find it?

5. The fourth perfect number is
   between 8120 and 8130. Can you
   find it?

6. Were any of the first 4 perfect
   numbers an odd number?

Concept of Factoring

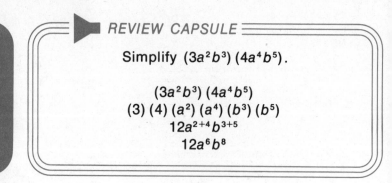

REVIEW CAPSULE

Simplify $(3a^2b^3)(4a^4b^5)$.

$(3a^2b^3)(4a^4b^5)$
$(3)(4)(a^2)(a^4)(b^3)(b^5)$
$12a^{2+4}b^{3+5}$
$12a^6b^8$

Numbers which are multiplied are *factors*.

24 can be factored into $8 \cdot 3$,
or $12 \cdot 2$,
or $2 \cdot 3 \cdot 4$,
or $2 \cdot 2 \cdot 2 \cdot 3$.

In the last case, none of the factors can be factored further except for itself and 1.

The only factors of 3 are 3 and 1.

itself and 1

2 is a prime number.
3 is also a prime number.

Definition of prime number ⟶ A *prime number* is a whole number greater than 1 whose only factors are itself and 1.

EXAMPLE 1   Factor 40 into primes.

Three ways to begin

$40 = 20 \cdot 2$ $40 = 8 \cdot 5$ $40 = 10 \cdot 4$
$= 5 \cdot 4 \cdot 2$ $= 4 \cdot 2 \cdot 5$
Each gives the same 4 factors. ⟶ $= 5 \cdot 2 \cdot 2 \cdot 2$ $= 2 \cdot 2 \cdot 2 \cdot 5$ $= 5 \cdot 2 \cdot 2 \cdot 2$

Each factor is prime. ⟶ **Thus,** $40 = 5 \cdot 2 \cdot 2 \cdot 2$.

$5 \cdot 2 \cdot 2 \cdot 2$ is the prime factorization of 40.

EXAMPLE 2   Factor 32 into primes.

Begin with any factorization.
16 is NOT prime.
 8 is NOT prime.
 4 is NOT prime.

$$32 = 16 \cdot 2$$
$$= 8 \cdot 2 \cdot 2$$
$$= 4 \cdot 2 \cdot 2 \cdot 2$$
$$= 2 \cdot 2 \cdot 2 \cdot 2 \cdot 2$$

EXAMPLE 3   Find the missing factor.
$$(a^5)\,(?) = a^8$$

$x^m \cdot x^n = x^{m+n}$ ⟶

$8 = 5 + \boxed{3}$ ⟶

$(a^5)\,(a^\square)$

$a^{5+\underset{\downarrow}{\square}}$

$a^{5+\boxed{3}}$

$(a^5)\,(a^{\boxed{3}})$

$(a^5)\,(a^3) = a^{5+3}$, or a^8 ⟶ **Thus,** the missing factor is a^3.

EXAMPLE 4   Find the missing factor.
$$(5a^4)\,(?) = -20a^7$$

We need a number factor and a
factor $a^\square$. ⟶

$-20 = (5)(-4)$

$a^7 = (a^4)(a^{\boxed{3}})$ ⟶

Check by multiplying.

$(5a^4)(-4a^3) = -20a^7$ ⟶ **Thus,** $-4a^3$ is the missing factor.

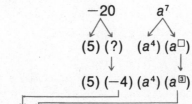

ORAL EXERCISES

Tell whether each is prime.

1. 8	**2.** 19	**3.** 21	**4.** 37
5. 7	**6.** 49	**7.** 15	**8.** 41
9. 52	**10.** 2	**11.** 27	**12.** 31
13. 40	**14.** 5	**15.** 29	**16.** 25

Factor each as the product of two factors in three different ways.

17. 12	**18.** 60	**19.** 28	**20.** 30
21. 36	**22.** 52	**23.** 42	**24.** 20
25. 18	**26.** 48	**27.** 32	**28.** 44

EXERCISES

PART A

Factor into primes.

1. 12	**2.** 24	**3.** 18	**4.** 28
5. 45	**6.** 60	**7.** 26	**8.** 35
9. 50	**10.** 72	**11.** 44	**12.** 30
13. 80	**14.** 42	**15.** 48	**16.** 27

Find the missing factor.

17. $(4x^2)(?) = 28x^4$

18. $(2a^3)(?) = 30a^8$

19. $(6m^5)(?) = 36m^8$

20. $(4a^3)(?) = 32a^7$

21. $(-3x^5)(?) = 27x^7$

22. $(-3x^3)(?) = 18x^6$

23. $(?)(5x^5) = 35x^{10}$

24. $(?)(4m^5) = 8m^9$

25. $(?)(3x^3) = -30x^7$

26. $(?)(-20a^8) = 40a^{13}$

27. $(3b^2)(?) = 3b^7$

28. $(?)(5b^9) = 5b^{12}$

29. $(-8b^5)(?) = 16b^6$

30. $(-b^7)(?) = 5b^8$

PART B

EXAMPLE

Find the missing factor.
$$(2a^2b^3)(?) = 8a^7b^9$$

We need a number factor, a factor $a^\square$, and a factor $b^\triangle$. ⟶

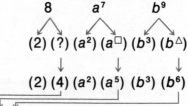

Check by multiplying.
$(2a^2b^3)(4a^5b^6) = 8a^7b^9$ ⟶ **Thus, $4a^5b^6$ is the missing factor.**

Find the missing factor.

31. $(3a^2b^3)(?) = 27a^5b^4$

32. $(4a^3m^5)(?) = 24a^7m^9$

33. $(?)(4a^3m^7) = -32a^5m^9$

34. $(3a^2b^5)(?) = 39a^4b^7$

35. $(?)(2a^2b^5) = -2a^3b^6$

36. $(?)(4x^3y^2) = -8x^4y^3$

37. $(?)(3x^3y^4) = -3x^5y^8$

38. $(2ab^2)(?) = -16a^2b^3$

39. $(3x^3y)(?) = 3x^4y$

40. $(8a^3m)(?) = -8a^7m$

PART C

Find the missing factor.

41. $(a^{2m})(?) = a^{5m}$

42. $(x^{3a})(?) = x^{8a}$

43. $(a^{2m+5})(?) = a^{4m+9}$

Factoring Out a Common Monomial

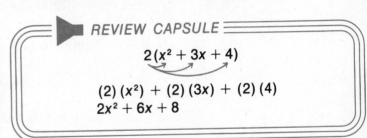

REVIEW CAPSULE

$$2(x^2 + 3x + 4)$$

$$(2)(x^2) + (2)(3x) + (2)(4)$$
$$2x^2 + 6x + 8$$

Use the distributive property in reverse. →

We can rewrite $2m^3 - 6m^2 + 10m - 8$
as $2(m^3 - 3m^2 + 5m - 4)$.

2 is a common monomial factor.

EXAMPLE 1 Factor a common monomial factor from $3b^2 + 9b + 6$.

3 divides each term evenly. Use 3 as a factor of each term.

$$3b^2 + \quad 9b \quad + 6$$
$$3(b^2) + 3(3b) + 3(2)$$

Use the distributive property in reverse. →

$$3(b^2 + 3b + 2)$$

EXAMPLE 2 Factor the greatest common factor from $4x^2 - 8x + 4$.

4 is the greatest number that divides each term evenly. Use 4 as a factor of each term.

$$4x^2 - \quad 8x \quad + 4$$
$$4(x^2) + 4(-2x) + 4(1)$$

Distributive property in reverse →

$$4(x^2 - 2x + 1)$$

4 is the GCF (short for greatest common factor) of $4x^2 - 8x + 4$.

EXAMPLE 3 Find the GCF of $6x^2 + 12$.

Factor 6 and 12 into primes. →

$$(3)(2)(x^2) \quad + \quad (2)(3)(2)$$

one 3, one 2   two 2's, one 3

At most, one 2 and one 3 are common to each term.

Thus, the GCF is $(2)(3)$, or 6.

Example 3 shows a technique for finding the GCF. You need not use that process if you can recognize the GCF immediately.

EXAMPLE 4 Factor the GCF from $20b^2 - 24b + 48$.

Factor into primes. $\longrightarrow$ $(2)(2)(5)(b^2) - (2)(2)(2)(3)(b) + (2)(2)(2)(2)(3)$

At most, two 2's are common to each term, so the GCF is $(2)(2)$, or 4.

$$20b^2 - 24b + 48$$

Use 4 as a factor of each term. $\longrightarrow$ $4(5b^2) + 4(-6b) + 4(12)$
Distributive property in reverse $\longrightarrow$ $4(5b^2 - 6b + 12)$

EXAMPLE 5 Factor $x^3 + x^2 + x$.

x means x^1. $\longrightarrow$

$$x^3 \quad + \quad x^2 \quad + \quad x^1$$
$$\uparrow \qquad\qquad \uparrow \qquad\qquad \uparrow$$

Think. $\longrightarrow$ three x's   two x's   one x

At most, one x is common to each term, so the GCF is x^1.

$$x^3 + x^2 + x^1$$

Use x^1 as a factor of each term. $\longrightarrow$ $x^1(x^2) + x^1(x^1) + x^1(1)$
$x^1 = x$ $x^1(x^2 + x^1 + 1)$, or $x(x^2 + x + 1)$

EXAMPLE 6 Factor $2x^4 + 4x^3 + 6x^2$.

First step $\longrightarrow$ Look for the greatest common whole number factor.

Factor coefficients into primes. $\longrightarrow$ $(2)(x^4) + (2)(2)(x^3) + (2)(3)(x^2)$
2 is common to each term. $\longrightarrow$ 2 is the greatest common whole number factor.

Second step $\longrightarrow$ Now look for the greatest common variable factor.

$$2x^4 \quad + \quad 4x^3 \quad + \quad 6x^2$$
$$\uparrow \qquad\qquad \uparrow \qquad\qquad \uparrow$$

Think. $\longrightarrow$ four x's   three x's   two x's
x^2 is common to each term. $\longrightarrow$ x^2 is the greatest common variable factor.
$2x^2$ divides each term evenly. $\longrightarrow$ The GCF of $2x^4 + 4x^3 + 6x^2$ is $2x^2$.
Use $2x^2$ as a factor of each term. $\longrightarrow$ $2x^2(x^2) + 2x^2(2x^1) + 2x^2(3)$
Distributive property in reverse $\longrightarrow$ $2x^2(x^2 + 2x + 3)$

Thus, $2x^4 + 4x^3 + 6x^2 = 2x^2(x^2 + 2x + 3)$.

EXAMPLE 7   Factor $5x^6 - 20x^4 + x^3$.

First step $\longrightarrow$ Look for a common whole number factor.

$$(5)(x^6) - (5)(4)(x^4) + 1(x^3)$$

1 is the common whole number factor. We do not bother to factor out the 1.

Second step $\longrightarrow$ Now look for the greatest common variable factor.

$$5x^6 \quad - \quad 20x^4 \quad + \quad 1x^3$$
$$\uparrow \qquad\qquad \uparrow \qquad\qquad \uparrow$$

Think. $\longrightarrow$ six x's   four x's   three x's

x^3 is common to each term. $\longrightarrow$ x^3 is the greatest common variable factor.

$$5x^6 - 20x^4 + 1x^3$$

Use x^3 as a factor of each term. $\longrightarrow$ $x^3(5x^3) + x^3(-20x^1) + x^3(1)$

Distributive property in reverse $\longrightarrow$ $x^3(5x^3 - 20x^1 + 1)$, or $x^3(5x^3 - 20x + 1)$

SUMMARY   **To factor out the greatest common monomial factor:**
First, factor out the greatest common whole number factor other than 1, if any. | **Second, factor out the greatest common variable factor, if any.**

EXERCISES

PART A

Factor.

1. $3x^2 + 27x + 9$ 2. $4a^2 + 32a + 20$ 3. $6b^2 + 18b + 30$ 4. $2m^2 - 10m + 4$
5. $7a^2 - 21a + 49$ 6. $m^3 + m^2 + m$ 7. $x^5 + x^4 - x^3$ 8. $b^4 - 2b^3 + b^2$
9. $2a^3 - a^2 + a$ 10. $y^3 - 7y^2 + y$ 11. $7a^2 - 28a$ 12. $3x^2 - 9x$
13. $4a^3 + 8a^2$ 14. $5b^3 - 10b$ 15. $6a^2 - 24a$ 16. $4a^3 - 16a^2 + 32a$
17. $4a^3 - 12a^2 + 8a$ 18. $7b^3 - 14b^2 + 49b$ 19. $12x^3 - 6x^2 + 18x$ 20. $4m^3 - 24m$
21. $4m^2 - 20$ 22. $3a^3 - 5a^2$ 23. $4m^3 - 32m^2$ 24. $5a^3 - 35a$

PART B

Factor.

25. $7a^5 - 35a^4 + 21a^3$ 26. $6a^4 - 12a^3 + 24a^2 + 3a$
27. $3a^2 + 12ab + 36b^2$ 28. $39a^3 - 52a^2 + 26a$
29. $18m^4 - 27m^3 - 45m^2 + 36m$ 30. $6y^3 - 18y^2 - 12y$

Chapter Five Review

Evaluate for the given values of the variables. [p. 119]

1. a^3 if $a = -2$
2. $-3x^2$ if $x = -2$
3. $-2a^3$ if $a = -2$
4. $2m^3$ if $m = -4$
5. x^2y^2 if $x = 2, y = -3$
6. $-2a^3b$ if $a = -1, b = -3$
7. $(-2a)^3$ if $a = -2$
8. $(3m)^2$ if $m = -2$
9. $(x^3y^2)^2$ if $x = -2, y = 1$

Simplify. [p. 121]

10. $(x^3)(x^7)$
11. $(a^7)(a^9)$
12. $(2a^3)(5a^4)$
13. $(3b^2)(5b)$
14. $(-3a^2)(4a^5)$
15. $(-5b^2)(-3b^6)$
16. $(-2a)(7a^5)$
17. $(5x^2y^3)(4x^7y^4)$
18. $(3a^2b)(7ab^6)$
19. $(3a^2)^3$
20. $(4b)^2$
21. $(-2m^2n^3)^3$

Classify each polynomial. [p. 124]

22. $a^2 + 7a$
23. $4x^3$
24. $6x^2 - 4x + 2$
25. $m^2 + 4$
26. $7a^2 - 4a + 5$
27. 5

Simplify. Then write the result in descending order of exponents. [p. 124]

28. $2x^2 + 7x + 3x + 5$
29. $5a^2 - 4a + 2a + 8$
30. $-3 + 5m^2 - 8 - 2m^2$
31. $4a^2 - 5 - 7a^2 + 15$
32. $1 + 7x - 3x^2 + x^2 - 8x + 2$
33. $5b^3 - 3b - b^2 + 8b + 5 + 4b^2 + 2 + 4b^3$

Simplify. [p. 128]

34. $a^2(a^3 + a^2)$
35. $b^5(b^3 + b^2 + b)$
36. $3a^2(4a^3 - 6a^2)$
37. $2m^3(3m^2 + 5m)$
38. $a(a^2 - 2a + 3)$
39. $-m(-m^2 - 5m - 2)$
40. $-(-a^2 - a - 1)$
41. $(a^4 - 3a^2 - 5a) - (-3a^3 + 6a - 7)$
42. $x^4 - 3x^2 + 5 + 3(x^5 - x^4 + 2x^3)$
43. $c^2 + 8c + 9 + 2(c^2 - 3c - 5)$
44. $3ab(a^2 - 5ab + 4b^2)$
45. $-3ac(a^3 - 2a^2c + ac^2 - c^3)$

Add. [p. 128]

46. $(x^3 - 2x^2 + 9) + (x^4 - 3x^3 + x^2)$
47. $(a^2 - 5a + 6) + (-4a^2 - a - 1)$
48. Subtract $x^2 - 5x$ from $2x^3 - 5x^2 + 3x - 2$.
49. Subtract $-y^3 - 3y$ from $y^3 + 2y^2 - 5y + 4$.

Find the missing factor. [p. 132]

50. $(a^2)(?) = a^7$
51. $(x^4)(?) = x^9$
52. $(?)(5a^3) = 5a^4$
53. $(4a)(?) = 20a^2$
54. $(-5a)(?) = -15a^2$
55. $(-x^5y^2)(?) = x^7y^6$

Factor. [p. 135]

56. $4a^2 - 8a + 6$
57. $6x - 2$
58. $4x^2 - 7x$
59. $a^3 - 7a^2 + 3a$
60. $4y^3 - 8y^2 + 12y$
61. $5a^4 - 30a^3 + 20a^2 - 15a$

Chapter Five Test

Evaluate for the given values of the variables.

1. $-3a^3$ if $a = -3$ **2.** $-2m^3n^3$ if $m = -3$, $n = -2$ **3.** $(2ab^2)^3$ if $a = -2$, $b = -1$

Simplify.

4. $(3b^2)(7b)$ **5.** $(-3a^2b)(4ab^3)$ **6.** $(3x^2y^3)^2$

Classify each polynomial.

7. $5a^2 + 2a$ **8.** $7a$ **9.** $4a^2 - 6a + 5$

Simplify. Then write the result in descending order of exponents.

10. $4x^2 - 8x + 5x + 7$ **11.** $3a^2 - 7 + 5a^2 + 9$ **12.** $-3 - 2a + 3a^2 - 5a - 7a^2 + 9$

Simplify.

13. $2a^2(4a^3 - 5a^2)$ **14.** $m^3(m^2 + 7m - 5)$ **15.** $-(-e^2 - 2e - 5)$

16. $(a^2 - 5a + 1) - (-a^2 + 2a^2 - a + 1)$ **17.** $4a^3 - 5a^2 + a + 2(a^2 - 3a^2 - a)$

18. $c^2 + 2a + 5 + 3(c^2 - 2a - 4)$ **19.** $-8ac(a^3 - 3a^2c + 2ac^2 + c^3)$

Add.

20. $(x^4 - 2x^3 + 3x) + (5x^3 - x + 2)$ **21.** $(c^3 - c^2 - c) + (-2c^3 - c^2 - 3c)$

22. Subtract $x^2 - 3x$ from $4x^3 - 6x^2 + 5x - 1$.   **23.** Subtract $-y^3 - 2y$ from $y^3 + 3y^2 - 4y + 2$.

Find the missing factor.

24. $(x^4)(?) = x^{10}$ **25.** $(x^5)(?) = x^6$

26. $(4m^2)(?) = 32m^9$ **27.** $(?)(-3a^2) = 18a^5$

28. $(?)(-5a) = 35a^2$ **29.** $(-2a^2b^3)(?) = 8a^3b^7$

Factor.

30. $3a^2 - 18$ **31.** $5a^2 - 10a$

32. $8a^2 - 16a + 40$ **33.** $a^3 - a^2 - 7a$

34. $m^3 - m^2 - m$ **35.** $6x^3 - 12x^2 + 18x$

36. $3a^2 - 7a - 25$ **37.** $4a^4 - 24a^3 + 12a^2 - 28a$

Using Exponents

Scientific notation is used to write very large numbers.

The distance from the sun to earth is
9.3×10^7 miles.

$9.3 \times 10^7 = 9.3 \times \underbrace{10,000,000}_{\text{7 zeros}}$

$= \underbrace{93,000,000}_{\text{Standard notation}}$ miles

The diameter of the earth
is approximately 7,900 miles.
$7,900 = 7.9 \times 1,000$
$\underbrace{= 7.9 \times 10^3 \text{ miles}}_{\text{Scientific Notation}}$

Scientific notation can be used to multiply numbers.

$$36,000 \qquad \times \qquad 25$$

$$3.6 \times 10^4 \quad \times \quad 2.5 \times 10^1$$

$$\underbrace{(3.6 \times 2.5)}_{9.0} \quad \times \quad \underbrace{(10^4 \times 10^1)}_{10^5,}$$

or 900,000

Write in standard notation.
1. 4×10^2
2. 5.8×10^6
3. 2.63×10^7

Write in scientific notation.
4. 400,000,000
5. 63,000
6. 23,200,000,000

Multiply. Use scientific notation.
7. $250 \times 7,000$
8. $9,300 \times 30$
9. $54,200 \times 8,100$

Multiplying Polynomials

▶ REVIEW CAPSULE

Simplify $4x(x + 2)$.

$$4x(x + 2) = (4x)(x) + (4x)(2)$$
$$= 4x^2 + 8x$$

EXAMPLE 1   Multiply $(3x + 5)(2x + 4)$.

$(3x + 5)(2x + 4)$

Think. ⟶ $(\boxed{})(2x + 4)$

Distribute $\boxed{}$. ⟶ $(\boxed{})(2x) + (\boxed{})(4)$

$\boxed{}$ is $3x + 5$. ⟶ $(3x + 5)(2x) + (3x + 5)(4)$

Distribute $2x$. Then distribute 4.

Multiply. ⟶ $(3x)(2x) + (5)(2x) + (3x)(4) + (5)(4)$

Combine like terms. ⟶ $6x^2 + 10x + 12x + 20$

$6x^2 + 22x + 20$

There is a more convenient way to arrange the work.

Rewrite in vertical form.

$\left.\begin{array}{l}(3x)(2x) = 6x^2 \\ (5)(4) = 20\end{array}\right\}$

$$
\begin{array}{ccc}
3x & & +5 \\
2x & & +4 \\
\hline
6x^2 & & +20
\end{array}
$$
end terms

Find the middle term by multiplying along the diagonals and adding.

$$
\begin{array}{cc}
3x & +5 \\
2x & +4 \\
\end{array}
$$

$(2x)(5) = 10x$

$(4)(3x) = 12x$

$+10x + 12x = +22x$

$$
\begin{array}{ccc}
 & +10x & \\
6x^2 & +12x & +20 \\
\hline
 & +22x &
\end{array}
$$

Thus, $(3x + 5)(2x + 4) = 6x^2 + 22x + 20$.

EXAMPLE 2   Multiply $(2x - 5)(3x + 4)$.

Rewrite in vertical form.
Find the end terms.
$(3x)(2x) = 6x^2$; $(4)(-5) = -20$ ⟶

$$\begin{array}{ll} 2x & -5 \\ 3x & +4 \\ \hline 6x^2 & -20 \end{array}$$

More compact form

$$\begin{array}{cc} 2x & -5 \\ 3x & +4 \end{array}$$
$$6x^2 \quad \begin{array}{c} -15x \\ +8x \\ \hline -7x \end{array} \quad -20$$

Find the middle term.
$(3x)(-5) = -15x$
$(4)(2x) = +8x$
$-15x + 8x = -7x$

$$\begin{array}{cc} 2x & -5 \\ 3x & +4 \end{array}$$
$$6x^2 \quad \begin{array}{c} -15x \\ +8x \\ \hline -7x \end{array} \quad -20$$

Thus, $(2x - 5)(3x + 4) = 6x^2 - 7x - 20$.

EXAMPLE 3   Multiply $(x + 5)(x - 5)$.

Write x as $1x$.
Find the middle term.
$(1x)(5) = +5x$
$(-5)(1x) = -5x$
$+5x - 5x = 0x$
$0x = 0$; $1x^2 = x^2$ ⟶
The product of two binomials
may be a binomial.

$$\begin{array}{cc} 1x & +5 \\ 1x & -5 \end{array}$$
$$1x^2 \quad \begin{array}{c} +5x \\ -5x \\ \hline 0x \end{array} \quad -25$$
$$1x^2 + 0 - 25, \text{ or } x^2 - 25$$

Thus, $(x + 5)(x - 5) = x^2 - 25$.

EXAMPLE 4   Simplify $(2x - 3)^2$.

$(2x - 3)^2 = (2x - 3)(2x - 3)$
Find the middle term.
$(2x)(-3) = -6x$
$(-3)(2x) = -6x$
$-6x - 6x = -12x$

$$\begin{array}{cc} 2x & -3 \\ 2x & -3 \end{array}$$
$$4x^2 \quad \begin{array}{c} -6x \\ -6x \\ \hline -12x \end{array} \quad +9$$

Thus, $(2x - 3)^2 = 4x^2 - 12x + 9$.

EXAMPLE 5   Multiply $(4a - b)(a - 2b)$.

Write $-b$ as $-1b$.
Write a as $1a$.
$(1a)(-1b) = (1)(-1)(a)(b)$, or $-1ab$
$(-2b)(4a) = (-2)(4)(a)(b)$, or $-8ab$
$-1ab - 8ab = -9ab$

$$\begin{array}{cc} 4a & -1b \\ 1a & -2b \end{array}$$
$$4a^2 \quad \begin{array}{c} -1ab \\ -8ab \\ \hline -9ab \end{array} \quad +2b^2$$

Thus, $(4a - b)(a - 2b) = 4a^2 - 9ab + 2b^2$.

EXERCISES

PART A

Multiply.

1. $(3x + 2)(2x + 7)$
2. $(4x + 5)(5x + 3)$
3. $(3m + 5)(2m + 1)$
4. $(2x - 1)(3x + 1)$
5. $(2a - 1)(4a + 7)$
6. $(2b - 5)(3b + 5)$
7. $(m - 5)(m + 5)$
8. $(y - 4)(y + 4)$
9. $(2r - 3)(2r + 3)$
10. $(3x - 1)(x + 2)$
11. $(3a - 2)(a - 1)$
12. $(2m - 6)(2m - 6)$
13. $(2y - 5)(y + 4)$
14. $(3t - 1)(3t + 1)$
15. $(2b - 5)(b + 2)$
16. $(4d - 1)(d + 2)$
17. $(3x + 5)(x - 7)$
18. $(2n - 1)(n + 8)$
19. $(3y - 1)(3y + 1)$
20. $(7a - 1)(2a + 3)$
21. $(6a - 5)(a + 2)$
22. $(3a - 8b)(a - 5b)$
23. $(2y - m)(2y + 9m)$
24. $(3p + q)(2p + 3q)$

Simplify.

25. $(3y - 5)^2$
26. $(4x - 1)^2$
27. $(2x + 3)^2$
28. $(5n + 1)^2$

PART B

EXAMPLE   Multiply $(2x + 3)(3x^2 + 2x - 5)$.

Rewrite in vertical form.

$2x(3x^2 + 2x - 5)$ ⟶

$3(3x^2 + 2x - 5)$ ⟶

Combine like terms. ⟶

$$\begin{array}{r} 3x^2 + 2x - 5 \\ 2x + 3 \\ \hline 6x^3 + 4x^2 - 10x \\ 9x^2 + 6x - 15 \\ \hline 6x^3 + 13x^2 - 4x - 15 \end{array}$$

Multiply.

29. $(3x - 1)(2x^2 + 4x + 3)$
30. $(2x + 7)(4x^2 - 3x + 2)$
31. $(x + 7)(3x^2 - x + 5)$
32. $(x - 5)(x^2 - 7x + 1)$
33. $(3x + 2)(x^3 - 7x^2 + 3x)$
34. $(2x + 3)(x^3 - 2x^2 + x - 3)$

PART C

EXAMPLE   Simplify $(a + b)^2$. Apply the pattern to $(x + 4)^2$.

Think: $(a + b)^2 = (a + b)(a + b)$.

$$\begin{array}{ccc} a & & +b \\ a & & +b \\ \hline & +1ab & \\ a^2 & +1ab & +b^2 \\ \hline & +2ab & \end{array}$$

Pattern for squaring a binomial ⟶ **Thus,** $(a + b)^2 = a^2 + 2ab + b^2$

Replace a with x and b with 4. ⟶ $(x + 4)^2 = x^2 + 2(x)(4) + (4)^2$, or

$$x^2 + 8x + 16.$$

Simplify by using $(a + b)^2 = a^2 + 2ab + b^2$.

35. $(x - 7)^2$
36. $(2x + 3)^2$
37. $(2m - 1)^2$
38. $(3a - 4b)^2$

Rectangle Products

Areas of rectangles and squares can be used to show the product of two binomials.

$(a+7)(a+1)$

Area = length x width
= $(a + 7)(a + 1)$.

$a + 7$

$a + 1$

a 7

a a

1 1

a 7

But, the area of the rectangle is the sum of the areas of all of its parts.

a	7		a		7
a	a	1		1	1

$(a)(a)$ + $7(a)$ + $1(a)$ + $7(1)$

↓   ↓   ↓   ↓

a^2 + $7a$ + $1a$ + 7

Thus, $(a + 7)(a + 1) = a^2 + 8a + 7$.

Use the rectangle method to multiply the binomials.

1. $(a + 2)(a + 3)$ 2. $(x + 8)(x + 5)$ 3. $(x + 2)(x + 5)$

Factoring Trinomials

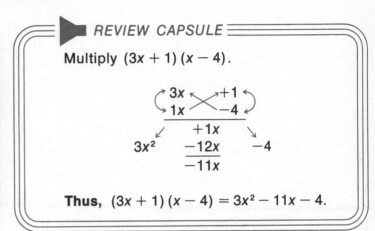

▶ REVIEW CAPSULE

Multiply $(3x + 1)(x - 4)$.

$$3x^2 \quad -11x \quad -4$$

Thus, $(3x + 1)(x - 4) = 3x^2 - 11x - 4$.

EXAMPLE 1   Factor $2x^2 + 5x + 3$ into two binomials.

Write a pattern to test factors.

$\left.\begin{array}{c}2\\1\end{array}\right\}$Factors of 2 $\left.\begin{array}{c}3\\1\end{array}\right\}$Factors of 3

$\begin{array}{cc} 2x & \square 3 \\ 1x & \square 1 \end{array}$ → Omit signs for now.

Does choice of factors give correct middle term?

$(1x)(\square 3) = \square 3x$
$(\square 1)(2x) = \square 2x$

$$2x^2 \quad \square 2x \quad +3$$
$$+5x$$

Check all sign combinations. ⟶

$+3x$	$+3x$	$-3x$	$-3x$
$+2x$	$-2x$	$+2x$	$-2x$
$+5x$	$+1x$	$-1x$	$-5x$

└─One sign combination works.

Check by multiplying.

$(1x)(\boxplus 3) = +3x$ $\Big\}$
$(\boxplus 1)(2x) = +2x$
$+3x + 2x = +5x$

$$2x^2 \quad +2x \quad +3$$
$$+5x$$

The factors are $(2x + 3)$ and $(1x + 1)$. ⟶ **Thus, $2x^2 + 5x + 3 = (2x + 3)(x + 1)$.**

EXAMPLE 2   Factor $6x^2 - 7x + 2$.

$\left.\begin{matrix}2\\3\end{matrix}\right\}$Factors of 6 $\left.\begin{matrix}2\\1\end{matrix}\right\}$Factors of 2

$(3x)\,(\square 2) = \square 6x$

$(\square 1)\,(2x) = \square 2x$

No sign combination works.

Try reversing factors of 2 $\left\{\begin{matrix}1\\2\end{matrix}\right.$.

$(3x)\,(\square 1) = \square 3x$

$(\square 2)\,(2x) = \square 4x$

One sign combination works.
Check by multiplying.

$\left.\begin{matrix}(3x)\,(\boxminus 1) = -3x\\(\boxminus 2)\,(2x) = -4x\\-3x - 4x = -7x\end{matrix}\right\}$

Write factors horizontally. ──────⟶

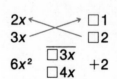

$$
\begin{matrix}
2x & \longrightarrow & \square 2\\
3x & \longrightarrow & \square 1
\end{matrix}
$$
$$6x^2 \quad \begin{matrix}\square 6x\\\square 2x\\\hline -7x\end{matrix} \quad +2$$

$$
\begin{matrix}
2x & \longrightarrow & \square 1\\
3x & \longrightarrow & \square 2
\end{matrix}
$$
$$6x^2 \quad \begin{matrix}\square 3x\\\square 4x\\\hline -7x\end{matrix} \quad +2$$

Check sign combinations.

$+6x$	$+6x$	$-6x$	$-6x$
$+2x$	$-2x$	$+2x$	$-2x$
$+8x$	$+4x$	$-4x$	$-8x$

None gives $-7x$.

Check sign combinations.

$+3x$	$+3x$	$-3x$	$-3x$
$+4x$	$-4x$	$+4x$	$-4x$
$+7x$	$-1x$	$+1x$	$-7x$

One gives $-7x$.

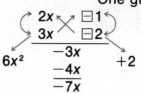

Thus, $6x^2 - 7x + 2 = (2x - 1)\,(3x - 2)$.

EXAMPLE 3   Factor $x^2 + x - 20$.

$x^2 = 1x^2,\ x = 1x$ ──────────⟶

$\left.\begin{matrix}1\\1\end{matrix}\right\}$Factors of 1 $\left.\begin{matrix}10\\2\end{matrix}\right\}$Factors of 20

$(1x)\,(\square 10) = \square 10x$

$(\square 2)\,(1x) = \square\,2x$

No sign combination works.

Try $\left.\begin{matrix}5\\4\end{matrix}\right\}$Factors of 20.

One sign combination works.
Check by multiplying.

$\left.\begin{matrix}(1x)\,(\boxplus 5) = +5x\\(\boxminus 4)\,(1x) = -4x\\+5x - 4x = +1x\end{matrix}\right\}$

The factors are
$(x + 5)$ and $(x - 4)$. ──────⟶

$$1x^2 \quad +1x \quad -20$$
$$
\begin{matrix}
1x & \longrightarrow & \square 10\\
1x & \longrightarrow & \square 2
\end{matrix}
$$
$$1x^2 \quad \begin{matrix}\square 10x\\\square 2x\\\hline +1x\end{matrix} \quad -20$$

$$
\begin{matrix}
1x & \longrightarrow & \square 5\\
1x & \longrightarrow & \square 4
\end{matrix}
$$
$$1x^2 \quad \begin{matrix}\square 5x\\\square 4x\\\hline +1x\end{matrix} \quad -20$$

Check sign combinations.

$+10x$	$+10x$	$-10x$	$-10x$
$+2x$	$-2x$	$+2x$	$-2x$
$+12x$	$+8x$	$-8x$	$-12x$

None gives $+1x$.

Check sign combinations.

$+5x$	$+5x$
$+4x$	$-4x$
$+9x$	$+1x$

One gives $+1x$.

$$
\begin{matrix}
1x & \times & \boxplus 5\\
1x & & \boxminus 4
\end{matrix}
$$
$$1x^2 \quad \begin{matrix}+5x\\-4x\\\hline +1x\end{matrix} \quad -20$$

Thus, $x^2 + x - 20 = (x + 5)\,(x - 4)$.

EXAMPLE 4   Factor $2x^2 - 5x - 12$.

$\left.\begin{array}{c} 2 \\ 1 \end{array}\right\}$ factors of 2 $\left.\begin{array}{c} 6 \\ 2 \end{array}\right\}$ factors of 12

$(1x)(\square 6) = \square 6x$

$(\square 2)(2x) = \square 4x$

No sign combination works.

$\text{Try } \left.\begin{array}{c} 2 \\ 6 \end{array}\right\}$ factors of 12.

No sign combination works.

$\text{Try } \left.\begin{array}{c} 3 \\ 4 \end{array}\right\}$ factors of 12.

$(1x)(\square 3) = \square 3x$

$(\square 4)(2x) = \square 8x$

One sign combination works.

Check by multiplying.

$(1x)(\boxplus 3) = +3x$

$(\boxminus 4)(2x) = -8x$

$+3x - 8x = -5x$

We can also write $(x - 4)(2x + 3)$.

$2x \diagdown \square 6$
$1x \diagup \square 2$
$\overline{}$
$2x^2 \;\begin{array}{c}\square 6x \\ \square 4x\end{array}\; -12$
$\overline{-5x}$

Check sign combinations.

$+6x$	$+6x$	$-6x$	$-6x$
$+4x$	$-4x$	$+4x$	$-4x$
$+10x$	$+2x$	$-2x$	$-10x$

None gives $-5x$.

$2x \diagdown \square 2$
$1x \diagup \square 6$
$\overline{}$
$2x^2 \;\begin{array}{c}\square 2x \\ \square 12x\end{array}\; -12$
$\overline{-5x}$

Check sign combinations.

$+2x$	$+2x$	$-2x$	$-2x$
$+12x$	$-12x$	$+12x$	$-12x$
$+14x$	$-10x$	$+10x$	$-14x$

None gives $-5x$.

$2x \diagdown \square 3$
$1x \diagup \square 4$
$\overline{}$
$2x^2 \;\begin{array}{c}\square 3x \\ \square 8x\end{array}\; -12$
$\overline{-5x}$

Check sign combinations.

$+3x$	$+3x$
$+8x$	$-8x$
$+11x$	$-5x$

One gives $-5x$.

$2x \diagdown \boxplus 3$
$1x \diagup \boxminus 4$
$2x^2 \;\begin{array}{c}+3x \\ -8x\end{array}\; -12$
$\overline{-5x}$

Thus, $2x^2 - 5x - 12 = (2x + 3)(x - 4)$.

ORAL EXERCISES

Find the sign combination that will give the indicated sum.

1. $\begin{array}{r}\square 2x \\ \square 5x \\ \hline -7x\end{array}$
2. $\begin{array}{r}\square 1x \\ \square 5x \\ \hline +4x\end{array}$
3. $\begin{array}{r}\square 3x \\ \square 2x \\ \hline +5x\end{array}$
4. $\begin{array}{r}\square 2x \\ \square 3x \\ \hline -1x\end{array}$
5. $\begin{array}{r}\square 12x \\ \square\; 3x \\ \hline -9x\end{array}$

6. $\begin{array}{r}\square 6x \\ \square 2x \\ \hline -8x\end{array}$
7. $\begin{array}{r}\square 5x \\ \square 2x \\ \hline -3x\end{array}$
8. $\begin{array}{r}\square 7x \\ \square 8x \\ \hline -1x\end{array}$
9. $\begin{array}{r}\square 4x \\ \square 3x \\ \hline +x\end{array}$
10. $\begin{array}{r}\square 8x \\ \square 9x \\ \hline -x\end{array}$

Find the sign combination, if any, that will give the indicated sum.

11. $\square 6x$
    $\square 2x$
    $\overline{-5x}$

12. $\square 3x$
    $\square 4x$
    $\overline{-x}$

13. $\square 10x$
    $\square \ 2x$
    $\overline{+7x}$

14. $\square 7x$
    $\square 3x$
    $\overline{-3x}$

15. $\square 9x$
    $\square 6x$
    $\overline{+3x}$

Find the sign combination, if any, that will give the indicated product.

16. $(2x)(\square 4) = -8x$

17. $(6x)(\square 3) = 18x$

18. $(3x)(\square 1) = -3x$

19. $(8x)(\square 4) = +32x$

20. $(5x)(\square 6) = -30x$

21. $(4x)(\square 2) = +8x$

22. $(7x)(\square 3) = -21x$

23. $(3x)(\square 4) = -12x$

24. $(6x)(\square 4) = -24x$

EXERCISES

PART A

Factor.

1. $2x^2 + 7x + 5$
2. $3x^2 + 10x + 7$
3. $5x^2 + 7x + 2$
4. $8x^2 - 10x + 3$
5. $6x^2 - 17x + 5$
6. $10x^2 - 19x + 7$
7. $x^2 + x - 6$
8. $x^2 + x - 12$
9. $x^2 + x - 30$
10. $2a^2 - 7a - 4$
11. $3x^2 - 10x - 25$
12. $2x^2 - x - 3$
13. $x^2 + 7x + 10$
14. $b^2 + 5b + 6$
15. $a^2 + 4a + 3$
16. $y^2 - 10y + 16$
17. $m^2 - 9m + 20$
18. $d^2 - 11d + 30$
19. $a^2 - a - 20$
20. $y^2 - 2y - 15$
21. $a^2 - 7a - 18$
22. $x^2 + 2x + 1$
23. $b^2 - 6b + 9$
24. $k^2 + 12k + 36$
25. $2a^2 - 7a + 6$
26. $2x^2 + 5x - 3$
27. $2a^2 - 7a - 4$
28. $2m^2 + 9m - 5$
29. $2a^2 + 13a + 15$
30. $3b^2 - 11b + 6$
31. $3x^2 + 10x - 25$
32. $2m^2 + 11m + 15$
33. $2m^2 - 7m + 5$
34. $6a^2 + a - 1$
35. $3y^2 + 7y - 20$
36. $2p^2 - 15p + 25$
37. $2b^2 + 17b + 30$
38. $2x^2 + 5x + 2$
39. $12y^2 + 7y + 1$
40. $3x^2 + 13x - 10$
41. $2a^2 - 3a - 14$
42. $2p^2 + 5p - 12$

PART B

Factor.

43. $2x^2 - 11x - 40$
44. $2x^2 + 23x + 45$
45. $3x^2 + 10x - 48$
46. $2a^2 - 25a + 50$
47. $3a^2 + 8a - 35$
48. $2b^2 - 29b + 60$
49. $3m^2 + 29m + 40$
50. $5x^2 - 42x - 27$
51. $3y^2 - 31y + 56$

PART C

Factor.

52. $15d^2 - 19d + 6$
53. $15y^2 + 17y - 18$
54. $14b^2 - 15b - 9$
55. $4a^2 - 20a + 25$
56. $9a^2 - 12a + 4$
57. $6a^2 - a - 15$
58. $15x^2 - 29x + 12$
59. $16y^2 + 14y - 15$
60. $18a^2 - 9a - 35$

Using a Flow Chart to Solve a Simple Equation

A flowchart for solving the equation $a\,x + b = c$

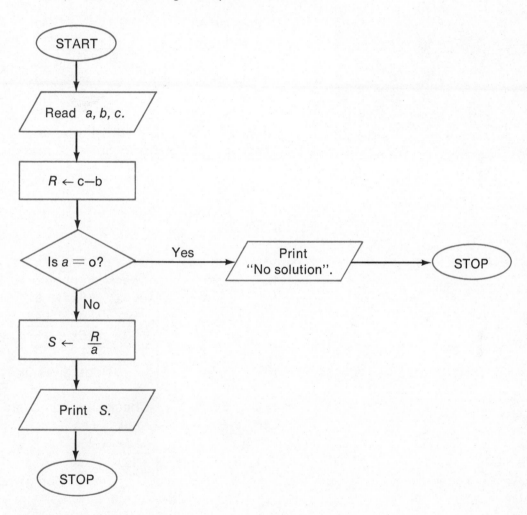

1. Follow the flow chart to solve $2\,x + 7 = 13$.

2. Write a flow chart to solve an equation of the form $a\,x + b = c\,x + d$. Use it to solve $5\,x + 3 = 3\,x + 13$.

The Difference of Two Squares

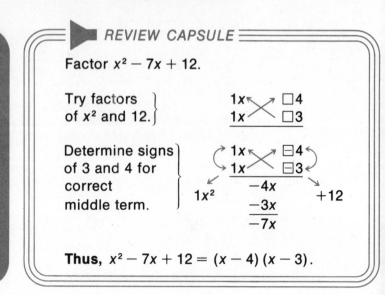

▶ REVIEW CAPSULE

Factor $x^2 - 7x + 12$.

Try factors of x^2 and 12.

Determine signs of 3 and 4 for correct middle term.

$$1x \quad \square 4$$
$$1x \quad \square 3$$

$$1x \quad \boxminus 4$$
$$1x \quad \boxminus 3$$

$$1x^2 \qquad \begin{array}{c} -4x \\ -3x \\ \hline -7x \end{array} \qquad +12$$

Thus, $x^2 - 7x + 12 = (x - 4)(x - 3)$.

EXAMPLE 1   Factor $x^2 - 36$.

Think of $x^2 - 36$ as a disguised trinomial with middle term $0x$.

$\left.\begin{array}{c} 1 \\ 1 \end{array}\right\}$ factors of 1; $\left.\begin{array}{c} 9 \\ 4 \end{array}\right\}$ factors of 36

$(1x)(\square 9) = \square 9x$
$(\square 4)(1x) = \square 4x$

No sign combination works.

Rewrite $x^2 - 36$ as $x^2 + 0x - 36$.

$$\begin{array}{c} 1x \quad \square 9 \\ 1x \quad \square 4 \end{array}$$

$$1x^2 \quad \begin{array}{c} \square 9x \\ \square 4x \\ \hline 0x \end{array} \quad -36$$

Check sign combinations.

+9x	+9x	−9x	−9x
+4x	−4x	+4x	−4x
+13x	+5x	−5x	−13x

None gives $0x$.

Try $\left.\begin{array}{c} 6 \\ 6 \end{array}\right\}$ factors of 36.

$(1x)(\square 6) = \square 6x$
$(\square 6)(1x) = \square 6x$

One sign combination works.
Check by multiplying.

$$\begin{array}{c} 1x \quad \square 6 \\ 1x \quad \square 6 \end{array}$$

$$1x^2 \quad \begin{array}{c} \square 6x \\ \square 6x \\ \hline 0x \end{array} \quad -36$$

Check sign combinations.

+6x	+6x
+6x	−6x
+12x	0x

One gives $0x$.

$\left.\begin{array}{l} (1x)(\boxplus 6) = +6x \\ (\boxminus 6)(1x) = -6x \\ +6x - 6x = \quad 0x \end{array}\right\}$

$$\begin{array}{c} 1x \quad \boxplus 6 \\ 1x \quad \boxminus 6 \end{array}$$

$$1x^2 \quad \begin{array}{c} +6x \\ -6x \\ \hline 0x \end{array} \quad -36$$

The factors are $(x + 6)$ and $(x - 6)$.

Thus, $x^2 - 36 = (x + 6)(x - 6)$.

$x^2 = (x)(x)$, or $(x)^2$
$36 = (6)(6)$, or $(6)^2$ ⟶

Since $x^2 - 36$

$(x)^2 - (6)^2$

$x^2 - 36$ is the difference of two squares.

EXAMPLE 2 Factor $4m^2 - 25$.

Rewrite as a trinomial. ⟶

$4m^2 + 0m - 25$

$\left.\begin{array}{l}2\\2\end{array}\right\}$ factors of 4; $\left.\begin{array}{l}5\\5\end{array}\right\}$ factors of 25

$(2m)(\square 5) = \square 10m$
$(\square 5)(2m) = \square 10m$
One sign combination works.

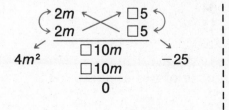

Check sign combinations.

+10m	+10m
+10m	−10m
+20m	↗ 0

One gives 0.

Check by multiplying.

$(2m)(\boxplus 5) = +10m$
$(\boxminus 5)(2m) = -10m$
$+10m - 10m = 0$

We can also write $(2m - 5)(2m + 5)$.

Thus, $4m^2 - 25 = (2m + 5)(2m - 5)$.

$4m^2 - 25$
$(2m)^2 - (5)^2$
$\ \ \smallsmile$ difference

$4m^2 - 25$ is also the difference of two squares.
$$(2m)^2 - (5)^2$$

Observe a pattern for factoring the difference of two squares.

Rewrite. ⟶
Factor. ⟶

$x^2 - 36$		$4m^2 - 25$
$(x)^2 - (6)^2$		$(2m)^2 - (5)^2$
$(x - 6)(x + 6)$		$(2m - 5)(2m + 5)$

EXAMPLE 3 Factor $x^2 - 4$.

Rewrite. ⟶
Factor. ⟶

$(x)^2 - (2)^2$
$(x - 2)(x + 2)$

EXAMPLE 4 Factor $36 - y^2$.

Rewrite. ⟶
Factor. ⟶

$(6)^2 - (y)^2$
$(6 - y)(6 + y)$

EXAMPLE 5 Factor $144b^2 - 49$.

Rewrite. ————————————→ $(12b)^2 - (7)^2$

Factor. ————————————→ $(12b - 7)(12b + 7)$

ORAL EXERCISES

Express each term in the form $(a)^2$.

1. 9
2. 64
3. 36
4. 100
5. 16
6. 144
7. $16b^2$
8. $81x^2$
9. $121x^2$
10. $49m^2$
11. c^2
12. $100x^2$
13. $9t^2$
14. $25b^2$
15. $225k^2$

Tell which are differences of two squares.

16. $x^2 - 16$
17. $m^2 + 49$
18. $y^2 - 35$
19. $25a^2 - 121$
20. $100x^2 - 50$
21. $64 - 49t^2$
22. $81k^2 + 225$
23. $625 + 10x^2$
24. $169 - 13y^2$

EXERCISES

PART A

Factor.

1. $x^2 - 16$
2. $m^2 - 49$
3. $b^2 - 25$
4. $a^2 - 81$
5. $b^2 - 1$
6. $m^2 - 100$
7. $m^2 - 64$
8. $x^2 - 36$
9. $4b^2 - 49$
10. $9a^2 - 25$
11. $25a^2 - 36$
12. $16x^2 - 25$
13. $49y^2 - 4$
14. $16m^2 - 1$
15. $25m^2 - 4$
16. $36a^2 - 25$
17. $4t^2 - 25$
18. $4b^2 - 1$
19. $25 - x^2$
20. $64 - y^2$
21. $81 - t^2$
22. $36 - a^2$
23. $49 - b^2$
24. $100 - c^2$
25. $1 - y^2$
26. $100 - 49x^2$
27. $64 - 81c^2$
28. $1 - 9x^2$
29. $16 - 81y^2$
30. $64 - 49b^2$

PART B

Factor.

31. $144a^2 - 81$
32. $100x^2 - 49$
33. $25m^2 - 144$
34. $4m^2 - 169$
35. $36x^2 - 25$
36. $25 - 144b^2$
37. $169p^2 - 16$
38. $x^2 - 196$
39. $49^2 - 225$
40. $121 - 16b^2$
41. $16t^2 - 225$
42. $100a^2 - 49$
43. $225a^2 - 169$
44. $36a^2 - 169$
45. $121m^2 - 225$

Combined Types of Factoring

 REVIEW CAPSULE

Factor the GCF from $4x^3 - 12x^2 + 8x$.

$$4(x^3) + 4(-3x^2) + 4(2x)$$

4 is the greatest common whole number factor.

$$4x^3 \quad - \quad 12x^2 \quad + \quad 8x$$
$$\uparrow \qquad\qquad \uparrow \qquad\qquad \uparrow$$

three x's   two x's one x

x is the greatest common variable factor. The GCF is $4x$.

$$4x^3 - 12x^2 + 8x$$
$$4x(x^2) + 4x(-3x) + 4x(2)$$
$$4x(x^2 - 3x + 2)$$

We have factored out the GCF from a polynomial. We have factored a polynomial into two binomials. Now, we combine these two types of factoring to factor a polynomial completely.

EXAMPLE 1 Factor $4x^3 - 12x^2 + 8x$ completely.

Use the steps in the Review to factor out the GCF. ─────────────────►

Factor $x^2 - 3x + 2$ into two binomials.

$(1x)(\square 2) = \square 2x$
$(\square 1)(1x) = \square 1x$

$$4x(x^2 - 3x + 2)$$

$$\begin{array}{l} 1x \searrow\nearrow \square 2 \\ 1x \nearrow\searrow \square 1 \\ \hline 1x^2 \quad \begin{array}{c} \square 2x \\ \square 1x \\ \hline -3x \end{array} \quad +2 \end{array}$$

Check sign combinations.

$+2x$	$+2x$	$-2x$	$-2x$
$+1x$	$-1x$	$+1x$	$-1x$
$+3x$	$+1x$	$-1x$	$-3x$

One gives $-3x$.

Check by multiplying.

$(1x)(\boxminus 2) = -2x$
$(\boxminus 1)(1x) = -1x$
$-2x - 1x = -3x$

$$\begin{array}{l} 1x \searrow\nearrow \boxminus 2 \\ 1x \nearrow\searrow \boxminus 1 \\ \hline 1x^2 \quad \begin{array}{c} -2x \\ -1x \\ \hline -3x \end{array} \quad +2 \end{array}$$

$$x^2 - 3x + 2 = (x - 2)(x - 1)$$

Put all factors together. ─────────────► **Thus,** $4x^3 - 12x^2 + 8x = 4x(x - 2)(x - 1)$.

EXAMPLE 2   Factor $2x^3 - 4x^2 - 48x$ completely.

Find the GCF.
Greatest common whole number factor is 2.
Greatest common variable factor, x
GCF is $2x$.
Factor out the GCF. ⟶

$$2(x^3) + 2(-2x^2) + 2(-24x)$$

   ↑   ↑   ↑

three x's   two x's   one x

$$2x(x^2) + 2x(-2x) + 2x(-24)$$
$$2x(x^2 - 2x - 24)$$

Factor $x^2 - 2x - 24$ into two binomials.

$$
\begin{array}{c}
1x \searrow \square 6 \\
1x \times \square 4 \\
\hline
\square 6x \\
\square 4x \\
\hline
-2x
\end{array}
\qquad 1x^2 \qquad -24
$$

Check sign combinations.		
$+6x$	$+6x$	$-6x$
$+4x$	$-4x$	$+4x$
$+10x$	$+2x$	$-2x$

One gives $-2x$. ⟶

Check by multiplying.

$(1x)(\boxminus 6) = -6x$
$(\boxplus 4)(1x) = +4x$
$-6x + 4x = -2x$

$$
\begin{array}{c}
1x \searrow \boxminus 6 \\
1x \times \boxplus 4 \\
\hline
-6x \\
+4x \\
\hline
-2x
\end{array}
\qquad 1x^2 \qquad -24
$$

$$x^2 - 2x - 24 = (x - 6)(x + 4)$$

Put all factors together. ⟶   **Thus,** $2x^3 - 4x^2 - 48x = 2x(x - 6)(x + 4)$.

EXAMPLE 3   Factor $3x^3 - 3x$ completely.

Find the GCF.
Greatest common whole number factor is 3.
Greatest common variable factor: x
GCF is $3x$. Factor it out.
$x^2 - 1 = (x)^2 - (1)^2$; factor. ⟶

$$3(x^3) + 3(-1x)$$

    ↑   ↑

three x's   one x

$$3x(x^2 - 1)$$
$$3x(x - 1)(x + 1)$$

Put all factors together. ⟶   **Thus,** $3x^3 - 3x = 3x(x - 1)(x + 1)$.

EXAMPLE 4   Factor $x^2 - 6x + 8$ completely.

Find the GCF.
No common whole number factor, other than 1
No common variable factor

$$1(x^2) + 2(-3x) + 2(4)$$

   ↑   ↑   ↑

two x's   one x no x's

The GCF is one. Don't bother to factor it out.

Factor $x^2 - 6x + 8$ into two binomials.

$$
\begin{array}{c}
1x \searrow \square 4 \\
1x \times \square 2 \\
\hline
\square 4x \\
\square 2x \\
\square 6x
\end{array}
$$

Check sign combinations.			
$+4x$	$+4x$	$-4x$	$-4x$
$+2x$	$-2x$	$+2x$	$-2x$
$+6x$	$+2x$	$-2x$	$-6x$

One gives $-6x$. ⟶

Check by multiplying. ⟶   **Thus,** $x^2 - 6x + 8 = (x - 4)(x - 2)$.

EXERCISES

PART A

Factor completely.

1. $2a^2 - 10a + 8$ **2.** $2b^2 - 6b + 4$ **3.** $2a^2 + 4a - 70$
4. $2m^3 - 5m^2 + 3m$ **5.** $3x^3 + 4x^2 - 4x$ **6.** $m^3 - 9m$
7. $2x^3 - 2x$ **8.** $3a^3 - 27a$ **9.** $8m^3 - 50m$
10. $2x^3 - 14x^2 + 24x$ **11.** $2m^3 - 20m^2 + 18m$ **12.** $3x^3 - 24x^2 + 36x$
13. $4a^3 - 12a^2 - 40a$ **14.** $6x^3 - 28x^2 - 10x$ **15.** $6b^3 - 3b^2 - 30b$
16. $4a^2 - 24a + 20$ **17.** $2a^3 + 16a^2 + 30a$ **18.** $12m^2 + 33m - 9$
19. $2a^2 + 13a - 7$ **20.** $4y^2 + 7y - 2$ **21.** $2a^2 + 3a + 1$

PART B

Factor completely.

22. $18x^2 - 98$ **23.** $6x^2 + 9x - 105$ **24.** $169a - 25a^3$
25. $3y^4 - 7y^3 - 20y^2$ **26.** $30e^3 - 32e^2 - 14e$ **27.** $12a^3 - 72a^2 + 33a$
28. $15a^2 - 57a + 54$ **29.** $9a^3 + 66a^2 - 48a$ **30.** $18m^3 - 512m$

PART C

EXAMPLE   Factor $am + bm + an + bn$.

$$a(m) + b(m) + a(n) + b(n)$$

Treat $(a + b)$ as a single common factor. Factor it out.

$$m(a + b) + n(a + b)$$
$$(a + b)(m + n)$$

Thus, $am + bm + an + bn = (a + b)(m + n)$.

EXAMPLE   Factor $x^2m + x^2 - 4m - 4$.

$$x^2(m) + x^2(1) + (-4)(m) + (-4)(1)$$
$$x^2(m + 1) - 4(m + 1)$$

Factor out $(m + 1)$. ⟶ $(m + 1)(x^2 - 4)$
Factor $x^2 - 4$. ⟶ $(m + 1)(x - 2)(x + 2)$

Thus, $x^2m + x^2 - 4m - 4 = (m + 1)(x - 2)(x + 2)$.

Factor.

31. $xm + xn - am - an$ **32.** $4x + 4y + bx + by$
33. $pr + pt - 2r - 2t$ **34.** $x^2a + x^2b - 16a - 16b$
35. $p^2y + p^2 - 25y - 25$ **36.** $16a + 16 - y^2a - y^2$

Factoring Polynomials in Two Variables

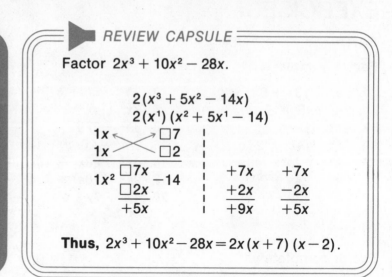

REVIEW CAPSULE

Factor $2x^3 + 10x^2 - 28x$.

$$2(x^3 + 5x^2 - 14x)$$
$$2(x^1)(x^2 + 5x^1 - 14)$$

		+7x	+7x
		+2x	−2x
		+9x	+5x

Thus, $2x^3 + 10x^2 - 28x = 2x(x+7)(x-2)$.

EXAMPLE 1   Factor $x^2 + 3xy + 2y^2$ completely.

Check for GCF. ⟶ 1 is the GCF of $x^2 + 3xy + 2y^2$.

$\left. \begin{matrix} 1x \\ 1x \end{matrix} \right\}$ factors of x^2 $\left. \begin{matrix} 2y \\ 1y \end{matrix} \right\}$ factors of $2y^2$

Check sign combinations.

$(1x)(\square 2y) = \square 2xy$ +2xy
$(\square y)(1x) = \square 1xy$ +1xy
                                   +3xy

This one works.

Check by multiplying.

$(1x)(\boxplus 2y) = +2xy$
$(\boxplus 1y)(1x) = +1xy$
$+2xy + 1xy = +3xy$

Thus, $x^2 + 3xy + 2y^2 = (x + 2y)(x + y)$.

EXAMPLE 2   Factor $5x^2 - 20y^2$ completely.

The GCF is 5. ⟶

$x^2 - 4y^2$
$\downarrow \quad\quad \downarrow$
$(x)^2 - (2y)^2$
difference of two squares

$5(x^2 - 4y^2)$
$5[(x)^2 - (2y)^2]$
$5(x - 2y)(x + 2y)$

Thus, $5x^2 - 20y^2 = 5(x - 2y)(x + 2y)$.

EXAMPLE 3   Factor $2a^2 - 4ab - 70b^2$ completely.

The GCF is 2. ————————————————→ $2(a^2 - 2ab - 35b^2)$

$\left.\begin{array}{l} 1a \\ 1a \end{array}\right\} a^2 \qquad \left.\begin{array}{l} 7b \\ 5b \end{array}\right\} 35b^2$

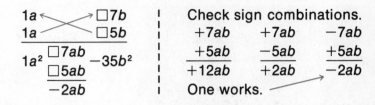

Check sign combinations.

$+7ab$	$+7ab$	$-7ab$
$+5ab$	$-5ab$	$+5ab$
$+12ab$	$+2ab$	$-2ab$

One works.

Check by multiplying.

$(1a)(\boxminus 7b) = -7ab$
$(\boxplus 5b)(1a) = +5ab$
$-7ab + 5ab = -2ab$

Thus, $2a^2 - 4ab - 70b^2 = 2(a - 7b)(a + 5b)$.

EXERCISES

PART A

Factor completely.

1. $a^2 + 4ab + 3b^2$
2. $x^2 + 5xy + 4y^2$
3. $c^2 + 7cd + 6d^2$
4. $4a^2 - 36b^2$
5. $5x^2 - 45y^2$
6. $4a^2 - 100b$
7. $2m^2 - mb - 10b^2$
8. $2a^2 - 5ab - 3b^2$
9. $2a^2 - 9ab - 5b^2$
10. $a^2 - ab - 42b^2$
11. $a^2 - 3ab + 2b^2$
12. $x^2 - 13xy + 42y^2$
13. $2a^2 + 20ab + 42b^2$
14. $8x^2 + 24xy + 18y^2$
15. $2y^2 + 20yz + 18z^2$
16. $2m^2 - 2mn - 40n^2$
17. $6x^2 - 26xy - 20y^2$
18. $3x^2 - 9xy - 30y^2$

PART B

Factor completely.

19. $a^2b^3 - 25b$
20. $x^3 - 3x^2y + 2xy^2$
21. $a^3b - ab^3$
22. $7x^2 + 19xy - 6y^2$
23. $6x^2 - 57xy + 105y^2$
24. $2m^2 + 17mn + 30n^2$
25. $4k^2 - 42kr + 80r^2$
26. $12m^2 - 75y^2$
27. $3a^2 + 13ab - 30b^2$

PART C

Factor completely.

28. $20m^2 + 60mn + 45n^2$
29. $6a^2 + 5ab - 21b^2$
30. $12x^2 + xy - 6y^2$
31. $10x^2 + 21xy + 9y^2$
32. $2a^3b + 11a^2b^2 - 21ab^3$
33. $6x^3y + 7x^2y^2 - 20xy^3$

Quadratic Equations

<table>
<tr><td>

OBJECTIVE

■ To solve equations like
$2x^2 + 9x - 5 = 0$
by factoring

</td></tr>
</table>

EXAMPLE 1 Find the missing factor. Then draw a conclusion.

Multiplying by 0 gives 0. ⟶

$(4)(?) = 0$	$(?)(-7) = 0$	$(0)(?) = 0$
$(4)(0) = 0$	$(0)(-7) = 0$	$(0)(0) = 0$

If a product is 0, then at least one factor must
be 0.

Either factor or both factors must be 0.

> If $a \cdot b = 0$, then $a = 0$ or $b = 0$.
> If a product is 0, then at least one factor is 0.

EXAMPLE 2 For what values of x will $(2x - 8)(x - 7) = 0$
be true?

If $a \cdot b = 0$, then $a = 0$ or $b = 0$.
Solve each equation for x.

$$2x - 8 = 0 \quad \text{or} \quad x - 7 = 0$$
$$\underline{\ 8\ \ 8} \qquad \quad \underline{7\ \ 7}$$
$$2x = 8 \qquad \qquad x = 7$$

Divide each side by 2. ⟶
$$x = 4$$

Check. ⟶

$$
\begin{array}{c|c}
(2x-8)\ \ (x-7)\,|\,0 \\
x=4 \quad (2 \cdot 4-8)\,(4-7)\,|\,0 \\
(8-8) \quad (-3) \\
(0) \quad (-3) \\
0
\end{array}
\quad
\begin{array}{c}
(2x-8)\ \ (x-7)\,|\,0 \\
x=7 \quad (2 \cdot 7-8)\,(7-7)\,|\,0 \\
(14-8) \quad (0) \\
(6) \quad (0) \\
0
\end{array}
$$

$(2x - 8)(x - 7)$ is 0. ⟶

Thus, $(2x - 8)(x - 7) = 0$ if $x = 4$ or $x = 7$.

Each equation contains an x^2 term.

Equations like $2x^2 + 9x - 5 = 0$, $x^2 - 36 = 0$,
and $x^2 - 3x = 0$ are quadratic equations.

EXAMPLE 3   Solve $x^2 - 8x + 12 = 0$.

Factor. Use the method you
have already learned. $\Big\}$

If $ab = 0$, then $a = 0$ or $b = 0.$ ⟶
Solve each equation for x.

$$x^2 - 8x + 12 = 0$$
$$(x - 6)(x - 2) = 0$$
$$x - 6 = 0 \quad \text{or} \quad x - 2 = 0$$

$$\begin{array}{cc} \underline{6 \quad 6} & \underline{2 \quad 2} \\ x = 6 & x = 2 \end{array}$$

Check. ⟶

$$x = 6 \quad \begin{array}{l|l} x^2 - 8x + 12 & 0 \\ \hline 6^2 - 8 \cdot 6 + 12 & 0 \\ 36 - 48 + 12 & \\ -12 + 12 & \\ 0 & \end{array} \quad x = 2 \quad \begin{array}{l|l} x^2 - 8x + 12 & 0 \\ \hline 2^2 - 8 \cdot 2 + 12 & 0 \\ 4 - 16 + 12 & \\ -12 + 12 & \\ 0 & \end{array}$$

Thus, the solutions are 2 and 6.

The solutions are also called roots.

A quadratic equation may have two solutions.

EXAMPLE 4   Find the solution set of $2x^2 + 5x - 3 = 0$.

$$2x^2 + 5x - 3 = 0$$

Factor. ⟶

If $a \cdot b = 0$, then $a = 0$ or $b = 0.$ ⟶
Solve each equation for x.

$$(2x - 1)(x + 3) = 0$$
$$2x - 1 = 0 \quad \text{or} \quad x + 3 = 0$$

$$\begin{array}{cc} \underline{1 \quad 1} & \underline{-3 \quad -3} \\ 2x = 1 & x = -3 \\ x = \dfrac{1}{2} & \end{array}$$

Check on your own. ⟶ The solutions are $\dfrac{1}{2}$ and -3.

Thus, the solution set is $\left\{ \dfrac{1}{2}, -3 \right\}$.

EXAMPLE 5   Solve $x^2 - 7x = 0$.

$$x^2 - 7x = 0$$

Factor out the GCF. ⟶

If $a \cdot b = 0$, then $a = 0$ or $b = 0.$ ⟶
Solve each equation for x.

$$x(x - 7) = 0$$
$$x = 0 \quad \text{or} \quad x - 7 = 0$$

$$\begin{array}{c} \underline{7 \quad 7} \\ x = 7 \end{array}$$

Check on your own. ⟶ **Thus,** the solutions are 0 and 7.

ORAL EXERCISES

For what values of x will each be true?

1. $(2x - 4)(x + 3) = 0$
2. $x(x + 5) = 0$
3. $5x(x - 7) = 0$
4. $(3x - 1)(2x - 4) = 0$
5. $(x - 3)(x - 3) = 0$
6. $(x - 5)(x + 5) = 0$

EXERCISES

PART A
Solve.

1. $x^2 - 5x + 6 = 0$
2. $x^2 - 7x + 10 = 0$
3. $x^2 - 9x + 8 = 0$
4. $x^2 - 6x = 0$
5. $x^2 - 36 = 0$
6. $x^2 + 8x + 12 = 0$

Find the solution set.

7. $2a^2 + 9a - 5 = 0$
8. $3m^2 + 8m - 3 = 0$
9. $2p^2 + 5p - 3 = 0$
10. $3x^2 + 14x - 5 = 0$
11. $2t^2 + 7t - 15 = 0$
12. $2b^2 + 3b - 9 = 0$
13. $3a^2 - 22a + 7 = 0$
14. $a^2 - 10a + 16 = 0$
15. $2y^2 - 11y + 5 = 0$
16. $2g^2 - 15g - 8 = 0$
17. $4a^2 - 25 = 0$
18. $x^2 - 64 = 0$
19. $2n^2 - 13n + 15 = 0$
20. $m^2 + 17m = 0$
21. $3k^2 - 5k = 0$

PART B
Solve.

22. $2x^2 + 13x - 24 = 0$
23. $3y^2 + 16y - 35 = 0$
24. $5a^2 + 34a - 7 = 0$
25. $2a^2 + 5a - 42 = 0$
26. $5a^2 - 22a + 21 = 0$
27. $2a^2 + 23a + 56 = 0$
28. $3b^2 - 31b + 36 = 0$
29. $a^2 - 20a + 100 = 0$
30. $x^2 + 18x + 81 = 0$

PART C

EXAMPLE   Solve $x^3 - 25x = 0$.

Factor out the GCF. $\longrightarrow$ $x(x^2 - 25) = 0$

$x^2 - 25 = (x)^2 - (5)^2$; factor. $\longrightarrow$ $x(x - 5)(x + 5) = 0$

If $a \cdot b \cdot c = 0$, then $a = 0$ $\longrightarrow$ $x = 0$ or $x - 5 = 0$ or $x + 5 = 0$
or $b = 0$ or $c = 0$.

$$\underline{ 5 5} \qquad \underline{-5 -5}$$
$$x = 5 \qquad\qquad x = -5$$

Thus, the solutions are 0, 5, and −5.

Solve.

31. $x^3 - 9x = 0$
32. $x^3 - 4x = 0$
33. $4b^3 - 16b = 0$
34. $x^3 - 2x^2 = 0$
35. $m^3 - 49m = 0$
36. $3x^3 - 75x = 0$

Computing Mentally

We can use our ability to multiply binomials to find the squares of two-digit numbers mentally!

We can find $(73)^2$ by rewriting 73 as $(70 + 3)$.

$$(a + b)^2 = a^2 + 2(a \cdot b) + b^2$$

$$(70 + 3)^2 = 70^2 + 2(70 \cdot 3) + 3^2$$

$$4900 + 420 + 9$$

$$\begin{array}{r} 4900 \\ 420 \\ 9 \\ \hline 5329 \end{array}$$

So, $(73)^2 = 5{,}329$

The above method suggests this shortcut:

To find $(73)^2$, write

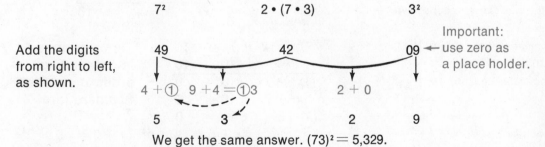

| 7^2 | $2 \cdot (7 \cdot 3)$ | 3^2 |

Add the digits from right to left, as shown.

49   42   09 ← Important: use zero as a place holder.

$4 + ①$ $9 + 4 = ①3$ $2 + 0$

5   3   2   9

We get the same answer. $(73)^2 = 5{,}329$.

Use the shortcut to find each of the following.

1. $(26)^2$ 2. $(57)^2$ 3. $(81)^2$ 4. $(34)^2$

Quadratic Equations: Standard Form

This quadratic equation is in standard form.

$$2x^2 - 5x + 2 = 0$$

A quadratic equation is in standard form if it meets all three of these conditions.

Coefficient of the x^2 term ($2x^2$) is positive.
Polynomial ($2x^2 - 5x + 2$) is equal to 0.
Terms are arranged in descending order of exponents.

EXAMPLE 1 Solve $7x = -x^2 - 10$.

Get coefficient of x^2 term positive.
Add $1x^2$ to each side.
Coefficient of x^2 term is positive.

$$7x = -1x^2 - 10$$
$$\underline{1x^2 \qquad\quad 1x^2}$$
$$1x^2 + 7x = \qquad -10$$

Get polynomial equal to 0.
Add 10 to each side.
Polynomial is equal to 0.

$$1x^2 + 7x = -10 \qquad \text{Terms arranged}$$
$$\underline{\qquad\quad 10 \quad 10} \qquad \text{in descending}$$
$$1x^2 + 7x + 10 = \quad 0 \quad \leftarrow \text{order of exponents}$$
$$x^2 + 7x + 10 = \quad 0 \quad \leftarrow \text{Standard form}$$

Factor. ————————————→ $(x + 5)(x + 2) = \quad 0$

Set each factor = 0. —————————→ $x + 5 = \quad 0 \quad \text{or} \quad x + 2 = \quad 0$

Solve each equation for x.

$$\underline{-5 \quad -5} \qquad\qquad \underline{-2 \quad -2}$$
$$x = -5 \qquad\qquad\quad x = -2$$

Thus, the solutions are -5 and -2.

EXAMPLE 2   Solve and check $5 - 9x = 2x^2$.

x^2 term is already positive.

Get polynomial equal to 0. ⎫
Add $9x$ to each side.   ⎬
Add -5 to each side.   ⎭
Polynomial is equal to 0.

Factor. ───────────────→

Set each factor $= 0$. ───────────→

Solve each equation for x.

$$5 - 9x = 2x^2$$

$$\underline{9x \quad 9x}$$

$$5 = 2x^2 + 9x \qquad \text{Terms arranged}$$

$$\underline{-5 \quad -5} \qquad \text{in descending}$$

$$0 = 2x^2 + 9x - 5 \quad \leftarrow \text{order of exponents}$$

$$0 = (2x - 1)(x + 5)$$

$$2x - 1 = 0 \quad \text{or} \quad x + 5 = 0$$

$$\underline{1 \quad 1} \qquad \underline{-5 \quad -5}$$

$$2x = 1 \qquad\qquad x = -5$$

$$x = \frac{1}{2}$$

Check. ──────────────────────→

$$x = \frac{1}{2} \quad \begin{array}{c|c} 5 - 9x & 2x^2 \\ \hline 5 - 9\left(\frac{1}{2}\right) & 2\left(\frac{1}{2}\right)^2 \\ 5 - \ 4\frac{1}{2} & 2\left(\frac{1}{4}\right) \\ \frac{1}{2} & \frac{1}{2} \end{array}$$

$$x = -5 \quad \begin{array}{c|c} 5 - 9x & 2x^2 \\ \hline 5 - 9(-5) & 2(-5)^2 \\ 5 + \ 45 & 2(25) \\ 50 & 50 \end{array}$$

Thus, the solutions are $\frac{1}{2}$ and -5.

EXAMPLE 3   Find the solution set of $-x^2 = 3x$.

Get x^2 term positive. ⎫
Add $1x^2$ to each side. ⎬
x^2 term is positive.   ⎭
Polynomial is equal to 0. ────────→
Factor out the GCF. ────────────→
Set each factor $= 0$. ───────────→
Solve each equation for x.

$$-1x^2 = 3x$$

$$\underline{1x^2 \quad 1x^2} \qquad \text{Terms arranged in descending}$$

$$0 \ = 1x^2 + 3x \quad \leftarrow \text{order of exponents}$$

$$0 \ = x^2 + 3x$$

$$0 \ = x(x + 3)$$

$$x = 0 \quad \text{or} \quad x + 3 = 0$$

$$\underline{-3 \quad -3}$$

$$x = -3$$

Check. ──────────────────→

$$x = 0 \quad \begin{array}{c|c} -x^2 & 3x \\ \hline -(0)^2 & 3(0) \\ 0 & 0 \end{array}$$

$$x = -3 \quad \begin{array}{c|c} -x^2 & 3x \\ \hline -(-3)^2 & 3(-3) \\ -1(9) & -9 \\ -9 & \end{array}$$

The solutions are 0 and -3.

Thus, the solution set is $\{0, -3\}$.

EXERCISES

Solve and check.

1. $8x = -x^2 - 15$ 2. $9x = -x^2 - 20$ 3. $12m = -m^2 - 32$
4. $18 - 7b = b^2$ 5. $12 - 4m = m^2$ 6. $6 - 5p = p^2$
7. $-x^2 = 9x$ 8. $-x^2 = 10x$ 9. $-x^2 = 7x$

Find the solution sets.

10. $x^2 + 4x = 5$ 11. $9m^2 = 4$ 12. $a^2 - 10 = 3a$
13. $13g = -g^2$ 14. $2a^2 + a = 10$ 15. $b^2 = 49$
16. $2a^2 + 3a = -1$ 17. $5b - 2 = 3b^2$ 18. $n^2 - 7n = 18$
19. $2x^2 + x = 1$ 20. $2a^2 + 7 = 15a$ 21. $3k^2 = -2k + 1$
22. $4n^2 = 1$ 23. $2x^2 - 21 = 11x$ 24. $3a^2 - 22a = 16$
25. $2p^2 = -11p + 6$ 26. $3x - 20 = -2x^2$ 27. $25 = 4b^2$

Solve.

28. $12x^2 = 35 - x$ 29. $19a - 6 = 15a^2$ 30. $4m^2 - 42 = 17m$
31. $11b - 10 = -6b^2$ 32. $12y^2 + 15 = 29y$ 33. $6x^2 = 35 - 11x$
34. $4m^2 = 225$ 35. $4a + 35 = 4a^2$ 36. $6b^2 + 13b = 28$
37. $24b = -3b^2$ 38. $17x - 14 = -6x^2$ 39. $10a^2 - 29a = -10$

EXAMPLE   Solve $(2x + 3)(x - 5) = x^2 + 9x - 43$.

$$
\begin{aligned}
2x^2 - 7x - 15 &= x^2 + 9x - 43 \\
-x^2 \qquad\qquad &\quad -x^2 \\
\hline
x^2 - 7x - 15 &= 9x - 43 \\
-9x \qquad\qquad &\quad -9x \\
\hline
x^2 - 16x - 15 &= -43 \\
43 \qquad &\quad 43 \\
\hline
x^2 - 16x + 28 &= 0 \\
(x - 14)(x - 2) &= 0 \\
x - 14 = 0 \quad &\text{or} \quad x - 2 = 0 \\
x = 14 \qquad &\qquad x = 2
\end{aligned}
$$

Check on your own. ⟶ **Thus,** the solutions are 14 and 2.

Solve.

40. $(3x - 2)(2x + 5) = 5x^2 + 5x - 18$ 41. $(x - 3)(x + 3) = 2x^2 - 18$

Consecutive Integers

REVIEW CAPSULE

Even integers have 2 as a factor.
For example: −4, 0, 28, 40, 90.

Odd integers do not have 2 as a factor.
For example: −5, 3, 15, 35, 47.

EXAMPLE 1   Write the next two consecutive integers.

Answers

Add 1 to get the next consecutive
integer.
$(a + 2) + 1 = a + 3$

7, 8, 9, 10, . . .   11, 12
−2, −1, 0, 1, 2, . . .   3, 4
$a, a + 1, a + 2, . . .$ $a + 3, a + 4$

Example 1 suggests this. ————→ $x, x + 1, x + 2, . . .$ represent consecutive integers
for each integer x.

EXAMPLE 2   Write three consecutive integers, beginning with
the given integer.
−28   7 n

Begin with. ————————————→   −28   7 n
$-28 + 1 = -27$ ————————→   −27   8 $n + 1 \quad = n + 1$
$-28 + 1 + 1 = -26$ ——————→   −26   9 $n + 1 + 1 = n + 2$

EXAMPLE 3   Write the next two consecutive even integers.

Answers

Add 2 to an even integer to get the next
consecutive even integer.

0, 2, 4, . . .   6, 8
−8, −6, −4, . . .   −2, 0
$b, b + 2, b + 4, . . .$ $b + 6, b + 8$

Example 3 suggests this. ————→ $x, x + 2, x + 4, . . .$ represent consecutive even
integers, for each even integer x.

EXAMPLE 4   Write three consecutive even integers, beginning with the given even integer.

$$n \qquad\qquad -8$$

Begin with ⟶

Add 2 to get the next consecutive even integer.

$$n \qquad\qquad\qquad\qquad -8$$
$$n + 2 \quad = n + 2 \qquad -8 + 2 \quad = -6$$
$$n + 2 + 2 = n + 4 \qquad -8 + 2 + 2 = -4$$

EXAMPLE 5   Write the next two consecutive odd integers.

Add 2 to an odd integer to get the next consecutive odd integer.

	Answers
5, 7, 9, . . .	11, 13
$-9, -7, -5, \ldots$	$-3, -1$
$c, c + 2, c + 4, \ldots$	$c + 6, c + 8$

Example 5 suggests this. ⟶

$x, x + 2, x + 4, \ldots$ represent consecutive odd integers, for each odd integer x.

EXAMPLE 6   Write three consecutive odd integers, beginning with the given odd integer.

$$-9 \qquad\qquad 5 \qquad n$$

Add 2 to get the next consecutive odd integer.

$$-9 \qquad 5 \qquad\qquad n$$
$$-9 + 2 = -7 \qquad 7 \qquad n + 2 \quad = n + 2$$
$$-7 + 2 = -5 \qquad 9 \qquad n + 2 + 2 = n + 4$$

EXAMPLE 7   Write an equation.
The sum of three consecutive integers is 21.

Represent the integers. Add 1 to get the next consecutive integer.

Sum means add. ⟶

Write the equation. ⟶

Let $x =$ first integer
$x + 1 =$ second integer
$x + 2 =$ third integer
Their sum is 21.
$$x + (x + 1) + (x + 2) = 21$$

EXAMPLE 8   Write an equation.
The product of two consecutive odd integers is 15.

Represent the integers. Add 2 to get the next odd integer.

Product is 15. ⟶

Let $x =$ first odd integer
$x + 2 =$ second odd integer
$$x(x + 2) = 15$$

ORAL EXERCISES

Give three consecutive integers, beginning with the given integer.

1. 7 **2.** 11 **3.** 26 **4.** −2 **5.** −6 **6.** −40 **7.** a

Give four consecutive even integers, beginning with the given integer.

8. 8 **9.** 6 **10.** 38 **11.** −4 **12.** −10 **13.** n **14.** $n + 8$

Give five consecutive odd integers beginning with the given integer.

15. 7 **16.** 19 **17.** 53 **18.** −5 **19.** −23 **20.** b **21.** $b + 6$

EXERCISES

PART A

Write an equation.

1. The sum of three consecutive integers is 27.

2. The sum of three consecutive integers is 33.

3. The sum of three consecutive integers is −15.

4. The sum of three consecutive integers is −21.

5. The product of two consecutive odd integers is 35.

6. The product of two consecutive odd integers is 99.

7. The product of three consecutive odd integers is 48.

8. The product of three consecutive even integers is 192.

9. The sum of four consecutive odd integers is 40.

10. The sum of four consecutive even integers is 36.

PART B

Write an equation.

11. Twice the second of two consecutive integers, decreased by the first is 5.

12. Twice the second of two consecutive even integers, decreased by the first is 10.

13. Twice the second of two consecutive odd integers, decreased by the first is 11.

14. Three times the second of two consecutive integers, decreased by three times the first is 3.

15. Three times the second of two consecutive even integers, decreased by twice the first is 48.

16. Three times the first of two consecutive odd integers, decreased by twice the second is 21.

17. The product of three consecutive integers is the same as 8 times their sum.

18. The product of three consecutive even integers is the same as 4 times their sum.

Consecutive Integer Problems

REVIEW CAPSULE

Write an equation.
The sum of three consecutive odd
integers is 27.

$$x + (x + 2) + (x + 4) = 27$$

EXAMPLE 1   Find two consecutive integers whose sum is 67.

Represent the integers. }
Add 1 to get the next integer. }

Sum means add. ─────────→

Write an equation. ─────────→

Combine like terms. ─────────→

Solve for x.

First integer ─────────→

Second integer ─────────→

Let x = first integer
       $x + 1$ = second integer
Their sum is 67.

$$x + (x + 1) = 67$$
$$2x + 1 = 67$$
$$2x = 66$$
$$x = 33$$
$$x + 1 = 33 + 1, \text{ or } 34$$

Check: $33 + 34 = 67$.

Thus, the integers are 33 and 34.

EXAMPLE 2   Find two consecutive integers whose product is 20.

Represent the integers.

Product means multiply. ─────────→

Write an equation. ─────────→

$x(x + 1) = x(x) + x(1)$ ─────────→

Get equation in standard form. }
Add -20 to each side. }

Factor. ─────────→

Set each factor = 0. ─────────→

First integer ─────────→

Second integer ─────────→

There are two pairs of integers.

Let x = first integer
       $x + 1$ = second integer
Their product is 20.

$$x(x + 1) = 20$$
$$x^2 + x = 20$$
$$\underline{ -20 \quad -20}$$
$$x^2 + x - 20 = 0$$
$$(x + 5)(x - 4) = 0$$
$$x + 5 = 0 \quad \text{or} \quad x - 4 = 0$$
$$x = -5 \quad \text{or} \qquad x = 4$$
$$x + 1 = -5 + 1, \text{ or } -4 \quad \text{or} \quad x + 1 = 4 + 1, \text{ or } 5$$

Check the first solution in the problem. ──→

-5 and -4 are consecutive integers, since
$-5 + 1 = -4$.
Their product is 20, since $(-5)(-4) = 20$.

Check 4 and 5 in the problem. There are
two pairs of solutions. ─────────→

Thus, the integers are -5 and -4, or 4 and 5.

EXAMPLE 3 Find two consecutive integers such that the sum of the first and the square of the second is 19.

Represent the integers algebraically.

Let $x =$ first integer
$x + 1 =$ second integer

Sum of the first and the square of the second is 19.

$(x + 1)^2 = (x + 1)(x + 1)$
$\qquad = x^2 + 2x + 1$ ⟶

Combine like terms. ⟶
Add -19 to each side. ⟶
Factor. ⟶
Set each factor $= 0$. ⟶
First integer ⟶
Second integer ⟶
Check both solutions in the problem.

$$x + (x + 1)^2 = 19$$
$$x + x^2 + 2x + 1 = 19$$
$$x^2 + 3x + 1 = 19$$
$$x^2 + 3x - 18 = 0$$
$$(x + 6)(x - 3) = 0$$
$$x + 6 = 0 \quad \text{or } x - 3 = 0$$
$$x = -6 \text{ or} \qquad x = 3$$
$$x + 1 = -6 + 1, \text{ or } -5 \text{ or } x + 1 = 3 + 1 = 4$$

Sum of the first and square of the second is 19.

$-6 + (-5)^2$	19
$-6 + \quad 25$	19
19	

$3 + (4)^2$	19
$3 + 16$	19
19	

Two pairs of solutions ⟶ **Thus,** the two consecutive integers are -6 and -5, or 3 and 4.

EXAMPLE 4 Find two consecutive odd integers such that the square of the second, decreased by the first is 22.

Represent the integers algebraically.

Let $x =$ first integer
$x + 2 =$ second integer

Square of second, decreased by first is 22.

Write the equation. ⟶
$(x + 2)^2 = x^2 + 4x + 4$ ⟶
Combine like terms. ⟶
Standard form ⟶
Factor. ⟶
Set each factor $= 0$. ⟶
First integer ⟶
Second integer ⟶
There is only one pair of integers.

$$(x + 2)^2 - x = 22$$
$$x^2 + 4x + 4 - x = 22$$
$$x^2 + 3x + 4 = 22$$
$$x^2 + 3x - 18 = 0$$
$$(x - 3)(x + 6) = 0$$
$$x - 3 = 0 \qquad \text{or} \qquad x + 6 = 0$$
$$x = 3 \qquad\qquad\qquad x = -6$$
$$x + 2 = 3 + 2, \text{ or } 5$$

first integer, x cannot be -6, since -6 is not odd.

Check 3 and 5 in the problem.

Square of second decreased by first is 22.

$(5)^2 - 3$	22
$25 - 3$	22
22	

There is only one solution. ⟶ **Thus,** the two consecutive odd integers are 3 and 5.

EXERCISES

PART A

1. Find two consecutive integers whose sum is 45.
2. Find three consecutive odd integers whose sum is 63.
3. Find five consecutive integers whose sum is 155.
4. Find three consecutive even integers whose sum is 120.
5. Find three consecutive integers such that twice the first added to the last is 23.
6. Find four consecutive odd integers such that twice the second added to the last is 25.
7. Find three consecutive odd integers such that twice the first, decreased by the second is 35.
8. Find three consecutive integers such that three times the second, increased by the last is 81.
9. Find two consecutive integers whose product is 12.
10. Find two consecutive integers whose product is 30.
11. Find two consecutive even integers whose product is 24.
12. Find two consecutive odd integers whose product is 35.
13. Find two consecutive odd integers such that the sum of their squares is 130.
14. Find two consecutive even integers such that the sum of their squares is 52.
15. Find three consecutive integers such that the square of the first, added to the last is 8.
16. Find three consecutive integers such that the square of the first, decreased by the last is 18.
17. Find three consecutive integers such that the square of the first is 18 more than the last.
18. Find three consecutive integers such that the square of the first is equal to the third.
19. Find two consecutive odd integers such that the square of the second, decreased by the first is 14.
20. Find two consecutive even integers such that the square of the second increased by twice the first is 44.

PART B

21. Find four consecutive integers such that 3 times the third, decreased by the second is the last.
22. Find four consecutive even integers such that the sum of the squares of the first and second is 12 more than the last.
23. Find four consecutive integers such that the sum of the squares of the second and third is 61.
24. Find five consecutive integers such that the square of the third, decreased by the square of the second is 3 times the first.

Complement of a Set

$U = \{1, 2, 3, 4, 5, 6\}$
$A = \{2, 4, 6\}$
$\overline{A} = \{1, 3, 5\}$

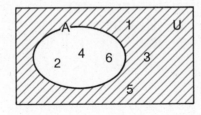

Read: complement of A

$\overline{A} = $ ///////

all elements of U that are not in A.

$U = \{1, 2, 3, 4, 5, 6, 7, 8\}$
$A = \{2, 4, 6\}$
$B = \{6, 7, 8\}$

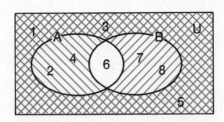

$\overline{A} = $ ///////
$= \{1, 3, 5, 7, 8\}$
$\overline{B} = $ \\\\\\\
$= \{1, 2, 3, 4, 5\}$

$A \cap B = \{6\}$

$\overline{A} \cup \overline{B} = \{1, 2, 3, 4, 5, 7, 8\}$

$\overline{A \cap B} = \overline{\{6\}} = \{1, 2, 3, 4, 5, 7, 8\}$

Same set

Thus, $\overline{A} \cup \overline{B} = \overline{A \cap B}$.

This is one of De Morgan's laws of complementation. De Morgan's laws have been proved for all sets. The algebra of sets is called Boolean Algebra.
A similar principle holds for $\overline{A} \cap \overline{B}$.
Use a Venn diagram to show $\overline{A} \cap \overline{B} = \overline{A \cup B}$.

Draw a diagram for each. Then use your diagrams to show that De Morgan's laws $\overline{A} \cap \overline{B} = \overline{A \cup B}$ and $\overline{A} \cup \overline{B} = \overline{A \cap B}$ hold.

1. $U = \{2, 4, 6, 8, 10, 12\}$ $A = \{4, 8, 10\}$ $B = \{6, 8, 10, 12\}$
2. $U = \{1, 3, 5, 7, 9, 11\}$ $A = \{3, 5, 11\}$ $B = \{3, 9, 11\}$

Chapter Six Review

Multiply. [*p. 141*]

1. $(x + 5)(x + 3)$
2. $(x - 7)(x + 9)$
3. $(2x + 3)(x + 5)$
4. $(3x - 1)(x + 6)$
5. $(2b - 3)(b + 4)$
6. $(m - 1)(m + 1)$
7. $(4z - 1)(3z - 2)$
8. $(3x - 5)(x + 5)$
9. $(3x - 1)(5x + 4)$
10. $(x - 5)(x^2 + 7x + 3)$
11. $(2x - 3)(x^2 + 3x - 4)$
12. $(3x - 1)(x^2 + 2x - 4)$

Simplify. [*p. 141*]

13. $(3a - 5)^2$
14. $(4x - 1)^2$
15. $(2x + 3)^2$
16. $(7x + 1)^2$

Factor completely. [*p. 145, 150, 153, 156*]

17. $x^2 - 7x + 12$
18. $p^2 + 7p + 10$
19. $2a^2 + 9a - 5$
20. $x^2 - 5x + 6$
21. $3y^2 + 17y + 10$
22. $3x^2 + 16x - 12$
23. $2m^2 + 3m - 20$
24. $2m^2 + 7m + 6$
25. $2x^2 - 9x + 9$
26. $4a^2 + 2a - 2$
27. $6x^2 - x - 1$
28. $12b^2 + 5b - 2$
29. $a^2 - 4$
30. $x^2 - 36$
31. $4a^2 - 25$
32. $49x^2 - 36y^2$
33. $3x^2 + 21x + 36$
34. $2a^2 - 8a + 6$
35. $2a^2 - 2a - 40$
36. $3b^2 + 6b - 45$
37. $3k^3 + 3k^2 - 90k$
38. $3b^2 - 21b - 90$
39. $6x^3 - 24x^2 + 18x$
40. $b^3 - 49b$
41. $x^2 + 3xy + 2y^2$
42. $a^2 - 9b^2$
43. $a^2 - 3ab - 28b^2$
44. $2p^2 + 13\,pq + 15\,q^2$
45. $144x^2 - 169y^2$
46. $4y^2 - 14yb - 30b^2$
47. $3x^2 - 31xy + 56y^2$
48. $yx^2 - 4y^3$
49. $2x^2 + 12x + 18$
50. $12x^2 - 60x + 75$

Solve. [*p. 158, 162*]

51. $a^2 - 3a + 2 = 0$
52. $x^2 - 4 = 0$
53. $a^2 - 9a - 36 = 0$
54. $4 = a^2$
55. $24 + p^2 = 10p$
56. $-9r + 14 = -r^2$

Find the solution set. [*p. 158, 162*]

57. $x^2 - 13x + 42 = 0$
58. $9m^2 - 49 = 0$
59. $9a - 5 = -2a^2$
60. $2x^2 = 13x - 21$
61. $45 + 19n = -2n^2$
62. $2a^2 = -15a - 28$

Solve these problems. [*p. 165, 168*]

63. Find two consecutive integers whose product is 72.

64. Find two consecutive integers such that the sum of the squares is 41.

65. Find three consecutive integers such that the square of the first, decreased by 5 times the second is 9.

66. Find three consecutive even integers such that the square of the first, added to the sum of the second and third is 30.

Chapter Six Test

Multiply.

1. $(x + 5)(x + 8)$
3. $(3x - 2)(3x + 2)$

2. $(2x - 1)(3x + 4)$
4. $(2a + 3)(a^2 - 7a + 4)$

Simplify.

5. $(3a - 2)^2$

6. $(4x + 1)^2$

Factor completely.

7. $a^2 - 7a + 10$
9. $4m^2 + 18m - 36$
11. $2b^3 - 8b^2 - 64b$
13. $2x^2 + 5xy - 3y^2$

8. $x^2 - 2x - 35$
10. $p^2 - 49$
12. $16a^3 - 25a$
14. $8b^2 - 8bc - 6c^2$

Solve.

15. $x^2 - 5x + 4 = 0$
17. $a^2 - 7a = 0$
19. $3p + 28 = p^2$

16. $a^2 - 4a - 12 = 0$
18. $m^2 - 10m = -24$
20. $x^2 = 64$

Find the solution set.

21. $m^2 + 14m = 0$
23. $-11m - 21 = -2m^2$
25. $2b^2 - 9b = 5$

22. $a^2 - 25 = 0$
24. $2k^2 = -21k - 40$
26. $2m^2 - 21 = -m$

Solve these problems.

27. Find two consecutive integers such that the sum of the second and the square of the first is 31.
29. Find two consecutive odd integers such that the square of the second increased by 4 times the first is 37.

28. Find two consecutive integers whose product is 56.

30. Find two consecutive even integers such that the square of the first increased by the second is 22.

Mathematics in Music

The distance from middle *C* to the next *C* is one octave.

The frequency of a note is its number of vibrations per second.

Note	Frequency
middle *C*	264
D	297
E	330
F	352

Note	Frequency
G	396
A	440
B	495
higher *C*	528

$$\frac{\text{frequency of higher } C}{\text{frequency of middle } C} = \frac{528}{264} \text{, or } \frac{2}{1} \leftarrow \begin{array}{l} \text{All octaves are} \\ \text{in this ratio.} \end{array}$$

Simple frequency ratios can indicate pleasing combinations of notes.

$$\frac{E}{C} = \frac{330}{264} \text{, or } \frac{5}{4}$$

pleasing

Can you find some other combinations which would be pleasing?

Fractions

OBJECTIVES

- To find products of the form $a\left(\dfrac{1}{b}\right)$
- To find reciprocals of fractions
- To find the values of x for which fractions like $\dfrac{x-3}{x+2}$ are undefined

▶ REVIEW CAPSULE

3(2) means $2 + 2 + 2$, or 6
$2(-5)$ means $-5 + (-5)$, or -10
$4(x)$ means $x + x + x + x$, or $4x$
$3(-a)$ means $-a + (-a) + (-a)$, or $-3a$

Fractions on a Number Line

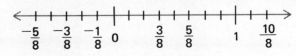

$\dfrac{3}{8}$ ⟵ Numerator
    ⟵ Denominator

EXAMPLE 1 Give the coordinates of points A and B.

Each subdivision is $\dfrac{1}{5}$.

Count from 0.

Count $-\dfrac{1}{5}, -\dfrac{2}{5}, -\dfrac{3}{5}$. ————————⟶

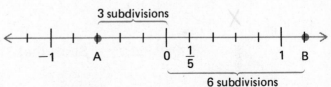

Point A	Point B
3 subdivisions	6 subdivisions
left of 0	*right* of 0
$-\dfrac{3}{5}$	$\dfrac{6}{5}$

EXAMPLE 2 Show that $\dfrac{16}{8} = 2$.

$\dfrac{16}{8}$ means $16 \div 8$.

$16 \div 8 = 2$ **Thus,** $\dfrac{16}{8} = 2$.

EXAMPLE 3 Show that $\frac{6}{0}$ is undefined, or meaningless.

Think. ⟶

$\frac{6}{0}$ means $6 \div 0$.   Let $6 \div 0 = x$.

Check. ⟶

Then $0 \cdot x = 6$.

$0 \cdot a = 0$, for each number a. ⟶

But $0 \cdot x = 0$.

There is no number that can be
multiplied by 0 to get 6. ⟶ **Thus,** $\frac{6}{0}$ is undefined, or meaningless.

Definition of rational number ⟶

A *rational number* is a number which can be
written in the form $\frac{a}{b}$, where a and b are
integers and $b \neq 0$.

$\frac{4}{5}, \frac{-7}{8}, \frac{24}{8}$ are rational numbers.

EXAMPLE 4 Write each in the form $\frac{a}{b}$.

Think. ⟶

$5 \div 1$ $16 \div 4$ $-2 \div 8$

$\frac{5}{1}$ $\frac{16}{4}$ $\frac{-2}{8}$

EXAMPLE 5 Show that $3\left(\frac{1}{6}\right) = \frac{3}{6}$.

$3\left(\frac{1}{6}\right)$ means $\frac{1}{6} + \frac{1}{6} + \frac{1}{6}$.

Mark off sixths on a number line.

Count 3 subdivisions from 0 to $\frac{3}{6}$.

Thus, $3\left(\frac{1}{6}\right) = \frac{3}{6}$.

Example 5 suggests this. ⟶

$a\left(\frac{1}{b}\right) = \frac{a}{b}, b \neq 0.$

EXAMPLE 6   Multiply $-2\left(\frac{1}{7}\right)$.   Multiply $(x+3)\left(\frac{1}{x-5}\right)$.

$a\left(\frac{1}{b}\right)=\frac{a}{b}$, $b\neq 0$ ──────────────→ $-2\left(\frac{1}{7}\right)=\frac{-2}{7}$ $(x+3)\left(\frac{1}{x-5}\right)=\frac{x+3}{x-5}$

EXAMPLE 7   Multiply $4\left(\frac{1}{4}\right)$.

$$4\left(\frac{1}{4}\right)=\frac{4}{4}$$

$\frac{4}{4}$ means $4\div 4$ and $4\div 4=1$.

Thus, $4\left(\frac{1}{4}\right)=1$.

Example 7 suggests this. ──────────→

Reciprocals are sometimes called *multiplicative inverses*.

$$a\left(\frac{1}{a}\right)=1.$$

a and $\frac{1}{a}$ are *reciprocals* of each other if $a\neq 0$.

EXAMPLE 8   Find the reciprocal of each of the following:
$$6, \frac{1}{7}, 0, -8$$

$6(?)=1$, $6\left(\frac{1}{6}\right)=1$

$\left(\frac{1}{7}\right)(?)=1$, $\left(\frac{1}{7}\right)(7)=1$

$(-8)(?)=1$, $(-8)\left(-\frac{1}{8}\right)=1$

Number	Reciprocal
6	$\frac{1}{6}$
$\frac{1}{7}$	7
0	No reciprocal
-8	$-\frac{1}{8}$

EXAMPLE 9   Find the missing factor or product.

$(?)\left(\frac{1}{a}\right)=\frac{b}{a}$ $\quad a(?)=\frac{a}{m}$ $\quad (x-2)\left(\frac{1}{x+4}\right)=?$

$b\left(\frac{1}{a}\right)=\frac{b}{a}$ $\quad a\left(\frac{1}{m}\right)=\frac{a}{m}$ $\quad (x-2)\left(\frac{1}{x+4}\right)=\frac{x-2}{x+4}$

ORAL EXERCISES

Find the products.

1. $3\left(\dfrac{1}{7}\right)$ **2.** $4\left(\dfrac{1}{5}\right)$ **3.** $m\left(\dfrac{1}{n}\right)$ **4.** $(a-3)\left(\dfrac{1}{a+5}\right)$

Find the missing factor.

5. $4\,(?) = \dfrac{4}{7}$ **6.** $p\,(?) = \dfrac{p}{q}$ **7.** $(?)\,(y) = \dfrac{y}{x}$ **8.** $(?)\,(-7) = \dfrac{-7}{13}$

9. Give the reciprocal of $-3,\ 0,\ 1,\ -1,$ and $-\dfrac{1}{5}$.

EXERCISES

PART A

Give the coordinate of each point A.

1. 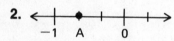   **2.**   **3.**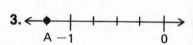

Write each in the form $\dfrac{a}{b}$.

4. 6 **5.** -3 **6.** $12 \div 3$ **7.** $-8 \div 2$ **8.** $-6 \div 12$

Multiply.

9. $4\left(\dfrac{1}{5}\right)$ **10.** $-5\left(\dfrac{1}{17}\right)$ **11.** $(x+5)\left(\dfrac{1}{x-4}\right)$ **12.** $(a-4)\left(\dfrac{1}{a+2}\right)$

PART B

EXAMPLE   For what value of x is $\dfrac{x+2}{2x-4}$ undefined?

$\dfrac{a}{b}$ is undefined for $b=0$. $\longrightarrow$ $\dfrac{x+2}{2x-4}$ is undefined when $2x-4=0$.

Solve.
$$2x - 4 = 0$$
$$2x = 4$$
$$x = 2 \quad \text{Thus, } \dfrac{x+2}{2x-4} \text{ is undefined when } x = 2.$$

Find the value(s) of x for which the fraction is undefined.

13. $\dfrac{2x-1}{x-7}$ **14.** $\dfrac{3x+2}{2x-10}$ **15.** $\dfrac{7x+1}{3x-12}$ **16.** $\dfrac{x+5}{x^2-9}$ **17.** $\dfrac{3x+2}{x^2-7x+12}$

Zero and Negative Exponents

Look at the powers of 2 as the exponents decrease from 5 to 0.

Exponents decrease by 1.

$2^5 = 2 \times 2 \times 2 \times 2 \times 2 = 32$
$2^4 = 2 \times 2 \times 2 \times 2 \quad\quad = 16$
$2^3 = 2 \times 2 \times 2 \quad\quad\quad = 8$
$2^2 = 2 \times 2 \quad\quad\quad\quad = 4$
$2^1 = 2 \quad\quad\quad\quad\quad\quad = 2$
$2^0 = \longrightarrow \quad\quad\quad = 1$

Powers are divided by 2.

Thus, $2^0 = 1$.

> For any $a \neq 0$, $\quad a^0 = 1$
> 0^0 is undefined.

Go back to the pattern and continue dividing by 2.

$2^2 = 2 \times 2 = 4$
$2^1 = 2 \quad\quad = 2$
$2^0 = \longrightarrow = 1$
$2^{-1} = \dfrac{1}{2} = \dfrac{1}{2}$
$2^{-2} = \dfrac{1}{2 \times 2} = \dfrac{1}{4}$
$2^{-3} = \dfrac{1}{2 \times 2 \times 2} = \dfrac{1}{8}$

> For any $a \neq 0$, $\quad a^{-n} = \dfrac{1}{a^n}$

Find the value of each of the following.

1. 4^0

2. 3^{-2}

3. $(-2)^0$

4. 5^{-3}

5. 6^{-1}

6. $\dfrac{1}{2^{-1}}$

7. $\dfrac{2^0}{3}$

8. $3^{-2} \times 5^0$

9. $(2 \times 3)^0$

10. $5^{-1} + 2^{-1}$

Multiplying Fractions

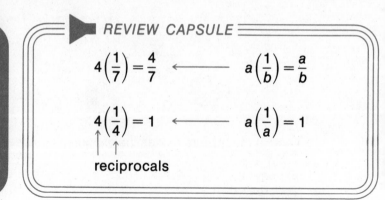

EXAMPLE 1 Show that $\dfrac{1}{3} \cdot \dfrac{1}{4} = \dfrac{1}{12}$.

A number has exactly one reciprocal.

First show the reciprocal of 12 as $\dfrac{1}{3} \cdot \dfrac{1}{4}$.

$$12 \cdot \dfrac{1}{3} \cdot \dfrac{1}{4}$$

Factor: $12 = 3 \cdot 4$. ⟶

$$3 \cdot 4 \cdot \dfrac{1}{3} \cdot \dfrac{1}{4}$$

Regroup. ⟶

$$\left(3 \cdot \dfrac{1}{3}\right)\left(4 \cdot \dfrac{1}{4}\right)$$

$a \cdot \dfrac{1}{a} = 1$ ⟶

$$1 \cdot 1$$
$$1$$

Two numbers whose product is 1 are reciprocals. ⎫

Since $12 \cdot \dfrac{1}{3} \cdot \dfrac{1}{4} = 1$, $\dfrac{1}{3} \cdot \dfrac{1}{4}$ is the reciprocal of 12.

$12 \cdot \dfrac{1}{12} = 1$ ⟶

But, $\dfrac{1}{12}$ is also the reciprocal of 12.

Thus, $\dfrac{1}{3} \cdot \dfrac{1}{4} = \dfrac{1}{12}$.

A technique for multiplying fractions like $\dfrac{1}{5} \cdot \dfrac{1}{4}$ ⟶

$$\dfrac{1}{a} \cdot \dfrac{1}{b} = \dfrac{1}{ab}, \; a \neq 0, \, b \neq 0$$

EXAMPLE 2 Multiply $\frac{1}{5} \cdot \frac{1}{6}$. Multiply $\frac{1}{3}\left(-\frac{1}{8}\right)$. Multiply $\frac{1}{x^2} \cdot \frac{1}{x^3}$.

$\frac{1}{a} \cdot \frac{1}{b} = \frac{1}{ab}$ ⟶

$$\begin{aligned} \frac{1}{5} \cdot \frac{1}{6} &= \frac{1}{5 \cdot 6} \\ &= \frac{1}{30} \end{aligned}$$

$$\begin{aligned} \frac{1}{3}\left(-\frac{1}{8}\right) &= -\frac{1}{3 \cdot 8} \\ &= -\frac{1}{24} \end{aligned}$$

$$\begin{aligned} \frac{1}{x^2} \cdot \frac{1}{x^3} &= \frac{1}{x^2 \cdot x^3} \\ &= \frac{1}{x^5} \end{aligned}$$

EXAMPLE 3 Multiply $\frac{4}{5} \cdot \frac{3}{7}$.

$\frac{a}{b} = a \cdot \frac{1}{b}$ ⟶

Multiplication can be done in any order}

$\frac{1}{a} \cdot \frac{1}{b} = \frac{1}{ab}$ ⟶

$a \cdot \frac{1}{b} = \frac{a}{b}$ ⟶

$$\begin{aligned} \frac{4}{5} \cdot \frac{3}{7} &= 4 \cdot \frac{1}{5} \cdot 3 \cdot \frac{1}{7} \\ &= (4 \cdot 3)\left(\frac{1}{5} \cdot \frac{1}{7}\right) \\ &= 12 \cdot \frac{1}{35} \\ &= \frac{12}{35} \end{aligned}$$

Thus, $\frac{4}{5} \cdot \frac{3}{7} = \frac{12}{35}$.

Product of Two Fractions

$$\frac{a}{b} \cdot \frac{c}{d} = \frac{ac}{bd}, \ b \neq 0, \ d \neq 0.$$

$\frac{\text{Product of numerators}}{\text{Product of denominators}}$ ⟶

EXAMPLE 4 Multiply $5 \cdot \frac{3}{7}$.   Multiply $\left(-\frac{2}{5}\right)\left(-\frac{6}{11}\right)$.

$5 = \frac{5}{1}$ ⟶

$\frac{a}{b} \cdot \frac{c}{d} = \frac{ac}{bd}$ ⟶

$$\begin{aligned} 5 \cdot \frac{3}{7} &= \frac{5}{1} \cdot \frac{3}{7} \\ &= \frac{5 \cdot 3}{1 \cdot 7} \\ &= \frac{15}{7} \end{aligned}$$

$$\left(-\frac{2}{5}\right)\left(-\frac{6}{11}\right)$$

$$+\frac{12}{55} \longleftarrow (-)(-) = +$$

$$\text{or } \frac{12}{55}$$

EXAMPLE 5 Multiply $\frac{7}{9}\left(-\frac{2}{3}\right)$.   Multiply $\frac{4}{5}\left(\frac{2}{3}\right)$.

$(+)(-) = -$ ⟶

$$-\frac{7 \cdot 2}{9 \cdot 3} = -\frac{14}{27}$$

$$\frac{4 \cdot 2}{5 \cdot 3} = \frac{8}{15}$$

EXAMPLE 6   Multiply $\frac{1}{2} \cdot \frac{3}{4} \cdot \frac{3}{2}$.

Extend rule for multiplication.

$$\frac{a}{b} \cdot \frac{c}{d} \cdot \frac{e}{f} = \frac{ace}{bdf}$$

$$\frac{1}{2} \cdot \frac{3}{4} \cdot \frac{3}{2} = \frac{1 \cdot 3 \cdot 3}{2 \cdot 4 \cdot 2}, \text{ or } \frac{9}{16}$$

EXAMPLE 7   Multiply $\frac{3a^2}{2b^3} \cdot \frac{4a^3}{5b^6}$.

$$\frac{3a^2}{2b^3} \cdot \frac{4a^3}{5b^6} = \frac{3a^2 \cdot 4a^3}{2b^3 \cdot 5b^6}$$

$$= \frac{3 \cdot 4 \cdot a^2 \cdot a^3}{2 \cdot 5 \cdot b^3 \cdot b^6}$$

$a^2 \cdot a^3 = a^{2+3}, \text{ or } a^5$
$b^3 \cdot b^6 = b^{3+6}, \text{ or } b^9$ $\Big\}$ $\longrightarrow$

$$= \frac{12a^5}{10b^9}$$

EXAMPLE 8   Multiply $\left(\frac{x+1}{x+3}\right)\left(-\frac{2x-1}{2x+1}\right)$.

$$\left(\frac{x+1}{x+3}\right)\left(-\frac{2x-1}{2x+1}\right) = -\frac{(x+1)(2x-1)}{(x+3)(2x+1)}$$

$$= -\frac{2x^2 + x - 1}{2x^2 + 7x + 3}$$

$$\frac{x \quad +1}{2x \quad -1} \qquad \frac{x \quad +3}{2x \quad +1}$$
$$\overline{2x^2 + x - 1} \qquad \overline{2x^2 + 7x + 3}$$

EXAMPLE 9   Multiply $2\left(\frac{x-1}{x+3}\right)$.

Rewrite 2 as $\frac{2}{1}$. $\longrightarrow$

$$2\left(\frac{x-1}{x+3}\right) = \frac{2}{1}\left(\frac{x-1}{x+3}\right)$$

$$= \frac{2(x-1)}{1(x+3)}$$

$2(x-1) = 2x - 2 \longrightarrow$

$$= \frac{2x-2}{x+3}$$

EXAMPLE 10   Multiply $(x-1)\left(\frac{2x+5}{x-3}\right)$.

$x - 1 = \frac{x-1}{1}$ $\longrightarrow$

$$(x-1)\left(\frac{2x+5}{x-3}\right) = \left(\frac{x-1}{1}\right)\left(\frac{2x+5}{x-3}\right)$$

$$= \frac{(x-1)(2x+5)}{1(x-3)}$$

$$\frac{x \quad -1}{2x \quad +5}$$
$$\overline{2x^2 + 3x - 5}$$

$$= \frac{2x^2 + 3x - 5}{x - 3}$$

ORAL EXERCISES

Multiply.

1. $\dfrac{1}{8} \cdot \dfrac{1}{2}$ **2.** $\dfrac{1}{5} \cdot \dfrac{1}{6}$ **3.** $\dfrac{1}{m^2} \cdot \dfrac{1}{m^3}$ **4.** $\dfrac{1}{a^5} \cdot \dfrac{1}{a^3}$ **5.** $\dfrac{1}{3} \cdot \dfrac{1}{2a}$

6. $5 \cdot \dfrac{1}{2a}$ **7.** $\dfrac{1}{5} \cdot \dfrac{1}{46}$ **8.** $\left(-\dfrac{2}{3}\right)\left(-\dfrac{4}{7}\right)$ **9.** $-\dfrac{3}{5} \cdot \dfrac{1}{2}$ **10.** $4 \cdot \dfrac{2}{3}$

11. $-7 \cdot \dfrac{2}{5}$ **12.** $\dfrac{a^2}{b^3} \cdot \dfrac{a^7}{b^5}$ **13.** $\dfrac{m^4}{n^7} \cdot \dfrac{m^2}{n^5}$ **14.** $\dfrac{a}{b^4}\left(-\dfrac{a^3}{b^2}\right)$ **15.** $-5 \cdot \dfrac{2}{a}$

EXERCISES

PART A
Multiply.

1. $\dfrac{1}{4} \cdot \dfrac{2}{3} \cdot \dfrac{3}{4}$ **2.** $\dfrac{1}{5} \cdot \dfrac{4}{3} \cdot \dfrac{2}{5}$ **3.** $\left(\dfrac{2}{3}\right)\left(\dfrac{4}{5}\right)\left(-\dfrac{1}{3}\right)$ **4.** $\left(\dfrac{2}{5}\right)\left(\dfrac{2}{3}\right)\left(-\dfrac{1}{2}\right)$

5. $\dfrac{2a^2}{3b^3} \cdot \dfrac{5a^3}{6b^6}$ **6.** $\dfrac{7x^2}{3y^4} \cdot \dfrac{4x^5}{5y^2}$ **7.** $-\dfrac{5a^2}{3b^5} \cdot \dfrac{4a^3}{3b^4}$ **8.** $\dfrac{6x^3}{5y^2}\left(-\dfrac{3x^5}{2y^5}\right)$

9. $\dfrac{x^3}{y^7} \cdot \left(-\dfrac{x^2}{y^4}\right)$ **10.** $\dfrac{a^2}{b^3} \cdot \dfrac{1}{b^4}$ **11.** $\dfrac{x^2}{y^3} \cdot \dfrac{x^4}{y^2} \cdot \dfrac{x^5}{y}$ **12.** $\dfrac{a^3}{b^2} \cdot \dfrac{a^2}{b^4} \cdot \dfrac{a}{b^5}$

13. $\dfrac{(x+1)}{(x+2)}\left(-\dfrac{2x-3}{2x+3}\right)$ **14.** $\left(\dfrac{x+2}{x+1}\right)\left(-\dfrac{3x-1}{3x+1}\right)$ **15.** $\left(\dfrac{x+3}{x+5}\right)\left(-\dfrac{2x-5}{2x+5}\right)$

16. $3\left(\dfrac{x-1}{x+5}\right)$ **17.** $5\left(\dfrac{2x-1}{x+4}\right)$ **18.** $6\left(\dfrac{x+2}{2x-5}\right)$

19. $(x-7)\left(\dfrac{2x+3}{x-4}\right)$ **20.** $\left(\dfrac{-a-4}{a+3}\right)(2a-1)$ **21.** $(2a-3)\left(\dfrac{a+5}{3a-7}\right)$

22. $a^3 \cdot \dfrac{a^7}{b^6}$ **23.** $\left(-\dfrac{x^2}{m^3}\right)(-x^5)$ **24.** $\left(-\dfrac{a-4}{a+3}\right)\left(-\dfrac{1}{2a-1}\right)$

25. $\left(\dfrac{x-2}{x+5}\right)\left(\dfrac{x+1}{x+4}\right)$ **26.** $\left(\dfrac{3a+1}{a+2}\right)\left(-\dfrac{3a-1}{a-2}\right)$ **27.** $\left(-\dfrac{2b+1}{b-4}\right)\left(-\dfrac{b+5}{b+4}\right)$

PART B
Multiply.

28. $\left(\dfrac{a+b}{x-y}\right)\left(\dfrac{a-b}{x+2y}\right)$ **29.** $\left(\dfrac{2m-n}{m+3n}\right)\left(\dfrac{3m+n}{2m+n}\right)$ **30.** $\left(\dfrac{3r-t}{r+t}\right)\left(\dfrac{4r+t}{r+2t}\right)$

31. $(x+2y)\left(\dfrac{x-y}{x+y}\right)$ **32.** $\left(\dfrac{a-2b}{x-y}\right)\left(-\dfrac{a+2b}{x+y}\right)$ **33.** $\left(\dfrac{2x+3y}{m+n}\right)^2$

34. $\left(-\dfrac{3a+b}{2a+b}\right)^2$ **35.** $\left(\dfrac{a+b}{2a-3b}\right)(a-b)$ **36.** $\left(-\dfrac{4a-b}{a+b}\right)\left(\dfrac{a+3b}{2a-b}\right)$

37. $\left(\dfrac{5a-b}{3a-b}\right)^2$ **38.** $\left(\dfrac{x-y}{2x+3y}\right)(x+y)$ **39.** $\left(-\dfrac{3a+2b}{x+5y}\right)\left(\dfrac{3a-2b}{x-5y}\right)$

Rewriting Fractions in Simplest Form

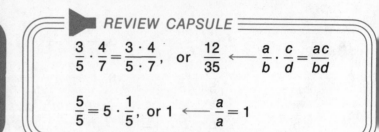

▶ REVIEW CAPSULE

$$\frac{3}{5} \cdot \frac{4}{7} = \frac{3 \cdot 4}{5 \cdot 7}, \text{ or } \frac{12}{35} \longleftarrow \frac{a}{b} \cdot \frac{c}{d} = \frac{ac}{bd}$$

$$\frac{5}{5} = 5 \cdot \frac{1}{5}, \text{ or } 1 \longleftarrow \frac{a}{a} = 1$$

EXAMPLE 1   Write $\frac{6}{15}$ as a product of two fractions.

Factor 6. ⟶
Factor 15. ⟶

$$\frac{6}{15} = \frac{3 \cdot 2}{5 \cdot 3}$$

$$= \frac{3}{5} \cdot \frac{2}{3}$$

or

$$\frac{6}{15} = \frac{2 \cdot 3}{5 \cdot 3}$$

$$= \frac{2}{5} \cdot \frac{3}{3}$$

We can use the second product to rewrite $\frac{6}{15}$ in a different form.

$\frac{3}{3} = 1$ ⟶ $\frac{2}{5} \cdot \frac{3}{3} = \frac{2}{5} \cdot 1, \text{ or } \frac{2}{5}$ **Thus,** $\frac{6}{15} = \frac{2}{5}.$

EXAMPLE 2   Write $\frac{20}{30}$ in simplest form.

Factor 20 into primes. ⟶
Factor 30 into primes. ⟶

Rearrange so like factors are over each other. ⟶

$\frac{a}{b} \cdot \frac{c}{d} \cdot \frac{e}{f} = \frac{ace}{bdf}$

$\frac{2}{2} = 1$ $\frac{5}{5} = 1$

$$\frac{20}{30} = \frac{2 \cdot 2 \cdot 5}{5 \cdot 3 \cdot 2}$$

$$= \frac{2 \cdot 2 \cdot 5}{3 \cdot 2 \cdot 5}$$

$$= \frac{2}{3} \cdot \frac{2}{2} \cdot \frac{5}{5}$$

$$= \frac{2}{3} \cdot 1 \cdot 1$$

$$= \frac{2}{3}$$

More Compact Form

$$\frac{20}{30} = \frac{2 \cdot 2 \cdot 5}{5 \cdot 3 \cdot 2}$$

$$= \frac{2 \cdot \overset{1}{2} \cdot \overset{1}{5}}{\underset{1}{5} \cdot 3 \cdot \underset{1}{2}} \longleftarrow \frac{2}{2} = \frac{1}{1} \quad \frac{5}{5} = \frac{1}{1}$$

$$= \frac{2 \cdot 1 \cdot 1}{1 \cdot 3 \cdot 1}$$

$$= \frac{2}{3}$$

The GCF of 2 and 3 is 1, so 2 and 3 are relatively prime.

$\frac{2}{3}$ is in simplest form, or lowest terms.

EXAMPLE 3   Simplify. (Write in simplest form.)

$$\frac{x^2 - 7x + 12}{2x^2 - 9x + 9}$$

$x^2 - 7x + 12 = (x - 3)(x - 4)$ ⟶

$2x^2 - 9x + 9 = (2x - 3)(x - 3)$ ⟶

$$\frac{(x - 3)(x - 4)}{(2x - 3)(x - 3)} \quad \left\{ \begin{array}{l} \text{Factor numerator} \\ \text{and denominator.} \end{array} \right.$$

$\dfrac{x - 3}{x - 3} = \dfrac{1}{1}$ ⟶

$$\frac{\overset{1}{\cancel{(x - 3)}}(x - 4)}{(2x - 3)\underset{1}{\cancel{(x - 3)}}} \quad \left\{ \begin{array}{l} \text{Divide out} \\ \text{common factors.} \end{array} \right.$$

$1(x - 4) = x - 4$ ⟶

$(2x - 3)1 = 2x - 3$ ⟶

$$\frac{x - 4}{2x - 3}$$

EXAMPLE 4   Simplify $\dfrac{a - 4}{2a - 8}$.

$a - 4$ is not factorable.

$2a - 8 = 2(a - 4)$

$$\frac{a - 4}{2a - 8} = \frac{\overset{1}{\cancel{a - 4}}}{2\underset{1}{\cancel{(a - 4)}}} \quad \left\{ \begin{array}{l} \text{Factor and divide} \\ \text{out common factors.} \end{array} \right.$$

The remaining factor 2 is in the denominator.

$$= \frac{1}{2 \cdot 1}, \text{ or } \frac{1}{2}$$

EXAMPLE 5   Show that $\dfrac{x + 3}{x + 4}$ cannot be simplified to $\dfrac{3}{4}$.

Let $x = 2$ in $\dfrac{x + 3}{x + 4}$. ⟶

$$\frac{2 + 3}{2 + 4} = \frac{5}{6}$$

But

$$\frac{5}{6} \neq \frac{3}{4}$$

Thus, $\dfrac{x + 3}{x + 4}$ cannot be simplified to $\dfrac{3}{4}$.

$\dfrac{x + 3}{x + 4} \neq \dfrac{3}{4}$

$\dfrac{x + 3}{x + 4}$ is already in simplest form.

EXAMPLE 6   Simplify $-\dfrac{3x^3 - 27x}{2x^2 - 6x}$.

$3x^3 - 27x = 3(x^3 - 9x) = 3 \cdot x(x^2 - 9)$ ⟶

$2x^2 - 6x = 2(x^2 - 6x) = 2 \cdot x(x - 3)$ ⟶

$$-\frac{3x^3 - 27x}{2x^2 - 6x} = -\frac{3x(x^2 - 9)}{2x(x - 3)}$$

Factor $x^2 - 9$. Then divide out common factors.

$$= -\frac{3 \cdot \overset{1}{\cancel{x}}\,\overset{1}{\cancel{(x - 3)}}(x + 3)}{2 \cdot \underset{1}{\cancel{x}}\quad \underset{1}{\cancel{(x - 3)}}}$$

$3\overparen{(x + 3)} = 3x + 9$

$$= -\frac{3(x + 3)}{2}, \text{ or } -\frac{3x + 9}{2}$$

ORAL EXERCISES

Tell whether the fraction is in simplest form.

1. $\dfrac{3}{8}$
2. $-\dfrac{5}{10}$
3. $\dfrac{7}{8}$
4. $\dfrac{4}{6}$
5. $\dfrac{a+3}{a+7}$

6. $\dfrac{4}{12}$
7. $\dfrac{x+5}{x+2}$
8. $\dfrac{5(x-4)}{7(x-4)}$
9. $\dfrac{14}{21}$
10. $\dfrac{3(m+1)}{5(m+1)}$

EXERCISES

PART A

Simplify.

1. $\dfrac{4}{12}$
2. $\dfrac{8}{16}$
3. $-\dfrac{15}{36}$
4. $-\dfrac{8}{30}$

5. $\dfrac{a^2-8a+15}{2a^2-7a+3}$
6. $\dfrac{m^2-3m-10}{2m^2-9m-5}$
7. $\dfrac{b^2-25}{b^2-7b+10}$
8. $-\dfrac{x^2-9x+14}{x^2-5x-14}$

9. $\dfrac{x-4}{4x-16}$
10. $\dfrac{a-8}{a^2-8a}$
11. $\dfrac{3b-15}{b^2-7b+10}$
12. $-\dfrac{x^2-5x+4}{2x-8}$

13. $\dfrac{4b-12}{b^2-9}$
14. $\dfrac{a^2-7a+12}{2a-8}$
15. $\dfrac{y^2+3y-28}{y^2+7y}$
16. $\dfrac{m^2+6m-16}{m^2+8m}$

17. $\dfrac{-3x^3-12x}{2x^2-4x}$
18. $\dfrac{2x^3-50x}{3x^2-15x}$
19. $\dfrac{b^2-7b}{b^2-49}$
20. $\dfrac{2x^2+3x-20}{8x-20}$

21. $\dfrac{3p^2+5p-2}{5p+10}$
22. $\dfrac{2n^2+3n-2}{n^2-4}$
23. $\dfrac{x^2+8x+16}{x^2-16}$
24. $\dfrac{a^2+2a}{a^2-5a-14}$

PART B

EXAMPLE   Find the quotient $(x^2+7x+12)\div(x+4)$.

$\dfrac{a}{b}$ means $a \div b$ $\longrightarrow$

Factor. Then divide out common factors.

$$(x^2+7x+12)\div(x+4) = \dfrac{x^2+7x+12}{x+4}$$

$$= \dfrac{\overset{1}{\cancel{(x+4)}}(x+3)}{\underset{1}{\cancel{x+4}}}$$

$$= \dfrac{x+3}{1}, \text{ or } x+3$$

Thus, the quotient is $x+3$.

Find the quotient when the first polynomial is divided by the second.

25. $x^2+x-12;\ x-3$
26. $z^2-3z-40;\ z+5$
27. $2x^2+9x-5;\ 2x-1$
28. $2a^2-ab-3b^2;\ 2a-3b$

What is the Navigator's Name?
or
The Great Airplane Mystery

On an airplane, three passengers got into a conversation with a stewardess. The following facts evolved.

1. The names of the passengers were Miller, Adams, and Baker.

2. The stewardess said that these were the names of the flight crew, which consisted of a pilot, a copilot, and a navigator.

3. Mr. Adams said that he earned $14,000 a year.

4. Mr. Baker said that he lived in Cleveland.

5. The stewardess said that the pilot lived halfway between Cleveland and St. Louis.

6. One of the passengers lived next door to the pilot and received exactly three times as much salary as the navigator.

7. The stewardess said that the copilot often played bridge with Miller, one of the crew members.

8. The pilot had the same name as the passenger who lived in St. Louis.

What is the navigator's name? Prove your answer.

Using The −1 Technique

 REVIEW CAPSULE

Rewrite each polynomial in descending order of exponents.

$$-2 + 3x \qquad -3x - 2 - x^2 \qquad -4 + x^2$$
$$\downarrow \qquad\qquad \downarrow \qquad\qquad\qquad \downarrow$$
$$3x - 2 \qquad -x^2 - 3x - 2 \qquad x^2 - 4$$

EXAMPLE 1 Rewrite $5x - x^2 + 4$ as a polynomial in descending order of exponents and whose first coefficient is positive.

$$5x - x^2 + 4$$

Descending order $\longrightarrow$ $-x^2 + 5x + 4$

$-x^2 = -1x^2$ $\longrightarrow$ $-1x^2 + 5x + 4$

Factor out −1. $\longrightarrow$ $-1(x^2 - 5x - 4)$

This form is useful when factoring polynomials and simplifying fractions.

Convenient Form of a Polynomial
$$5x - x^2 + 4$$
$$-1\underbrace{(1x^2 - 5x - 4)}$$

first coefficient positive   descending order

EXAMPLE 2 Simplify $\dfrac{x - 3}{9 - x^2}$.

Descending order $\longrightarrow$

$$\frac{x - 3}{9 - x^2} = \frac{x - 3}{-x^2 + 9}$$

Convenient form $\longrightarrow$

$$= \frac{x - 3}{-1(x^2 - 9)}$$

Factor $x^2 - 9$. Then divide out common factors.

$$= \frac{\overset{1}{\cancel{x - 3}}}{-1(\cancel{x - 3})(x + 3)}$$

$$= \frac{1}{-1(x + 3)}$$

EXAMPLE 3   Show that $-\dfrac{12}{3} = \dfrac{-1(12)}{3} = \dfrac{12}{-1(3)}.$

$$
\begin{array}{c|c|c}
-\dfrac{12}{3} & \dfrac{-1(12)}{3} & \dfrac{12}{-1(3)} \\[2mm]
-(12 \div 3) & \dfrac{-12}{3} & \dfrac{12}{-3} \\[2mm]
-4 & -4 & -4
\end{array}
$$

Same answers ⟶

Thus, $-\dfrac{12}{3} = \dfrac{-1(12)}{3} = \dfrac{12}{-1(3)}.$

Example 3 suggests this. ⟶

$$-\frac{a}{b} = \frac{-1(a)}{b} = \frac{a}{-1(b)}, \ b \neq 0$$

EXAMPLE 4   Rewrite $\dfrac{1}{-1(x+3)}$ in two other ways.

$\dfrac{a}{-1(b)} = -\dfrac{a}{b} = \dfrac{-1(a)}{b}$ ⟶

$$\frac{1}{-1(x+3)} = -\frac{1}{x+3} = \frac{-1(1)}{x+3}$$

Any one of the three is acceptable. Generally, we use the form $-\dfrac{a}{b}.$

EXAMPLE 5   Simplify $\dfrac{-3x^2 - 5x + 2}{2 - 6x}.$

Rewrite denominator in descending order.

Factor out -1 from both numerator and denominator. }

Factor numerator and denominator.

Divide out common factors.

$$\frac{-3x^2 - 5x + 2}{-6x + 2}$$

$$\frac{-1(3x^2 + 5x - 2)}{-1(6x - 2)}$$

$$\frac{-1(3x - 1)(x + 2)}{-1(2)(3x - 1)}$$

$$\frac{\overset{1}{\cancel{-1}}(3x\cancel{-1})(x + 2)}{\cancel{-1}(2)(3x\cancel{-1})}$$

$$\frac{x + 2}{2}$$

EXAMPLE 6   Simplify $\dfrac{b^2 - 2b - 15}{30 - b - b^2}$.

$$30 - b - b^2 = -b^2 - b + 30$$
$$= -1(b^2 + b - 30)$$

Factor. Then divide out common factors.

$$\frac{a}{-1(b)} = -\frac{a}{b}$$

$$\frac{b^2 - 2b - 15}{-1(b^2 + b - 30)}$$

$$\frac{\overset{1}{(b - 5)}(b + 3)}{-1(b + 6)\underset{1}{(b - 5)}}$$

$$\frac{b + 3}{-1(b + 6)}, \text{ or } -\frac{b + 3}{b + 6}$$

EXERCISES

PART A

Simplify.

1. $\dfrac{x - 4}{16 - x^2}$

2. $\dfrac{a + 5}{25 - a^2}$

3. $\dfrac{5 - b}{2b - 10}$

4. $\dfrac{8 - b}{2b - 16}$

5. $\dfrac{-a^2 - 2a + 15}{12 - 4a}$

6. $\dfrac{-m^2 + m + 20}{2m - 10}$

7. $\dfrac{x^2 - 7x + 12}{3 - x}$

8. $\dfrac{p^2 - 2p - 15}{5 - p}$

9. $\dfrac{2m - 8}{4 - m}$

10. $\dfrac{14 - 2x}{x^2 - 49}$

11. $\dfrac{3 - c}{c^2 - 5c + 6}$

12. $\dfrac{6 - 2b}{b^2 - 6b + 9}$

13. $\dfrac{a^2 - 2a - 8}{4 - a}$

14. $\dfrac{16 + 6m - m^2}{m^2 + 5m + 6}$

15. $\dfrac{9 - a^2}{a^2 + 5a - 24}$

16. $\dfrac{c^2 + 8c - 20}{16 - 8c}$

17. $\dfrac{y^2 - y - 42}{14 + 5y - y^2}$

18. $\dfrac{a^2 + 10a + 25}{40 + 3a - a^2}$

19. $\dfrac{x^2 - 8x - 20}{-x^2 + 14x - 40}$

20. $\dfrac{36 - m^2}{2m^2 - 8m - 24}$

PART B

Simplify.

21. $\dfrac{12 + n - n^2}{2n^2 - 18}$

22. $\dfrac{2x^2 - 6x}{24 - 2x - 2x^2}$

23. $\dfrac{-a^2 + b^2}{a^2 + 3ab + 2b^2}$

24. $\dfrac{2x^2 + xy - y^2}{-2x - 2y}$

25. $\dfrac{a^2 - b^2}{-2a^2 - ab + b^2}$

26. $\dfrac{-10 + 22a - 4a^2}{3a^2 - 16a + 5}$

PART C

Simplify.

27. $\dfrac{-a^4 + b^4}{a^3 + ab^2}$

28. $\dfrac{a^6 - a^2 b^6}{a^2 b^2 - b^5}$

29. $\dfrac{x^4 - 8x^2 + 15}{3x - x^3}$

30. $\dfrac{a^2 - a^3}{a^2 - a}$

31. $\dfrac{-36 + 13b^2 - b^4}{b^2 - 5b + 6}$

32. $\dfrac{5 + 4m - m^2}{m^4 - 26m^2 + 25}$

Fractions with Common Monomial Factors

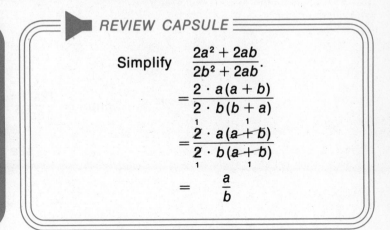

▶ REVIEW CAPSULE

Simplify $\dfrac{2a^2 + 2ab}{2b^2 + 2ab}$.

$$= \frac{2 \cdot a(a + b)}{2 \cdot b(b + a)}$$

$$= \frac{\overset{1}{2} \cdot a\overset{1}{(a + b)}}{\underset{1}{2} \cdot b\underset{1}{(a + b)}}$$

$$= \frac{a}{b}$$

EXAMPLE 1   Simplify $\dfrac{a^3}{a^7}$.

Write numerator and denominator in factored form. Then divide out common factors.

$a \cdot a \cdot a \cdot a = a^4$ ⟶

$$\frac{a^3}{a^7} = \frac{\overset{1}{a} \cdot \overset{1}{a} \cdot \overset{1}{a}}{\underset{1}{a} \cdot \underset{1}{a} \cdot \underset{1}{a} \cdot a \cdot a \cdot a \cdot a}$$

$$= \frac{1}{a^4}$$

EXAMPLE 2   Simplify $\dfrac{x^5}{x^7}$.

Shorten the work by thinking of factored form in your head.

$$\frac{\overset{1}{x} \cdot \overset{1}{x} \cdot \overset{1}{x} \cdot \overset{1}{x} \cdot \overset{1}{x}}{\underset{1}{x} \cdot \underset{1}{x} \cdot \underset{1}{x} \cdot \underset{1}{x} \cdot \underset{1}{x} \cdot x \cdot x}$$

$$\frac{x^5}{x^7} = \frac{\overset{1}{x^5}}{\underset{x^2}{x^7}}$$

$$= \frac{1}{x^2}$$

EXAMPLE 3   Simplify $\dfrac{b^5}{b^2}$.

b is a factor two times in both numerator and denominator.

$$\frac{\overbrace{b \cdot b \cdot b \cdot b \cdot b}}{\underbrace{b \cdot b}}$$

$$\frac{b^5}{b^2} = \frac{\overset{b^3}{b^5}}{\underset{1}{b^2}}$$

$$= \frac{b^3}{1}, \text{ or } b^3$$

EXAMPLE 4   Simplify $\dfrac{x^7}{x}$.

x is a factor one time in both numerator and denominator.

$$\frac{x^7}{x^1} = \frac{\overset{x^6}{\cancel{x^7}}}{\underset{1}{\cancel{x^1}}}$$

$$= \frac{x^6}{1}, \text{ or } x^6$$

EXAMPLE 5   Simplify $\dfrac{12a^3b^5}{18ab^7}$.

Factor 12 and 18 into primes. a means a^1.

$$\frac{12a^3b^5}{18ab^7} = \frac{2 \cdot 2 \cdot 3 \cdot a^3 \cdot b^5}{3 \cdot 3 \cdot 2 \cdot a^1 \cdot b^7}$$

$\dfrac{a^3}{a^1} = \dfrac{a^2}{1}; \dfrac{b^5}{b^7} = \dfrac{1}{b^2}$

$$= \frac{2 \cdot 2 \cdot 3 \cdot \overset{a^2}{\cancel{a^3}} \cdot \overset{1}{\cancel{b^5}}}{3 \cdot 3 \cdot 2 \cdot \underset{1}{\cancel{a^1}} \cdot \underset{b^2}{\cancel{b^7}}}$$

$2 \cdot 1 \cdot 1 \cdot a^2 \cdot 1 = 2a^2$
$3 \cdot 1 \cdot 1 \cdot 1 \cdot b^2 = 3b^2$

$$= \frac{2a^2}{3b^2}$$

EXAMPLE 6   Simplify $\dfrac{a^3b^4(y^2 + 7y + 10)}{a^6b^2(-5 - y)}$.

Write $-5 - y$ in convenient form.
$-5 - y = -y - 5$
Factor out -1.
$-y - 5 = -1(y + 5)$

$\dfrac{a^3b^4(y^2 + 7y + 10)}{a^6b^2(-y - 5)} \leftarrow$ Descending order

$\dfrac{a^3b^4(y^2 + 7y + 10)}{a^6b^2(-1)(y + 5)}$

Factor $y^2 + 7y + 10$.
Divide out common factors.

$\dfrac{\overset{1}{\cancel{a^3}}\overset{b^2}{\cancel{b^4}}(y + 2)(\cancel{y + 5})}{\underset{a^3}{\cancel{a^6}}\underset{1}{\cancel{b^2}}(-1)(\cancel{y + 5})}$

$\dfrac{a}{-1(b)} = -\dfrac{a}{b}$

$\dfrac{b^2(y + 2)}{-1(a^3)}, \text{ or } -\dfrac{b^2(y + 2)}{a^3}$

EXAMPLE 7   Simplify $\dfrac{a^2b(3x^2 - 12x + 9)}{ab^2(6x - 18)}$.

$3x^2 - 12x + 9 = 3(x^2 - 4x + 3)$
$6x - 18 = 6(x - 3)$

$\dfrac{a^2b(3)(x^2 - 4x + 3)}{ab^2(6)(x - 3)}$

Factor $x^2 - 4x + 3$.
Divide out common factors.

$\dfrac{\overset{a}{\cancel{a^2}}\overset{1}{\cancel{b}}(\overset{1}{\cancel{3}})(\cancel{x - 3})(x - 1)}{\underset{1\,b}{\cancel{ab^2}}(\underset{2}{\cancel{6}})(\underset{1}{\cancel{x - 3}})}$

$\dfrac{a(x - 1)}{2b}$

ORAL EXERCISES

Simplify.

1. $\dfrac{a^4}{a^7}$ 2. $\dfrac{m^9}{m^3}$ 3. $\dfrac{a^{10}}{a^{12}}$ 4. $\dfrac{b^6}{b^5}$ 5. $\dfrac{b^8}{b^9}$ 6. $\dfrac{a^2b^3}{a^4b^7}$ 7. $\dfrac{x^3y^3}{xy^2}$ 8. $\dfrac{m^4n^6}{m^2n^3}$

EXERCISES

PART A

Simplify.

1. $\dfrac{4m^5n^7}{6m^2n^9}$

2. $\dfrac{10x^6y^4}{15x^3y^8}$

3. $\dfrac{4a^9b^5}{8a^4b^6}$

4. $\dfrac{x^2y^3(a^2+7a+10)}{xy^5(-2-a)}$

5. $\dfrac{m^2n^4(n^2-2n+1)}{m^7n^2(1-n)}$

6. $\dfrac{3a^2b^3(x^2+6x-16)}{9ab^5(2-x)}$

7. $\dfrac{a^8b^5(6x^2-30x+36)}{a^5b^3(3x-9)}$

8. $\dfrac{m^6(4x^2-64)}{m^9(2x-8)}$

9. $\dfrac{x^3(5b^2-20)}{x^4(10b+20)}$

10. $\dfrac{y^4(a+1)}{y^3(a^2+6a+5)}$

11. $\dfrac{k^4(a-8)}{k^5(a^2-4a-32)}$

12. $\dfrac{m^5(y^2-8y-20)}{m^2(y-10)}$

13. $\dfrac{n^4(a^2-4)}{n^5(a^2-3a+2)}$

14. $\dfrac{c^2(y^2-7y+12)}{c^3(2y-8)}$

15. $\dfrac{b^5(x^2-9)}{b^2(x^2-4x+3)}$

16. $\dfrac{a^3b^5(c^2-49)}{a^4b^7(c-7)}$

17. $\dfrac{a^3b^7(2x^2+9x-5)}{a^2b^9(2x^2+7x-15)}$

18. $\dfrac{a^7(3-x)}{a^5(x^2-9)}$

PART B

EXAMPLE Simplify $\dfrac{a^2b-a^2}{a^5}$.

$$\frac{a^2b-a^2}{a^5}=\frac{a^2(b-1)}{a^5}$$

$$=\frac{\overset{1}{\cancel{a^2}}(b-1)}{\underset{a^3}{\cancel{a^5}}}$$

$$=\frac{b-1}{a^3}$$

Simplify.

19. $\dfrac{x^2y-x^2}{x^6}$

20. $\dfrac{a^4}{a^3b-a^3}$

21. $\dfrac{x^7}{x^2b+x^2y}$

22. $\dfrac{a^2(x-3)}{a^4x^2-9a^4}$

23. $\dfrac{b^2x^2-b^2x-2b^2}{b^5(x+1)}$

24. $\dfrac{a^4(5-m)}{a^4m^2-7a^4m+10a^4}$

Simplifying Products of Fractions

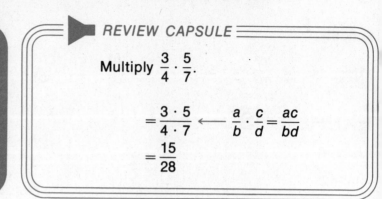

▶ REVIEW CAPSULE

Multiply $\dfrac{3}{4} \cdot \dfrac{5}{7}$.

$$= \frac{3 \cdot 5}{4 \cdot 7} \longleftarrow \frac{a}{b} \cdot \frac{c}{d} = \frac{ac}{bd}$$

$$= \frac{15}{28}$$

EXAMPLE 1   Multiply $\dfrac{x^2 - 3x + 2}{x + 5} \cdot \dfrac{2x + 10}{x - 2}$.

$\dfrac{a}{b} \cdot \dfrac{c}{d} = \dfrac{ac}{bd}$ ⟶

$$\frac{(x^2 - 3x + 2)(2x + 10)}{(x + 5)(x - 2)}$$

Look for common monomial factors.⎤
$2x + 10 = 2(x + 5)$ ⎦

$$\frac{(x^2 - 3x + 2)(2)(x + 5)}{(x + 5)(x - 2)}$$

$x^2 - 3x + 2 = (x - 2)(x - 1)$ ⟶

$$\frac{(x - 2)(x - 1)(2)(x + 5)}{(x + 5)(x - 2)}$$

Divide out common factors.

$$\frac{(\overset{1}{\cancel{x - 2}})(x - 1)(2)(\overset{1}{\cancel{x + 5}})}{(\underset{1}{\cancel{x + 5}})(\underset{1}{\cancel{x - 2}})}$$

Multiply remaining factors.

$$\frac{2(x - 1)}{1}$$

$2(\overset{\frown}{x - 1}) = 2x - 2$

$$\frac{2x - 2}{1}, \text{ or } 2x - 2$$

EXAMPLE 2   Multiply $(b + 5)\left(\dfrac{2b + 14}{4b^2 + 12b - 40}\right)$.

Rewrite $(b + 5)$ as $\left(\dfrac{b + 5}{1}\right)$.

$$\left(\frac{b + 5}{1}\right)\left(\frac{2b + 14}{4b^2 + 12b - 40}\right)$$

$\dfrac{a}{b} \cdot \dfrac{c}{d} = \dfrac{ac}{bd}$ ⟶

$$\frac{(b + 5)(2b + 14)}{1(4b^2 + 12b - 40)}$$

$2b + 14 = 2(b + 7)$ ⎤
$4b^2 + 12b - 40 = 4(b^2 + 3b - 10)$ ⎦

$$\frac{(b + 5)(2)(b + 7)}{1(4)(b^2 + 3b - 10)}$$

$4 = 2 \cdot 2$ ⎤
$b^2 + 3b - 10 = (b + 5)(b - 2)$ ⎬
Divide out common factors. ⎦

$$\frac{(\overset{1}{\cancel{b + 5}})(\overset{1}{\cancel{2}})(b + 7)}{1 \cdot \underset{1}{\cancel{2}} \cdot 2(\underset{1}{\cancel{b + 5}})(b - 2)}, \text{ or } \frac{b + 7}{2(b - 2)}$$

EXAMPLE 3   Multiply $\dfrac{4x^6b^5}{5} \cdot \dfrac{15}{8x^7b^4}$.

$$\frac{4x^6b^5 \cdot 15}{5 \cdot 8x^7b^4}$$

Factor 4, 15, and 8 into primes. Then
divide out common factors.

$$\frac{\overset{1}{2} \cdot \overset{1}{2} \cdot \overset{1}{x^6} \cdot \overset{b^1}{b^5} \cdot 3 \cdot \overset{1}{5}}{5 \cdot \underset{1}{2} \cdot \underset{1}{2} \cdot 2 \cdot \underset{x^1}{x^7} \cdot \underset{1}{b^4}}$$

$$\frac{3b}{2x}$$

EXAMPLE 4   Multiply $\dfrac{y^2 - 3y + 2}{3x^2y^5} \cdot \dfrac{12xy^3}{6 - 6y}$

$\dfrac{a}{b} \cdot \dfrac{c}{d} = \dfrac{ac}{bd}$ $\longrightarrow$

$$\frac{(y^2 - 3y + 2) \cdot 12xy^3}{3x^2y^5(6 - 6y)}$$

Write $6 - 6y$ in convenient form.
$(6 - 6y) = (-6y + 6) = -1(6y - 6)$

$$\frac{(y^2 - 3y + 2) \cdot 12 \cdot x \cdot y^3}{3 \cdot x^2 \cdot y^5(-1)(6y - 6)} \qquad \begin{cases} 12\,xy^3 = 12 \cdot x \cdot y^3 \\ 3x^2y^5 = 3 \cdot x^2 \cdot y^5 \end{cases}$$

Factor.
$6y - 6 = 6(y - 1)$
$\quad 12 = 2 \cdot 2 \cdot 3$
$\quad\;\; 6 = 2 \cdot 3$
$y^2 - 3y + 2 = (y - 2)(y - 1).$

$$\frac{(y^2 - 3y + 2) \cdot 12 \cdot x \cdot y^3}{3 \cdot x^2 \cdot y^5(-1)(6)(y - 1)}$$

$$\frac{(y^2 - 3y + 2) \cdot 2 \cdot 2 \cdot 3 \cdot x \cdot y^3}{3 \cdot x^2 \cdot y^5(-1) \cdot 2 \cdot 3(y - 1)}$$

$$\frac{(y - 2)(y - 1) \cdot 2 \cdot 2 \cdot 3 \cdot x \cdot y^3}{3 \cdot x^2 \cdot y^5(-1) \cdot 2 \cdot 3(y - 1)}$$

Divide out common factors.
$\dfrac{x}{x^2} = \dfrac{x^1}{x^2} = \dfrac{1}{x}, \dfrac{y^3}{y^5} = \dfrac{1}{y^2}, \dfrac{y-1}{y-1} = 1$

$$\frac{(y - 2)\overset{1}{(y - 1)} \cdot \overset{1}{2} \cdot 2 \cdot \overset{1}{3}\overset{1}{x}\overset{1}{y^3}}{3 \cdot x^2 \cdot y^5(-1) \cdot 2 \cdot 3(y - 1)}$$

$\dfrac{a}{-1(b)} = -\dfrac{a}{b}$

$$\frac{2(y - 2)}{3 \cdot x \cdot y^2(-1)}, \text{ or } -\frac{2(y - 2)}{3xy^2}$$

ORAL EXERCISES

Give in simplest form.

1. $\dfrac{x^3y^2}{2} \cdot \dfrac{4}{x^6y}$

2. $(b + 3)\left(\dfrac{x}{b + 3}\right)$

3. $\dfrac{5(x - 3)}{10(x + 2)} \cdot \dfrac{(x + 2)}{x - 5}$

4. $\dfrac{a^2b^3}{2(x - 7)} \cdot \dfrac{6(x - 7)}{ab^4}$

5. $\dfrac{15x^5y^6}{5(2x - 5)} \cdot \dfrac{8(2x + 5)}{16x^6y}$

6. $\dfrac{a - 2}{a - 3} \cdot \dfrac{2(a - 3)}{a - 5}$

7. $\dfrac{(b - 4)(b - 3)}{(b - 5)(b - 2)} \cdot \dfrac{4(b - 5)}{2(b - 3)}$

8. $\dfrac{(2x - 5)(2x + 5)}{(x + 8)(x + 2)} \cdot \dfrac{6(x + 2)}{2(2x - 5)}$

9. $\dfrac{-1(x - 5)}{(x - 5)(x + 4)} \cdot \dfrac{(x + 4)(x + 4)}{(x + 4)(x + 3)}$

10. $\dfrac{(c - 3)(c - 2)}{c(c + 3)} \cdot \dfrac{4(c + 3)}{-1(c - 3)}$

EXERCISES

PART A

Multiply.

1. $\dfrac{b^2 - 7b + 12}{b^2 - 7b + 10} \cdot \dfrac{4b - 20}{2b - 6}$

2. $\dfrac{x^2 - 2x - 15}{x - 6} \cdot \dfrac{3x - 18}{x^2 + 10x + 21}$

3. $\dfrac{b^2 - b - 20}{b^2 - 49} \cdot \dfrac{2b + 14}{2b + 8}$

4. $\dfrac{m^2 - m - 6}{m^2 + 6m + 8} \cdot \dfrac{m + 4}{3m - 9}$

5. $\dfrac{a - 2}{a - 5} \cdot \dfrac{a^2 - 25}{2a - 4}$

6. $\dfrac{6a - 9}{a - 1} \cdot \dfrac{a^2 - 1}{2a - 3}$

7. $(x - 4)\left(\dfrac{3x - 3}{x^2 - 5x + 4}\right)$

8. $(m - 7)\left(\dfrac{5m - 30}{m^2 - 49}\right)$

9. $(m + 2)\left(\dfrac{m - 8}{m^2 + 2m}\right)$

10. $\dfrac{4a^4 b^7}{5} \cdot \dfrac{15}{8a^5 b^6}$

11. $\dfrac{2x^2}{3y} \cdot \dfrac{6y^2}{4x^4}$

12. $\dfrac{a^2 b^3}{4a + 8} \cdot \dfrac{a + 2}{a^5 b}$

13. $\dfrac{a^2 - 2a}{a - 5} \cdot \dfrac{6a - 30}{3a}$

14. $\dfrac{3b - 9}{b} \cdot \dfrac{b^2 + 5b}{b^2 - 6b + 9}$

15. $\dfrac{2k^2 + 5k + 3}{2k + 2} \cdot \dfrac{k}{2k^2 + 3k}$

16. $\dfrac{7x^3 y^4}{2a^2 + 5a + 3} \cdot \dfrac{4a + 4}{21x^2 y^7}$

17. $\dfrac{4x^2 - 25}{x^2 + 10x + 16} \cdot \dfrac{6x + 12}{4x - 10}$

18. $\dfrac{2a^2 + 5a + 2}{a + 5} \cdot \dfrac{3a + 15}{2a^2 + 7a + 3}$

19. $\dfrac{3x^2 + 13x - 10}{4x - 12} \cdot \dfrac{8x - 12}{27x^2 - 12}$

20. $\dfrac{10x^2 + 13x - 3}{9x - 9} \cdot \dfrac{3x^2 - 6x + 3}{20x^2 + 26x - 6}$

21. $\dfrac{6a^2 + 15a + 6}{6a + 30} \cdot \dfrac{6a + 30}{6a^2 + 21a + 9}$

22. $\dfrac{12x^2 - 75}{2x^2 + 20x + 32} \cdot \dfrac{24x + 48}{12x - 30}$

PART B

Multiply.

23. $\dfrac{5 - x}{x^2 - x - 20} \cdot \dfrac{x^2 + 8x + 16}{x^2 + 7x + 12}$

24. $\dfrac{c^2 - 5c - 6}{c^2 + 3c} \cdot \dfrac{4c + 12}{12 - 2c}$

25. $\dfrac{2n^2 - 13n - 7}{n} \cdot \dfrac{6n}{21 - 3n}$

26. $\dfrac{2a^2 - 4a - 16}{a^2 - a - 12} \cdot \dfrac{a^2 + a - 6}{a^2 - 6a + 8}$

27. $\dfrac{a^2 - 5a + 6}{a^2 - 7a + 10} \cdot \dfrac{5 + 4a - a^2}{a^2 - 2a - 3}$

28. $\dfrac{c + d}{c} \cdot \dfrac{c^2}{c^2 + 2cd + d^2}$

29. $\dfrac{35 - 2x - x^2}{x^3 - 9x} \cdot \dfrac{x^2 + 3x}{x + 7}$

30. $\dfrac{x^2 + 5xy + 6y^2}{a^5 b^2} \cdot \dfrac{4a^3 b}{2x + 6y}$

31. $\dfrac{4m^2 - n^2}{2m^2 + 3m - 35} \cdot \dfrac{m + 5}{n - 2m}$

32. $\dfrac{a^2 - 7ab - 18b^2}{-a + 9b} \cdot \dfrac{3a + 9b}{a^2 - 4b^2}$

33. $\dfrac{2c^2 - 10cd + 12d^2}{3c^2 - 21cd + 30d^2} \cdot \dfrac{15c^2 + 12cd - 3d^2}{4c^2 - 8cd - 12d^2}$

PART C

Multiply.

34. $\dfrac{10 + m - 2m^2}{4m^2 - 1} \cdot \dfrac{2m^2 - 3m + 1}{2m^2 - 7m + 5}$

35. $\dfrac{10 - 16a - 8a^2}{2a^2 - 3a - 20} \cdot \dfrac{3a^2 - 12a}{12a^2 - 6a}$

36. $\dfrac{m^4 - 50m^2 + 49}{m^2 + 6m - 7} \cdot \dfrac{2}{28 - 4m}$

37. $\dfrac{x^6 - y^6}{x^6 - 3x^3 y^3 - 4y^6} \cdot \dfrac{4x^3 - 16y^3}{4x^3 - 4y^3}$

Puzzlers

Fill in the missing numbers for this
multiplication problem.

```
        *  *  3
        2  *  *
     ─────────────
     *  1  *  7
     *  *  *
  *  1  4  *
  ─────────────────
  *  *  *  *  *  *
```

Division puzzlers are even harder.
Fill in the numbers.

```
              1  *  *
         ─────────────
  2  1  5 │ *  *  *  *  *
           *  *  *
           ─────────
           *  *  *  *
           *  5  *  *
           ─────────
              *  4  *
              *  *  *
              ─────────
```

```
           *  8  *
        ─────────────
  2  * │ *  *  8  *
        *  8
        ──────
        *  *  *
        *  *  8
        ──────
        *  *  *
        *  *  *
        ──────
```

Dividing Fractions

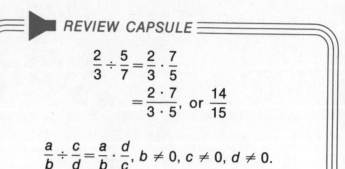

EXAMPLE 1   Divide $\dfrac{x^2 - 7x + 12}{x^2 - 25} \div \dfrac{2x - 8}{x - 5}$.

$\dfrac{a}{b} \div \dfrac{c}{d} = \dfrac{a}{b} \cdot \dfrac{d}{c}$ ⟶

$\dfrac{x^2 - 7x + 12}{x^2 - 25} \cdot \dfrac{x - 5}{2x - 8}$

$\dfrac{a}{b} \cdot \dfrac{d}{c} = \dfrac{ad}{bc}$ ⟶

$\dfrac{(x^2 - 7x + 12)(x - 5)}{(x^2 - 25)(2x - 8)}$

Look for common monomial factors.⎤
$2x - 8 = 2(x - 4)$ ⎦

$\dfrac{(x^2 - 7x + 12)(x - 5)}{(x^2 - 25)(2)(x - 4)}$

Factor $x^2 - 7x + 12$ and $x^2 - 25$.⎤
Then divide out common factors.⎦

$\dfrac{(x - 3)\,\overset{1}{\cancel{(x - 4)}}\,\overset{1}{\cancel{(x - 5)}}}{\underset{1}{\cancel{(x - 5)}}\,(x + 5)(2)\,\underset{1}{\cancel{(x - 4)}}}$

$\dfrac{x - 3}{2(x + 5)}$

EXAMPLE 2   Divide $\dfrac{k^2 - 7k - 18}{k^5} \div \dfrac{2k^2 - 18k}{6k^3}$.

$\dfrac{a}{b} \div \dfrac{c}{d} = \dfrac{a}{b} \cdot \dfrac{d}{c}$ ⟶

$\dfrac{k^2 - 7k - 18}{k^5} \cdot \dfrac{6k^3}{2k^2 - 18k}$

$\dfrac{a}{b} \cdot \dfrac{d}{c} = \dfrac{ad}{bc}$ ⟶

$\dfrac{(k^2 - 7k - 18)(6k^3)}{k^5(2k^2 - 18k)}$

$k^2 - 7k - 18 = (k - 9)(k + 2)$,⎤
$6 = 2 \cdot 3, \, 2k^2 - 18k = 2 \cdot k(k - 9)$⎥
Divide out common factors.   ⎦

$\dfrac{\overset{1}{\cancel{(k - 9)}}\,(k + 2) \cdot \overset{1}{\cancel{2}} \cdot 3 \cdot \overset{1}{\cancel{k^3}}}{\underset{k^2}{\cancel{k^5}} \cdot \underset{1}{\cancel{2}} \cdot k\,\underset{1}{\cancel{(k - 9)}}}$

$\dfrac{3(k + 2)}{k^3}$

EXAMPLE 3   Divide $\dfrac{3a^2b^3}{6a - 2a^2} \div \dfrac{ab^4}{4a - 12}$.

$\dfrac{a}{b} \div \dfrac{c}{d} = \dfrac{a}{b} \cdot \dfrac{d}{c}$ $\longrightarrow$ $\dfrac{3a^2b^3}{6a - 2a^2} \cdot \dfrac{4a - 12}{ab^4}$

$\dfrac{a}{b} \cdot \dfrac{d}{c} = \dfrac{ad}{bc}$ $\longrightarrow$ $\dfrac{3a^2b^3(4a - 12)}{(6a - 2a^2)ab^4}$

$6a - 2a^2 = -2a^2 + 6a = -1(2a^2 - 6a)$ $\longrightarrow$ $\dfrac{3 \cdot a^2 \cdot b^3(4a - 12)}{-1(2a^2 - 6a)ab^4}$

$4a - 12 = 4(a - 3)$ $\longrightarrow$ $\dfrac{3 \cdot a^2 \cdot b^3 \cdot 4(a - 3)}{-1 \cdot 2 \cdot a(a - 3)ab^4}$

$2a^2 - 6a = 2a(a - 3)$ $\longrightarrow$

Factor 4 into primes. Multiplication can be done in any order. Divide out common factors. $\Big\}$ $\dfrac{3 \cdot \overset{1}{\cancel{a^2}} \cdot \overset{1}{\cancel{b^3}} \cdot \overset{1}{\cancel{2}} \cdot 2\overset{1}{\cancel{(a - 3)}}}{-1 \cdot \underset{1}{\cancel{2}} \cdot \underset{1}{\cancel{a}} \cdot \underset{1}{\cancel{a}} \cdot \underset{b}{\cancel{b^4}} \underset{1}{\cancel{(a - 3)}}}$

$\dfrac{a}{-1(b)} = -\dfrac{a}{b}$ $\dfrac{6}{-1(b)}$, or $-\dfrac{6}{b}$

EXERCISES

PART A

Divide.

1. $\dfrac{x - 3}{5} \div \dfrac{2x - 6}{10}$

2. $\dfrac{4a - 28}{6} \div \dfrac{a^2 - 49}{3a - 21}$

3. $\dfrac{a^2 - 25}{a + 1a} \div \dfrac{2a + 10}{4a + 4}$

4. $\dfrac{m^2 - 4m + 3}{m^2 - 1} \div \dfrac{2m - 6}{m^2 + 2m + 1}$

5. $\dfrac{5b^2 - 20}{b^2 - 5b + 6} \div \dfrac{6b + 12}{3b - 6}$

6. $\dfrac{m}{m^2 + 6m + 9} \div \dfrac{1}{m + 3}$

7. $\dfrac{x^2 - 3x + 2}{x^2 - 1} \div \dfrac{2 - x}{x - 1}$

8. $\dfrac{y}{5 - y} \div \dfrac{y^3}{2y - 10}$

9. $\dfrac{3 - m}{m - 6} \div \dfrac{m^2 + 2m - 15}{m^2 - m - 30}$

10. $\dfrac{a^2 + 4a}{3a^2} \div \dfrac{6a + 24}{9a^3}$

11. $\dfrac{m^2 - 2m + 1}{4m^3} \div \dfrac{4m - 4}{8m^2}$

12. $\dfrac{k^2 + k}{k^2} \div \dfrac{2k + 2}{8k^3}$

13. $\dfrac{b^2 + 3b - 4}{b^2 + 6b + 8} \div \dfrac{b^2 + 4b + 3}{b^2 + 3b + 2}$

14. $\dfrac{a^2 + 3a - 10}{a^2 + 9a + 20} \div \dfrac{a^2 + 2a - 8}{a^2 + 7a + 12}$

15. $\dfrac{4a^3b^2}{3a^2 + 5a} \div \dfrac{6a^5b^7}{3a^2 + 17a + 20}$

16. $\dfrac{8x^7y^5}{5x^2 - 10x} \div \dfrac{4x^8y^4}{5x^2 + 15x - 50}$

PART B

Divide.

17. $\dfrac{4b^3c^5}{x^2 - 2x - 35} \div \dfrac{24b^4c^4}{49 - x^2}$

18. $\dfrac{2a^2 - a}{4a^2 - 1} \div \dfrac{a^2}{4a^2 + 4a + 1}$

19. $\dfrac{4b - b^2}{3b} \div \dfrac{b^2 - 8b + 16}{b^2 - b}$

20. $\dfrac{3a^2b^3}{6 - 2x} \div \dfrac{ab^4}{4x - 12}$

21. $\dfrac{4m^2 + 8m + 3}{6m^3 + 3m^2} \div \dfrac{4m^2 - 9}{2m^2 + m}$

22. $\dfrac{m^3 - m}{4m^2} \div \dfrac{2 - 2m}{m^8}$

Chapter Seven Review

Give the coordinate of point A. $[p.\ 175]$

1.
0   A 1

2.
−1   A 0   1

3.
0   1   A

Find the missing factor. $[p.\ 175]$

4. $(7)(?) = \dfrac{7}{12}$

5. $(a-3)(?) = \dfrac{a-3}{a+7}$

6. $(?)\left(\dfrac{1}{3m+2}\right) = \dfrac{m}{3m+2}$

Find the value(s) of x for which the fraction is undefined. $[p.\ 175]$

7. $\dfrac{7}{x-5}$

8. $\dfrac{3x+5}{2x-8}$

9. $\dfrac{7x-8}{x^2-10x+24}$

Multiply. $[p.\ 180]$

10. $\left(\dfrac{3a^2}{5b^2}\right)\left(\dfrac{2a^3}{7b^7}\right)$

11. $(x-3)\left(\dfrac{x+5}{2x-3}\right)$

12. $\left(-\dfrac{a-2b}{a+b}\right)\left(\dfrac{a+2b}{a+3b}\right)$

Simplify. $[p.\ 184]$

13. $\dfrac{3a-15}{4a-20}$

14. $\dfrac{b^2-b}{2b-2}$

15. $\dfrac{12p^2+26p-10}{3p^2+11p-4}$

Find the quotient when the first polynomial is divided by the second. $[p.\ 184]$

16. $x^2-8x+12;\ x-6$

17. $z^2-3z-10;\ z-5$

Simplify. $[p.\ 188,\ 191]$

18. $\dfrac{3m-12}{4-m}$

19. $\dfrac{16-y^2}{y^2-8y+16}$

20. $\dfrac{10+a-3a^2}{a^2+5a-14}$

21. $\dfrac{a^3}{a^{10}}$

22. $\dfrac{8a^5b^9}{20a^7b^6}$

23. $\dfrac{6x^2y^7(a^2-3a-40)}{14xy^8(16+6a-a^2)}$

Multiply. $[p.\ 194]$

24. $\dfrac{a+4}{a-7}\cdot\dfrac{3a-21}{2a+8}$

25. $(a-3)\left(\dfrac{a+6}{a^2+2a-15}\right)$

26. $\dfrac{a+3b}{9}\cdot\dfrac{3a-6b}{a^2+ab-6b^2}$

27. $\dfrac{81-m^4}{3m^2+27}\cdot\dfrac{2m^2+m-21}{2m^2+13m+21}$

Divide. $[p.\ 198]$

28. $\dfrac{x-8}{4}\div\dfrac{2x-16}{8}$

29. $\dfrac{a^2+2a}{a^3}\div\dfrac{2a+4}{6a^7}$

30. $\dfrac{k^2-6k+9}{8-2k}\div\dfrac{4k-12}{3k^2-10k-8}$

31. $\dfrac{9a^7m^6}{3y^2-16y-12}\div\dfrac{30a^5m^2}{36-y^2}$

Chapter Seven Test

Give the coordinate of point A.

1.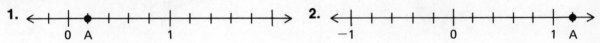

2.

Find the missing factor.

3. $(x - 2)\,(?) = \dfrac{x - 2}{3x + 1}$

4. $(?)\left(\dfrac{1}{5x - 1}\right) = \dfrac{2x - 9}{5x - 1}$

Find the value(s) of m for which the fraction is undefined.

5. $\dfrac{3}{2m - 8}$

6. $\dfrac{2m - 3}{m^2 - 7m + 12}$

Multiply.

7. $\left(\dfrac{4m^3}{7b^6}\right)\left(\dfrac{3m^9}{5b^4}\right)$

8. $\left(\dfrac{m - 4}{2m - 7}\right)(m + 3)$

Simplify.

9. $\dfrac{5p - 35}{4p - 28}$

10. $\dfrac{a^2 + 11a + 28}{a^2 - 2a - 24}$

11. $\dfrac{5k - 25}{5 - k}$

12. $\dfrac{49 - y^2}{2y^2 - 11y - 21}$

13. $\dfrac{8b^7}{12b^9}$

14. $\dfrac{24m^3y^8(t^2 - 13t + 42)}{16my^9(28 + 3t - t^2)}$

Find the quotient when the first polynomial is divided by the second.

15. $a^2 + 7a + 10;\ a + 5$

16. $m^2 - 6m - 16;\ m - 8$

Multiply.

17. $\dfrac{b - 8}{b + 3} \cdot \dfrac{b^2 - 9}{5b - 40}$

18. $(x - 7)\left(\dfrac{2x - 3}{x^2 - 2x - 35}\right)$

19. $\dfrac{2t^2 - 4t - 30}{t^2 + 3t} \cdot \dfrac{t^3}{6t - 30}$

20. $\dfrac{3a^2 - 4a}{2a^2 - 3a - 20} \cdot \dfrac{2a + 5}{9a^2 - 16}$

21. $\dfrac{2k^2(2k + 5)}{8k^4} \cdot \dfrac{3 - k}{2k^2 - k - 15}$

22. $\dfrac{a^2 - 3ab + 2b^2}{a^2 - ab} \cdot \dfrac{a^3}{2b - a}$

Divide.

23. $\dfrac{m^2 - 8m + 12}{m^2 - 2m} \div \dfrac{4m - 24}{m}$

24. $\dfrac{r^2 - 6r}{5} \div \dfrac{r^2 - 36}{5r + 30}$

25. $\dfrac{r^2 - 7r + 12}{r^2 - 25} \div \dfrac{2r - 8}{5 - r}$

26. $\dfrac{a^2 + 4a - 12}{4 - 2a} \div \dfrac{a^2 + 8a + 12}{2}$

Two Games

Game 1.

Start with a pile of 15 toothpicks. Each player in turn may take 1, 2, or 3 toothpicks from the pile. The player who must take the last object is the loser.

Game 2.

Arrange the numbers 1, 2, 3, 4, 5, 6, 7, 8, 9 so that there are exactly three numbers in each circle and the sum of the numbers in each circle is 15.

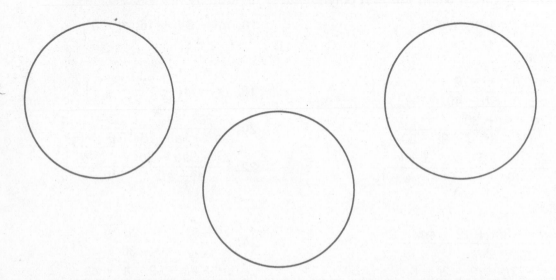

Adding Fractions: Same Denominator

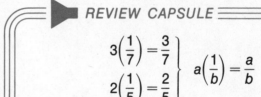

▶ *REVIEW CAPSULE*

$$\left.\begin{array}{l} 3\left(\dfrac{1}{7}\right) = \dfrac{3}{7} \\[2mm] 2\left(\dfrac{1}{5}\right) = \dfrac{2}{5} \end{array}\right\} \quad a\left(\dfrac{1}{b}\right) = \dfrac{a}{b}$$

EXAMPLE 1   Add $\dfrac{3}{7} + \dfrac{2}{7}$.

$\dfrac{a}{b} = a\left(\dfrac{1}{b}\right)$ ⟶

Use the distributive property.
$ac + bc = (a + b)c$ ⎫

$a\left(\dfrac{1}{b}\right) = \dfrac{a}{b}$ ⟶

$$\frac{3}{7} + \frac{2}{7} = 3\left(\frac{1}{7}\right) + 2\left(\frac{1}{7}\right)$$
$$= (3 + 2)\left(\frac{1}{7}\right)$$
$$= 5\left(\frac{1}{7}\right)$$
$$= \frac{5}{7}$$

Example 1 suggests this. ⟶

$$\frac{a}{b} + \frac{c}{b} = \frac{a + c}{b}, \, b \neq 0.$$

EXAMPLE 2   Add $\dfrac{5}{18} + \dfrac{1}{18}$.

$\dfrac{a}{b} + \dfrac{c}{b} = \dfrac{a + c}{b}$ ⟶

Factor into primes.
Divide out common factors. ⎫

Simplest form ⟶

$$\frac{5}{18} + \frac{1}{18} = \frac{5 + 1}{18}$$
$$= \frac{6}{18}$$
$$= \frac{\overset{1}{\cancel{3}} \cdot \overset{1}{\cancel{2}}}{\underset{1}{\cancel{3}} \cdot 3 \cdot \underset{1}{\cancel{2}}}$$
$$= \frac{1}{3}$$

EXAMPLE 3   Add $\dfrac{2y}{y-4}+\dfrac{3y}{y-4}$.

$\dfrac{a}{b}+\dfrac{c}{b}=\dfrac{a+c}{b}$ ─────────→

$\dfrac{2y}{y-4}+\dfrac{3y}{y-4}=\dfrac{2y+3y}{y-4}$

Combine like terms. ─────────→
The result is in simplest form.

$=\dfrac{5y}{y-4}$

EXAMPLE 4   Add $\dfrac{x^2}{2x+14}+\dfrac{-49}{2x+14}$.

$\dfrac{a}{b}+\dfrac{c}{b}=\dfrac{a+c}{b}$ ─────────→

$\dfrac{x^2}{2x+14}+\dfrac{-49}{2x+14}=\dfrac{x^2-49}{2x+14}$

Factor. $x^2-49=(x+7)(x-7)$ ────→
          $2x+14=2(x+7)$ ────→

$=\dfrac{\overset{1}{\cancel{(x+7)}}(x-7)}{2\underset{1}{\cancel{(x+7)}}}$

Simplest form ─────────→

$=\dfrac{x-7}{2}$

EXAMPLE 5   Add $\dfrac{-3}{x^2-7x+12}+\dfrac{x}{x^2-7x+12}+\dfrac{-1}{x^2-7x+12}$.

$\dfrac{a}{b}+\dfrac{c}{b}+\dfrac{d}{b}=\dfrac{a+c+d}{b}$ ────→

$\dfrac{-3+x-1}{x^2-7x+12}$

$\dfrac{x-4}{x^2-7x+12}$

Factor the denominator.
Divide out common factors. $\Big\}$ ──→

$\dfrac{\overset{1}{\cancel{x-4}}}{\underset{1}{\cancel{(x-4)}}(x-3)}$

Simplest form ─────────→

$\dfrac{1}{x-3}$

ORAL EXERCISES

Add.

1. $\dfrac{3}{5}+\dfrac{1}{5}$ 2. $\dfrac{5}{9}+\dfrac{3}{9}$ 3. $\dfrac{3}{13}+\dfrac{7}{13}$ 4. $\dfrac{5}{14}+\dfrac{4}{14}$

5. $\dfrac{3}{m}+\dfrac{2}{m}$ 6. $\dfrac{3}{a}+\dfrac{-7}{a}$ 7. $\dfrac{x}{5}+\dfrac{3}{5}+\dfrac{2x}{5}$ 8. $\dfrac{7m}{2}+\dfrac{5}{2}+\dfrac{-9m}{2}$

EXERCISES

PART A

Add.

1. $\dfrac{5}{9} + \dfrac{1}{9}$

2. $\dfrac{3}{18} + \dfrac{6}{18}$

3. $\dfrac{4}{7} + \dfrac{3}{7}$

4. $\dfrac{3}{10} + \dfrac{5}{10}$

5. $\dfrac{2a}{3} + \dfrac{5a}{3} + \dfrac{4a}{3}$

6. $\dfrac{5}{3t} + \dfrac{2}{3t} + \dfrac{4}{3t}$

7. $\dfrac{7}{4x} + \dfrac{-1}{4x} + \dfrac{3}{4x}$

8. $\dfrac{x}{x^2 - 4} + \dfrac{2}{x^2 - 4}$

9. $\dfrac{b}{b^2 - 9} + \dfrac{-3}{b^2 - 9}$

10. $\dfrac{a}{a^2 - 16} + \dfrac{4}{a^2 - 16}$

11. $\dfrac{a}{a^2 - a - 20} + \dfrac{-5}{a^2 - a - 20}$

12. $\dfrac{2a}{2a^2 - 5a - 3} + \dfrac{1}{2a^2 - 5a - 3}$

13. $\dfrac{x}{x^2 - 5x} + \dfrac{-5}{x^2 - 5x}$

14. $\dfrac{6}{m^2 + m - 30} + \dfrac{m}{m^2 + m - 30}$

15. $\dfrac{-15}{x^2 - 36} + \dfrac{x}{x^2 - 36} + \dfrac{9}{x^2 - 36}$

16. $\dfrac{-10}{a^2 + 7a} + \dfrac{a + 17}{a^2 + 7a}$

PART B

Add.

17. $\dfrac{3}{26} + \dfrac{5}{26} + \dfrac{5}{26}$

18. $\dfrac{2}{21} + \dfrac{7}{21} + \dfrac{5}{21}$

19. $\dfrac{3a}{28} + \dfrac{5b}{28} + \dfrac{9a}{28} + \dfrac{3b}{28}$

20. $\dfrac{5a}{32} + \dfrac{3b}{32} + \dfrac{7a}{32} + \dfrac{7b}{32}$

21. $\dfrac{2x}{2x^2 + 13x + 15} + \dfrac{3}{2x^2 + 13x + 15}$

22. $\dfrac{3a}{6a^2 + a - 12} + \dfrac{-4}{6a^2 + a - 12}$

23. $\dfrac{2a^2}{6a^2 - 5a - 25} + \dfrac{(a - 15)}{6a^2 - 5a - 25}$

24. $\dfrac{4b}{6b^2 + 11b - 35} + \dfrac{-15}{6b^2 + 11b - 35} + \dfrac{3b^2}{6b^2 + 11b - 35}$

PART C

Add.

25. $\dfrac{a^3}{a^2 + a} + \dfrac{4a^2}{a^2 + a} + \dfrac{3a}{a^2 + a}$

26. $\dfrac{4b^3 + 14b^2}{8b^2 - 12b} + \dfrac{-30b}{8b^2 - 12b}$

27. $\dfrac{8x^2 - 15y^2}{2x - 5y} + \dfrac{-14xy}{2x - 5y}$

28. $\dfrac{2x^2}{3x + 6y} + \dfrac{7xy}{3x + 6y} + \dfrac{6y^2}{3x + 6y}$

Age Problems

	Now	3 Years from Now	5 Years Ago
Manuel's age	14	$14 + 3$, or 17	$14 - 5$, or 9
Judy's age	x	$x + 3$	$x - 5$
Ed's age	$4y$	$4y + 3$	$4y - 5$
Sue's age	$z + 2$	$(z + 2) + 3$, or $z + 5$	$(z + 2) - 5$, or $z - 3$

Practice Problem 1   Amy is 4 years older than Mario. Write an algebraic expression for each of their ages 6 years from now.

Represent the ages algebraically } Let x = Mario's age now
$x + 4$ = Amy's age now

Make a chart ⟶

	Now	6 Years from Now
Mario's age	x	$x + 6$
Amy's age	$x + 4$	$(x + 4) + 6$, or $x + 10$

Thus, $x + 6$ represents Mario's age 6 years from now and $x + 10$ represents Amy's age 6 years from now.

| Practice Problem 2 | Jane is 3 years older than Gary. The sum of their ages is 25. Find their ages. |

Represent the ages algebraically. } Let x = Gary's age
$x + 3$ = Jane's age

Write an equation. → Sum of their ages is 25
$$x + (x + 3) = 25$$

Solve. → $$2x + 3 = 25$$
$$2x = 22$$

Gary's age → $$x = 11$$
Jane's age → $$x + 3 = 14$$

Thus, Gary is 11 and Jane is 14.

| Practice Problem 3 | Ralph is 3 times as old as Peg. In 6 years, Ralph will be only twice as old as Peg will be. Find their ages now. |

Represent the ages algebraically. } Let x = Peg's age now
$3x$ = Ralph's age now

Make a chart. →

	Now	6 Years from Now
Peg's age	x	$x + 6$
Ralph's age	$3x$	$3x + 6$

Write an equation. → (Ralph's age in 6 yr.) is 2 times (Peg's age in 6 yr.)

Substitute. → $$3x + 6 = 2(x + 6)$$
Solve. → $$3x + 6 = 2x + 12$$

Peg's age → $$x = 6$$
Ralph's age → $$3x = 3(6), \text{ or } 18$$

Check.

Ralph's age is 3 times Peg's age.

18	3 (6)
	18

$18 + 6 = 24$,
$6 + 6 = 12$. →

Ralph's age in 6 yr. is 2 times Peg's age in 6 yr.

24	2 (12)
	24

Thus, Peg is 6 and Ralph is 18.

| Practice Problem 4 | Mrs. Schrader is 36 and her son is 9. In how many years will Mrs. Schrader be exactly twice as old as her son? |

Represent the ages algebraically. } Let x = number of years until Mrs. Schrader is exactly twice as old as her son.

Make a chart. →

	Now	x Years from Now
Mrs. Schrader's age	36	$36 + x$
Son's age	9	$9 + x$

Write an equation. →

$$\left(\begin{array}{c}\text{Mrs. Schrader's age}\\ \text{in } x \text{ yr.}\end{array}\right) = 2 \text{ times} \left(\begin{array}{c}\text{Son's age}\\ \text{in } x \text{ yr.}\end{array}\right)$$

Substitute. →
Solve. →

$$36 + x = 2(9 + x)$$
$$36 + x = 18 + 2x$$
$$36 = 18 + x$$
$$18 = x$$

Thus, in 18 years, Mrs. Schrader will be exactly twice as old as her son.

Practice Problem 5 | Betty is 8 years younger than Larry. Two years ago, Larry was 3 times as old as Betty. Find their ages now.

Represent the ages algebraically. } Let x = Larry's age now
$x - 8$ = Betty's age now

Make a chart. →

	Now	2 Years Ago
Larry's age	x	$x - 2$
Betty's age	$x - 8$	$(x - 8) - 2$, or $x - 10$

Write an equation. →

$$\left(\begin{array}{c}\text{Larry's age}\\ \text{2 yr. ago}\end{array}\right) = 3 \text{ times} \left(\begin{array}{c}\text{Betty's age}\\ \text{2 yr. ago}\end{array}\right)$$

Substitute. →
Solve. →

$$x - 2 = 3(x - 10)$$
$$x - 2 = 3x - 30$$
$$-2x - 2 = -30$$
$$-2x = -28$$

Larry's age. →
Betty's age. →

$$x = 14$$
$$x - 8 = 14 - 8, \text{ or } 6$$

Thus, Larry is 14 and Betty is 6.

Exercises

1. Pedro is twice as old as Mona. Four years ago, Pedro was four times as old as Mona. Find their ages now.

2. Debbie is 20 and Rita is 13. How many years ago was Debbie exactly twice as old as Rita?

3. Steve is 16 years older than Grace. In three years he will be exactly 3 times as old as Grace. Find their ages now.

4. Eileen is 29 and her son is 7. In how many years will Eileen be exactly three times as old as her son?

5. Tom is 7 years older than Joe. The sum of their ages is 37. Find their ages.

6. Beth is twice as old as Donna. The sum of their ages is 54. Find their ages.

7. Cathy is 16 years younger than Mary. In five years, Mary will be twice as old as Cathy. Find their ages now.

8. John is 29 and his sister, Dianna is 18. How many years ago was John exactly twice as old as his sister?

9. Mr. Davis is 39 and his daughter Alice is 11. In how many years will Mr. Davis be exactly 3 times as old as Alice?

10. Sue and Jeff are twins. They have a brother, Tony, who is 5 years older. If the sum of the ages of all three is 23, find their ages.

11. Dot is 4 times as old as Lou. In 6 years, she will be twice as old as Lou. Find their ages now.

12. Jim is 7 years older than Phil. Eleven years ago, Jim was twice as old as Phil. Find their ages now.

13. Ruby is 37 and Eva is 21. How many years ago was Ruby exactly 3 times as old as Eva?

14. Marge is 16 and her grandfather is 70. In how many years will Marge's grandfather be 3 times as old as she?

Adding: Different Denominators

REVIEW CAPSULE

$$\frac{2a}{5}+\frac{7a}{5}=\frac{2a+7a}{5}$$

$$=\frac{9a}{5}$$

same denominator

To add fractions with the same denominator, add the numerators.

EXAMPLE 1   Show that $\dfrac{2}{5}=\dfrac{2\cdot3}{5\cdot3}$.

$\dfrac{2}{5}$	$\dfrac{2\cdot3}{5\cdot3}$
$\dfrac{2}{5}$	$\dfrac{2}{5}\cdot\dfrac{3}{3}$
	$\dfrac{2}{5}\cdot1$
	$\dfrac{2}{5}$

$\dfrac{3}{3}=1$

Thus, $\dfrac{2}{5}=\dfrac{2\cdot3}{5\cdot3}.$

Example 1 suggests this. ⟶

$$\frac{a}{b}=\frac{a\cdot c}{b\cdot c},\ c\neq0.$$
Multiplying both numerator and denominator of a fraction by the same number does not change its value.

EXAMPLE 2   Add $\dfrac{5}{6}+\dfrac{1}{3}$.

Denominators are not the same. Factor 6 into primes, $6=2\cdot3$.

$$\frac{5}{2\cdot3}+\frac{1}{3}\longleftarrow \begin{cases}\text{This denominator needs the}\\ \text{factor 2 to be like }2\cdot3.\end{cases}$$

Multiply both numerator and denominator of $\frac{1}{3}$ by 2.

$$\frac{5}{2\cdot3}+\frac{1\cdot2}{3\cdot2}=\frac{5}{6}+\frac{2}{6}$$

$\dfrac{5}{6}+\dfrac{2}{6}=\dfrac{5+2}{6}$, or $\dfrac{7}{6}$ ⟶

Thus, $\dfrac{5}{6}+\dfrac{1}{3}=\dfrac{7}{6}.$

In Example 2, $3 \cdot 2$ is the *least common denominator* (LCD).

EXAMPLE 3   Add $\dfrac{7}{12} + \dfrac{2}{3} + \dfrac{1}{6}$.

First find the LCD.

$$\dfrac{7}{2 \cdot 2 \cdot 3} + \dfrac{2}{3} + \dfrac{1}{3 \cdot 2}$$

Factor the denominators. ————————————→

The only factors present are 2 and 3. To have a common denominator, we must have exactly the same factors in each denominator.

$$\underset{\substack{\uparrow \quad \uparrow \\ \text{two 2's, one 3}}}{2 \cdot 2 \cdot 3} \qquad \underset{\substack{\uparrow \\ \text{one 3}}}{3} \qquad \underset{\substack{\nearrow \quad \nwarrow \\ \text{one 3, one 2}}}{3 \cdot 2}$$

$$\text{LCD} = \underset{\substack{\nearrow \quad \nwarrow \\ \text{two 2's, one 3}}}{2 \cdot 2 \cdot 3}$$

In each denominator, there are at most two 2's and one 3.

$$\underset{\substack{\text{has two 2's,} \\ \text{one 3}}}{\dfrac{7}{2 \cdot 2 \cdot 3}} + \underset{\substack{\text{needs} \\ \text{two 2's}}}{\dfrac{2}{3}} + \underset{\substack{\text{needs} \\ \text{one 2}}}{\dfrac{1}{3 \cdot 2}}$$

In each fraction, multiply by the missing factors.

$$\dfrac{7}{2 \cdot 2 \cdot 3} + \dfrac{2 \cdot 2 \cdot 2}{3 \cdot 2 \cdot 2} + \dfrac{1 \cdot 2}{3 \cdot 2 \cdot 2}$$

$$\dfrac{7}{12} + \dfrac{8}{12} + \dfrac{2}{12}$$

The denominators are the same. ————→
Add the numerators. ————————→

$$\dfrac{7 + 8 + 2}{12}$$

$$\dfrac{17}{12}$$

EXAMPLE 4   Add $\dfrac{5a}{6} + \dfrac{a}{3}$.

Denominators are not the same. Factor 6.

$$\dfrac{5a}{2 \cdot 3} + \dfrac{a}{3} \longleftarrow \begin{cases} \text{This denominator needs the factor} \\ \text{2 to be like 6.} \end{cases}$$

Rewrite each fraction with the LCD, $2 \cdot 3$.

$$\dfrac{5a}{2 \cdot 3} + \dfrac{a \cdot 2}{3 \cdot 2}$$

The denominators are the same. Add the numerators.

$$\dfrac{5a}{6} + \dfrac{2a}{6}$$

$$\dfrac{7a}{6}$$

EXAMPLE 5   Add $\dfrac{7a}{18} + \dfrac{5a}{6} + \dfrac{7}{2}$.

Find the LCD.
Factor the denominators. }

$$\dfrac{7a}{3 \cdot 3 \cdot 2} + \dfrac{5a}{3 \cdot 2} + \dfrac{7}{2}$$

{ At most two 3's, one 2 in any denominator

$$LCD = 3 \cdot 3 \cdot 2$$

In each fraction, multiply
by the missing factors. }

$$\dfrac{7a}{3 \cdot 3 \cdot 2} + \dfrac{5a \cdot 3}{3 \cdot 2 \cdot 3} + \dfrac{7 \cdot 3 \cdot 3}{2 \cdot 3 \cdot 3}$$

needed one 3   needed two 3's

$5a \cdot 3 = 5 \cdot 3 \cdot a$, or $15a$

$$\dfrac{7a}{18} + \dfrac{15a}{18} + \dfrac{63}{18}$$

Combine numerators. $\longrightarrow$

$$\dfrac{7a + 15a + 63}{18}$$

$7a + 15a = 22a$ $\longrightarrow$

$$\dfrac{22a + 63}{18}$$

EXAMPLE 6   Add $\dfrac{2b + 3}{8b} + \dfrac{3b + 5}{2b}$.

Find the LCD.
Factor the denominators. }

$$\dfrac{2b + 3}{2 \cdot 2 \cdot 2 \cdot b} + \dfrac{3b + 5}{2 \cdot b}$$

{ At most three 2's, one b in any denominator

$$LCD = 2 \cdot 2 \cdot 2 \cdot b$$

In each fraction, multiply
by the missing factors. }

$$\dfrac{2b + 3}{2 \cdot 2 \cdot 2 \cdot b} + \dfrac{(3b + 5) \cdot 2 \cdot 2}{2 \cdot b \cdot 2 \cdot 2}$$ $\longleftarrow$ needed two 2's

$$\dfrac{2b + 3}{8b} + \dfrac{(3b + 5)4}{8b}$$

$(3b + 5)4 = 12b + 20$ $\longrightarrow$

$$\dfrac{2b + 3}{8b} + \dfrac{12b + 20}{8b}$$

Combine numerators. $\longrightarrow$

$$\dfrac{14b + 23}{8b}$$

EXAMPLE 7   Add $\dfrac{2x - 3}{6x} + \dfrac{4x - 1}{2x}$.

Rewrite each fraction with
the LCD: $2 \cdot 3 \cdot x$. }

$$\dfrac{2x - 3}{2 \cdot 3 \cdot x} + \dfrac{(4x - 1) \cdot 3}{2 \cdot x \cdot 3}$$

$(4x - 1) \cdot 3 = 12x - 3$ $\longrightarrow$

$$\dfrac{2x - 3}{6x} + \dfrac{12x - 3}{6x}$$

Combine numerators. $\longrightarrow$

$$\dfrac{14x - 6}{6x}$$

Write in simplest form. Factor. Then
divide out common factors.

$$\dfrac{\overset{1}{2}(7x - 3)}{\underset{3}{6x}} = \dfrac{7x - 3}{3x}$$

ORAL EXERCISES

Find the LCD.

1. $\dfrac{2}{3} + \dfrac{5}{3 \cdot 2}$

2. $\dfrac{3}{5} + \dfrac{7}{5 \cdot 2}$

3. $\dfrac{7a}{3} + \dfrac{5a}{3 \cdot 2} + \dfrac{7a}{3 \cdot 3 \cdot 2}$

4. $\dfrac{3m}{2} + \dfrac{5m}{7 \cdot 2} + \dfrac{3m}{2 \cdot 7 \cdot 2}$

5. $\dfrac{3}{5 \cdot 2 \cdot 2} + \dfrac{3a}{2 \cdot 2 \cdot 2} + \dfrac{1}{2 \cdot 5}$

6. $\dfrac{3a}{2 \cdot 5 \cdot 7} + \dfrac{2a}{5 \cdot 5} + \dfrac{11a}{7 \cdot 2}$

7. $\dfrac{3k+1}{2 \cdot 3 \cdot 3} + \dfrac{3k-4}{3 \cdot 3 \cdot 3} + \dfrac{2k-6}{2 \cdot 2}$

8. $\dfrac{7b+5}{8a} + \dfrac{3b+2}{4a}$

9. $\dfrac{2m+1}{3m} + \dfrac{3m+2}{27m}$

EXERCISES

PART A

Add.

1. $\dfrac{2}{3} + \dfrac{5}{6}$

2. $\dfrac{1}{8} + \dfrac{3}{4}$

3. $\dfrac{4}{5} + \dfrac{7}{10}$

4. $\dfrac{2}{3} + \dfrac{1}{2} + \dfrac{5}{6}$

5. $\dfrac{2b}{7} + \dfrac{3b}{14}$

6. $\dfrac{7m}{9} + \dfrac{2m}{3}$

7. $\dfrac{3a}{8} + \dfrac{5a}{2}$

8. $\dfrac{7k}{15} + \dfrac{3k}{5}$

9. $\dfrac{2}{3m} + \dfrac{7}{18m}$

10. $\dfrac{4}{9x} + \dfrac{2}{3x}$

11. $\dfrac{2m}{9} + \dfrac{3}{2} + \dfrac{5m}{18}$

12. $\dfrac{9a+5}{2} + \dfrac{5a}{6}$

13. $\dfrac{4}{5} + \dfrac{2m-3}{10}$

14. $\dfrac{7}{9} + \dfrac{2a+5}{3}$

15. $\dfrac{2b-3}{6b} + \dfrac{4b+1}{2b}$

16. $\dfrac{2m-3}{5m} + \dfrac{4m-1}{25m}$

17. $\dfrac{m-1}{8} + \dfrac{3m-1}{4}$

PART B

Add.

18. $\dfrac{2a-5}{6} + \dfrac{1}{3} + \dfrac{5a+2}{2}$

19. $\dfrac{4x-1}{3} + \dfrac{2x}{15} + \dfrac{3x-2}{5}$

20. $\dfrac{9m-2}{18} + \dfrac{6-5m}{27} + \dfrac{5}{9}$

21. $\dfrac{4a+1}{3a} + \dfrac{5}{6a} + \dfrac{7a-3}{2a}$

22. $\dfrac{t+1}{2} + \dfrac{3t-5}{14} + \dfrac{4t-3}{21}$

23. $\dfrac{3a^2-1}{2a} + \dfrac{5a^2-4a-3}{18a}$

24. $\dfrac{3x^2-9}{5x} + \dfrac{2x-10}{15x} + \dfrac{x+1}{3x}$

25. $\dfrac{4a^2-2a+3}{24} + \dfrac{a^2-1}{24}$

26. $\dfrac{2m^2-5m+3}{28} + \dfrac{3m-1}{7} + \dfrac{m^2}{4}$

27. $\dfrac{2a^2+a-30}{3a} + \dfrac{5a+4}{5a} + \dfrac{a^2-9}{30a}$

Adding: Polynomial Denominators

▶ *REVIEW CAPSULE*

Add $\quad \dfrac{3a + 2}{5a} + \dfrac{2}{15a}.$

$$\frac{3a + 2}{5a} + \frac{2}{5 \cdot 3 \cdot a} \quad \text{LCD} =$$

$$\frac{(3a + 2) \cdot 3}{5a \cdot 3} + \frac{2}{5 \cdot 3 \cdot a} \qquad 5 \cdot 3 \cdot a$$

$$\frac{9a + 6}{15a} + \frac{2}{15a}$$

$$\frac{9a + 8}{15a}$$

EXAMPLE 1   Add $\dfrac{3}{x - 3} + \dfrac{2}{x^2 - 9} + \dfrac{5}{x + 3}$

Factor $x^2 - 9$.   ⟶

$$\frac{3}{x - 3} + \frac{2}{(x + 3)(x - 3)} + \frac{5}{x + 3}$$
$$\text{LCD} = (x + 3)(x - 3)$$

$$\frac{3(x + 3)}{(x - 3)(x + 3)} + \frac{2}{(x + 3)(x - 3)} + \frac{5(x - 3)}{(x + 3)(x - 3)}$$

$$\uparrow \qquad\qquad\qquad\qquad\qquad \nearrow$$

$$\text{needed } (x + 3) \qquad\qquad \text{needed } (x - 3)$$

$3(x + 3) = 3x + 9$
$5(x - 3) = 5x - 15$

$$\frac{3x + 9}{(x - 3)(x + 3)} + \frac{2}{(x + 3)(x - 3)} + \frac{5x - 15}{(x + 3)(x - 3)}$$

$\dfrac{a}{b} + \dfrac{c}{b} + \dfrac{d}{b} = \dfrac{a + c + d}{b}$ ⟶

$$\frac{3x + 9 + 2 + 5x - 15}{(x + 3)(x - 3)}$$

Combine like terms.   ⟶

$$\frac{8x - 4}{(x + 3)(x - 3)}$$

Factor the numerator. See if the fraction can be simplified.

$$\frac{4(2x - 1)}{(x + 3)(x - 3)}$$

There are no common factors other ⟶ **Thus,** the sum is $\dfrac{4(2x - 1)}{(x + 3)(x - 3)}$ in simplest form.
than 1.

EXAMPLE 2 Add $\dfrac{8x + 15}{x^2 + 5x} + \dfrac{x}{x + 5}$.

$x^2 + 5x = x(x + 5)$ ⟶
$$\frac{8x + 15}{x(x + 5)} + \frac{x}{x + 5}$$
LCD $= x(x + 5)$
$$\underset{\text{needs } x}{\nwarrow}$$

$$\frac{8x + 15}{x(x + 5)} + \frac{x \cdot x}{(x + 5) \cdot x}$$

$x \cdot x = x^2$ ⟶
$$\frac{8x + 15}{x(x + 5)} + \frac{x^2}{(x + 5)x}$$

Combine numerators. ⎫
Write in descending order. ⎬
$$\frac{x^2 + 8x + 15}{x(x + 5)}$$

Factor the numerator. ⎫
$x^2 + 8x + 15 = (x + 5)(x + 3)$ ⎬
$$\frac{(x + 5)(x + 3)}{x(x + 5)}$$

Divide out common factors. ⟶
$$\frac{\overset{1}{\cancel{(x + 5)}}(x + 3)}{x\underset{1}{\cancel{(x + 5)}}}$$

Thus, the sum is $\dfrac{x + 3}{x}$ in simplest form.

EXAMPLE 3 Add $\dfrac{2}{x^2 - 12x + 27} + \dfrac{3}{x - 3} + \dfrac{5}{x - 9}$.

$x^2 - 12x + 27 = (x - 9)(x - 3)$ ⟶
$$\frac{2}{(x - 9)(x - 3)} + \frac{3}{x - 3} + \frac{5}{x - 9}$$
LCD $= (x - 9)(x - 3)$
$$\underset{\text{needs }(x - 9)}{\nearrow} \qquad \underset{\text{needs }(x - 3)}{\nwarrow}$$

$$\frac{2}{(x - 9)(x - 3)} + \frac{3(x - 9)}{(x - 3)(x - 9)} + \frac{5(x - 3)}{(x - 9)(x - 3)}$$

$3(x - 9) = 3x - 27$ ⎫
$5(x - 3) = 5x - 15$ ⎬
$$\frac{2}{(x - 9)(x - 3)} + \frac{3x - 27}{(x - 3)(x - 9)} + \frac{5x - 15}{(x - 9)(x - 3)}$$

Combine numerators. ⟶
$$\frac{2 + 3x - 27 + 5x - 15}{(x - 9)(x - 3)}$$

Combine like terms. ⟶
$$\frac{8x - 40}{(x - 9)(x - 3)}$$

Factor. See if the fraction can be simplified.
$$\frac{8(x - 5)}{(x - 9)(x - 3)}$$

There are no common factors ⟶ **Thus,** the sum is $\dfrac{8(x - 5)}{(x - 9)(x - 3)}$ in simplest form.
other than 1.

EXERCISES

PART A

Add.

1. $\dfrac{7}{a-4} + \dfrac{3}{a^2-16} + \dfrac{2}{a+4}$

2. $\dfrac{5}{b+5} + \dfrac{2}{b^2-25} + \dfrac{4}{b-5}$

3. $\dfrac{9x+14}{x^2+7x} + \dfrac{x}{x+7}$

4. $\dfrac{a}{a-5} + \dfrac{-3a-10}{a^2-5a}$

5. $\dfrac{7}{x^2+5x} + \dfrac{3}{x}$

6. $\dfrac{4}{m} + \dfrac{3}{m^2-4m}$

7. $\dfrac{2}{x-3} + \dfrac{5}{x^2-9}$

8. $\dfrac{7}{m-4} + \dfrac{2}{m^2-m-12}$

9. $\dfrac{5}{x^2-6x-16} + \dfrac{3}{x-8}$

10. $\dfrac{7}{m-7} + \dfrac{3}{m^2-2m-35}$

11. $\dfrac{5}{a+1} + \dfrac{2}{a^2-1} + \dfrac{4}{a-1}$

12. $\dfrac{2}{a-5} + \dfrac{3}{a^2-7a+10} + \dfrac{4}{a-2}$

13. $\dfrac{2}{a+3} + \dfrac{4}{2a^2+a-15} + \dfrac{6}{2a-5}$

14. $\dfrac{4}{k^2-k-20} + \dfrac{2}{k-5} + \dfrac{3}{k+4}$

PART B

EXAMPLE Add $\dfrac{x+1}{x^2-5x+6} + \dfrac{x+4}{x-3}$.

LCD $= (x-3)(x-2)$.
Second fraction needs $(x-2)$. $\longrightarrow$

$\dfrac{x+1}{(x-3)(x-2)} + \dfrac{x+4}{x-3}$

$\dfrac{x+1}{(x-3)(x-2)} + \dfrac{(x+4)(x-2)}{(x-3)(x-2)}$

$\dfrac{x+1}{(x-3)(x-2)} + \dfrac{x^2+2x-8}{(x-3)(x-2)}$

$\dfrac{x^2+3x-7}{(x-3)(x-2)}$

$\begin{array}{c} x \quad + \quad 4 \\ x \quad - \quad 2 \\ \hline x^2 + 2x - 8 \end{array}$

Add.

15. $\dfrac{4k-3}{k^2-5k+6} + \dfrac{k+1}{k-3}$

16. $\dfrac{2a+1}{a^2+3a+2} + \dfrac{a-4}{a+2}$

17. $\dfrac{4m-1}{2m^2+5m} + \dfrac{m-2}{m}$

Rings

Three-Minute Clock Addition

$\oplus$	0	1	2
0	0	1	2
1	1	2	0
2	2	0	1

Three-Minute Clock Multiplication

$\otimes$	0	1	2
0	0	0	0
1	0	1	2
2	0	2	1

- Commutative Groups Under $\oplus$

Closed	yes
Associative	yes
Identity	0
Inverses	for 0 is 0
	1 is 2
	2 is 1
Commutative	yes

- Closure for $\otimes$
  Yes. The answers are
  either 0, 1, or 2

  Associative for $\otimes$

$$(2 \otimes 1) \otimes 2 \overset{?}{=} 2 \otimes (1 \otimes 2)$$

$$2 \otimes 2 \overset{?}{=} 2 \otimes 2$$
$$1 = 1$$
$$\llcorner\text{same}\lrcorner$$

- Distributive

$$1 \otimes (2 \oplus 1) \overset{?}{=} (1 \otimes 2) \oplus (1 \otimes 1)$$

$$1 \otimes 0 \overset{?}{=} 2 \oplus 1$$
$$0 \qquad\qquad 0$$
$$\llcorner\text{——same——}\lrcorner$$

If we check all possible number combinations we see that the associative, commutative and distributive properties hold for each case.

So, three-minute clock arithmetic forms a **ring**

> A set with two operations
> $\oplus$ and $\otimes$ forms a RING if
> • the set is a commutative group under $\oplus$
> • the set is closed and associative for $\otimes$
> • $\otimes$ is distributive over $\oplus$ in the set

Does four-minute clock arithmetic form a ring?

More on Adding Fractions

 REVIEW CAPSULE

Find the LCD.
$$\frac{5x+1}{2} + \frac{2x+1}{9} + \frac{2x+9}{8}$$
$$\frac{5x+1}{2} + \frac{2x+1}{3 \cdot 3} + \frac{2x+9}{2 \cdot 2 \cdot 2}$$
The LCD is $2 \cdot 2 \cdot 2 \cdot 3 \cdot 3$.

EXAMPLE 1 Add $4 + \frac{5}{3m}$.

Rewrite 4 as $\frac{4}{1}$. ⟶ $\quad \frac{4}{1} + \frac{5}{3m}$

LCD = $3 \cdot m$ $\qquad$ needs $3 \cdot m$

$$\frac{4 \cdot 3 \cdot m}{1 \cdot 3 \cdot m} + \frac{5}{3 \cdot m}$$

$4 \cdot 3 \cdot m = 12m$ ⟶

$1 \cdot 3 \cdot m = 3m$ ⟶ $\qquad \frac{12m}{3m} + \frac{5}{3m}$

There are no common factors. ⟶ **Thus,** the sum is $\dfrac{12m+5}{3m}$ in simplest form.

EXAMPLE 2 Add $\dfrac{9}{y+4} + \dfrac{6}{y-4}$.

$\left.\begin{matrix} y+4 \\ y-4 \end{matrix}\right\}$ cannot be factored. ⟶ $\qquad$ LCD = $(y+4)(y-4)$

In each fraction, multiply by the $\Big\}$
missing factors.
$$\frac{9(y-4)}{(y+4)(y-4)} + \frac{6(y+4)}{(y-4)(y+4)}$$

$\left.\begin{matrix} 9(y-4) = 9y - 36 \\ 6(y+4) = 6y + 24 \end{matrix}\right\}$
$$\frac{9y-36}{(y+4)(y-4)} + \frac{6y+24}{(y-4)(y+4)}$$

$\dfrac{a}{b} + \dfrac{c}{b} = \dfrac{a+c}{b}$ ⟶
$$\frac{15y-12}{(y+4)(y-4)}$$

Factor $15y - 12$. See if the fraction
can be simplified.
$$\frac{3(5y-4)}{(y+4)(y-4)}$$

Thus, the sum is $\dfrac{3(5y-4)}{(y+4)(y-4)}$ in simplest form.

EXAMPLE 3 Add $\dfrac{6}{5x^2} + \dfrac{-7}{3x} + \dfrac{2}{15x^3}$.

Find the LCD.
Factor the denominators.
At most one 3, one 5, three x's in any denominator

$$\dfrac{6}{5 \cdot x \cdot x} + \dfrac{-7}{3 \cdot x} + \dfrac{2}{3 \cdot 5 \cdot x \cdot x \cdot x}$$

$$\text{LCD} = 3 \cdot 5 \cdot x \cdot x \cdot x, \text{ or } 15x^3$$

In each fraction, multiply by the missing factors.

$$\dfrac{6 \cdot 3 \cdot x}{5 \cdot x \cdot x \cdot 3 \cdot x} + \dfrac{-7 \cdot 5 \cdot x \cdot x}{3 \cdot x \cdot 5 \cdot x \cdot x} + \dfrac{2}{3 \cdot 5 \cdot x \cdot x \cdot x}$$

$6 \cdot 3 \cdot x = 18x, -7 \cdot 5 \cdot x \cdot x = -35x^2 \longrightarrow$

$$\dfrac{18x}{15x^3} \quad + \quad \dfrac{-35x^2}{15x^3} \quad + \quad \dfrac{2}{15x^3}$$

Combine numerators.
Write in descending order.

$$\dfrac{-35x^2 + 18x + 2}{15x^3}$$

EXAMPLE 4 Add $\dfrac{2}{3y} + \dfrac{7 - 4y}{6y^3} + \dfrac{3 + 2y}{4y^2}$.

Find the LCD.
Factor the denominators.
At most two 2's, one 3, three y's in any denominator.

$$\dfrac{2}{3 \cdot y} + \dfrac{7 - 4y}{2 \cdot 3 \cdot y \cdot y \cdot y} + \dfrac{3 + 2y}{2 \cdot 2 \cdot y \cdot y}$$

$$\text{LCD} = 2 \cdot 2 \cdot 3 \cdot y \cdot y \cdot y, \text{ or } 12y^3$$

In each fraction, multiply by the missing factors.

$$\dfrac{2 \cdot 2 \cdot 2 \cdot y \cdot y}{3 \cdot y \cdot 2 \cdot 2 \cdot y \cdot y} + \dfrac{(7 - 4y) \cdot 2}{2 \cdot 3 \cdot y \cdot y \cdot y \cdot 2} + \dfrac{(3 + 2y) \cdot 3 \cdot y}{2 \cdot 2 \cdot y \cdot y \cdot 3 \cdot y}$$

$(7 - 4y)2 = 14 - 8y$
$(3 + 2y)3y = 9y + 6y^2$

$$\dfrac{8y^2}{12y^3} \quad + \quad \dfrac{14 - 8y}{12y^3} \quad + \quad \dfrac{9y + 6y^2}{12y^3}$$

$\dfrac{a}{b} + \dfrac{c}{b} + \dfrac{d}{b} = \dfrac{a + c + d}{b} \longrightarrow$

$$\dfrac{8y^2 + 14 - 8y + 9y + 6y^2}{12y^3}$$

Combine like terms. $\longrightarrow$

$$\dfrac{14y^2 + y + 14}{12y^3}$$

ORAL EXERCISES

Find the LCD.

1. $\dfrac{3}{y^2} + \dfrac{7}{y} + \dfrac{8}{y^3}$

2. $\dfrac{7}{a^2} + \dfrac{2}{a^3} + \dfrac{4}{a}$

3. $\dfrac{3}{p^2} + \dfrac{4}{p} + \dfrac{2}{p^5}$

EXERCISES

PART A

Add.

1. $\dfrac{3}{m} + 2$

2. $8 + \dfrac{3}{7b}$

3. $3 + \dfrac{2}{m}$

4. $\dfrac{7}{a-1} + \dfrac{4}{a+2}$

5. $\dfrac{4}{x+2} + \dfrac{3}{x-4}$

6. $\dfrac{2}{3a-1} + \dfrac{4}{2a+5}$

7. $\dfrac{5}{a-3} + \dfrac{7}{2a+5}$

8. $\dfrac{3}{b-7} + \dfrac{-2}{2b+3}$

9. $\dfrac{8}{x^2} + \dfrac{7}{x} + \dfrac{3}{x^3}$

10. $\dfrac{7}{15y} + \dfrac{-3}{5y^3} + \dfrac{2}{3y^2}$

11. $\dfrac{3}{2a^2} + \dfrac{5}{3a^3} + \dfrac{7}{6a}$

12. $\dfrac{5}{x} + \dfrac{3}{x^2} + \dfrac{2}{x^3}$

13. $\dfrac{3}{m} + \dfrac{2}{m^2} + 5$

14. $6k + \dfrac{5}{3k}$

15. $\dfrac{3}{a^2} + \dfrac{2}{a} + 1$

16. $\dfrac{7}{2a} + \dfrac{2-a}{3a^2} + \dfrac{3+5a}{6a^3}$

17. $\dfrac{2}{5b} + \dfrac{4-3b}{3b^2} + \dfrac{2b-3}{b^3}$

18. $\dfrac{7-x}{2x^2} + \dfrac{3+2x}{10x^3} + \dfrac{2-5x}{5x}$

19. $\dfrac{2a+5}{4a} + \dfrac{a-1}{6a^3} + \dfrac{3-a}{3a^2}$

PART B

EXAMPLE   Add $x + 3 + \dfrac{7}{x-2}$.

$$\dfrac{x+3}{1} + \dfrac{7}{x-2}$$

$$\dfrac{(x+3)(x-2)}{1 \cdot (x-2)} + \dfrac{7}{x-2}$$

LCD $= 1 \cdot (x-2)$, or $x-2$.

$(x+3)(x-2) = x^2 + x - 6 \longrightarrow$

$$\dfrac{x^2+x-6}{x-2} + \dfrac{7}{x-2}$$

Combine numerators.

$$\dfrac{x^2+x+1}{x-2}$$

Add.

20. $a - 2 + \dfrac{4}{a+5}$

21. $2m - 1 + \dfrac{3}{m+5}$

22. $\dfrac{5}{3a+1} + a - 4$

23. $2x - 1 + \dfrac{x-7}{2x-1}$

24. $\dfrac{a-5}{2a+3} + a - 2$

25. $x - 5 + \dfrac{7}{3x+2}$

PART C

Add.

26. $\dfrac{2}{mn} + \dfrac{7}{3n}$

27. $\dfrac{4}{a^2b} + \dfrac{3}{ab^2}$

28. $\dfrac{2}{a^3b^2} + \dfrac{5}{a^2b^2}$

Subtracting Fractions

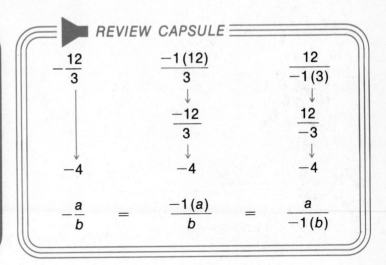

▶ *REVIEW CAPSULE*

$$-\frac{12}{3}\qquad\qquad \frac{-1(12)}{3}\qquad\qquad \frac{12}{-1(3)}$$

$$\downarrow\qquad\qquad\qquad \downarrow\qquad\qquad\qquad \downarrow$$

$$\qquad\qquad\qquad \frac{-12}{3}\qquad\qquad \frac{12}{-3}$$

$$\qquad\qquad\qquad \downarrow\qquad\qquad\qquad \downarrow$$

$$-4\qquad\qquad\qquad -4\qquad\qquad\qquad -4$$

$$-\frac{a}{b}\;=\;\frac{-1(a)}{b}\;=\;\frac{a}{-1(b)}$$

EXAMPLE 1 Rewrite $-\dfrac{2x-3}{x+5}$.

$$-\frac{a}{b}=\frac{-1(a)}{b}\longrightarrow \qquad -\frac{2x-3}{x+5}=\frac{-1(2x-3)}{x+5}$$

$$-1(2x-3)=-1(2x)+(-1)(-3) \qquad\qquad\qquad =\frac{-2x+3}{x+5}$$

EXAMPLE 2 Simplify $\dfrac{x}{x^2-4x+3}-\dfrac{2}{x-3}$.

Rewrite as addition.
$$-\frac{2}{x-3}=\frac{-1(2)}{x-3}\longrightarrow \qquad \frac{x}{x^2-4x+3}+\frac{-1(2)}{x-3}$$

Factor: $x^2-4x+3=(x-3)(x-1)$.
LCD $=(x-3)(x-1)$
$$\frac{x}{(x-3)(x-1)}+\frac{-2}{x-3}$$
$$\text{needs } (x-1)$$

$$-2(x-1)=-2x+2\longrightarrow \qquad \frac{x}{(x-3)(x-1)}+\frac{-2(x-1)}{(x-3)(x-1)}$$

$$\frac{x}{(x-3)(x-1)}+\frac{-2x+2}{(x-3)(x-1)}$$

$$\frac{a}{b}+\frac{c}{b}=\frac{a+c}{b}\longrightarrow \qquad \frac{x-2x+2}{(x-3)(x-1)}$$

$$x-2x=1x-2x=-1x,\text{ or }-x \qquad\qquad \frac{-x+2}{(x-3)(x-1)}$$

EXAMPLE 3 Simplify $3 - \dfrac{3x - 1}{2x}$.

Rewrite as addition.

$-\dfrac{3x - 1}{2x} = \dfrac{-1(3x - 1)}{2x}$ ⟶ $\dfrac{3}{1} + \dfrac{-1(3x - 1)}{2x}$

$-1(3x - 1) = -3x + 1$ ⟶ $\dfrac{3}{1} + \dfrac{-3x + 1}{2x}$

$\searrow$ needs $2 \cdot x$

LCD $= 2 \cdot x$, or $2x$

$\dfrac{3 \cdot 2 \cdot x}{1 \cdot 2 \cdot x} + \dfrac{-3x + 1}{2 \cdot x}$

$3 \cdot 2 \cdot x = 6x$ ⟶ $\dfrac{6x}{2x} + \dfrac{-3x + 1}{2x}$

$1 \cdot 2 \cdot x = 2x$ ⟶

$\dfrac{a}{b} + \dfrac{c}{b} = \dfrac{a + c}{b}$ ⟶ $\dfrac{6x - 3x + 1}{2x}$

Thus, the result is $\dfrac{3x + 1}{2x}$.

EXAMPLE 4 Simplify $\dfrac{x^2 + 2}{x^2 - 5x + 4} - \dfrac{x - 2}{x - 1}$.

Rewrite as addition.

$\dfrac{x^2 + 2}{x^2 - 5x + 4} + \dfrac{-1(x - 2)}{x - 1}$

$-1(x - 2) = -1x + 2$ ⟶ $\dfrac{x^2 + 2}{x^2 - 5x + 4} + \dfrac{-1x + 2}{x - 1}$

Find the LCD.

$x^2 - 5x + 4 = (x - 4)(x - 1)$
LCD $= (x - 4)(x - 1)$

$\dfrac{x^2 + 2}{(x - 4)(x - 1)} + \dfrac{-1x + 2}{x - 1}$

$\nwarrow$ needs $x - 4$

$\dfrac{-1x \quad + \quad 2}{1x \quad - \quad 4}$

$-1x^2 + 6x - 8$ ⟶

$\dfrac{x^2 + 2}{(x - 4)(x - 1)} + \dfrac{(-1x + 2)(x - 4)}{(x - 1)(x - 4)}$

$\dfrac{x^2 + 2}{(x - 4)(x - 1)} + \dfrac{-1x^2 + 6x - 8}{(x - 1)(x - 4)}$

$\dfrac{a}{b} + \dfrac{c}{b} = \dfrac{a + c}{b}$ ⟶ $\dfrac{x^2 + 2 - 1x^2 + 6x - 8}{(x - 4)(x - 1)}$

Combine like terms. ⟶ $\dfrac{6x - 6}{(x - 4)(x - 1)}$

Factor the numerator:
$6x - 6 = 6(x - 1)$.
Divide out common factors.

$\dfrac{6(x \overset{1}{-} 1)}{(x - 4)(x \underset{1}{-} 1)}$

$\dfrac{6}{x - 4}$

Thus, the result is $\dfrac{6}{x - 4}$.

EXERCISES

Rewrite.

1. $-\dfrac{2}{a+5}$

2. $-\dfrac{2a+5}{a^2-9}$

3. $-\dfrac{x^2-3x}{x^2+5x+1}$

Simplify.

4. $\dfrac{5}{x^2-4}-\dfrac{2}{x-2}$

5. $\dfrac{7}{a^2-7a+10}-\dfrac{3}{a-5}$

6. $\dfrac{4}{b^2+4b+3}-\dfrac{3}{b+3}$

7. $5-\dfrac{3}{2x}$

8. $8-\dfrac{7}{5x}\quad\dfrac{40x-7}{5x}$

9. $4-\dfrac{2a+3}{a-2}$

10. $\dfrac{5}{x-7}-\dfrac{x+3}{x^2-49}$

11. $\dfrac{3}{x-2}-\dfrac{2x-3}{x^2-6x+8}$

12. $\dfrac{2}{b-4}-\dfrac{b+5}{b^2-3b-4}$

13. $\dfrac{5}{3b-1}-\dfrac{4}{2b+7}$

14. $\dfrac{3}{5x-2}-\dfrac{2}{3x+4}$

15. $\dfrac{3}{8y^2}-\dfrac{5}{12y^3}$

PART B

Simplify.

16. $\dfrac{m^2-8}{m^2-8m+12}-\dfrac{m+1}{m-6}$

17. $\dfrac{a^2-22}{a^2-9a+20}-\dfrac{a-2}{a-5}$

18. $\dfrac{m^2-5}{m^2-5m}-\dfrac{m+3}{m}$

19. $\dfrac{5}{a+3}-\dfrac{2a+1}{a+2}$

20. $\dfrac{2a-3}{a^2-4}-\dfrac{a+1}{a-2}$

21. $\dfrac{3a^2}{2a^2-7a-15}-\dfrac{2a-5}{2a+3}$

22. $\dfrac{y+3}{y-6}-\dfrac{y+1}{y^2-4y-12}$

23. $\dfrac{2a+1}{a}-\dfrac{3a+1}{a^2-5a}$

24. $\dfrac{4}{y-4}-\dfrac{2y-1}{y-2}$

PART C

Simplify.

25. $\dfrac{a-2}{a+4}-\dfrac{a-3}{2a-5}$

26. $\dfrac{x-5}{2x-5}-\dfrac{2x+1}{x-7}$

27. $\dfrac{3}{2y^2-5y-12}-\dfrac{y+1}{2y+3}+\dfrac{y-5}{y-4}$

28. $\dfrac{2m^2-5}{4m^3-9m}-\dfrac{3}{2m-3}+\dfrac{2m-1}{2m^2+3m}$

Simplifying Fractions: -1 Technique

OBJECTIVE

■ To simplify fractions like
$$\frac{7}{x^2 - 4x + 4} - \frac{2}{2 - x}$$

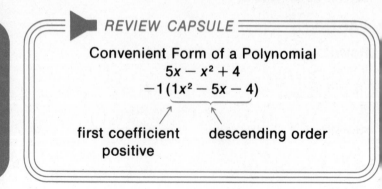

▶ *REVIEW CAPSULE*

Convenient Form of a Polynomial
$$5x - x^2 + 4$$
$$-1(1x^2 - 5x - 4)$$

first coefficient positive   descending order

EXAMPLE 1   Simplify $\dfrac{4x}{x^2 - 4} + \dfrac{2}{2 - x}$.

Get $2 - x$ in convenient form.
Arrange in descending order.

$$\frac{4x}{x^2 - 4} + \frac{2}{-x + 2}$$

Factor out -1.
$2 - x$ is now in convenient form.

$$\frac{4x}{x^2 - 4} + \frac{2}{-1(x - 2)}$$

$$\frac{a}{-1(b)} = \frac{-1(a)}{b}$$

$$\frac{4x}{x^2 - 4} + \frac{-1(2)}{x - 2}$$

$$\frac{4x}{x^2 - 4} + \frac{-2}{x - 2}$$

Find the LCD.
Factor: $x^2 - 4 = (x - 2)(x + 2)$.
LCD $= (x - 2)(x + 2)$

$$\frac{4x}{(x - 2)(x + 2)} + \frac{-2}{x - 2}$$

↖ needs $x + 2$

$$\frac{4x}{(x - 2)(x + 2)} + \frac{-2(x + 2)}{(x - 2)(x + 2)}$$

Use the distributive property.
$-2(x + 2) = -2x - 4$

$$\frac{4x}{(x - 2)(x + 2)} + \frac{-2x - 4}{(x - 2)(x + 2)}$$

$$\frac{a}{b} + \frac{c}{b} = \frac{a + c}{b}$$

$$\frac{4x - 2x - 4}{(x - 2)(x + 2)}$$

Combine like terms.

$$\frac{2x - 4}{(x - 2)(x + 2)}$$

Factor: $2x - 4 = 2(x - 2)$.
Divide out common factors.

$$\frac{2\overset{1}{\cancel{(x - 2)}}}{\underset{1}{\cancel{(x - 2)}}(x + 2)}$$

The result is in simplest form.

$$\frac{2}{x + 2}$$

EXAMPLE 2 Simplify $\dfrac{-6}{x^2 - 7x + 12} - \dfrac{x+2}{4-x}$.

Rewrite as addition:

$-\dfrac{x+2}{4-x} = \dfrac{-1(x+2)}{4-x}$

$$\dfrac{-6}{x^2-7x+12} + \dfrac{-1(x+2)}{4-x}$$

$4 - x = -x + 4 = -1(x-4) \longrightarrow$

$\dfrac{\overset{1}{\cancel{-1}}(x+2)}{\underset{1}{\cancel{-1}}(x-4)} = \dfrac{x+2}{x-4} \longrightarrow$

$$\dfrac{-6}{x^2-7x+12} + \dfrac{-1(x+2)}{-1(x-4)}$$

$$\dfrac{-6}{x^2-7x+12} + \dfrac{x+2}{x-4}$$

LCD $= (x-3)(x-4)$

$$\dfrac{-6}{(x-3)(x-4)} + \dfrac{x+2}{x-4}_{\nwarrow}$$

$\quad\quad\quad\quad\quad\quad\quad$ needs $(x-3)$

$\dfrac{x \quad + \quad 2}{x \quad - \quad 3}$

$\overline{x^2 - x - 6} \longrightarrow$

$$\dfrac{-6}{(x-3)(x-4)} + \dfrac{(x+2)(x-3)}{(x-4)(x-3)}$$

Combine numerators. $\Big\}$
Write in descending order.

$$\dfrac{-6}{(x-3)(x-4)} + \dfrac{x^2-x-6}{(x-4)(x-3)}$$

$$\dfrac{x^2 - x - 12}{(x-3)(x-4)}$$

Factor: $x^2 - x - 12 = (x-4)(x+3)$
Divide out common factors.

$$\dfrac{\overset{1}{\cancel{(x-4)}}(x+3)}{(x-3)\underset{1}{\cancel{(x-4)}}}$$

$$\dfrac{x+3}{x-3}$$

EXAMPLE 3 Simplify $\dfrac{3}{m-1} + \dfrac{3m+2}{m-m^2} + \dfrac{3}{m}$.

Get $m - m^2$ in convenient form. $\Big\}$
$m - m^2 = -m^2 + m = -1(m^2 - m)$

$$\dfrac{3}{m-1} + \dfrac{3m+2}{-1(m^2-m)} + \dfrac{3}{m}$$

$\dfrac{3m+2}{-1(m^2-m)} = \dfrac{-1(3m+2)}{m^2-m} \longrightarrow$

$$\dfrac{3}{m-1} + \dfrac{-3m-2}{m^2-m} + \dfrac{3}{m}$$

Factor: $m^2 - m = m(m-1) \longrightarrow$

$$\dfrac{3}{m-1} + \dfrac{-3m-2}{m(m-1)} + \dfrac{3}{m}$$

LCD $= m(m-1) \longrightarrow$
$3(m-1) = 3m - 3 \longrightarrow$

$$\dfrac{3 \cdot m}{(m-1)\cdot m} + \dfrac{-3m-2}{m(m-1)} + \dfrac{3(m-1)}{m(m-1)}$$

$$\dfrac{3m}{(m-1)m} + \dfrac{-3m-2}{m(m-1)} + \dfrac{3m-3}{m(m-1)}$$

$\dfrac{a}{b} + \dfrac{c}{b} = \dfrac{a+c}{b} \longrightarrow$

$$\dfrac{3m - 3m - 2 + 3m - 3}{m(m-1)}$$

The result is in simplest form. $\longrightarrow$

$$\dfrac{3m - 5}{m(m-1)}$$

EXERCISES

PART A

Simplify.

1. $\dfrac{7}{x^2 - 49} + \dfrac{3}{7 - x}$

2. $\dfrac{6}{5a - 10} + \dfrac{2}{2 - a}$

3. $\dfrac{7b - 9}{b^2 - 3b + 2} + \dfrac{5}{2 - b}$

4. $\dfrac{3a + 6}{4a - 8} + \dfrac{3}{2 - a}$

5. $\dfrac{3b - 1}{b^2 - b - 2} + \dfrac{4}{2 - b}$

6. $\dfrac{3a - 5}{7a - 21} + \dfrac{2a - 5}{3 - a}$

7. $\dfrac{7y}{y^2 - 7y + 10} - \dfrac{3}{5 - y}$

8. $\dfrac{-15}{x^2 - 9x + 14} - \dfrac{3}{7 - x}$

9. $\dfrac{-7a}{a^2 - 3a - 10} - \dfrac{a}{5 - a}$

10. $\dfrac{-2a}{a^2 - 12a + 35} - \dfrac{a}{7 - a}$

11. $\dfrac{5}{m - 2} + \dfrac{2m - 1}{4 - m^2} + \dfrac{7}{m + 2}$

12. $\dfrac{5}{a - 4} + \dfrac{2a - 1}{4a - a^2} + \dfrac{7}{a}$

13. $\dfrac{k + 2}{k^2 - 8k + 12} + \dfrac{k}{6 - k}$

14. $\dfrac{2}{a + 2} - \dfrac{3}{8 - a} + \dfrac{2a}{a^2 - 6a - 16}$

15. $\dfrac{-2m}{m^2 - 12m + 35} - \dfrac{m}{7 - m}$

16. $\dfrac{x^2 + 3x + 15}{x^2 + 5x - 24} + \dfrac{-2}{3 - x} + \dfrac{5}{x + 8}$

PART B

Simplify.

17. $\dfrac{2m}{m^2 - 7m + 10} + \dfrac{2m - 1}{5 - m}$

18. $\dfrac{3a + 1}{a^2 - 25} - \dfrac{2a + 1}{5 - a}$

19. $\dfrac{2n - 1}{n + 3} - \dfrac{4n^2}{9 - n^2} + \dfrac{2}{n - 3}$

20. $\dfrac{2m + 1}{4 - m} - \dfrac{3m^2}{m^2 - 16} + \dfrac{7}{m + 4}$

PART C

Simplify.

21. $\dfrac{7}{a^2 - b^2} - \dfrac{2}{b - a} + \dfrac{a + 3b}{a + b}$

22. $\dfrac{7}{a^2 - 2ab} - \dfrac{3a - 2b}{4b^2 - a^2}$

23. $\dfrac{b - c}{b + c} - \dfrac{3bc}{c^2 - b^2}$

24. $\dfrac{4b}{b + 1} - \dfrac{2 + b}{1 - b} - \dfrac{4}{1 - b^2}$

Fields

Three-Minute Clock Addition

$\oplus$	0	1	2
0	0	1	2
1	1	2	0
2	2	0	1

Three-Minute Clock Multiplication

$\otimes$	0	1	2
0	0	0	0
1	0	1	2
2	0	2	1

- Commutative Group Under $\oplus$
  Closed — Yes
  Associative — Yes
  Identity — 0
  Inverses — for 0 is 0
             1 is 2
             2 is 1

- Commutative Group Under $\otimes$
  (0 is removed)
  Closure — yes
  Associative — Yes
  Identity — 1
  Inverses:

Number		Inverse	
1	$\otimes$	1	$= 1$
2	$\otimes$	2	$= 1$

- Distributive

$$2 \otimes (2 \oplus 0) \overset{?}{=} (2 \otimes 2) \oplus (2 \otimes 0)$$

$$2 \otimes 2 \overset{?}{=} 1 \oplus 0$$

$$1 = 1$$

└─── same ───┘

We can show that the commutative, associative and distributive properties hold.

So, three-minute clock arithmetic forms a **field.**

> A set with two operations
> $\oplus$ and $\otimes$ forms a FIELD if
> • the set is a commutative group under $\oplus$
> • the set is a commutative group under $\otimes$ (0 removed)
> • $\otimes$ is distributive over $\oplus$

Does seven-minute clock arithmetic form a field?

Chapter Eight Review

Add. [*p. 203, 210, 214, 218*]

1. $\dfrac{m}{m^2 - 10m + 16} + \dfrac{-8}{m^2 - 10m + 16}$

2. $\dfrac{x}{x^2 - 36} + \dfrac{-6}{x^2 - 36}$

3. $\dfrac{5b}{2} + \dfrac{7b}{4}$

4. $\dfrac{7m}{9} + \dfrac{5m}{3} + \dfrac{4m}{27}$

5. $\dfrac{5}{a + 1} + \dfrac{3}{a^2 - 7a - 8}$

6. $\dfrac{7b - 5}{b + 3} + \dfrac{2}{3b + 9}$

7. $\dfrac{4}{y^2 - 5y} + \dfrac{3}{y - 5}$

8. $\dfrac{2a + 1}{a^2 - 7a + 12} + \dfrac{a + 1}{a - 3}$

9. $\dfrac{4}{a} + 3$

10. $\dfrac{7}{5b} + \dfrac{3}{2b}$

11. $\dfrac{3}{m + 4} + 2$

12. $9 + \dfrac{2}{b + 5}$

13. $\dfrac{2}{3a^2} + \dfrac{5}{2a} + \dfrac{3}{4a^3}$

14. $\dfrac{3}{a} + \dfrac{5}{a^3} + \dfrac{7}{a^2}$

15. $\dfrac{3}{4x} + \dfrac{6 - x}{6x^3} + \dfrac{3 + 2x}{3x^2}$

16. $\dfrac{3x + 2}{10x^3} + \dfrac{x - 3}{2x} + \dfrac{4 - x}{5x^2}$

Simplify. [*p. 221, 224*]

17. $\dfrac{2m - 1}{2m^2 + 9m - 18} - \dfrac{5}{2m - 3}$

18. $\dfrac{5}{x^2 - 9} - \dfrac{5}{x - 3}$

19. $\dfrac{3n - 1}{n^2 - 6n - 7} + \dfrac{2}{7 - n}$

20. $\dfrac{5}{x^2 - 36} - \dfrac{2}{x - 6} + \dfrac{3}{x + 6}$

21. $\dfrac{5}{x^2 - 9x} - \dfrac{7}{9 - x} + \dfrac{5}{x}$

22. $\dfrac{7}{x^2 - 9} + \dfrac{4}{3 - x}$

23. $\dfrac{7}{b^2 - 7b + 10} - \dfrac{3}{b - 5}$

24. $\dfrac{2a}{2a^2 - 13a - 24} - \dfrac{3}{8 - a}$

25. $\dfrac{6}{b + 3} - \dfrac{b + 2}{b - 1}$

26. $\dfrac{2}{a - 5} + \dfrac{7}{3 - a} - \dfrac{4}{a^2 - 8a + 15}$

27. $\dfrac{3}{a^2 - 25} - \dfrac{a}{25 - a^2} + \dfrac{4}{a + 5}$

28. $\dfrac{2x - 1}{x^2 - 7x + 10} + \dfrac{5}{5 - x} - \dfrac{2}{x - 2}$

Chapter Eight Test

Add.

1. $\dfrac{a}{a^2 - 8a - 20} + \dfrac{2}{a^2 - 8a - 20}$

2. $\dfrac{b}{b^2 - 49} + \dfrac{7}{b^2 - 49}$

3. $\dfrac{a^2}{a + 2} + \dfrac{3a}{a + 2} + \dfrac{2}{a + 2}$

4. $\dfrac{5k}{4} + \dfrac{7k}{2}$

5. $\dfrac{7a}{6} + \dfrac{3a}{2} + \dfrac{5a}{3}$

6. $\dfrac{2n - 1}{12n} + \dfrac{3n + 2}{4n} + \dfrac{2n - 5}{3n}$

7. $\dfrac{4}{y^2 + 3y} + \dfrac{2}{y + 3}$

8. $\dfrac{7b - 3}{b^2 - 3b - 10} + \dfrac{4}{b + 2}$

9. $\dfrac{2}{a + 6} + \dfrac{3a + 4}{a^2 + 3a - 18} + \dfrac{7}{a - 3}$

10. $\dfrac{x + 4}{x^2 - 7x + 10} + \dfrac{x + 1}{x - 5}$

11. $\dfrac{3}{a + 7} + 2$

12. $a + 5 + \dfrac{3}{a - 2}$

13. $\dfrac{6}{5x^2} + \dfrac{2}{15x^3} + \dfrac{5}{3x}$

14. $\dfrac{2m + 1}{3m^2} + \dfrac{m - 3}{4m} + \dfrac{2 - m}{6m^3}$

Simplify.

15. $\dfrac{x + 2}{x^2 - 7x + 12} - \dfrac{4}{x - 4}$

16. $\dfrac{5}{a + 1} - \dfrac{7}{a + 2}$

17. $\dfrac{x + 1}{x + 5} + \dfrac{7}{x^2 - 25} - \dfrac{2}{x - 5}$

18. $\dfrac{2n - 1}{n^2 - 7n - 8} + \dfrac{3}{8 - n}$

19. $\dfrac{4}{x^2 - 36} + \dfrac{5}{6 - x}$

20. $\dfrac{3b - 5}{b^2 + 2b - 35} - \dfrac{3}{5 - b} + \dfrac{4}{b + 7}$

The Great Swami

A	B	C	D	E	F
1	2	3	6	9	18
4	5	4	7	10	19
7	8	5	8	11	20
10	11	12	15	12	21
13	14	13	16	13	22
16	17	14	17	14	23
19	20	21	24	15	24
22	23	22	25	16	25
25	26	23	26	17	26

Have a friend tell the letter of each column that contains his age. The sum of the first numbers in each column will give his age. For example, if he answers column B, C, and E, then his age is 2 + 3 + 9, or 14.

Absolute Value

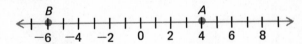

REVIEW CAPSULE

Points A and B are graphed on a number line.

Point A is 4 units from the origin.
Point B is 6 units from the origin.

EXAMPLE 1   Find the distance between city A and city D.

A —— 80 mi —— B —— 100 mi —— C —— 150 mi —— D

$$80 + 100 + 150 = 330$$
Thus, the distance from A to D is 330 miles, and the distance from D to A is 330 miles.

EXAMPLE 2   Find the points on a number line whose distance is 4 units from the origin.

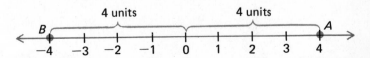

Absolute values can be found by measuring distances on a number line.

We say that $\left.\begin{array}{l}\text{the absolute value of 4}\\\text{the absolute value of } -4\end{array}\right\}$ is 4.

An absolute value is associated with each number.

Number ————————————→   3   −3   5   −5   0

Absolute value ———————→   3   5   0

EXAMPLE 3   Find the absolute value of 13 and of −13.

Say. ──────────────────────────→   The absolute value │ The absolute value
                                       of 13 is 13.   │   of −13 is 13.
Write. ─────────────────────────→ $|13| = 13$ │ $|-13| = 13$

Definition of absolute value ──────→
  $13 > 0$ $|13| = 13$
  $-13 < 0$ $|-13| = -(-13)$ or 13 }

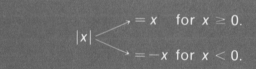

$$|x| \begin{cases} = x & \text{for } x \geq 0. \\ = -x & \text{for } x < 0. \end{cases}$$

EXAMPLE 4   Find $|7|$.   │ Find $|0|$.   │ Find $|-3|$.

                  $|7| = 7$ │ $|0| = 0$ │ $|-3| = 3$

EXAMPLE 5   Find $|-8 + 4|$.   Find $|-7 + 9|$.

Simplify the expression inside the $|-8 + 4| = |-4|$ │ $|-7 + 9| = |2|$
absolute value symbol first. $= 4$ │ $= 2$

EXAMPLE 6   Find $|3x - 2|$ if $x = -4$.

Substitute −4 for x. ───────────→ $|3(-4) - 2|$
$3(-4) = -12$ ─────────────────→ $|-12 - 2|$
                                        $|-14|$
                                        14

EXAMPLE 7   Solve $|a| = 6$.

                  We must find numbers with absolute value 6.
                                $|a| = 6$

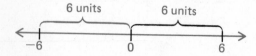

6 units   6 units

−6   0   6

Both −6 and 6 are 6 units from the origin.
                        $a = -6$ or $a = 6$
                  Thus, the solutions are 6 and −6.

ORAL EXERCISES

Give the absolute value.

1. $|6|$ 2. $|-5|$ 3. $|-19|$ 4. $|9|$
5. $|-8 + 2|$ 6. $|4 - 3|$ 7. $|7 - 9|$ 8. $|3 - 4 - 1|$

EXERCISES

PART A

Find each.

1. $|x - 5|$ if $x = 2$ **2.** $|a - 7|$ if $a = -4$ **3.** $|m - 5|$ if $m = -1$
4. $|4 - 3a|$ if $a = -2$ **5.** $|2 - m|$ if $m = 3$ **6.** $|5 - 4m|$ if $m = 3$
7. $|4x - 2|$ if $x = 5$ **8.** $|6k - 3|$ if $k = -2$ **9.** $|3y - 6|$ if $y = 1$
10. $|5a - 3|$ if $a = -7$ **11.** $|6 - 4b|$ if $b = -3$ **12.** $|5 - 3t|$ if $t = -3$

Solve.

13. $|a| = 4$ **14.** $|m| = 1$ **15.** $|p| = 2$ **16.** $|r| = 3$

PART B

Find each.

17. $\left|\dfrac{3a}{2} - \dfrac{3}{5}\right|$ if $a = -2$ **18.** $\left|\dfrac{2m - 1}{3} + \dfrac{m}{2}\right|$ if $m = -3$

19. $\left|\dfrac{5}{a^2 - 4} + \dfrac{3}{a - 2}\right|$ if $a = -1$ **20.** $\left|\dfrac{1}{2} - \dfrac{3x}{x^2 - 3x + 1}\right|$ if $x = 0$

PART C

EXAMPLE   Graph the solution set of $|x| < 3$ on a number line.

The solution set contains all numbers which are less than 3 units from the origin.

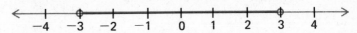

−3 and 3 are not solutions. The solutions are the numbers between −3 and 3. ⟶   The solution set is $\{x \,|\, -3 < x < 3\}$.

EXAMPLE   Graph the solution set of $|x| > 3$.

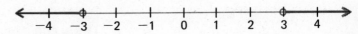

Numbers which are more than 3 units from the origin are solutions. ⟶   The solution set is $\{x \,|\, x < -3 \text{ or } x > 3\}$.

Find and graph the solution set.

21. $|x| < 2$ **22.** $|x| \leq 4$ **23.** $|x| < 1$
24. $|x| > 0$ **25.** $|x| \geq 2$ **26.** $|x| > 5$

Equations with Absolute Value

OBJECTIVE
- To solve equations like $|3x - 2| = 4$

▶ *REVIEW CAPSULE*

Solve $|x| = 4$.

$x = -4$ or $x = 4$

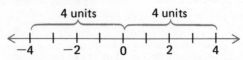

Both -4 and 4 are 4 units from origin.
Thus, -4 and 4 are the solutions.

EXAMPLE 1   Solve $|3x - 3| = 6$.

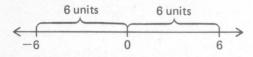

$|6| = 6$ or $|-6| = 6$

Think of $3x - 3$ as some number a.

$$|3x - 3| = 6$$
$$\downarrow$$
$$|a| = 6$$

$$a = -6 \text{ or } a = 6$$

So, $3x - 3 = -6 \qquad 3x - 3 = 6$

Add 3 to each side. $3x = -3 \qquad\qquad 3x = 9$
Divide each side by 3. $x = -1 \qquad\qquad x = 3$

Check. ⟶

Let $x = -1$

$$\frac{|3x - 3|}{|3(-1) - 3|} \bigg|\, \frac{6}{6}$$
$$|-3 - 3|$$
$$|-6|$$
$$6$$

Let $x = 3$

$$\frac{|3x - 3|}{|3(3) - 3|} \bigg|\, \frac{6}{6}$$
$$|9 - 3|$$
$$|6|$$
$$6$$

Thus, the solutions are -1 and 3.

EXAMPLE 2   Solve $|x + 2| = 7$.

$x + 2 = -7$ or $x + 2 = 7$
$x = -9 \qquad\qquad x = 5$

Thus, the solutions are -9 and 5.

EXAMPLE 3   Find the solution set of $|2 - 3x| = 10$.

$$|2 - 3x| = 10$$

$$2 - 3x = -10 \quad \text{or} \quad 2 - 3x = 10$$

Add -2 to each side. $\longrightarrow$

$$\begin{array}{cc} -2 \qquad -2 & -2 \qquad -2 \\ \hline -3x = -12 & -3x = 8 \end{array}$$

Divide each side by -3. $\longrightarrow$

$$x = 4 \qquad\qquad x = -\dfrac{8}{3}$$

Thus, the solution set is $\{-\frac{8}{3}, 4\}$.

EXERCISES

PART A

Solve and check.

1. $|x - 3| = 4$
2. $|4 - x| = 7$
3. $|2m - 2| = 4$
4. $|2x - 5| = 7$
5. $|2m + 1| = 5$
6. $|3x| = 12$
7. $|7 - b| = 6$
8. $|4 - b| = 2$
9. $|5 + m| = 4$

Find the solution set.

10. $|2x - 6| = 4$
11. $|4 - 3x| = 7$
12. $|a + 4| = 7$
13. $|3 - 7k| = 5$
14. $|3x - 5| = 7$
15. $|5 - p| = 19$
16. $|3 - 2r| = 6$
17. $|5 + y| = 20$
18. $|3a - 4| = 2$
19. $|4 + 3b| = 3$
20. $|7 - 5k| = 5$
21. $|5 - 3b| = 4$
22. $|2m - 14| = 1$
23. $|7y - 13| = 2$
24. $|2b - 7| = 5$

PART B

EXAMPLE   Solve $3|x - 5| + 4 = 7$.

$$3|x - 5| + 4 = 7$$

Add -4 to each side. $\longrightarrow$

$$\begin{array}{c} -4 \quad -4 \\ \hline 3|x - 5| = 3 \end{array}$$

Divide each side by 3.

$$|x - 5| = 1$$

$$x - 5 = -1 \quad \text{or} \quad x - 5 = 1$$

Add 5 to each side.

$$x = 4 \qquad\qquad x = 6$$

Thus, the solutions are 4 and 6.

Solve.

25. $2|a - 3| + 7 = 13$
26. $3|2x - 7| - 4 = 17$
27. $4 + 3|2x - 5| = 19$
28. $8 - 4|3 - 2a| = -32$

Directed Distance on a Number Line

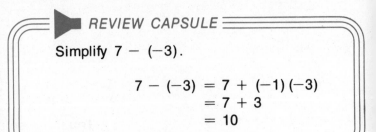

▶ *REVIEW CAPSULE*

Simplify $7 - (-3)$.

$$7 - (-3) = 7 + (-1)(-3)$$
$$= 7 + 3$$
$$= 10$$

No direction is indicated. ─────────→

$$\underbrace{50 \text{ miles}}_{\uparrow \atop \text{distance}}$$

Distance and direction
↓   ↓
50 mi   right

$$\underbrace{50 \text{ miles to the right}}_{\uparrow \atop \text{directed distance}}$$

EXAMPLE 1 Find the directed distance *from A to B*.

The coordinate of A is 6.⎫
The coordinate of B is 8.⎭

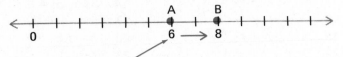

Start at *A*. Move 2 units to the *right* to *B*.

$\vec{d}(AB)$ means directed distance *from A to B.* ─────────→ **Thus, $\vec{d}(AB) = +2$.**

Example 1 suggests this. ─────────→ A directed distance to the right is positive.

EXAMPLE 2 Find $\vec{d}(QP)$.

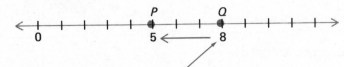

Start at *Q*. Move 3 units to the *left* to *P*.

$\vec{d}(QP)$ means directed distance *from Q to P.* ─────────→

left   distance
↘ −3 ↙

Thus, $\vec{d}(QP) = -3$.

Example 2 suggests this. ─────────→ A directed distance to the left is negative.

We now look for a formula to find directed distances.

EXAMPLE 3 Find $\vec{d}(RS)$.

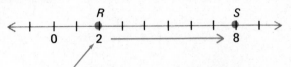

Start at R. Move 6 units to the *right* to S.

Directed distance to the right is positive. ————————————→ **Thus, $\vec{d}(RS) = +6$.**

Notice that
$$\vec{d}(RS) = \text{coordinate of } S - \text{coordinate of } R$$
$$\qquad\qquad\qquad 8 \qquad\qquad - \qquad\qquad 2$$

$8 - 2 = 6$

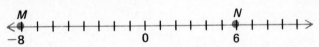

Directed distance from P to Q

$\vec{d}(PQ) = \text{coordinate of } Q - \text{coordinate of } P$

Example 3 suggests this. ————————→

EXAMPLE 4 Find $\vec{d}(MN)$ and $\vec{d}(NM)$.

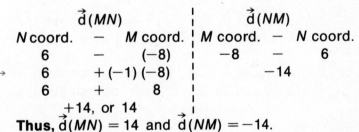

$\vec{d}(MN)$			$\vec{d}(NM)$		
N coord.	$-$	M coord.	M coord.	$-$	N coord.
6	$-$	(-8)	-8	$-$	6
6	$+(-1)(-8)$			-14	
6	$+$	8			
	$+14$, or 14				

$a - b$ means $a + (-1)(b)$. ————————→
$\vec{d}(MN)$ is to the right.
$\vec{d}(NM)$ is to the left.

Thus, $\vec{d}(MN) = 14$ and $\vec{d}(NM) = -14$.

$+14 = -(-14)$ ————————————→ Observe that $\vec{d}(MN) = -\vec{d}(NM)$.

EXAMPLE 5 Find $\vec{d}(PQ)$.

coordinate of P: -3
coordinate of Q: -5

$$\begin{aligned}
\vec{d}(PQ) &= Q \text{ coord.} \quad - \quad P \text{ coord.}\\
&= \quad -5 \qquad - \qquad (-3)\\
&= \quad -5 \qquad + (-1)(-3)\\
&= \quad -5 \qquad +3\\
&= \quad -2
\end{aligned}$$

$a - b$ means $a + (-1)(b)$. ————————→

ORAL EXERCISES

Tell whether the directed distance is positive or negative.

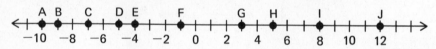

1. $\vec{d}(CE)$
2. $\vec{d}(BA)$
3. $\vec{d}(JB)$
4. $\vec{d}(FE)$
5. $\vec{d}(FC)$
6. $\vec{d}(AD)$
7. $\vec{d}(IG)$
8. $\vec{d}(HF)$
9. $\vec{d}(AE)$
10. $\vec{d}(FJ)$
11. $\vec{d}(DB)$
12. $\vec{d}(EJ)$

Use the number line above to find each directed distance.

13. $\vec{d}(CE)$
14. $\vec{d}(BA)$
15. $\vec{d}(JB)$
16. $\vec{d}(FE)$
17. $\vec{d}(FC)$
18. $\vec{d}(AD)$
19. $\vec{d}(IG)$
20. $\vec{d}(HF)$

EXERCISES

PART A

Find $\vec{d}(PQ)$.

1. coordinate of P: 4
   coordinate of Q: 8

2. coordinate of P: -8
   coordinate of Q: -4

3. coordinate of P: -6
   coordinate of Q: 4

4. coordinate of P: -8
   coordinate of Q: 10

5. coordinate of P: -2
   coordinate of Q: 4

6. coordinate of P: 7
   coordinate of Q: 18

7. coordinate of P: -16
   coordinate of Q: 2

8. coordinate of P: -8
   coordinate of Q: -3

9. coordinate of P: -18
   coordinate of Q: -14

PART B

Find $\vec{d}(AB)$.

10. coordinate of A: $-3\frac{1}{2}$

    coordinate of B: $4\frac{1}{4}$

11. coordinate of A: $-\frac{1}{3}$

    coordinate of B: $\frac{1}{2}$

12. coordinate of A: $-\frac{2}{3}$

    coordinate of B: $\frac{5}{9}$

PART C

Find each. Use the number line at the top of the page.

13. $\vec{d}(AB) + \vec{d}(BC)$

14. $\vec{d}(BD) + \vec{d}(DC)$

15. $\vec{d}(GF) + \vec{d}(GH)$

Fun for Philatelists

$$1 + 1 = 2$$

The two stamps illustrated are from a group of ten stamps issued by Nicaragua in 1971.

By counting on his fingers an ancient man worked out the elementary equation, $1 + 1 = 2$. This equation brought an end to inexact tallying. It is the basis of our system of counting.

$$A^2 + B^2 = C^2$$

This geometric theorem, named after Pythagoras, compares the squares of the lengths of sides of a right triangle.

The series gives the ten equations that changed the face of the earth. Each represents a major turning point in mathematics or science. On the back of each stamp is a brief history of the equation.

Reprinted by permission of Oficina de Control de Especies, Postales y Filatella, Managua, Nicaragua.

Locating Points in a Plane

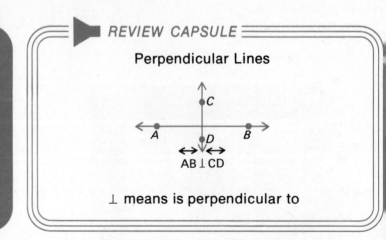

REVIEW CAPSULE

Perpendicular Lines

AB ⊥ CD

⊥ means is perpendicular to

A plane is a flat surface.

Points are located in a plane by using two perpendicular number lines.

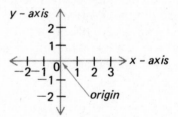

EXAMPLE 1 Describe the location of point P.

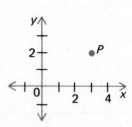

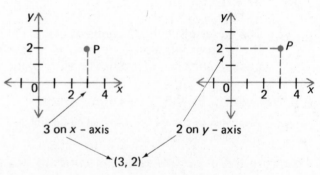

3 on x – axis

2 on y – axis

(3, 2)

The position of P is described by an ordered pair.

x-coordinate   y-coordinate

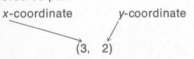

(3,   2)

The x-coordinate is always first.

EXAMPLE 2   Give the ordered pair for *P*, *Q*, *R*, and *S*.

For *P*: Read 4 on *x*-axis. }
       Read 2 on *y*-axis. }

For *Q*: Read −3 on *x*-axis. }
       Read −2 on *y*-axis. }

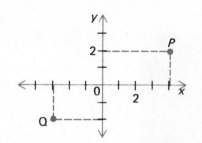

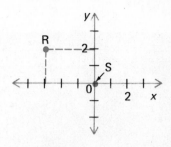

Point *S* is the origin. The coordinates are (0, 0).

    P(4, 2)   *Q*(−3, −2)   *R*(−3, 2)   *S*(0, 0)

EXERCISES

PART A

Give the ordered pair for each point.

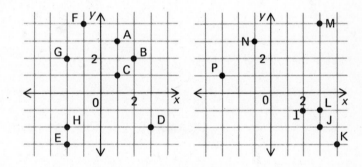

1. *A*
2. *B*
3. *C*
4. *D*
5. *E*
6. *F*
7. *G*
8. *H*
9. *I*
10. *J*
11. *K*
12. *L*
13. *M*
14. *N*
15. *P*

PART B

The axes divide the plane into four quadrants.

Each point except the origin is located in one of the quadrants or on one of the axes. The origin is on both axes.

Second Quadrant	*y*	First Quadrant
Third Quadrant		Fourth Quadrant

Give the quadrant in which each point lies.

16. (−1, −5)
17. (6, 10)
18. (2, −8)
19. (−7, −3)
20. (1, −8)
21. (−6, 5)
22. Describe the coordinates of all points in the second quadrant.

Plotting Points in a Plane

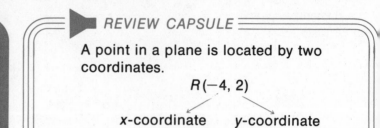

▶ *REVIEW CAPSULE*

A point in a plane is located by two coordinates.

R(−4, 2)

x-coordinate   *y*-coordinate

EXAMPLE 1   Plot the point (2, 3).

Draw and mark axes on graph paper.

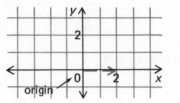 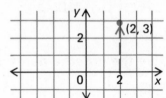

Start at the origin. ————————————→

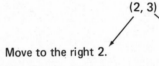

(2, 3)

Move to the right 2.   Then move up 3.

EXAMPLE 2   Plot the point (−4, 2).

Start at the origin.

(−4, 2)

Move left 4.   Move up 2.

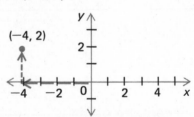

Examples 1 and 2 show that the signs of the coordinates tell in which directions to move from the origin.

(x   y)

right or left   up or down

+   −   +   −

(2, 3)	(−4, 2)	(−1, −3)	(4, −3)
(+, +)	(−, +)	(−, −)	(+, −)
↓ ↓	↓ ↓	↓ ↓	↓ ↓
right up	left up	left down	right down

EXAMPLE 3

Plot the points.
$A(-2,-1)$, $B(-1,3)$, $C(3,-3)$, $D(-2,-4)$

Draw and mark axes on graph paper.

left 2   down 1

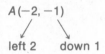

left 1   up 3

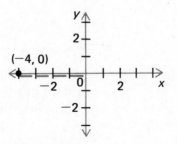

EXAMPLE 4

Plot $(-4, 0)$.   Plot $(0, -2)$.

Begin at the origin.   Begin at the origin.
$(-4,\quad 0)$ $(0,\qquad -2)$

left 4   neither up   neither right   down 2
          nor down   nor left

$(-4, 0)$ lies on the x-axis.
$(0, -2)$ lies on the y-axis.

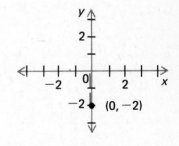

Any point on the   Any point on the
x-axis has y-axis has
y-coordinate 0. x-coordinate 0.

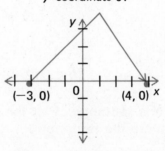   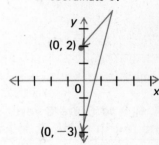

ORAL EXERCISES

Tell in which directions to move in order to plot each point.

1. $A(3, 4)$ **2.** $B(2, -5)$ **3.** $C(-3, 7)$ **4.** $D(-2, -5)$ **5.** $E(-8, 2)$
6. $M(0, 2)$ **7.** $N(4, 0)$ **8.** $P(-5, 0)$ **9.** $Q(0, -4)$ **10.** $R(-1, -3)$
11. $I(4, -3)$ **12.** $G(-7, 0)$ **13.** $K(0, -14)$ **14.** $R(-1, -5)$ **15.** $A(4, -5)$

EXERCISES

PART A

Plot each point.

1. $A(2, 3)$ **2.** $B(-4, 1)$ **3.** $C(-3, -1)$ **4.** $D(2, -3)$ **5.** $E(3, 0)$
6. $F(0, 6)$ **7.** $G(-3, 0)$ **8.** $H(0, -4)$ **9.** $I(-3, -1)$ **10.** $J(-5, 2)$
11. $K(4, -1)$ **12.** $L(-5, 1)$ **13.** $M(0, 3)$ **14.** $N(6, 0)$ **15.** $P(-8, 0)$
16. $Q(0, 0)$ **17.** $R(0, -7)$ **18.** $S(8, 0)$ **19.** $T(-1\frac{1}{2}, 2\frac{1}{2})$ **20.** $U(4\frac{1}{2}, -5\frac{1}{2})$

PART B

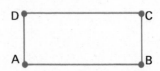

Points A, B, C, and D are the vertices of the rectangle.

EXAMPLE A, B, and C are 3 vertices of a rectangle. Plot the points. Find the coordinates of the fourth point, D, to complete the rectangle.

$$A(2, 1), B(6, 1), C(6, 4)$$

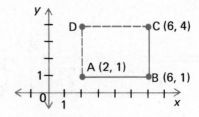

D has the same x-coord. as A and the same y-coord. as C. ⟶ **Thus, $D(2, 4)$ is the fourth point.**

A, B, and C are 3 vertices of a rectangle. Plot the points. Find the coordinates of the fourth point, D, to complete the rectangle.

21. $A(2, 3), B(7, 3), C(7, 5)$ **22.** $A(-4, 2), B(7, 2), C(7, 8)$

Equivalence Relations

Jane ℛ Jane
Jane "is as tall as" Jane

Jane ℛ Joe
and
Joe ℛ Jane
Jane "is as tall as" Joe
and
Joe "is as tall as" Jane.

If Jane ℛ Joe and Joe ℛ Fred then Jane ℛ Fred.
If Jane "is as tall as" Joe and Joe "is as tall as" Fred then Jane "is as tall as" Fred.

ℛ is a relation
(above ℛ is "as tall as")
a relation compares elements of a set
(above the elements are "people in a class")

EQUIVALENCE RELATION
A relation which is
- Reflexive: a ℛ a
- Symmetric: If a ℛ b, then b ℛ a
- Transitive: If a ℛ b and b ℛ c, then a ℛ c

"is as tall as" is an equivalence relation.

Which of the following are equivalence relations?

1. ℛ : "is shorter than"
2. ℛ : "is a friend of"
3. ℛ : "lives on the same block as"
4. ℛ : "is a brother of"

Lines Parallel to the Axes

▶ REVIEW CAPSULE

Give the coordinates of points A, B, and C.

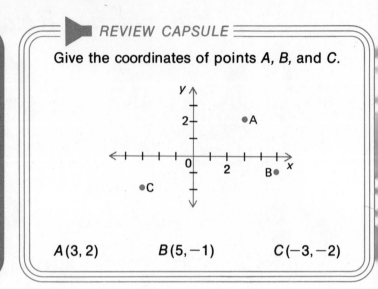

$A(3, 2)$ $B(5, -1)$ $C(-3, -2)$

EXAMPLE 1

The line containing A, B, and C is horizontal. The line containing D, E, and F is vertical. Give the coordinates for each point A, B, C, D, E, F.

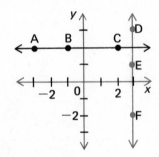

$A(-3, 2)$, $B(-1, 2)$, $C(2, 2)$

same y-coordinate

$D(3, 3)$, $E(3, 1)$, $F(3, -2)$

same x-coordinate

Example 1 suggests this. ----------→

Every point on a horizontal line has the same y-coordinate.

Every point on a vertical line has the same x-coordinate.

EXAMPLE 2 Determine to which axis the line joining $M(-3, 5)$ and $N(7, 5)$ is parallel.

$$M(-3, 5) \qquad N(7, 5)$$

same y-coordinate

$\overleftrightarrow{MN}$ is a horizontal line.

Thus, $\overleftrightarrow{MN}$ is parallel to the x-axis.

EXAMPLE 3 Determine to which axis the line joining $R(2, -5)$ and $S(2, 3)$ is parallel.

$$R(2, -5) \qquad S(2, 3)$$

same x-coordinate

$\overleftrightarrow{RS}$ is a vertical line.

Thus, $\overleftrightarrow{RS}$ is parallel to the y-axis.

ORAL EXERCISES

Determine, without sketching, to which axis the line joining M and N is parallel.

1. $M(2, 7)$, $N(-5, 7)$ **2.** $M(1, 4)$, $N(1, -3)$ **3.** $M(2, -6)$, $N(3, -6)$
4. $M(-1, 5)$, $N(-1, 3)$ **5.** $M(6, -4)$, $N(-2, -4)$ **6.** $M(-2, -2)$, $N(-2, 6)$

EXERCISES

PART A

Determine, without sketching, to which axis the line joining M and N is parallel. Then sketch to check.

1. $M(3, 7)$, $N(-2, 7)$ **2.** $M(-2, 4)$, $N(-2, -1)$ **3.** $M(3, -5)$, $N(4, -5)$
4. $M(-2, 4)$, $N(-2, -4)$ **5.** $M(-3, 3)$, $N(-3, 2)$ **6.** $M(-5, -3)$, $N(-1, -3)$
7. $M(-6, -2)$, $N(6, -2)$ **8.** $M(5, 1)$, $N(5, -8)$ **9.** $M(-7, 3)$, $N(-7, -3)$

PART B

For what value of b will the line joining P and Q be parallel to the indicated axis?

10. $P(-4, 3)$, $Q(b, 1)$; y-axis   **11.** $P(-5, 2)$, $Q(7, b)$; x-axis
12. $P(5, 12)$, $Q(-4, 3b)$; x-axis   **13.** $P(8, 5)$, $Q(2b, 4)$; y-axis
14. $P(3b - 1, 5)$, $Q(8, 4)$; y-axis   **15.** $P(-6, 2b + 1)$, $Q(2, 7)$; x-axis

Directed Distances

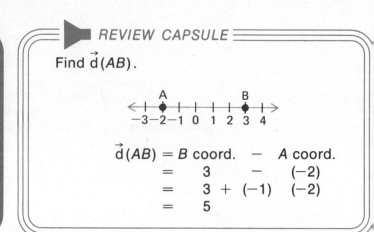

Find $\vec{d}(AB)$.

$$
\begin{aligned}
\vec{d}(AB) &= B \text{ coord.} \quad - \quad A \text{ coord.} \\
&= \quad 3 \quad\quad - \quad (-2) \\
&= \quad 3 + (-1) \quad (-2) \\
&= \quad 5
\end{aligned}
$$

EXAMPLE 1 Find $\vec{d}(PQ)$.

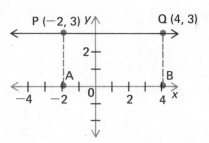

Use points directly below P and Q on the x-axis.

A and B are points on a number line. ⟶

$$
\begin{aligned}
\vec{d}(AB) &= B \text{ coord.} \quad - \quad A \text{ coord.} \\
&= \quad 4 \quad\quad - \quad (-2) \\
&= \quad 4 \quad + (-1)(-2) \\
&= \quad 4 \quad + \ 2 \ \text{ or } 6.
\end{aligned}
$$

$a - b = a + (-1)b.$ ⟶

A and B are directly below P and Q.

But, $\vec{d}(PQ) = \vec{d}(AB)$.

Thus, $\vec{d}(PQ) = 6$.

$\left. \begin{array}{l} P(-2, 3) \quad Q(4, 3) \\ \vec{d}(PQ) = 4 - (-2) \end{array} \right\}$

$\vec{d}(PQ)$ is determined only by the x-coordinates of P and Q.

Example 1 suggests this. ⟶

If $\overleftrightarrow{PQ}$ is a horizontal line,
$\vec{d}(PQ) = (x\text{-coord. of } Q) - (x\text{-coord. of } P)$.

EXAMPLE 2   Find $\vec{d}(ST)$ for $S(2,5)$ and $T(-7,5)$.

Both *y*-coord. are the same.

$\overleftrightarrow{ST}$ is a horizontal line.
So, $\vec{d}(ST) = (x\text{-coord. of } T) - (x\text{-coord. of } S)$
$$= \quad -7 \quad - \quad 2$$
$$= \quad -9$$

Thus, $\vec{d}(ST) = -9$.

EXAMPLE 3   Find $\vec{d}(RS)$.

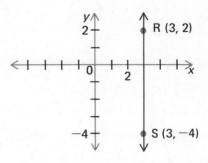

$\overleftrightarrow{RS}$ is a vertical line, since the *x*-coordinates of *R* and *S* are the same.

Find points directly across from *R* and *S* on the *y*-axis.

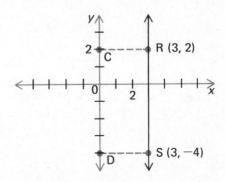

C and *D* are points on a number line. ⟶

$$d(CD) = D \text{ coord.} - C \text{ coord.}$$
$$= \quad -4 \quad - \quad 2$$
$$= \quad -6$$

$\vec{d}(RS)$ is determined only by the *y*-coord. of *R* and *S*.

But, $\vec{d}(RS) = \vec{d}(CD)$.
Thus, $\vec{d}(RS) = -6$.

Example 3 suggests this. ──────⟶

If $\overleftrightarrow{PQ}$ is a vertical line,
$\vec{d}(PQ) = (y\text{-coord. of } Q) - (y\text{-coord. of } P)$.

EXAMPLE 4   Find $\vec{d}(GH)$ for $G(-3,-4)$ and $H(-3,7)$.

Both *x*-coord. are the same.

$\overleftrightarrow{GH}$ is a vertical line.
So, $\vec{d}(GH)$ = (*y*-coord. of *H*) $-$ (*y*-coord. of *G*)

$$\begin{array}{ccc} 7 & - & (-4) \end{array}$$
$$= 7 + (-1)(-4)$$
$$= 11$$

Thus, $\vec{d}(GH) = 11$.

EXERCISES

PART A

Find $\vec{d}(MN)$.

1. $M(2,-7)$, $N(-5,-7)$ **2.** $M(1,4)$, $N(1,-3)$ **3.** $M(2,-6)$, $N(3,-6)$

4. $M(-1,5)$, $N(-1,-3)$ **5.** $M(6,-4)$, $N(-2,-4)$ **6.** $M(-8,-2)$, $N(-8,-5)$

7. $M(-2,-3)$, $N(-5,-3)$ **8.** $M(0,-4)$, $N(3,-4)$ **9.** $M(1,2)$, $N(1,-9)$

10. $M(0,-8)$, $N(-3,-8)$ **11.** $M(-3,0)$, $N(-3,8)$ **12.** $M(4,0)$, $N(4,-3)$

13. $M(4,0)$, $N(4,-6)$ **14.** $M(-3,-3)$, $N(5,-3)$ **15.** $M(-4,6)$, $N(-4,-17)$

16. $M(-5,3)$, $N(42,3)$ **17.** $M(0,-15)$, $N(0,14)$ **18.** $M(-17,0)$, $N(6,0)$

PART B

Find $\vec{d}(PQ)$.

19. $P(3\frac{1}{2},-5)$, $Q(2\frac{1}{4},-5)$ **20.** $P(\frac{5}{6},4)$, $Q(-\frac{2}{3},4)$

21. $P(6,-\frac{4}{3})$, $Q(6,\frac{5}{6})$ **22.** $P(3\frac{1}{8},-\frac{3}{4})$, $Q(3\frac{1}{8},\frac{5}{12})$

23. $P(-\frac{4}{5},5)$, $Q(\frac{7}{15},5)$ **24.** $P(3.8,2)$, $Q(-1.7,2)$

25. $P(-4,1.6)$, $Q(-3.2,1.6)$ **26.** $P(7,-5.3)$, $Q(7,4.9)$

27. $P(1\frac{1}{8},4)$, $Q(-1\frac{3}{4},4)$ **28.** $P(-\frac{4}{9},5)$, $Q(\frac{1}{27},5)$

PART C

Express $\vec{d}(RT)$ in terms of variables.

29. $R(3a,2b)$, $T(-5a,2b)$ **30.** $R(2m,5n)$, $T(2m,-7n)$

31. $R(3m,-2k)$, $T(3m,-5k)$ **32.** $R(2a-3,b)$, $T(-4a+3,b)$

33. $R(\frac{3m}{2},5)$, $T(\frac{2m}{3},5)$ **34.** $R(-4,\frac{5}{m^2})$, $T(-4,\frac{3}{m^2})$

Slopes of Line Segments

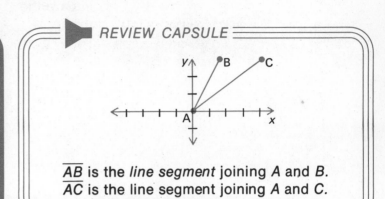

$\overline{AB}$ is the *line segment* joining A and B.
$\overline{AC}$ is the line segment joining A and C.

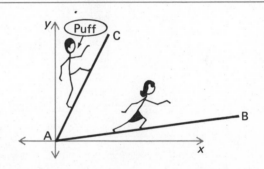

$\overline{AC}$ and $\overline{AB}$ are not parallel to either axis.

If the *x*-axis represents level ground and $\overline{AB}$ and $\overline{AC}$ represent paths up a hill, $\overline{AC}$ would be more difficult to climb than $\overline{AB}$.

Think of slope of a hill.

We say that $\overline{AC}$ has greater *slope* than $\overline{AB}$.

EXAMPLE 1 Find $\dfrac{\vec{d}(AE)}{\vec{d}(EB)}$.

$\vec{d}(AE)$ measures the vertical, or rise. ⟶ $\vec{d}(AE) = 5 - 1$
$\phantom{\vec{d}(AE) } = 4$

$\vec{d}(EB)$ measures the horizontal, or run. ⟶ $\vec{d}(EB) = 7 - 2$
$\phantom{\vec{d}(EB) } = 5$

Thus, $\dfrac{\vec{d}(AE)}{\vec{d}(EB)} = \dfrac{4}{5}$.

$\text{Slope} = \dfrac{\text{rise}}{\text{run}}$. ⟶ We say that the slope of $\overline{AB}$ is $\frac{4}{5}$.

EXAMPLE 2 Find the slopes of $\overline{AB}$ and $\overline{AC}$. Compare the slopes.

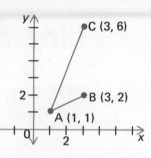

Draw the graph of each line segment separately.

Form a right triangle. ————————→

Slope $= \dfrac{\text{rise}}{\text{run}}$. ————————————→

Vertical directed distance————————→
Horizontal directed distance ——————→

Slope of $\overline{AB} = \dfrac{\vec{d}(AD)}{\vec{d}(DB)}$

$= \dfrac{2-1}{3-1}$, or $\dfrac{1}{2}$

Slope of $\overline{AC} = \dfrac{\vec{d}(AE)}{\vec{d}(EC)}$

$= \dfrac{6-1}{3-1}$, or $\dfrac{5}{2}$

Thus, the slope of $\overline{AC}$ is greater than the slope of $\overline{AB}$.

EXAMPLE 3 Find the slope of the line segment joining $A(2, 1)$ and $B(5, 3)$.

Draw a diagram.

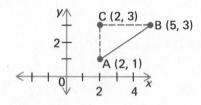

Build a right triangle by drawing a vertical line segment through A and a horizontal line segment through B.

Slope $= \dfrac{\text{rise}}{\text{run}}$. ————————————→

Slope of $\overline{AB} = \dfrac{\vec{d}(AC)}{\vec{d}(CB)}$

$= \dfrac{3-1}{5-2}$, or $\dfrac{2}{3}$

Thus, the slope of $\overline{AB}$ is $\frac{2}{3}$.

In Example 3, for $A(2, 1)$ and $B(5, 3)$ we found:

$$\frac{\text{Difference of } y\text{-coordinates}}{\text{Difference of } x\text{-coordinates}}$$

$$\text{Slope of } \overline{AB} = \frac{\overset{\text{y-coord. of } B}{3} - \overset{\text{y-coord. of } A}{1}}{\underset{\text{x-coord. of } B}{5} - \underset{\text{x-coord. of } A}{2}}$$

We can find the slope of a segment directly from the coordinates of its endpoints.

$$\text{Slope} = \frac{\text{difference of the } y\text{-coordinates}}{\text{difference of the } x\text{-coordinates}}.$$

EXAMPLE 4   Find the slope of $\overline{AB}$ for $A(6, 3)$, $B(-1, -4)$.

First way

$\dfrac{\text{Difference of } y\text{-coordinates}}{\text{Difference of } x\text{-coordinates}} \longrightarrow$

$$\text{Slope} = \frac{y\text{-coord. of } B - y\text{-coord. of } A}{x\text{-coord. of } B - x\text{-coord. of } A}$$

$$= \frac{-4 - 3}{-1 - 6}$$

$$= \frac{-7}{-7}$$

$$= 1$$

Second way

$\dfrac{\text{Difference of } y\text{-coordinates}}{\text{Difference of } x\text{-coordinates}} \longrightarrow$

$$\text{Slope} = \frac{y\text{-coord. of } A - y\text{-coord. of } B}{x\text{-coord. of } A - x\text{-coord. of } B}$$

$$= \frac{3 - (-4)}{6 - (-1)}$$

$$= \frac{3 + (-1)(-4)}{6 + (-1)(-1)}$$

$$= \frac{3 + 4}{6 + 1}$$

$$= \frac{7}{7}, \text{ or } 1$$

Both ways give the same slope. $\longrightarrow$ **Thus, the slope of $\overline{AB}$ is 1.**

EXAMPLE 5 Find the slope of $\overline{CD}$ for $C(8, 2)$ and $D(-2, 6)$.

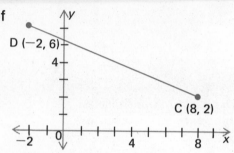

Also, $\dfrac{2-6}{8-(-2)} = \dfrac{-4}{10}$.

The slope of a line segment can be negative. ─────────────→

Slope of $\overline{CD} = \dfrac{6-2}{-2-8}$, or $\dfrac{4}{-10}$.

Thus, the slope of $\overline{CD}$ is $-\frac{4}{10}$, or $-\frac{2}{5}$.

EXAMPLE 6 Find the slope of $\overline{AB}$ for $A(3, 5)$ and $B(6, 5)$.

$\overline{AB}$ is a horizontal line segment.

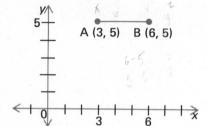

Also, $\dfrac{5-5}{3-6} = \dfrac{0}{-3} = 0$.

The slope of a line segment can be zero. ─────────────→

Slope of $\overline{AB} = \dfrac{5-5}{6-3}$, or $\dfrac{0}{3}$.

Thus, the slope of $\overline{AB}$ is 0.

EXERCISES

PART A

Find the slope of $\overline{AB}$.

1. $A(0, 0)$, $B(4, 3)$
2. $A(3, 5)$, $B(7, 6)$
3. $A(2, 5)$, $B(5, 7)$
4. $A(-3, -4)$, $B(8, 2)$
5. $A(-4, -1)$, $B(6, 2)$
6. $A(5, 3)$, $B(1, 8)$
7. $A(-8, 3)$, $B(7, -1)$
8. $A(-1, 1)$, $B(7, 4)$
9. $A(0, 4)$, $B(7, 0)$

PART B

Express the slope of $\overline{AB}$ in terms of variables.

10. $A(2b, 5k)$, $B(4b, 8k)$
11. $A(3i, 5t)$, $B(-4i, 7t)$
12. $A(2c, -4d)$, $B(-5c, 7d)$
13. $A(-3b, 5k)$, $B(b, k)$

Slope of Lines

OBJECTIVES

■ To find the slope of a line
■ To determine if lines are parallel from their slopes
■ To determine the slant of a line from its slope

▶ REVIEW CAPSULE

Find the slope of $\overline{PQ}$ for
$P(-4,-2)$ and $Q(7,6)$.

$$\frac{y\text{-coord. of }Q - y\text{-coord. of }P}{x\text{-coord. of }Q - x\text{-coord. of }P}$$

$$\frac{6 - (-2)}{7 - (-4)}$$

$$\frac{6 + (-1)(-2)}{7 + (-1)(-4)}, \text{ or } \frac{8}{11}$$

EXAMPLE 1

A, B, C, and D are points on the same line. Find the slopes of $\overline{AB}$ and $\overline{CD}$.

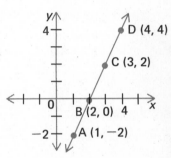

The slope of both segments is the same. ───────────────▶

$$\text{Slope of } \overline{AB} = \frac{0 - (-2)}{2 - 1} \qquad \text{Slope of } \overline{CD} = \frac{4 - 2}{4 - 3}$$

$$= \frac{2}{1}, \text{ or } 2 \qquad\qquad = \frac{2}{1}, \text{ or } 2$$

We say that the slope of $\overleftrightarrow{AB}$ is 2.

Use any two points on the line to find the slope.

> The slope of a line is the slope of any line segment on the line.

EXAMPLE 2

Find the slope of $\overleftrightarrow{PQ}$ for $P(4,1)$ and $Q(1,3)$.

$$\text{Slope of } \overleftrightarrow{PQ} = \frac{3 - 1}{1 - 4}$$

diff. of y-coords. ───────────▶
diff. of x-coords.

$$= \frac{2}{-3}, \text{ or } -\frac{2}{3}$$

EXAMPLE 3 Find the slope of $\overleftrightarrow{AB}$.

$\overleftrightarrow{AB}$ is a horizontal line.

$$\text{Slope of } \overleftrightarrow{AB} = \frac{2-2}{4-(-1)}$$

$$= \frac{0}{5}, \text{ or } 0$$

A (−1, 2) B (4, 2)

EXAMPLE 4 Find the slope of $\overleftrightarrow{CD}$.

$$\text{Slope of } \overleftrightarrow{CD} = \frac{3-(-1)}{4-4}$$

A fraction cannot have 0 in the denominator.

$$= \frac{4}{0}$$

↰undefined

C (4, 3)

D (4, −1)

Thus, the slope of the vertical line $\overleftrightarrow{CD}$ is undefined.

Examples 3 and 4 suggest this. ⟶

> The slope of a horizontal line is zero.
> The slope of a vertical line is undefined.

See Examples 1–4. ⟶ **The slope of a line determines its slant.**

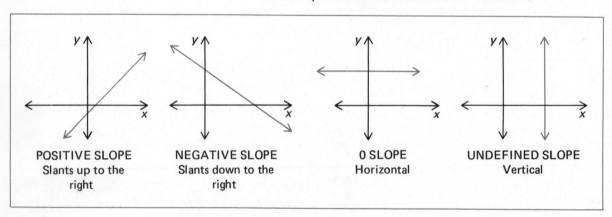

| POSITIVE SLOPE | NEGATIVE SLOPE | 0 SLOPE | UNDEFINED SLOPE |
| Slants up to the right | Slants down to the right | Horizontal | Vertical |

EXAMPLE 5 Find the slope of $\overleftrightarrow{CD}$ for $C(-2, -4)$ and $D(5, 8)$. Then describe the slant of $\overleftrightarrow{CD}$.

$\dfrac{\text{Difference of } y\text{-coordinates}}{\text{Difference of } x\text{-coordinates}}$

$$\text{Slope of } \overleftrightarrow{CD} = \frac{8-(-4)}{5-(-2)} = \frac{12}{7}.$$

Thus, the slope of $\overleftrightarrow{CD}$ is $\frac{12}{7}$.

The slope of $\overleftrightarrow{CD}$ is positive. ⟶ $\overleftrightarrow{CD}$ slants up to the right.

EXAMPLE 6 $\overleftrightarrow{PQ}$ is parallel to $\overleftrightarrow{AB}$.
Find the slope of each.

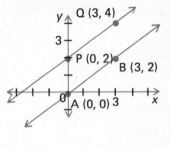

Slope of $\overleftrightarrow{AB}$ Slope of $\overleftrightarrow{PQ}$

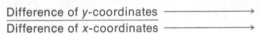

$$\frac{2-0}{3-0} \quad | \quad \frac{4-2}{3-0}$$

$$\frac{2}{3} \quad | \quad \frac{2}{3}$$

Thus, the slope of each line is $\frac{2}{3}$.

Example 6 suggests this. ⟶ Parallel lines have the same slope.

ORAL EXERCISES

Describe the slant of the line whose slope is given.

1. $\frac{2}{3}$ **2.** $-\frac{4}{5}$ **3.** $\frac{0}{4}$ **4.** $\frac{5}{0}$ **5.** $-\frac{1}{2}$

EXERCISES

PART A

Find the slope of $\overleftrightarrow{PQ}$ and describe its slant.

1. $P(3,4)$, $Q(3,7)$ **2.** $P(3,2)$, $Q(-2,5)$ **3.** $P(2,5)$, $Q(3,5)$
4. $P(-5,-3)$, $Q(7,-4)$ **5.** $P(0,0)$, $Q(-8,-5)$ **6.** $P(-6,1)$, $Q(7,5)$
7. $P(-3,-4)$, $Q(-3,6)$ **8.** $P(-6,1)$, $Q(7,5)$ **9.** $P(1,-2)$, $Q(-5,-2)$

Determine whether $\overleftrightarrow{PQ}$ is parallel to $\overleftrightarrow{RS}$.

10. $P(2,5)$, $Q(3,7)$ **11.** $P(3,7)$, $Q(6,9)$ **12.** $P(1,3)$, $Q(2,5)$
   $R(2,7)$, $S(0,5)$ $R(3,1)$, $Q(9,5)$ $R(0,1)$, $S(2,11)$

PART B

Determine whether A, B, and C lie on the same line. [Hint: Check if the slope of $\overline{AB}$ = the slope of $\overline{BC}$.]

13. $A(1,1)$, $B(-3,-7)$, $C(5,9)$ **14.** $A(0,3)$, $B(-2,5)$, $C(1,0)$
15. $A(2,-3)$, $B(-2,-7)$, $C(0,-3)$ **16.** $A(4,3)$, $B(-6,-2)$, $C(8,5)$
17. $A(0,0)$, $B(1,-3)$, $C(-2,4)$ **18.** $A(3,-3)$, $B(-1,2)$, $C(6,-2)$
19. $A(10,5)$, $B(-5,-1)$, $C(0,1)$ **20.** $A(2,1)$, $B(-4,-8)$, $C(6,7)$

Chapter Nine Review

Find each. [*p. 231*]

1. $|-6|$
2. $|-7 + 5|$
3. $|3a - 2|$ if $a = -4$
4. $|4b + 3|$ if $b = 2$

Solve. [*p. 231, 234*]

5. $|x| = 7$
6. $|5 - 2x| = 1$
7. $|2x - (5 - x)| = 4$
8. $2|x - 4| + 3 = 9$

Find $\vec{d}(MN)$. [*p. 236*]

9. coordinate of M: -5
   coordinate of N: 4

10. coordinate of M: 6
    coordinate of N: -3

11. coordinate of M: $\frac{5}{6}$
    coordinate of N: $-\frac{2}{3}$

Give the ordered pair for each point. [*p. 240*]

12. A
13. B
14. C
15. D
16. E

17. F
18. G
19. H
20. I
21. J

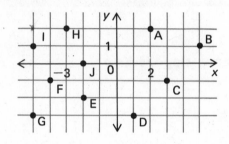

Give the quadrant in which each point lies. Then plot the point. [*p. 240, 242*]

22. $A(3, 5)$
23. $B(-3, 2)$
24. $C(-5, 0)$
25. $D(0, 3)$

[*p. 246*]

Determine, without sketching, to which axis the line joining P and Q is parallel.

26. $P(3, 5)$, $Q(-7, 5)$
27. $P(4, 8)$, $Q(4, -8)$
28. $P(a, b)$, $Q(c, b)$

[*p. 246*]

For what value of b will the line joining P and Q be parallel to the indicated axis?

29. $P(-5, 2)$, $Q(b, 1)$; y-axis
30. $P(6, 3b + 1)$, $Q(2, 4)$; x-axis

Find $\vec{d}(MN)$. [*p. 248*]

31. $M(-4, 3)$, $N(7, 3)$
32. $M(2, -6)$, $N(2, 8)$
33. $M(-1, -5)$, $N(4, -5)$

Find the slope of $\overleftrightarrow{PQ}$. Then describe its slant. [*p. 251, 253*]

34. $P(1, 5)$, $Q(2, 9)$
35. $P(4, 3)$, $Q(7, 3)$
36. $P(-2, 5)$, $Q(5, -2)$

Determine whether $\overleftrightarrow{PQ}$ is parallel to $\overleftrightarrow{RS}$. [*p. 255*]

37. $P(1, -5)$, $Q(4, 1)$
    $R(6, 13)$, $S(-4, -7)$

38. $P(5, 2)$, $Q(-5, -4)$
    $R(10, 7)$, $S(-15, -8)$

39. $P(3, 1)$, $Q(-6, -2)$
    $R(9, 5)$, $S(6, 2)$

Chapter Nine Test

Find each.

1. $|-4|$

2. $|2 - 8|$

3. $|3a - 5|$ if $a = -4$

Solve.

4. $|x| = 6$

5. $|3x - 4| = 7$

6. $3|x - 2| + 5 = 14$

Find $\vec{d}(MN)$.

7. coordinate of M: -6
    coordinate of N: 1

8. coordinate of M: $\frac{1}{8}$
    coordinate of N: $-\frac{3}{4}$

Give the ordered pair for each point.

9. A
10. B
11. C
12. D
13. E

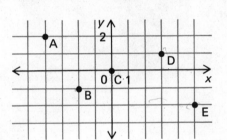

Plot each point.

14. $A(5, 2)$

15. $B(-3, -6)$

16. $C(0, -4)$

Determine, without sketching, to which axis the line joining P and Q is parallel.

17. $P(-2, 4)$, $Q(8, 4)$

18. $P(-3, -4)$, $Q(-3, 2)$

For what value of b will the line joining P and Q be parallel to the indicated axis?

19. $P(-6, 3)$, $Q(b, 4)$; y-axis

20. $P(5, 6)$, $Q(12, 2b + 1)$; x-axis

Find $\vec{d}(MN)$.

21. $M(-5, 3)$, $N(7, 3)$

22. $M(5, 2\frac{1}{2})$, $N(5, 3\frac{3}{4})$

Find the slope of $\overleftrightarrow{PQ}$. Then describe its slant.

23. $P(2, 3)$, $Q(7, 9)$

24. $P(-4, 2)$, $Q(3, 2)$

Determine whether $\overleftrightarrow{PQ}$ is parallel to $\overleftrightarrow{RS}$.

25. $P(6, 3)$, $Q(-3, -3)$
    $R(0, 4)$, $S(3, 6)$

26. $P(0, 0)$, $Q(-6, -15)$
    $R(2, 6)$, $S(4, 9)$

Mathematics in Construction

Construction workers must make careful plans in the form of cost budgets, time schedules and blueprints (scale drawing of project). Pictured above is a foreman preparing a time schedule. Shown here is a carpenter measuring lumber to the specifications on the blueprints.

Ratio and Proportion

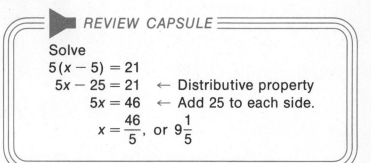

REVIEW CAPSULE

Solve
$$5(x - 5) = 21$$
$$5x - 25 = 21 \quad \leftarrow \text{Distributive property}$$
$$5x = 46 \quad \leftarrow \text{Add 25 to each side.}$$
$$x = \frac{46}{5}, \text{ or } 9\frac{1}{5}$$

EXAMPLE 1 John can paint a house in 4 days. He works 3 days. Write a fraction which compares the number of days actually worked with the number of days needed to do the entire job.

$\frac{3}{4}$ is a *ratio*.

$$\frac{\text{Number of days worked}}{\text{Number of days to do entire job}} = \frac{3}{4}$$

Numbers being compared should represent the same units. In Example 1, 3 and 4 represent days.

The comparison of two numbers by division is a *ratio*.

Two ways to write the ratio 3 to 4

$$\frac{3}{4} \qquad 3:4$$

EXAMPLE 2 Write the ratio 5 to 7 in two ways.

Compare 5 to 7. $\longrightarrow \quad \dfrac{5}{7}, \text{ or } 5:7$

EXAMPLE 3 Write an equation.

The ratio is the same as the ratio

| 3 to 4 | | a to 16 |

$$\frac{3}{4} = \frac{a}{16}$$

The ratios are equal.
The equation is a proportion.

or 3:4 $\quad = \quad$ a:16

A *proportion* is an equation which states that two ratios are equal.

$$\frac{a}{b} = \frac{c}{d} \qquad \text{or} \qquad a:b = c:d$$

extremes

means

a and d are *extremes*.
b and c are *means*.

EXAMPLE 4 Identify the extremes and means.

$$\frac{7}{10} = \frac{14}{20}$$

$7:10 = 14:20$

means

extremes

Extremes are 7 and 20. Means are 10 and 14.

EXAMPLE 5 Solve the proportion $\frac{3}{4} = \frac{x}{16}$.

Multiply each side by the product of the denominators: $4 \cdot 16 = 64$.

$$\overset{16}{\cancel{64}} \cdot \frac{3}{\underset{1}{\cancel{4}}} = \frac{x}{\underset{1}{\cancel{16}}} \cdot \overset{4}{\cancel{64}}$$

$$3 \cdot 16 = 4 \cdot x$$
$$48 = 4x$$
$$12 = x$$

$\frac{3}{4} = \frac{12}{16}.$ ────────────→ **Thus,** the solution is 12.

Example 4 suggests this. ───────→

$\left. \begin{array}{c} \dfrac{3}{4} = \dfrac{12}{16} \\ 3 \cdot 16 = 4 \cdot 12 \end{array} \right\}$

In a proportion $\dfrac{a}{b} = \dfrac{c}{d}$,

$$ad = bc$$

product of extremes = product of means

EXAMPLE 6 Solve the proportion $\frac{x}{3} = \frac{2}{5}$.

$\dfrac{a}{b} = \dfrac{c}{d}$ ────────────────→

$a \cdot d = b \cdot c$ ────────────────→

$$\frac{x}{3} = \frac{2}{5}$$
$$x \cdot 5 = 3 \cdot 2$$
$$5x = 6$$

Thus, $x = \dfrac{6}{5}$ and the solution is $\dfrac{6}{5}$, or $1\dfrac{1}{5}$.

EXAMPLE 7 Solve $\dfrac{x-5}{7} = \dfrac{3}{5}$.

Use
prod. of extremes = prod. of means.
$5(x-5) = 5 \cdot x + 5 \cdot -5$, or $5x - 25$

$$5(x-5) = 7 \cdot 3$$
$$5x - 25 = 21$$
$$5x = 46$$

Divide each side by 5.

Thus, $x = \dfrac{46}{5}$ and the solution is $\dfrac{46}{5}$, or $9\dfrac{1}{5}$.

EXAMPLE 8 If one out of five people use Cavity Toothpaste, how many people can be expected to use this brand in a city of 30,000 population?

Let t = number of people using Cavity

Write a proportion by setting the ratios equal.

$$\dfrac{t}{30,000} = \dfrac{\text{Cavity users}}{\text{total population}}$$

But, $\dfrac{1}{5} = \dfrac{\text{Cavity users}}{\text{total population}}$

$$\dfrac{t}{30,000} = \dfrac{1}{5}$$
$$5t = 30,000$$
$$t = 6,000$$

Thus, 6,000 people use Cavity Toothpaste.

ORAL EXERCISES

Identify the means and extremes of each proportion.

1. $\dfrac{3}{5} = \dfrac{6}{10}$

2. $7:14 = 21:42$

3. $\dfrac{a}{b} = \dfrac{m}{n}$

4. $\dfrac{3}{5} = \dfrac{x}{4}$

5. $2:5 = 7:5a$

6. $\dfrac{5}{9} = \dfrac{2m}{3}$

7. $\dfrac{3m}{2b} = \dfrac{7x}{5y}$

8. $x:b = 2y:t$

EXERCISES

PART A

Solve.

1. $\dfrac{5}{3} = \dfrac{a}{2}$

2. $\dfrac{3}{10} = \dfrac{x}{4}$

3. $\dfrac{7}{14} = \dfrac{m}{21}$

4. $\dfrac{2}{m} = \dfrac{3}{7}$

5. $\dfrac{3}{x} = \dfrac{7}{x+5}$

6. $\dfrac{m+4}{2} = \dfrac{m-3}{5}$

7. $\dfrac{a+3}{5} = \dfrac{14}{10}$

8. $\dfrac{x-2}{3} = \dfrac{2x+7}{5}$

9. $\dfrac{5}{2m+5} = \dfrac{2}{4m-1}$

10. In Centerville, 3 out of 5 people belong to a union. How many union members can we find if the population is 70,000?

11. A batter's batting average is .385 (385:1,000). How many hits should he get in 6,000 times at bat?

12. One out of 4 people earn less than $2,000 per year. How many people in a city of 40,000 earn less than $2,000 per year?

13. Four out of 5 freshmen study algebra. How many study algebra in a freshman class of 400?

PART B

EXAMPLE Solve $\dfrac{m}{3} = \dfrac{2}{m+5}$

Prod of extremes = prod. of means. $m(m+5) = 3 \cdot 2$

$m(m+5) = m^2 + 5m \longrightarrow$ $m^2 + 5m = 6$

Add -6 to each side. $\longrightarrow$ $m^2 + 5m - 6 = 0$

Factor. $\longrightarrow$ $(m+6)(m-1) = 0$

Set each factor equal to 0. $\longrightarrow$ $m+6 = 0$ or $m-1 = 0$

$m = -6$ or $m = 1 \longrightarrow$ **Thus,** the solutions are -6 and 1.

Solve.

14. $\dfrac{4}{x} = \dfrac{x}{9}$

15. $\dfrac{a}{2} = \dfrac{32}{a}$

16. $\dfrac{x}{2} = \dfrac{2}{x+3}$

17. $\dfrac{y-4}{1} = \dfrac{2}{y-3}$

PART C

EXAMPLE Find two numbers in the ratio $2:3$ whose sum is 15.

$\dfrac{2x}{3x} = \dfrac{\overset{1}{\cancel{2x}}}{\underset{1}{\cancel{3x}}} = \dfrac{2}{3} \longrightarrow$ Let $2x =$ one of the numbers

                      $3x =$ the other number

                        $2x + 3x = 15$

                           $5x = 15$

                             $x = 3$

Check: $\dfrac{6}{9} = \dfrac{2}{3}$ and $6 + 9 = 15.$

Thus, first number, $2x$, is $2 \cdot 3$, or 6 and second number, $3x$, is $3 \cdot 3$, or 9.

18. Find two numbers whose ratio is $3:5$ and whose sum is 24.

19. Find two numbers whose ratio is $7:3$ and whose difference is 28.

20. Find two numbers whose ratio is $3:8$ and whose sum is 33.

21. Find three numbers whose ratio is $2:3:5$ and whose sum is 30.

Equation of a Line

Given two points, only one line can be drawn through them.

(x, y) represents the coordinates of a general point (G) on the line.

The line through the points $R(-2,-7)$ and $S(3,8)$ is shown. $G(x,y)$ represents any other point on the same line.

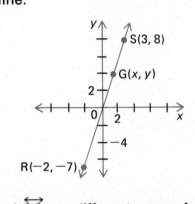

$\overleftrightarrow{RS}$, $\overleftrightarrow{RG}$, and $\overleftrightarrow{SG}$ are different names for the same line. The slope of the line is the slope of any segment on it.

EXAMPLE 1 Write an equation of the line through $R(-2,-7)$ and $S(3,8)$.

$\text{Slope} = \dfrac{\text{diff. of } y\text{-coordinates}}{\text{diff. of } x\text{-coordinates}}$

$$\text{Slope of } \overline{RS} = \frac{8-(-7)}{3-(-2)} = \frac{8+7}{3+2} = \frac{15}{5} = \frac{3}{1}.$$

$$\text{Slope of } \overline{SG} = \frac{y-8}{x-3}.$$

R, S, and G are on the same line. ⟶ But, slope of $\overline{SG}$ = slope of $\overline{RS}$.

Set the two slopes equal. ⟶ **Thus,** $\dfrac{y-8}{x-3} = \dfrac{3}{1}$ is an equation of the line.

EXAMPLE 2 Solve the equation $\dfrac{y-8}{x-3}=\dfrac{3}{1}$ for y (from Example 1).

The equation is a proportion.

$$\dfrac{y-8}{x-3}=\dfrac{3}{1}$$

Prod. of extremes = prod. of means. $\longrightarrow$ $1(y-8)=3(x-3)$

$3(x-3)=3x-9$ $\longrightarrow$ $y-8=3x-9$

Add 8 to each side. $\longrightarrow$ $y=3x-1$

An equation of the line in Example 1 is $y=3x-1$. It describes every point on the line.

EXAMPLE 3   Show that the point $P(-5,-16)$ lies on the line $\overleftrightarrow{RS}$ in Example 1.

To show that a point is on a line, we show that its coordinates satisfy an equation of the line.

Substitute in the equation.

Let $\left.\begin{array}{l}x=-5\\y=-16\end{array}\right\}$

y	$3x-1$
-16	$3(-5)-1$
	$-15-1$
	-16

Thus, $P(-5,-16)$ lies on $\overleftrightarrow{RS}$.

EXAMPLE 4   Write an equation for $\overleftrightarrow{PQ}$ given $P(-1,4)$ and $Q(2,-5)$.

Let $G(x,y)$ represent any point on the line.

Slope of $\overline{PG}$ = Slope of $\overline{QP}$

$$\dfrac{y-4}{x-(-1)}=\dfrac{4-(-5)}{-1-2}$$

$$\dfrac{y-4}{x+1}=\dfrac{9}{-3}$$

Solve the proportion.

Use the distributive property.

$$-3(y-4)=9(x+1)$$
$$-3y+12=9x+9$$
$$\underline{-12-12}$$
$$-3y=9x-3$$
$$y=\dfrac{9x-3}{-3}$$

Divide each side by -3. $\longrightarrow$

$\dfrac{9x-3}{-3}=\dfrac{9}{-3}x+\dfrac{-3}{-3}$ $\longrightarrow$ $y=-3x+1$

Thus, an equation of $\overleftrightarrow{PQ}$ is $y=-3x+1$.

EXAMPLE 5   Show that $R(5,-14)$ is on $\overleftrightarrow{PQ}$ of Example 4.

See if the coordinates of R
satisfy an equation of $\overleftrightarrow{PQ}$.

$$\text{Let } \left. \begin{array}{l} x = 5 \\ y = -14 \end{array} \right\}$$

y	$-3x + 1$
-14	$-3(5) + 1$
	$-15 + 1$
	-14

Thus, $R(5,-14)$ is on $\overleftrightarrow{PQ}$.

ORAL EXERCISES

Give an expression for the slope of $\overleftrightarrow{PG}$.

1. $P(1,3)$, $G(x,y)$
4. $P(-3,-5)$, $G(x,y)$

2. $P(4,3)$, $G(x,y)$
5. $P(1,-2)$, $G(x,y)$

3. $P(-3,1)$, $G(x,y)$
6. $P(-1,-1)$, $G(x,y)$

EXERCISES

PART A

Write an equation for $\overleftrightarrow{PQ}$.

1. $P(1,1)$, $Q(2,3)$
4. $P(2,-1)$, $Q(5,2)$
7. $P(-2,-10)$, $Q(1,2)$
10. $P(-3,8)$, $Q(2,-7)$
13. $P(0,4)$, $Q(2,-2)$

2. $P(1,5)$, $Q(3,11)$
5. $P(-1,3)$, $Q(1,5)$
8. $P(-1,15)$, $Q(2,6)$
11. $P(1,7)$, $Q(-2,-2)$
14. $P(0,1)$, $Q(2,-9)$

3. $P(3,1)$, $Q(4,3)$
6. $P(-2,-6)$, $Q(5,8)$
9. $P(-1,0)$, $Q(3,-8)$
12. $P(-3,-13)$, $Q(4,1)$
15. $P(4,0)$, $Q(3,-2)$

Show that P lies on the line with the given equation.

16. $P(-1,-1)$ $y = 2x + 1$
17. $P(-3,1)$ $y = -2x - 5$
18. $P(-3,-1)$ $y = -x - 4$

PART B

Write an equation for $\overleftrightarrow{PQ}$. Show that R lies on $\overleftrightarrow{PQ}$.

19. $P(1,4)$, $Q(2,8)$, $R(3,12)$
21. $P(0,-5)$, $Q(2,1)$, $R(3,4)$

20. $P(0,4)$, $Q(2,-2)$, $R(3,-5)$
22. $P(-1,5)$, $Q(1,1)$, $R(3,-3)$

PART C

Write an equation of the line through the given point and having the given slope.

23. $P(-2,1)$; slope 2
25. $P(0,0)$; slope 1

24. $P(0,5)$; slope -3
26. $P(1,6)$; slope 0

More Difficult Equations

 REVIEW CAPSULE

Write an equation of the line through $P(2, 7)$ and $Q(4, 13)$.

Let $G(x, y)$ represent any point on the line.

Slope of $\overline{QG}$ = Slope of $\overline{PQ}$

$$\frac{y - 13}{x - 4} = \frac{13 - 7}{4 - 2}$$

$$\frac{y - 13}{x - 4} = \frac{6}{2}$$

$$2(y - 13) = 6(x - 4)$$

$$2y - 26 = 6x - 24$$

$$y = 3x + 1$$

EXAMPLE 1 Write an equation for $\overleftrightarrow{AB}$ given $A(1, -1)$ and $B(7, 3)$.

$G(x, y)$ represents any point on the line. ⟶

Slope of $\overline{BG}$ = Slope of $\overline{AB}$

$$\frac{y - 3}{x - 7} = \frac{3 - (-1)}{7 - 1}$$

$3 - (-1) = 3 + (-1)(-1) = 3 + 1$

$$\frac{y - 3}{x - 7} = \frac{4}{6}$$

Prod. of extremes = prod. of means. ⟶

Use the distributive property. ⟶

Add 18 to each side. ⟶

$$6(y - 3) = 4(x - 7)$$

$$6y - 18 = 4x - 28$$

$$6y = 4x - 10$$

Divide each side by 6. ⟶

$$y = \frac{4x - 10}{6}$$

$$y = \frac{4}{6}x - \frac{10}{6}$$

Rewrite each fraction in simplest form. ⟶

$$y = \frac{2}{3}x - \frac{5}{3}$$

EXAMPLE 2 Write an equation for $\overleftrightarrow{AB}$ given $A(3,3)$ and $B(0,5)$.

Let $G(x,y)$ represent any point on the line.
Slope of $\overline{AG}$ = Slope of $\overline{AB}$

Find the slope of each segment. $\longrightarrow$
$$\frac{y-3}{x-3} = \frac{5-3}{0-3}$$
$$\frac{y-3}{x-3} = \frac{2}{-3}$$

Prod. of means = prod. of extremes $\longrightarrow$
$$-3(y-3) = 2(x-3)$$
$$-3y + 9 = 2x - 6$$

Add -9 to each side. $\longrightarrow$
$$-3y = 2x - 15$$

Divide each side by -3. $\longrightarrow$
$$y = \frac{2x-15}{-3}$$

$$\frac{2x-15}{-3} = \frac{2}{-3}x + \frac{-15}{-3} \longrightarrow$$
$$y = -\frac{2}{3}x + 5$$

EXAMPLE 3 $C(6,y)$ lies on $\overleftrightarrow{AB}$ of Example 2. Find y.

$C(6,y)$

$\uparrow$

x

Use the equation of $\overleftrightarrow{AB}$.

$$y = -\frac{2}{3}x + 5$$

Let $x = 6$ in the equation. $\longrightarrow$
$$y = -\frac{2}{3}(6) + 5$$

$-\frac{2}{3}(6) = \frac{-2}{3} \cdot \frac{6}{1}$

$\qquad = \frac{-2 \cdot \overset{1}{3} \cdot 2}{\underset{1}{3} \cdot 1} = -4$

$$y = -4 + 5$$
$$y = 1$$

The point $C(6,1)$ lies on $\overleftrightarrow{AB}$.

Check by drawing the line joining $A(3,3)$ and $B(0,5)$.

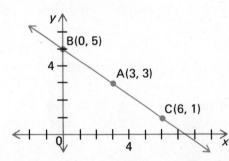

ORAL EXERCISES
Rename each.

1. $\dfrac{3x-5}{2}$

2. $\dfrac{-2x+5}{7}$

3. $\dfrac{4x-8}{5}$

4. $\dfrac{-3x+5}{2}$

EXERCISES

PART A

Write an equation for $\overleftrightarrow{PQ}$.

1. $P(1, 2)$, $Q(3, 5)$
2. $P(3, 5)$, $Q(8, 7)$
3. $P(2, 5)$, $Q(6, 6)$
4. $P(0, 5)$, $Q(4, 6)$
5. $P(3, 3)$, $Q(-2, 5)$
6. $P(-2, -3)$, $Q(-7, -5)$
7. $P(-2, 0)$, $Q(3, 4)$
8. $P(0, 8)$, $Q(3, 0)$
9. $P(-2, 0)$, $Q(0, 5)$

Write an equation for $\overleftrightarrow{AB}$. Then use the equation to find the y-coordinate of point C on $\overleftrightarrow{AB}$.

10. $A(0, 2)$, $B(-4, -1)$, $C(4, y)$
11. $A(-3, -5)$, $B(3, -1)$, $C(6, y)$
12. $A(0, 1)$, $B(-5, -1)$, $C(-5, y)$
13. $A(2, 5)$, $B(6, 11)$, $C(-2, y)$

PART B

EXAMPLE An equation of $\overleftrightarrow{MN}$ is $y = 3x - 2$. Write a table of values and give the coordinates of three points on the line.

Choose any three numbers for x. Use numbers that will make the arithmetic easy.

x	$3x - 2$	y
1	$3(1) - 2$	1
0	$3(0) - 2$	-2
-1	$3(-1) - 2$	-5

Thus, $(1, 1)$, $(0, -2)$, and $(-1, -5)$ are three points on $\overrightarrow{MN}$.

Write a table of values and give the coordinates of three points on the line whose equation is given.

14. $y = x + 1$
15. $y = 2x - 3$
16. $y = -3x + 4$
17. $y = \frac{1}{2}x - 2$
18. $y = \frac{2}{3}x + 3$
19. $y = -\frac{1}{4}x - 1$

Write an equation for $\overleftrightarrow{PQ}$. Then use the equation to set up a table of values and give the coordinates of three other points on the line.

20. $P(0, 1)$, $Q(2, 7)$
21. $P(6, 8)$, $Q(12, 11)$
22. $P(-9, -11)$, $Q(15, 5)$
23. $P(0, -6)$, $Q(10, -1)$
24. $P(-16, 10)$, $Q(0, 6)$ ↘
25. $P(0, 1)$, $Q(12, 9)$ ↘

PART C

Find the value of b so that the given point lies on the line.

26. $y = bx - 3$; $(3, -1)$
27. $y = bx + 1$; $(4, -1)$
28. $y = bx + 4$; $(10, 8)$
29. $y = bx - \frac{1}{2}$; $(12, -2)$

Pascal's Triangle

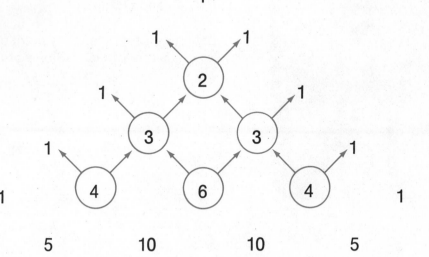

1

1   1

1   2   1

1   3   3   1

1   4   6   4   1

1   5   10   10   5   1

Pascal's Triangle is an arrangement of numbers. Each number is the sum of the two numbers just above it. Each row begins and ends with 1.

This list shows the powers of $(a + b)$.

$(a + b)^0 =$ 1

$(a + b)^1 =$ $^1a + {}^1b$

$(a + b)^2 =$ $^1a^2 + {}^2a\,b + {}^1b^2$

$(a + b)^3 =$ $^1a^3 + {}^3a^2b + {}^3a\,b^2 + {}^1b^3$

$(a + b)^4 =$ $^1a^4 + {}^4a^3b + {}^6a^2b^2 + {}^4a\,b^3 + {}^1b^4$

$(a + b)^5 =$ $^1a^5 + {}^5a^4b + {}^{10}a^3b^2 + {}^{10}a^2b^3 + {}^5a\,b^4 + {}^1b^5$

Do you see Pascal's Triangle?

What do the numerals of Pascal's Triangle represent?

1. Write the next two rows of Pascal's Triangle.

2. Write the expansions for $(a + b)^6$ and $(a + b)^7$.

$y = mx + b$

OBJECTIVES

■ To determine slope and y-intercept from an equation of a line
■ To write an equation given the slope and y-intercept
■ To graph a line given its slope and y-intercept

► REVIEW CAPSULE

Write an equation for the line through $P(3, 4)$ and $Q(7, 5)$.

Let $G(x, y)$ represent any point on the line.
$$\text{Slope of } \overline{QG} = \text{Slope of } \overline{PQ}$$
$$\frac{y - 5}{x - 7} = \frac{5 - 4}{7 - 3}$$
$$\frac{y - 5}{x - 7} = \frac{1}{4}$$
$$4(y - 5) = 1(x - 7)$$
$$y = \tfrac{1}{4}x + \tfrac{13}{4}$$

$$\text{Slope} = \frac{\text{diff. of } y\text{-coord.}}{\text{diff. of } x\text{-coord.}}$$

Use the steps in the Review Capsule to write the equation. ⟶

$P(5, 6), Q(10, 4)$
Slope of
$$\overleftrightarrow{PQ} = \frac{4 - 6}{10 - 5} = -\frac{2}{5}$$
Equation for $\overleftrightarrow{PQ}$
$$y = -\tfrac{2}{5}x + 8$$

$A(4, -3), B(8, 0)$
Slope of
$$\overleftrightarrow{AB} = \frac{0 - (-3)}{8 - 4} = \frac{3}{4}$$
Equation for $\overleftrightarrow{AB}$
$$y = \tfrac{3}{4}x - 6$$

EXAMPLE 1   Give the slope of each line.
$$y = \tfrac{4}{7}x - 3$$ $$y = -\tfrac{3}{5}x + 8$$

The slope is the coefficient of x. ⟶

Slope is $\tfrac{4}{7}$.

Slope is $-\tfrac{3}{5}$.

Graphing $\overleftrightarrow{PQ}$ and $\overleftrightarrow{AB}$ reveals another pattern.

The x-coordinate of any point on the y-axis is 0.

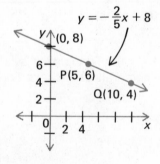

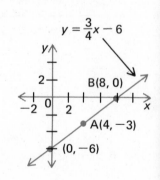

The *y*-coordinate of the point of intersection of a line with the *y*-axis is the *y*-intercept.

EXAMPLE 2   Find the *y*-intercept.

$$y = \frac{4}{7}x - 3 \qquad\qquad y = -\frac{3}{5}x + 8$$

Let $x = 0$ to find *y*.

$$y = \frac{4}{7}x - 3 \qquad\qquad y = -\frac{3}{5}x + 8$$

$$y = \frac{4}{7}(0) - 3 \qquad\qquad y = -\frac{3}{5}(0) + 8$$

$$y = -3 \qquad\qquad\qquad y = 8$$

Examples 1 and 2 suggest this.

If $y = mx + b$ is an equation of a line,
then
slope is *m*   and   *y*-intercept is *b*.

EXAMPLE 3   Give the slope and the *y*-intercept.

$$y = \frac{4}{5}x - 12$$

The line crosses the *y*-axis at $(0, -12)$.

Slope is $\frac{4}{5}$.   *y*-intercept is -12.

EXAMPLE 4   Write an equation for the line whose slope is *m* and whose *y*-intercept is *b*.

b is the *y*-intercept, $x = 0$.

The slope of a line is the slope of any segment on it.

$P(0, b)$ is a point on the line.
Let $G(x, y)$ represent any point on the line.

Slope of $\overline{PG} = m$

$$\frac{y - b}{x - 0} = \frac{m}{1}$$

Prod. of extremes = prod. of means.

Get *y* alone on one side. }
Add *b* to each side.

$$1(y - b) = mx$$
$$y - b = mx$$
$$y = mx + b$$

A line with slope *m* and *y*-intercept *b* has
equation $y = mx + b$.

EXAMPLE 5   Write an equation for the line whose slope is −5 and whose y-intercept is −3.

m is the slope.
b is the y-intercept.

$$m = -5 \qquad b = -3$$

$$y = mx + b$$

Thus, $y = -5x - 3$ is the equation.

EXAMPLE 6   Graph $y = \dfrac{2}{3}x + 1$.

The y-intercept is 1. ⟶   Plot $P(0, 1)$.   Use the slope to locate another point Q.

Slope $= \dfrac{2}{3}$ ⟵ up 2
⟵ right 3

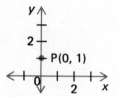

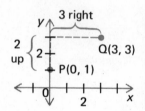

Connect P and Q.

Graph of $y = \dfrac{2}{3}x + 1$ ⟶

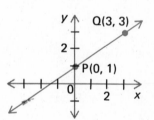

Read: the set of points (x, y) such that $y = \dfrac{2}{3}x + 1$. ⟶ The graph shows $\left\{(x, y)\,|\,y = \dfrac{2}{3}x + 1\right\}$.

Each point on a line satisfies its equation.

See the graph. ⟶ For example, $(-3, -1)$ is on $\overleftrightarrow{PQ}$,

y	$\dfrac{2}{3}x + 1$
-1	$\dfrac{2}{3}(-3) + 1$
	$-2 + 1$
	-1

Plot $(0, 1)$, $(3, 3)$, and $(-3, -1)$
to check that all three points are on
the same line.

since $(-3, -1)$ satisfies the equation.

EXAMPLE 7 Graph $\left\{(x,y) \mid y = -\dfrac{2}{5}x + 3\right\}$.

Rewrite $-\dfrac{2}{5}$ as $\dfrac{-2}{5}$.

$$y = \dfrac{-2}{5}x + 3$$

slope   y-intercept

The y-intercept is 3. $\longrightarrow$ Plot $(0,3)$.
Then use the slope.   Draw $\overleftrightarrow{PQ}$.

Slope $= \dfrac{-2}{5}$ $\longleftarrow$ down 2
 $\longleftarrow$ right 5

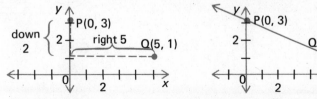

ORAL EXERCISES

Give the slope and the y-intercept.

1. $y = \frac{1}{2}x - 7$ **2.** $y = \frac{2}{3}x + 4$ **3.** $y = -\frac{4}{5}x + 7$ **4.** $y = -\frac{2}{3}x - \frac{4}{5}$
5. $y = 3x + 2$ **6.** $y = -2x - 6$ **7.** $y = 2x$ **8.** $y = -x - 1$

EXERCISES

PART A

Write an equation for the line.

1. slope $= 2$ **2.** slope $= -3$ **3.** slope $= 5$
   y-intercept $= 4$ y-intercept $= -5$ y-intercept $= 0$
4. slope $= \frac{1}{2}$ **5.** slope $= -\frac{2}{3}$ **6.** slope $= \frac{1}{8}$
   y-intercept $= 2$ y-intercept $= -4$ y-intercept $= 2$

Graph.

7. $y = \frac{2}{3}x + 1$ **8.** $y = -\frac{3}{4}x + 2$ **9.** $y = -\frac{2}{5}x - 4$
10. $y = 3x + 1$ (Hint: Write the slope as $\frac{3}{1}$.)   **11.** $y = 4x - 3$
12. $y = -2x + 4$ **13.** $y = -3x - 1$ **14.** $y = -4x + 5$
15. $\{(x,y) \mid y = \frac{2}{3}x + 6\}$ **16.** $\{(x,y) \mid y = -\frac{5}{3}x + 2\}$ **17.** $\{(x,y) \mid y = \frac{3}{4}x - 2\}$

PART B

Graph.

18. $y = 2x$ (Hint: Crosses y-axis at $(0,0)$.)   **19.** $y = 3x$ **20.** $y = -3x$

Graphing A Line

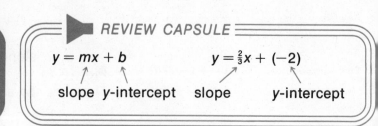

REVIEW CAPSULE

$y = mx + b$

slope y-intercept

$y = \frac{2}{3}x + (-2)$

slope y-intercept

EXAMPLE 1

Give the slope and y-intercept.
$$3x - 2y = 10$$

Put the equation in $y = mx + b$ form.

Solve for y

Get y alone on one side.
Add $-3x$ to each side.
Divide each side by -2.

$$3x - 2y = \qquad 10$$
$$\underline{-3x \qquad\qquad -3x}$$
$$-2y = -3x + 10$$
$$y = \frac{-3x + 10}{-2}$$

$$\frac{-3x + 10}{-2} = \frac{-3}{-2}x + \frac{10}{-2} \longrightarrow$$

$$y = \frac{3}{2}x - 5$$

Thus, the slope is $\frac{3}{2}$ and the y-intercept is -5.

EXAMPLE 2

Graph $\{(x, y) \,|\, -y - x = 2\}$.

Put the equation in $y = mx + b$ form.
Add x to each side. ⟶

$$-y - x = \qquad 2$$
$$\underline{+x \quad +x}$$
$$-y \quad = \quad x + 2$$

Divide each side by -1. ⟶

$$y \quad = -x - 2$$

$-x$ means $-1x$. ⟶

Slope is $\frac{-1}{1}$. y-intercept is -2.

Plot $(0, -2)$.
Then use the slope.

Draw $\overleftrightarrow{PQ}$.

Slope $= \dfrac{-1}{1}$ ← down 1
← right 1

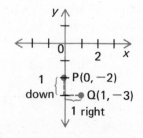

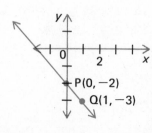

EXAMPLE 3 Graph $x + 3y = 0$.

Solve for y.
Add $-1x$ to each side.
Divide each side by 3.

$$1x + 3y = 0$$
$$3y = -1x$$
$$y = \tfrac{-1}{3}x, \text{ or } y = \tfrac{-1}{3}x + 0$$

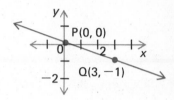

Slope is $\tfrac{-1}{3}$. y-intercept is 0.

Since the y-intercept is 0, the line passes through the origin. ⟶ Plot $(0, 0)$.
Then use the slope.

Draw $\overleftrightarrow{PQ}$.

Slope $= \dfrac{-1}{3}$ ⟵ down 1
⟵ right 3

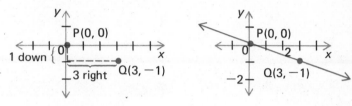

EXAMPLE 4 Graph $\{(x, y) \mid y = -2\}$.

Rewrite: $0x = 0 \cdot x = 0$ ⟶

$$y = 0x - 2$$
$$y = \frac{0}{1}x - 2$$

Slope is $\tfrac{0}{1}$ y-intercept is -2.

Plot $(0, -2)$.
Then use the slope.

Draw $\overleftrightarrow{PQ}$.

Slope $= \dfrac{0}{1}$ ⟵ neither up nor down
⟵ right 1

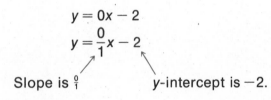

A horizontal line has 0 slope. ⟶ $\overleftrightarrow{PQ}$ is a horizontal line.

$y = -2$ represents a horizontal line.
$P(0, -2)$ $Q(1, -2)$

Same y-coordinate

Instead of the method shown in Example 4, we can graph a horizontal line like this.

First plot the y-intercept.
Then plot any other point with the same y-coordinate and draw the line through these points.

EXAMPLE 5 Graph $3y - 9 = 0$.

Solve for y.
Add 9 to each side.
Divide each side by 3.

$$3y - 9 = 0$$
$$3y = 9$$
$$y = 3, \text{ or } y = 0x + 3$$

The y-intercept is 3. ⟶ Plot $P(0, 3)$.

Then, use any other point with y-coordinate 3 like $Q(4, 3)$.

Draw the horizontal line. ⟶

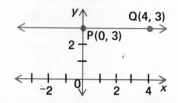

EXERCISES

PART A

Graph.

1. $3x - 2y = 3$
2. $4y + 3x = 8$
3. $5y + 2x = -10$
4. $y - 1 = x$
5. $y = 6$
6. $2y + 6 = 0$

Graph.

7. $\{(x, y) \mid 3y - 2x = 12\}$
8. $\{(x, y) \mid y - 2x = 0\}$
9. $\{(x, y) \mid 4x + 2y = 8\}$
10. $\{(x, y) \mid y = 4\}$
11. $\{(x, y) \mid 2y - 5x = 10\}$
12. $\{(x, y) \mid x + y = 2\}$

PART B

EXAMPLE Graph $y = 2x - 1$. Use a table of values.

Choose any 3 numbers for x.
Find the y-coordinates.
Plot the 3 points.
Draw the line.

x	$2x - 1$	y
1	$2(1) - 1$	1
0	$2(0) - 1$	-1
-1	$2(-1) - 1$	-3

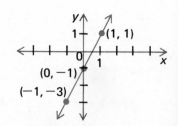

Graph. Use a table of values.

13. $y = x + 3$
14. $y = -3x + 1$
15. $y = -2x$
16. $2x + y = 1$
17. $2x - 3y = 4$
18. $6x - y = 1$

Vertical Lines

OBJECTIVES
- To write an equation of a vertical line
- To graph a vertical line given its equation

 REVIEW CAPSULE

Find the slope of $\overleftrightarrow{PQ}$ for $P(3, 2)$, $Q(3, -1)$.

$$\text{Slope of } \overleftrightarrow{PQ} = \frac{2 - (-1)}{3 - 3}$$

$$= \frac{3}{0} \leftarrow \begin{array}{l} \text{Division by 0} \\ \text{is undefined.} \end{array}$$

Thus, the slope of $\overleftrightarrow{PQ}$ is undefined.

EXAMPLE 1

Graph $\overleftrightarrow{PQ}$ for $P(3, 2)$, $Q(3, -1)$. Identify the slope and the y-intercept.

See the Review Capsule. ⟶ The slope of $\overleftrightarrow{PQ}$ is undefined.

It does not cross the y-axis. ⟶ $\overleftrightarrow{PQ}$ has no y-intercept.
It is parallel to the y-axis.

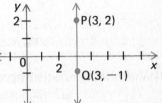

$\overleftrightarrow{PQ}$ in Example 1 is a vertical line.
A vertical line does not have an equation of the form.

$$y = mx + b.$$

A vertical line (other than the y-axis) has no y-intercept.

undefined slope ⟶   ⟵ no y-intercept

EXAMPLE 2

Write an equation for $\overleftrightarrow{PQ}$ in Example 1.

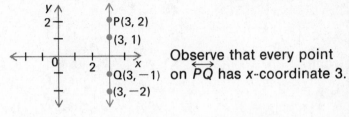

$\overleftrightarrow{PQ}$ is parallel to the y-axis and 3 units to the right of the y-axis.

Observe that every point on $\overleftrightarrow{PQ}$ has x-coordinate 3.

$\overleftrightarrow{PQ}$ is the set of all points (x, y) such that $x = 3$.

$$\{(x, y) \mid x = 3\}$$

y is not mentioned in the equation. It can be any number. But x is always 3. ⟶ **Thus,** an equation is $x = 3$.

EXAMPLE 3   Graph $\{(x, y) \mid x = -6\}$.

y is not mentioned in $x = -6$. ⟶ The graph is a vertical line.

y is any number. x is -6. ⟶ The line is the set of all points with x-coordinate -6.

Use any two points with x-coordinate -6 to graph.
For example, $P(-6, 0)$ and $Q(-6, 2)$.

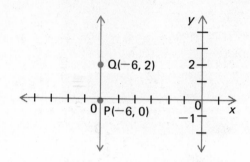

EXAMPLE 4   Graph $x = 5$.

y is not mentioned in $x = 5$.
The graph is a vertical line.

The line will be the set of all points whose x-coordinate is 5.

y can be any number.
x is always 5.

Use any two points with x-coordinate 5 like $P(5, 2)$ and $Q(5, -1)$ to draw the graph.

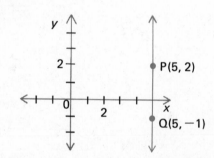

EXERCISES

PART A

Graph.

1. $x = -2$ 2. $x = 1$ 3. $x = -3$ 4. $x = 9$
5. $\{(x, y) \mid x = 3\}$ 6. $\{(x, y) \mid x = -4\}$ 7. $\{(x, y) \mid x = 7\}$ 8. $\{(x, y) \mid 8 = x\}$

PART B

Graph. (Hint: Solve for x.)

9. $\{(x, y) \mid 3x - 9 = 0\}$ 10. $\{(x, y) \mid 8 + 2x = 0\}$ 11. $\{(x, y) \mid 6 - x = 0\}$

Diophantus

HERE YOU SEE THE TOMB CONTAINING THE REMAINS OF DIOPHANTUS. ONE SIXTH OF HIS LIFE GOD GRANTED HIM YOUTH. AFTER A TWELFTH MORE HIS CHEEKS WERE BEARDED. AFTER AN ADDITIONAL SEVENTH HE KINDLED THE LIGHT OF MARRIAGE AND IN THE FIFTH YEAR HE FATHERED A SON. ALAS THE UNFORTUNATE SON'S LIFE SPAN WAS ONLY HALF THAT OF HIS FATHER WHO CONSOLED HIS GRIEF IN THE REMAINING FOUR YEARS OF HIS LIFE. BY THIS DEVICE OF NUMBERS TELL THE EXTENT OF HIS LIFE...

According to legend the above is the inscription on Diophantus' tomb. He was a Greek mathematician who lived in Alexandria in the 3rd century A.D. Diophantus is thought to be one of the originators of algebra. He was probably the first to use symbols for unknowns and operations. He also developed analytical approaches to solve problems.

Diophantus was dedicated to algebra as his epitaph indicates. Can you find how old he was when he died?

Chapter Ten Review

Identify the means and extremes. Solve. [_p. 261_]

1. $\dfrac{x}{6} = \dfrac{4}{3}$

2. $\dfrac{2}{5} = \dfrac{x}{10}$

3. $\dfrac{x+2}{4} = \dfrac{x-5}{3}$

4. $\dfrac{3}{2x-1} = \dfrac{4}{x+4}$

5. $\dfrac{2x+1}{5} = \dfrac{x}{4}$

6. $\dfrac{3x+1}{2} = \dfrac{4x-3}{5}$

7. $\dfrac{x}{9} = \dfrac{1}{x}$

8. $\dfrac{x+5}{4} = \dfrac{-1}{x}$

Solve. [_p. 261_]

9. Two out of 9 people use Gum toothbrushes. How many use this brand in a town of 27,000 people?

10. A batter's batting average is .675. How many hits should he score, if he goes to bat 5,000 times?

Write an equation for $\overleftrightarrow{PQ}$. [_p. 265, 268_]

11. $P(3,1)$, $Q(5,5)$

12. $P(0,1)$, $Q(2,7)$

13. $P(1,4)$, $Q(3,0)$

14. $P(1,1)$, $Q(5,3)$

15. $P(-2,3)$, $Q(1,4)$

16. $P(-3,-2)$, $Q(1,1)$

Write an equation for $\overleftrightarrow{PQ}$. Show that R lies on $\overleftrightarrow{PQ}$. [_p. 265_]

17. $P(2,4)$, $Q(3,6)$, $R(4,8)$

18. $P(1,2)$, $Q(2,5)$, $R(3,8)$

Write an equation for the line. [_p. 272_]

19. slope $= \dfrac{2}{3}$

    y-intercept $= -5$

20. slope $= -\dfrac{3}{7}$

    y-intercept $= 6$

21. slope $= 3$

    y-intercept $= -1$

Give the slope and y-intercept. Graph the line. [_p. 272, 276_]

22. $y = \dfrac{2}{3}x - 4$

23. $y = -\dfrac{4}{5}x + 2$

24. $y = -2x$

25. $\{(x,y)\,|\,y = 2x + 1\}$

26. $\{(x,y)\,|\,x - 3y = 6\}$

27. $\{(x,y)\,|\,y = -6\}$

Graph. Use a table of values. [_p. 276_]

28. $y = 2x - 1$

29. $y = x + 4$

30. $2x - 3y = 15$

Graph. [_p. 279_]

31. $x = 3$

32. $x = -4$

33. $x = 7$

34. $\{(x,y)\,|\,x = 1\}$

35. $\{(x,y)\,|\,2x + 4 = 0\}$

36. $\{(x,y)\,|\,4 - x = 0\}$

Chapter Ten Test

Identify the means and extremes. Solve.

1. $\dfrac{x}{14} = \dfrac{1}{7}$

2. $\dfrac{2x + 1}{3} = \dfrac{x - 4}{5}$

3. $\dfrac{x + 2}{6} = \dfrac{-2}{x - 5}$

Solve.

4. Two out of 5 men shave with Dull blades. How many use this brand in a town of 20,000?

5. A batter's batting average is .125. How many hits should he expect if he goes to bat 2,000 times?

Write an equation for $\overleftrightarrow{PQ}$.

6. $P(4, 9)$, $Q(6, 13)$

7. $P(0, 1)$, $Q(2, -3)$

8. $P(2, 3)$, $Q(5, 1)$

9. $P(0, 2)$, $Q(5, 0)$

Write an equation for $\overleftrightarrow{PQ}$. Show that R lies on $\overleftrightarrow{PQ}$.

10. $P(3, 4)$, $Q(5, 5)$, $R(7, 6)$

11. $P(0, 3)$, $Q(2, 10)$, $R(4, 17)$

Write an equation for the line.

12. slope $= \dfrac{3}{4}$

    y-intercept $= -7$

13. slope $= 2$

    y-intercept $= 3$

Give the slope and y-intercept. Graph the line.

14. $y = \dfrac{2}{3}x - 4$

15. $y = -\dfrac{4}{5}x + 2$

16. $y = 8$

17. $x + y = 5$

18. $\{(x, y) \mid y = 3x + 2\}$

19. $\{(x, y) \mid 2x - 3y = 6\}$

Graph. Use a table of values.

20. $y = 2x - 7$

21. $x - 2y = -16$

Graph.

22. $x = -2$

23. $\{(x, y) \mid x = 3\}$

24. $\{(x, y) \mid 5x + 20 = 0\}$

Linear Programming

The shaded region of the graph below is called a *polygonal region*. It represents the intersection of the solution of the system of inequalities listed below.

$$x \geq 0$$
$$y \geq 0$$
$$x \leq 4$$
$$x + y \leq 8$$

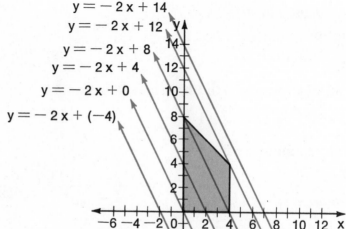

$$y = -2x + 14$$
$$y = -2x + 12$$
$$y = -2x + 8$$
$$y = -2x + 4$$
$$y = -2x + 0$$
$$y = -2x + (-4)$$

The lines
are the graphs of

$$y = -2x + K \text{ for}$$

$$K = \{-4, 0, 4, 8, 12, 14\}$$

The graphs of inequalities and equations as shown above are useful in solving problems in industry. This technique is called *linear programming*.

The graph tells us the maximum (12) and minimum (0) values of *K* that the equation may use and still have a solution in the polygonal region.

In an industrial situation *K* might represent the number of shoes to make per hour to gain the maximum profit. The polygonal region represents the physical limitations of the factory, employees, and so on.

Systems of Equations: Graphing

REVIEW CAPSULE

The intersection of two sets is the set of all elements common to both sets.

$$\{3, 4, 5, 6\} \cap \{2, 4, 5, 8\} = \{4, 5\}$$

The graph of $\{(x, y) \mid y = 3x + 2\}$ is the line whose equation is $y = 3x + 2$.

EXAMPLE 1

Graph $\{(x, y) \mid y = 3x - 9\}$ and $\{(x, y) \mid y = -4x + 5\}$ on the same set of axes.

Use the slope-intercept method to graph each line:

$y = 3x - 9$

slope $\dfrac{3}{1}$ y-intercept -9

$y = -4x + 5$

slope $\dfrac{-4}{1}$ y-intercept 5

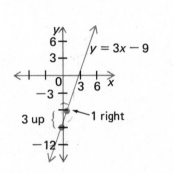

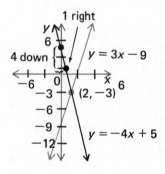

From the graph, $(2, -3)$ is a point common to both lines.

EXAMPLE 2

Find $\{(x, y) \mid y = 3x - 9\} \cap \{(x, y) \mid y = -4x + 5\}$.

Each set of points is graphed in Example 1. $(2, -3)$ is in both sets.

Intersection is the set of points in common. ⟶ **Thus,** $\{(2, -3)\}$ **is the intersection of the two sets.**

The two equations in Example 1 ⟶ form a *system* of equations.

(2, −3) satisfies both equations. ⟶

A System of Equations

$$y = 3x - 9$$
$$y = -4x + 5$$

$(2, -3)$ is a solution of the system.

EXAMPLE 3 Verify that $(2, -3)$ satisfies both $y = 3x - 9$ and $y = -4x + 5$ in Example 1.

$(2, -3)$ (x, y)

Let $x = 2$ and $y = -3$.

y	$3x - 9$
-3	$3(2) - 9$
	$6 - 9$
	-3

y	$-4x + 5$
-3	$-4(2) + 5$
	$-8 + 5$
	-3

Thus, $(2, -3)$ satisfies both equations.

EXAMPLE 4 Solve the system by graphing.
$$3x - 2y = 4$$
$$y = -2x + 5$$

Put the equations in $y = mx + b$ form.
Add $-3x$ to each side.
Divide each side by -2.

$$3x - 2y = 4$$
$$-2y = -3x + 4$$
$$y = \frac{3}{2}x - 2$$

slope y-intercept

$$y = -2x + 5$$

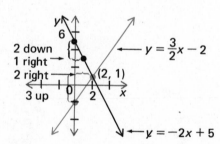

2 down
1 right →
2 right →
3 up

$(2, 1)$

$y = \frac{3}{2}x - 2$

$y = -2x + 5$

From the graph, find the solution.
The two lines intersect at $(2, 1)$. ⟶ **$(2, 1)$ is a solution of the system.**

Check by letting $x = 2$ and $y = 1$ in each ⟶ **Thus, $(2, 1)$ is a solution of both $3x - 2y = 4$**
equation.   **and $y = -2x + 5$.**

SUMMARY   To solve a system of equations by graphing:

Graph each equation on the same | Then read the coordinates of the point
set of axes. | of intersection from the graph.

EXERCISES

Find the intersection.

1. $\{(x, y) \mid y = -2x + 1\} \cap \{(x, y) \mid y = \frac{1}{2}x - 4\}$
2. $\{(x, y) \mid y = \frac{1}{2}x + 6\} \cap \{(x, y) \mid y = -2x + 11\}$
3. $\{(x, y) \mid y = -2x + 4\} \cap \{(x, y) \mid y = 3x + 4\}$

Find the intersection. Verify that its coordinates satisfy both equations.

4. $\{(x, y) \mid y = 3x - 6\} \cap \{(x, y) \mid y = -\frac{2}{3}x + 5\}$
5. $\{(x, y) \mid y = x + 4\} \cap \{(x, y) \mid y = -\frac{3}{2}x + 9\}$
6. $\{(x, y) \mid 3x - 2y = 4\} \cap \{(x, y) \mid 3x + 2y = 8\}$

Solve each system by graphing.

7. $y = 2x + 1$
   $y = -\frac{3}{2}x + 8$
8. $3x - 2y = 6$
   $x - y = 2$
9. $y = 2x$
   $x + y = 9$
10. $x = 3y + 6$
    $x + 3y = 6$
11. $3x + 4y = 8$
    $x - y = -2$
12. $2x + y = 6$
    $2x - y = 10$
13. $y = 3x$
    $x + y = 8$
14. $x + y = 9$
    $y = 2x - 3$

PART B

EXAMPLE   Find $\{(x, y) \mid y = 3x + 5\} \cap \{(x, y) \mid y = 3x - 2\}$.

The lines are parallel. They never intersect.

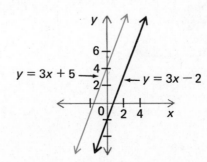

The lines have no points in common.

$$\{(x, y) \mid y = 3x + 5\} \cap \{(x, y) \mid y = 3x - 2\} = \phi$$

We call this an *inconsistent system.*
A *consistent system* is one which has a solution.

Determine whether each system is consistent or inconsistent.

15. $3x - 2y = 14$
    $6x - 4y = 8$
16. $x + y = 8$
    $x - y = 10$
17. $y = 3x - 2$
    $y - 3x = 4$
18. $y = 4$
    $y = -2$

Ordering Numbers Using a Flow Chart

A computer can be programmed to arrange a set of numbers in order from smallest to largest.

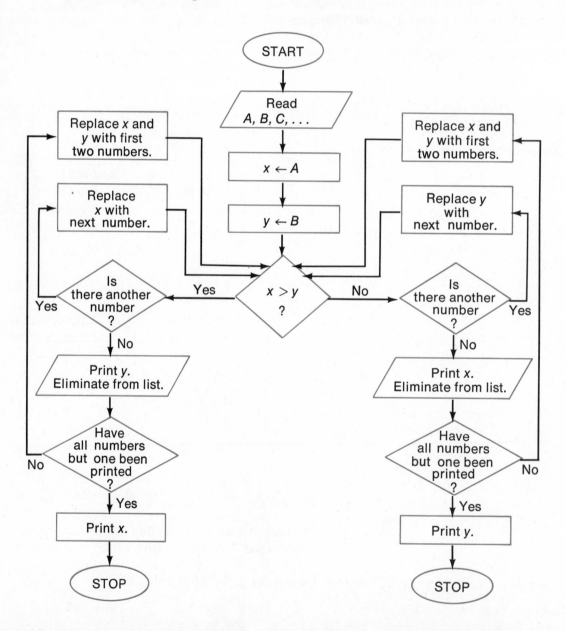

Follow the steps on the flow chart to list the numbers
17, 6, 1, 100 in order from smallest to largest.

Start

Read 17, 6, 1, 100
$x = 17$ $y = 6$
$x > y$? Yes
Is there another number? Yes.
Replace x with the next number.

$x = 1$ $y = 6$
$x > y$? No
Is there another number? Yes.
Replace y with next number.

$x = 1$ $y = 100$
$x > y$? No
Is there another number? No.
Print x.   *Machine prints 1. 1 is removed
                                      from list. New List 17, 6, 100.

$x = 17$ $y = 6$
$x > y$? Yes
Is there another number? Yes.
Replace x with next number.

$x = 100$ $y = 6$
$x > y$? Yes.
Is there another number? No.
Print y.   *Machine prints 6. 6 is removed.
                                      New List 17, 100.

$x = 17$ $y = 100$
$x > y$? No
Is there another number? No.
Print x.   *Machine prints 17.
                                      17 is removed from list.

Have all the numbers but one
been printed? Yes.
Print y.   *Machine prints 100.

Stop

Write the steps in using the flow chart to list each sequence of
numbers in order from smallest to largest.

1. 8, 6, 10   2. 7, 2, 38, 14   3. − 8, 20, 6, − 2   4. 59, 26, − 3, 18, 3

5. Write a flow chart for listing a sequence of numbers in order from
largest to smallest.

Systems of Equations: Substitution

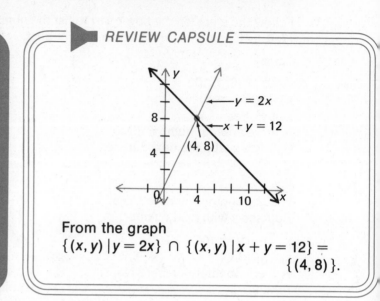

▶ REVIEW CAPSULE

From the graph
$$\{(x, y) \,|\, y = 2x\} \cap \{(x, y) \,|\, x + y = 12\} = \{(4, 8)\}.$$

EXAMPLE 1 Solve the system algebraically.
$$y = 2x$$
$$x + y = 12$$

We want values of x and y that satisfy both equations. y must be the same in both equations.

$$y = 2x$$

$$x + y = 12$$
$$\downarrow$$

Replace y by $2x$ in $x + y = 12$. ⟶
Solve the equation for x.

{ Substitute for y to get an equation with one variable.

$$x + 2x = 12$$
$$3x = 12$$
$$x = 4$$

To find y, let $x = 4$ in either equation.

Replace x by 4 in one of the equations. ⟶
Solve for y.

$$y = 2x \qquad\qquad \text{or} \qquad x + y = 12$$
$$y = 2(4) \qquad\qquad\qquad\qquad 4 + y = 12$$
$$y = 8 \qquad\qquad\qquad\qquad\qquad y = 8$$

So, $x = 4$ and $y = 8$.

Check. ⟶
Let $x = 4$ and $y = 8$ in each equation. ⟶

y	$2x$
8	$2(4)$
	8

$x + y$	12
$4 + 8$	12
12	

Thus, $(4, 8)$ is a solution of the system.

EXAMPLE 2   Solve.

$$3x + 2y = 13$$
$$2x - y = 4$$

Choose a variable whose coefficient is 1 or −1. $\longrightarrow$ First solve $2x - y = 4$ for y.

$-y = -1y$ $\longrightarrow$

Add $-2x$ to each side. $\longrightarrow$

$$2x - 1y = 4$$
$$-1y = -2x + 4$$

Divide each side by −1. $\dfrac{-2}{-1} = 2;$

$\dfrac{+4}{-1} = -4$

$$y = \frac{-2x + 4}{-1}, \text{ or } \frac{-2}{-1}x + \frac{4}{-1}$$
$$y = 2x - 4$$

The other equation $\longrightarrow$

$$3x + 2y = 13$$

Replace y by $2x - 4$. $\longrightarrow$

$2(2x - 4) = 4x - 8$ $\longrightarrow$

Combine like terms. $\longrightarrow$

Add 8 to each side. $\longrightarrow$

$$3x + 2(2x - 4) = 13$$
$$3x + 4x - 8 = 13$$
$$7x - 8 = 13$$
$$\underline{\quad 8 \quad 8}$$
$$7x = 21$$

Divide each side by 7. $\longrightarrow$

$$x = 3$$

Any of the equations could be used. $y = 2x - 4$ is easiest to use, since it is already solved for y.

To find y, let $x = 3$ in $y = 2x - 4$.

$$y = 2x - 4$$
$$y = 2 \cdot 3 - 4$$
$$y = 6 - 4$$
$$y = 2$$

So, $x = 3$ and $y = 2$.

Check by letting $x = 3$ and $y = 2$ in both equations. $\longrightarrow$

Thus, $(3, 2)$ is a solution of the system.

$2x - y = 4$, or

$2x - 1y = 4$

coefficient is −1

The method of substitution is easy to use when one equation contains a variable with a coefficient of 1 or −1.

SUMMARY   **To solve a system of equations by substitution:**

Solve one equation for one of its variables. | **Then substitute for that variable in the other equation.**

ORAL EXERCISES

Identify the variable for which it is easier to solve.

1. $2x - y = 7$
$3x + 7y = 8$

2. $3x - 4y = 6$
$x + 2y = 8$

3. $x + 3y = 9$
$2x - 5y = 6$

4. $3x - 7y = 1$
$2x - y = 4$

EXERCISES

PART A

Solve.

1. $y = 2x$
$x + y = 9$

2. $x + y = 6$
$y = x - 4$

3. $y = 2x - 5$
$x - y = 2$

4. $x + y = 7$
$y = x + 1$

5. $3x - 2y = 9$
$x + 2y = 3$

6. $2x - 3y = 8$
$x + y = 4$

7. $x - 3y = 2$
$3x - 2y = 6$

8. $x - 2y = 6$
$x + 2y = 2$

PART B

Solve.

9. $x - y = 6$
$x + y = 5$

10. $x + y = 8$
$2x - y = -6$

11. $y = 2x$
$2x + y = 10$

12. $x + y = 1$
$y = x$

PART C

EXAMPLE Solve by substitution.

$$3y = 5 - 2x$$
$$4x + 3y = 11$$

Replace $3y$ by $5 - 2x$. $\longrightarrow$

Combine like terms. $\longrightarrow$

$$4x + 3y = 11$$
$$4x + (5 - 2x) = 11$$
$$2x + 5 = 11$$
$$x = 3$$

Use $3y = 5 - 2x$ and find y. $\longrightarrow$

Let $x = 3$. $\longrightarrow$

$$3y = 5 - 2x$$
$$3y = 5 - 2 \cdot 3$$
$$y = -\tfrac{1}{3}$$

Thus, $(3, -\tfrac{1}{3})$ is a solution.

Solve.

13. $5y = x - 1$
$2x = 5y$

14. $4x = 2y - 5$
$2y - 5 + 3x = 14$

15. $2x - 5y = 2$
$5y = 3x + 1$

16. $7y = 3x - 2$
$2x + 7y = 13$

Systems of Equations: $ax + by = c$ $dx - by = e$

OBJECTIVE

■ To solve a system of equations like

$$5x + 2y = 12$$
$$3x - 2y = 4$$

by addition

▶ REVIEW CAPSULE

The addition property for equations

$3 + 1 = 4$	$x - 5 = 3x$	$3x = 12$
$5 + 2 = 7$	$-x \quad = -x$	$2x = 18$
$8 + 3 = 11$	$-5 = 2x$	$5x = 30$

EXAMPLE 1   Add the equations.

$$5x + 2y = 12$$
$$3x - 2y = 4$$

Solve the resulting equation.

$+2y$ ⟵
$-2y$ ⟵ opposites

Equation with only one variable

Divide each side by 2. ⟶

$$5x + 2y = 12 \longleftarrow \text{first equation (1)}$$
$$3x - 2y = 4 \longleftarrow \text{second equation (2)}$$
$$8x + 0 = 16 \longleftarrow \text{third, or resulting equation (3)}$$
$$x = 2$$

EXAMPLE 2   Let $x = 2$ in $5x + 2y = 12$ in Example 1. Solve for the corresponding value of y.

Replace x with 2. ⟶

Solve for y.

Add −10 to each side.

Divide each side by 2.

$$5x + 2y = 12$$
$$5 \cdot 2 + 2y = 12$$
$$10 + 2y = 12$$
$$2y = 2$$
$$y = 1$$

Show that (2, 1) is a solution of the system.

$$5x + 2y = 12$$
$$3x - 2y = 4$$

Check in both equations.

Let $x = 2$ and $y = 1$. ⟶

$5x + 2y$	12	$3x - 2y$	4
$5 \cdot 2 + 2 \cdot 1$	12	$3 \cdot 2 - 2 \cdot 1$	4
$10 + 2$		$6 - 2$	
12		4	

Thus, (2, 1) is a solution of the system.

EXAMPLE 3   Solve.

$$4x - 3y = 6$$
$$2x + 3y = 12$$

Get an equation with one variable.
Add the two equations.
An equation with only one variable
Solve $6x = 18$ for x.

$$
\begin{array}{ll}
4x - 3y = 6 & (1) \\
2x + 3y = 12 & (2) \\
\hline
6x \quad\quad = 18 & (3) \\
\quad\quad x = 3 &
\end{array}
$$

To find y, let $x = 3$ in either equation (1) or (2).

Replace x with 3.

Solve for y.

Add -12 to each side.

Divide each side by -3.

$4x - 3y = 6$		$2x + 3y = 12$
$4 \cdot 3 - 3y = 6$		$2 \cdot 3 + 3y = 12$
$12 \ - 3y = 6$		$6 \ + 3y = 12$
$-3y = -6$		$3y = 6$
$y = 2$		$y = 2$

So, $x = 3$ and $y = 2$.

Check in both equations. ⟶ **Thus,** $(3, 2)$ is a solution of the system.

$-3y$
$3y$ ⟵ opposites

A system of equations like
$$4x - 3y = 6$$
$$2x + 3y = 12$$
can be solved by addition.

EXAMPLE 4   Solve by addition.

$$x + 3y = -7$$
$$-x - 7y = 19$$

x
$-x$ ⟵ opposites

Equation with only one variable y

$$
\begin{array}{ll}
x + 3y = -7 & (1) \\
-x - 7y = 19 & (2) \\
\hline
-4y = 12 & (3) \\
y = -3 &
\end{array}
$$

To find x, let $y = -3$ in either equation (1) or (2).

$$x + 3y = -7 \quad (1)$$

Replace y with -3. ⟶
$$x + 3(-3) = -7$$
$$x - 9 = -7$$

Add 9 to each side. ⟶
$$x = 2$$

So, $x = 2$ and $y = -3$.

Check in both equations. ⟶ **Thus,** $(2, -3)$ is a solution of the system.

ORAL EXERCISES

Give the equation resulting from adding the two equations.

1. $3x - 5y = 4$
$2x + 5y = 7$

2. $x - y = 7$
$x + y = 8$

3. $-3x + 2y = 6$
$-4x - 2y = 9$

4. $-8x - 7y = 9$
$8x + 4y = 10$

EXERCISES

PART A

Solve.

1. $x + y = 8$
$x - y = 4$

2. $-2x + y = 6$
$2x + 3y = 10$

3. $3x - 2y = 2$
$5x + 2y = 14$

4. $-7x + y = 1$
$7x + 3y = 3$

5. $3x - y = 5$
$2x + y = 5$

6. $2x - 3y = 3$
$x + 3y = 3$

7. $5x - 2y = 6$
$x + 2y = 6$

8. $-2x + 5y = -3$
$2x + 3y = 11$

PART B

EXAMPLE   Solve.

$$4x - 3y = 14 \quad (1)$$
$$5x = -3y + 31 \quad (2)$$

The variables are not on one side in
$5x = -3y + 31$.
Add $3y$ to each side. The variables are now
on one side. ⟶

Add the two equations. ⟶

The addition method works best if both variables
are on one side in each equation.

$$5x = -3y + 31 \quad (2)$$
$$5x + 3y = 31 \quad (2)$$
$$\underline{4x - 3y = 14} \quad (1)$$
$$9x \qquad = 45 \quad (3)$$
$$x = 5$$

To find y, let $x = 5$ in either equation (1) or (2).

$$5x = -3y + 31 \quad (2)$$
$$5 \cdot 5 = -3y + 31$$

Substitute 5 for x. ⟶

Add -31 to each side. ⟶

$$25 = -3y + 31$$
$$-6 = -3y$$
$$2 = y$$

So, $x = 5$ and $y = 2$.

Check $(5, 2)$ in both equations. ⟶ **Thus,** $(5, 2)$ is a solution of the system.

Solve.

9. $5x + 8y = 31$
$4y = 5x - 7$

10. $x - 4y = 5$
$2x = -4y - 2$

11. $2x = -9y + 24$
$-9y + 4x = -6$

12. $3x + 2y = 13$
$5x = 2y + 11$

Systems of Equations: $ax + by = c$
$\ dx + ey = f$

OBJECTIVE

■ To solve systems like
$$3x + 2y = 13$$
$$2x + 5y = 16$$
by addition

 REVIEW CAPSULE

Transform $3x + 2y = 8$ into another equation by multiplying each side by 2.

$$2(3x + 2y) = 2 \cdot 8$$
$$6x + 4y = 16$$

Both $3x + 2y = 8$ and $6x + 4y = 16$ have the same solutions.

EXAMPLE 1   Solve by addition.
$$3x + 2y = 13 \quad (1)$$
$$2x + 5y = 16 \quad (2)$$

Adding (1) and (2) does not give an equation in one variable.

$$
\begin{array}{ll}
3x + 2y = 13 & (1) \\
\underline{2x + 5y = 16} & (2) \\
5x + 7y = 29 & (3)
\end{array}
$$

Multiply each side by 5. ⟶

Multiply each side by −2. ⟶

$+10y$ ↙
$-10y$ ↙ opposites

An equation in one variable ⟶

Transform each equation so that adding them gives an equation in one variable.

$$5(3x + 2y) = 5 \cdot 13$$
$$-2(2x + 5y) = -2 \cdot 16$$
$$
\begin{array}{r}
15x + 10y = 65 \\
\underline{-4x - 10y = -32} \\
11x = 33 \\
x = 3
\end{array}
$$

To find y, let $x = 3$ in either equation (1) or (2).

Replace x with 3. ⟶

Solve for y.
Add −9 to each side. ⎫
Divide each side by 2. ⎭

$$
\begin{array}{l}
3x + 2y = 13 \quad (1) \\
3 \cdot 3 + 2y = 13 \\
9 + 2y = 13 \\
2y = 4 \\
y = 2
\end{array}
$$

So, $x = 3$ and $y = 2$.

Check $(3, 2)$ in both equations. ⟶ **Thus,** $(3, 2)$ is a solution of the system.

EXAMPLE 2   Solve.

$$3x - 2y = 6 \quad (1)$$
$$5x + 7y = 41 \quad (2)$$

Two ways

Make the coefficients of y opposites.	Make the coefficients of x opposites.
$7(3x - 2y) = 7 \cdot 6$	$5(3x - 2y) = 5 \cdot 6$
$2(5x + 7y) = 2 \cdot 41$	$-3(5x + 7y) = -3 \cdot 41$

$-14y$ ← opposites → $+15x$
$+14y$ ← → $-15x$

$21x - 14y = 42$	$15x - 10y = 30$
$\underline{10x + 14y = 82}$	$\underline{-15x - 21y = -123}$
$31x \qquad = 124$	$-31y = -93$
$x = 4$	$y = 3$

We can solve for the other variable by using either equation.

To find y, let $x = 4$ in either (1) or (2).	To find x, let $y = 3$ in either (1) or (2).
$5x + 7y = 41 \quad (2)$	$3x - 2y = 6 \quad (1)$
$5 \cdot 4 + 7y = 41$	$3x - 2 \cdot 3 = 6$
$20 + 7y = 41$	$3x - 6 = 6$
$7y = 21$	$3x = 12$
$y = 3$	$x = 4$

Both ways give the same solution. ⟶ **Thus,** $(4, 3)$ is a solution of the system.

EXAMPLE 3   Solve.

$$x + y = -2 \quad (1)$$
$$x - 2y = 7 \quad (2)$$

Make the coefficients of x opposites.
Multiply each side of equation (1) by -1.
Leave equation (2) alone.

$$-1(x + y) = -1(-2)$$
$$-1x - 1y = 2$$

$-1x$ ← opposites
$+1x$ ←

$$-1x - 1y = 2$$
$$\underline{1x - 2y = 7}$$
$$-3y = 9$$

Divide each side by -3. ⟶
$$y = -3$$

To find x, let $y = -3$ in either equation (1) or (2).
$$x + y = -2 \quad (1)$$

Replace y by -3. ⟶
$$x + (-3) = -2$$
$$x - 3 = -2$$
$$x = 1$$

Check $(1, -3)$ in both equations. ⟶ **Thus,** $(1, -3)$ is a solution of the system.

ORAL EXERCISES

Select a multiplier for each equation so that addition leads to an equation in one variable.

1. $3x + 2y = 4$
   $2x + 5y = 2$

2. $2x - 7y = 1$
   $3x + 4y = 2$

3. $3x + 5y = 2$
   $2x + 7y = 1$

4. $3x - 7y = 2$
   $4x - 3y = 8$

5. $2x + 6y = 8$
   $5x - 2y = 9$

6. $3x - 8y = 2$
   $2x + 8y = 2$

7. $3x + 2y = 5$
   $6x + 9y = 2$

8. $7x - 3y = 9$
   $3x - 5y = 4$

EXERCISES

PART A

Solve.

1. $3x + 2y = 8$
   $2x + 5y = 9$

2. $5x - 2y = 3$
   $2x + 7y = 9$

3. $2x + 2y = 8$
   $5x - 3y = 4$

4. $5x - 3y = 2$
   $4x + 2y = 6$

5. $5x + 4y = 29$
   $3x - 2y = 13$

6. $3x - 5y = 1$
   $2x + 10y = 14$

7. $7x + 2y = 9$
   $3x + 8y = 11$

8. $4x - 7y = 5$
   $2x + 8y = 14$

9. $8x - 6y = 10$
   $4x - 5y = 3$

10. $-12x + y = 14$
    $-7x + y = -11$

11. $11x - 3y = 16$
    $4x + 2y = 12$

12. $7x + 5y = 31$
    $-14x + 6y = -30$

13. $x + y = 4$
    $2x + y = 2$

14. $x - 7y = 4$
    $x - 7y = 16$

15. $6x - 2y = -7$
    $13x - 2y = 0$

16. $5x - y = 13$
    $x - y = -1$

PART B

EXAMPLE   Solve.

$$3x - 2y = 6$$
$$5x = -7y + 41$$

Add $7y$ to each side to get both variables on one side. ⟶

$$5x = -7y + 41$$
$$5x + 7y = 41$$

Solve as in Example 2.

$$3x - 2y = 6$$
$$5x + 7y = 41$$

Thus, $(4, 3)$ is a solution of the system.

Solve.

17. $3x - 2y = 5$
    $2x = 5y - 4$

18. $2x - 5y = 1$
    $3x = 4y - 2$

19. $3x = -7y + 2$
    $2x + 5y = 4$

20. $3y = -2x + 7$
    $4x + 3y = 1$

Men of Mathematics

René Descartes
(1596-1650)

René Descartes was known not only as a great mathematician but as a great scientist and philosopher as well. He was very sickly as a child and throughout his life. Because of his condition, he would spend the morning hours in bed and would often use this time to think. Sometimes he would watch a fly walking on the ceiling and try to derive a mathematical equation for its path. Descartes, also called Cartesius, is regarded as the founder of analytic geometry which defines geometric functions using algebraic expressions. Whenever ordered pairs of real numbers are assigned to points in the plane, we have a Cartesian coordinate system.

Descartes was a founder of modern philosophy and one of the Western world's most influential thinkers. His famous statement, "Cogito, ergo sum" (I think, therefore I am) provided a basis for his philosophical system, Cartesianism.

Dry Mixtures: Representing Costs

 REVIEW CAPSULE

Find the cost in cents of 5 lb of gumdrops at $1.25 per lb.

$1.25 = 125$ cents $5(125) = 625$ cents

$$\left(\begin{array}{c}\text{number}\\\text{of lb}\end{array}\right)\left(\begin{array}{c}\text{cost in cents}\\\text{of 1 lb}\end{array}\right) = \left(\begin{array}{c}\text{cost}\\\text{in cents}\end{array}\right)$$

EXAMPLE 1   Butter costs 89¢ per lb. Find the cost in cents of 4 lb. Find the cost in cents of x lb.

$$\left(\begin{array}{c}\text{number}\\\text{of lb}\end{array}\right)\left(\begin{array}{c}\text{cost in cents}\\\text{of 1 lb}\end{array}\right) = \left(\begin{array}{c}\text{cost}\\\text{in cents}\end{array}\right)$$

$4 \cdot 89 = 356$ cents   ¦ $x \cdot 89 = 89x$ cents

EXAMPLE 2   Find the cost in cents of a mixture of 3 lb of coffee at $1.15 per lb and 5 lb of coffee at $.95 per lb.

Use $\left(\begin{array}{c}\text{number}\\\text{of lb}\end{array}\right)\left(\begin{array}{c}\text{cost in cents}\\\text{of 1 lb}\end{array}\right)$ twice. ⟶

$3(115) + 5(95) = 345 + 475$, or 820

Thus, the cost of the mixture is 820 cents.

EXAMPLE 3   Find the cost in cents of a mixture of x lb of candy at $1.35 per lb and y lb of candy at $.85 per lb.

Use $\left(\begin{array}{c}\text{number}\\\text{of lb}\end{array}\right)\left(\begin{array}{c}\text{cost in cents}\\\text{of 1 lb}\end{array}\right)$ twice. ⟶

$x(135) + y(85)$

Thus, the cost of the mixture is $(135x + 85y)$ cents.

EXAMPLE 4   Complete the chart.

	Number of lb	Cost per lb	Cost in Cents
Brand A	x	$1.45	?
Brand B	y	$1.95	?
Total cost in cents			

$1.45 = 145$ cents }
$1.95 = 195$ cents }

	Number of lb	Cost per lb	Cost in Cents
Brand A	x	$1.45	$145x$
Brand B	y	$1.95	$195y$
Total cost in cents			$145x + 195y$

EXAMPLE 5   Three lb of candy at $.85 per lb are to be mixed with 5 lb of candy at $1.10 per lb to form an 8-lb box. Find the cost of the 8-lb box.

Use a chart to display the information. Then use $\left(\begin{matrix}\text{number}\\\text{of lb}\end{matrix}\right)\left(\begin{matrix}\text{cost in cents}\\\text{of 1 lb}\end{matrix}\right)=\left(\begin{matrix}\text{cost}\\\text{in cents}\end{matrix}\right).$

	Number of lb	Cost per lb	Cost in Cents
1st Brand	3	85	$3 \cdot 85 = 255$
2nd Brand	5	110	$5 \cdot 110 = 550$
		Total cost in cents	805

805 cents = $8.05 ————————→ **Thus,** $8.05 is the cost of the 8-lb box.

EXAMPLE 6 x lb of candy at $.75 per lb are to be mixed with y lb of candy at $.95 per lb. Find the number of lb in the mixture and the total cost.

Use a chart to display the information. Then use $\left(\begin{matrix}\text{number}\\\text{of lb}\end{matrix}\right)\left(\begin{matrix}\text{cost in cents}\\\text{of 1 lb}\end{matrix}\right)=\left(\begin{matrix}\text{cost}\\\text{in cents}\end{matrix}\right).$

	Number of lb	Cost per lb	Cost in Cents
1st Brand	x	75	$x \cdot 75 = 75x$
2nd Brand	y	95	$y \cdot 95 = 95y$
		Total cost in cents	$75x + 95y$

Thus, $(x + y)$ lb cost $(75x + 95y)$ cents.

ORAL EXERCISES

Give the cost in cents.

1. 5 lb at 15¢ per lb

2. 6 lb at $2.00 per lb

3. x lb at 85¢ per lb

EXERCISES

PART A

Find the number of pounds and the total cost in cents of the combined mixture.

1. 5 lb at $.45 per lb
6 lb at $1.35 per lb

2. 7 lb at $.85 per lb
9 lb at $1.35 per lb

3. x lb at $.79 per lb
y lb at $2.10 per lb

4. x lb at $2.15 per lb
y lb at $3.35 per lb

5. x lb at $.04 per lb
y lb at $.78 per lb

6. x lb at $1.41 per lb
y lb at $2.10 per lb

PART B

Find the number of pounds and the total cost in cents of the combined mixture.

7. x lb at $1.35 per lb
y lb at m¢ per lb

8. x lb at $1.40 per lb
$(y + 3)$ lb at $.75 per lb

9. x lb at p¢ per lb
y lb at q¢ per lb

Solving Dry Mixture Problems

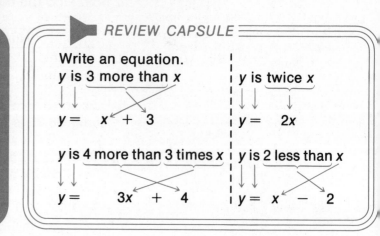

REVIEW CAPSULE

Write an equation.

y is 3 more than x

$y = x + 3$

y is twice x

$y = 2x$

y is 4 more than 3 times x

$y = 3x + 4$

y is 2 less than x

$y = x - 2$

EXAMPLE 1

One brand of candy costs $.85 per lb. Another costs $.75 per lb. The two brands are to be mixed to form a 5-lb gift box that will cost $4.05. How many lb of each should be included?

Use a chart to display the information. Then use

$$\binom{\text{number}}{\text{of lb}} \binom{\text{cost in cents}}{\text{of 1 lb}} = \binom{\text{cost}}{\text{in cents}}.$$

	Number of lb	Cost per lb	Cost in Cents
1st Brand	x	85	$x \cdot 85 = 85x$
2nd Brand	y	75	$y \cdot 75 = 75y$
		Total cost in cents	$85x + 75y$

The total number of pounds is 5. Write an equation. The total cost is 405 (cents). Write an equation.

Solve the system by substitution. Solve for x in $x + y = 5$.

total lb: $x + y = 5$ cost in cents: $85x + 75y = 405$

$x = -y + 5$ (1)   { The two equations
$85x + 75y = 405$ (2)   { form a system.

Replace x by $-y + 5$. ⟶ $85(-y + 5) + 75y = 405$

Distribute the 85. ⟶ $-85y + 425 + 75y = 405$

$$-10y + 425 = 405$$
$$-10y = -20$$
$$y = 2$$

To find x, let $y = 2$ in equation (1).
$$x = -y + 5$$
$$x = -2 + 5$$
$$x = 3$$

Thus, 3 lb at $.85 per lb and 2 lb at $.75 per lb should be included in the mixture.

EXAMPLE 2

Jean wants to make up packs of $.25 comic books mixed with $.15 comic books to sell at $2.45 per pack. If the number of $.15 books is 3 more than the number of $.25 books, write a system of equations which can be used to find the number of each type in a pack.

Use a chart to display the information. Then use
$$\binom{\text{no. of}}{\text{books}}\binom{\text{cost in cents}}{\text{of 1 book}} = \binom{\text{cost}}{\text{in cents}}.$$

No. of Books	Cost per Book	Cost in Cents
x	25	$x \cdot 25 = 25x$
y	15	$y \cdot 15 = 15y$
Total cost in cents		$25x + 15y$

No. of 15¢ books is 3 more than no. of 25¢ books.

Write an equation. $\longrightarrow$

$2.45 = 245$ cents $\longrightarrow$

$$y = x + 3$$

Total cost is 245 cents.

Write an equation. $\longrightarrow$

$$25x + 15y = 245$$

The two equations form a system. Solve the system on your own.

Thus, a system which can be used is $y = x + 3$
$$25x + 15y = 245.$$

EXAMPLE 3

A wholesaler wants to mix pencils costing $.05 each with those costing $.04 each to make a single pack of pencils that will cost $1.04. How many of each type should be in the pack if the number at $.04 is twice the number at $.05?

Use a chart to display the information. Then use
$$\binom{\text{no. of}}{\text{pencils}}\binom{\text{cost in cents}}{\text{of 1 pencil}} = \binom{\text{cost}}{\text{in cents}}.$$

No. of Pencils	Cost per Pencil	Cost in Cents
x	5	$x(5) = 5x$
y	4	$y(4) = 4y$
Total cost in cents		$5x + 4y$

No. of 4¢ pencils is twice no. of 5¢ pencils.

Write an equation. $\longrightarrow$

$1.04 = 104$ cents $\longrightarrow$

$$y = 2 \cdot x$$

Total cost is 104 cents.

$$5x + 4y = 104$$

Write an equation. $\longrightarrow$

Solve the system by substitution. Replace y by $2x$.

$$y = 2x \quad (1)$$
$$5x + 4y = 104 \quad (2)$$

{ The two equations form a system.

$$5x + 4(2x) = 104$$
$$5x + 8x = 104$$
$$x = 8$$

To find y, let $x = 8$ in equation (1).
$$y = 2x = 2 \cdot 8, \text{ or } 16$$
Thus, no. of $.04 pencils is 16; no. of $.05 pencils is 8.

EXAMPLE 4   Show the check for Example 3.

No. of $.04 pencils: 16 ⎱
No. of $.05 pencils: 8 ⎰

$\left(\begin{matrix}\text{No. of}\\\text{pencils}\end{matrix}\right)\left(\begin{matrix}\text{Cost in cents}\\\text{of 1 pencil}\end{matrix}\right) = \left(\begin{matrix}\text{cost}\\\text{in cents}\end{matrix}\right).$

No. of $.04 pencils is twice no. of $.05 pencils.

16	2(8)
	16

Cost of 4¢ pencils + cost of 5¢ pencils is 104¢.

16 (4)	+	8 (5)	104
64	+	40	
	104		

EXERCISES

PART A

Write a system of equations which can be used to solve the problem.

1. Bill wants to mix candy costing $.45 per lb with candy costing $.65 per lb to form a 7-lb box that will cost $3.75. How many lb of each should he use?

2. Candy costing $1.30 per lb is to be mixed with candy costing $1.45 per lb to form a 5-lb box that will cost $6.65. How many lb of each should be used?

3. Lois wants to mix pencils costing $.05 each with pencils costing $.15 each to make a single pack that will cost $1.30. How many of each type should be in the pack if the number of $.15 pencils is 2 more than the number of $.05 ones?

4. Two varieties of cards are to be mixed to form an assortment that will cost $3.65. One kind costs $.45 each and the other $.25 each. How many of each kind should be included if the number of $.45 cards is 1 more than 3 times the number of $.25 cards?

5. Assorted creams cost $1.15 per lb. Caramels cost $.85 per lb. How many lb of each type should be mixed to make a box that will cost $3.70 if the number of lb of creams is 2 less than the number of lb of caramels?

6. A $3.00 gift box of nuts contains two varieties. One type costs $.70 per lb and the other $.90 per lb. Find the number of lb of each if the number of lb at $.70 per lb is 3 times the number of lb at $.90 per lb.

Solve.

7. Jan sold a 9-lb box of candy that contained two varieties. One sold at $.25 per lb and the other at $.35 per lb. How many lb of each type were included if the mixture sold at $2.65?

8. Two brands of candy, one costing $1.50 per lb, the other costing $1.35 per lb were mixed in a 10-lb gift box that cost $14.55. How many lb of each were included?

9. Mr. Lead wants to mix pencils costing $.15 each with pencils costing $.35 each in a single pack that will cost $3.45. How many of each type should be in the pack if the number of $.35 pencils is 7 more than the number of $.15 pencils?

10. Cashews cost $1.25 per lb. Pecans cost $1.35 per lb. How many lb of each should be mixed to make a box to sell at $14.35 if the number of lb of cashews is 1 less than the number of lb of pecans?

11. A $10.40 gift box of candy contains two varieties. One type costs $.80 per lb, and the other costs $.90 per lb. Find the number of lb of each if the number of lb at $.90 per lb is twice the number of lb at $.80 per lb.

12. Two types of gift-wrap paper are to be mixed in an assortment that will cost $2.90. One type sells at $.25 per sheet, the other at $.30 per sheet. How many of each type should be included if the number of sheets of $.30 paper is 2 more than 3 times the number of sheets of $.25 paper?

PART B

13. Ribbons costing $.20 each are to be mixed with ribbons costing $.15 each to make a box that will cost $1.20. If the number of $.20 ribbons is $\frac{3}{4}$ the number of $.15 ribbons, find the number of each type in the box.

14. Party decorations costing $.20 each are to be mixed with decorations costing $.30 each in an assortment that will cost $4.30. If the number of $.30 ones is 5 more than $\frac{1}{2}$ the number of $.20 ones, find the number of each type in the assortment.

15. Meg wants to sell a box of candy which contains two varieties for $7.20. If the number of lb at $.80 per lb is 1 less than $\frac{3}{4}$ the number of lb at $.40 per lb, find the number of lb of each kind.

16. A $1.60 assortment of pads contains $.20 pads and $.15 pads. The number of $.20 pads is 2 less than $\frac{1}{2}$ the number of $.15 pads. Find the number of each type of pad.

17. A grocer sells pecans for $1.05 per lb, almonds for $1.80 per lb, and cashews for $2.10 per lb. He made a mixture of 10 lb to sell for $1.50 per lb. He used $\frac{1}{2}$ as many lb of cashews as pecans. How many lb of each kind did he use?

18. Three pounds of cheese and 2 pounds of meat cost $3.55. Two pounds of the same cheese and 1 pound of the meat cost $2.15. How much does a pound of cheese cost? How much does a pound of meat cost?

19. A 5-lb beef roast and a 6-lb pork roast cost $19.59. A 6-lb beef roast and a 5-lb pork roast cost $19.79. How much per lb was the beef roast? How much per lb was the pork roast?

20. Three bunches of carrots and 4 bunches of scallions cost $.97. Two bunches of carrots and 3 bunches of scallions cost $.68. How much does a bunch of carrots cost? How much does a bunch of scallions cost?

Digit Problems

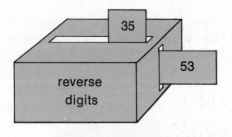 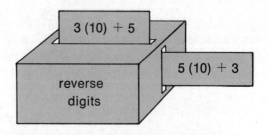

$$35 = 3\,(10) + 5$$
$$\downarrow \qquad \downarrow$$
tens   units
digit   digit

let $3 = t$ and $5 = u$;
then $35 = t\,(10) + u$.

If t is the tens digit and u is the units digit of a two-digit number, then $10\,t + u$ is the number.

Practice Problem 1

If $10\,t + u$ represents a two-digit number, express in algebraic terms the sum of the digits.

$10\,t + u$ is the number

t is the tens digit
u is the units digit

Thus, the sum of the digits is $t + u$.

Practice Problem 2

If $10\,t + u$ represents a two-digit number, express 13 less than the number in algebraic terms.

13 less than the number

$(10\,t + u) - 13$

Thus, the expression is $(10\,t + u) - 13$.

Practice Problem 3

Reverse the digits.

$$65 \qquad\qquad 10\,t + u$$

$$65 = 6\,(10) + 5 \qquad\qquad 10\,t + u$$

$$56 = 5\,(10) + 6 \qquad\qquad 10\,u + t$$

Thus, 56 is the result of reversing the digits of 65 and $10\,u + t$ is the result of reversing the digits of $10\,t + u$.

Practice Problem 4

The sum of the digits of a two-digit number is 10. If the digits of the number are reversed, the new number is 18 less than the original number. Find the original number.

Represent the digits algebraically.

$$\text{Let } t = \text{tens digit of original number}$$
$$u = \text{units digit of original number}$$
$$10\,t + u = \text{original number}$$
$$10\,u + t = \text{number with digits reversed}$$

Write two equations.
First →

Sum of the digits is 10.
$$t + u = 10$$

Second →

New number is 18 less than original.
$$10\,u + t = (10\,t - u) - 18$$

Simplify →

$$9\,t - 9\,u = 18$$

Solve the system. (Use substitution.)
$$t + u = 10$$
$$9\,t - 9\,u = 18$$

First solve $t + u = 10$ for t.

Subtract u from each side.

$$t = 10 - u$$

Replace t by $10 - u$. →
Simplify. →
Solve. →

$$9\,(10 - u) - 9\,u = 18$$
$$18\,u = 72$$
$$u = 4$$

Find t. Substitute for u in one of the equations

$$t + u = 10$$
$$t + 4 = 10$$
$$t = 6$$

$10\,t + u = 10\,(6) + 4$ →   Thus, the original number is 64.

Practice Problem 5	Three times the tens digit of a two-digit number increased by the units digit is 21. If the digits are reversed, the new number is 9 more than the original number. Find the original number.
Represent the digits algebraically. $\}$	Let $t =$ tens digit of original number, $u =$ units digit of original number, $10\,t + u =$ original number, $10\,u + t =$ number with digits reversed.
Write two equations. First $\rightarrow$	Three times tens digit increased by units digit is 21. $3\,t + u = 21$
Second $\rightarrow$ Simplify $\rightarrow$	New number is 9 more than original number. $10\,u + t = (10\,t + u) + 9$ $9\,u - 9\,t = 9$
	Solve the system. $\quad 3\,t + u = 21 \qquad (1)$ $\quad 9\,u - 9\,t = 9 \qquad (2)$
Divide each side of (2) by -9. $\}$	$-u + t = -1 \qquad (3)$
Rearrange the variables in equation (3). $\}$	$t - u = -1$
Add (1) to (3). $\rightarrow$	$\begin{array}{r} 3\,t + u = 21 \\ t - u = -1 \\ \hline 4\,t = 20 \end{array}$
Divide each side by 4. $\rightarrow$	$t = 5$
Find u, Substitute for t in (1). $\rightarrow$	$3\,(t) + y = 21 \qquad (1)$ $3\,(5) + u = 21$ $\qquad u = 21 - 15$ $\qquad u = 6$
$10\,(t) + u = 10\,(5) + 6$	Thus, 56 is the original number

Oral Exercises

If the digits of each of the following are reversed, give the new number.

1. 76   2. $10\,x + y$ 3. $10\,a + b$

EXERCISES

1. The sum of the digits of a two-digit number is 15. If the digits are reversed, the new number is 27 less than the original number. Find the original number.

2. The sum of the digits of a two-digit number is 6. If the digits are reversed, the new number is 18 more than the original number. Find the original number.

3. The tens digit of a two-digit number is twice the units digit. If the digits are reversed, the new number is 36 less than the original number. Find the original number.

4. The units digit of a two-digit number is twice the tens digit. If the digits are reversed, the new number is 18 more than the original number. Find the original number.

5. The sum of the digits of a two-digit number is 13. If the digits are reversed, the new number is 4 less than twice the original number. Find the original number.

6. The sum of the digits of a two-digit number is 8. If the digits are reversed, the new number is 3 more than 4 times the original number. Find the original number.

7. The tens digit of a two-digit number is three times the units digit. If the digits are reversed, the new number is 54 less than the original number. Find the original number.

8. The units digit of a two-digit number is 3 times the tens digit. If the digits are reversed, the new number is 36 more than the original number. Find the original number.

9. The sum of the digits of a two-digit number is 11. If the digits are reversed, the new number is 7 more than twice the original number. Find the original number.

10. The sum of the digits of a two-digit number is 6. If the digits are reversed, the new number is 9 less than 4 times the original number. Find the original number.

11. The units digit of a two-digit number is 1 more than 3 times the tens digit. If the digits are reversed, the new number is 9 less than three times the original number. Find the new number.

12. The tens digit of a two-digit number is 7. If the digits are reversed, the new number is 9 less than the original number. Find the new number.

Solving Number Relation Problems

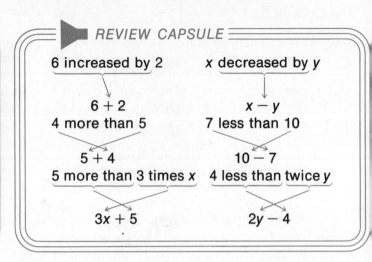

▶ *REVIEW CAPSULE*

6 increased by 2   x decreased by y

$6 + 2$ $x - y$

4 more than 5   7 less than 10

$5 + 4$ $10 - 7$

5 more than 3 times x   4 less than twice y

$3x + 5$ $2y - 4$

EXAMPLE 1   The sum of two numbers is 42. One number is 5 times the other number. Find the numbers.

Let x = one number
   y = other number
The sum of the numbers is 42.

Write an equation.⎫
Sum means add. ⎭

$x + y$ $= 42$
One number is 5 times the other number.

Write another equation. ⟶

$x = 5 \cdot y$
$x + y = 42$ (1)   ⎰ The two equations
$x = 5y$ (2)   ⎱ form a system.

Solve the system by substitution.⎫
Replace x by 5y in equation (1). ⎭

$5y + y = 42$
$6y = 42$
$y = 7$

Use either equation to find x.
Equation (2) is already solved for x.

To find x, let $y = 7$ in equation (2).
$x = 5y$
$x = 5 \cdot 7$
$x = 35$

Check. ⟶

Sum is 42.		One is 5 times the other.	
7 + 35	42	35	5 · 7
	42		35

Thus, the two numbers are 35 and 7.

EXAMPLE 2 One number is 5 times another number. Their difference is 8. Find the numbers.

Let x = larger number
y = smaller number
One number is 5 times another number.

$$x = 5 \cdot y$$

Their difference is 8.

The problem tells us that one number is larger than the other. ————————→ Larger − smaller = 8.

$$x - y = 8$$

$x = 5y$ (1)

The two equations form a system.
Replace x by $5y$ in equation (2). ————→

$x - y = 8$ (2)
$5y - y = 8$
$4y = 8$
$y = 2$

To find x, let $y = 2$ in equation (1).

$$x = 5y$$
$$x = 5 \cdot 2$$
$$x = 10$$

Thus, the two numbers are 2 and 10.

EXAMPLE 3 The sum of two numbers is 50. One number is 5 less than 4 times the other number. Find the numbers.

Let x = one number
y = other number
Their sum is 50.

$$x + y = 50$$

One number is 5 less than 4 times the other.

$$x = 4y - 5$$

$x + y = 50$ (1)
$x = 4y - 5$ (2)

Replace x by $4y - 5$ in equation (1). ————→
$4y - 5 + y = 50$
$5y - 5 = 50$
$5y = 55$
$y = 11$

To find x, let $y = 11$ in (2).
$x = 4y - 5$
$x = 4(11) - 5$
$x = 44 - 5$, or 39

Thus, the two numbers are 39 and 11.

EXAMPLE 4   One number is 3 less than another number. If twice the smaller number is increased by the larger number, the result is 18. Find the numbers.

Let x = smaller number
y = larger number

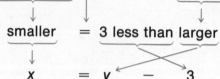

One number is 3 less than another.

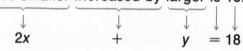

$x = y - 3$

Twice smaller increased by larger is 18.

$2x \qquad + \qquad y = 18$

The problem tells us that one number is smaller than the other. ⟶

$$x = y - 3 \quad (1)$$
$$2x + y = 18 \quad (2)$$

Solve by substitution. Replace x by $y - 3$ in equation (2). ⟶

$$2(y - 3) + y = 18$$

Distribute the 2. Solve the equation.

$$3y - 6 = 18$$
$$3y = 24$$
$$y = 8$$

To find x, let $y = 8$ in equation (1).

$$x = y - 3$$
$$x = 8 - 3$$
$$x = 5$$

Check. ⟶   Smaller is 3 less than larger.

5	8 − 3
	5

Twice smaller increased by larger is 18.

2 · 5	+	8	18
10	+	8	
	18		

Thus, the two numbers are 5 and 8.

EXERCISES

PART A

Find the numbers.

1. The sum of two numbers is 50. One number is 4 times the other.

2. One number is 3 more than twice another. Their sum is 24.

3. The sum of two numbers is 18. Their difference is 6.

4. The sum of two numbers is 72. One number is 8 more than the other.

5. One number is 9 more than another. If the larger is increased by 7, the result is 5 times the smaller.

6. One number is 3 less than another. If the larger is decreased by twice the smaller, the result is −7.

7. The sum of two numbers is 22. One number is 2 more than three times the other.

8. One number is 9 less than twice another. The sum of the number is 12.

9. One number is 4 more than another. If twice the smaller is added to the larger, the result is 28.

10. One number is 2 less than another. If twice the larger is decreased by 3 times the smaller, the result is −10.

PART B

EXAMPLE The length of a rectangle is 5 feet more than the width. The perimeter is 38 feet. Find the length and width.

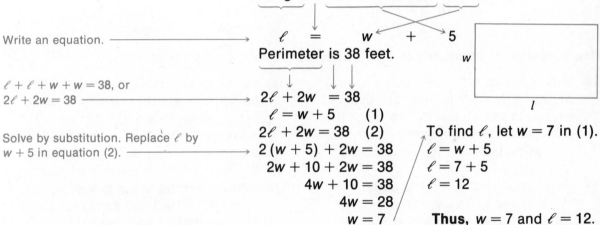

Length is 5 feet more than width.

Write an equation. $\longrightarrow$ $\ell = w + 5$

Perimeter is 38 feet.

$\ell + \ell + w + w = 38$, or
$2\ell + 2w = 38$ $\longrightarrow$ $2\ell + 2w = 38$

$\ell = w + 5$ (1)

Solve by substitution. Replace ℓ by $w + 5$ in equation (2). $\longrightarrow$

$2\ell + 2w = 38$ (2)

$2(w + 5) + 2w = 38$

$2w + 10 + 2w = 38$

$4w + 10 = 38$

$4w = 28$

$w = 7$

To find ℓ, let $w = 7$ in (1).

$\ell = w + 5$

$\ell = 7 + 5$

$\ell = 12$

Thus, $w = 7$ and $\ell = 12$.

Solve.

11. The length of a rectangle is twice the width. The perimeter is 42 feet. Find the length and width.

12. The perimeter of a rectangle is 68 feet. The length is 2 feet less than 3 times the width. Find the length and width.

13. The length of a rectangle is 8 yards more than 6 times the width. Find the length and width if the perimeter is 156 yards.

14. A rectangle is 4 times as long as it is wide. Find the length and width if the perimeter is 50 centimeters.

Chapter Eleven Review

Find the intersection. Verify that its coordinates satisfy both equations. $[\,p.\,285\,]$

1. $\{(x,y)\,|\,x+y=8\}\cap\{(x,y)\,|\,x-y=2\}$
2. $\{(x,y)\,|\,y=3x\}\cap\{(x,y)\,|\,x+y=8\}$
3. $\{(x,y)\,|\,3x-2y=4\}\cap\{(x,y)\,|\,y=x\}$
4. $\{(x,y)\,|\,y=3x+2\}\cap\{(x,y)\,|\,y+x=10\}$

Determine whether each system is consistent or inconsistent. $[\,p.\,285\,]$

5. $x+y=4$	6. $2x-y=5$	7. $x-y=2$	8. $3y=2x-15$
$x+y=6$	$x+y=4$	$3x+3y=4$	$2x-3y=-2$

Solve by addition. $[\,p.\,293,\,296\,]$

9. $x+y=4$	10. $x-5y=6$	11. $2x+5y=5$	12. $3x=4y+5$
$x-y=2$	$-x=y+6$	$3x+3y=12$	$2x+2y=8$

Solve by substitution. $[\,p.\,290\,]$

13. $y=2x$	14. $x-y=8$	15. $x-5y=6$	16. $x+y=1$
$x+y=9$	$x+y=12$	$x+y=6$	$x-y=4$

Use a system of equations to solve each of the following problems. $[\,p.300,\,302,\,310\,]$

17. Nan wants to sell a 5-lb box of candy containing two varieties. One sells at $.75 per lb, the other at $.95 per lb. How many lb of each should be included if the mixture is to cost $4.15?

18. Pedro mixes candy selling at $1.10 per lb with another selling at $1.20 per lb to make a $5.80 gift box. The number of lb at $1.10 per lb is 1 less than the number of lb at $1.20 per lb. Find the number of lb of each.

19. Two varieties of gift-wrap paper are to be mixed in an assortment that will cost $2.00. One sells at $.40 per sheet, the other at $.30 per sheet. How many of each type should be included if the number of sheets at $.30 per sheet is twice the number of sheets at $.40 per sheet?

20. Diane wants to sell a box of two varieties of birthday cards for $5.80. The number of $.30 cards is 6 more than $\frac{1}{2}$ the number of $.35 cards. Find the number of cards of each type.

21. The sum of two numbers is 40. One number is 8 more than the other. Find the numbers.

22. The sum of two numbers is 24. Their difference is 8. Find the numbers.

23. One number is 3 more than twice another. If the larger is increased by the smaller, the result is 18. Find the numbers.

24. The perimeter of a rectangle is 36. The length is 6 more than twice the width. Find the length and width.

Chapter Eleven Test

Find the intersection. Verify that its coordinates satisfy both equations.

1. $\{(x, y) \mid x + y = 4\} \cap \{(x, y) \mid x - y = 6\}$
2. $\{(x, y) \mid y = 3x\} \cap \{(x, y) \mid 3x + y = 6\}$

Determine whether each system is consistent or inconsistent.

3. $x + y = 7$
   $x + y = 5$

4. $3x - y = 4$
   $x + y = 4$

5. $2x = y + 3$
   $2x - y = 6$

Solve by substitution.

6. $y = 3x$
   $x + y = 8$

7. $x - y = 8$
   $x + y = 4$

8. $2x + y = 3$
   $y = 2x + 1$

Solve by addition.

9. $2x + y = 4$
   $x - y = 8$

10. $2x - 3y = 1$
   $3x - 5y = 1$

11. $2x = 7y + 1$
   $5x + 3y = 23$

Use a system of equations to solve each of the following problems.

12. Ed wants to sell a 7-lb box of candy containing two varieties. One sells at $.65 per lb, the other at $.85 per lb. How many lb of each should be included if the mixture is to cost $5.15?

13. Tanya mixes candy selling at $1.40 per lb with another selling at $1.20 per lb to make a $13.20 gift box. The number of lb at $1.40 per lb is 2 more than the number of lb at $1.20 per lb. Find the number of lb of each.

14. The sum of two numbers is 60. One number is 20 less than the other. Find the numbers.

15. One number is 5 less than twice another. Their sum is 16. Find the numbers.

16. One number is 7 more than 3 times another. If the larger is decreased by twice the smaller, the result is 9. Find the numbers.

17. The perimeter of a rectangle is 28. The width is 2 less than the length. Find the length and the width of the rectangle.

Galileo and Freefall

Galileo Galilei, the renowned Italian astronomer and physicist, made a remarkable discovery in 1585. He timed an object as it fell from a given height, discovering the "free fall" equation.

$$y = 16\, t^2$$

distance of the fall in feet

elapsed time in seconds after the start of the fall

According to legend, Galileo dropped small cannon balls from the colonnades of the Leaning Tower of Pisa, timing their fall.
Even though the cannon balls were of different sizes and weights, they all took the same number of seconds to hit the ground.

1. Stand on a chair and drop a book and a pencil at the same time. What happens?
2. Drop a pencil and a large piece of paper. What happens? Crumble the paper into a ball and then drop it at the same time with a pencil. What happens?
3. Using Galileo's formula, how long will it take an object to fall 144 ft.?

Relations and Functions

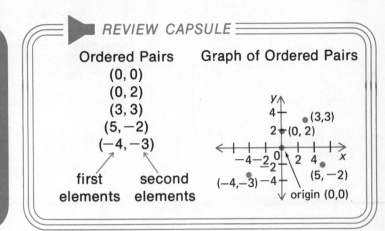

REVIEW CAPSULE

Ordered Pairs   Graph of Ordered Pairs
(0, 0)
(0, 2)
(3, 3)
(5, −2)
(−4, −3)

first   second
elements   elements

origin (0,0)

Set C is a relation. ⟶ $C = \{(-1, 3), (2, 4), (0, -2), (-1, -5)\}.$

Definition of relation ⟶ A *relation* is a set of ordered pairs.

Domain of relation $C = \{-1, 2, 0\}.$
Range of relation $C = \{3, 4, -2, -5\}.$

Definition of domain and range ⟶ The set of all first elements of the ordered pairs in a relation is the *domain*. The set of all second elements is the *range*.

EXAMPLE 1   Graph $A = \{(5, 0), (-3, 4), (-3, -1), (-2, 4)\}.$
Then give the domain and the range of relation A.

Graph of relation A ⟶

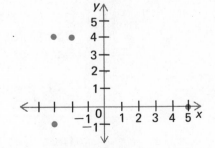

In the domain, list −3 only once.

In the range, list 4 only once.

Domain of A:
$\{5, -3, -2\}$

Range of A:
$\{0, 4, -1\}$

Set S is a function. ────────────→ $S = \{(4, 8),\ (2, -1),\ (-6, 7),\ (5, 7)\}.$

A function is a special kind of a relation. No two first elements   Second elements
                                            are the same.   may be the same.

Definition of function. ────────────→ | A *function* is a relation in which no two ordered pairs have the same first element.

EXAMPLE 2   Graph
$B = \{(0, -3),\ (3, 1),\ (4, -3),\ (-3, -5),\ (-6, 6)\}.$
Give the domain and the range of relation B. Is B a function?

Graph of relation B ────────────→

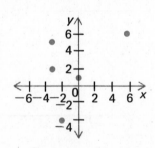

Domain of B:
$\{0, 3, 4, -3, -6\}$

Range of B:
$\{-3, 1, -5, 6\}$

No two first elements are the same in a function.

B is a function.

EXAMPLE 3   List the ordered pairs in relation C graphed below. Give the domain and the range of C. Is C a function?

Graph of relation C ────────────→

Ordered pairs in relation C ────────────→ $C = \{(-3, 2),\ (-3, 5),\ (-2, -4),\ (0, 1),\ (6, 6)\}.$
Domain of $C = \{-3, -2, 0, 6\}.$
Range of $C = \{2, 5, -4, 1, 6\}.$

Both $(-3, 2)$ and $(-3, 5)$ are in C. ────────────→ -3 is the first element in two of the ordered pairs in C.

Two first elements are the same. **Thus, C is not a function.**

EXERCISES

List the ordered pairs in each relation graphed below. Give the domain and the range of the relation. Is the relation a function?

1.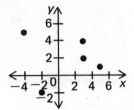

2.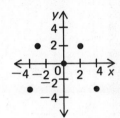

3.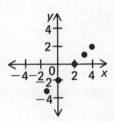

Graph each relation. Give the domain and the range. Is the relation a function?

4. $\{(0, 1), (-1, 1), (3, -2), (-4, 4)\}$ **5.** $\{(3, 2), (4, 2), (-1, 2), (0, 2)\}$

6. $\{(2, -2), (2, -3), (2, -1), (2, 0)\}$ **7.** $\{(3, 0), (-3, 0), (0, 3), (0, -3)\}$

8. $\{(-1, 1), (-2, 2), (0, 0), (1, -1), (2, -2)\}$

9. $\{(-1, -1), (-2, -2), (0, 0), (1, 1), (2, 2)\}$

10. $\{(3, 0), (-1, 2), (2, 4), (3, -4), (0, -2)\}$

11. $\{(0, 0), (1, -1), (1, 1), (4, -2), (4, 2)\}$

12. $\{(-3, 1), (-2, 1), (-1, 1), (0, 1), (1, -1), (2, -1)\}$

13. $\{(-4, -5), (-3, -4), (-1, -3), (0, -3), (2, -4), (3, -5), (4, -5), (5, -3)\}$

PART B

| EXAMPLE | $A = \{(1, 3), (2, 0), (-1, 3)\}$ |

The inverse of relation A is relation B. ⟶ $B = \{(3, 1), (0, 2), (3, -1)\}$

The first and second elements of the ordered pairs in A are interchanged to form B.

B is the inverse of A. Also, A is the inverse of B.
Is A a function? Is B a function?

A is a function. B is not a function.

Give the inverse of each relation. Is the relation a function? Is its inverse a function?

14. $\{(-2, 4), (-1, 1), (0, 4)\}$ **15.** $\{(2, 3), (1, -2), (2, -4), (3, 0)\}$

16. $\{(-1, 1), (-2, 1), (0, 1), (1, 1), (2, 1)\}$

17. $\{(-2, 0), (-1, 1), (0, 2), (1, 3), (2, 4)\}$

18. $\{(1, 0), (-1, 0), (3, 2), (2, 1), (3, -1)\}$

Types of Functions

OBJECTIVES
- To determine if a relation is a function by applying the vertical line test to its graph
- To identify linear and constant functions

▶ *REVIEW CAPSULE*

Graph of Relation A

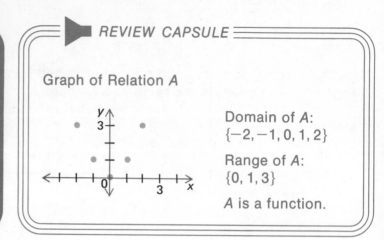

Domain of A:
$\{-2, -1, 0, 1, 2\}$

Range of A:
$\{0, 1, 3\}$

A is a function.

EXAMPLE 1 Is the following the graph of a function?

The dashed vertical line crosses the graph in two points:

$(4, 2)$ and $(4, -2)$.

_____
same first element

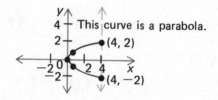

This curve is a parabola.

Two ordered pairs have the same first element. ⟶ **Thus,** the graph is not the graph of a function.

Vertical Line Test

A *relation* is a function if no vertical line crosses its graph in more than one point.

EXAMPLE 2 Is $\{(x, y) \mid y = 2x + 1\}$ a function?

Use the slope-intercept method to graph $y = 2x + 1$.

Slope $\frac{2}{1}$ y-intercept 1

No vertical line will cross the graph in more than one point.

No two ordered pairs have the same first element. ⟶ **Thus,** $\{(x, y) \mid y = 2x + 1\}$ is a function.

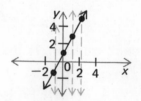

Definition of linear function ⟶

> A *linear function* is a function whose graph is a line or a subset of a line which is neither vertical nor horizontal.

EXAMPLE 3 Is $\{(x, y) \mid y = -3\}$ a function? If so, is it a linear function?

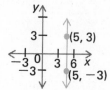

$y = -3$ $(0, -3)$ $(5, -3)$

Plot $(0, -3)$, since the y-intercept is -3.
Then plot any other point with y-coord.
-3 like $(5, -3)$.
Draw the horizontal line.
No two ordered pairs have the same first element. ⟶ **Thus, $\{(x, y) \mid y = -3\}$ is a function.**

Its graph is a horizontal line. ⟶ $\{(x, y \mid y = -3\}$ **is not a linear function.**

Definition of constant function ⟶
Example 3 shows a constant function.

> A *constant function* is a function whose graph is a horizontal line or a subset of a horizontal line.

EXAMPLE 4 Is $\{(x, y) \mid x = 5\}$ a function? If so, is it a linear function or a constant function?

y is not mentioned in $x = 5$. The graph is a vertical line. Use any two points with x-coordinate 5 like $(5, 3)$ and $(5, -3)$.

The graph is a vertical line. ⟶ **Thus, $\{(x, y) \mid x = 5\}$ is not a function.**

ORAL EXERCISES

Which relations are functions? Which functions are linear functions? Which functions are constant functions?

1.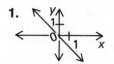
2.
3.
4.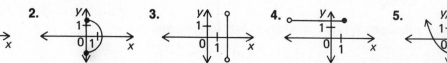
5.

EXERCISES

PART A

Graph each relation. Which relations are functions? Which functions are linear functions? Which functions are constant functions?

1. $\{(x, y \mid y = 3x\}$
2. $\{(x, y) \mid y = -2x\}$
3. $\{(x, y) \mid y = x\}$
4. $\{(x, y) \mid y = 5\}$
5. $\{(x, y) \mid x = -4\}$
6. $\{(x, y) \mid -2 = y\}$
7. $\{(x, y) \mid 3 = x\}$
8. $\{(x, y) \mid y = x + 1\}$
9. $\{(x, y) \mid y = 2x - 3\}$
10. $\{(x, y) \mid x = 4y\}$
11. $\{(x, y) \mid x = 3y - 1\}$
12. $\{(x, y) \mid x = 0\}$
13. $\{(x, y) \mid y = 0\}$
14. $\{(x, y) \mid y = -2x - 4\}$
15. $\{(x, y) \mid y = 3x - 2\}$
16. $\{(x, y) \mid 2x + y = 3\}$
17. $\{(x, y) \mid x + 2y = -1\}$
18. $\{(x, y) \mid y = -x\}$
19. $\{(x, y) \mid x + y = 4\}$
20. $\{(x, y) \mid x - y = -6\}$
21. $\{(x, y) \mid x = 4\}$
22. $\{(x, y) \mid y = -3\}$
23. $\{(x, y) \mid 2x + 4y = -1\}$
24. $\{(x, y) \mid 3x = y - 1\}$
25. $\{(x, y) \mid 3y = 4 + x\}$
26. $\{(x, y) \mid x + 1 = 0\}$
27. $\{(x, y) \mid 3 + y = 0\}$
28. $\{(x, y) \mid 2x = y - 1\}$
29. $\{(x, y) \mid -3x + y = 5\}$
30. $\{(x, y) \mid -y - x = -4\}$

PART B

EXAMPLE Graph $\{(x, y) \mid y = -x^2\}$. Is the relation a function?

Find some ordered pairs. ⎫
Choose any numbers for x. ⎬
Find the y-coordinates. ⎭

Draw a smooth curve through the points.

The curve is a parabola.

No vertical line will cross the graph in more than one point. ⟶ **Thus, $\{(x, y) \mid y = -x^2\}$ is a function.**

x	$-x^2$	y
0	$-(0)^2$	0
1	$-(1)^2$	-1
-1	$-(-1)^2$	-1
2	$-(2)^2$	-4
-2	$-(-2)^2$	-4
3	$-(3)^2$	-9
-3	$-(-3)^2$	-9

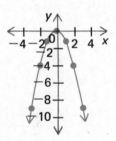

Graph each relation. Which relations are functions?

31. $\{(x, y) \mid y = x^2\}$
32. $\{(x, y) \mid y = x^2 + 1\}$
33. $\{(x, y) \mid y = x^2 - 3\}$
34. $\{(x, y) \mid y = 2x^2\}$
35. $\{(x, y) \mid y = -3x^2\}$
36. $\{(x, y) \mid 4x^2 = -2y\}$
37. $\{(x, y) \mid x = y^2\}$
38. $\{(x, y) \mid x = -1y^2\}$
39. $\{(x, y) \mid x = 3y^2\}$
40. $\{(x, y) \mid 2y^2 = -1x\}$
41. $\{(x, y) \mid x = y^2 + 2\}$
42. $\{(x, y) \mid x = y^2 - 1\}$

PART C

Graph each relation. Which relations are functions?

43. $\{(x, y) \mid y = x^3\}$
44. $\{(x, y) \mid y = x^3 + 2\}$
45. $\{(x, y) \mid y = 3x^3\}$
46. $\{(x, y) \mid y = -1x^3\}$
47. $\{(x, y) \mid x = y^4\}$
48. $\{(x, y) \mid y = -1x^4\}$

$f(x)$ Notation

OBJECTIVE

■ To find the range of a function for a given domain

 REVIEW CAPSULE

Small letters are used to name functions.

$$f = \{(0, 1),\ (-4, 3),\ (2, -3)\}$$

Domain of f: $\{0, -4, 2\}$.
Range of f: $\{1, 3, -3\}$.

EXAMPLE 1

In the function above, what value of y is paired with each of these values of x: $0, -4, 2$?

Examine each ordered pair:
$(0, 1),\ (-4, 3),\ (2, -3)$.

When x is 0, y is 1.
When x is -4, y is 3.
When x is 2, y is -3.

Definition of value of f at x ⟶

Read $f(x) = y$ as the value of f at x is y, or as f at x is y.

If (x, y) is an ordered pair in function f, then the value of f at x is y.
$$f(x) = y$$

For function f above,
$f(0) = 1$	$f(-4) = 3$	$f(2) = -3$.
f at 0 is 1.	f at -4 is 3.	f at 2 is -3.

EXAMPLE 2

$f = \{(x, y)\,|\,y = 2x - 1\}$. Find $f(2)$, $f(-1)$, and $f(20)$.

Substitute 2, -1, and 20 for x.

Find $f(2)$.

$$f(x) = 2x - 1$$
$$f(2) = 2 \cdot 2 - 1$$
$$= 4 - 1$$
$$= 3$$

f at 2 is 3.

Find $f(-1)$.

$$f(x) = 2x - 1$$
$$f(-1) = 2(-1) - 1$$
$$= -2 - 1$$
$$= -3$$

f at -1 is -3.

Find $f(20)$.

$$f(x) = 2x - 1$$
$$f(20) = 2 \cdot 20 - 1$$
$$= 40 - 1$$
$$= 39$$

f at 20 is 39.

EXAMPLE 3 $h(x) = x^2 - 2$, and the domain of h is $\{-1, 0, 1\}$.
Determine the range of h.

Substitute −1, 0, and 1 for x.

Find $h(-1)$.	Find $h(0)$.	Find $h(1)$.
$h(x) = x^2 - 2$	$h(x) = x^2 - 2$	$h(x) = x^2 - 2$
$h(-1) = (-1)^2 - 2$	$h(0) = 0^2 - 2$	$h(1) = 1^2 - 2$
$= 1 - 2$	$= 0 - 2$	$= 1 - 2$
$= -1$	$= -2$	$= -1$

List −1 only once. ⟶ **Thus, the range of h is $\{-1, -2\}$.**

EXERCISES

PART A

$f = \{(x, y) \,|\, y = 3x - 2\}$. **Find each.**

1. $f(0)$ **2.** $f(4)$ **3.** $f(-2)$ **4.** $f(15)$ **5.** $f(-22)$

$g = \{(x, y) \,|\, y = -4x + 7\}$. **Find each.**

6. $g(-1)$ **7.** $g(5)$ **8.** $g(13)$ **9.** $g(-7)$ **10.** $g(30)$

$h(x) = x^2 - 5$. **Find each.**

11. $h(0)$ **12.** $h(-4)$ **13.** $h(4)$ **14.** $h(15)$ **15.** $h(-20)$

D **is the domain of each function. Determine the range.**

16. $f(x) = 4x - 3$ $D = \{0, 1, 2\}$
17. $h(x) = 6x + 2$ $D = \{-3, 1, 4\}$
18. $g(x) = -2x - 9$ $D = \{2, 4, 6\}$
19. $r(x) = -7x + 4$ $D = \{-2, -4, -6\}$
20. $f(x) = x^2 + 1$ $D = \{-3, 0, 9\}$
21. $g(x) = 2x^2 + 3$ $D = \{-8, -7, -6\}$
22. $k(x) = x^2 + x - 1$ $D = \{2, 1, 0\}$
23. $r(x) = 2x^2 - 3x - 2$ $D = \{1, 3, 6\}$

PART B

D **is the domain of each function. Determine the range.**

24. $f(x) = 2x - 8$ $D = \{\frac{1}{2}, \frac{1}{4}, \frac{1}{3}\}$
25. $g(x) = -3x + 7$ $D = \{.5, .6, .7\}$
26. $f(x) = (x + 1)^2$ $D = \{0, 2, 4\}$
27. $k(x) = (2x - 3)^2$ $D = \{-1, -2, -3\}$
28. $r(x) = (x^2 - 2)^2$ $D = \{-2, 0, 2\}$
29. $j(x) = x^2 - 5$ $D = \{-\frac{1}{2}, \frac{1}{2}, \frac{1}{4}\}$

PART C

$f(x) = 4x - 5$ and $g(x) = x^2 + 3$. **Find each.**

30. $f(2) + g(2)$ **31.** $g(6) - f(6)$ **32.** $f(7) - g(-3)$ **33.** $g(-8) + f(-2)$
34. $g[f(1)]$ **35.** $g[f(-2)]$ **36.** $f[g(4)]$ **37.** $f[g(-6)]$

The Greatest Integer Function

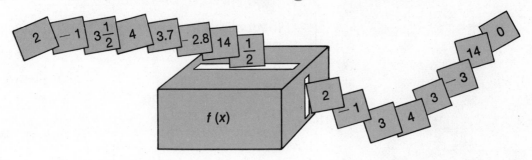

Can you see a pattern here?

x	f (x)
$35\frac{3}{4}$	35
21	21
3.2	3
$\frac{1}{3}$	0
0	0
$-2\frac{1}{4}$	-3
-7	-7

In each case, f (x) is the nearest integer to x which is less than or equal to x. This is called the greatest integer function, and is written [x].

$$\left.\begin{array}{l} 13 \\ 13.1 \\ 13\frac{1}{2} \\ 13.23 \\ 13\frac{2}{7} \\ 13.99 \end{array}\right\} \longrightarrow \mathbf{13}$$

For any number n, [n] is the greatest integer less than or equal to n.

$$\left[34\frac{1}{2}\right] = 34 \qquad \left[2.3\right] = 2 \qquad \left[-\frac{1}{4}\right] = -1$$

Draw the graph of the greatest integer function.

Graphing Inequalities in Two Variables

 REVIEW CAPSULE

Inequalities in one variable can be graphed on a number line.

$$-2x + 4 \leq 10$$

Add -4 to each side. ⟶ $\quad -2x \leq 6$
Divide each side by -2.
Reverse the order. ⟶ $\quad\quad x \geq -3$

Graph. ⟶

EXAMPLE 1   Graph $y < 2$ on a plane.

First graph $y = 2$ with a dashed line.

Graph of $y = 2$ is a horizontal line. The
y-coordinate of every point is 2. }

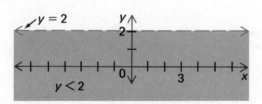

The y-coordinate of every point below
the line is less than 2. ⟶ The graph of $y < 2$ is *below* the line. The shaded
region is the graph of $y < 2$.

EXAMPLE 2   Graph $y > 2$ on a plane.

First graph $y = 2$ with a dashed line.

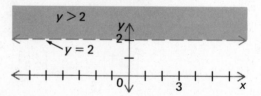

The y-coordinate of every point above
the line is greater than 2.

The graph of $y > 2$ is the shaded region *above*
the line.

EXAMPLE 3 Graph $y = 2x - 1$ with a dashed line. Show that $(-2, 1)$ satisfies the inequality $y > 2x - 1$. Show that $(3, -4)$ satisfies the inequality $y < 2x - 1$.

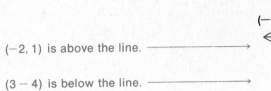

(−2, 1) is above the line. ────────────→

(3 − 4) is below the line. ────────────→

Test $(-2, 1)$.

$y >$	$2x - 1$
1	$2(-2) - 1$
	$-4 \ -1$
	-5

$1 > -5$
True

Test $(3, -4)$.

$y <$	$2x - 1$
-4	$2(3) - 1$
	$6 \ -1$
	5

$-4 < 5$
True

Example 3 suggests this. ────────────→

The graph of $y = mx + b$ is a line.
The graph of $y > mx + b$ is the region *above* the line.
The graph of $y < mx + b$ is the region *below* the line.

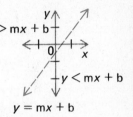

EXAMPLE 4 Graph $-3x - 2y > 6$.

Solve for y.
Add $3x$ to each side. ────────────→
Divide each side by -2.⎱
Reverse the order. ⎰

$$-3x - 2y > 6$$
$$-2y > 3x + 6$$
$$y < \frac{3x + 6}{-2}$$
$$y < -\frac{3}{2}x - 3$$

Graph $y = -\dfrac{3}{2}x - 3$ with a dashed line.

$$y = -\frac{3}{2}x - 3$$

slope $-\dfrac{3}{2}$ y-intercept -3

To graph $y < -\dfrac{3}{2}x - 3$, shade the region

below the line. ────────────→

Thus, the graph of $-3x - 2y > 6$ is the shaded region *below* the line.

EXAMPLE 5   Graph $\{(x,y)\,|\,y \geq 3x - 1\}$

Graph $y = 3x - 1$.

Slope $\dfrac{3}{1}$ y-intercept -1

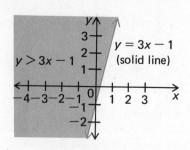

$\geq$ means is greater than or equal to. The graph must include the line $y = 3x - 1$. Draw a solid line.

Thus, the graph of $\{(x,y)\,|\,y \geq 3x - 1\}$ is the *line* and the shaded region *above* the line.

EXAMPLE 6   Graph $\{(x,y)\,|\,x > 3\}$. Then graph $\{(x,y)\,|\,x < 3\}$.

First graph $x = 3$ with a dashed line.

Graph of $x = 3$ is a vertical line. The x-coordinate of every point is 3.

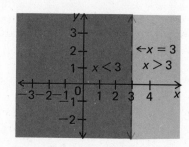

The x-coordinate of every point to the *right* of the line is *greater* than 3.

The x-coordinate of every point to the *left* of the line is less than 3.

The graph of $\{(x,y)\,|\,x > 3\}$ is the shaded portion to the *right* of the line.
The graph of $\{(x,y)\,|\,x < 3\}$ is the shaded portion to the *left* of the line.

Example 6 suggests this. ⟶

The graph of $x = a$ is a vertical line.
The graph of $x > a$ is the region to the right of the line.
The graph of $x < a$ is the region to the left of the line.

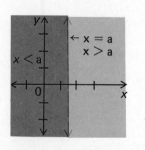

ORAL EXERCISES

Give the equation of the line which must be graphed in order to graph each inequality. Tell whether the shaded region will be above, below, to the left, or to the right of the line. Tell whether the line will be included in the graph.

1. $y \leq 3x + 2$ 2. $y > x + 5$ 3. $y \leq 4$ 4. $y < x + 3$ 5. $y \geq 2x - 1$ 6. $x \geq 5$
7. $x < 2$ 8. $y > 7$ 9. $y \leq 4x + 1$ 10. $y > x$ 11. $x \leq 3$ 12. $y < 3$
13. $y \geq x + 4$ 14. $x < 1$ 15. $y > 2$ 16. $x \geq 3$ 17. $y < x + 4$ 18. $y < x - 9$

EXERCISES

PART A

Solve for y.

1. $x + y < 3$ 2. $x - y > 8$ 3. $x + 3 > -y$ 4. $2x - y \leq 4$
5. $3x + 2y > 0$ 6. $4x + y \geq 6$ 7. $-3x + y < 4$ 8. $3y < x$
9. $5x > 2y$ 10. $2x + 3y < 6$ 11. $x > 4y - 8$ 12. $6x - 2y \leq 12$

Graph each inequality.

13. $y > 3$ 14. $x < -1$ 15. $y \leq -4$ 16. $\{(x, y) \mid x \geq 2\}$
17. $y < 3x$ 18. $y > 2x$ 19. $y \leq x$ 20. $\{(x, y) \mid y \geq -2x\}$
21. $y \leq x + 5$ 22. $y \geq 2x - 3$ 23. $y < -x - 3$ 24. $\{(x, y) \mid y > 3x - 4\}$
25. $y \leq 2x + 1$ 26. $y \geq 3x - 2$ 27. $x < 0$ 28. $\{(x, y) \mid y \geq 0\}$
29. $y < \frac{2}{3}x + 1$ 30. $y \geq \frac{3}{5}x - 2$ 31. $y \leq \frac{1}{2}x + 1$ 32. $\{(x, y) \mid y > \frac{2}{3}x - 2\}$
33. $x + y > 2$ 34. $x - y \leq 3$ 35. $2x - y > 4$ 36. $\{(x, y) \mid 2x + 3y < 6\}$

Graph each inequality. Then determine which of the given points belong to the graph.

37. $y > 1$; (3, 1), (3, 7)   38. $x \leq 4$; (−5, 3), (7, 3)
39. $y > x - 6$; (3, −3), (3, 8)   40. $y \geq x - 6$; (8, 2), (8, 1)
41. $y \geq x + 2$; (4, 1), (4, 6)   42. $y > 2x + 1$; (2, 3), (2, 7)
43. $y \leq 3x + 1$; (3, 11), (3, 0)   44. $y < 3x - 4$; (3, 5), (3, 2)

PART B

Graph each inequality.

45. $2y < 8$ 46. $-3x \leq 9$ 47. $3x \geq 2y$ 48. $\{(x, y) \mid -4y \geq 8\}$
49. $3x - 2y \leq 6$ 50. $2x - 3y \geq 9$ 51. $4x - 3y \geq 6$ 52. $\{(x, y) \mid 2x - 5y \geq 10\}$
53. $4x \leq 3y + 6$ 54. $2x + 5y \leq 20$ 55. $5x - 2y < 8$ 56. $\{(x, y) \mid 3x - 5y > 20\}$
57. $3x - 5y \leq 15$ 58. $3x \leq 4y + 12$ 59. $8x + 4y > 2$ 60. $\{(x, y) \mid 6x - 3y < 9\}$
61. $x + 6y < 2$ 62. $4 > 3x + 2y$ 63. $7x \leq 3y - 9$ 64. $\{(x, y) \mid 12 \geq 6x - 4y\}$

Direct Variation

OBJECTIVES
- To determine if a relation is a direct variation
- To find the constant of proportionality in a direct variation
- To solve direct variation problems

Formula for the perimeter of an equilateral triangle:

$$p = 3s$$

If $s = 2$, then
$$p = 3 \cdot 2 = 6.$$

If $s = 5$, then
$$p = 3 \cdot 5 = 15.$$

EXAMPLE 1

The table shows ordered pairs, $(2, 6)$, $(4, 12)$, $(5, 15)$, etc.

Find the ratio $\dfrac{p}{s}$ for each pair of numbers in the table below.

s	p
2	6
4	12
5	15
6	18
10	30

$$\frac{p}{s} = \frac{6}{2} = 3$$

$$\frac{p}{s} = \frac{12}{4} = 3$$

$$\frac{p}{s} = \frac{15}{5} = 3$$

Thus, the ratio $\dfrac{p}{s} = 3$ in all cases.

$\{(s, p) \mid p = 3s\}$ is a function.

The formula $\dfrac{p}{s} = 3$ describes a direct variation.

Definition of direct variation ———→

A *direct variation* is a function in which the ratio y to x is always the same.

Table of values for graph of $y = 3x$

x	y
2	6
1	3
−1	−3
−2	−6

Slope is 3.

3 is the constant of variation.

For a direct variation,
$$\frac{y}{x} = k,$$
or $y = kx$, where k is a constant.
y varies directly as x
or
y is directly proportional to x.

k is the constant of variation, or constant of proportionality. ⟶

We say. ⟶

EXAMPLE 2 From the table, determine if y varies directly as x. If so, find the constant of proportionality.

x	y
2	−10
3	−15
−1	5
−4	20

See if $\frac{y}{x} = k$, a constant.

$$\frac{-10}{2} = -5 \qquad \frac{-15}{3} = -5$$

$$\frac{5}{-1} = -5 \qquad \frac{20}{-4} = -5$$

$\frac{y}{x} = -5$ for all pairs (x, y).

$\frac{y}{x} = k$, where $k = -5$. ⟶ **Thus,** y varies directly as x. The constant of proportionality is -5.

EXAMPLE 3 y varies directly as x, and $y = 32$ when $x = 4$. Find y when $x = 9$.

(x_1, y_1)

x-sub-one, y-sub-one

$\frac{y}{x} = k$ for all (x, y). ⟶

Let $y = kx$ be the direct variation.
Let (x_1, y_1) and (x_2, y_2) be any two ordered pairs that satisfy $y = kx$.

$$\frac{y_1}{x_1} = k \qquad \frac{y_2}{x_2} = k$$

Therefore,

$$\frac{y_1}{x_1} = \frac{y_2}{x_2}$$

Let $(x_1, y_1) = (4, 32)$ and $(x_2, y_2) = (9, y_2)$.

Solve the proportion.

$$\frac{32}{4} = \frac{y_2}{9}$$

$$4 \cdot y_2 = 32 \cdot 9$$

Divide each side by 4. ⟶

$$\frac{\overset{1}{\cancel{4}} \cdot y_2}{\underset{1}{\cancel{4}}} = \frac{\overset{8}{\cancel{32}} \cdot 9}{\underset{1}{\cancel{4}}}$$

$$y_2 = 72$$

Thus, $y = 72$ when $x = 9$.

ORAL EXERCISES

Which formulas describe direct variations? For each direct variation, give the constant of proportionality.

1. $d = 30t$ 2. $xy = -6$ 3. $p = 5s$ 4. $lw = 24$ 5. $x = -7y$

6. $s = \dfrac{1}{4}p$ 7. $c = 6.28r$ 8. $d = \dfrac{1}{r}$ 9. $r = \dfrac{d}{2}$ 10. $-5x = y$

EXERCISES

PART A

Which tables express direct variations? For each direct variation, give the constant of proportionality.

1.

x	y
1	6
2	12
3	18
4	24

2.

x	y
1	2
3	4
5	6
7	8

3.

x	y
-2	8
-1	4
1	-4
2	-8

4.

x	y
5	20
10	15
15	10
20	5

5.

x	y
-1	2
-2	4
-3	6
-4	8

y varies directly as x.

6. y is 24 when x is 3. Find y when x is 4.
7. y is -12 when x is -6. Find y when x is 7.
8. y is 3 when x is 21. Find y when x is 35.
9. y is -4 when x is 36. Find x when y is 6.

PART B

EXAMPLE   On a map, 50 miles are represented by $\frac{3}{4}$ inch. How many miles are represented by 2 inches?

The relationship between inches and miles describes a direct variation.

$$\dfrac{\text{inches}}{\text{miles}} = \dfrac{\text{inches}}{\text{miles}} \longrightarrow$$

Use
prod. of extremes = prod. of means
twice.

Let $x =$ no. of mi. represented by 2 in.

$$\dfrac{\frac{3}{4}}{50} = \dfrac{2}{x}$$

$$\dfrac{3x}{4} = 100$$

$$3x = 400$$

$$x = \tfrac{400}{3}, \text{ or } 133\tfrac{1}{3}$$

Thus, 2 inches represent $133\tfrac{1}{3}$ miles.

10. The ratio of flour to milk in a recipe is 5:2. If 6 cups of milk are to be used, how much flour should be used?

11. The cost of a certain metal varies directly as its weight. If 6 ounces cost $9, how much will 15 ounces cost?

12. A map is scaled so that $\frac{5}{8}$ inch represents 20 miles. What length represents 10 miles?

13. There are 2 rods in 11 yards. How many yards are there in 5 rods?

14. At a given time and place, the height of an object varies directly as the length of the shadow it casts. A building casts a 500-foot shadow while a 20-foot flagpole casts a 30-foot shadow. How tall is the building?

15. In a recipe, the amount of flour varies directly as the amount of sugar. Three cups of flour are used for every 2 cups of sugar. How much sugar is used with 15 cups of flour?

16. The ratio of an object's weight on Earth to its weight on Mars is 5:2. A girl weighs 110 pounds on Earth. How much would she weigh on Mars?

17. In an election, Jones beat Smith by a margin of 6 to 5. Jones got 5,142 votes. How many votes did Smith get?

18. A man 6 feet 4 inches tall casts a shadow 9 feet 8 inches while a tree casts a shadow 36 feet 3 inches. How tall is the tree?

19. Two yards of a certain cable weigh .54 pound. What is the weight of 200 feet of this cable?

20. A farmer can sell 5 bushels of produce for $16. How much will he receive for 35 bushels of the same produce?

21. On a blueprint, a 14-foot hallway is represented by $3\frac{1}{2}$ inches. Find the dimensions of a room represented by a rectangle 4 inches by $4\frac{1}{2}$ inches.

PART C

22. On a map, Wyoming is represented by a rectangle approximately $2\frac{5}{8}$ inches by $2\frac{3}{16}$ inches. If $\frac{7}{16}$ inch represents 60 miles, find the approximate area of Wyoming.

23. There are approximately 2 inches in 5.08 centimeters. How many square centimeters are there in 7 square inches?

24. The distance needed to stop a car varies directly as the square of its speed. It requires 550 feet to stop a car at 50 miles per hour. What distance is needed to stop a car at 70 miles per hour? $\left(\text{Hint: } \frac{550}{50^2} = \frac{x}{70^2}\right)$

25. The distance which a freely falling body falls varies directly as the square of the time it falls. A brick falls 64 feet in 2 seconds. How far will it fall in 10 seconds?

Inverse Variation

▶ *REVIEW CAPSULE*

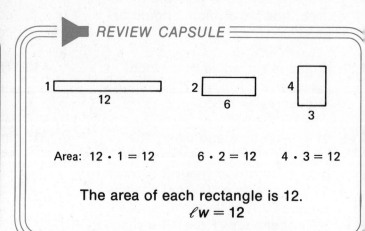

Area: $12 \cdot 1 = 12$ $6 \cdot 2 = 12$ $4 \cdot 3 = 12$

The area of each rectangle is 12.
$$\ell w = 12$$

EXAMPLE 1

Find the product ℓw for each pair of numbers in the table below.

The table shows ordered pairs, (12, 1), (6, 2), (4, 3), etc.

ℓ	w	
12	1	← $12 \cdot 1 = 12$
6	2	← $6 \cdot 2 = 12$
4	3	← $4 \cdot 3 = 12$
24	$\frac{1}{2}$	← $24 \cdot \frac{1}{2} = 12$

Thus, the product $\ell w = 12$ in all cases.

$\{(\ell, w) \mid \ell w = 12\}$ is a function.

The formula $\ell w = 12$ describes an inverse variation.

Definition of inverse function ⟶ An *inverse variation* is a function in which the product xy is always the same.

Table of values for graph of $xy = 12$

Other ordered pairs are (3, 4), (2, 6), (1, 12).

x	y
12	1
6	2
4	3
−1	−12
−2	−6
−3	−4
−6	−2
−12	−1

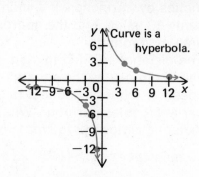

Curve is a hyperbola.

k is the constant of variation.

Also, $y = k \cdot \dfrac{1}{x}$.

We say.

For an inverse variation,
$$x\,y = k,$$
or $\quad y = \dfrac{k}{x},$ where k is a constant.

y varies inversely as x
or
y is inversely proportional to x.

EXAMPLE 2   From the table, determine if y varies inversely as x. If so, find the constant of variation.

x	y
2	9
6	3
−1	−18
−9	−2

See if $x \cdot y = k$, a constant.

$2 \cdot 9 = 18$

$6 \cdot 3 = 18$

$−1\,(−18) = 18$

$−9\,(−2) = 18$

$x \cdot y = 18$ for all pairs (x, y).

$x \cdot y = k$, where $k = 18$. ⟶ **Thus,** y varies inversely as x. The constant of variation is 18.

EXAMPLE 3 y varies inversely as x, and $y = 5$ *when* $x = 12$. Find x when $y = -4$.

Let $x \cdot y = k$ be the inverse variation.
Let (x_1, y_1) and (x_2, y_2) be any two ordered pairs that satisfy $x \cdot y = k$.

$x \cdot y = k$, for all (x, y). ⟶ $\qquad x_1 \cdot y_1 = k \qquad x_2 \cdot y_2 = k$

Let $(x_1, y_1) = (12, 5)$ and
$(x_2, y_2) = (x_2, -4)$. ⟶

Therefore, $\quad x_1 \cdot y_1 = x_2 \cdot y_2$

$12 \cdot 5 = x_2\,(-4)$

$60 = -4x_2$

Divide each side by -4. ⟶ $\quad \dfrac{60}{-4} = \dfrac{-4x_2}{-4}$

$-15 = x_2$

Thus, $x = -15$ when $y = -4$.

ORAL EXERCISES

Which formulas describe inverse variations? For each inverse variation, give the constant of variation.

1. $r \cdot t = 60$ **2.** $c = 3.14d$ **3.** $x \cdot y = -8$ **4.** $36 = b \cdot h$ **5.** $x \cdot y = 1$

6. $\dfrac{20}{y} = x$ **7.** $r = \dfrac{s}{-6}$ **8.** $\dfrac{-22}{b} = a$ **9.** $\dfrac{p}{4} = s$ **10.** $\dfrac{1}{5} \cdot y = x$

EXERCISES

PART A

Which tables express inverse variations? For each inverse variation, give the constant of variation.

1.

x	y
3	6
-2	-9
36	$\frac{1}{2}$
-18	-1

2.

x	y
1	1
-1	-1
0	0
2	2

3.

x	y
3	6
6	12
-3	-6
-6	-12

4.

x	y
5	20
-10	-10
-4	-25
$\frac{1}{2}$	200

5.

x	y
$\frac{1}{2}$	-2
-1	1
$-\frac{3}{4}$	$\frac{4}{3}$
1	-1

y varies inversely as x.

6. y is 24 when x is 8. Find y when x is 4.

7. y is 30 when x is 2. Find y when x is 15.

8. y is -7 when x is 8. Find y when x is 4.

PART B

EXAMPLE   Jane weighs 100 lb and is sitting 8 ft from the fulcrum of a seesaw. John weighs 120 lb. How far from the fulcrum must he sit to balance the seesaw?

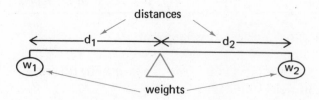

distances

weights

Law of the Lever ⟶

	Jane	John
weight	w_1	w_2
distance	d_1	d_2

The lever is in balance if $w_1 \cdot d_1 = w_2 \cdot d_2$.

$$100 \cdot 8 = 120 \cdot d_2$$
$$800 = 120 \cdot d_2$$
$$6\tfrac{2}{3} = d_2$$

Thus, John must sit $6\tfrac{2}{3}$ ft from the fulcrum.

9. How far from the fulcrum of a seesaw must Bill sit to balance Laurie who sits 6 feet from it and weighs 120 pounds, if Bill weighs 110 pounds?

10. Jack, sitting $6\frac{1}{2}$ feet from the fulcrum of a seesaw, balances Mary who weighs 130 pounds and sits 7 feet from the fulcrum. How heavy is Jack?

11. The dimensions of a rectangle are 6 feet and 18 feet. Find the width of another rectangle with the same area and a length of 12 feet.

12. The volume of a gas is 60 cubic feet under 6 pounds of pressure. What is its volume at the same temperature under 9 pounds of pressure?

13. A trip takes 5 hours at 30 miles per hour. How long does it take at 40 miles per hour?

14. It takes 8 women 6 hours to do a job. How long will it take 12 women working at the same rate?

15. What amount invested at 6% yields the same yearly income as $1,000 invested at $4\frac{1}{2}$%?

16. At what rate does $15,000 yield the same annual income as $12,000 invested at 5%?

17. The base of a triangle is 16 centimeters and the altitude is 9 centimeters. Find the base of a triangle of equal area whose altitude is 6 centimeters.

18. Nancy weighs 144 pounds, and Sylvia weighs 120. Nancy is sitting $5\frac{1}{2}$ feet from the fulcrum of a seesaw. How far from Nancy should Sylvia sit to balance the seesaw?

19. Sophia has enough money to buy 3 yards of fabric priced at $6.40 per yard. How many yards of fabric priced at $3.60 per yard can she buy with the same amount of money?

20. The current through a circuit is 25 amperes when the resistance is 16 ohms. What is the current when the resistance is increased to 20 ohms?

PART C

21. Tina and Wilt are sitting 11 feet apart on a seesaw. Tina weighs 135 pounds, and Wilt weighs 162. How far from the fulcrum must Tina be sitting if the seesaw is in balance?

22. Jill drove a round trip between cities A and B in $7\frac{1}{2}$ hours. From A to B she averaged 35 mph, and from B back to A she averaged 40 mph. How far apart are A and B?

23. Cylinders A and B have the same volume. Their altitudes vary inversely as the squares of the radii of their bases. The altitude of cylinder A is 8 feet, and the radius of its base is 6 feet. Find the altitude of cylinder B if the radius of its base is 4 feet.

24. The weight of a body at or above the earth's surface varies inversely as the square of the body's distance from the earth's center. What does a 441-pound object weigh when it is 200 miles above the earth's surface? (Use 4,000 miles as the earth's radius.)

Chapter Twelve Review

List the ordered pairs in each relation graphed below. Give the domain and the range. Is the relation a function? [*p. 317*]

1.
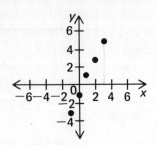

2.
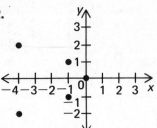

3.
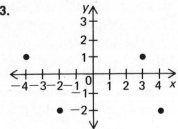

Graph each relation. Give the domain and range. Is the relation a function? [*p. 317*]

4. $\{(-1,-1),\ (-2,-2),\ (0,0),\ (-1,1),\ (-2,2)\}$
5. $\{(-2,1),\ (-1,1),\ (0,1),\ (1,1),\ (2,1)\}$

Graph each relation. Which relations are functions? Which functions are linear functions? Which functions are constant functions? [*p. 320*]

6. $\{(x,y)\,|\,y=2x\}$
7. $\{(x,y)\,|\,x=4\}$
8. $\{(x,y)\,|\,y=x+2\}$
9. $\{(x,y)\,|\,y-3x=-1\}$
10. $\{(x,y)\,|\,y=-1\}$
11. $\{(x,y)\,|\,y=2x^2+1\}$

$f=\{(x,y)\,|\,y=x^2+3\}$. **Find each.** [*p 323*]

12. $f(0)$
13. $f(3)$
14. $f(-2)$
15. $f(6)$
16. $f(-12)$

D is the domain of each function. Determine the range. [*p. 323*]

17. $f(x)=3x-2 \quad D=\{0,1,-1\}$
18. $g(x)=-x^2+3 \quad D=\{-3,-2,-1\}$

Graph each inequality. Then determine which of the given points belong to the graph.

19. $y>3x+1;\ (2,0),\ (2,9)$
20. $y-2x\le-5;\ (3,-2),\ (3,5)$ [*p. 326*]

Which tables express direct variations? Which express inverse variations? For each variation give the constant of variation. [*p. 330, 334*]

21.

x	y
-3	-9
-1	-3
1	3
2	6

22.

x	y
2	3
-1	-6
-3	-2
12	$\frac{1}{2}$

23.

x	y
-1	-3
0	-1
1	1
2	3

24.

x	y
-2	4
5	-10
-3	6
4	-8

25.

x	y
2	-6
-3	-4
-1	12
4	3

26. y varies directly as x, and y is -4 when x is 12. Find y when x is -18. [*p. 330*]

27. y varies inversely as x, and y is 5 when x is 4. Find x when y is -2. [*p. 334*]

Chapter Twelve Test

List the ordered pairs in each relation graphed below. Give the domain and the range. Is the relation a function?

1.

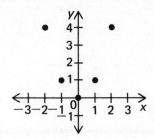

2.

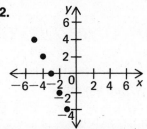

3.

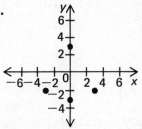

Graph each relation. Which relations are functions? Which functions are linear functions? Which functions are constant functions?

4. $\{(x, y) \mid x = -2\}$

5. $\{(x, y) \mid y = 3\}$

6. $\{(x, y) \mid y = x^2 + 1\}$

$f = \{(x, y) \mid y = 2x - 3\}$. Find each.

7. $f(3)$

8. $f(0)$

9. $f(-10)$

D is the domain of each function. Find the range.

10. $f(x) = 2x^2 - 1 \quad D = \{-1, 0, 1\}$

11. $h(x) = -3x + 4 \quad D = \{-2, 0, 2\}$

Graph each inequality. Then determine which of the given points belong to the graph.

12. $y \geq x - 3$; $(0, 3)$, $(2, -5)$

13. $y < 3x - 1$; $(-2, 5)$, $(5, -3)$

Which tables express direct variations? Which express inverse variations? For each variation, give the constant of variation.

14.

x	y
-1	4
0	3
1	2
2	1

15.

x	y
8	-8
-2	32
-4	16
-8	8

16.

x	y
2	-6
1	-3
-1	3
-2	6

17. y varies directly as x, and y is 24 when x is 6. Find y when x is -8.

18. y varies inversely as x, and y is 8 when x is -4. Find x when y is -2.

Continued Fractions

The number below is called a simple *continued fraction.*

$$1 + \cfrac{1}{3 + \cfrac{1}{2 + \cfrac{1}{5}}}$$

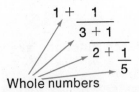

Whole numbers

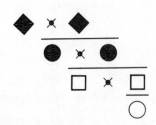

Every simple continued fraction names a rational number.

To find a name of the form $\frac{a}{b}$, begin combining terms at the bottom.

$$1 + \cfrac{1}{3 + \cfrac{1}{\boxed{2 + \cfrac{1}{5}}}} \qquad = 1 + \cfrac{1}{3 + \cfrac{1}{\boxed{\frac{11}{5}}}}$$

$$= 1 + \cfrac{1}{\frac{38}{11}} \qquad \longleftarrow \quad 3 + \cfrac{1}{\frac{11}{5}} = 3 + \frac{5}{11} = \frac{38}{11}$$

$$= 1 + \frac{11}{38}$$

$$= 1\frac{11}{38}, \text{ or } \frac{49}{38}$$

Write $2 + \cfrac{1}{4 + \cfrac{1}{3}}$ in the form $\frac{a}{b}$.

Give an explanation as to why every simple continued fraction names a rational number.

Solving Fractional Equations

REVIEW CAPSULE

Find the least common denominator (LCD).

$$\frac{x}{10} + \frac{x}{4} + \frac{3x + 1}{5}$$

$$\frac{x}{5 \cdot 2} + \frac{x}{2 \cdot 2} + \frac{3x + 1}{5}$$

The LCD is $5 \cdot 2 \cdot 2$.

Two equations which have the same solution are equivalent equations.

We can use the equation properties to transform an equation into another equation which has the same solution.

$a = b$	$a = b$	$a = b$
$a + c = b + c$	$ac = bc$	$\dfrac{a}{c} = \dfrac{b}{c}$
Add the same number to each side.	Multiply each side by the same number.	Divide each side by the same number.

EXAMPLE 1 Rewrite $\dfrac{x}{2} + \dfrac{2}{3} = \dfrac{x}{6}$ as an equation with no fractions.

Find the LCD by factoring the denominators. ⟶

$$\frac{x}{2} + \frac{2}{3} = \frac{x}{3 \cdot 2} \quad \text{The LCD is } 3 \cdot 2.$$

Multiply each side by the LCD, $3 \cdot 2$. ⟶

$$3 \cdot 2\left(\frac{x}{2} + \frac{2}{3}\right) = 3 \cdot 2 \cdot \frac{x}{3 \cdot 2}$$

Use the distributive property. ⟶

$$3 \cdot 2 \cdot \frac{x}{2} + 3 \cdot 2 \cdot \frac{2}{3} = 3 \cdot 2 \cdot \frac{x}{3 \cdot 2}$$

Do multiplications. ⟶

$$3 \cdot \overset{1}{2} \cdot \frac{x}{\underset{1}{2}} + \overset{1}{3} \cdot 2 \cdot \frac{2}{\underset{1}{3}} = \overset{1}{3} \cdot \overset{1}{2} \cdot \frac{x}{\underset{1}{3} \cdot \underset{1}{2}}$$

This equation has no fractions. It is a simpler equation to solve. ⟶

$$3x \quad + \quad 4 \quad = x$$

EXAMPLE 2 Solve $3x + 4 = x$, the resulting equation in Example 1. Then show that the solution also satisfies the original fractional equation $\frac{x}{2} + \frac{2}{3} = \frac{x}{6}$.

$x = 1x$ ────────────────────→

$$\begin{aligned} 3x + 4 &= 1x \\ -3x \qquad\quad &\ \ -3x \\ \hline 4 &= -2x \end{aligned}$$

Add $-3x$ to each side. ─────→

Divide each side by -2. ────→

$$-2 = x$$

Check -2 in $\frac{x}{2} + \frac{2}{3} = \frac{x}{6}$.

Replace x by -2. ──────────→

$$\frac{-1}{1} + \frac{2}{3} = \frac{-3}{3} + \frac{2}{3}$$
$$= -\frac{1}{3}$$

$$\begin{array}{c|c} \dfrac{x}{2} + \dfrac{2}{3} & \dfrac{x}{6} \\[2ex] \hline \dfrac{-2}{2} + \dfrac{2}{3} & \dfrac{-2}{6} \\[2ex] \dfrac{-1}{1} + \dfrac{2}{3} & -\dfrac{1}{3} \\[2ex] -\dfrac{1}{3} & \end{array}$$

Thus, -2 is the solution of $\frac{x}{2} + \frac{2}{3} = \frac{x}{6}$.

> **To solve a fractional equation:**
> First, find the LCD for all fractions.
> Next, multiply each side by the LCD.
> Then, solve the resulting equation.

EXAMPLE 3 Find the solution set of $\dfrac{3a}{5} + \dfrac{3}{2} = \dfrac{7a}{10}$.

Find the LCD by factoring the denominators. ───────────→

$$\frac{3a}{5} + \frac{3}{2} = \frac{7a}{5 \cdot 2} \quad \text{The LCD is } 5 \cdot 2.$$

Multiply each side by the LCD, $5 \cdot 2$.

$$5 \cdot 2 \left(\frac{3a}{5} + \frac{3}{2} \right) = 5 \cdot 2 \cdot \frac{7a}{5 \cdot 2}$$

Distribute the $5 \cdot 2$. ───────→

$$5 \cdot 2 \cdot \frac{3a}{5} + 5 \cdot 2 \cdot \frac{3}{2} = 5 \cdot 2 \cdot \frac{7a}{5 \cdot 2}$$

Do multiplications. ──────────→

$$\overset{1}{5} \cdot 2 \cdot \frac{3a}{\underset{1}{5}} + 5 \cdot \overset{1}{2} \cdot \frac{3}{\underset{1}{2}} = \overset{1}{5} \cdot \overset{1}{2} \cdot \frac{7a}{\underset{1}{5} \cdot \underset{1}{2}}$$

$2 \cdot 3a = 6a$; $5 \cdot 3 = 15$ ──→

$$6a + 15 = 7a$$

Add $-6a$ to each side. ──────→

$$15 = a$$

Check on your own. ─────────→ **Thus,** the solution set is $\{15\}$.

EXAMPLE 4 Solve $\dfrac{3a}{4} - \dfrac{2a-1}{2} = \dfrac{a-7}{6}$.

$-\dfrac{2a-1}{2} = \dfrac{-1(2a-1)}{2}$ ───────────→ $\dfrac{3a}{4} + \dfrac{-1(2a-1)}{2} = \dfrac{a-7}{6}$

$-1(2a-1) = -2a+1$ ───────────→ The LCD is $\dfrac{3a}{2\cdot 2} + \dfrac{-2a+1}{2} = \dfrac{a-7}{2\cdot 3}$

Factor the denominators. ──────→ $3\cdot 2\cdot 2$.

Multiply each side by the LCD. ───────→ $3\cdot 2\cdot 2\left(\dfrac{3a}{2\cdot 2} + \dfrac{-2a+1}{2}\right) = 3\cdot 2\cdot 2\cdot \dfrac{a-7}{2\cdot 3}$

Use the distributive property. ────→ $3\cdot 2\cdot 2\cdot \dfrac{3a}{2\cdot 2} + 3\cdot 2\cdot 2\cdot \dfrac{-2a+1}{2} = 3\cdot 2\cdot 2\cdot \dfrac{a-7}{2\cdot 3}$

$$3\cdot \overset{1}{\cancel{2}}\cdot \overset{1}{\cancel{2}}\cdot \dfrac{3a}{\underset{1}{\cancel{2}}\cdot \underset{1}{\cancel{2}}} + 3\cdot 2\cdot \overset{1}{\cancel{2}}\cdot \dfrac{-2a+1}{\underset{1}{\cancel{2}}} = \overset{1}{\cancel{3}}\cdot \overset{1}{\cancel{2}}\cdot 2\cdot \dfrac{a-7}{\underset{1}{\cancel{2}}\cdot \underset{1}{\cancel{3}}}$$

Simplify. ─────────────→ $3\cdot 3a + 6(-2a+1) = 2(a-7)$

$\left.\begin{array}{l}6(-2a+1) = -12a+6\\ 2(a-7) = 2a-14\end{array}\right\}$ → $\quad 9a \quad -12a\ +6\ = 2a-14$

Add $3a$ to each side. ─────────→ $-3a\ +6\ = 2a-14$

Add 14 to each side. ─────────→ $6 = 5a-14$

$20 = 5a$

Check by letting $a = 4$ in the original equation. ─────────→ $4 = a$

Thus, the solution is 4.

EXAMPLE 5 Solve $\dfrac{4}{5} + \dfrac{3}{a} = 2$.

$2 = \dfrac{2}{1}$; the denominators are already factored. ─────────→ $\dfrac{4}{5} + \dfrac{3}{a} = \dfrac{2}{1}$ The LCD is $5\cdot a$.

Multiply each side by the LCD, $5\cdot a$. ─────────→ $5\cdot a\left(\dfrac{4}{5} + \dfrac{3}{a}\right) = 5\cdot a\cdot \dfrac{2}{1}$

Distributive property ────────→ $5\cdot a\cdot \dfrac{4}{5} + 5\cdot a\cdot \dfrac{3}{a} = 5\cdot a\cdot \dfrac{2}{1}$

$$\overset{1}{\cancel{5}}\cdot a\cdot \dfrac{4}{\underset{1}{\cancel{5}}} + 5\cdot \overset{1}{\cancel{a}}\cdot \dfrac{3}{\underset{1}{\cancel{a}}} = 5\cdot a\cdot 2$$

$a\cdot 4 = 4\cdot a = 4a$;
$5\cdot a\cdot 2 = 5\cdot 2\cdot a = 10a$ ────→ $4a + 15 = 10a$

Add $-4a$ to each side. ─────→ $15 = 6a$

$\dfrac{15}{6} = a$

$\dfrac{15}{6} = \dfrac{5}{2}$ ─────────────→ **Thus,** the solution is $\dfrac{5}{2}$, or $2\dfrac{1}{2}$.

EXAMPLE 6 Solve the proportion $\dfrac{3x-1}{2}=\dfrac{5x+1}{4}$.

In a proportion, $\dfrac{a}{b}=\dfrac{c}{d}$, $a\cdot d=b\cdot c$;

prod. of extremes = prod. of means. $\longrightarrow$

First Method	Second Method

First Method

$$\frac{3x-1}{2}=\frac{5x+1}{4}$$

$$4(3x-1)=2(5x+1)$$

$$12x-4=10x+2$$

$$\underline{-10x-10x}$$

$$2x-4=2$$

$$\underline{44}$$

$$2x=6$$

$$x=3$$

Second Method

$$\frac{3x-1}{2}=\frac{5x+1}{2\cdot2}$$

$$\overset{1}{2}\cdot 2\cdot\frac{3x-1}{\underset{1}{2}}=\overset{1}{2}\cdot\overset{1}{2}\cdot\frac{5x+1}{\underset{1}{2}\cdot\underset{1}{2}}$$

$$2(3x-1)=5x+1$$

$$6x-2=5x+1$$

$$\underline{-5x-5x}$$

$$x-2=1$$

$$x=3$$

Both methods give the same solution.

A proportion can be solved in two ways:

One way $\longrightarrow$ Product of the extremes = product of the means.

Second way $\longrightarrow$ Multiply each side of the equation by the LCD.

EXERCISES

PART A
Solve.

1. $\dfrac{2a-3}{6}=\dfrac{2a}{3}+\dfrac{1}{2}$

2. $\dfrac{3a}{5}+\dfrac{3}{2}=\dfrac{7a}{10}$

3. $\dfrac{3m}{2}+\dfrac{5}{4}=\dfrac{5m}{2}$

4. $\dfrac{5}{4x}+\dfrac{1}{x}=3$

5. $\dfrac{3}{5b}+\dfrac{7}{2b}=1$

6. $\dfrac{1}{m}+\dfrac{2}{3}=1$

7. $\dfrac{3r+4}{12}-\dfrac{5}{3}=\dfrac{2r-1}{2}$

8. $\dfrac{2x-3}{7}-\dfrac{x}{2}=\dfrac{x+3}{14}$

9. $\dfrac{a}{4}-\dfrac{a}{3}=7$

Find the solution set.

10. $\dfrac{3a+2}{6}=\dfrac{2a+2}{3}$

11. $\dfrac{2m-5}{3}=\dfrac{m+1}{2}$

12. $\dfrac{2a-3}{5}=\dfrac{3a+1}{7}$

PART B
Find the solution set.

13. $\dfrac{2}{3}(x-2)+\dfrac{x+3}{2}=\dfrac{5x+3}{6}$

14. $\dfrac{3}{5}(a-3)+\dfrac{a+1}{15}=\dfrac{1}{3}$

15. $\dfrac{2}{3}b-\dfrac{5}{6}(3-b)=\dfrac{2b-5}{3}$

16. $\dfrac{3m}{5}+\dfrac{1-2m}{3}=\dfrac{m+1}{15}$

A Step Function

Suppose you are working in a post office and some one comes in to mail a package. The rates might be something like this.

8¢ up to 1 oz
16¢ over 1 oz to 2 oz
24¢ over 2 oz to 3 oz
32¢ over 3 oz to 4 oz

This is called a step function because of the appearance of its graph.

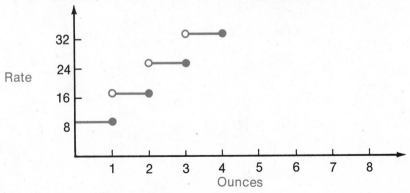

How much would it cost to mail these letters?

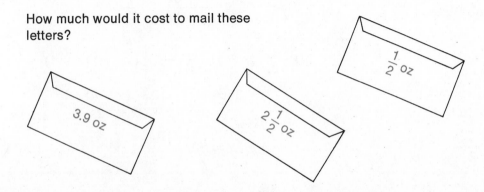

3.9 oz

$2\frac{1}{2}$ oz

$\frac{1}{2}$ oz

More Fractional Equations

OBJECTIVE

■ To solve equations like

$$\frac{6}{a+2} + \frac{3}{a^2-4} = \frac{2a-7}{a-2}$$

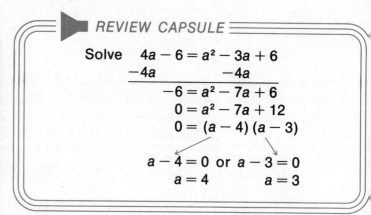

▶ REVIEW CAPSULE

Solve $4a - 6 = a^2 - 3a + 6$

$\quad \underline{-4a \qquad\qquad -4a}$

$\qquad -6 = a^2 - 7a + 6$

$\qquad\quad 0 = a^2 - 7a + 12$

$\qquad\quad 0 = (a-4)(a-3)$

$\qquad a - 4 = 0$ or $a - 3 = 0$

$\qquad\quad a = 4 \qquad\qquad a = 3$

EXAMPLE 1 Solve $\dfrac{3x}{x^2 - 5x + 4} = \dfrac{2}{x-4} + \dfrac{3}{x-1}$.

Factor $x^2 - 5x + 4$; LCD is $(x-4)(x-1)$. →
$$\frac{3x}{(x-4)(x-1)} = \frac{2}{x-4} + \frac{3}{x-1}$$

Multiply each side by the LCD, $(x-4)(x-1)$. }
$$(x-4)(x-1) \cdot \frac{3x}{(x-4)(x-1)} =$$
$$(x-4)(x-1)\left(\frac{2}{x-4} + \frac{3}{x-1}\right)$$

$$(x-4)(x-1) \cdot \frac{3x}{(x-4)(x-1)} =$$

Use the distributive property. ⟶
$$(x-4)(x-1) \cdot \frac{2}{x-4} + (x-4)(x-1) \cdot \frac{3}{x-1}$$

Do multiplications. ⟶
$$(x \overset{1}{-} 4)(x \overset{1}{-} 1) \cdot \frac{3x}{(x-4)(x-1)} =$$

$$(x \overset{1}{-} 4)(x-1) \cdot \frac{2}{x-4} + (x-4)(x \overset{1}{-} 1) \cdot \frac{3}{x-1}$$

$(x-1)2 = 2x - 2$;

$(x-4)3 = 3x - 12$ ⟶
$$3x = (x-1)2 + (x-4)3$$
Combine like terms. ⟶
$$3x = 2x - 2 + 3x - 12$$
$$3x = 5x - 14$$
Add $-5x$ to each side. ⟶
$$-2x = -14$$
Divide each side by -2. ⟶
$$x = 7$$

Thus, the solution is 7.

EXAMPLE 2 Show that 7 is the solution of

$$\frac{3x}{x^2 - 5x + 4} = \frac{2}{x - 4} + \frac{3}{x - 1}.$$

$\dfrac{3x}{x^2 - 5x + 4}$	$\dfrac{2}{x - 4} + \dfrac{3}{x - 1}$
$\dfrac{3 \cdot 7}{7^2 - 5 \cdot 7 + 4}$	$\dfrac{2}{7 - 4} + \dfrac{3}{7 - 1}$
$\dfrac{21}{18}$	$\dfrac{2}{3} + \dfrac{3}{6}$
$\dfrac{7}{6}$	$\dfrac{4}{6} + \dfrac{3}{6},$ or $\dfrac{7}{6}$

Replace x by 7.

$7^2 - 5 \cdot 7 + 4 = 49 - 35 + 4 = 18 \longrightarrow$

$\dfrac{21}{18} = \dfrac{7}{6}; \dfrac{2}{3} = \dfrac{4}{6}$ _____

Thus, 7 is the solution of $\dfrac{3x}{x^2 - 5x + 4} = \dfrac{2}{x - 4} + \dfrac{3}{x - 1}.$

EXAMPLE 3 Find the solution set of $\dfrac{7}{m^2 - 5m} + \dfrac{3}{5 - m} = \dfrac{4}{m}.$

Put $5 - m$ in convenient form.

$5 - m = -1m + 5 = -1(m - 5) \longrightarrow$ $\dfrac{7}{m^2 - 5m} + \dfrac{3}{-1(m - 5)} = \dfrac{4}{m}$

↖ descending order

$\dfrac{3}{-1(m - 5)} = \dfrac{-1 \cdot 3}{m - 5} = \dfrac{-3}{m - 5} \longrightarrow$ $\dfrac{7}{m^2 - 5m} + \dfrac{-3}{m - 5} = \dfrac{4}{m}$

Factor $m^2 - 5m$; LCD is $m(m - 5)$. $\longrightarrow$ $\dfrac{7}{m(m - 5)} + \dfrac{-3}{m - 5} = \dfrac{4}{m}$

Multiply each side by the LCD, $m(m - 5)$.

$m(m - 5)\left[\dfrac{7}{m(m - 5)} + \dfrac{-3}{m - 5}\right] = m(m - 5) \cdot \dfrac{4}{m}$

Distribute $m(m - 5)$. Do multiplications.

$\overset{1}{m}(\overset{1}{m - 5}) \cdot \dfrac{7}{\underset{1}{m}(\underset{1}{m - 5})} + m(\overset{1}{m - 5}) \cdot \dfrac{-3}{\underset{1}{m - 5}} =$

$\overset{1}{m}(m - 5) \cdot \dfrac{4}{\underset{1}{m}}$

$m(-3) = -3m;$

$(m - 5)4 = 4m - 20 \longrightarrow$

Add $3m$ to each side. $\longrightarrow$

Add 20 to each side. $\longrightarrow$

Divide each side by 7. $\longrightarrow$

$7 + m(-3) = (m - 5)4$

7	$-3m$	$= 4m - 20$
	$3m$	$3m$
7		$= 7m - 20$
20		20
27		$= 7m$
$\dfrac{27}{7}$		$= m$

Thus, the solution set is $\{\tfrac{27}{7}\}.$

EXAMPLE 4   Solve $\dfrac{6}{a+2}+\dfrac{3}{a^2-4}=\dfrac{2a-7}{a-2}$.

Factor a^2-4; LCD is $(a-2)(a+2)$. $\longrightarrow$ $\dfrac{6}{a+2}+\dfrac{3}{(a-2)(a+2)}=\dfrac{2a-7}{a-2}$

Multiply each side by the LCD, $(a-2)(a+2)$.

$$(a-2)(a+2)\left[\dfrac{6}{a+2}+\dfrac{3}{(a-2)(a+2)}\right]=$$

$$(a-2)(a+2)\cdot\dfrac{2a-7}{a-2}$$

Distribute $(a-2)(a+2)$. $\longrightarrow$ $(a-2)(a+2)\cdot\dfrac{6}{a+2}+(a-2)(a+2)\cdot$

$$\dfrac{3}{(a-2)(a+2)}=(a-2)(a+2)\cdot\dfrac{2a-7}{a-2}$$

$(a-2)\overset{1}{(a+2)}\cdot\dfrac{6}{\underset{1}{a+2}}+\overset{1}{(a-2)}\overset{1}{(a+2)}\cdot$

$\dfrac{3}{\underset{1}{(a-2)}\underset{1}{(a+2)}}=\overset{1}{(a-2)}(a+2)\cdot\dfrac{2a-7}{\underset{1}{a-2}}$

$(a-2)6+3=(a+2)(2a-7)$
$6a-12+3=(a+2)(2a-7)$
$\qquad 6a-9=2a^2-3a-14$

$(a-2)6=6a-12$

$\begin{array}{r} a \quad + \quad 2 \\ 2a \quad - \quad 7 \\ \hline 2a^2 \quad -3a \quad -14 \end{array}$

Put the quadratic equation in standard form.

$6a-9=2a^2-3a-14$

Coefficient of a^2 term is positive.
Get polynomial $=0$. Add $-6a$, then 9 to each side.

$\qquad -9=2a^2-9a-14$ **Terms are arranged in**
$\qquad 0=2a^2-9a-5$ $\longleftarrow$ **descending order**

Factor. $\longrightarrow$ $\qquad 0=(2a+1)(a-5)$

Set each factor $=0$. $\longrightarrow$ $2a+1=0$ $\qquad$ or $\qquad a-5=0$

Solve each equation for a. $\longrightarrow$

$\quad 2a=-1$
$\quad a=-\tfrac{1}{2}$ $\qquad\qquad\qquad\qquad\qquad a=5$

Thus, the solutions are $-\tfrac{1}{2}$ and 5.

EXERCISES

PART A

Solve.

1. $\dfrac{3}{x^2-4}+\dfrac{5}{x-2}=\dfrac{7}{x+2}$

2. $\dfrac{8}{x^2-7x+12}=\dfrac{5}{x-3}+\dfrac{2}{x-4}$

3. $\dfrac{9}{a^2 - 5a} + \dfrac{3}{a - 5} = \dfrac{2}{a}$

4. $\dfrac{4}{x - 5} = \dfrac{2x - 30}{x^2 - 25} + \dfrac{4}{x + 5}$

5. $\dfrac{5}{n^2 - 3n} - \dfrac{3}{n - 3} = \dfrac{2}{n}$

6. $\dfrac{2}{b^2 - 5b - 14} = \dfrac{3}{b - 7} - \dfrac{4}{b + 2}$

Find the solution set.

7. $\dfrac{4}{y + 5} - \dfrac{2}{y - 8} = \dfrac{3}{y^2 - 3y - 40}$

8. $\dfrac{7}{a^2 - 5a} - \dfrac{2}{a - 5} = \dfrac{4}{a}$

9. $\dfrac{8}{4 - x} + \dfrac{2x + 3}{x^2 - 2x - 8} = \dfrac{7}{x + 2}$

10. $\dfrac{7}{m^2 - 3m} - \dfrac{4}{m} = \dfrac{5}{3 - m}$

11. $\dfrac{4}{a + 3} + \dfrac{2}{3 - a} = \dfrac{4}{a^2 - 9}$

12. $\dfrac{2x + 3}{x^2 - 5x + 6} = \dfrac{2}{x - 2} - \dfrac{5}{x - 3}$

13. $\dfrac{-7}{b^2 - 9b + 20} = \dfrac{b}{b - 4} + \dfrac{1}{b - 5}$

14. $\dfrac{x + 3}{x + 5} + \dfrac{2}{x - 9} = \dfrac{-20}{x^2 - 4x - 45}$

PART B

EXAMPLE   Solve $\dfrac{x + 1}{x - 3} = \dfrac{3}{x} + \dfrac{12}{x^2 - 3x}$.

Multiply each side by the LCD, $x(x - 3)$. ⟶ $x(x - 3) \cdot \dfrac{x + 1}{x - 3} = x(x - 3) \cdot \dfrac{3}{x} + x(x - 3) \cdot \dfrac{12}{x(x - 3)}$

$x(x + 1) = x^2 + x;$
$(x - 3)3 = 3x - 9$ ⟶ $x(x + 1) = (x - 3)3 + 12$

$x^2 + x = 3x - 9 + 12$

Write the equation in standard form.

$x^2 - 2x - 3 = 0$

$(x - 3)(x + 1) = 0$

$x - 3 = 0 \qquad\qquad \text{or} \qquad\qquad x + 1 = 0$

$x = 3 \qquad\qquad\qquad\qquad\qquad\qquad x = -1$

If we replace x with 3 in the original equation $\dfrac{x + 1}{x - 3} = \dfrac{3 + 1}{3 - 3}$, or $\dfrac{4}{0}$ which is undefined.

The fraction $\dfrac{x + 1}{x - 3}$ is undefined when $x = 3$.

So, 3 cannot be a solution.

Thus, the solution is -1.

In the example, 3 is an extraneous solution.

An *extraneous solution* of an equation is an apparent solution that does not check.

Solve and check for extraneous solutions.

15. $\dfrac{4}{y^2 - 8y + 12} = \dfrac{y}{y - 2} + \dfrac{1}{y - 6}$

16. $\dfrac{2}{a + 2} - \dfrac{a}{a - 2} = \dfrac{-13}{a^2 - 4}$

17. $x - \dfrac{5x}{x - 2} = \dfrac{-10}{x - 2}$

18. $\dfrac{x^2 + 7x}{x - 2} = 4 + \dfrac{36}{2x - 4}$

Representing Amounts of Work

 REVIEW CAPSULE

Fractions are used to compare parts of an object with the whole.

What part of the diagram is shaded?

Four of the 5 squares are shaded.

Thus, $\frac{4}{5}$ of the diagram is shaded.

EXAMPLE 1   Sheila can mow a lawn in 3 hours. What part of the lawn can she mow in 1 hour?

Lawn
3 hours

1 hour
3 hours

In 1 hour, she can mow $\frac{1}{3}$ of the lawn.

EXAMPLE 2   Pedro can paint a house in 5 days. What part will he paint in 1 day? in 3 days? in 4 days? in x days?

He will have finished in

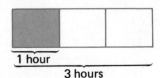

1 day		$\frac{1}{5}$ of the job.
3 days	$3 \cdot \frac{1}{5} = \frac{3}{5}$	of the job.
4 days	$4 \cdot \frac{1}{5} = \frac{4}{5}$	of the job.
x days	$x \cdot \frac{1}{5} = \frac{x}{5}$	of the job.

3 days

4 days

Example 2 shows this. ⟶

Number of hours to do the job	Part of job done in 1 hour	Part of job done in h hours
x	$\dfrac{1}{x}$	$h\left(\dfrac{1}{x}\right) = \dfrac{h}{x}$

EXAMPLE 3

Emma can mow a lawn in 8 hours. If John helps her they can finish in 5 hours. What part of the job will Emma do?

$a\left(\dfrac{1}{b}\right) = \dfrac{a}{b}$

Emma will do

in 1 hour } $\dfrac{1}{8}$ of the job. in 5 hours } $5 \cdot \dfrac{1}{8}$, or $\dfrac{5}{8}$ of the job.

EXAMPLE 4

Morris can build a fence in 5 days. Helen can build the same fence in x days. If they work together, they can finish in 3 days. What part of the fence is built by each if they work together?

Morris completes

in 1 day } $\dfrac{1}{5}$ of the work. in 3 days } $3 \cdot \dfrac{1}{5}$, or $\dfrac{3}{5}$ of the work.

Helen completes

in 1 day } $\dfrac{1}{x}$ of the work. in 3 days } $3 \cdot \dfrac{1}{x}$, or $\dfrac{3}{x}$ work.

Thus, in 3 days, Morris does $\dfrac{3}{5}$ of the work and

Helen does $\dfrac{3}{x}$ of the work.

EXAMPLE 5

Robert and Sandra sewed costumes for a school play. Working together, they completed a costume in 5 hours. By himself, Robert could sew the costume in 9 hours. Working together, what part of the job did Sandra complete?

Robert completes

in 1 hour } $\dfrac{1}{9}$ of the job. in 5 hours } $5\left(\dfrac{1}{9}\right)$, or $\dfrac{5}{9}$

$\dfrac{5}{9} + \dfrac{4}{9} = 1$ ⟶ **Thus,** Sandra completed $\dfrac{4}{9}$ of the job.

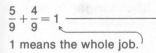
1 means the whole job.

ORAL EXERCISES

What fractional part of the work is completed by each?

		Hours for Entire Job	Hours Worked
1.	Joel	5	1
2.	Peg	4	3
3.	Mary	7	5

		Hours for Entire Job	Hours Worked
4.	José	7	2
5.	Linda	$5a$	4
6.	Jeff	$3x + 1$	3

EXERCISES

PART A

What fractional part of the job is completed by each when they work together?

1. It takes Jake 5 hours and Bill x hours to do a job. Working together, they finish in 3 hours.

2. It takes Janet m hours and Paula 8 hours to wallpaper a room. Working together, they finish the job in 5 hours.

3. It takes Maria x hours and Todd $2x$ hours to do a job. Working together, they finish in 12 hours.

4. It takes Rudy $3x + 1$ hours and Jane $2x + 4$ hours to repair a radio. Working together, they complete the job in 6 hours.

5. It takes Lester $2m$ hours and Jim $m + 1$ hours to put up a shed. Working together, they finish in 14 hours.

6. It takes Shirley $2x + 3$ days and Ruth x days to paint a kitchen. Working together, they finish the work in 2 days.

7. It takes Mark $3m + 1$ days and Stuart $m - 4$ days to plant a field. Working together, they finish in 3 days.

8. It takes Joyce $a - 2$ hours and Lee $3a + 4$ hours to wax a floor. Working together, they complete the work in 3 hours.

9. It takes Helene and Joan 5 days to complete a job if they work together. Joan can do it alone in 7 days.

10. Working together, it takes Mark and Tina 10 hours to clean a house. Mark can clean it in 30 hours.

PART B

What fractional part of the job is completed by each when they work together?

11. It takes Eleanor 5 hours and Ted twice as long to do a job. Working together, they complete the job in x hours.

12. It takes Martha 4 days and Chris 3 days longer than Martha to do a job. Working together, they finish in x days.

13. It takes Donald x hours and Merv 3 times as long to do a job. Working together, they finish in 5 hours.

14. It takes Hank x hours to do a job. It takes Sylvia 1 hour longer to do the job. Working together, they finish in 6 hours.

Work Problems

REVIEW CAPSULE

John can paint a house in 5 days.

Part of Job Done in 1 Day	Number of Days Worked	Part of Job Completed
$\frac{1}{5}$	x	$x \cdot \frac{1}{5} = \frac{x}{5}$

EXAMPLE 1   It takes Jack 5 hours and Joan 10 hours to paint a shed. How long will it take them to do the job if they work together?

Let x = hours worked together. ⟶

	Part of Job Done in 1 Hour	Number Hours Working Together	Part of Job Completed
Jack	$\frac{1}{5}$	x	$x \cdot \frac{1}{5} = \frac{x}{5}$
Joan	$\frac{1}{10}$	x	$x \cdot \frac{1}{10} = \frac{x}{10}$

The sum of the fractional parts of a job is 1 whole job. ⟶

$$\underbrace{\text{Part Jack did}}_{\downarrow} + \underbrace{\text{part Joan did}}_{\downarrow} = \underbrace{\text{whole job.}}_{\downarrow}$$

$$\frac{x}{5} \qquad + \qquad \frac{x}{10} \qquad = \qquad 1$$

$$\frac{x}{5} + \frac{x}{5 \cdot 2} = 1$$

Factor 10; LCD is $5 \cdot 2$. ⟶

Multiply each side by $5 \cdot 2$. ⟶

$$5 \cdot 2 \left(\frac{x}{5} + \frac{x}{5 \cdot 2} \right) = 5 \cdot 2 \cdot \frac{1}{1}$$

Distribute $5 \cdot 2$; do multiplications. ⟶

$$\overset{1}{5} \cdot 2 \cdot \frac{x}{\underset{1}{5}} + \overset{1}{5} \cdot \overset{1}{2} \cdot \frac{x}{\underset{1}{5} \cdot \underset{1}{2}} = 5 \cdot 2 \cdot 1$$

$$2x + 1x = 10$$

$$3x = 10$$

$$x = \frac{10}{3}$$

Thus, it takes $3\frac{1}{3}$ hours if they work together.

EXAMPLE 2

Mike can build a fence in twice the time it would take Henry. Working together, they can build the fence in 7 hours. How long would it take each?

	Part of Job Done in 1 Hour	Number Hours Working Together	Part of Job Completed
Henry	$\dfrac{1}{x}$	7	$7 \cdot \dfrac{1}{x} = \dfrac{7}{x}$
Mike	$\dfrac{1}{2x}$	7	$7 \cdot \dfrac{1}{2x} = \dfrac{7}{2x}$

Let x = hours for Henry alone. ⟶

$2x$ = hours for Mike alone. ⟶

Part Henry did + part Mike did = 1.

$$\frac{7}{x} + \frac{7}{2x} = 1$$

Multiply each side by the LCD, $2 \cdot x$.

$$2 \cdot x\left(\frac{7}{x} + \frac{7}{2 \cdot x}\right) = 2 \cdot x \cdot \frac{1}{1}$$

Distribute $2 \cdot x$; do multiplications.

$$2 \cdot \overset{1}{x} \cdot \frac{7}{\underset{1}{x}} + 2 \cdot \overset{1}{x} \cdot \frac{7}{\underset{1}{2 \cdot x}} = 2 \cdot x \cdot 1$$

$$14 + 7 = 2x$$
$$21 = 2x$$
$$10\tfrac{1}{2} = x$$

Hours for Mike alone ⟶
Hours for Henry alone ⟶

Thus, it would take Henry $10\tfrac{1}{2}$ hours and Mike 21 hours.

EXAMPLE 3

Working together, Pat and Pam can paint a house in 14 hours. If it takes Pam 30 hours alone, how long would it take Pat alone?

	Part of Job Done in 1 Hour	Number Hours Working Together	Part of Job Completed
Pam	$\dfrac{1}{30}$	14	$14 \cdot \dfrac{1}{30} = \dfrac{14}{30}$
Pat	$\dfrac{1}{x}$	14	$14 \cdot \dfrac{1}{x} = \dfrac{14}{x}$

Let x = hours for Pat alone. ⟶

Part Pam did + part Pat did = 1.

$$\frac{14}{30} + \frac{14}{x} = 1$$

Multiply each side by the LCD, $30 \cdot x$.

$$30 \cdot x\left(\frac{14}{30} + \frac{14}{x}\right) = 30 \cdot x \cdot \frac{1}{1}$$

Distribute $30 \cdot x$; do multiplications.

$$\overset{1}{30} \cdot x \cdot \frac{14}{\underset{1}{30}} + 30 \cdot \overset{1}{x} \cdot \frac{14}{\underset{1}{x}} = 30 \cdot x \cdot 1$$

$$14x + 420 = 30x$$

Add $-14x$ to each side. ⟶

$$420 = 16x$$

$\dfrac{420}{16} = \dfrac{105}{4}$, or $26\tfrac{1}{4}$ ⟶

$$26\tfrac{1}{4} = x$$

Thus, it would take Pat $26\tfrac{1}{4}$ hours.

EXERCISES

1. Fay can prepare surgical equipment in 3 hours. Another nurse, Carol, can do it in 4 hours. How long will it take if they work together?

2. A mason can put up a tile wall in 6 days. His helper can do it alone in 8 days. How long will it take them if they work together?

3. Together, Stanley and Elsie can mow a lawn in 3 hours. It would take Elsie 5 hours to do it alone. How long would it take Stanley?

4. Together, Pat and Pam can prepare a turkey dinner in 6 hours. It would take Pam 8 hours by herself. How long would it take Pat?

5. George can address envelopes in 4 hours. If Flora helps him, they can complete the job in 1 hour. How long would it take Flora alone?

6. Noah can deliver papers in twice the time it would take Jake. How long would it take each if they can do the job together in 3 hours?

7. Working together, Josephine and Lois can clean a house in 6 hours. It takes Lois 3 times longer than Josephine to do it alone. How long would it take each girl alone?

8. Working together, two men can build a house in 5 months. It takes one of them twice as long as the other to do it along. How long would it take each by himself?

9. To do a job alone, it would take Rose 4 hours, Bill 3 hours, and Marc 5 hours. How long would it take if they all work together?

10. To do a job alone, it would take Jane 3 hours, Mary 5 hours, and Jerry 6 hours. How long would it take if they all work together?

11. Eva can mow a lawn in 4 hours. It would take Bob 3 hours. How long would it take Ted if, working together, all three can do the job in 1 hour?

12. Martha can build a desk in 3 weeks. It would take Joe 5 weeks. How long would it take Kim if, working together, all three can do the job in 1 week?

13. Mary can make a suit in 5 hours. It would take Jane twice as long as Jerome. How long would it take Jane if, working together, all three can do it in 2 hours?

14. Bill can repair a transmission in 8 hours. It would take Henry 3 times as long as Clara. How long would it take Clara if, working together, all three can do it in 4 hours?

Zeller's Congruence

ON WHAT DAY OF THE WEEK DID
JULY 4, 1776 FALL?

Almanacs have perpetual calendars to answer this question.
A mathematical formula can also be used.

Zeller's Congruence

$$f = \left\{ [2.6\,m - 0.2] + k + D + \left[\frac{D}{4}\right] + \left[\frac{C}{4}\right] - 2\,C \right\} \bmod 7$$

m = month code number C = first two digits of the year
k = date of month D = last two digits of the year
f = day of the week code number

Chart 1: Code Number for Month

Month	Code Number (m)
January	11*
February	12*
March	1
April	2
May	3
June	4
July	5
August	6
September	7
October	8
November	9
December	10

Chart 2: Code Number for Day

Day of Week	Code Number (f)
Sunday	0
Monday	1
Tuesday	2
Wednesday	3
Thursday	4
Friday	5
Saturday	6

*Use the last two digits
of the preceding year.

JULY	4	17	76
↓	↓	↓	↓
$m = 5$	$K = 4$	$C = 17$	$D = 76$
(See Chart 1)			

$$[2.6\,m - 0.2] + k + D + \left[\frac{D}{4}\right] + \left[\frac{C}{4}\right] - 2C$$

$$[2.6\,(5) - 0.2] + 4 + 76 + \left[\frac{76}{4}\right] + \left[\frac{17}{4}\right] - 2 \cdot 17$$

$$[13.0 - 0.2] + 4 + 76 + \left[\frac{76}{4}\right] + \left[\frac{17}{4}\right] - 34$$

[ ] means the greatest integer less than or equal to the number. →

$$[12.8] + 4 + 76 + \left[\frac{76}{4}\right] + \left[\frac{17}{4}\right] - 34$$

$$12 \qquad + 4 + 76 + 19 + 4 - 34$$

$$81$$

$$\begin{array}{r} 11 \\ 7\,\overline{)81} \\ \underline{77} \\ 4 \end{array} \rightarrow \text{remainder}$$

The { } mod 7 around the formula means that we must find the remainder from dividing 81 by 7.

Now, use Chart 2.
July 4, 1776 fell on a Thursday.

Use Zeller's Congruence:

1. to see if it works for today's date;

2. to find out what day of the week you were born on.

Equations with Decimals

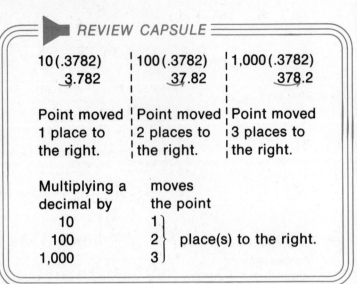

REVIEW CAPSULE

$10(.3782)$	$100(.3782)$	$1,000(.3782)$
3.782	37.82	378.2

Point moved 1 place to the right.	Point moved 2 places to the right.	Point moved 3 places to the right.

Multiplying a decimal by	moves the point
10	1
100	2 } place(s) to the right.
1,000	3

EXAMPLE 1

Rewrite $.3x + .45 = .984$ as an equation which has only whole numbers.

First rewrite all decimals as fractions.

$.3 = \dfrac{3}{10}; .45 = \dfrac{45}{100}; .984 = \dfrac{984}{1,000}$

$$\frac{3}{10}x + \frac{45}{100} = \frac{984}{1,000} \leftarrow \text{LCD is 1,000.}$$

Multiply each side by 1,000. ⟶

$$1,000\left(\frac{3}{10}x + \frac{45}{100}\right) = 1,000\left(\frac{984}{1,000}\right)$$

Distribute 1,000; do multiplications. ⟶

$$\overset{100}{1,000}\left(\frac{3}{\underset{1}{10}}x\right) + \overset{10}{1,000}\left(\frac{45}{\underset{1}{100}}\right) = \overset{1}{1,000}\left(\frac{984}{\underset{1}{1,000}}\right)$$

Equation with only whole numbers

$$300x + 450 = 984$$

.3	.45	.984
↓	↓	↓
$\frac{3}{10}$	$\frac{45}{100}$	$\frac{984}{1,000}$

LCD = 1,000

$1,000(.3) = 300.$ $1,000(.45) = 450.$
$1,000(.984) = 984.$

Here is a more convenient technique.

$$.3x + .45 = .984$$

$$1,000(.3x + .45) = 1,000(.984)$$
$$1,000(.3x) + 1,000(.45) = 1,000(.984)$$
$$300x + 450 = 984$$

Notice that this is the same equation as the resulting equation in Example 1.

For the equation,

$$.3x \quad + \quad .45 \quad = \quad .984$$

one digit   two digits   three digits
past point   past point   past point

The greatest number of digits past any decimal point is three. LCD = 1,000.

the LCD is 1,000.

three zeros

EXAMPLE 2

Give the LCD for each equation.

$$.03x - .004 = .72x + 1.8 \qquad .2x + .04 = 5x - .36$$

$$.03x - .004 = .72x + 1.8 \quad | \quad .2x + .04 = 5(x) - .36$$

Number of digits past decimal point

two   three   two   one | one   two   none   two

LCD is 1,000. | LCD is 100.

EXAMPLE 3

Solve $.5x - 1.2 = 6.4$.

The greatest number of digits past any decimal point is one. LCD = 10.

To multiply by 10, move the decimal point one place to the right. $\longrightarrow$

Add 12 to each side. $\longrightarrow$

Divide each side by 5. $\longrightarrow$

$$10(.5x - 1.2) = 10(6.4)$$
$$10(.5x) - 10(1.2) = 10(6.4)$$
$$5x - 12 = 64$$
$$5x = 76$$
$$x = \frac{76}{5}, \text{ or } 15\frac{1}{5}$$

$\frac{1}{5} = 1 \div 5 = .2$ $\longrightarrow$ **Thus,** the solution is $15\frac{1}{5}$, or 15.2.

EXAMPLE 4

Solve $.15x - 7.2 = 8.5$.

The greatest number of digits past any decimal point is two. LCD = 100.

Multiply each side by 100. $\longrightarrow$

To multiply by 100, move the decimal point two places to the right. $\longrightarrow$

Add 720 to each side. $\longrightarrow$

Divide each side by 15. $\longrightarrow$

$$.15x - 7.2 = 8.5$$

two   one   one

$$100(.15x - 7.2) = 100(8.5)$$
$$100(.15x) - 100(7.2) = 100(8.5)$$
$$15x - 720 = 850$$
$$15x = 1,570$$
$$x = \frac{1,570}{15}, \text{ or } 104\frac{2}{3}$$

Thus, the solution is $104\frac{2}{3}$.

ORAL EXERCISES

Give the LCD for each equation.

1. $.38x = .246 + .2x$

2. $.712x - 24 = .06$

3. $2.08x - 2 = .1$

4. $2.1x = .7x - .008$

5. $4.1 = 20x - .27$

6. $.002 = 7.1x - 8.2$

EXERCISES

PART A

Solve. Answers may be written in fraction or decimal form.

1. $.03x = .2$

2. $.016 = .32x$

3. $.004x - 7.1 = .12$

4. $.1x - 2.4 = 1.17$

5. $.007 = .7x - .21$

6. $2.1x = .72 + 1.8x$

7. $.18x - 24 = .1x + .6$

8. $5 - .03x = .7x - .11$

9. $.7x - .2 = .13x - 80$

10. $.012x - 4 = .112x + 1$

11. $.7x - 1 = .6x + .002$

12. $.5 - .08x = .004x + .2$

PART B

EXAMPLE Solve $.02(4 - .3x) = .15x + 3.2$.

Distribute .02. ⟶

$.02(.3) = \dfrac{2}{100}\left(\dfrac{3}{10}\right) = \dfrac{6}{1,000} = .006$

$.02(4) - .02(.3x) = .15x + 3.2$

$\underbrace{.08} - \underbrace{.006x} = \underbrace{.15x} + \underbrace{3.2}$

   ↑   ↑   ↑   ↑

   two   three   two   one

Multiply each side by the LCD, 1,000. ⟶

$1,000(.08 - .006x) = 1,000(.15x + 3.2)$

$1,000(.08) - 1,000(.006x) = 1,000(.15x) + 1,000(3.2)$

$80 \quad - \quad 6x \quad = \quad 150x \quad + \quad 3,200$

$-156x = 3,120$

$x = \dfrac{3,120}{-156}, \text{ or } -20$

Thus, the solution is -20.

Solve. Answers may be written in fraction or decimal form.

13. $.03(4 - .2x) = .17x - 1.2$

14. $.01(5 - .2x) = .75 + .198x$

15. $.3x - 2.91 = 5 - .2(3 - .01x)$

16. $47.582 - .01(.2 + 3x) = 7.9x$

17. $.04(.2 - .1x) = 7.12 + .02x$

18. $.1(2 - 7x) = 7.1 - 3x$

Rational Numbers

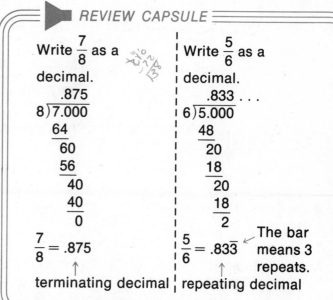

▶ *REVIEW CAPSULE*

Write $\frac{7}{8}$ as a decimal.

$$
\begin{array}{r}
.875 \\
8\overline{)7.000} \\
64 \\
\overline{60} \\
56 \\
\overline{40} \\
40 \\
\overline{0}
\end{array}
$$

$\frac{7}{8} = .875$

↑ terminating decimal

Write $\frac{5}{6}$ as a decimal.

$$
\begin{array}{r}
.833\ldots \\
6\overline{)5.000} \\
48 \\
\overline{20} \\
18 \\
\overline{20} \\
18 \\
\overline{2}
\end{array}
$$

$\frac{5}{6} = .83\bar{3}$

The bar means 3 repeats.

↑ repeating decimal

Definition of rational number ⟶

A *rational number* is a number which can be written in the form $\frac{a}{b}$, where a and b are integers and $b \neq 0$.

EXAMPLE 1

Show that the integers -16, 0, 1, and 23 are rational numbers.

Write each as $\frac{a}{b}$, where a is the integer itself and b is 1.

$$-16 = \frac{-16}{1} \quad 0 = \frac{0}{1} \quad 1 = \frac{1}{1} \quad 23 = \frac{23}{1}$$

Thus, -16, 0, 1, and 23 are rational numbers.

Every integer is a rational number.

EXAMPLE 2

Show that $\frac{2}{3}$, $\frac{5}{2}$, and $-\frac{9}{16}$ are rational numbers.

$-\frac{9}{16} = \frac{-9}{16}$

All are in the form $\frac{a}{b}$, where a and b are integers.

$$\frac{2}{3} \qquad \frac{5}{2} \qquad \frac{-9}{16}$$

Thus, $\frac{2}{3}$, $\frac{5}{2}$, and $-\frac{9}{16}$ are rational numbers.

EXAMPLE 3

EXAMPLE 3 Show that these decimals are rational numbers.

.7		−.06		2.591
↓		↓		↓
$\dfrac{7}{10}$		$\dfrac{-6}{100}$		$\dfrac{2{,}591}{1{,}000}$

Write each as $\dfrac{a}{b}$, where b is 10, 100, and 1,000. ⟶

Thus, .7, −.06, and 2.591 are rational numbers.

Every terminating decimal is a rational number.

EXAMPLE 4 Show that $.3\overline{3}$ is a rational number.

The bar means 3 repeats.
$.3\overline{3} = .3333\ldots$ ⟶ Let $n = .3\overline{333}$ (1)

Multiply each side by 10; the decimal point moves one place. ⟶

Multiply each side of equation (1) by −1. Add equations (2) and (3). ⟶

$$\begin{array}{rl} 10n = & 3.333\overline{3} \ \ (2) \\ -\ \ 1n = - & .333\overline{3} \ \ (3) \\ \hline 9n = & 3.0000 \end{array}$$

or $\quad 9n = 3$

Divide each side by 9. ⟶ $\quad n = \dfrac{3}{9}$, or $\dfrac{1}{3}$

$\dfrac{3}{9} = \dfrac{1}{3}$ ↙ integer ⟶ **Thus,** $.3\overline{3}$ is the rational number $\dfrac{1}{3}$.

EXAMPLE 5 Show that $.94\overline{4}$ is a rational number.

Let $n = .94\overline{4}$ (1)

Multiply each side by 10; the decimal point moves one place. ⟶

Multiply each side of equation (1) by −1. Add equations (2) and (3). ⟶

$$\begin{array}{rl} 10n = & 9.444\overline{4} \ \ (2) \\ -\ \ 1n = - & .944\overline{4} \ \ (3) \\ \hline 9n = & 8.5000 \end{array}$$

or $\quad 9n = 8.5$

Divide each side by 9. ⟶ $\quad n = \dfrac{8.5}{9}$

$\dfrac{8.5}{9} = \dfrac{8.5(10)}{9(10)} = \dfrac{85}{90}$ ↙ integer ⟶ $\quad n = \dfrac{85}{90}$, or $\dfrac{17}{18}$

Check. $\quad \dfrac{.94\overline{4}}{18\,\overline{)\,17.000}}$ ⟶ **Thus,** $.94\overline{4}$ is the rational number $\dfrac{17}{18}$.

Every repeating decimal is a rational number.

EXAMPLE 6   Show that $2.6\overline{6}$ is a rational number.

Let $n = 2.666\overline{6}$ (1)

Multiply each side by 10; the decimal point moves one place. ————→

Multiply each side of equation (1) by −1.
Add equations (2) and (3). ————→

$$10n = 26.666\overline{6} \quad (2)$$
$$-\ 1n = -\ 2.666\overline{6} \quad (3)$$
$$9n = 24.0000$$

or $9n = 24$

Divide each side by 9. ————→

$$n = \frac{24}{9}, \text{ or } \frac{8}{3}$$

Thus, $2.6\overline{6}$ is the rational number $\frac{8}{3}$.

EXERCISES

PART A

Show that each is a rational number.

1. -1 2. 32 3. -16 4. 0 5. $-\dfrac{24}{36}$ 6. $.00706$ 7. -3.64

8. $.7\overline{7}$ 9. $.4\overline{4}$ 10. $.62\overline{2}$ 11. $.75\overline{5}$ 12. $1.2\overline{2}$ 13. $3.5\overline{5}$ 14. $.48\overline{8}$

15. $.72\overline{2}$ 16. $.36\overline{6}$ 17. $.59\overline{9}$ 18. $4.23\overline{3}$ 19. $.39\overline{9}$ 20. $.16\overline{6}$ 21. $5.7\overline{7}$

PART B

EXAMPLE   Show that $1.78\overline{78}$ is a rational number.

Let $n = 1.7878\overline{78}$ (1)

Multiply each side by 100; the decimal point moves two places. ————→

Multiply each side of equation (1) by −1.
Add equations (2) and (3). ————→

$$100n = 178.7878\overline{78} \quad (2)$$
$$-\ 1n = -\ 1.7878\overline{78} \quad (3)$$
$$99n = 177$$

Divide each side by 99. ————→

$$n = \frac{177}{99}, \text{ or } \frac{59}{33}$$

Thus, $1.78\overline{78}$ is the rational number $\frac{59}{33}$.

Show that each is a rational number.

22. $.16\overline{16}$ 23. $.24\overline{24}$ 24. $.83\overline{83}$ 25. $.75\overline{75}$ 26. $.98\overline{98}$

27. $.123\overline{123}$ 28. $.671\overline{671}$ 29. $.976\overline{976}$ 30. $.149\overline{149}$ 31. $5.7812\overline{812}$

Investment and Loan Problems

If John invested $400 for one year at 5% interest, how much interest did he earn?

$i = ?$
$p = 400$
$r = 5\%$
$t = 1$ yr

$i = p\,r\,t$
$i = 400\,(.05)\,(1)$
$i = 20$ Change the percent to a decimal.

Thus, he earned $20 interest.

Practice Problem 1

Mrs. Lee borrowed *x* dollars at 7½ % interest for one year. Write an algebraic representation for the amount of interest she paid.

Use formula   → $i = p\,r\,t$
Substitute; 7½ % = .075   → $i = x\,(.075)\,(1)$

                 Thus, .075 *x* represents Mrs. Lee's interest.

Practice Problem 2

Ellen invested one sum of money at 5½% and another sum at 6%. She invested $300 more at the 6% rate than at the 5½% rate. If her total interest for 1 year was $133, find each principal she invested.

Represent the amounts } invested algebraically. }

Let x = principal invested at 5½% (in dollars),
$x + 300$ = principal invested at 6% (in dollars).

Make a chart. →

	Principal	Rate	Time	Interest ($i = prt$)
At 5½%	x	.055	1 yr.	.055 x
At 6%	$x + 300$	.06	1 yr.	.06 ($x + 300$)

Write an equation. →

(Interest at 5½%) + (Interest at 6%) = (Total interest)

Substitute. →

$$.055x + .06(x + 300) = 133$$
$$.055x + .06x + 18 = 133$$

Multiply each side by 1,000.

$$55x + 60x + 18,000 = 133,000$$
$$115x = 115,000$$

Principal invested at 5½%
Principal invested at 6%

$$x = 1,000$$
$$x + 300 = 1,300$$

Thus, Ellen invested $1,000 at 5½% and $1,300 at 6%.

Practice Problem 3

Mike borrowed part of the $1,900 from a bank at an interest rate of 8% and the rest from his father at 5%. At the end of 6 months he owed $64 in interest. How much did he borrow from each.

Represent the amounts } invested algebraically. }

Let x = principal borrowed at 8%
$1,900 - x$ = principal borrowed at 5%

Make a chart. →
6 months = .5 yr.

	Principal	Rate	Time	Interest ($i = prt$)
At 8%	x	.08	.5 yr.	.04 x
At 5%	$1,900 - x$	.05	.5 yr.	.025 ($1,900 - x$)

Write an equation. →

(Interest at 8%) + (Interest at 5%) = (Total interest)

Substitute. →

$$.04x + .025(1,900 - x) = 64$$
$$.04x + 47.5 - .025x = 64$$

Multiply each side by 1,000.

$$40x + 47,500 - 25x = 64,000$$
$$15x = 16,500$$

Principal invested at 8%
Principal invested at 5%

$$x = 1,100$$
$$1,900 - x = 1,900 - 1,100, \text{ or } 800$$

Thus, Mike borrowed $800 at 5% and $1,100 at 8%.

| Practice Problem 4 | Alba invested one-half of her money at 5¾ % and one-fourth of her money at 5½ %. If her total interest at the end of one year was $136, write an equation to find her original sum of money. |

Represent the amounts invested algebraically.

Let x = amount of original sum,
$\frac{1}{2}x$ = amount invested at 5¾ %,
$\frac{1}{4}x$ = amount invested at 5½ %.

Make a chart. →

5¾ % = 5.75% →

5½ % = 5.5% →

	Principal	Rate	Time	Interest ($i = prt$)
At 5¾ %	½ x	.0575	1 yr	$\frac{.0575}{2}x$
At 5½ %	¼ x	.055	1 yr	$\frac{.055}{4}x$

Write an equation. → (Interest at 5¾ %) + (Interest at 5½ %) = (Total Interest)

Substitute →

$$\frac{.0575}{2}x \quad + \quad \frac{.055}{4}x \quad = \quad 136$$

Multiply each side by 4 and simplify.

$$.115x \quad + \quad .055x \quad = \quad 544$$

| Practice Problem 5 | Jane had $600. She invested part of this in one bank at 6% interest, the rest in a second bank at 5%. Her total return from these two investments was $34 at the end of 1 year. How much did she invest at each rate? |

Represent the amounts invested algebraically.

Let x = amount invested at 6%,
$600 - x$ = amount invested at 5%.

Make a chart. →

	Principal	Rate	Time	Interest ($i=prt$)
At 6%	x	.06	1 yr	.06x
At 5%	600 − x	.05	1 yr	.05 (600 − x)

Write an equation. → (Interest at 6%) + (Interest at 5%) = (Total Interest)

Substitute →

$$.06x \quad + \quad .05(600 - x) \quad = \quad 34$$
$$.06x \quad + \quad 30 - .05x \quad = \quad 34$$

Multiply each side by 100.

$$6x \quad + \quad 3{,}000 - 5x \quad = \quad 3{,}400$$
$$1x \quad = \quad 400$$
$$x \quad = \quad 400$$

Principal invested at 6%
Principal invested at 5%

$$600 - x \quad = 600 - 400, \text{ or } 200$$

Thus, Jane invested $400 at 6% and $200 at 5%.

EXERCISES

1. Bill borrowed some money at 7½% interest for 3 months. If his total interest was $11.25, how much did he borrow?

2. Liz invested $1,800, part of it at 5½% and the rest at 6%. If her total interest at the end of 1 year was $103, find the amount of each investment.

3. Susan had $2,500, she invested part of it at 4% and the rest at 5%. If her total income after 3 years was $348, find the amount of each investment.

4. Melba had $1,300. She invested part of it at 5% and the rest at 6%. If her total income after 1 year was $73, how much did she invest at each rate?

5. Doris invested part of her money at 4½% and part at 5%. She invested $1,200 more at the higher interest rate than at the lesser rate. If her total interest after 18 months was $209 find the amount of each investment.

6. Tony borrowed some of his money at 4% and some at 6%. The principal borrowed at 6% was twice as much as that borrowed at 4%. If the total interest after 1 year was $96, how much did he borrow at each rate?

7. Ann had $500 to invest. She invested part of this sum at 5% and the rest at 5½%. If her interest after 1 year was $26, find the amount of each investment.

8. Bob invested $800, part of it at 4% and the rest at 5%. If his total interest at the end of 3 years was $111, find the amount of each investment.

9. Evelyn invested one-half of her money at 5% and one-fourth at 6%. At the end of 2 years, she had earned $120 in interest. What was the original sum of money?

10. Sylvia had $2,100. She invested part of it at 5% and the rest at 5¼%. If her total income after 1 year was $108, how much did she invest at each rate?

Complex Fractions

OBJECTIVE

■ To simplify fractions like

$$\frac{\dfrac{3}{a}+\dfrac{5}{2}}{\dfrac{7}{3}+\dfrac{4}{a^2}}$$

▶ *REVIEW CAPSULE*

Simplify $6a^2\left(\dfrac{3}{a}+\dfrac{5}{2}\right)$.

$$6a^2\cdot\frac{3}{a}+6a^2\cdot\frac{5}{2}$$

$$3\cdot2\cdot\overset{1}{\cancel{a}}\cdot a\cdot\frac{3}{\underset{1}{\cancel{a}}}+3\cdot\overset{1}{\cancel{2}}\cdot a\cdot a\cdot\frac{5}{\underset{1}{\cancel{2}}}$$

$$18a+15a^2$$

or $\qquad 15a^2+18a$

Complex Fractions

$$\left.\dfrac{\dfrac{1}{2}}{6}\right\} \begin{array}{l}\text{numerator}\\[6pt]\text{denominator}\end{array} \qquad \left.\dfrac{\dfrac{2}{3}}{\dfrac{1}{5}}\right\} \begin{array}{l}\text{numerator}\\[6pt]\text{denominator}\end{array}$$

$$\left.\dfrac{x+3}{\dfrac{2}{x}}\right\} \begin{array}{l}\text{numerator}\\[6pt]\text{denominator}\end{array}$$

Definition of complex fraction ⟶ | A *complex fraction* is one whose numerator or denominator or both contain a fraction.

EXAMPLE 1

Simplify $\dfrac{\dfrac{2}{3}}{\dfrac{1}{5}}$.

The LCD of $\dfrac{2}{3}$ and $\dfrac{1}{5}$ is $3\cdot5$.

Multiply both numerator and denominator by $3\cdot5$; $\dfrac{a}{b}=\dfrac{a\cdot c}{b\cdot c}$

$$\frac{3\cdot5\cdot\dfrac{2}{3}}{3\cdot5\cdot\dfrac{1}{5}}=\frac{\overset{1}{\cancel{3}}\cdot5\cdot\dfrac{2}{\underset{1}{\cancel{3}}}}{3\cdot\overset{1}{\cancel{5}}\cdot\dfrac{1}{\underset{1}{\cancel{5}}}}$$

$$=\frac{10}{3}$$

EXAMPLE 2 Simplify $\dfrac{3a + \dfrac{2}{3}}{\dfrac{a}{2} + \dfrac{5}{6}}$.

$3a = \dfrac{3a}{1}$ ⟶

$$\dfrac{\dfrac{3a}{1} + \dfrac{2}{3}}{\dfrac{a}{2} + \dfrac{5}{3 \cdot 2}}$$

Factor the denominators. ⟶

The LCD of $\dfrac{3a}{1}, \dfrac{2}{3}, \dfrac{a}{2}, \dfrac{5}{3 \cdot 2}$ is $3 \cdot 2$.

Multiply both numerator and denominator by $3 \cdot 2$.

$$\dfrac{3 \cdot 2\left(\dfrac{3a}{1} + \dfrac{2}{3}\right)}{3 \cdot 2\left(\dfrac{a}{2} + \dfrac{5}{3 \cdot 2}\right)}$$

Distribute $3 \cdot 2$. Divide out common factors in each product.

$$\dfrac{3 \cdot 2 \cdot \dfrac{3a}{1} + \overset{1}{3} \cdot 2 \cdot \dfrac{2}{\underset{1}{3}}}{3 \cdot \overset{1}{2} \cdot \dfrac{a}{\underset{1}{2}} + \overset{1}{3} \cdot \overset{1}{2} \cdot \dfrac{5}{\underset{1}{3} \cdot \underset{1}{2}}}$$

Multiply remaining factors in each product.

$$\dfrac{18a + 4}{3a + 5}$$

EXAMPLE 3 Simplify $\dfrac{\dfrac{3}{a} - \dfrac{5}{2}}{\dfrac{7}{3} + \dfrac{4}{a^2}}$.

$\dfrac{3}{a} - \dfrac{5}{2} = \dfrac{3}{a} + \dfrac{-1 \cdot 5}{2} = \dfrac{3}{a} + \dfrac{-5}{2}$ ⟶

$$\dfrac{\dfrac{3}{a} + \dfrac{-5}{2}}{\dfrac{7}{3} + \dfrac{4}{a \cdot a}}$$

Factor the denominators. ⟶

The LCD of $\dfrac{3}{a}, \dfrac{-5}{2}, \dfrac{7}{3}, \dfrac{4}{a \cdot a}$ is $3 \cdot 2 \cdot a \cdot a$.

Multiply both numerator and denominator by the LCD.

$$\dfrac{3 \cdot 2 \cdot a \cdot a\left(\dfrac{3}{a} + \dfrac{-5}{2}\right)}{3 \cdot 2 \cdot a \cdot a\left(\dfrac{7}{3} + \dfrac{4}{a \cdot a}\right)}$$

Distribute $3 \cdot 2 \cdot a \cdot a$. Divide out common factors in each product.

$$\dfrac{3 \cdot 2 \cdot \overset{1}{a} \cdot a \cdot \dfrac{3}{\underset{1}{a}} + 3 \cdot \overset{1}{2} \cdot a \cdot a \cdot \dfrac{-5}{\underset{1}{2}}}{\overset{1}{3} \cdot 2 \cdot a \cdot a \cdot \dfrac{7}{\underset{1}{3}} + 3 \cdot 2 \cdot \overset{1}{a} \cdot \overset{1}{a} \cdot \dfrac{4}{\underset{1}{a} \cdot \underset{1}{a}}}$$

Multiply remaining factors in each product.

$$\dfrac{18a - 15a^2}{14a^2 + 24}, \text{ or } \dfrac{-15a^2 + 18a}{14a^2 + 24}$$

EXERCISES

PART A

Simplify.

1. $\dfrac{\dfrac{2}{3}+\dfrac{1}{2}}{\dfrac{1}{6}+\dfrac{1}{2}}$

2. $\dfrac{\dfrac{2}{5}+\dfrac{1}{10}}{\dfrac{1}{2}+\dfrac{3}{5}}$

3. $\dfrac{\dfrac{3m}{5}+\dfrac{1}{3}}{\dfrac{m}{15}+\dfrac{1}{5}}$

4. $\dfrac{\dfrac{2}{3}+\dfrac{5}{m}}{\dfrac{7}{m}+\dfrac{4}{3}}$

5. $\dfrac{\dfrac{5}{4}+3}{\dfrac{1}{2}+2}$

6. $\dfrac{\dfrac{3a}{2}+1}{\dfrac{a}{4}+2}$

7. $\dfrac{4a+\dfrac{1}{3}}{2a+\dfrac{1}{3}}$

8. $\dfrac{\dfrac{3b}{5}+\dfrac{2}{3}}{\dfrac{b}{15}+\dfrac{3}{5}}$

9. $\dfrac{5a+\dfrac{1}{4}}{2a+\dfrac{1}{8}}$

10. $\dfrac{\dfrac{3k}{7}-\dfrac{5}{14}}{3k+\dfrac{1}{2}}$

11. $\dfrac{\dfrac{3}{a^2}-\dfrac{5}{a}}{\dfrac{2}{a}+\dfrac{1}{a^2}}$

12. $\dfrac{\dfrac{4}{b^2}+\dfrac{3}{b}}{\dfrac{2}{b}+\dfrac{5}{3b^2}}$

PART B

EXAMPLE

Simplify $\dfrac{1-\dfrac{5}{m}+\dfrac{4}{m^2}}{1-\dfrac{16}{m^2}}$.

$$\dfrac{m^2\left(1-\dfrac{5}{m}+\dfrac{4}{m^2}\right)}{m^2\left(1-\dfrac{16}{m^2}\right)}=\dfrac{m^2+\overset{m}{\cancel{m^2}}\cdot\dfrac{-5}{\underset{1}{\cancel{m}}}+\overset{1}{\cancel{m^2}}\cdot\dfrac{4}{\underset{1}{\cancel{m^2}}}}{m^2+\overset{1}{\cancel{m^2}}\cdot\dfrac{-16}{\underset{1}{\cancel{m^2}}}}$$

$$=\dfrac{m^2-5m+4}{m^2-16}$$

$$=\dfrac{(\overset{1}{\cancel{m-4}})(m-1)}{(\underset{1}{\cancel{m-4}})(m+4)},\text{ or }\dfrac{m-1}{m+4}$$

Simplify.

13. $\dfrac{1+\dfrac{3}{x}+\dfrac{2}{x^2}}{\dfrac{1}{x}+\dfrac{2}{x^2}}$

14. $\dfrac{1-\dfrac{9}{x}+\dfrac{14}{x^2}}{\dfrac{1}{x}-\dfrac{7}{x^2}}$

15. $\dfrac{\dfrac{1}{m}+\dfrac{2}{m^2}}{1-\dfrac{6}{m}-\dfrac{16}{m^2}}$

More Complex Fractions

▶ REVIEW CAPSULE

Simplify $\dfrac{\dfrac{c}{2} + \dfrac{3}{5}}{\dfrac{c}{10} + \dfrac{1}{2}}$.

$$\dfrac{5 \cdot 2\left(\dfrac{c}{2} + \dfrac{3}{5}\right)}{5 \cdot 2\left(\dfrac{c}{5 \cdot 2} + \dfrac{1}{2}\right)}$$

$$\dfrac{5 \cdot \overset{1}{2} \cdot \dfrac{c}{\underset{1}{2}} + \overset{1}{5} \cdot 2 \cdot \dfrac{3}{\underset{1}{5}}}{\overset{1}{5} \cdot \overset{1}{2} \cdot \dfrac{c}{\underset{1}{5} \cdot \underset{1}{2}} + 5 \cdot \overset{1}{2} \cdot \dfrac{1}{\underset{1}{2}}} = \dfrac{5c + 6}{c + 5}$$

EXAMPLE 1

Simplify $\dfrac{\dfrac{5}{m - 3} + \dfrac{7}{m + 2}}{\dfrac{7}{m^2 - m - 6} + \dfrac{1}{m - 3}}$.

$m^2 - m - 6 = (m - 3)(m + 2)$;
LCD $= (m - 3)(m + 2)$. ⟶

$$\dfrac{\dfrac{5}{m - 3} + \dfrac{7}{m + 2}}{\dfrac{7}{(m - 3)(m + 2)} + \dfrac{1}{m - 3}}$$

Multiply both numerator and denominator by the LCD, $(m - 3)(m + 2)$. ⎤

$$\dfrac{(m - 3)(m + 2)\left(\dfrac{5}{m - 3} + \dfrac{7}{m + 2}\right)}{(m - 3)(m + 2)\left[\dfrac{7}{(m - 3)(m + 2)} + \dfrac{1}{m - 3}\right]}$$

Use the distributive property. Divide out common factors in each product. ⎤

$$\dfrac{(\overset{1}{m - 3})(m + 2) \cdot \dfrac{5}{\underset{1}{m - 3}} + (m - 3)(\overset{1}{m + 2}) \cdot \dfrac{7}{\underset{1}{m + 2}}}{\overset{1}{(m-3)}\overset{1}{(m+2)} \cdot \dfrac{7}{\underset{1}{(m-3)(m+2)}} + \overset{1}{(m-3)}(m+2) \cdot \dfrac{1}{\underset{1}{m-3}}}$$

Multiply remaining factors in each product. Combine like terms. ⎤

$$\dfrac{5m + 10 + 7m - 21}{7 + m + 2} = \dfrac{12m - 11}{m + 9}$$

EXAMPLE 2

Simplify $\dfrac{\dfrac{2}{a} + \dfrac{-16}{a^2 + 6a}}{\dfrac{4}{a+6} - \dfrac{1}{a}}$.

Factor: $a^2 + 6a = a(a+6)$.

$\dfrac{4}{a+6} - \dfrac{1}{a} = \dfrac{4}{a+6} + \dfrac{-1 \cdot 1}{a}$

$\quad = \dfrac{4}{a+6} + \dfrac{-1}{a}$

$$\dfrac{\dfrac{2}{a} + \dfrac{-16}{a(a+6)}}{\dfrac{4}{a+6} + \dfrac{-1}{a}} \quad \leftarrow \text{LCD is } a(a+6).$$

Multiply both numerator and denominator by the LCD, $a(a+6)$.

$$\dfrac{a(a+6)\left[\dfrac{2}{a} + \dfrac{-16}{a(a+6)}\right]}{a(a+6)\left(\dfrac{4}{a+6} + \dfrac{-1}{a}\right)}$$

Use the distributive property. Divide out common factors in each product.

$$\dfrac{\cancel{a}(a+6) \cdot \dfrac{2}{\cancel{a}_1} + \cancel{a}\cancel{(a+6)} \cdot \dfrac{-16}{_1\cancel{a(a+6)}_1}}{a\cancel{(a+6)} \cdot \dfrac{4}{\cancel{a+6}_1} + \cancel{a}(a+6) \cdot \dfrac{-1}{\cancel{a}_1}}$$

Multiply remaining factors in each product. Combine like terms.

$$\dfrac{2a + 12 - 16}{4a - 1a - 6}, \text{ or } \dfrac{2a - 4}{3a - 6}$$

Factor numerator and denominator. Then write in simplest form.

$$\dfrac{2\cancel{(a-2)}^1}{3\cancel{(a-2)}_1} = \dfrac{2}{3}$$

EXAMPLE 3

Simplify $\dfrac{b + 8 + \dfrac{5}{b-3}}{1 + \dfrac{-1}{b-3}}$.

$b - 3$ cannot be factored. Multiply both numerator and denominator by the LCD, $b - 3$.

$$\dfrac{(b-3)\left(\dfrac{b+8}{1} + \dfrac{5}{b-3}\right)}{(b-3)\left(1 + \dfrac{-1}{b-3}\right)}$$

Use the distributive property. Divide out common factors in each product.

$$\dfrac{(b-3)(b+8) + \cancel{(b-3)}^1 \cdot \dfrac{5}{\cancel{b-3}_1}}{b-3 + \cancel{(b-3)}^1 \cdot \dfrac{-1}{\cancel{b-3}_1}}$$

$$\dfrac{b^2 + 5b - 24 + 5}{b - 3 - 1}$$

Combine like terms.

$$\dfrac{b^2 + 5b - 19}{b - 4}$$

EXERCISES

Simplify.

1. $$\dfrac{\dfrac{3}{a^2 - 7a + 10} + \dfrac{2}{a - 5}}{\dfrac{4}{a - 5} + \dfrac{2}{a - 2}}$$

2. $$\dfrac{\dfrac{5}{x^2 - 9} + \dfrac{2}{x - 3}}{\dfrac{3}{x - 3} + \dfrac{2}{x + 3}}$$

3. $$\dfrac{\dfrac{5}{b^2 - 5b} + \dfrac{2}{b - 5}}{\dfrac{7}{b - 5} + \dfrac{3}{b}}$$

4. $$\dfrac{\dfrac{7}{a - 1} + \dfrac{2}{a}}{\dfrac{5}{a^2 - a}}$$

5. $$\dfrac{\dfrac{3}{b - 2} - \dfrac{2}{b - 3}}{\dfrac{7}{b^2 - 5b + 6}}$$

6. $$\dfrac{\dfrac{7}{x^2 - 7x + 12} + \dfrac{3}{x - 4}}{\dfrac{2}{x - 4} + \dfrac{7}{x - 3}}$$

7. $$\dfrac{\dfrac{3}{a - 2} - \dfrac{2}{a + 1}}{\dfrac{a + 7}{a^2 - a - 2}}$$

8. $$\dfrac{\dfrac{2}{a + 7} + \dfrac{-28}{a^2 + 7a}}{\dfrac{3}{a + 7} - \dfrac{2}{a}}$$

9. $$\dfrac{\dfrac{2}{a + 2} + \dfrac{1}{a + 5}}{\dfrac{a + 4}{a^2 + 7a + 10}}$$

10. $$\dfrac{\dfrac{4}{m + 5} + \dfrac{-20}{m^2 + 5m}}{\dfrac{2}{m + 5} - \dfrac{1}{m}}$$

11. $$\dfrac{5 + \dfrac{7}{x - 3}}{4 + \dfrac{3}{x - 3}}$$

12. $$\dfrac{\dfrac{6b}{3b - 1} + \dfrac{1}{2}}{\dfrac{5}{2} + \dfrac{4}{3b - 1}}$$

13. $$\dfrac{\dfrac{4}{x^2 - 6x - 16} - \dfrac{3}{x - 8}}{\dfrac{5}{x - 8} + \dfrac{2}{x + 2}}$$

14. $$\dfrac{\dfrac{4}{a - 2} + \dfrac{2}{2a + 1}}{\dfrac{5a}{2a^2 - 3a - 2}}$$

15. $$\dfrac{\dfrac{3x}{x^2 - 9}}{\dfrac{6}{x - 3} + \dfrac{6}{x + 3}}$$

Simplify.

16. $$\dfrac{\dfrac{x + 1}{x} - \dfrac{5}{x + 2}}{\dfrac{x + 1}{x^2 + 2x} + \dfrac{3}{x + 2}}$$

17. $$\dfrac{\dfrac{1}{x + 3} + \dfrac{1}{x - 7}}{\dfrac{2x^2 + x - 10}{x^2 - 4x - 21}}$$

18. $$\dfrac{\dfrac{x + 1}{x + 2} + \dfrac{x + 7}{x - 5}}{\dfrac{5}{x^2 - 3x - 10}}$$

Simplify.

19. $$\dfrac{\dfrac{a}{b} + 2 + \dfrac{b}{a}}{\dfrac{a^2 - b^2}{ab}}$$

20. $$\dfrac{\dfrac{x}{y} - 6 + \dfrac{7y}{6}}{\dfrac{x^2 - 49y^2}{xy}}$$

21. $$\dfrac{\dfrac{x - y}{x - 2y} + \dfrac{x + 7y}{x + 5y}}{\dfrac{3x}{x^2 + 3xy - 10y^2}}$$

Formulas

REVIEW CAPSULE

Solve for y. Then find y if $x = 3$.

$2x + 3y = 10$

$\underline{-2x \qquad\qquad -2x}$

$3y = 10 - 2x$

$y = \dfrac{10 - 2x}{3}$

If $x = 3$, then

$y = \dfrac{10 - 2(3)}{3}$

$= \dfrac{10 - 6}{3}$, or $\dfrac{4}{3}$.

EXAMPLE 1 Solve $ax = b$ for x.

Divide each side by a. ⟶

Similar to $3x = 17$

$x = \dfrac{17}{3}$

$ax = b$

$\dfrac{ax}{a} = \dfrac{b}{a}$

$x = \dfrac{b}{a}$

EXAMPLE 2 The formula for perimeter of a rectangle is
$p = \ell + w + \ell + w$, or
$p = 2\ell + 2w$.
Solve $p = 2\ell + 2w$ for ℓ.
Then find ℓ if $p = 46$ and
$w = 9$.

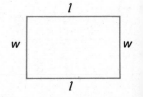

Get 2ℓ alone on one side.
Add $-2w$ to each side.
ℓ is alone on one side.
Divide each side by 2.
Formula is solved for ℓ.

$p = 2\ell + 2w$

$\underline{-2w \qquad\qquad -2w}$

$p - 2w = 2\ell$

$\dfrac{p - 2w}{2} = \ell$, or $\ell = \dfrac{p - 2w}{2}$

Now, find ℓ if $p = 46$ and $w = 9$.

Replace p with 46, w with 9. ⟶

$\ell = \dfrac{p - 2w}{2}$

$= \dfrac{46 - 2(9)}{2}$

$= \dfrac{46 - 18}{2}$, or 14

EXAMPLE 3   Solve $pkt - m = 5m$ for k.

Get pkt alone on one side.⎫
Add m to each side.   ⎭

Rewrite pkt as $(pt)k$, since we can
multiply in any order. ⟶

Divide each side by pt. ⟶

$$pkt - m = 5m$$
$$\underline{\qquad m \qquad m}$$
$$pkt = 6m$$
$$(pt)k = 6m$$
$$\frac{(pt)k}{pt} = \frac{6m}{pt}$$
$$k = \frac{6m}{pt}$$

EXAMPLE 4   Solve $F = \frac{9}{5}C + 32$ for C. Then find C if $F = 68$.

$$\frac{F}{1} = \frac{9}{5}C + \frac{32}{1} \leftarrow LCD \text{ is } 5.$$

Multiply each side by 5. ⟶

$$5 \cdot \frac{F}{1} = 5\left(\frac{9}{5}C + \frac{32}{1}\right)$$

Use the distributive property.⎫
Divide out common factors. ⎭

$$5F = \overset{1}{5} \cdot \frac{9}{\underset{1}{5}}C + 5 \cdot 32$$

Get $9c$ alone on one side.⎫
Add -160 to each side.   ⎭

$$5F = 9C + 160$$
$$\underline{-160 \qquad\qquad -160}$$
$$5F - 160 = 9C$$

Divide each side by 9. ⟶

$$\frac{5F - 160}{9} = C, \text{ or } C = \frac{5F - 160}{9}$$

Now find C if $F = 68$.

$$C = \frac{5F - 160}{9}$$

$$\left.\begin{array}{c}\dfrac{5(68) - 160}{9} = \dfrac{340 - 160}{9}\\[2mm] = 20\end{array}\right\}$$

$$= \frac{5(68) - 160}{9}$$
$$= 20$$

EXAMPLE 5   Solve $ax = c - bx$ for x.

Get all the x terms on one side.⎫
Add bx to each side.   ⎭

$$ax = c - bx$$
$$\underline{bx \qquad\qquad bx}$$
$$ax + bx = c$$

Factor out the common monomial, x. ⟶

Divide each side by $(a + b)$, since x is⎫
multiplied by $(a + b)$.   ⎭

$$x(a + b) = c$$
$$\frac{x(a + b)}{a + b} = \frac{c}{a + b}$$
$$x = \frac{c}{a + b}$$

EXERCISES

PART A

Solve for x.

1. $ax = 2$
2. $rx = 5$
3. $3x = 3a$
4. $bc = 2x$
5. $x + 3a = 0$
6. $2c + x = a$
7. $x - 4a = 0$
8. $5 = x - 3c$
9. $2x - c = d$
10. $bx - 7 = 3c$
11. $4a + 2x = 3b$
12. $7x + 2a = 6h$
13. $8 - 2x = kx$
14. $ax = 4 - cx$
15. $3ax = ax + b$
16. $mx = px - t$
17. $\dfrac{x}{3} = \dfrac{b}{2} + \dfrac{c}{6}$
18. $\dfrac{m}{5} + \dfrac{p}{3} = \dfrac{x}{15}$
19. $\dfrac{x}{2a} = \dfrac{b}{c}$
20. $\dfrac{x}{b} - c = a$

Solve each formula for the variable indicated. Then evaluate.

21. Solve $p = 4s$ for s. Then find s if $p = 28$.
22. Solve $A = pti$ for i. Then find i if $p = 180$, $A = 270$, and $t = \frac{1}{2}$.
23. Solve $p = 2s + b$ for s. Then find s if $p = 52$ and $b = 14$.
24. Solve $\ell = a + 15d$ for d. Then find d if $\ell = 125$ and $a = 35$.
25. Solve $C = 2\pi r$ for r. Then find r if $C = 12.56$ and $\pi \doteq 3.14$.
26. Solve $i = prt$ for r. Then find r if $i = 30$, $p = 200$, and $t = 4$.
27. Solve $V = \ell wh$ for h. Then find h if $V = 48$, $\ell = 2$, and $w = 6$.
28. Solve $C = \frac{1}{3}fd^2$ for f. Then find f if $C = 20$ and $d = 2$.

PART B

Solve for x.

29. $5a + 2bx = 3c$
30. $6x - 6a = 2x + 10a$
31. $ax - c = 2d + 3c$
32. $3b - 3c = 2bx - 3c$
33. $2 - 2bx = -4b + 3bx$
34. $7a + 3x = 6a + 4x$
35. $a^2 - ax + 4 = 2x - 4a$
36. $4x - ax = 16 - a^2$
37. $ax + bx = a^2 + 2ab + b^2$

PART C

Solve each formula for the variable indicated. Then evaluate.

38. Solve $C = \dfrac{5}{9}(F - 32)$ for F. Then find F if $C = 15$.
39. Solve $V = \dfrac{1}{3}\pi r^2 h$ for h. Then find h if $V = 157$, $\pi \doteq 3.14$, and $r = 5$.
40. Solve $T = \pi r(r + \ell)$ for ℓ. Then find ℓ if $T = 942$, $r = 10$, and $\pi \doteq 3.14$.
41. Solve $A = p + prt$ for p. Then find p if $A = 134.40$, $r = .06$, and $t = 2$.
42. Solve $T = 2\pi r(r + h)$ for h. Then find h if $T = 301.44$, $r = 4$, and $\pi \doteq 3.14$.
43. Solve $A = \dfrac{b + c + a}{3}$ for a. Then find a if $A = 34$, $b = 39$, and $c = 32$.

Mathematics in Pharmacy

As drugs are manufactured their quality is constantly checked.
Results of such tests are known immediately through the use of
computer-video systems as shown above.

Other aspects of a pharmacist's job are the development of new drugs
and the careful preparation of doctor's prescriptions.

Chapter Thirteen Review

Solve and check for extraneous solutions. $[p.\ 341,\ 346]$

1. $\dfrac{2a-3}{6} = \dfrac{4a}{3} + \dfrac{1}{2}$

2. $\dfrac{3}{5} + \dfrac{6}{x} = 1$

3. $\dfrac{2}{3}(x-4) + \dfrac{x+5}{2} = \dfrac{2x-1}{3}$

4. $\dfrac{7}{y+3} - \dfrac{4}{y-7} = \dfrac{2}{y^2-4y-21}$

5. $\dfrac{x}{x-7} + \dfrac{3}{x} = \dfrac{-23}{x^2-7x}$

6. $\dfrac{2}{b+2} + \dfrac{13}{b^2-4} = \dfrac{b}{b-2}$

$[p.\ 350,\ 353]$

7. Working together, Mona and Martin can mow a lawn in 5 hours. It would take Mona 9 hours to do it alone. How long would it take Martin?

8. George can repair a radio in 5 hours. If Tina helps him, they can complete the job in 2 hours. How long would it take Tina to do it alone?

9. Working together, two women can build a house in 7 months. It would take one of them 3 times as long as the other to do it alone. How long would it take each alone?

10. By herself, Jane can build a table in 2 weeks. It would take Juan 5 weeks. How long would it take Irv if, working together, all three can complete the job in 1 week?

Solve. $[p.\ 358]$

11. $.03x = 7$

12. $.6x + 3 = .21x + 18$

13. $.01(2 - .5x) = .48 - .003x$

Show that each is a rational number. $[p.\ 361]$

14. -18

15. 0

16. $7\frac{1}{2}$

17. $4.6\overline{6}$

18. $.32\overline{2}$

19. $.18\overline{18}$

Simplify. $[p.\ 368,\ 371]$

20. $\dfrac{\dfrac{3}{5} + \dfrac{1}{2}}{\dfrac{3}{10} + \dfrac{2}{5}}$

21. $\dfrac{\dfrac{3}{b^2} + \dfrac{5}{b}}{\dfrac{2}{b} + \dfrac{7}{3b^2}}$

22. $\dfrac{1 - \dfrac{2}{x} - \dfrac{15}{x^2}}{\dfrac{1}{x} - \dfrac{5}{x^2}}$

23. $\dfrac{\dfrac{6}{a-3} + \dfrac{4}{a}}{\dfrac{7}{a^2-3a}}$

24. $\dfrac{\dfrac{3}{a-4} + \dfrac{5}{2a+3}}{\dfrac{4a}{2a^2-5a-12}}$

25. $\dfrac{x-5 + \dfrac{3}{x-2}}{\dfrac{3}{x-2} + 2}$

Solve for x. $[p.\ 374]$

26. $bx - 8 = 3m$

27. $5a + mx = tr$

28. $8 - 5x = kx$

29. $6a + 5x = 4a + 3x$

Solve each formula for the variable indicated. Then evaluate. $[p.\ 374]$

30. Solve $a = mpq$ for p. Then find p if $a = 32$, $m = 2$, and $q = 7$.

31. Solve $k = \frac{1}{4}fd^2$ for f. Then find f if $k = 7$ and $d = 2$.

Chapter Thirteen Test

Solve and check for extraneous solutions.

1. $\dfrac{3a - 4}{15} = \dfrac{2a}{5} + \dfrac{1}{3}$

2. $\dfrac{2}{3} + \dfrac{6}{x} = 2$

3. $\dfrac{4}{y - 8} - \dfrac{3}{y + 2} = \dfrac{4}{y^2 - 6y - 16}$

4. $\dfrac{2}{7}(x - 2) + \dfrac{x + 4}{7} = \dfrac{x + 15}{14}$

5. Working together, Janice and Jack can mow a lawn in 4 hours. It would take Janice 7 hours to do it alone. How long would it take Jack?

6. Rodney can repair a T.V. set in 9 hours. If Lisa helps him, they can complete the job in 4 hours. How long would it take Lisa to do it alone?

7. Working together, two men can build a shed in 15 hours. It would take one of them 4 times as long as the other to do it alone. How long would it take each alone?

8. By herself, Joan can build a desk in 4 weeks. It would take José 5 weeks. How long would it take Sue if, working together, all three can complete the job in 2 weeks?

Solve.

9. $.05x = 4$

10. $.5x + 2 = .32x + 12$

11. $.01(3 - .4x) = .23 - .002x$

Show that each is a rational number.

12. -14

13. $8\frac{1}{3}$

14. $.4\overline{4}$

15. $.12\overline{12}$

Simplify.

16. $\dfrac{\dfrac{4}{7} + \dfrac{1}{3}}{\dfrac{2}{3} + \dfrac{5}{21}}$

17. $\dfrac{\dfrac{7}{a - 2} + \dfrac{5}{a}}{\dfrac{3}{a^2 - 2a}}$

18. $\dfrac{1 - \dfrac{5}{m} - \dfrac{14}{m^2}}{\dfrac{1}{m} - \dfrac{7}{m^2}}$

19. $\dfrac{x - 2 + \dfrac{5}{x + 3}}{\dfrac{7}{x + 3} + 5}$

Solve for x.

20. $mx - 4 = 2a$

21. $7 + 2x = tx$

22. $5x - 4b = 3x + 8b$

Solve each formula for the variable indicated. Then evaluate.

23. Solve $m = abd$ for b. Then find b if $m = 28$, $a = 2$, and $d = 7$.

24. Solve $I = \frac{1}{5}mp^2$ for m. Then find m if $p = 2$ and $I = 20$.

The Normal Curve

64 ninth grade boys were categorized according to their height. The results are given below.

Height	Number of boys
Under 5'	1
5'1" to under 5'3"	6
5'3" to under 5'5"	15
5'5" to under 5'7"	20
5'7" to under 5'9"	15
5'9" to under 5'11"	6
5'11" or over	1
Total	64 boys

The graph below, which is composed of rectangles, is called a *histogram.* It represents the data from the table.

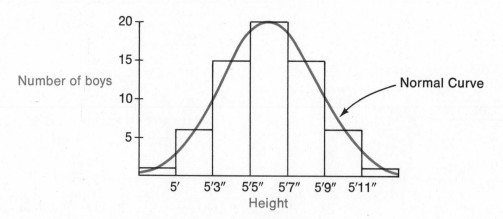

The smooth curve drawn through the graph is shaped like a bell. It is called the *normal curve.*

The Apex Lighting Company took a survey of 10,000 150-watt light bulbs to determine the number of hours each bulb would burn. The results are given below.

Mortality Rate of 150-watt light bulbs

Number of hours burned	Number of bulbs
100–299.9	3
300–499.9	321
500–699.9	1,108
700–899.9	2,193
900–1099.9	2,745
1100–1299.9	2,196
1300–1499.9	1,113
1500–1699.9	319
1700–1889.9	2
	Total 10,000 bulbs

These results fit the normal curve.

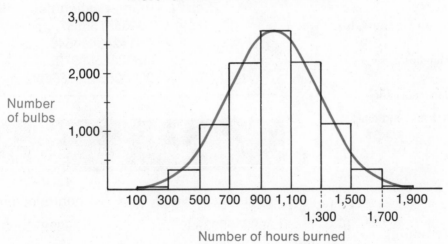

Number of bulbs

Number of hours burned

Actually, the normal curve describes the distribution of a great many seemingly unrelated sets of data.

* the batting averages of a large group of baseball players
* the velocity of molecules of gas

* the weights of thousands of apples

* the sizes of leaves of a tree

The Set of Real Numbers

OBJECTIVES
- To determine if a decimal is, or is not, a rational number
- To write decimals which are not rational numbers

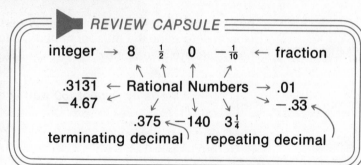

REVIEW CAPSULE

integer → 8 $\frac{1}{2}$ 0 $-\frac{1}{10}$ ← fraction

.31$\overline{31}$ ← Rational Numbers → .01

−4.67

.375 ←−140 $3\frac{1}{4}$ → −.3$\overline{3}$

terminating decimal   repeating decimal

EXAMPLE 1 If possible, write these decimals with a bar.
.311311311311. . .
.313113111311113111113. . .

This decimal repeats. → .311311311311. . . = .311$\overline{311}$

.313113111311113111113. . . cannot be written with a bar since no group of digits continues to repeat.

These cannot be written with a bar.

Decimal approximation for π →

Nonrepeating decimals cannot be written in the form $\frac{a}{b}$, where a and b are integers and $b \neq 0$.

These are nonrepeating decimals.
.57557555755557. . .
−7.40414243444546. . .
3.14159265358979. . .
43.0060066006660066600. . .

Nonrepeating decimals are *irrational* numbers.

repeating decimal
↓
.399939993999. . .
↓
rational number

nonrepeating decimal
↓
.3939939993. . .
↓
irrational number

EXAMPLE 2 Which are rational and which are irrational numbers?

		Answers
Terminating decimal →	−4.287	Rational
Nonrepeating decimal →	6.161161116. . .	Irrational
Repeating decimal →	37.237$\overline{237}$	Rational

{rationals} ∪ {irrationals} = {reals}.

The set of *real* numbers contains all the rational and all the irrational numbers.

EXERCISES

PART A

Which are rational and which are irrational numbers?

1. .424242. . .
2. .424424442. . .
3. −.5639
4. .68$\overline{68}$
5. −.31323334. . .
6. .308$\overline{383}$
7. .123123123. . .
8. −.00009
9. π
10. 7.1234$\overline{1234}$
11. $\frac{34}{3,434}$
12. 0
13. −2.101101110. . .
14. −.1121231234. . .
15. 456,456
16. 3.1416
17. −.438438
18. $\frac{22}{7}$
19. −.682$\overline{682}$
20. .20212223. . .

PART B

21. Make up five real numbers that are rational.
22. Make up decimal numerals for five real numbers that are irrational.
23. Name five real numbers that are integers.
24. Is every integer a real number? Why or why not?
25. A number called e is used in higher mathematics. $e \doteq 2.71828. \ldots$ At no time does a group of digits repeat, no matter how far the decimal is carried out. Is e rational or irrational?
26. Start with a decimal point. Flip a coin. If heads comes up, write 1. If tails comes up, write 2. Imagine doing this indefinitely. Does the numeral you are constructing name a rational or an irrational number?
27. Start with a decimal point. Toss a die. Record the number shown on the die. Imagine that this continues forever. Does the numeral you are constructing name a rational or an irrational number?
28. Start with a decimal point. Toss two dice. Record the number that is the sum of the numbers shown on the dice. Imagine that this continues forever. Does the numeral you are constructing name a rational or an irrational number?

PART C

True or false?

29. {rationals} ∩ {irrationals} = {reals}
30. {integers} ⊆ {reals}
31. {rationals} ∩ {irrationals} = ϕ
32. {reals} = {rationals}
33. {reals} ∩ {rationals} = {rationals}
34. {rationals} ∪ {reals} = {reals}

Square Roots

REVIEW CAPSULE

$$(2)(2) = 4$$
$$(-2)(-2) = 4$$

$$(15)(15) = 225$$
$$(-15)(-15) = 225$$

$$(3.1)(3.1) = 9.61$$
$$(-3.1)(-3.1) = 9.61$$

$$\left(\frac{3}{4}\right)\left(\frac{3}{4}\right) = \frac{9}{16}$$

$$\left(-\frac{3}{4}\right)\left(-\frac{3}{4}\right) = \frac{9}{16}$$

Definition of square root ⟶ If $x \cdot x = n$, then x is a square root of n.

Every positive real number has two square roots, one positive and one negative.

Number	Positive Square Root	Negative Square Root
4	2	−2
9.61	3.1	−3.1
$\frac{9}{16}$	$\frac{3}{4}$	$-\frac{3}{4}$

2 is a square root of 4, since $(2)(2) = 4$. Also, −2 is a square root of 4, since $(-2)(-2) = 4$.

Definition of principal square root ⟶ The positive square root of a number is called the *principal square root.* It is indicated by the symbol $\sqrt{}$.

The principal square root of 4 is 2.

$$\sqrt{4} = 2 \qquad \sqrt{9.61} = 3.1 \qquad \sqrt{225} = 15 \qquad \sqrt{\frac{9}{16}} = \frac{3}{4}$$

EXAMPLE 1 Are $\sqrt{16}$ and $\sqrt{33}$ whole numbers?

$(5)(5) = 25$ and $(6)(6) = 36$; so, $\sqrt{33}$ is not 5 or 6. ⟶ $\sqrt{16}$ is the whole number 4, since $(4)(4) = 16$.
$\sqrt{33}$ is not a whole number.

Definition of a perfect square ⟶   A *perfect square* is a number whose principal
16 is a perfect square   square root is a whole number.

The table on page 478 gives 3-decimal place values
for square roots of whole numbers from 1 to 100.

≐ means is approximately equal to.

$\sqrt{33} \doteq 5.745$ $(5.745)(5.745) = 33.005025 \doteq 33$
$\sqrt{65} \doteq 8.062$ $(8.062)(8.062) = 64.995844 \doteq 65$

EXAMPLE 2   The area of a square is 86 square inches. Find the
length of a side, to the nearest tenth of an inch.

Formula for area of a square ⟶ $s^2 = A$
Substitute 86 for *A*. ⟶ $s^2 = 86$
$s = \sqrt{86}$
From the table, $\sqrt{86} \doteq 9.274$. ⟶ $s \doteq 9.274$
Round to the nearest tenth. ⟶ $s \doteq 9.3$

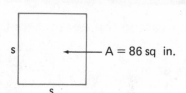
s   ⟵ A = 86 sq in.
s

Thus, the length of a side is 9.3 in., to the nearest
tenth.

EXAMPLE 3   The area of a rectangle is 48 square meters. The
length is 4 times the width. Find the length and
the width, to the nearest tenth of a meter.

Let x = width in meters
$4x$ = length in meters

Formula for area of a rectangle ⟶ $\ell \cdot w = A$
Substitute 4x, x, and 48. ⟶ $(4x)(x) = 48$
$4x^2 = 48$
Divide each side by 4. ⟶ $x^2 = 12$
$x = \sqrt{12}$
From the table, $\sqrt{12} \doteq 3.464$. ⟶ $x \doteq 3.464$
Round to the nearest tenth. ⟶ $x \doteq 3.5$
Find the length, 4x. ⟶ $4x \doteq 4(3.464)$
Multiply 3.464 by 4. ⟶ $4x \doteq 13.856$
Round to the nearest tenth. ⟶ $4x \doteq 13.9$

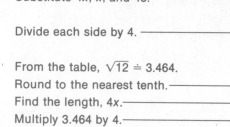
x   A = 48 sq m

Thus, the length is 13.9 m and the width is 3.5 m,
to the nearest tenth.

ORAL EXERCISES

Tell which are perfect squares. Then give the principal square root of each number. Approximate to the nearest tenth for nonperfect squares. Use the table on page 478.

1. 25   **2.** 6   **3.** 100   **4.** 26   **5.** 36
6. 38   **7.** 42   **8.** 49   **9.** 11   **10.** 59
11. 1   **12.** 67   **13.** 12   **14.** 64   **15.** 8
16. 74   **17.** 36   **18.** 78   **19.** 9   **20.** 92

EXERCISES

PART A

Give answers to the nearest tenth.

1.
s | A = 37 sq ft | s

Find s.

2.
s | A = 62 sq in. | s

Find s.

3.
A = 110 sq m | x / $2x$

Find x and $2x$.

4.
s | A = 94 sq cm | s

Find s.

5.
x | A = 90 sq yd / $3x$

Find x and $3x$.

6.
A = 255 sq cm | x / $5x$

Find x and $5x$.

7.
s | A = 28 sq in. / s

Find s.

8.
A = 102 sq m | $3x$ / $2x$

Find $2x$ and $3x$.

9. The length of a rectangle is 5 times the width. The area is 220 sq m. Find the length and the width.

10. The area of a rectangle is 166 sq ft. The length is twice the width. Find the length and the width.

PART B

Give answers to the nearest tenth.

Find r.
(Hint: $A = \pi r^2$.)
Use 3.14 for π.

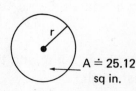

$A \doteq 25.12$ sq in.

Find $3x$ and $2x$.
(Hint: $A = \frac{1}{2}bh$.)

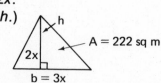

$A = 222$ sq m
$2x$
$b = 3x$
h

The Galton Board

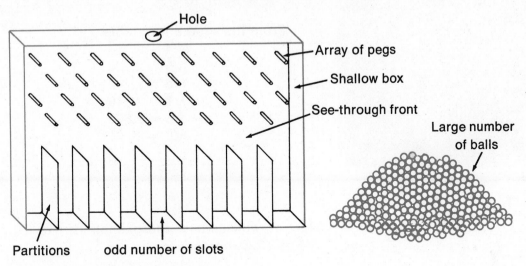

Build a model of the Galton Board.
(Suggested materials: wood, plastic, heavy cardboard)

If the balls are poured into the
hole, they will form a model
of the normal curve.

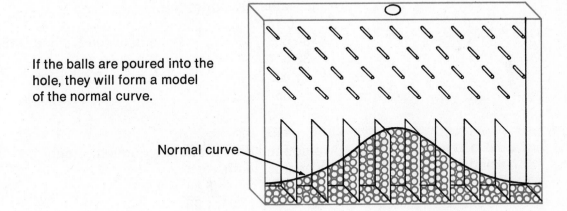

The board was invented by a British mathematician, Sir Francis Galton
(1822-1911).

Approximating Square Roots

<table>
<tr><td>

OBJECTIVES

■ To determine if numbers like $\sqrt{48}$ are irrational

■ To approximate the square root of a whole number, correct to the nearest tenth

</td><td>

▶ *REVIEW CAPSULE*

From the square root table:
$$\sqrt{4} = 2$$
$$\sqrt{5} \doteq 2.236$$
$$\sqrt{6} \doteq 2.449$$
$$\sqrt{7} \doteq 2.646$$
$$\sqrt{8} \doteq 2.828$$
$$\sqrt{9} = 3$$

</td></tr>
</table>

Now we will see how approximations like $\sqrt{5} \doteq 2.236$ are derived.

EXAMPLE 1   Approximate $\sqrt{34}$ to the nearest tenth.

Step 1 ⟶ Guess the square root.

$5 \times 5 = 25$ and $6 \times 6 = 36$ ⟶ $\sqrt{34}$ is between 5 and 6. GUESS: 5.5.

Step 2 ⟶ Divide the guess into the number. Carry to hundredths. Do not round.

Divide 5.5 into 34. Carry to two decimal places.

```
      6.18
5.5)34.000          √34 is between 5.5 and 6.18.
   33 0
    1 00                   5.5 < √34 < 6.18
      55
     450
     440
```

Step 3 ⟶ Average the divisor and the quotient. Round to the nearest tenth.

To average 5.5 and 6.18, add them and divide by 2. Then round to the nearest tenth.

```
              5.84 ≐ 5.8
  5.5       2)11.68
+6.18         10              5.8 is the average.
 11.68         1 6
               1 6
                 8
                 8
```

If they were the same, we would be finished. However, we must continue.

Check to see if the average is the same as the previous divisor: $5.8 \neq 5.5$.

Step 4	Divide the average into the number. Carry to hundredths. Do not round.

Divide 5.8 into 34. ───────────────→

$$
\begin{array}{r}
5.86 \\
5.8\,)\overline{34.000} \\
\underline{29\ 0} \\
5\ 00 \\
\underline{4\ 64} \\
360 \\
\underline{348}
\end{array}
$$

If they were not the same, we would have to repeat Step 3.

The divisor and the quotient are the same in the tenths place: 5.8   5.86

$5.8 < \sqrt{34} < 5.86$

Thus, $\sqrt{34} = 5.8$ to the nearest tenth.

This method of approximating square roots is called the divide and average method.

To approximate a square root to the nearest tenth:
Step 1   Guess the square root.
Step 2   Divide the guess into the number. Carry to hundredths. Do not round.
Step 3   Average the divisor and quotient. Round to the nearest tenth.
Step 4   Divide the average into the number. Carry to hundredths. Do not round.
Repeat Steps 3 and 4 until the average is the same as the divisor in Step 3 or until the divisor and quotient agree in the tenths place in Step 4.

EXAMPLE 2   Approximate $\sqrt{86}$ to the nearest tenth.

Step 1
$9 \times 9 = 81$ and $10 \times 10 = 100$
$9 < \sqrt{86} < 10$ ───────────→ GUESS: 9.5

Guess the square root.

Step 2

Divide the guess into the number. Carry to hundredths. Do not round.

Divide 9.5 into 86. Carry to two decimal places. }

$$
\begin{array}{r}
9.05 \\
9.5\,)\overline{86.000} \\
\underline{85\ 5} \\
500 \\
\underline{475}
\end{array}
$$

$\sqrt{86}$ is between 9.05 and 9.5.

$9.05 < \sqrt{86} < 9.5$

Step 3	Average the divisor and quotient. Round to the nearest tenth.

Add and divide by 2. Then round to the nearest tenth.

$$\begin{array}{r} 9.5 \\ +9.05 \\ \hline 18.55 \end{array}$$

$$\begin{array}{r} 9.27 \doteq 9.3 \\ 2\overline{)18.55} \\ 18 \\ \hline 5 \\ 4 \\ \hline 15 \end{array}$$

9.3 is the average.

$9.3 \neq 9.5$. We must continue.

Step 4

Divide the average into the number. Carry to hundredths. Do not round.

Divide 9.3 into 86. Carry to two decimal places. }

$$\begin{array}{r} 9.24 \\ 9.3\overline{)86.000} \\ 83\ 7 \\ \hline 2\ 30 \\ 1\ 86 \\ \hline 440 \\ 372 \\ \hline \end{array}$$

$\sqrt{86}$ is between 9.24 and 9.3.

$9.24 < \sqrt{86} < 9.3$

9.3 9.27 We must continue. ⟶
Repeat Step 3.

Divisor and quotient do not agree in the tenths place. Average divisor and quotient. Round to the nearest tenth.

Add and divide by 2. Then round to the nearest tenth.

$$\begin{array}{r} 9.3 \\ +9.24 \\ \hline 18.54 \end{array}$$

$$\begin{array}{r} 9.27 \doteq 9.3 \\ 2\overline{)18.54} \\ 18 \\ \hline 5 \\ 4 \\ \hline 14 \end{array}$$

9.3 is the average.

Average equals previous quotient.

Thus, $\sqrt{86} = 9.3$ to the nearest tenth.

The decimal for $\sqrt{86}$ is nonrepeating. $\sqrt{86}$ is an irrational number. ⟶

If the square root of a whole number is not a whole number, then it is an irrational number.

EXERCISES

Which are irrational numbers? For each irrational number, approximate the square root to the nearest tenth. Use the divide and average method.

1. $\sqrt{26}$ 2. $\sqrt{1}$ 3. $\sqrt{48}$ 4. $\sqrt{25}$ 5. $\sqrt{89}$ 6. $\sqrt{62}$ 7. $\sqrt{18}$
8. $\sqrt{49}$ 9. $\sqrt{52}$ 10. $\sqrt{7}$ 11. $\sqrt{12}$ 12. $\sqrt{36}$ 13. $\sqrt{37}$ 14. $\sqrt{78}$
15. $\sqrt{32}$ 16. $\sqrt{90}$ 17. $\sqrt{67}$ 18. $\sqrt{58}$ 19. $\sqrt{70}$ 20. $\sqrt{100}$ 21. $\sqrt{82}$
22. $\sqrt{28}$ 23. $\sqrt{40}$ 24. $\sqrt{72}$ 25. $\sqrt{61}$ 26. $\sqrt{92}$ 27. $\sqrt{38}$ 28. $\sqrt{2}$

Simplifying Radicals

▶ REVIEW CAPSULE

Factor 48 into primes.
$$48 = (2)(24)$$
$$= (2)(2)(12)$$
$$= (2)(2)(2)(6)$$
$$= (2)(2)(2)(2)(3)$$

Thus, $48 = (2)(2)(2)(2)(3)$.

EXAMPLE 1 Simplify $\sqrt{9} \cdot \sqrt{4}$. Then simplify $\sqrt{9 \cdot 4}$. What conclusion can you draw?

Results are the same. ————————→

$\sqrt{9} \cdot \sqrt{4}$		$\sqrt{9 \cdot 4}$
$3 \cdot 2$		$\sqrt{36}$
6		6

Thus, $\sqrt{9} \cdot \sqrt{4} = \sqrt{9 \cdot 4}$.

Example 1 suggests this. ————→
a is nonnegative if $a \geq 0$.

$\sqrt{a} \cdot \sqrt{b} = \sqrt{a \cdot b}$ and $\sqrt{a \cdot b} = \sqrt{a} \cdot \sqrt{b}$, for all nonnegative numbers a and b.

EXAMPLE 2 Simplify $\sqrt{5} \cdot \sqrt{11}$.

$\sqrt{a} \cdot \sqrt{b} = \sqrt{a \cdot b}$ ————————→ $\sqrt{5} \cdot \sqrt{11} = \sqrt{5 \cdot 11} = \sqrt{55}$

Thus, $\sqrt{5} \cdot \sqrt{11} = \sqrt{55}$.

EXAMPLE 3 Simplify $\sqrt{5} \cdot \sqrt{5}$.   Simplify $\sqrt{8} \cdot \sqrt{8}$.

Multiply first. ————————→
Then simplify. ————————→

$\sqrt{5} \cdot \sqrt{5} = \sqrt{5 \cdot 5}$		$\sqrt{8} \cdot \sqrt{8} = \sqrt{8 \cdot 8}$
$= \sqrt{25}$		$= \sqrt{64}$
$= 5$		$= 8$

Thus, $\sqrt{5} \cdot \sqrt{5} = 5$ and $\sqrt{8} \cdot \sqrt{8} = 8$.

Example 3 suggests this. ──────────────→ $\sqrt{x} \cdot \sqrt{x} = x$, for each nonnegative number x.

EXAMPLE 4   Simplify $\sqrt{36 \cdot 81}$.

$\sqrt{a \cdot b} = \sqrt{a} \cdot \sqrt{b}$ ──────────────→
$$\begin{aligned} \sqrt{36 \cdot 81} &= \sqrt{36} \cdot \sqrt{81} \\ &= 6 \cdot 9 \\ &= 54 \end{aligned}$$

Thus, $\sqrt{36 \cdot 81} = 54$.

EXAMPLE 5   Simplify $\sqrt{72}$.

One way Factor into primes.	Another way Find greatest perfect square factor.

$\sqrt{a \cdot b} = \sqrt{a} \cdot \sqrt{b}$ ──────────────→

$\sqrt{x} \cdot \sqrt{x} = x$ ──────────────→

$$\begin{aligned} \sqrt{72} &= \sqrt{3 \cdot 3 \cdot 2 \cdot 2 \cdot 2} \\ &= \underline{\sqrt{3} \cdot \sqrt{3}} \cdot \underline{\sqrt{2} \cdot \sqrt{2}} \cdot \sqrt{2} \\ &= \quad 3 \quad \cdot \quad 2 \quad \cdot \sqrt{2} \\ &= 6\sqrt{2} \end{aligned}$$

Thus, $\sqrt{72} = 6\sqrt{2}$.

$$\begin{aligned} \sqrt{72} &= \sqrt{36 \cdot 2} \\ &= \sqrt{36} \cdot \sqrt{2} \\ &= \underline{6\sqrt{2}} \end{aligned}$$

Simplest radical form

$\sqrt{72}$ is a *radical*. $\sqrt{}$ is the *radical sign*. 72 is the *radicand*. A radical is *simplified* when the radicand does not have a perfect square factor.

EXAMPLE 6   Simplify $-5\sqrt{147}$. Then approximate to the nearest tenth.

$147 = 49 \cdot 3$. 49 is the greatest perfect square factor of 147. ──────────────→
$$\begin{aligned} -5\sqrt{147} &= -5\sqrt{49 \cdot 3} \\ &= -5\sqrt{49} \cdot \sqrt{3} \\ &= \underline{-5 \cdot 7} \cdot \sqrt{3} \end{aligned}$$

Simplest radical form ──────────────→
From the table, $\sqrt{3} \doteq 1.732$. ──────────────→
$$\begin{aligned} &= -35\sqrt{3} \\ &\doteq -35(1.732) \\ &\doteq -60.620 \end{aligned}$$

Round to the nearest tenth. ──────────────→
$$\doteq -60.6$$

Thus, $-5\sqrt{147} = -35\sqrt{3} \doteq -60.6$.

ORAL EXERCISES

Give the greatest perfect square factor of each number.

1. 36   **2.** 12   **3.** 18   **4.** 50   **5.** 98   **6.** 20   **7.** 64   **8.** 48

Factor into primes.

9. 6   **10.** 12   **11.** 18   **12.** 27   **13.** 50   **14.** 28   **15.** 36   **16.** 42

EXERCISES

PART A

Simplify.

1. $\sqrt{2} \cdot \sqrt{5}$ **2.** $\sqrt{3} \cdot \sqrt{7}$ **3.** $\sqrt{5} \cdot \sqrt{6}$ **4.** $\sqrt{3} \cdot \sqrt{11}$ **5.** $\sqrt{7} \cdot \sqrt{2}$

6. $\sqrt{5} \cdot \sqrt{13}$ **7.** $\sqrt{10} \cdot \sqrt{11}$ **8.** $\sqrt{14} \cdot \sqrt{3}$ **9.** $\sqrt{6} \cdot \sqrt{7}$ **10.** $\sqrt{15} \cdot \sqrt{2}$

11. $\sqrt{2} \cdot \sqrt{3} \cdot \sqrt{5}$ **12.** $\sqrt{6} \cdot \sqrt{7} \cdot \sqrt{11}$ **13.** $\sqrt{3} \cdot \sqrt{5} \cdot \sqrt{7}$

14. $\sqrt{21} \cdot \sqrt{2} \cdot \sqrt{5}$ **15.** $\sqrt{10} \cdot \sqrt{3} \cdot \sqrt{11}$

Simplify.

16. $\sqrt{9 \cdot 25}$ **17.** $\sqrt{64 \cdot 16}$ **18.** $\sqrt{81 \cdot 4}$ **19.** $\sqrt{49 \cdot 25}$ **20.** $\sqrt{100 \cdot 121}$

21. $\sqrt{12}$ **22.** $\sqrt{80}$ **23.** $\sqrt{27}$ **24.** $\sqrt{50}$ **25.** $\sqrt{180}$

26. $\sqrt{98}$ **27.** $\sqrt{243}$ **28.** $\sqrt{600}$ **29.** $\sqrt{242}$ **30.** $\sqrt{192}$

31. $\sqrt{28}$ **32.** $\sqrt{99}$ **33.** $\sqrt{162}$ **34.** $\sqrt{112}$ **35.** $\sqrt{405}$

36. $2\sqrt{60}$ **37.** $-5\sqrt{48}$ **38.** $6\sqrt{90}$ **39.** $-7\sqrt{44}$ **40.** $10\sqrt{54}$

Simplify. Then approximate to the nearest tenth.

41. $\sqrt{200}$ **42.** $\sqrt{75}$ **43.** $\sqrt{117}$ **44.** $\sqrt{125}$ **45.** $\sqrt{432}$

46. $3\sqrt{150}$ **47.** $-2\sqrt{162}$ **48.** $7\sqrt{176}$ **49.** $-5\sqrt{225}$ **50.** $-\sqrt{324}$

PART B

EXAMPLE   Simplify $\sqrt{675}$.

$$\sqrt{675} = \sqrt{3 \cdot 3 \cdot 3 \cdot 5 \cdot 5}$$
$$= \sqrt{3} \cdot \sqrt{3} \cdot \sqrt{5} \cdot \sqrt{5} \cdot \sqrt{3}$$
$$= \quad 3 \quad \cdot \quad 5 \quad \cdot \sqrt{3}, \text{ or } 15\sqrt{3}$$

Simplify.

51. $\sqrt{550}$ **52.** $\sqrt{784}$ **53.** $\sqrt{847}$ **54.** $\sqrt{980}$ **55.** $\sqrt{684}$

56. $\sqrt{833}$ **57.** $\sqrt{891}$ **58.** $\sqrt{1,080}$ **59.** $\sqrt{832}$ **60.** $\sqrt{512}$

61. $-\sqrt{1,372}$ **62.** $5\sqrt{1,014}$ **63.** $-2\sqrt{1,805}$ **64.** $-17\sqrt{972}$ **65.** $6\sqrt{3,179}$

Even Exponents

REVIEW CAPSULE

$$a^2 \cdot a^2 = a^{2+2} = a^4$$
$$x^5 \cdot x^5 = x^{5+5} = x^{10}$$

Also, $\quad y^8 = y^{4+4} = y^4 \cdot y^4$
$$z^6 = z^{3+3} = z^3 \cdot z^3$$

EXAMPLE 1 Simplify $\sqrt{a^6 b^2}$.

$\sqrt{x \cdot y} = \sqrt{x} \cdot \sqrt{y}$ ⟶

a^6 and b^2 are perfect squares. ⟶

$\sqrt{x} \cdot \sqrt{x} = x$ ⟶

$$\begin{aligned}\sqrt{a^6 b^2} &= \sqrt{a^6} \cdot \sqrt{b^2} \\ &= \sqrt{a^3 \cdot a^3} \cdot \sqrt{b^1 \cdot b^1} \\ &= \sqrt{a^3} \cdot \sqrt{a^3} \cdot \sqrt{b} \cdot \sqrt{b} \\ &= a^3 b\end{aligned}$$

EXAMPLE 2 Simplify $-\sqrt{49x^{10}y^4z^{18}}$.

x^{10} is a perfect square;
$\sqrt{x^{10}} = \sqrt{x^5} \cdot \sqrt{x^5} = x^5.$ }

$$-\sqrt{49} \cdot \sqrt{x^{10}} \cdot \sqrt{y^4} \cdot \sqrt{z^{18}} = -7x^5y^2z^9$$

EXAMPLE 3 Try to express $\sqrt{-64}$ as a real number.

Neither product is -64. ⟶

8 and -8 are not the same. ⟶

No real number squared is -64. ⟶

$$(8)(8) = 64 \text{ and } (-8)(-8) = 64$$
$$(8)(-8) = -64$$
It seems that $\sqrt{-64}$ is not a real number.

The square root of a negative number is not a real number.

EXAMPLE 4 Simplify $\sqrt{-81}$ and $-\sqrt{81}$ if possible.

$\sqrt{-81}$ is not a real number.
$$-\sqrt{81} = -9$$

We will assume that variables under a radical sign represent only positive numbers or zero.

ORAL EXERCISES

Simplify, if possible.

1. $\sqrt{1}$

2. $\sqrt{-1}$

3. $-\sqrt{1}$

4. $-\sqrt{-1}$

5. $\sqrt{25}$

6. $-\sqrt{36}$

7. $\sqrt{-100}$

8. $\sqrt{49}$

9. $-\sqrt{-25}$

10. $\sqrt{-16}$

11. $-\sqrt{9}$

12. $\sqrt{121}$

EXERCISES

PART A

Simplify.

1. $\sqrt{x^8 y^4}$

2. $-\sqrt{a^6 b^{10}}$

3. $\sqrt{c^2 d^8}$

4. $\sqrt{25x^2}$

5. $-\sqrt{9y^4}$

6. $\sqrt{49a^{10}}$

7. $-\sqrt{81a^2 b^6}$

8. $\sqrt{64x^4 y^8}$

9. $-\sqrt{4c^{10} d^2}$

10. $-\sqrt{16x^8 y^{12}}$

11. $\sqrt{9a^6 b^8}$

12. $\sqrt{100x^4 y^{14}}$

13. $\sqrt{a^4 b^6 c^8}$

14. $\sqrt{x^2 y^6 z^{10}}$

15. $-\sqrt{c^4 d^2 e^{12}}$

16. $-\sqrt{4x^2 y^8 z^2}$

17. $\sqrt{9a^6 b^8 c^2}$

18. $-\sqrt{49x^4 y^8 z^2}$

19. $\sqrt{64a^4 b^{12} c^2}$

20. $-\sqrt{81x^8 y^{12} z^4}$

21. $\sqrt{36c^8 d^{10} e^{12}}$

22. $-\sqrt{100x^2 y^{12} z^{10}}$

23. $\sqrt{25a^{12} b^{10} c^4}$

24. $-\sqrt{16c^2 d^6 e^{14}}$

25. $\sqrt{121c^8 d^6 e^2}$

26. $-\sqrt{169x^8 y^2 z^{10}}$

27. $\sqrt{144a^8 b^2 c^{16}}$

PART B

EXAMPLE Simplify $\sqrt{12x^4 y^{16} z^2}$.

$$\sqrt{12x^4 y^{16} z^2} = \sqrt{12} \cdot \sqrt{x^4} \cdot \sqrt{y^{16}} \cdot \sqrt{z^2}$$
$$= 2\sqrt{3}\, x^2 y^8 z$$

$\sqrt{12} = 2\sqrt{3}$ ⟶

Simplify.

28. $\sqrt{20x^2 y^8}$

29. $-\sqrt{27a^4 b^{10}}$

30. $-\sqrt{28c^8 d^2}$

31. $-\sqrt{32a^6 b^{12}}$

32. $\sqrt{50x^2 y^6}$

33. $-\sqrt{48a^{10} b^{12}}$

34. $\sqrt{200x^4 y^2 z^6}$

35. $\sqrt{45a^{12} b^{14} c^2}$

36. $\sqrt{75c^8 d^2 e^{12}}$

37. $-\sqrt{98a^4 b^8 c^{16}}$

38. $\sqrt{128x^4 y^{10} z^8}$

39. $-\sqrt{243x^8 y^2 z^{18}}$

PART C

Simplify.

40. $\sqrt{.04x^2 y^8}$

41. $-\sqrt{1.69a^2 b^8 c^{20}}$

42. $\sqrt{.000016x^4 y^2 z^{18}}$

43. $\sqrt{\dfrac{1}{25} x^{10} y^2 z^{12}}$

44. $\sqrt{\dfrac{4}{49} x^8 y^{12} z^{24}}$

45. $-\sqrt{\dfrac{81}{16} a^2 b^{36} c^{100}}$

Odd Exponents

REVIEW CAPSULE

$$x^6 \cdot x = x^6 \cdot x^1 = x^{6+1} = x^7$$
$$a^{10} \cdot a = a^{10} \cdot a^1 = a^{10+1} = a^{11}$$

Also, $y^9 = y^{8+1} = y^8 \cdot y^1 = y^8 \cdot y$
$$z^5 = z^{4+1} = z^4 \cdot z^1 = z^4 \cdot z$$

EXAMPLE 1   Simplify $\sqrt{x^5}$.

x^4 is a perfect square. ⟶

$\sqrt{x^4} = \sqrt{x^2 \cdot x^2} = x^2$ ⟶

$$\sqrt{x^5} = \sqrt{x^4 \cdot x^1}$$
$$= \sqrt{x^4} \cdot \sqrt{x^1}$$
$$= x^2\sqrt{x}$$

EXAMPLE 2   Simplify $\sqrt{a^3b^7}$.

a^2 and b^6 are perfect squares. ⟶
Group perfect squares together. ⟶
$\sqrt{a^2b^6} = \sqrt{a^2} \cdot \sqrt{b^6} = ab^3$ ⟶

$$\sqrt{a^3b^7} = \sqrt{a^2 \cdot a^1 \cdot b^6 \cdot b^1}$$
$$= \sqrt{a^2 \cdot b^6} \cdot \sqrt{ab}$$
$$= ab^3\sqrt{ab}$$

EXAMPLE 3   Simplify $\sqrt{40xy^9}$.

The greatest perfect square factor of $40xy^9$ is $4y^8$.

$\sqrt{4y^8} = \sqrt{4} \cdot \sqrt{y^8} = 2y^4$ ⟶

$$\sqrt{40xy^9} = \sqrt{4 \cdot 10 \cdot x \cdot y^8 \cdot y^1}$$
$$= \sqrt{4y^8} \cdot \sqrt{10xy}$$
$$= 2y^4\sqrt{10xy}$$

EXAMPLE 4   Simplify $-4x^2y\sqrt{45x^3y^4}$.

The greatest perfect square factor of $45x^3y^4$ is $9x^2y^4$.

$$-4x^2y\sqrt{45x^3y^4} = -4x^2y\sqrt{9 \cdot 5 \cdot x^2 \cdot x^1 \cdot y^4}$$
$$= -4x^2y\sqrt{9x^2y^4} \cdot \sqrt{5x}$$
$$= -4x^2y(3xy^2)\sqrt{5x}$$
$$= -12x^3y^3\sqrt{5x}$$

Read: the cube root of 8 equals 2. ⟶

$\sqrt[3]{8} = 2$, since $2 \cdot 2 \cdot 2 = 8$. $[2^3 = 8]$

$\sqrt[3]{-64} = -4$, since $(-4)(-4)(-4) = -64$.

$[(-4)^3 = -64]$

EXAMPLE 5   Simplify $\sqrt[3]{24x^3y^7}$
$$= \sqrt[3]{2 \cdot 2 \cdot 2 \cdot 3 \cdot x^1 \cdot x^1 \cdot x^1 \cdot y^2 \cdot y^2 \cdot y^2 \cdot y^1}$$
$$= \sqrt[3]{2 \cdot 2 \cdot 2 \cdot x^1 \cdot x^1 \cdot x^1 \cdot y^2 \cdot y^2 \cdot y^2}\ \sqrt[3]{3y^1}$$

Read: $2xy^2$ times the cube root of $3y$. $\longrightarrow$ $= 2xy^2\sqrt[3]{3y}$

EXERCISES

PART A
Simplify.

1. $\sqrt{x^3}$
2. $-\sqrt{a^7}$
3. $\sqrt{9x^5}$
4. $\sqrt{25c}$

5. $\sqrt{8x^5}$
6. $\sqrt{18a^9}$
7. $\sqrt{7x^3}$
8. $-\sqrt{5x^{11}}$

9. $\sqrt{x^4y^7}$
10. $\sqrt{a^2b^5}$
11. $-\sqrt{c^6d^3}$
12. $\sqrt{m^8n}$

13. $\sqrt{x^5y^7}$
14. $\sqrt{a^9b^3}$
15. $\sqrt{c^3d}$
16. $\sqrt{mn^7}$

17. $\sqrt{a^5b^8}$
18. $-\sqrt{4cd^2}$
19. $\sqrt{5x^3y^4}$
20. $\sqrt{99m^3b^8}$

21. $\sqrt{36x^2y}$
22. $-\sqrt{16m^8n^7}$
23. $\sqrt{6x^6y^9}$
24. $\sqrt{20a^4b^3}$

25. $\sqrt{19x^5y^9}$
26. $\sqrt{40xy^3}$
27. $-\sqrt{50m^3n^4}$
28. $\sqrt{72ab^6}$

29. $4\sqrt{44xy^2z^6}$
30. $-7\sqrt{90a^3b^6c^7}$
31. $6\sqrt{28a^4bc^{12}}$

32. $x\sqrt{x^3yz^8}$
33. $-cd\sqrt{c^4d^5e^6}$
34. $-a^2bc\sqrt{a^3b^8c^9}$

35. $-3y\sqrt{x^3y^5z}$
36. $4xz\sqrt{x^4y^7z^2}$
37. $-5c^2d\sqrt{b^7c^3d^6}$

38. $4a^2b\sqrt{75a^6b^7}$
39. $-12xy^3\sqrt{32x^2y^5}$
40. $8e^3f^2\sqrt{128ef^2g^3}$

PART B
Simplify.

41. $\sqrt[3]{x^3y^9}$
42. $\sqrt[3]{a^6b^{12}}$
43. $-\sqrt[3]{c^3d^{12}}$

44. $\sqrt[3]{-x^6y^9}$
45. $\sqrt[3]{8a^3b^9}$
46. $\sqrt[3]{-27x^6y^3}$

47. $-\sqrt[3]{64a^4b^6}$
48. $\sqrt[3]{-125x^7y^9}$
49. $-\sqrt[3]{40a^2b^8}$

50. $\sqrt[3]{-56ab^6c^{10}}$
51. $-\sqrt[3]{-192x^7yz^{12}}$
52. $-\sqrt[3]{32x^9y^{10}z^{11}}$

PART C

Read:
The fourth root of 81 equals 3. $\longrightarrow$ $\sqrt[4]{81} = 3$, since $3 \cdot 3 \cdot 3 \cdot 3 = 81$. $[3^4 = 81]$
The fifth root of 32 equals 2. $\longrightarrow$ $\sqrt[5]{32} = 2$, since $2 \cdot 2 \cdot 2 \cdot 2 \cdot 2 = 32$. $[2^5 = 32]$

Simplify.

53. $\sqrt[4]{x^4y^{12}}$
54. $\sqrt[5]{a^5b^{10}}$
55. $-\sqrt[4]{16x^8y^4}$

56. $\sqrt[6]{64x^6y^{12}}$
57. $\sqrt[5]{243x^6y^{10}}$
58. $-\sqrt[4]{81a^3b^5}$

59. $\sqrt[5]{-96a^2b^7c^3}$
60. $\sqrt[4]{80x^3y^7z^{12}}$
61. $-2a\sqrt[5]{160c^5d^6e^7}$

62. $-3a^3b\sqrt[4]{162a^6bc^9}$
63. $6xy^2\sqrt[3]{54x^2yz^8}$
64. $-7c^2d^3\sqrt[4]{12c^9d^{21}e}$

Using a Flow Chart to Find Square Roots

This is a flow chart of a process used in computers to find square roots.

Find $\sqrt{x}$

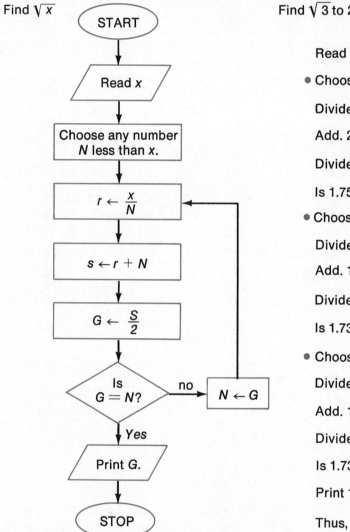

Find $\sqrt{3}$ to 2 decimal places.

Read 3.

● Choose 1.5. (1.5 < 3).

Divide. $\dfrac{3}{1.5} = 2$

Add. $2 + 1.5 = 3.5$

Divide. $\dfrac{3.5}{2} = 1.75$

Is $1.75 = 1.5$? No.

● Choose 1.75. (1.75 < 3)

Divide. $\dfrac{3}{1.75} = 1.71$

Add. $1.71 + 1.75 = 3.46$

Divide. $\dfrac{3.46}{2} = 1.73$

Is $1.73 = 1.75$? No.

● Choose 1.73. (1.73 < 3)

Divide. $\dfrac{3}{1.73} = 1.73$

Add. $1.73 + 1.73$

Divide. $\dfrac{3.46}{2} = 1.73$

Is $1.73 = 1.73$? Yes.

Print 1.73.

Thus, $\sqrt{3} = 1.73$.

1. Use the flow chart to find $\sqrt{5}$ to 2 decimal places. Carry all calculations to 2 decimal places. Do not round.

2. Use the flow chart to find $\sqrt{7}$ to 2 decimal places. Carry all calculations to 2 decimal places. Do not round.

The Pythagorean Theorem

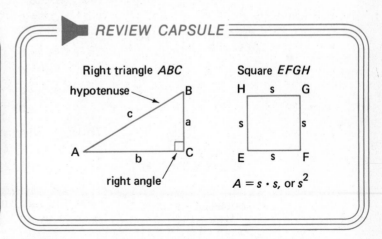

▶ *REVIEW CAPSULE*

Right triangle *ABC*

hypotenuse

Square *EFGH*

$A = s \cdot s$, or s^2

EXAMPLE 1 Examine right triangle *ABC* and the three squares shown. Find the area of each square. See what you can discover.

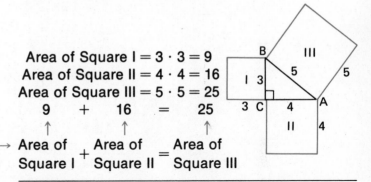

Area of Square I $= 3 \cdot 3 = 9$
Area of Square II $= 4 \cdot 4 = 16$
Area of Square III $= 5 \cdot 5 = 25$
$\quad 9 \quad + \quad 16 \quad = \quad 25$

This is true for all right triangles. ———→ $\underset{\text{Square I}}{\text{Area of}} + \underset{\text{Square II}}{\text{Area of}} = \underset{\text{Square III}}{\text{Area of}}$

Pythagoras, a Greek philosopher and mathematician, discovered the relationship above in 500 B.C.

c is the length of the hypotenuse.
a and *b* are the lengths of the other two sides.

If △*ABC* is a right triangle, then $a^2 + b^2 = c^2$.

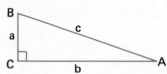

Pythagorean theorem ————————→
A *theorem* is a property which can be proved.

In any right triangle, the square of the length of the hypotenuse equals the sum of the squares of the lengths of the other two sides.

EXAMPLE 2

If the lengths of two sides of a right triangle are 5 meters and 12 meters, find the length of the hypotenuse.

Pythagorean theorem —————————→ $a^2 + b^2 = c^2$

Substitute 5 for a, 12 for b. —————→ $5^2 + 12^2 = c^2$

$25 + 144 = c^2$

$169 = c^2$

$\sqrt{169} = c$

$13 \cdot 13 = 169$ ———————————————→ $13 = c$

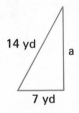

Thus, the length of the hypotenuse is 13 meters.

EXAMPLE 3

The length of the hypotenuse of a right triangle is 14 yards, and the length of one side is 7 yards. Find the length of the other side, in simplest radical form.

Pythagorean theorem —————————→ $a^2 + b^2 = c^2$

Substitute 7 for b, 14 for c. —————→ $a^2 + 7^2 = 14^2$

$a^2 + 49 = 196$

Add -49 to each side. ———————→ $a^2 = 147$

$a = \sqrt{147}$

$\sqrt{147} = \sqrt{7 \cdot 7 \cdot 3} = 7\sqrt{3}$ ————→ $a = 7\sqrt{3}$

Thus, the length of the other side is $7\sqrt{3}$ yards.

If $a^2 + b^2 = c^2$, then the triangle is a right triangle with c the hypotenuse.

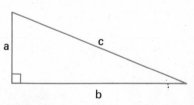

Converse of the Pythagorean theorem —→ If the sum of the squares of the lengths of two sides of a triangle equals the square of the length of the third side, then the triangle is a right triangle.

To form a converse of a statement, reverse the if and the then parts.

EXAMPLE 4

If the lengths of the sides of a triangle are 7, 24, and 25, is the triangle a right triangle?

See if $7^2 + 24^2 = 25^2$. ———————→ $7^2 = 49$ $24^2 = 576$ $25^2 = 625$ $49 + 576 = 625$

Thus, the triangle is a right triangle.

EXERCISES

PART A

Tell whether each triangle described is a right triangle. The lengths of the three sides are given.

1. 4, 5, 6   **2.** 6, 8, 10   **3.** 3, 5, 7   **4.** 12, 16, 20
5. 12, 14, 16   **6.** 9, 40, 41   **7.** 10, 24, 25   **8.** 10, 20, 30
9. 11, 60, 61   **10.** 6, 6, 9   **11.** 30, 40, 50   **12.** 14, 48, 50
13. 1, 2, $\sqrt{5}$ **14.** 1, 3, $\sqrt{11}$ **15.** 1, $\sqrt{3}$, 2   **16.** $\sqrt{2}$, $\sqrt{3}$, $\sqrt{5}$

For each triangle, find the missing length. Give answers in simplest radical form.

17. $a = 8, b = 6$ **18.** $a = 12, b = 16$ **19.** $a = 9, c = 15$
20. $a = 2, b = 6$ **21.** $b = 4, c = 8$ **22.** $b = 1, c = 3$
23. $a = 7, b = 7$ **24.** $a = 6, b = 12$ **25.** $a = 9, c = 18$
26. $b = 4, c = 12$ **27.** $a = 8, b = 8$ **28.** $a = 9, b = 40$
29. $a = 14, c = 50$ **30.** $b = 4, c = 4\sqrt{5}$ **31.** $a = 2\sqrt{2}, b = 2\sqrt{3}$

PART B

EXAMPLE   A rectangular field is 50 feet wide by 100 feet long. How long is a diagonal path connecting two opposite corners? Give the answer to the nearest tenth of a foot.

$$a^2 + b^2 = c^2$$
$$50^2 + 100^2 = c^2$$
$$2,500 + 10,000 = c^2$$
$$12,500 = c^2$$
$$\sqrt{12,500} = c$$
$$50\sqrt{5} = c$$
$$50(2.236) = c$$
$$111.800 = c$$

50 ft

c

100 ft

$\sqrt{12,500} = \sqrt{2,500} \cdot \sqrt{5} = 50\sqrt{5}$ ⟶

Round to the nearest tenth. ⟶   **Thus,** the diagonal path is approx. 111.8 feet long.

Give answers to the nearest tenth.

32. Paul walked 8 miles north and 3 miles west. How far was he from his starting point?

33. A 12-foot ramp covers 10 feet of ground. How high does it rise?

34. A T.V. screen is 15 inches by 12 inches. What is its diagonal length?

35. A 15-foot ladder is 5 feet from the base of a building. At what height does it touch the building?

Combining Radicals

OBJECTIVE
■ To combine like radicals

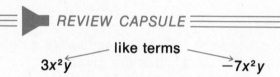

REVIEW CAPSULE

like terms

$3x^2y$ $-7x^2y$

Simplify by using the distributive property.
$$3x^2y - 7x^2y = (3 - 7)x^2y$$
$$= -4x^2y$$

$\sqrt{2}$ in each ⟶ $5\sqrt{2}$ and $2\sqrt{2}$ are *like radicals*.

EXAMPLE 1   Simplify $5\sqrt{2} + 2\sqrt{2}$.

Distributive Property ⟶
$$5\sqrt{2} + 2\sqrt{2} = (5 + 2)\sqrt{2} = 7\sqrt{2}$$

Illustration of $5\sqrt{2} + 2\sqrt{2} = 7\sqrt{2}$ ⟶

| $\sqrt{2}$ | $\sqrt{2}$ | $\sqrt{2}$ | $\sqrt{2}$ | $\sqrt{2}$ | $\sqrt{2}$ | $\sqrt{2}$ |

$5\sqrt{2}$ $2\sqrt{2}$

$7\sqrt{2}$

EXAMPLE 2   Simplify $5\sqrt{7} - 9\sqrt{13} + 6\sqrt{7}$.

Rearrange the terms. ⟶ $5\sqrt{7} - 9\sqrt{13} + 6\sqrt{7} = 5\sqrt{7} + 6\sqrt{7} - 9\sqrt{13}$
$$= (5 + 6)\sqrt{7} - 9\sqrt{13}$$
$11\sqrt{7}$ and $-9\sqrt{13}$ are unlike radicals. ⟶ $\qquad = 11\sqrt{7} - 9\sqrt{13}$

EXAMPLE 3   Simplify $\sqrt{75} - \sqrt{27} + \sqrt{12}$.

Simplify each radical. ⟶ $\sqrt{75} - \sqrt{27} + \sqrt{12}$
$$= \sqrt{25 \cdot 3} - \sqrt{9 \cdot 3} + \sqrt{4 \cdot 3}$$
$$= \sqrt{25} \cdot \sqrt{3} - \sqrt{9} \cdot \sqrt{3} + \sqrt{4} \cdot \sqrt{3}$$
$\sqrt{3}$ is common to each term. ⟶ $\qquad = 5\sqrt{3} - 3\sqrt{3} + 2\sqrt{3}$
Distributive property ⟶ $\qquad = (5 - 3 + 2)\sqrt{3}$
$$= 4\sqrt{3}$$

EXAMPLE 4   Simplify $2\sqrt{cd} - 5\sqrt{cd} + 9\sqrt{cd}$.

Distributive property ⟶ $2\sqrt{cd} - 5\sqrt{cd} + 9\sqrt{cd} = (2 - 5 + 9)\sqrt{cd}$
$$= 6\sqrt{cd}$$

EXAMPLE 5 Simplify $\sqrt{ab^3} + \sqrt{9ab^3} - 5b\sqrt{16ab}$.

$$\sqrt{ab^3} + \sqrt{9ab^3} - 5b\sqrt{16ab}$$
$$= \sqrt{b^2 \cdot ab} + \sqrt{9b^2 \cdot ab} - 5b\sqrt{16 \cdot ab}$$
$$= b\sqrt{ab} + 3b\sqrt{ab} - 5b(4)\sqrt{ab}$$
$$= b\sqrt{ab} + 3b\sqrt{ab} - 20b\sqrt{ab}$$
$$= (b + 3b - 20b)\sqrt{ab} = -16b\sqrt{ab}$$

$\sqrt{ab}$ is common to each term. $\longrightarrow$

Distributive Property $\longrightarrow$

EXERCISES

PART A

Simplify.

1. $2\sqrt{5} + 7\sqrt{5}$
2. $5\sqrt{3} - 2\sqrt{3}$
3. $7\sqrt{6} + 8\sqrt{6}$
4. $9\sqrt{2} - 8\sqrt{2}$
5. $4\sqrt{10} + 2\sqrt{10} - 5\sqrt{10}$
6. $6\sqrt{7} - 10\sqrt{7} - 4\sqrt{7}$
7. $5\sqrt{6} - 3\sqrt{6} + 6\sqrt{3}$
8. $4\sqrt{3} - 8\sqrt{2} - 7\sqrt{2}$
9. $4\sqrt{5} - 6\sqrt{7} + 8\sqrt{5}$
10. $6\sqrt{5} - \sqrt{11} + 5\sqrt{11} - 10\sqrt{5}$
11. $\sqrt{5} + 3\sqrt{2} - 6\sqrt{2} + 7\sqrt{5}$
12. $8\sqrt{7} - 7\sqrt{3} + 6\sqrt{7} + 9\sqrt{3}$
13. $3\sqrt{8} + \sqrt{2}$
14. $4\sqrt{3} + \sqrt{12}$
15. $2\sqrt{24} - 3\sqrt{54}$
16. $6\sqrt{27} - 3\sqrt{48}$
17. $3\sqrt{44} - 7\sqrt{11} + \sqrt{99}$
18. $-\sqrt{32} + 5\sqrt{18} - 7\sqrt{98}$
19. $\sqrt{a} + 8\sqrt{a}$
20. $6\sqrt{x} + 7\sqrt{x} - \sqrt{x}$
21. $4\sqrt{mn} - 2\sqrt{mn} + 5\sqrt{mn}$
22. $3\sqrt{xy} - \sqrt{xy} + 8\sqrt{xy} + \sqrt{xy}$
23. $\sqrt{xy} + \sqrt{4xy} - 2\sqrt{9xy}$
24. $-6\sqrt{9c} + 8\sqrt{16c} - 4c\sqrt{4c}$
25. $5x\sqrt{3z} + x\sqrt{5z} - x\sqrt{3z} - 2x\sqrt{5z}$
26. $2\sqrt{xy} - 5\sqrt{4xy} - \sqrt{25xy}$
27. $3\sqrt{a^3b^3} + 2b\sqrt{4a^3b} - 7a\sqrt{16ab^3}$
28. $c\sqrt{cd^3} + cd\sqrt{cd} + d\sqrt{c^3d}$

PART B

Simplify.

29. $\sqrt{27x} - \sqrt{48x} + \sqrt{75x}$
30. $2\sqrt{24y} - 5\sqrt{54y} + 7\sqrt{96y}$
31. $\sqrt{33a} + \sqrt{11a} - \sqrt{77a}$
32. $2\sqrt{98z} + \sqrt{18z} - 5\sqrt{32z}$
33. $2\sqrt{10x} + \sqrt{40x} - 5\sqrt{90x}$
34. $\sqrt{3xy} + \sqrt{27xy} - \sqrt{12xy}$
35. $2x\sqrt{5xy^2} + 3\sqrt{20x^3y^2}$
36. $7\sqrt{8a^2b^3} - 4b\sqrt{50a^2b}$

PART C

Simplify.

37. $\sqrt{.04xy^2} + y\sqrt{.16x}$
38. $3\sqrt{.25a^3b} + 4a\sqrt{.0001ab}$
39. $6x\sqrt{.0036xy^2} - 2yx\sqrt{.0049x}$
40. $2x\sqrt{.01xy^2} - 5\sqrt{.0025x^3y^2}$
41. $-2b\sqrt{.0004a^3b} + 6a\sqrt{.36ab^3}$
42. $7xy\sqrt{.64xy} - 8y\sqrt{.0081x^3y}$

Products of Radicals

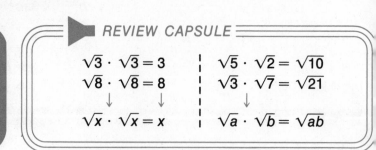

REVIEW CAPSULE

$$\sqrt{3} \cdot \sqrt{3} = 3 \qquad \sqrt{5} \cdot \sqrt{2} = \sqrt{10}$$
$$\sqrt{8} \cdot \sqrt{8} = 8 \qquad \sqrt{3} \cdot \sqrt{7} = \sqrt{21}$$
$$\downarrow \qquad \downarrow \qquad\qquad \downarrow$$
$$\sqrt{x} \cdot \sqrt{x} = x \qquad \sqrt{a} \cdot \sqrt{b} = \sqrt{ab}$$

EXAMPLE 1   Multiply $6\sqrt{5} \cdot 4\sqrt{3}$.

Rearrange factors. ⟶
$6 \cdot 4 = 24;\ \sqrt{5} \cdot \sqrt{3} = \sqrt{5 \cdot 3}$ ⟶
$\sqrt{5 \cdot 3} = \sqrt{15}$

$$6\sqrt{5} \cdot 4\sqrt{3} = 6 \cdot 4 \cdot \sqrt{5} \cdot \sqrt{3}$$
$$= 24 \cdot \sqrt{5 \cdot 3}$$
$$= 24\sqrt{15}$$

EXAMPLE 2   Multiply $-7\sqrt{6x} \cdot 2\sqrt{3x}$.

$$-7\sqrt{6x} \cdot 2\sqrt{3x} = -7 \cdot 2 \cdot \sqrt{6x} \cdot \sqrt{3x}$$
$$= -14\sqrt{6x \cdot 3x}$$
$$= -14\sqrt{2 \cdot 3x \cdot 3x}$$

$\sqrt{3x \cdot 3x} = 3x$ ⟶
$-14 \cdot 3 = -42$ ⟶

$$= -14 \cdot 3x \cdot \sqrt{2}$$
$$= -42x\sqrt{2}$$

EXAMPLE 3   Multiply $\sqrt{3}(\sqrt{5} + 4\sqrt{3})$.

Distribute the $\sqrt{3}$. ⟶
$\sqrt{3} \cdot 4\sqrt{3} = 4\sqrt{3} \cdot \sqrt{3}$ ⟶
$\sqrt{3 \cdot 5} = \sqrt{15};\ \sqrt{3} \cdot \sqrt{3} = 3$ ⟶

$$\sqrt{3}(\sqrt{5} + 4\sqrt{3}) = \sqrt{3} \cdot \sqrt{5} + \sqrt{3} \cdot 4\sqrt{3}$$
$$= \sqrt{3 \cdot 5} + 4\sqrt{3} \cdot \sqrt{3}$$
$$= \sqrt{15} + 4 \cdot 3$$
$$= \sqrt{15} + 12$$

EXAMPLE 4   Multiply $-6\sqrt{2}(\sqrt{10} - 7\sqrt{8})$.

Distribute the $-6\sqrt{2}$. ⟶

$\sqrt{a} \cdot \sqrt{b} = \sqrt{ab}$ ⟶
4 and 16 are perfect squares. ⟶
$\sqrt{4} = 2;\ \sqrt{16} = 4$ ⟶

$$-6\sqrt{2}(\sqrt{10} - 7\sqrt{8})$$
$$= (-6\sqrt{2})(\sqrt{10}) + (-6\sqrt{2})(-7\sqrt{8})$$
$$= -6\sqrt{20} + 42\sqrt{16}$$
$$= -6\sqrt{4 \cdot 5} + 42\sqrt{16}$$
$$= -6 \cdot 2\sqrt{5} + 42 \cdot 4$$
$$= -12\sqrt{5} + 168$$

EXAMPLE 5   Multiply $(2\sqrt{6} + \sqrt{5})(8\sqrt{6} - \sqrt{5})$.

Write vertically.
Multiply like two binomials.

$8\sqrt{6}(+\sqrt{5}) = +8 \cdot \sqrt{6} \cdot \sqrt{5} = +8\sqrt{30}$ ⟶
$-\sqrt{5}(2\sqrt{6}) = -2 \cdot \sqrt{5} \cdot \sqrt{6} = -2\sqrt{30}$ ⟶

$$2\sqrt{6} \qquad +\sqrt{5}$$
$$8\sqrt{6} \qquad -\sqrt{5}$$

$$2 \cdot 8 \cdot \underbrace{\sqrt{6} \cdot \sqrt{6}} \quad \begin{array}{c} +8\sqrt{30} \\ -2\sqrt{30} \end{array} \quad -\underbrace{\sqrt{5} \cdot \sqrt{5}}$$

$+8\sqrt{30} - 2\sqrt{30} = +6\sqrt{30}$ ⟶

$$16 \cdot 6 \qquad +6\sqrt{30} \qquad - \quad 5$$
$$96 \qquad\qquad +6\sqrt{30} \qquad - \quad 5$$

$96 - 5 = 91$ ⟶

$$91 + 6\sqrt{30}$$

EXAMPLE 6   Multiply $(7\sqrt{2} - 3\sqrt{10})(7\sqrt{2} + 3\sqrt{10})$.

$$7\sqrt{2} \qquad -3\sqrt{10}$$
$$7\sqrt{2} \qquad +3\sqrt{10}$$

$7\sqrt{2}(-3\sqrt{10}) = 7(-3)\sqrt{2} \cdot \sqrt{10} = -21\sqrt{20}$
$+3\sqrt{10}(7\sqrt{2}) = +3 \cdot 7 \cdot \sqrt{10} \cdot \sqrt{2} = +21\sqrt{20}$

$$7 \cdot 7 \cdot \underbrace{\sqrt{2} \cdot \sqrt{2}} \quad \begin{array}{c} -21\sqrt{20} \\ +21\sqrt{20} \end{array} \quad -3 \cdot 3 \cdot \underbrace{\sqrt{10} \cdot \sqrt{10}}$$

$-21\sqrt{20} + 21\sqrt{20} = 0$ ⟶

$$49 \cdot 2 \qquad + \quad 0 \qquad - \quad 9 \cdot 10$$
$$98 \qquad\qquad\qquad\qquad - \quad 90$$
$$8$$

EXAMPLE 7   Multiply $(2\sqrt{3} + \sqrt{6})^2$.

$(a + b)^2$ means $(a + b)(a + b)$.

$$2\sqrt{3} \qquad +\sqrt{6}$$
$$2\sqrt{3} \qquad +\sqrt{6}$$

$$2 \cdot 2 \cdot \underbrace{\sqrt{3} \cdot \sqrt{3}} \quad \begin{array}{c} +2\sqrt{18} \\ +2\sqrt{18} \end{array} \quad +\underbrace{\sqrt{6} \cdot \sqrt{6}}$$

$2\sqrt{18} + 2\sqrt{18} = 4\sqrt{18}$
$\sqrt{18} = \sqrt{9 \cdot 2} = 3\sqrt{2}$ ⟶
$4 \cdot 3\sqrt{2} = 12\sqrt{2}; \ 12 + 6 = 18$ ⟶

$$4 \cdot 3 \qquad +4\sqrt{18} \qquad + \quad 6$$
$$12 \qquad\qquad +4 \cdot 3\sqrt{2} \qquad + \quad 6$$
$$18 \qquad\qquad +12\sqrt{2}$$

ORAL EXERCISES

Multiply.

1. $\sqrt{7} \cdot \sqrt{7}$ **2.** $(\sqrt{8})^2$ **3.** $(-\sqrt{5})^2$

4. $2\sqrt{3} \cdot 2\sqrt{3}$ **5.** $(4\sqrt{6})^2$ **6.** $(-5\sqrt{2})^2$

7. $7\sqrt{5} \cdot 4\sqrt{5}$ **8.** $-8\sqrt{2} \cdot 3\sqrt{2}$ **9.** $-6\sqrt{3} \cdot 6\sqrt{3}$

10. $2 \cdot 4\sqrt{7}$ **11.** $5 \cdot (-6\sqrt{2})$ **12.** $4\sqrt{10} \cdot 6\sqrt{3}$

EXERCISES

PART A

Multiply.

1. $5\sqrt{6} \cdot 4\sqrt{2}$
2. $3\sqrt{7} \cdot 2\sqrt{5}$
3. $4\sqrt{10} \cdot 6\sqrt{3}$
4. $2\sqrt{7} \cdot 3\sqrt{14}$
5. $5\sqrt{5} \cdot 3\sqrt{10}$
6. $-8\sqrt{2} \cdot 4\sqrt{6}$
7. $4\sqrt{3} \cdot 9\sqrt{15}$
8. $-6\sqrt{11} \cdot 4\sqrt{22}$
9. $3\sqrt{8} \cdot (-2\sqrt{2})$

Multiply.

10. $2\sqrt{x} \cdot \sqrt{x}$
11. $5\sqrt{c} \cdot 3\sqrt{c}$
12. $(-\sqrt{y})^2$
13. $(6\sqrt{x})^2$
14. $(-2\sqrt{y})^2$
15. $\sqrt{4d} \cdot \sqrt{2d}$
16. $3\sqrt{2x} \cdot \sqrt{2x}$
17. $-4\sqrt{3y} \cdot 6\sqrt{3y}$
18. $8\sqrt{2x} \cdot 5\sqrt{6x}$
19. $2x\sqrt{5x} \cdot (-x\sqrt{10x})$
20. $4\sqrt{5a} \cdot 3\sqrt{15a}$
21. $7\sqrt{5z} \cdot (-2\sqrt{3z})$

Multiply.

22. $\sqrt{2}(5 + \sqrt{3})$
23. $7(\sqrt{5} + 9)$
24. $6(8 - 3\sqrt{3})$
25. $\sqrt{5}(4 + 2\sqrt{3})$
26. $-9(\sqrt{7} + 2\sqrt{3})$
27. $6(\sqrt{2} - 8\sqrt{5})$
28. $\sqrt{2}(\sqrt{5} + 3)$
29. $\sqrt{3}(4 + \sqrt{27})$
30. $\sqrt{8}(2\sqrt{2} - 5)$
31. $\sqrt{6}(\sqrt{12} - \sqrt{3})$
32. $\sqrt{2}(\sqrt{18} - 3\sqrt{2})$
33. $\sqrt{7}(2\sqrt{7} - \sqrt{14})$
34. $3\sqrt{3}(\sqrt{2} + 5\sqrt{6})$
35. $4\sqrt{2}(\sqrt{5} - 2\sqrt{2})$
36. $-5\sqrt{6}(2\sqrt{2} + 4\sqrt{3})$
37. $2\sqrt{5}(2\sqrt{2} + 8\sqrt{10})$
38. $(2\sqrt{5} + \sqrt{2})(3\sqrt{5} - \sqrt{2})$
39. $(3\sqrt{7} + \sqrt{3})(2\sqrt{7} + 5\sqrt{3})$
40. $(4\sqrt{6} + 2\sqrt{7})(\sqrt{6} - 3\sqrt{7})$
41. $(5\sqrt{2} + 6\sqrt{5})(\sqrt{2} - \sqrt{5})$
42. $(\sqrt{3} + \sqrt{2})^2$
43. $(2\sqrt{5} - \sqrt{6})(2\sqrt{5} - \sqrt{6})$
44. $(2\sqrt{3} - \sqrt{10})(2\sqrt{3} + \sqrt{10})$
45. $(4\sqrt{3} - \sqrt{7})^2$
46. $(\sqrt{8} - 3\sqrt{6})(\sqrt{8} + 3\sqrt{6})$
47. $(2\sqrt{3} + 7\sqrt{10})(2\sqrt{3} - 7\sqrt{10})$
48. $(6\sqrt{5} + \sqrt{8})^2$
49. $(5\sqrt{6} - 2\sqrt{3})^2$
50. $(2\sqrt{12} - \sqrt{5})(2\sqrt{12} + \sqrt{5})$
51. $(6\sqrt{5} + \sqrt{7})(6\sqrt{5} - \sqrt{7})$
52. $(7\sqrt{2} + 3\sqrt{6})^2$
53. $(8\sqrt{2} + 4\sqrt{3})^2$
54. $(9\sqrt{5} + 2\sqrt{3})(9\sqrt{5} - 2\sqrt{3})$
55. $(4\sqrt{6} - 8\sqrt{3})^2$
56. $(2\sqrt{8} + 8\sqrt{2})(2\sqrt{8} - 8\sqrt{2})$
57. $(3\sqrt{6} + 6\sqrt{3})^2$
58. $(4\sqrt{5} - 5\sqrt{4})^2$
59. $(7\sqrt{5} + 8\sqrt{2})(3\sqrt{5} - 4\sqrt{2})$

PART B

Multiply.

60. $\sqrt{x}(3 + \sqrt{x})$
61. $y(3\sqrt{y} + 2\sqrt{x})$
62. $2\sqrt{x}(2\sqrt{x} - 3)$
63. $(\sqrt{a} - 1)(\sqrt{a} + 1)$
64. $(\sqrt{2} + \sqrt{x})^2$
65. $(2\sqrt{x} - 3)^2$
66. $(\sqrt{y} - 2)(\sqrt{y} + 2)$
67. $(4\sqrt{x} + 6)(\sqrt{x} - 2)$
68. $(3\sqrt{y} - 3)(2\sqrt{y} + 1)$

Points for Irrational Numbers

Find a point corresponding to $\sqrt{2}$ on a number line.

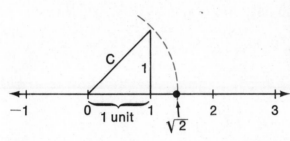

Construct a right triangle with each leg 1 unit in length. Use the Pythagorean Theorem to find the length of the hypotenuse.

$$C^2 = 1^2 + 1^2$$
$$C^2 = 1 + 1$$
$$C^2 = 2$$
So, $C = \sqrt{2}$

Thus, the hypotenuse is $\sqrt{2}$ units long. Mark off a segment the length of the hypotenuse on the number line. The endpoint is $\sqrt{2}$.

Find a point corresponding to $\sqrt{3}$ on a number line.

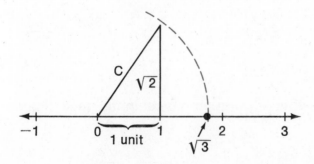

Construct a right triangle with legs 1 and $\sqrt{2}$ units long. Again, use the Pythagorean Theorem.

$$C^2 = 1^2 + (\sqrt{2})^2$$
$$C^2 = 1 + 2$$
$$C^2 = 3$$
So, $C = \sqrt{3}$

Thus, the hypotenuse is $\sqrt{3}$ units long. Mark off the length of the hypotenuse on the number line. The endpoint is $\sqrt{3}$.

1. Find a point corresponding to $\sqrt{5}$ on a number line.
   (Let one leg equal 1 unit and the other equal 2 units)
2. Find a point corresponding to $\sqrt{6}$ on a number line.

Rationalizing Denominators

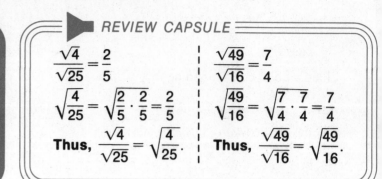

▶ REVIEW CAPSULE

$$\frac{\sqrt{4}}{\sqrt{25}} = \frac{2}{5} \qquad\qquad \frac{\sqrt{49}}{\sqrt{16}} = \frac{7}{4}$$

$$\sqrt{\frac{4}{25}} = \sqrt{\frac{2}{5} \cdot \frac{2}{5}} = \frac{2}{5} \qquad \sqrt{\frac{49}{16}} = \sqrt{\frac{7}{4} \cdot \frac{7}{4}} = \frac{7}{4}$$

Thus, $\dfrac{\sqrt{4}}{\sqrt{25}} = \sqrt{\dfrac{4}{25}}.$ **Thus,** $\dfrac{\sqrt{49}}{\sqrt{16}} = \sqrt{\dfrac{49}{16}}.$

The examples in the Review suggest this rule.

$$\frac{\sqrt{a}}{\sqrt{b}} = \sqrt{\frac{a}{b}}, \text{ for all positive numbers } a \text{ and } b.$$

EXAMPLE 1 Simplify $\dfrac{\sqrt{15}}{\sqrt{3}}.$ Simplify $\dfrac{\sqrt{32x^3}}{\sqrt{8x}}.$

$\dfrac{\sqrt{a}}{\sqrt{b}} = \sqrt{\dfrac{a}{b}}$ ──────

$$\frac{\sqrt{15}}{\sqrt{3}} = \sqrt{\frac{15}{3}} \qquad\qquad \frac{\sqrt{32x^3}}{\sqrt{8x}} = \sqrt{\frac{32x^3}{8x}}$$
$$= \sqrt{5} \qquad\qquad\qquad\qquad = \sqrt{4x^2}$$
$$= 2x$$

EXAMPLE 2 Rewrite $\dfrac{5}{\sqrt{7}}$ with no radical in the denominator.

$\dfrac{\sqrt{7}}{\sqrt{7}} = 1;$ multiply by $\dfrac{\sqrt{7}}{\sqrt{7}}.$ ──────→

$$\frac{5}{\sqrt{7}} = \frac{5}{\sqrt{7}} \cdot \frac{\sqrt{7}}{\sqrt{7}}$$
$$= \frac{5\sqrt{7}}{7}$$

There is no radical in the denominator. ──────→

Definition of rationalize ──────→

To *rationalize* the denominator of a fraction means to rewrite the fraction with no radical in the denominator.

EXAMPLE 3 Rationalize the denominator of $\dfrac{\sqrt{3}}{5\sqrt{6}}$. Then approximate to the nearest tenth.

Multiply by $\dfrac{\sqrt{6}}{\sqrt{6}}$.

$$\frac{\sqrt{3}}{5\sqrt{6}} = \frac{\sqrt{3}}{5\sqrt{6}} \cdot \frac{\sqrt{6}}{\sqrt{6}} = \frac{\sqrt{3}\cdot\sqrt{6}}{5\sqrt{6}\cdot\sqrt{6}} = \frac{\sqrt{3\cdot3\cdot2}}{5\cdot6}$$

$$= \frac{\overset{1}{3}\sqrt{2}}{\underset{10}{30}} = \frac{\sqrt{2}}{10}$$

From the table, $\sqrt{2} \doteq 1.414$. ⟶ $\dfrac{\sqrt{2}}{10} \doteq \dfrac{1.414}{10}$, or .1

Thus, $\dfrac{\sqrt{3}}{5\sqrt{6}} = .1$, to the nearest tenth.

EXAMPLE 4 Rationalize the denominator of $\dfrac{3ab}{\sqrt{a^2b}}$.

Multiply by $\dfrac{\sqrt{b}}{\sqrt{b}}$. Then a^2b^2 is a perfect square.

$$\frac{3ab}{\sqrt{a^2b}} = \frac{3ab}{\sqrt{a^2b}} \cdot \frac{\sqrt{b}}{\sqrt{b}} = \frac{3ab\sqrt{b}}{\sqrt{a^2b^2}} = \frac{3\overset{1}{a}\overset{1}{b}\sqrt{b}}{\underset{1\,1}{ab}} = 3\sqrt{b}$$

EXAMPLE 5 Rationalize the denominator of $\dfrac{8y^2}{\sqrt{12y}}$.

Multiply by $\dfrac{\sqrt{3y}}{\sqrt{3y}}$. Then 36 and y^2 are perfect squares.

$$\frac{8y^2}{\sqrt{12y}} = \frac{8y^2}{\sqrt{12y}} \cdot \frac{\sqrt{3y}}{\sqrt{3y}} = \frac{8y^2\sqrt{3y}}{\sqrt{36y^2}} = \frac{\overset{4y}{8y^2}\sqrt{3y}}{\underset{3\,1}{6y}} = \frac{4y\sqrt{3y}}{3}$$

ORAL EXERCISES

Simplify.

1. $\dfrac{\sqrt{18}}{\sqrt{2}}$ 2. $\dfrac{\sqrt{48}}{\sqrt{3}}$ 3. $\dfrac{\sqrt{20}}{\sqrt{5}}$ 4. $\dfrac{\sqrt{75}}{\sqrt{3}}$ 5. $\dfrac{\sqrt{250}}{\sqrt{25}}$

6. $\dfrac{\sqrt{75x^3}}{\sqrt{3x}}$ 7. $\dfrac{\sqrt{45x^2y}}{\sqrt{5y}}$ 8. $\dfrac{\sqrt{72a^3b}}{\sqrt{2ab}}$ 9. $\dfrac{\sqrt{12a^4b^3}}{\sqrt{3a^2b}}$ 10. $\dfrac{\sqrt{192x^4y}}{\sqrt{3x^2y}}$

EXERCISES

PART A

Rationalize the denominator. Then approximate to the nearest tenth.

1. $\dfrac{1}{\sqrt{2}}$ 2. $\dfrac{5}{\sqrt{3}}$ 3. $\dfrac{\sqrt{2}}{4}$ 4. $\dfrac{5}{\sqrt{5}}$ 5. $\dfrac{28}{\sqrt{7}}$

6. $\dfrac{\sqrt{2}}{\sqrt{3}}$ 7. $\dfrac{\sqrt{3}}{2\sqrt{2}}$ 8. $\dfrac{\sqrt{6}}{3\sqrt{7}}$ 9. $\dfrac{5\sqrt{7}}{2\sqrt{2}}$ 10. $\dfrac{7\sqrt{3}}{3\sqrt{7}}$

Rationalize the denominator.

11. $\dfrac{5xy}{\sqrt{x}}$ 12. $\dfrac{12ab}{\sqrt{a^2b}}$ 13. $\dfrac{3x}{\sqrt{x^2y}}$ 14. $\dfrac{5c^3d}{\sqrt{cd}}$ 15. $\dfrac{12x^3y^3}{\sqrt{xy}}$

16. $\dfrac{6x^2y}{\sqrt{xy^2}}$ 17. $\dfrac{8y}{\sqrt{2y}}$ 18. $\dfrac{3x^2}{\sqrt{3x}}$ 19. $\dfrac{4xy}{\sqrt{6x}}$ 20. $\dfrac{27x^3y^2}{\sqrt{3x^2y}}$

$\dfrac{3x^{?}\sqrt{3y}}{3x}$

$6x \dfrac{2}{3} y \sqrt{6x}$

PART B

EXAMPLE Rationalize the denominator of $\dfrac{\sqrt{6}+4}{\sqrt{2}}$.

Multiply by $\dfrac{\sqrt{2}}{\sqrt{2}}$. ⟶ $\dfrac{\sqrt{6}+4}{\sqrt{2}} \cdot \dfrac{\sqrt{2}}{\sqrt{2}} = \dfrac{(\sqrt{6}+4)\sqrt{2}}{\sqrt{2}\cdot 2}$

Distribute the $\sqrt{2}$. ⟶

$\sqrt{2}\cdot 2 = 2$ ⟶ $= \dfrac{\sqrt{6}\cdot\sqrt{2}+4\sqrt{2}}{2}$

$= \dfrac{\sqrt{12}+4\sqrt{2}}{2}$

Factor the numerator. Then divide out $\Big\}$ the common factor, 2.

$= \dfrac{2\sqrt{3}+4\sqrt{2}}{2}$

$= \dfrac{\overset{1}{\cancel{2}}(\sqrt{3}+2\sqrt{2})}{\underset{1}{\cancel{2}}} = \sqrt{3}+2\sqrt{2}$

Rationalize the denominator.

21. $\dfrac{\sqrt{6}+5}{\sqrt{3}}$ 22. $\dfrac{7-\sqrt{5}}{\sqrt{2}}$ 23. $\dfrac{-8+\sqrt{3}}{\sqrt{5}}$ 24. $\dfrac{-4-\sqrt{2}}{\sqrt{6}}$

25. $\dfrac{8+\sqrt{6}}{\sqrt{8}}$ 26. $\dfrac{\sqrt{2}+\sqrt{8}}{\sqrt{2}}$ 27. $\dfrac{\sqrt{3}+\sqrt{6}}{\sqrt{2}}$ 28. $\dfrac{\sqrt{5}-\sqrt{10}}{\sqrt{2}}$

29. $\dfrac{\sqrt{a^3}+6\sqrt{a}}{\sqrt{a}}$ 30. $\dfrac{\sqrt{y^3}-4\sqrt{y}}{\sqrt{y}}$ 31. $\dfrac{2\sqrt{x^3}+\sqrt{x}}{\sqrt{x}}$ 32. $\dfrac{\sqrt{z}-3\sqrt{z^3}}{\sqrt{z}}$

PART C

EXAMPLE Rationalize the denominator of $\dfrac{6}{3+\sqrt{5}}$.

$\dfrac{6}{3+\sqrt{5}} \cdot \dfrac{3-\sqrt{5}}{3-\sqrt{5}} = \dfrac{6(3-\sqrt{5})}{(3+\sqrt{5})(3-\sqrt{5})}$

$= \dfrac{\overset{3}{\cancel{6}}(3-\sqrt{5})}{\underset{2}{\cancel{4}}}$, or $\dfrac{3(3-\sqrt{5})}{2}$

Rationalize the denominator.

33. $\dfrac{5}{4+\sqrt{7}}$ 34. $\dfrac{1}{3-\sqrt{2}}$ 35. $\dfrac{-3}{\sqrt{7}-2}$ 36. $\dfrac{5}{2\sqrt{5}+1}$ 37. $\dfrac{-4}{1-\sqrt{5}}$

Fractional Radicands

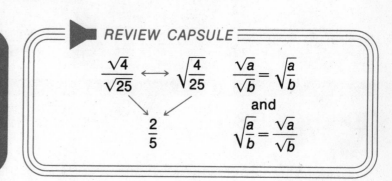

REVIEW CAPSULE

$$\frac{\sqrt{4}}{\sqrt{25}} \longleftrightarrow \sqrt{\frac{4}{25}} \qquad \frac{\sqrt{a}}{\sqrt{b}} = \sqrt{\frac{a}{b}}$$

$$\frac{2}{5}$$

and

$$\sqrt{\frac{a}{b}} = \frac{\sqrt{a}}{\sqrt{b}}$$

$\sqrt{10}$ ← radical
10 ← radicand

To simplify $\sqrt{\dfrac{3}{4}}$, rewrite it so that the radicand is not a fraction.

EXAMPLE 1 Simplify $\sqrt{\dfrac{3}{4}}$.

The radicand is 3; 3 is not a fraction. ⟶
$$\frac{\sqrt{3}}{\sqrt{4}} = \frac{\sqrt{3}}{2}$$

EXAMPLE 2 Simplify $\sqrt{\dfrac{24}{25}}$.

$\sqrt{24} = \sqrt{4 \cdot 6} = 2\sqrt{6}$ ⟶
$$\frac{\sqrt{24}}{\sqrt{25}} = \frac{2\sqrt{6}}{5}$$

EXAMPLE 3 Simplify $\sqrt{\dfrac{5}{8}}$.

Multiply by $\dfrac{\sqrt{2}}{\sqrt{2}}$, since $8 \cdot 2 = 16$, and 16 is a perfect square.

$$\frac{\sqrt{5}}{\sqrt{8}} = \frac{\sqrt{5}}{\sqrt{8}} \cdot \frac{\sqrt{2}}{\sqrt{2}}$$
$$= \frac{\sqrt{10}}{\sqrt{16}} = \frac{\sqrt{10}}{4}$$

EXAMPLE 4 Simplify $\sqrt{\dfrac{3}{2y^3}}$.

Rationalize the denominator of $\dfrac{\sqrt{3}}{\sqrt{2y^3}}$. ⟶

$$\frac{\sqrt{3}}{\sqrt{2y^3}} = \frac{\sqrt{3}}{\sqrt{2y^3}} \cdot \frac{\sqrt{2y}}{\sqrt{2y}}$$
$$= \frac{\sqrt{6y}}{\sqrt{4y^4}} = \frac{\sqrt{6y}}{2y^2}$$

EXAMPLE 5 Simplify $\sqrt{\dfrac{14x}{24x^2}}$.

$$\dfrac{14x}{24x^2} = \dfrac{\overset{1}{\cancel{2}} \cdot 7 \cdot \overset{1}{\cancel{x}}}{\underset{1}{\cancel{2}} \cdot 12 \cdot \underset{1}{\cancel{x}} \cdot x} = \dfrac{7}{12x} \longrightarrow \sqrt{\dfrac{7}{12x}} = \dfrac{\sqrt{7}}{\sqrt{12x}} = \dfrac{\sqrt{7}}{\sqrt{12x}} \cdot \dfrac{\sqrt{3x}}{\sqrt{3x}} = \dfrac{\sqrt{21x}}{\sqrt{36x^2}} = \dfrac{\sqrt{21x}}{6x}$$

EXERCISES

PART A

Simplify.

1. $\sqrt{\dfrac{9}{16}}$ 2. $\sqrt{\dfrac{25}{49}}$ 3. $\sqrt{\dfrac{100}{81}}$ 4. $\sqrt{\dfrac{64}{36}}$ 5. $\sqrt{\dfrac{121}{25}}$

6. $\sqrt{\dfrac{7}{4}}$ 7. $\sqrt{\dfrac{54}{25}}$ 8. $\sqrt{\dfrac{31}{49}}$ 9. $\sqrt{\dfrac{67}{81}}$ 10. $\sqrt{\dfrac{27}{16}}$

11. $\sqrt{\dfrac{63}{45}}$ 12. $\sqrt{\dfrac{44}{52}}$ 13. $\sqrt{\dfrac{12}{32}}$ 14. $\sqrt{\dfrac{5}{75}}$ 15. $\sqrt{\dfrac{21}{28}}$

16. $\sqrt{\dfrac{3}{8}}$ 17. $\sqrt{\dfrac{4}{27}}$ 18. $\sqrt{\dfrac{5}{12}}$ 19. $\sqrt{\dfrac{7}{20}}$ 20. $\sqrt{\dfrac{11}{40}}$

21. $\sqrt{\dfrac{5}{y}}$ 22. $\sqrt{\dfrac{16}{x^3}}$ 23. $\sqrt{\dfrac{7}{3z^2}}$ 24. $\sqrt{\dfrac{6}{5y^3}}$ 25. $\sqrt{\dfrac{27}{xy^3}}$

26. $\sqrt{\dfrac{54x}{y^5}}$ 27. $\sqrt{\dfrac{60}{x^2y^3}}$ 28. $\sqrt{\dfrac{x}{2x^4}}$ 29. $\sqrt{\dfrac{12z^2}{3yz}}$ 30. $\sqrt{\dfrac{5xz}{15x^3z^2}}$

31. $\sqrt{\dfrac{3y}{18y^4}}$ 32. $\sqrt{\dfrac{22y}{14y^3}}$ 33. $\sqrt{\dfrac{24a^2b^3}{6ab}}$ 34. $\sqrt{\dfrac{56y^4z}{4yz^2}}$ 35. $\sqrt{\dfrac{64a^2b^2}{20ab^3}}$

PART B

EXAMPLE Simplify $\sqrt{\dfrac{3y+2}{y}}$.

$$\dfrac{\sqrt{3y+2}}{\sqrt{y}} = \dfrac{\sqrt{3y+2}}{\sqrt{y}} \cdot \dfrac{\sqrt{y}}{\sqrt{y}} = \dfrac{\sqrt{(3y+2)y}}{\sqrt{y^2}} = \dfrac{\sqrt{3y^2+2y}}{y}$$

Simplify.

36. $\sqrt{\dfrac{2x+3}{2}}$ 37. $\sqrt{\dfrac{5z-3}{3}}$ 38. $\sqrt{\dfrac{4x+7}{7}}$ 39. $\sqrt{\dfrac{5x+5}{2}}$

40. $\sqrt{\dfrac{3-5z}{5}}$ 41. $\sqrt{\dfrac{4x^2-7}{2}}$ 42. $\sqrt{\dfrac{2z^2+3}{3}}$ 43. $\sqrt{\dfrac{6y^2-y}{2}}$

44. $\sqrt{\dfrac{2x+3}{3x}}$ 45. $\sqrt{\dfrac{1-5x}{5x}}$ 46. $\sqrt{\dfrac{7-8y}{y}}$ 47. $\sqrt{\dfrac{4x^2+1}{2x}}$

Venn Diagram of
the Real Number System

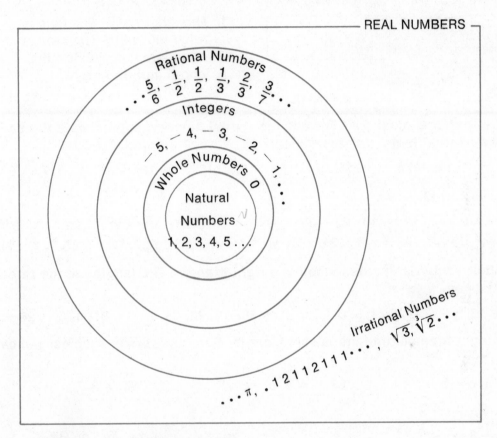

REAL NUMBERS

Rational Numbers

$\dots \frac{5}{6}, -\frac{1}{2}, \frac{1}{2}, \frac{1}{3}, \frac{2}{3}, \frac{3}{7} \dots$

Integers

$-5, -4, -3, -2, -1, \dots$

Whole Numbers 0

Natural Numbers

$1, 2, 3, 4, 5 \dots$

Irrational Numbers

$\sqrt{3}, \sqrt[3]{2} \dots$

$\dots \pi, .121121111 \dots$,

Make a Venn diagram similar to the one above. Place each of the following numbers in the appropriate place in your diagram.

$$\sqrt{144} \qquad\qquad -.9\overline{87} \qquad\qquad \frac{\sqrt{3}}{2}$$

$$-\left(\frac{7}{2}\right)^2 \qquad\qquad \sqrt{2}+3 \qquad\qquad .41$$

Do you know any numbers which do not fit into the diagram?

Chapter Fourteen Review

Which are rational and which are irrational numbers? $[p.\ 382]$

1. $.131131113\ldots$ **2.** $.13\overline{13}$ **3.** $.468$ **4.** $2\frac{7}{8}$
5. π **6.** $-\sqrt{81}$ **7.** $\sqrt{21}$ **8.** -3.6

Give answers to the nearest tenth. Use the table on page 478. $[p.\ 384]$

9.

s | A = 46 sq in. |
s

Find s.

10.

x | A = 159 sq m |
3x

Find x and 3x.

11. The length of a rectangle is twice the width. The area is 70 square inches. Find the length and the width.

Which are irrational numbers? For each irrational number, approximate the square root to the nearest tenth. Use the divide and average method. $[p.\ 388]$

12. $\sqrt{81}$ **13.** $\sqrt{74}$ **14.** $\sqrt{41}$ **15.** $\sqrt{16}$ **16.** $\sqrt{15}$ **17.** $\sqrt{62}$

Simplify. $[p.\ 391,\ 394,\ 396]$

18. $\sqrt{49}\cdot\sqrt{9}$ **19.** $\sqrt{16\cdot 81}$ **20.** $-\sqrt{48}$ **21.** $\sqrt{64a^4b^{10}}$ **22.** $-\sqrt{49x^8y^2z^{10}}$
23. $\sqrt{144c^2d^4e^{10}}$ **24.** $\sqrt{xy^3}$ **25.** $-2x^2y\sqrt{27x^7y^9}$ **26.** $\sqrt[3]{27x^6y^{11}}$ **27.** $-\sqrt[3]{-64x^4y^5z^6}$

Tell whether each triangle described is a right triangle. The lengths of the three sides are given. $[p.\ 399]$

28. $5, 12, 13$ **29.** $4, 5, 6$ **30.** $15, 20, 25$ **31.** $1, 5, \sqrt{26}$

For each right triangle, find the missing length. Give answers in simplest radical form. $[p.\ 399]$

32. $a = 15, b = 8$ **33.** $b = 6, c = 3\sqrt{5}$ **34.** $a = 7, c = 9$

Simplify. $[p.\ 402]$

35. $4\sqrt{5} - 8\sqrt{5} + 3\sqrt{5}$ **36.** $5x\sqrt{4y} + 7x\sqrt{y} - 3\sqrt{16x^2y}$

Multiply. $[p.\ 404]$

37. $5\sqrt{x}(3\sqrt{x} - 2)$ **38.** $(2\sqrt{2} - 3\sqrt{3})^2$ **39.** $(\sqrt{3} - \sqrt{5})(\sqrt{3} + \sqrt{5})$

Rationalize the denominator. $[p.\ 408]$

40. $\dfrac{1}{\sqrt{3}}$ **41.** $\dfrac{10x^2}{\sqrt{5x}}$ **42.** $\dfrac{24xy^4}{\sqrt{8xy^3}}$ **43.** $\dfrac{-3 + \sqrt{7}}{\sqrt{3}}$

Simplify. $[p.\ 411]$

44. $\dfrac{\sqrt{98}}{\sqrt{2}}$ **45.** $\dfrac{\sqrt{75x^3y}}{\sqrt{3xy}}$ **46.** $\sqrt{\dfrac{56a^2b^2}{4ab^3}}$ **47.** $\sqrt{\dfrac{4x + 2}{3}}$

Chapter Fourteen Test

Which are rational and which are irrational numbers?

1. 001

2. $\sqrt{64}$

3. $.123\overline{123}$

4. .123122312223. . .

5. -2.37

6. π

7. $-\sqrt{52}$

8. $-6\frac{5}{8}$

Give answers to the nearest tenth. Use the table on page 478.

9.

Find s.

10.

Find 3x and 4x.

11. The length of a rectangle is 3 times the width. The area is 216 square inches. Find the length and the width.

Which are irrational numbers? For each irrational number, approximate the square root to the nearest tenth. Use the divide and average method.

12. $\sqrt{10}$

13. $\sqrt{49}$

14. $\sqrt{52}$

15. $\sqrt{100}$

Simplify.

16. $\sqrt{5} \cdot \sqrt{13}$

17. $\sqrt{100 \cdot 16}$

18. $-\sqrt{80}$

19. $\sqrt{49a^4b^2}$

20. $-\sqrt{81x^6y^2z^{12}}$

21. $\sqrt{15cd^2}$

22. $-5x^2y\sqrt{54xy^3}$

23. $-\sqrt[3]{-27x^9y^{13}}$

Tell whether each triangle described is a right triangle. The lengths of the three sides are given.

24. 8, 6, 10

25. 7, 8, 9

26. 4, $4\sqrt{3}$, 8

For each right triangle, find the missing length. Give answers in simplest radical form.

27. $a = 2$, $b = 4$

28. $a = 12$, $c = 13$

29. $b = 6$, $c = 6\sqrt{2}$

Simplify.

30. $2\sqrt{3} - 9\sqrt{3} + 6\sqrt{3}$

31. $2x\sqrt{16y} + 5x\sqrt{y} - 7\sqrt{25x^2y}$

Multiply.

32. $(1 - \sqrt{2})^2$

33. $(\sqrt{5} + \sqrt{7})(\sqrt{5} - \sqrt{7})$

34. $3\sqrt{x}(2\sqrt{x} - 5)$

Rationalize the denominator.

35. $\dfrac{7}{\sqrt{3}}$

36. $\dfrac{15x^2}{\sqrt{5x}}$

37. $\dfrac{15cd^3}{\sqrt{3cd}}$

38. $\dfrac{2 + \sqrt{5}}{\sqrt{7}}$

Simplify.

39. $\dfrac{\sqrt{48}}{\sqrt{3}}$

40. $\dfrac{\sqrt{54xy^5}}{\sqrt{2xy^2}}$

41. $\sqrt{\dfrac{34xy^3}{4x^2y}}$

42. $\sqrt{\dfrac{3x - 5}{7}}$

EQUATIONS WITH REAL SOLUTIONS

Pythagorean Triples

A *Pythagorean triple* is a group of positive integers, *a*, *b* and *c*, which make the sentence $a^2 + b^2 = c^2$ true. For example, 3, 4, 5 is a Pythagorean triple because

$$3^2 + 4^2 = 5^2$$
$$9 + 16 = 25$$
$$25 = 25$$

Symbol of the Order of the Pythagoreans, a society of ancient Greek mathematicians.

Look at the list of triples below. Verify that each is a Pythagorean triple.

3	4	5
5	12	13
7	24	25
9	40	41
11	60	61
•	•	•
•	•	•
•	•	•

All of the triples above start with an odd number for *a*.

Can you see a pattern in the formation?
List the next three triples which fit the pattern.

Radical Equations

OBJECTIVES
- To solve radical equations like $x + 4 = \sqrt{2x + 8}$
- To solve word problems which result in radical equations

OBJECTIVES
- To solve radical equations like $x + 4 = \sqrt{2x + 8}$
- To solve word problems which result in radical equations

▶ *REVIEW CAPSULE*

	Equation	Solution set
Square each side of $x = 5$. →	$x = 5$	$\{5\}$
	$x^2 = 5^2$,	$\{5, -5\}$
	or $x^2 = 25$	
Square each side of $x = 7$. →	$x = 7$	$\{7\}$
	$x^2 = 7^2$,	$\{7, -7\}$
	or $x^2 = 49$	

The equations in the Review Capsule suggest this property. ⟶

The solution of the equation $x = a$ is a solution of the equation $x^2 = a^2$. But, a solution of $x^2 = a^2$ may not be a solution of $x = a$.

$\sqrt{x} = 6$ is a radical equation since the variable is in the radicand.

EXAMPLE 1   Find the solution set of $\sqrt{x} = 6$.

Square each side of $\sqrt{x} = 6$. ⟶
Always check the solutions for a radical equation.

$$\sqrt{x} = 6$$
$$(\sqrt{x})^2 = 6^2$$
$$x = 36$$

Check.	$\sqrt{x}$	6
	$\sqrt{36}$	6
	6	

Thus, the solution set is $\{36\}$.

EXAMPLE 2   Find the solution set of $\sqrt{2x - 5} + 8 = 7$.

Add -8 to each side. Now the radical is by itself. ⟶

Square each side. ⟶

Add 5 to each side. ⟶
Divide each side by 2. ⟶

$$\sqrt{2x - 5} + 8 = 7$$
$$\sqrt{2x - 5} = -1$$
$$(\sqrt{2x - 5})^2 = (-1)^2$$
$$2x - 5 = 1$$
$$2x = 6$$
$$x = 3$$

Check.		
$\sqrt{2x - 5} + 8$		7
$\sqrt{2(3) - 5} + 8$		7
$\sqrt{6 - 5} + 8$		
$\sqrt{1} + 8$		
$1 + 8$		
9		

3 doesn't check. $9 \neq 7$.
ϕ is the empty set. ⟶ **Thus,** the solution set is ϕ.

EXAMPLE 3   Solve $\sqrt{2y} = 4\sqrt{5}$.

Square each side. ⟶

$$\sqrt{2y} = 4\sqrt{5}$$
$$(\sqrt{2y})^2 = (4\sqrt{5})^2$$
$$2y = 80$$

Divide each side by 2. ⟶

$$y = 40$$

Check.	$\sqrt{2y}$	$4\sqrt{5}$
	$\sqrt{2 \cdot 40}$	$4\sqrt{5}$
	$\sqrt{80}$	
	$4\sqrt{5}$	

40 checks. ⟶ **Thus,** the solution is 40.

EXAMPLE 4   Solve $x - 2 = \sqrt{19 - 6x}$.

Square each side. ⟶
$(x - 2)^2 = (x - 2)(x - 2)$ ⟶
Add -19 and $6x$ to each side. ⟶
Factor. ⟶

$$x - 2 = \sqrt{19 - 6x}$$
$$(x - 2)^2 = (\sqrt{19 - 6x})^2$$
$$x^2 - 4x + 4 = 19 - 6x$$
$$x^2 + 2x - 15 = 0$$
$$(x - 3)(x + 5) = 0$$
$$x - 3 = 0 \text{ or } x + 5 = 0$$
$$x = 3 \text{ or } \qquad x = -5$$

Check 3.

$x - 2$	$\sqrt{19 - 6x}$
$3 - 2$	$\sqrt{19 - 6(3)}$
1	$\sqrt{19 - 18}$
	$\sqrt{1}$
	1

Check -5.

$x - 2$	$\sqrt{19 - 6x}$
$-5 - 2$	$\sqrt{19 - 6(-5)}$
-7	$\sqrt{19 + 30}$
	$\sqrt{49}$
	7
	$-7 \neq 7$

-5 doesn't check. ⟶ **Thus,** the solution is 3.

EXAMPLE 5   If 4 is added to 3 times a number, the square root is 5. Find the number.

Let x = the number.
Write an equation. ⟶
Square each side. ⟶

$$\sqrt{3x + 4} = 5$$
$$(\sqrt{3x + 4})^2 = 5^2$$
$$3x + 4 = 25$$
$$3x = 21$$
$$x = 7$$

Check 7 in the original problem; add 4 to 3 times 7. ⟶

$$3(7) + 4 = 21 + 4$$
$$= 25$$

7 checks. ⟶ Is $\sqrt{25} = 5$? Yes.

Thus, the number is 7.

EXERCISES

PART A

Find the solution set.

1. $\sqrt{y} = 3$ **2.** $\sqrt{x} = 8$ **3.** $\sqrt{5x} = 10$ **4.** $\sqrt{2y} = 24$

5. $\sqrt{4x} = \frac{1}{2}$ **6.** $\sqrt{3y} = \frac{1}{6}$ **7.** $\sqrt{18y} = 6$ **8.** $\sqrt{3x} = 3$

Solve.

9. $\sqrt{x} + 1 = 2$ **10.** $\sqrt{z} + 3 = 7$

11. $\sqrt{6x} + 5 = 2$ **12.** $\sqrt{2x} + 4 = 10$

13. $\sqrt{3x + 2} = 9$ **14.** $\sqrt{y + 2} = 4$

15. $\sqrt{2x - 1} = \sqrt{x + 3}$ **16.** $\sqrt{x - 3} = \sqrt{2x + 7}$

17. $\sqrt{x + 3} + 4 = 0$ **18.** $\sqrt{x - 5} - 8 = 0$

19. $\sqrt{y - 3} - 1 = 2$ **20.** $\sqrt{3x + 2} + 5 = 7$

21. $\sqrt{x} = 2\sqrt{3}$ **22.** $2\sqrt{x} = \sqrt{48}$

23. $3\sqrt{2x} = \sqrt{18}$ **24.** $5\sqrt{3y} = 3\sqrt{5}$

25. $\sqrt{3x + 10} = x + 4$ **26.** $\sqrt{x^2 - 9} = -4$

27. $\sqrt{x^2 + 11} = x + 1$ **28.** $\sqrt{2x - 20} = x - 1$

Solve each problem.

29. The square root of a number, decreased by 2 equals 3. Find the number.

30. Twice the square root of a number is equal to 20. Find the number.

31. A number is multiplied by 2 and 5 is added to the product. The square root of the result is equal to 3. Find the number.

32. A number is increased by 6. The square root of the sum is multiplied by 3, resulting in 12. Find the number.

PART B

EXAMPLE   Solve $\sqrt{x} + 2 = \sqrt{x + 20}$.

Square each side. $\longrightarrow$ $(\sqrt{x} + 2)^2 = (\sqrt{x + 20})^2$

$x + 4\sqrt{x} + 4 = x + 20$

Add $-x$ and -4 to each side. $\longrightarrow$ $4\sqrt{x} = 16$

Divide each side by 4. $\longrightarrow$ $\sqrt{x} = 4$

Square each side. $\longrightarrow$ $x = 16$

Check.	
$\sqrt{x} + 2$	$\sqrt{x + 20}$
$\sqrt{16} + 2$	$\sqrt{16 + 20}$
$4 + 2$	$\sqrt{36}$
6	6

Thus, the solution is 16.

Solve.

33. $\sqrt{x} - 5 = -\sqrt{x + 15}$ **34.** $\sqrt{x} + 3 = \sqrt{x - 9}$ **35.** $\sqrt{x} = \sqrt{x + 77} - 7$

(Hint: First add 7 to each side.)

The Solution Set of $x^2 = a$

▶ REVIEW CAPSULE

$$(\sqrt{25})^2 = \sqrt{25} \cdot \sqrt{25} = 5 \cdot 5 = 25$$
$$(-\sqrt{25})^2 = (-\sqrt{25})(-\sqrt{25}) = (-5)(-5)$$
$$= 25$$

$$(\sqrt{17})^2 = \sqrt{17} \cdot \sqrt{17} = 17$$
$$(-\sqrt{17})^2 = (-\sqrt{17})(-\sqrt{17}) = 17$$

$$\left.\begin{array}{l}(\sqrt{a})^2 = \sqrt{a} \cdot \sqrt{a} = a \\ (-\sqrt{a})^2 = (-\sqrt{a})(-\sqrt{a}) = a\end{array}\right\} \begin{array}{l}\text{for each} \\ a \geq 0.\end{array}$$

EXAMPLE 1 Find the solution set of $x^2 = 25$.

$$x^2 = 25$$

$$x = \sqrt{25} \quad \text{or} \quad x = -\sqrt{25}$$
$$x = 5 \quad \text{or} \quad x = -5$$

$(5)^2 = 25$ and $(-5)^2 = 25.$ ⟶ **Thus,** the solution set is $\{5, -5\}$.

EXAMPLE 2 Solve $x^2 = 17$.

$$x^2 = 17$$

$$x = \sqrt{17} \quad \text{or} \quad x = -\sqrt{17}$$

$(\sqrt{17})^2 = 17$ and $(-\sqrt{17})^2 = 17.$ ⟶ **Thus,** the solutions are $\sqrt{17}$ and $-\sqrt{17}$.

Examples 1 and 2 suggest this. ⟶ If $x^2 = a$, then $x = \sqrt{a}$ or $x = -\sqrt{a}$, for each $a \geq 0$.

EXAMPLE 3 Find the solution set of $y^2 = 12$.

$$y^2 = 12$$

If $x^2 = a$, then $x = \sqrt{a}$ or $x = -\sqrt{a}$. ⟶
$\sqrt{12} = \sqrt{4 \cdot 3} = 2\sqrt{3}$ ⟶

$$y = \sqrt{12} \quad \text{or} \quad y = -\sqrt{12}$$
$$y = 2\sqrt{3} \quad \text{or} \quad y = -2\sqrt{3}$$

Thus, the solution set is $\{2\sqrt{3}, -2\sqrt{3}\}$.

EXAMPLE 4   Solve $(y + 4)^2 = 49$.

$$(y + 4)^2 = 49$$

If $x^2 = a$, then $x = \sqrt{a}$ or $x = -\sqrt{a}$. $\longrightarrow$

Solve each equation.

Add -4 to each side. $\longrightarrow$

$y + 4 = \sqrt{49}$	or	$y = 4 = -\sqrt{49}$
$y + 4 = 7$		$y + 4 = -7$
$y = 3$	or	$y = -11$

Check 3 and -11 in $(y + 4)^2 = 49$. $\longrightarrow$ **Thus, the solutions are 3 and -11.**

EXAMPLE 5   Find the solution set of $(x - 3)^2 = 100$.

$$(x - 3)^2 = 100$$

$x - 3 = \sqrt{100}$	or	$x - 3 = -\sqrt{100}$

Solve each equation.

Add 3 to each side. $\longrightarrow$

$x - 3 = 10$		$x - 3 = -10$
$x = 13$	or	$x = -7$

Check 13 and -7 in $(x - 3)^2 = 100$. $\longrightarrow$ **Thus, the solution set is $\{13, -7\}$.**

EXAMPLE 6   Solve $3x^2 = 7$.

$$3x^2 = 7$$

Divide each side by 3. $\longrightarrow$

$$\frac{3x^2}{3} = \frac{7}{3}$$

$$x^2 = \frac{7}{3}$$

$x = \sqrt{\dfrac{7}{3}}$	or	$x = -\sqrt{\dfrac{7}{3}}$

$\sqrt{\dfrac{7}{3}} = \dfrac{\sqrt{7}}{\sqrt{3}} \cdot \dfrac{\sqrt{3}}{\sqrt{3}} = \dfrac{\sqrt{21}}{3}$ $\longrightarrow$

$x = \dfrac{\sqrt{21}}{3}$	or	$x = -\dfrac{\sqrt{21}}{3}$

Check $\dfrac{\sqrt{21}}{3}$ and $-\dfrac{\sqrt{21}}{3}$ in $3x^2 = 7$. $\longrightarrow$ **Thus, the solutions are $\dfrac{\sqrt{21}}{3}$ and $-\dfrac{\sqrt{21}}{3}$.**

EXERCISES

PART A

Find the solution set.

1. $x^2 = 1$
4. $x^2 = -16$
7. $x^2 = 9$
10. $x^2 = 100$
13. $x^2 = 400$

[Hint: What number squared equals -16?]

2. $x^2 = 36$
5. $x^2 = 49$
8. $x^2 = -36$
11. $x^2 = -100$
14. $x^2 = 900$

3. $x^2 = 4$
6. $x^2 = 0$
9. $x^2 = 64$
12. $x^2 = 144$
15. $x^2 = 121$

16. $x^2 = 169$
17. $x^2 = 225$
18. $x^2 = 196$
19. $x^2 - 9 = 0$ ←[Hint. Add 9
20. $x^2 - 25 = 0$
21. $x^2 - 81 = 0$
22. $x^2 + 9 = 0$ to each side.]
23. $x^2 - 36 = 0$
24. $x^2 + 144 = 0$
25. $(x - 2)^2 = 9$
26. $(x + 5)^2 = 16$
27. $(x - 8)^2 = 1$
28. $(x - 3)^2 = 4$
29. $(x + 7)^2 = -25$
30. $(x - 9)^2 = 0$
31. $(x + 4)^2 = 36$
32. $(x + 1)^2 = 100$
33. $(x - 3)^2 = 49$
34. $(x - 1)^2 = 81$
35. $(x + 2)^2 = 64$
36. $(x + 10)^2 = 25$
37. $(x - 8)^2 = 16$
38. $(x - 12)^2 = 144$
39. $(x + 5)^2 = 0$
40. $(x + 3)^2 + 8 = 24$ ↖
41. $(x - 4)^2 - 3 = 46$
42. $(x - 7)^2 - 5 =$
    [Hint: add -8 to each side.]
43. $(x + 8)^2 - 72 = -8$
44. $(x + 12)^2 + 4 = -20$
45. $(x - 6)^2 - 2 = 79$
46. $(x - 10)^2 - 8 = -4$
47. $(x + 1)^2 + 16 = 16$
48. $(x + 7)^2 - 8 = 8$
49. $2(x + 6)^2 = 32$
50. $5(x - 7)^2 = 80$
51. $-3(x + 5)^2 = -75$
    [Hint: Divide each side by 2.]

Solve. Simplify radicals, where possible.

52. $x^2 = 5$
53. $x^2 = 11$
54. $x^2 = 15$
55. $x^2 - 23 = 0$
56. $x^2 + 35 = 0$
57. $x^2 - 39 = 0$
58. $x^2 = 8$
59. $x^2 = 32$
60. $x^2 = -54$
61. $x^2 - 27 = 0$
62. $x^2 - 80 = 0$
63. $x^2 + 45 = 0$
64. $2x^2 = 12$
65. $3x^2 = 30$
66. $7x^2 = -14$
67. $3x^2 = 11$
68. $7x^2 = 23$
69. $5x^2 - 8 = 9$
70. $9x^2 = 8$
71. $16x^2 = -12$
72. $6x^2 - 4 = 14$
73. $10x^2 = -30$
74. $8x^2 = 3$
75. $12x^2 = 50$

PART B

EXAMPLE Find the solution set of $(x - 5)^2 = 3$.

$$(x - 5)^2 = 3$$
$$x - 5 = \sqrt{3} \quad \text{or} \quad x - 5 = -\sqrt{3}$$

Add 5 to each side. ⟶

$$\begin{array}{ll} \quad 5 \quad 5 & \quad 5 \quad 5 \\ \hline x \quad = 5 + \sqrt{3} & \text{or} \quad x \quad = 5 - \sqrt{3} \end{array}$$

$5 + \sqrt{3}$ and $5 - \sqrt{3}$ will check. ⟶ **Thus,** the solution set is $\{5 + \sqrt{3}, 5 - \sqrt{3}\}$.

Find the solution set. Simplify radicals, where possible.

76. $(x + 1)^2 = 5$
77. $(x - 3)^2 = 6$
78. $(x - 8)^2 = -8$
79. $(x + 3)^2 = 8$
80. $(x + 4)^2 = 32$
81. $(x - 9)^2 = 54$
82. $(x + 2)^2 = -18$
83. $(x - 1)^2 = 72$
84. $(x + 6)^2 = 28$
85. $(x - 8)^2 - 4 = 3$
86. $(x + 2)^2 - 8 = 3$
87. $(x + 12)^2 - 7 = -15$
88. $(x + 4)^2 - 6 = 6$
89. $(x - 9)^2 - 3 = 15$
90. $2(x + 6)^2 = 90$
91. $4(x + 7)^2 = 88$
92. $5(x - 3)^2 + 7 = -12$
93. $3(x - 8)^2 - 4 = 68$

Completing the Square

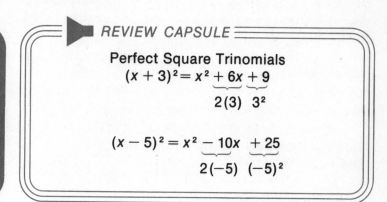

▶ REVIEW CAPSULE

Perfect Square Trinomials

$$(x + 3)^2 = x^2 + \underbrace{6x}_{2(3)} + \underbrace{9}_{3^2}$$

$$(x - 5)^2 = x^2 - \underbrace{10x}_{2(-5)} + \underbrace{25}_{(-5)^2}$$

The Review Capsule suggests this. ⟶ $(a + b)^2 = a^2 + \underbrace{2ba}_{2(b)} + \underbrace{b^2}_{b^2}$

twice b ⟶   ⟵ b squared

EXAMPLE 1   What number do we add to $x^2 + 14x$ to make a perfect square trinomial?

$$x^2 + \underbrace{14x}_{2(7)}$$

$14 = 2(7)$ ⟶

$7^2 = 49$ ⟶ Add 49: $x^2 + 14x + 49$

Check by squaring $(x + 7)$. ⟶ $(x + 7)^2 = x^2 + 14x + 49$, a perfect square trinomial.

EXAMPLE 2   What number do we add to $x^2 - 20x$ to make a perfect square trinomial?

$$x^2 - \underbrace{20x}_{2(-10)}$$

$-20 = 2(-10)$ ⟶

$(-10)^2 = 100$ ⟶ Add 100: $x^2 - 20x + 100$

$(x - 10)^2 = x^2 - 20x + 100$, a perfect square trinomial.

In Example 3, we show a method called *completing the square* for finding the solution set of a quadratic equation.

EXAMPLE 3   Find the solution set of $x^2 - 6x = 27$ by completing the square.

Adding 9 to $x^2 - 6x$ will make a perfect square trinomial.

$x^2 - 6x \quad -6 = 2(-3)$ and $(-3)^2 = 9$

Add 9 to each side. ──────────⟶

$$\begin{array}{rcl} x^2 - 6x & = & 27 \\ 9 & & 9 \\ \hline x^2 - 6x + 9 & = & 36 \\ (x - 3)^2 & = & 36 \end{array}$$

$(x - 3)^2 = x^2 - 6x + 9$ ──────⟶

$$x - 3 = \sqrt{36} \quad \text{or} \quad x - 3 = -\sqrt{36}$$

Solve each equation.
Add 3 to each side. ──────────⟶

$$\begin{array}{rcl} x - 3 & = & 6 \\ 3 & & 3 \\ \hline x & = & 9 \end{array} \quad \text{or} \quad \begin{array}{rcl} x - 3 & = & -6 \\ 3 & & 3 \\ \hline x & = & -3 \end{array}$$

Check 9 and -3 in $x^2 - 6x = 27$. ───⟶ **Thus,** the solution set is $\{9, -3\}$.

EXAMPLE 4   Find the solution set of $x^2 + 16x + 55 = 0$ by completing the square.

To get $x^2 + 16x$ by itself on the left, add -55 to each side. ──────────⟶

$16 = 2(8)$ and $8^2 = 64$; add 64 to each side. ──────────⟶

$$\begin{array}{rcl} x^2 + 16x + 55 & = & 0 \\ -55 & & -55 \\ \hline x^2 + 16x & = & -55 \\ 64 & & 64 \\ \hline x^2 + 16x + 64 & = & 9 \\ (x + 8)^2 & = & 9 \end{array}$$

$$x + 8 = \sqrt{9} \quad \text{or} \quad x + 8 = -\sqrt{9}$$

Add -8 to each side. ──────────⟶

$$\begin{array}{rcl} x + 8 & = & 3 \\ x & = & -5 \end{array} \quad \text{or} \quad \begin{array}{rcl} x + 8 & = & -3 \\ x & = & -11 \end{array}$$

Check -5 and -11 in
$x^2 + 16x + 55 = 0$. ──────────⟶ **Thus,** the solution set is $\{-5, -11\}$.

EXAMPLE 5   Find the solution set of $x^2 + 10x - 4 = 0$ by completing the square.

$$\begin{array}{rcl} x^2 + 10x - 4 & = & 0 \\ 4 & & 4 \end{array}$$

Add 4 to each side. ──────────⟶
Now $x^2 + 10x$ is by itself. ──────⟶

$$\begin{array}{rcl} \hline x^2 + 10x & = & 4 \\ 25 & & 25 \end{array}$$

Add 25 to each side. ──────────⟶
$x^2 + 10x + 25$ is a perfect square. ──⟶

$$\begin{array}{rcl} \hline x^2 + 10x + 25 & = & 29 \\ (x + 5)^2 & = & 29 \end{array}$$

$$x + 5 = \sqrt{29} \quad \text{or} \quad x + 5 = -\sqrt{29}$$

Add -5 to each side. ──────────⟶

$$x = -5 + \sqrt{29} \quad \text{or} \quad x = -5 - \sqrt{29}$$

Thus, the solution set is $\{-5 + \sqrt{29}, -5 - \sqrt{29}\}$.

ORAL EXERCISES

What number should be added to each expression to make a perfect square trinomial?

1. $x^2 + 2x$
2. $x^2 - 6x$
3. $x^2 + 10x$
4. $x^2 - 4x$
5. $x^2 + 16x$
6. $x^2 - 8x$
7. $x^2 - 12x$
8. $x^2 + 18x$

EXERCISES

PART A

Find the solution set by completing the square.

1. $x^2 + 10x = -16$
2. $x^2 + 2x = 3$
3. $x^2 + 16x = -15$
4. $x^2 + 2x = 8$
5. $x^2 - 8x = -5$
6. $x^2 - 6x = 27$
7. $x^2 + 10x + 15 = 0$
8. $x^2 + 12x - 13 = 0$
9. $x^2 - 4x - 21 = 0$
10. $x^2 + 8x + 3 = 0$
11. $x^2 - 4x + 4 = 0$
12. $x^2 + 6x - 7 = 0$
13. $x^2 + 4x - 77 = 0$
14. $x^2 + 6x - 3 = 0$
15. $x^2 - 16x + 28 = 0$
16. $x^2 - 2x - 48 = 0$
17. $x^2 - 18x + 72 = 0$
18. $x^2 + 16x + 60 = 0$
19. $x^2 - 10x - 39 = 0$
20. $x^2 + 4x - 3 = 0$
21. $x^2 + 20x + 51 = 0$
22. $x^2 + 2x - 5 = 0$
23. $x^2 - 16x + 60 = 0$
24. $x^2 + 18x + 77 = 0$
25. $x^2 - 20x - 21 = 0$
26. $x^2 - 24x + 80 = 0$
27. $x^2 + 30x + 155 = 0$

PART B

EXAMPLE Find the solution set of $x^2 + 3x - 40 = 0$ by completing the square.

$\left(\frac{1}{2}\right)(3) = \frac{3}{2}; \quad \left(\frac{3}{2}\right)^2 = \frac{9}{4}$

$x^2 + 3x - 40 = 0$

$x^2 + 3x = 40$

Add $\frac{9}{4}$ to each side. $\longrightarrow$ $x^2 + 3x + \frac{9}{4} = 40 + \frac{9}{4}$

$40\frac{9}{4} = \frac{169}{4}$ $\left(x + \frac{3}{2}\right)^2 = \frac{169}{4}$

$x + \frac{3}{2} = \sqrt{\frac{169}{4}}$ or $x + \frac{3}{2} = -\sqrt{\frac{169}{4}}$

$x + \frac{3}{2} = \frac{13}{2}$ $x + \frac{3}{2} = -\frac{13}{2}$

Add $-\frac{3}{2}$ to each side. $\longrightarrow$ $x = \frac{13}{2} - \frac{3}{2}$ $x = -\frac{13}{2} - \frac{3}{2}$

$x = \frac{10}{2}$ $x = -\frac{16}{2}$

Check 5 and -8 in $x = 5$ or $x = -8$

$x^2 + 3x - 40 = 0.$ $\longrightarrow$ **Thus,** the solution set is $\{5, -8\}$.

Find the solution set by completing the square.

28. $x^2 - 3x = 10$ 29. $x^2 + 9x = -8$ 30. $x^2 - 7x = -6$

31. $x^2 + 5x = 50$ 32. $x^2 - 3x = 4$ 33. $x^2 - x = 6$

34. $x^2 - 11x + 28 = 0$ 35. $x^2 + x - 30 = 0$ 36. $x^2 + 5x + 6 = 0$

37. $x^2 + x - 12 = 0$ 38. $x^2 - 9x - 10 = 0$ 39. $x^2 - 5x - 14 = 0$

40. $x^2 + 15x + 36 = 0$ 41. $x^2 - 17x + 30 = 0$ 42. $x^2 - 3x + 2 = 0$

43. $x^2 + x - 56 = 0$ 44. $x^2 - 7x - 8 = 0$ 45. $x^2 + 11 + 28 = 0$

46. $x^2 - 13x + 36 = 0$ 47. $x^2 - 19x + 84 = 0$ 48. $x^2 - 15x + 54 = 0$

49. $x^2 - 21x + 38 = 0$ 50. $x^2 + 17x + 72 = 0$ 51. $x^2 + 15x - 34 = 0$

52. $x^2 + 23x + 60 = 0$ 53. $x^2 - 25x + 100 = 0$ 54. $x^2 - 21x - 46 = 0$

PART C

EXAMPLE   Find the solution set of $x^2 + 7x - 2 = 0$ by completing the square.

$$x^2 + 7x - 2 = 0$$
$$x^2 + 7x = 2$$

$\left(\frac{1}{2}\right)(7) = \frac{7}{2}$; $\left(\frac{7}{2}\right)^2 = \frac{49}{4}$ ⟶

Add $\frac{49}{4}$ to each side.

$$x^2 + 7x + \frac{49}{4} = 2 + \frac{49}{4}$$

$$\left(x + \frac{7}{2}\right)^2 = \frac{57}{4}$$

$\sqrt{\frac{57}{4}} = \frac{\sqrt{57}}{\sqrt{4}} = \frac{\sqrt{57}}{2}$ ⟶

$$x + \frac{7}{2} = \sqrt{\frac{57}{4}} \qquad \text{or} \quad x + \frac{7}{2} = -\sqrt{\frac{57}{4}}$$

$$x + \frac{7}{2} = \frac{\sqrt{57}}{2} \qquad\qquad x + \frac{7}{2} = -\frac{\sqrt{57}}{2}$$

Add $-\frac{7}{2}$ to each side. ⟶

$$x = -\frac{7}{2} + \frac{\sqrt{57}}{2} \qquad\qquad x = -\frac{7}{2} - \frac{\sqrt{57}}{2}$$

$$x = \frac{-7 + \sqrt{57}}{2} \quad \text{or} \qquad x = \frac{-7 - \sqrt{57}}{2}$$

We may show the solution set as $\left\{\frac{-7 \pm \sqrt{57}}{2}\right\}$.

Thus, the solution set is $\left\{\dfrac{-7 + \sqrt{57}}{2}, \dfrac{-7 - \sqrt{57}}{2}\right\}$.

Find the solution set by completing the square.   [HINT: Divide each side by 2.]

55. $x^2 + 7x + 3 = 0$ 56. $x^2 + 11x + 20 = 0$ 57. $2x^2 + 4x + 1 = 0$

58. $3x^2 - 6x - 1 = 0$ 59. $2x^2 + 10x + 15 = 0$ 60. $4x^2 - 8x + 5 = 0$

61. $2x^2 + 6x - 3 = 0$ 62. $4x^2 + 4x - 3 = 0$ 63. $2x^2 - 2x - 1 = 0$

64. $x^2 - 3x - 5 = 0$ 65. $x^2 + 5x - 1 = 0$ 66. $x^2 - 7x - 2 = 0$

67. $x^2 - x - 3 = 0$ 68. $x^2 + 2x + 2 = 0$ 69. $x^2 + 7x + 4 = 0$

70. $x^2 + 3x - 1 = 0$ 71. $x^2 - x + 1 = 0$ 72. $2x^2 + 2x + 5 = 0$

The Quadratic Formula

 REVIEW CAPSULE

Determine a, b, and c in $x^2 - 5x + 2 = 0$.

Standard form: $\quad ax^2 \; + \; bx \; + c = 0$

$$(1)x^2 + (-5)x + 2 = 0$$

Thus, $a = 1$, $b = -5$, and $c = 2$.

EXAMPLE 1   Find the solution set of $2x^2 + 3x - 1 = 0$ by completing the square.

$$2x^2 + 3x - 1 = 0$$

Add 1 to each side. $\longrightarrow$ $\quad 2x^2 + 3x \quad = 1$

Divide each side by 2. $\longrightarrow$ $\quad \dfrac{2x^2 + 3x}{2} = \dfrac{1}{2}$

$\left(\dfrac{1}{2}\right)\left(\dfrac{3}{2}\right) = \dfrac{3}{4}$; $\left(\dfrac{3}{4}\right)^2 = \dfrac{9}{16}$; $\qquad x^2 + \dfrac{3}{2}x \quad = \dfrac{1}{2}$

Add $\dfrac{9}{16}$ to each side. $\longrightarrow$ $\quad x^2 + \dfrac{3}{2}x + \dfrac{9}{16} = \dfrac{1}{2} + \dfrac{9}{16}$

$$\left(x + \dfrac{3}{4}\right)^2 = \dfrac{17}{16}$$

Solve each equation. $\qquad x + \dfrac{3}{4} = \sqrt{\dfrac{17}{16}} \qquad$ or $\quad x + \dfrac{3}{4} = -\sqrt{\dfrac{17}{16}}$

$\sqrt{\dfrac{17}{16}} = \dfrac{\sqrt{17}}{\sqrt{16}} = \dfrac{\sqrt{17}}{4}$ $\longrightarrow$ $\quad x + \dfrac{3}{4} = \dfrac{\sqrt{17}}{4} \qquad\qquad x + \dfrac{3}{4} = -\dfrac{\sqrt{17}}{4}$

Add $-\dfrac{3}{4}$ to each side. $\longrightarrow$ $\quad x = -\dfrac{3}{4} + \dfrac{\sqrt{17}}{4} \qquad\quad x = -\dfrac{3}{4} - \dfrac{\sqrt{17}}{4}$

4 is the common denominator. $\quad x = \dfrac{-3 + \sqrt{17}}{4} \quad$ or $\qquad x = \dfrac{-3 - \sqrt{17}}{4}$

We may write the solution set as

$\left\{\dfrac{-3 \pm \sqrt{17}}{4}\right\}$. $\longrightarrow$ **Thus,** the solution set is $\left\{\dfrac{-3 + \sqrt{17}}{4}, \dfrac{-3 - \sqrt{17}}{4}\right\}$.

We now use this process to derive a formula for solving a quadratic equation.

EXAMPLE 2

Solve $ax^2 + bx + c = 0$, $(a > 0)$ by completing the square.

$$ax^2 + bx + c = 0$$

Add $-c$ to each side. ───────→
$$ax^2 + bx = -c$$

Divide each side by a. ───────→
$$\frac{ax^2 + bx}{a} = \frac{-c}{a}$$

$\left(\frac{1}{2}\right)\left(\frac{b}{a}\right) = \frac{b}{2a}$; $\left(\frac{b}{2a}\right)^2 = \frac{b^2}{4a^2}$;
$$x^2 + \frac{b}{a}x = \frac{-c}{a}$$

Add $\frac{b^2}{4a^2}$ to each side. ───────→
$$x^2 + \frac{b}{a}x + \frac{b^2}{4a^2} = \frac{-c}{a} + \frac{b^2}{4a^2}$$

$4a^2$ is a common denominator on the right. ───────→
$$\left(x + \frac{b}{2a}\right)^2 = \frac{-4ac + b^2}{4a^2}$$

$$\left(x + \frac{b}{2a}\right)^2 = \frac{b^2 - 4ac}{4a^2}$$

$$x + \frac{b}{2a} \qquad\qquad \text{or} \quad x + \frac{b}{2a}$$

$$= \sqrt{\frac{b^2 - 4ac}{4a^2}} \qquad\qquad = -\sqrt{\frac{b^2 - 4ac}{4a^2}}$$

Add $-\frac{b}{2a}$ to each side; $\sqrt{4a^2} = 2a$. ──→
$$x = -\frac{b}{2a} + \frac{\sqrt{b^2 - 4ac}}{2a} \qquad x = -\frac{b}{2a} - \frac{\sqrt{b^2 - 4ac}}{2a}$$

$2a$ is a common denominator. ───────→
$$x = \frac{-b + \sqrt{b^2 - 4ac}}{2a} \quad \text{or} \quad x = \frac{-b - \sqrt{b^2 - 4ac}}{2a}$$

$\pm$ means $+$ or $-$. ───────→
Thus, $x = \dfrac{-b \pm \sqrt{b^2 - 4ac}}{2a}$.

A similar proof can be shown for $a < 0$.

Example 2 gives this formula. ───────→

The Quadratic Formula
The solutions of a quadratic equation of the form
$$ax^2 + bx + c = 0$$
may be found by the formula
$$x = \frac{-b \pm \sqrt{b^2 - 4ac}}{2a}$$

EXAMPLE 3

Rewrite $5x = 6x^2 - 7$ in standard form. Then determine a, b, and c.

$$5x = 6x^2 - 7$$

Add $-5x$ to each side. ───────→
$$0 = 6x^2 - 7 - 5x$$

Rearrange in descending order. ───────→
$$0 = 6x^2 - 5x - 7$$

Standard form ───────→
$$0 = ax^2 + bx + c$$

$a = 6$, $b = -5$, and $c = -7$.

EXAMPLE 4 Solve $x^2 - 9x + 14 = 0$ by using the quadratic formula.

Determine a, b, and c. $\longrightarrow$ $a = 1$, $b = -9$, $c = 14$

Quadratic formula $\longrightarrow$
$$x = \frac{-b \pm \sqrt{b^2 - 4ac}}{2a}$$

Substitute for a, b, and c. $\longrightarrow$
$$x = \frac{-(-9) \pm \sqrt{(-9)^2 - 4(1)(14)}}{2(1)}$$

$-(-9) = 9$ $\longrightarrow$
$$x = \frac{9 \pm \sqrt{81 - 56}}{2}$$

$$x = \frac{9 \pm \sqrt{25}}{2}$$

$$x = \frac{9 \pm 5}{2}$$

$\pm$ means $+$ or $-$. $\longrightarrow$
$$x = \frac{9 + 5}{2} \quad \text{or} \quad x = \frac{9 - 5}{2}$$

$x = \frac{14}{2}$ or $x = \frac{4}{2}$ $\longrightarrow$ $\quad x = 7 \quad\quad$ or $\quad x = 2$

Check 7 and 2 in $x^2 - 9x + 14 = 0$. $\longrightarrow$ **Thus,** the solutions are 7 and 2.

EXERCISES

PART A

Rewrite each equation in standard form. Then determine a, b, and c.

1. $2x^2 + 6x + 5 = 0$
2. $4x^2 + 3x + 2 = 0$
3. $2x^2 - 4x - 8 = 0$
4. $2x^2 - 4x = 0$
5. $x^2 + 2x = 0$
6. $3x^2 + 7 = 0$
7. $x^2 - 5 = 0$
8. $x^2 = 6x - 3$
9. $3x^2 - 6x = 2$
10. $x^2 = 4$
11. $5x^2 = 3x$
12. $2 + 6x = 4x^2$
13. $5x - x^2 = 3$
14. $7 = -4x^2$
15. $-3x = x^2 + 2$
16. $6x^2 = -1 + x$
17. $5x^2 = -3x$
18. $7 + 2x = -8x^2$

Solve by using the quadratic formula.

19. $x^2 + 4x + 3 = 0$
20. $x^2 - 5x + 6 = 0$
21. $x^2 - 2x + 1 = 0$
22. $x^2 + 3x - 10 = 0$
23. $x^2 - 4x - 21 = 0$
24. $x^2 - 2x - 24 = 0$
25. $x^2 + 3x - 40 = 0$
26. $x^2 - 12x - 13 = 0$
27. $x^2 - 8x + 16 = 0$

PART B

Find the solution set by using the quadratic formula.

28. $x^2 = 6 - x$
29. $x^2 - 11 = -10x$
30. $-12x = 45 - x^2$
31. $-30 = x - x^2$
32. $x^2 = -2x + 3$
33. $5x = -x^2 - 4$

Wet Mixture Problems

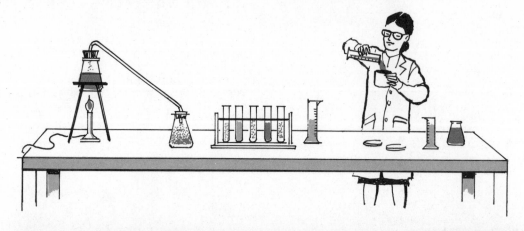

A 40 pint solution is made up of iodine and alcohol.
The solution is 20% iodine.

$$\binom{\text{Number of pints}}{\text{of iodine}} = \binom{\text{Percent}}{\text{iodine}} \cdot \binom{\text{Total number of pints}}{\text{in the solution}}$$

Pints of iodine = .20 • 40

= 8.00 ——— Decimal is used for percent

Thus, there are 8 pints of iodine in the solution

Practice Problem 1

A solution of 60 quarts contains a mixture of alcohol and water. If 30% of the solution is alcohol, how many quarts are water?

Total quarts, 60 is 100% → If 30% is alcohol, 100% —30% is water, or 70% is water.

Quarts of water = Percent water • Total quarts

= .70 (60)

= 42.00

Thus, there are 42 quarts of water in the solution.

Practice Problem 2	How many gallons of water must be added to 32 gallons of a 25% sulfuric acid solution to reduce it to a 20% acid solution?

Represent the amount needed algebraically. } Let x = number of gallons of water to be added.

Make a chart. →
Total gal in new solution:
original total, 32
+
water added, x }

	Total Gal	Gal of Acid	Gal of Water
25% solution	32	.25 (32)	.75 (32)
20% solution	32 + x	.20 (32 + x)	.80 (32 + x)

Only water is added; amounts of acid are the same in each solution.

Write an equation. →

$$\left(\begin{array}{c}\text{Acid in 25\%}\\ \text{solution}\end{array}\right) = \left(\begin{array}{c}\text{Acid in 20\%}\\ \text{solution}\end{array}\right)$$

Substitute. →
$$.25 (32) = .20 (32 + x)$$
$$8 = 6.4 + .2 x$$

Multiply each side by 10.
$$80 = 64 + 2 x$$
$$16 = 2 x$$
$$8 = x$$

Thus, 8 gallons of water must be added.

Practice Problem 3	A solution is made of an antiseptic and distilled water. How many ounces of antiseptic must be added to 80 oz of a 5% antiseptic solution to make it a 24% solution?

Represent the amount needed algebraically. } Let x = number of ounces of antiseptic to be added.

Make a chart. →
Total oz in new solution:
original total, 80
+
antiseptic added, x }

	Total Oz	Oz of Antiseptic	Oz of Water
5% solution	80	.05 (80)	.95 (80)
24% solution	80 + x	.24 (80 + x)	.76 (80 + x)

Write an equation. →
(Only antiseptic is added)

$$\left(\begin{array}{c}\text{Water in}\\ \text{5\% solution}\end{array}\right) = \left(\begin{array}{c}\text{Water in}\\ \text{24\% solution}\end{array}\right)$$

Substitute. →
$$.95 (80) = .76 (80 + x)$$
$$76 = 60.8 + .76 x$$

Multiply each side by 100.
$$7,600 = 6,080 + 76 x$$
$$1,520 = 76 x$$
$$20 = x$$

Thus, 20 ounces of antiseptic must be added.

| Practice Problem 4 | How many pints of antifreeze must be added to 20 pints of a 15% antifreeze solution (antifreeze and water), to make a 40% antifreeze solution? |

Represent the amount need algebraically. }   Let x = number of pints of antifreeze to be added.

Make a chart. →

	Total Pt	Pt of Antifreeze	Pt of Water
15% solution	20	.15 (20)	.85 (20)
40% solution	20 + x	.40 (20 + x)	.60 (20 + x)

Write an equation. (Since only antifreeze is added, amount of water in each stays the same.) }

$$\begin{pmatrix} \text{Pt of water in} \\ \text{15\% solution} \end{pmatrix} = \begin{pmatrix} \text{Pt of water in} \\ \text{40\% solution} \end{pmatrix}$$

$$.85\ (20) = .60\ (20 + x)$$
$$17.00 = 12.00 + .60x$$

Multiply each side by 100.

$$1700 = 1200 + 60x$$
$$500 = 60x$$
$$8\tfrac{1}{3} = x$$

Thus, $8\tfrac{1}{3}$ pints of antifreeze are needed.

| Practice Problem 5 | A chemist has 8 pints of a solution that is 20% alcohol. She also has a more concentrated solution that is 85% alcohol. How much of the more concentrated solution must she add to her original solution to obtain a solution that is 45% alcohol? |

Represent the amount needed algebraically. }   Let x = number of pints of 85% solution to be added.

Make a chart. →

Total pt in the new solution: } original total 8 + added concentrate x

	Total Pt	Pt of Alcohol
20% solution	8	.20 (8)
85% solution	x	.85 (x)
45% solution	8 + x	.45 (8 + x)

Write an equation. →

$$\begin{pmatrix} \text{Alcohol in} \\ \text{20\% solution} \end{pmatrix} + \begin{pmatrix} \text{Alcohol in} \\ \text{85\% solution} \end{pmatrix} = \begin{pmatrix} \text{Alcohol in} \\ \text{45\% solution} \end{pmatrix}$$

Substitute →
Multiply each side by 100. →

$$.20\ (8) + .85\ (x) = .45\ (8 + x)$$
$$1.6 + .85\ x = 3.6 + .45\ x$$
$$160 + 85\ x = 360 + 45\ x$$
$$40\ x = 200$$
$$x = 50$$

Thus, 50 pints of the 85% solution must be added.

EXERCISES

1. How many quarts of water must be added to 9 quarts of a 40% solution of hydrochloric acid to make it a 30% acid solution?

2. A nurse has 4 quarts of a mixture that is 20% medicine. How much more medicine must he add to make it a 36% mixture?

3. Dr. Rivers has 3 gallons of a 60% salt solution. How many gallons of water must she add to obtain a 20% solution?

4. If a pharmacist has 100 pints of a 10% peroxide in water solution, how much peroxide must he add to obtain a 20% solution?

5. A farmer has 200 quarts of milk that tests 9.2% butterfat. How many quarts of skimmed milk (without butterfat) must he add to obtain milk that tests 6.4% butterfat?

6. A chemist has a solution of alcohol and water. How many cubic centimeters of alcohol must be added to 60 cc. of a 28% solution to make it a 46% solution?

7. How many quarts of water must a chemist add to 24 quarts of a sulfuric acid solution that is 30% acid to obtain a solution that is 10% acid?

8. A pharmacist has 3 pints of cough medicine that is 10% water. For children, it must be 40% water. How much water must she add?

9. How many cubic centimeters of a solution that is 75% alcohol must be added to 50 cc. of a 25% alcohol solution to make a 40% solution?

10. How many quarts of water must be added to 26 quarts of a 15% antifreeze solution to dilute it to a 12% solution?

11. How many ounces of a 50% iodine solution must be added to 4 ounces of a 20% iodine solution in order to obtain a 30% iodine solution?

12. How many grams of water must be added to 40 grams of a 50% acid solution to dilute it to a 30% acid solution?

Applying the Quadratic Formula

 REVIEW CAPSULE

Quadratic Equation	Standard Form	a	b	c
$x^2 - 7x + 2 = 0$	same	1	−7	2
$5x^2 = 3x$	$5x^2 - 3x + 0 = 0$	5	−3	0
$-x - 8 = -x^2$	$x^2 - x - 8 = 0$	1	−1	−8

Quadratic Formula

$$x = \frac{-b \pm \sqrt{b^2 - 4ac}}{2a}$$

EXAMPLE 1   Find the solution set of $2x^2 + x = 6$ by using the quadratic formula.

Add −6 to each side to get standard form. ⟶
$$2x^2 + x = 6$$
$$2x^2 + x - 6 = 0$$

Determine a, b, and c. ⟶
$$a = 2 \qquad b = 1 \qquad c = -6$$

Quadratic formula ⟶
$$x = \frac{-b \pm \sqrt{b^2 - 4ac}}{2a}$$

Substitute for a, b, and c. ⟶
$$x = \frac{-1 \pm \sqrt{1^2 - 4(2)(-6)}}{2(2)}$$

$-4(2)(-6) = 48$ ⟶
$$x = \frac{-1 \pm \sqrt{1 + 48}}{4}$$

$$x = \frac{-1 \pm \sqrt{49}}{4}$$

$$x = \frac{-1 \pm 7}{4}$$

$$x = \frac{-1 + 7}{4} \quad \text{or} \quad x = \frac{-1 - 7}{4}$$

$$x = \frac{6}{4} \quad \text{or} \quad x = \frac{-8}{4}$$

$$x = \frac{3}{2} \quad \text{or} \quad x = -2$$

Rational solutions ⟶ **Thus,** the solution set is $\left\{\frac{3}{2}, -2\right\}$.

EXAMPLE 2 Find the solution set of $3x^2 + x - 1 = 0$ by using the quadratic formula.

$$x = \frac{-b \pm \sqrt{b^2 - 4ac}}{2a}$$

$a = 3, b = 1, c = -1$ ⟶
$$x = \frac{-1 \pm \sqrt{1^2 - 4(3)(-1)}}{2(3)}$$

$$x = \frac{-1 \pm \sqrt{1 + 12}}{6}$$

Irrational solutions ⟶
$$x = \frac{-1 \pm \sqrt{13}}{6}$$

Thus, the solution set is $\left\{ \dfrac{-1 \pm \sqrt{13}}{6} \right\}$.

EXAMPLE 3 Find the solution set of $3x^2 - x + 1 = 0$ by using the quadratic formula.

$$x = \frac{-b \pm \sqrt{b^2 - 4ac}}{2a}$$

$a = 3, b = -1, c = 1.$ ⟶
$$x = \frac{-(-1) \pm \sqrt{(-1)^2 - 4(3)(1)}}{2(3)}$$

$$x = \frac{1 \pm \sqrt{1 - 12}}{6}$$

$\sqrt{-11}$ is not a real number. ⟶
$$x = \frac{1 \pm \sqrt{-11}}{6}$$

No real solutions ⟶ **Thus,** the solution set is ϕ.

EXAMPLE 4 Find the solution set of $x^2 - 2x - 1 = 0$ by using the quadratic formula.

$$x = \frac{-b \pm \sqrt{b^2 - 4ac}}{2a}$$

$a = 1, b = -2, c = -1.$ ⟶
$$x = \frac{-(-2) \pm \sqrt{(-2)^2 - 4(1)(-1)}}{2(1)}$$

$$x = \frac{2 \pm \sqrt{4 + 4}}{2}$$

$$x = \frac{2 \pm \sqrt{8}}{2}$$

$\sqrt{8} = \sqrt{2 \cdot 2 \cdot 2} = 2\sqrt{2}$ ⟶
$$x = \frac{2 \pm 2\sqrt{2}}{2}$$

Factor numerator and denominator.⎤
Simplify.   ⎦
$$x = \frac{\overset{1}{\cancel{2}}(1 \pm \sqrt{2})}{\underset{1}{\cancel{2}}}$$

$$x = 1 \pm \sqrt{2}$$

Irrational solutions ⟶ **Thus,** the solution set is $\{1 \pm \sqrt{2}\}$.

EXERCISES

Find the solution set by using the quadratic formula.

1. $2x^2 + 5x - 3 = 0$ 2. $3x^2 - 7x + 2 = 0$ 3. $6x^2 - x - 2 = 0$

4. $2x^2 - 7x + 3 = 0$ 5. $2x^2 - 11x + 12 = 0$ 6. $8x^2 - 22x + 15 = 0$

7. $3x^2 + 5x - 2 = 0$ 8. $2x^2 - 3x - 9 = 0$ 9. $9x^2 - 60x + 100 = 0$

10. $x^2 - 5x - 2 = 0$ 11. $x^2 - 7x + 3 = 0$ 12. $x^2 - 7x - 3 = 0$

13. $2x^2 + 4x + 3 = 0$ 14. $x^2 + x - 1 = 0$ 15. $x^2 + 5x - 3 = 0$

16. $x^2 + x - 5 = 0$ 17. $3x^2 - 7x + 9 = 0$ 18. $x^2 - 3x + 1 = 0$

19. $5x^2 - 3x + 2 = 0$ 20. $x^2 - 6x - 2 = 0$ 21. $x^2 - 4x - 10 = 0$

22. $x^2 - 10x = -5$ 23. $x^2 = 8x - 3$ 24. $x^2 + 2x + 7 = 0$

25. $2x^2 - 12 = -5x$ 26. $15x = 9x^2 + 4$ 27. $x^2 + 1 = -4x$

28. $x^2 + 8 = 3x$ 29. $x^2 = 7x - 11$ 30. $2x^2 + 9 = 9x$

PART B

EXAMPLE   Find the solutions to the nearest tenth.

$$x^2 - \frac{10}{3}x - 4 = 0$$

Multiply each side by 3. $\longrightarrow$ $3\left(x^2 - \frac{10}{3}x - 4\right) = 3(0)$

Distributive property $\longrightarrow$ $3x^2 - 10x - 12 = 0$

$a = 3$, $b = -10$, $c = -12$; substitute in the quadratic formula. $\Big\}$ $x = \dfrac{10 \pm \sqrt{244}}{6}$

$\sqrt{244} = \sqrt{4 \cdot 61} = 2\sqrt{61}$; $\Big\}$
2 is a common factor. $x = \dfrac{2 \cdot 5 \pm 2\sqrt{61}}{2 \cdot 3}$

Simplify. $\longrightarrow$ $x = \dfrac{5 \pm \sqrt{61}}{3}$

From the table, $\sqrt{61} \doteq 7.81$. $\longrightarrow$ $x = \dfrac{5 + \sqrt{61}}{3} \doteq \dfrac{5 + 7.81}{3} = \dfrac{12.81}{3} \doteq 4.3$, or

$$x = \frac{5 - \sqrt{61}}{3} \doteq \frac{5 - 7.81}{3} = \frac{-2.81}{3} \doteq -.9$$

Thus, the solutions are 4.3 and $-.9$ to the nearest tenth.

Find the solutions to the nearest tenth.

31. $x^2 + \dfrac{5}{2}x + 1 = 0$ 32. $x^2 - \dfrac{8}{3}x - 1 = 0$ 33. $x^2 + \dfrac{11}{3}x + 2 = 0$

34. $x^2 - \dfrac{x}{3} + 2 = 0$ 35. $x^2 - \dfrac{4}{5}x - 1 = 0$ 36. $x^2 + \dfrac{4}{3}x - 1 = 0$

Area Problems

REVIEW CAPSULE

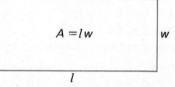

$A = lw$ w

l

Find the area of a rectangle whose length is 7 inches and whose width is 3 inches.

$A = \ell w$

$= 7 \cdot 3$, or 21 square inches

EXAMPLE 1 The length of a rectangle is 3 inches more than the width. The area is 70 square inches. Find the length and the width.

Represent length and width algebraically; draw a rough sketch. ──────→

Let x = width in inches
$x + 3$ = length in inches

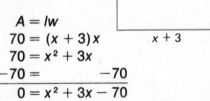

x

x + 3

Formula for area ──────────→
Substitute for A, l, and w. ────→
$(x + 3)x = x \cdot x + 3 \cdot x = x^2 + 3x$ ──→

$A = lw$
$70 = (x + 3)x$
$70 = x^2 + 3x$

Add -70 to each side to get standard form. ──────────→

$\begin{array}{r} -70 = -70 \\ \hline 0 = x^2 + 3x - 70 \end{array}$

Two ways to solve $x^2 + 3x - 70$

Factor   Quadratic formula

$0 = (x + 10)(x - 7)$ $x = \dfrac{-b \pm \sqrt{b^2 - 4ac}}{2a}$

$a = 1, b = 3, c = 70.$

$x + 10 = 0$ or $x - 7 = 0$
$x = -10$ or $x = 7$

$x = \dfrac{-3 \pm \sqrt{9 + 280}}{2}$

-10 is an extraneous solution. ──────→

Reject -10, since a rectangle cannot have a negative number as its width.

$x = \dfrac{-3 \pm \sqrt{289}}{2}$

$x = \dfrac{-3 \pm 17}{2}$

$\dfrac{-3 \pm 17}{2}$ means $\dfrac{-3 + 17}{2}$ or $\dfrac{-3 - 17}{2}$

Width, x is 7.
Length, $x + 3$ is 10.

$x = \frac{14}{2}$ or $x = \frac{-20}{2}$
$x = 7$ or $x = -10$

Check: $A = lw$

$= 10 \cdot 7 = 70.$ ──────→

Thus, the length is 10 in. and the width is 7 in.

EXAMPLE 2 The length of a rectangle is twice the width. The area is 50 sq ft. Find the length and the width.

Represent length and width algebraically; draw a rough sketch. ———————→

Let x = width in ft
$2x$ = length in ft
$A = lw$

Substitute for A, l, and w. ———————→ $50 = 2x(x)$
$50 = 2x^2$

Divide each side by 2. ———————→ $25 = x^2$

It $x^2 = a$, then $x = \sqrt{a}$ or $x = -\sqrt{a}$. ———————→ $x = \sqrt{25}$ or $x = -\sqrt{25}$
$x = 5$ or $x = -5$ ← Extraneous solution
Width, x is 5.
Length, $2x$ is 10.

Check: $A = lw$
= $10 \cdot 5 = 50$. ———————→ **Thus,** the length is 10 ft and the width is 5 ft.

EXAMPLE 3 The length of a rectangle is 8 cm more than the width. The area is 50 sq cm. Find the length and the width.

Represent length and width algebraically; draw a rough sketch. ———————→

Let x = width in cm
$x + 8$ = length in cm
$A = lw$

Substitute for A, l, and w. ———————→ $50 = (x + 8)x$
Distribute x. ———————→ $50 = x^2 + 8x$
Add -50 to each side. ———————→ $0 = x^2 + 8x - 50$

$$x = \frac{-b \pm \sqrt{b^2 - 4ac}}{2a}$$

Replace a with 1, b with 8, and c with 50.

$$x = \frac{-8 \pm \sqrt{(8)^2 - 4(1)(-50)}}{2(1)}$$

$(8)^2 = 64. \ -4(1)(-50) = 200;$
$64 + 200 = 264$ }

$$x = \frac{-8 \pm \sqrt{264}}{2}$$

$$x = \frac{-8 \pm \sqrt{4(66)}}{2}$$

$$x = \frac{-8 \pm 2\sqrt{66}}{2}$$

Divide numerator and denominator by the common factor, 2. ———————→ $x = -4 \pm \sqrt{66}$

From the table, $\sqrt{66} \doteq 8.12$. ———————→ $x = -4 + \sqrt{66} \doteq -4 + 8.12 = 4.12 \doteq 4.1$, or

Extraneous solution. ———————→ $x = -4 - \sqrt{66} \doteq -4 - 8.12 = -12.12$
Width, x is 4.1.
Length, $x + 8$ is 12.1.

Check: $(12.1)(4.1) = 49.61$, which is 50 to the nearest whole number. ———————→ **Thus,** the length is 12.1 cm and the width is 4.1 cm, to the nearest tenth.

ORAL EXERCISES

Give the area of each rectangle in terms of x.

1. $\ell = 7x$; $w = 2x$ **2.** $\ell = x + 1$; $w = x$ **3.** $\ell = 3x$; $w = x + 5$

4. $\ell = x + 3$; $w = x - 3$ **5.** $\ell = 2x + 5$; $w = 2x - 5$ **6.** $\ell = 3x + 2$; $w = 2x - 3$

EXERCISES

PART A

Find the length and the width of each rectangle.

1. The length is 3 more than the width. The area is 40 square inches.

2. The length is 5 less than 3 times the width. The area is 50 square feet.

3. The length is twice the width. The area is 32 square meters.

4. The length is 3 times the width. The area is 27 square yards.

5. The length is 3 more than twice the width. The area is 44 square feet.

6. The length is 2 more than twice the width. The area is 60 sq cm.

7. The length is 3 less than twice the width. The area is 20 square feet.

8. The length is 1 less than twice the width. The area is 28 square meters.

9. The length is 6 more than the width. The area is 20 sq cm.

10. The length is 15 more than the width. The area is 50 square meters.

11. The width is 2 less than the length. the area is 44 square feet.

12. The width is 4 less than the length. The area is 6 square miles.

PART B

Find the length and the width of each rectangle.

13. The length is 4 less than twice the width. The area is 96 square inches.

14. The length is 5 less than 3 times the width. The area is 152 square feet.

15. The length is 3 greater than twice the width. The area is 90 sq km.

16. The length is 1 less than twice the width. The area is 91 square inches.

17. The length is 2 more than 4 times the width. The area is 72 square miles.

18. The length is twice the width. The area is 128 sq cm.

19. The width is 5 less than the length. The area is 25 square meters.

20. The width is 3 less than twice the length. The area is 4 sq km.

PART C

Find the length and the width of each rectangle.

21. The perimeter is 24. The area is 35.

22. The perimeter is 44. The area is 120.

A Flow Chart for the Quadratic Formula

Quadratic Formula

$$x = \frac{-b \pm \sqrt{b^2 - 4\,ac}}{2\,a}$$

gives the solutions to the quadratic equation $a\,x^2 + b\,x + c = 0$.

b^2-4ac is the *discriminant*.

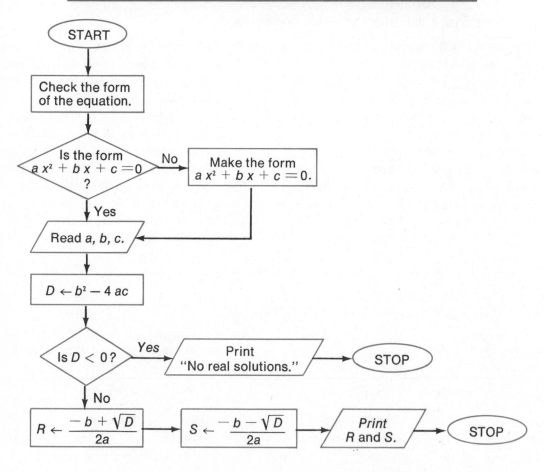

Use the flow chart to solve each quadratic equation.

1. $2\,x^2 + 3\,x + 4 = 0$
2. $x^2 - 5\,x + 6 = 0$
3. $x^2 + x - 5 = 0$
4. $9\,x^2 - 30\,x + 25 = 0$

The discriminant can also be used to describe the kind of solutions to a quadratic equation.

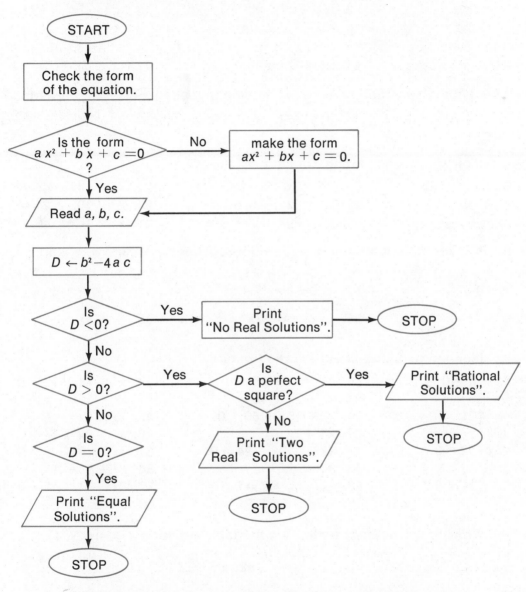

Use the flow chart to evaluate the discriminant and describe the kind of solutions for each equation.

5. $2x^2 + 3x + 4 = 0$ 6. $25x^2 - 4 = 0$
7. $x^2 + 2x + 1 = 0$ 8. $x^2 + 5x + 3 = 0$

Chapter Fifteen Review

Find the solution set. $[p.\ 417,\ 420]$

1. $\sqrt{3x} = 15$
2. $\sqrt{y} + 5 = 11$
3. $\sqrt{4x - 5} = -2$
4. $4\sqrt{3x} = \sqrt{96}$
5. $\sqrt{x^2 - 4} = -8$
6. $\sqrt{19 + 3x} = x + 3$
7. $x^2 = 100$
8. $x^2 = -49$
9. $x^2 - 36 = 0$
10. $(x - 4)^2 = 64$
11. $(x + 8)^2 = 144$
12. $(x - 3)^2 + 6 = 42$

What number should be added to each expression to make a perfect square trinomial?

13. $x^2 + 8x$
14. $x^2 - 14x$
15. $x^2 - 2x$ $\quad [p.\ 423]$
16. $x^2 + 20x$
17. $x^2 + 5x$
18. $x^2 - 15x$

Find the solution set by completing the square. $[p.\ 423]$

19. $x^2 - 12x - 13 = 0$
20. $x^2 + 2x - 3 = 0$
21. $x^2 - 14x + 45 = 0$
22. $x^2 + 8x - 48 = 0$
23. $x^2 - 4x - 21 = 0$
24. $x^2 - 10x + 24 = 0$
25. $x^2 + 6x + 8 = 0$
26. $x^2 - 20x + 51 = 0$
27. $x^2 + 16x + 60 = 0$

Rewrite each quadratic equation in standard form. Then determine *a*, *b*, and *c*.

28. $3x^2 - 5x + 4 = 0$
29. $x^2 - x + 6 = 0$
30. $3x^2 + 6x = 0$ $\quad [p.\ 427]$
31. $x^2 - 7 = 0$
32. $4x^2 = 3x$
33. $7 = 5x^2 - 4$
34. $-4x + 3x^2 = 8$
35. $1 - 2x = -7x^2$
36. $\dfrac{x^2}{2} + 4x = \dfrac{1}{6}$

Find the solution set by using the quadratic formula. $[p.\ 434]$

37. $x^2 - 6x + 8 = 0$
38. $x^2 + 2x - 15 = 0$
39. $x^2 - 7x + 12 = 0$
40. $x^2 - 5x - 6 = 0$
41. $x^2 + 7x + 10 = 0$
42. $x^2 - 10x - 11 = 0$
43. $x^2 + 4x - 21 = 0$
44. $x^2 - 15x + 50 = 0$
45. $2x - 3 = -x^2$
46. $x^2 - 10x = -24$
47. $x^2 = 7x$
48. $x^2 = 3x + 54$
49. $3x^2 + 5x - 2 = 0$
50. $4x^2 - 10x - 24 = 0$
51. $4x^2 + 8x - 5 = 0$
52. $x^2 + 3x + 10 = 0$
53. $3x^2 + 2x - 4 = 0$
54. $x^2 + 6x - 1 = 0$
55. $x^2 - 7x + 11 = 0$
56. $2x^2 - x + 7 = 0$
57. $2x^2 - 4x - 7 = 0$
58. $x^2 = 1 - x$
59. $-5x + 1 = -2x^2$
60. $3 + 2x^2 = -5x$

Find the solutions to the nearest tenth. Use the table on page 478. $[p.\ 434]$

61. $x^2 - \dfrac{5}{3}x - 2 = 0$
62. $x^2 - \dfrac{2}{7}x = \dfrac{1}{7}$

Solve each problem. $[p.\ 437]$

63. The length of a rectangle is 3 feet less than twice the width. The area is 20 square feet. Find the length and the width.

64. The length of a rectangle is 5 times the width. The area is 80 square meters. Find the length and the width.

Chapter Fifteen Test

Find the solution set.

1. $\sqrt{7x - 3} = 5$

2. $\sqrt{3y} + 8 = 2$

3. $x - 2 = \sqrt{x + 10}$

4. $x^2 = 36$

5. $x^2 - 100 = 0$

6. $(x + 5)^2 - 8 = 73$

What number should be added to each expression to make a perfect square trinomial?

7. $x^2 + 10x$

8. $x^2 - 4x$

9. $x^2 - 18x$

10. $x^2 + 7x$

Find the solution set by completing the square.

11. $x^2 + 4x + 3 = 0$

12. $x^2 - 10x - 39 = 0$

13. $x^2 + 6x - 16 = 0$

14. $x^2 - 18x - 19 = 0$

Rewrite each quadratic equation in standard form. Then determine *a*, *b*, and *c*.

15. $2x^2 - 5x + 4 = 0$

16. $x^2 = x + 8$

17. $-3x = 7 - 2x^2$

18. $\dfrac{x^2}{3} = 6x + \dfrac{1}{9}$

Find the solution set by using the quadratic formula.

19. $x^2 + 9x + 18 = 0$

20. $x^2 + x - 30 = 0$

21. $x^2 + 7x - 2 = 0$

22. $6x^2 - 7x + 2 = 0$

23. $2x^2 - x - 3 = 0$

24. $3x^2 - 2x = 4$

25. $7x^2 + 15 = 2x$

26. $6x^2 + 3x + 5 = 0$

Find solutions to the nearest tenth. Use the table on page 478.

27. $x^2 - \dfrac{2}{3}x - 1\ 0$

Solve each problem.

28. The length of a rectangle is 5 meters less than twice the width. The area is 12 square meters. Find the length and the width.

29. The length of a rectangle is 3 times the width. The area is 12 square kilometers. Find the length and the width.

Approximating Cube Roots

Approximate $\sqrt[3]{100}$ correct to one decimal place.

$n = 100$
Let R = 4. $(4)^3 < 100$

Divide by $(4)^2 = 16$

$$\begin{array}{r} 6.2 = 6.\,3 \leftarrow \\ 16\overline{)100.0} \\ 96 \\ \hline 40 \\ 32 \\ \hline 8 \end{array}$$ divide to one decimal place

Average. $\dfrac{4 + 4 + 6.3}{3} = \dfrac{14.3}{3}$ or 4.8

Is $(4.8)^3 = 100$? No

Divide by $(4.8)^2 = 23.04$

$$\begin{array}{r} 4.34 \leftarrow \\ 23.04_\wedge\overline{)100.00_\wedge00} \\ 9216 \\ \hline 7840 \\ 6912 \\ \hline 9280 \\ 9216 \end{array}$$ divide to two decimal places

Average $\dfrac{4.8 + 4.8 + 4.34}{3} = \dfrac{13.94}{3}$

$\phantom{Average \frac{4.8+4.8+4.34}{3}} = 4.65$

$4.65^3 \doteq 100.5$

Thus, $\sqrt[3]{100} = 4.7$ correct to one decimal place.

Approximate $\sqrt[3]{n}$ to one decimal place
1. 89   2. 21   3. 180   4. 300

To approximate the cube root of a number n to one decimal place.

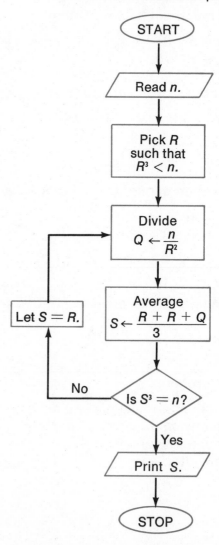

Angles and Triangles

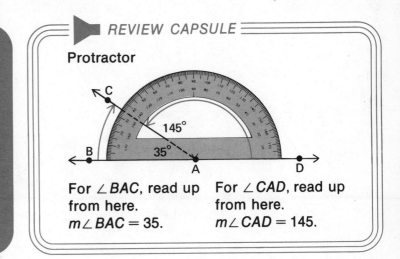

▶ REVIEW CAPSULE

Protractor

For ∠*BAC*, read up from here.
$m\angle BAC = 35$.

For ∠*CAD*, read up from here.
$m\angle CAD = 145$.

Pairs of complementary angles ⟶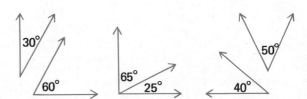

30° 60°   65° 25°   50° 40°

Definition of complementary angles ⟶

Complementary angles are two angles the sum of whose measures is 90°. Each is the *complement* of the other.

EXAMPLE 1

An angle is 12° greater in measure than its complement. Find the measure of the angle and its complement.

Let x = degree measure of the complement
$x + 12$ = degree measure of the angle

Write an equation: The sum of the degree measures is 90. ⟶

$$x + (x + 12) = 90$$
$$2x + 12 = 90$$
$$2x = 78$$
$$x = 39$$
$$x + 12 = 51$$

Measure of complement ⟶
Measure of angle ⟶
Check: $39 + 51 = 90$. ⟶

Thus, the angle measures 51° and its complement measures 39°.

EXAMPLE 2	Try this experiment. Cut a triangle out of paper. Tear off the three corners and fit them together, as shown below.

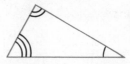 

This is true for every triangle. ──────→ The three angles form a straight line, or 180°.

This can be proved in a geometry course. ──────→

> The sum of the measures of the three angles of a triangle is 180°.

EXAMPLE 3 The second angle of a triangle measures twice the first. The third angle measures 8 degrees more than the first. Find the measures of the three angles.

Let x = degree measure of first angle
$2x$ = degree measure of second angle
$x + 8$ = degree measure of third angle

Sum of the measures of the three angles of a triangle is 180°. ──────→
$$x + 2x + (x + 8) = 180$$
$$4x + 8 = 180$$

Add −8 to each side. ──────→ $4x = 172$
Measure of first angle ──────→ $x = 43$
Measure of second angle ──────→ $2x = 86$
Measure of third angle ──────→ $x + 8 = 51$

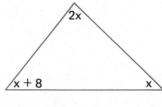

Thus, the angles measure 43°, 86°, and 51°.

EXAMPLE 4 In right triangle ABC, $m\angle C = 90$, and $m\angle A = 32$. Find $m\angle B$.

Sum of the measures of the angles of a triangle is 180°. ──────→
$$m\angle A + m\angle B + m\angle C = 180$$
Let $x = m\angle B$. ──────→ $32 + x + 90 = 180$
$32 + 90 = 122$ ──────→ $122 + x = 180$
Add −122 to each side. ──────→ $x = 58$

Thus, $m\angle B = 58$.

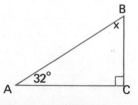

In Example 4,
$m\angle A + m\angle B = 32 + 58 = 90$. ──────→

An acute angle has a measure of less than 90°.

> $$m\angle A + m\angle B = 90$$
> *The acute angles of a right triangle are complementary.*

ORAL EXERCISES

Find the measure of the complement of the angle whose measure is given.

1. 20°   **2.** 35°   **3.** 15°   **4.** 60°   **5.** 85°   **6.** x°

In right triangle ABC, $m \angle C = 90$. Find $m \angle A$ for the given $m \angle B$.

7. 30°   **8.** 45°   **9.** 75°   **10.** 2°   **11.** 82°   **12.** y°

EXERCISES

PART A

1. An angle measures 24° less than its complement. Find the measure of the angle and its complement.

2. All three angles of an equilateral triangle have the same measure. What is the measure of each?

3. An angle measures 15° more than twice its complement. Find the measure of each angle.

4. The measures of the angles of a triangle are in the ratio 1:2:3. Find the measures.

5. The acute angles of a right triangle have the same measure. Find the measure of the acute angles.

6. One of two complementary angles measures 20° more than 4 times the other. Find the measures of the two angles.

7. Two angles of a triangle have the same measure. The third angle measures 20° more than 8 times the first, or second. Find the measures of the two acute angles.

8. The degree-measures of the angles of a triangle are consecutive even integers. Find the measures of the three angles.

9. One acute angle of a right triangle measures 30° more than 3 times the other acute angle. Find the measures of the two acute angles.

10. One of two complementary angles has $\frac{2}{3}$ the degree-measure of the other. Find the measures of the two angles.

PART B

11. One angle of a triangle measures 5° less than the second. The third angle measures 20° more than the complement of the second angle. Find the measures of the three angles.

12. One angle of a triangle measures 6° more than the second. The third angle measures 4° less than 3 times the sum of the measures of the first two angles. Find the measures of the three angles.

Similar Triangles

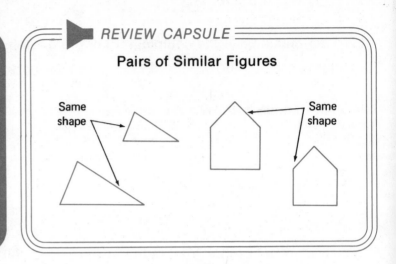

REVIEW CAPSULE

Pairs of Similar Figures

Same shape

Same shape

Read.

Write.

$\triangle ABC \sim \triangle DEF$

$\triangle ABC$ is similar to $\triangle DEF$.

$\triangle ABC \sim \triangle DEF$

$m\angle A = m\angle D$, $m\angle B = m\angle E$, $m\angle C = m\angle F$. The angles of each triangle are congruent, equal in measure, in the order given. $\cong$ means is congruent to.

In $\triangle ABC$, $\overline{BC}$ is opposite $\angle A$.
In $\triangle DEF$, $\overline{EF}$ is opposite $\angle D$.

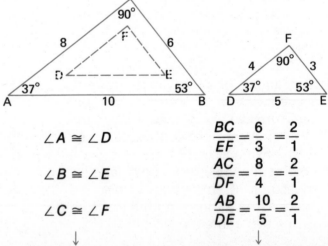

$\angle A \cong \angle D$

$\angle B \cong \angle E$

$\angle C \cong \angle F$

$\dfrac{BC}{EF} = \dfrac{6}{3} = \dfrac{2}{1}$

$\dfrac{AC}{DF} = \dfrac{8}{4} = \dfrac{2}{1}$

$\dfrac{AB}{DE} = \dfrac{10}{5} = \dfrac{2}{1}$

Corresponding sides are opposite corresponding angles in similar triangles.

Corresponding angles are congruent.

Lengths of corresponding sides have the same ratio.

Definition of similar triangles

First condition

Second condition

Two triangles are similar if the corresponding angles are congruent and the lengths of the corresponding sides have the same ratio.

EXAMPLE 1 △*ABC* ~ △*DEF*. Find *x* and *y*.

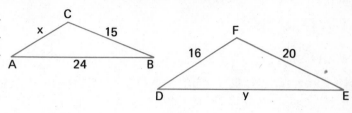

$\overline{AB}$ corresponds to $\overline{DE}$. ——————⟶
$\overline{BC}$ corresponds to $\overline{EF}$. ——————⟶
$\overline{AC}$ corresponds to $\overline{DF}$. ——————⟶

Lengths of corresponding sides have the same ratio. Write and solve these proportions. ——————⟶

$$\frac{x}{16} = \frac{15}{20}$$

Simplify $\frac{15}{20}$ to $\frac{3}{4}$. ——————⟶

$$\frac{x}{16} = \frac{3}{4}$$
$$4x = 3 \cdot 16$$
$$4x = 48$$
$$x = 12$$

$$\frac{y}{24} = \frac{20}{15}$$
$$\frac{y}{24} = \frac{4}{3}$$
$$3y = 4 \cdot 24$$
$$3y = 96$$
$$y = 32$$

Thus, *x* is 12 and *y* is 32.

EXAMPLE 2 △*ABC* ~ △*DEF*. *AC* = 9, *BC* = 10, and *DF* = 6. Find *EF*.

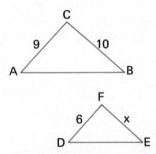

△*ABC* ~ △*DEF*
$\overline{AB}$ corresponds to $\overline{DE}$.
$\overline{BC}$ corresponds to $\overline{EF}$.
$\overline{AC}$ corresponds to $\overline{DF}$.

Let $x = EF$

$$\frac{x}{10} = \frac{6}{9}$$
$$\frac{x}{10} = \frac{2}{3}$$
$$3x = 2 \cdot 10$$
$$3x = 20$$
$$x = 6\tfrac{2}{3}$$

Thus, *EF* is $6\tfrac{2}{3}$.

EXAMPLE 3 A boy 5 feet tall cast a shadow 8 feet long. How tall is a nearby flagpole if its shadow is 50 feet long?

Two similar triangles are formed.

x

5 ft

8 ft

50 ft

Let *x* = height of flagpole

$$\frac{x}{5} = \frac{50}{8}$$
$$\frac{x}{5} = \frac{25}{4}$$
$$4x = 125$$
$$x = 31\tfrac{1}{4}$$

Thus, the flagpole is $31\tfrac{1}{4}$ feet long.

EXERCISES

PART A

In Exercises 1–8, $\triangle ABC \sim \triangle DEF$. Find the indicated measures.

1.

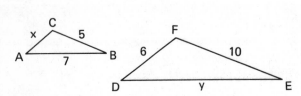

2.

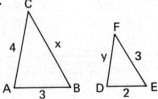

3. $AB = 12$, $AC = 13$, $BC = 5$ and $DE = 8$. Find DF and EF.

4. $DE = 15$, $EF = 6$. $AB = 10$, $AC = 9$. Find BC and DF.

5. $AB = 7$, $AC = 9$, $BC = 12$, and $DF = 15$. Find DE and EF.

6. $AC = 5$, $CB = 8$, $DF = 15$, and $DE = 18$. Find AB and FE.

7. $AB = 12$, $AC = 10$, $DE = 18$, and $FE = 20$. Find CB and DF.

8. $DE = 16$, $FE = 14$, $DF = 11$, and $AB = 24$. Find CB and AC.

9. A vertical yardstick casts a 4-foot shadow while a flagpole casts a 24-foot shadow. How tall is the flagpole?

10. A girl 5 feet 4 inches tall casts a shadow 4 feet long while a tower casts a shadow 90 feet long. How tall is the tower?

11. A 10-foot ladder touches the side of a building at a height of 8 feet. At what height would a 12-foot ladder touch the building if it makes the same angle with the ground?

12. Use the similar triangles pictured to find the width of the river.

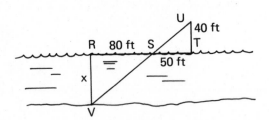

PART B

13. Jim walked 8 feet up a ramp and was 3 feet above the ground. If he walked 12 feet further up the ramp, how far above the ground would he be?

14. Mary was standing 12 feet from the base of a 10-foot tree. She could spot the top of a 500-foot building just beyond the top of the tree. How far was she from the base of the building?

Trigonometric Ratios

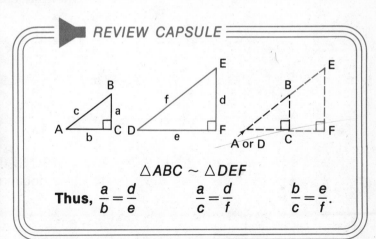

▶ REVIEW CAPSULE

$$\triangle ABC \sim \triangle DEF$$

Thus, $\dfrac{a}{b} = \dfrac{d}{e}$ $\dfrac{a}{c} = \dfrac{d}{f}$ $\dfrac{b}{c} = \dfrac{e}{f}$.

From the Greek language ⟶ **Trigonometry means *triangle measurement*. We will work with right triangles.**

Words associated with right triangles.

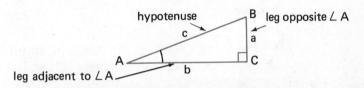

leg adjacent to ∠A

All right triangles with a given $m\angle A$ are similar: The ratios, $\dfrac{a}{b}, \dfrac{a}{c}$, and $\dfrac{b}{c}$ are the same for each $m\angle A$.

Ratio	Abbreviation
tangent of $m\angle A =$ $\dfrac{\text{measure of opposite leg}}{\text{measure of adjacent leg}}$	$\tan A = \dfrac{a}{b}$
sine of $m\angle A =$ $\dfrac{\text{measure of opposite leg}}{\text{measure of hypotenuse}}$	$\sin A = \dfrac{a}{c}$
cosine of $m\angle A =$ $\dfrac{\text{measure of adjacent leg}}{\text{measure of hypotenuse}}$	$\cos A = \dfrac{b}{c}$

EXAMPLE 1 For $\triangle ABC$, find $\tan A$, $\sin A$, and $\cos A$.

$\tan = \dfrac{\text{opp.}}{\text{adj.}}$; opp. means opposite. adj. means adjacent.

$\sin = \dfrac{\text{opp.}}{\text{hyp.}}$; hyp. means hypotenuse.

$\cos = \dfrac{\text{adj.}}{\text{hyp.}}$

$\tan A = \dfrac{3}{4}$, or .75

$\sin A = \dfrac{3}{5}$, or .6

⟶ $\cos A = \dfrac{4}{5}$, or .8

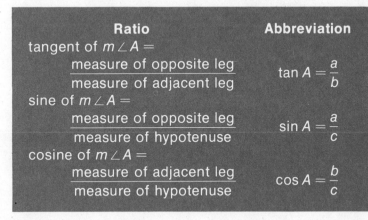

EXAMPLE 2   For △ABC, find tan B, sin B, and cos B, to three decimal places.

$\tan = \dfrac{\text{opp.}}{\text{adj.}}$ ───────────→ $\tan B = \dfrac{12}{5} = 2.400$

$\sin = \dfrac{\text{opp.}}{\text{hyp.}}$ ───────────→ $\sin B = \dfrac{12}{13} = .923$

$\cos = \dfrac{\text{adj.}}{\text{hyp.}}$ ───────────→ $\cos B = \dfrac{5}{13} = .385$

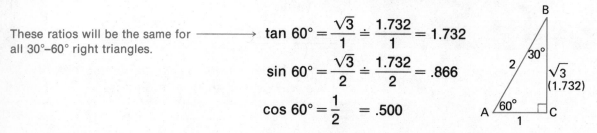

EXAMPLE 3   Use △ABC to find tan 60°, sin 60°, and cos 60°, to three decimal places.

These ratios will be the same for ───→ $\tan 60° = \dfrac{\sqrt{3}}{1} \doteq \dfrac{1.732}{1} = 1.732$
all 30°–60° right triangles.

$$\sin 60° = \dfrac{\sqrt{3}}{2} \doteq \dfrac{1.732}{2} = .866$$

$$\cos 60° = \dfrac{1}{2} = .500$$

EXAMPLE 4   Use the figure in Example 3 to find tan 30°, sin 30°, cos 30° to three decimal places.

First rationalize the denominator. ───→ $\tan 30° = \dfrac{1}{\sqrt{3}} = \dfrac{1}{\sqrt{3}} \cdot \dfrac{\sqrt{3}}{\sqrt{3}} = \dfrac{\sqrt{3}}{3} \doteq \dfrac{1.732}{3} \doteq .577$

$$\sin 30° = \dfrac{1}{2} = .500$$

$$\cos 30° = \dfrac{\sqrt{3}}{2} \doteq \dfrac{1.732}{2} = .866$$

ORAL EXERCISES

Refer to the figure at the right.

1. Name the leg adjacent to ∠P.
2. Name the leg opposite ∠Q.
3. Name the hypotenuse.
4. Name the leg opposite ∠P.
5. Name the leg adjacent to ∠Q.
6. What is sin P?
7. What is cos Q?
8. What is tan Q?
9. What is cos P?
10. What is sin Q?

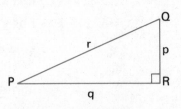

EXERCISES

PART A

Find tan *A*, sin *A*, cos *A*, tan *B*, sin *B*, and cos *B* to three decimal places.

1.

2.
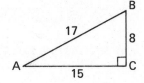

3.
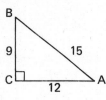

4.
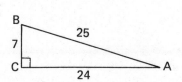

5.

6.
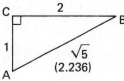

Find the value of each, to three decimal places.
Use the figure at the right.

7. tan 45°   **8.** sin 45°   **9.** cos 45°

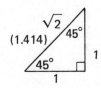

PART B

Show that each statement is true. Use the figure at the right.

10. sin *A* = cos *B*

11. sin *B* = cos *A*

12. $\tan A = \dfrac{1}{\tan B}$

13. (sin *A*)² + (cos *A*)² = 1 (Hint: Use the Pythagorean theorem.)

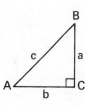

PART C

Find tan *A*, sin *A*, cos *A*, tan *B*, sin *B*, and cos *B*, to three decimal places.

14.
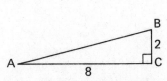

15.
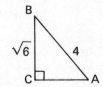

16.

17. Show that the sine of an angle is equal to the cosine of its complement.

18. Explain why the sine of an angle is between 0 and 1.

Graphing in Space

We add a z-axis perpendicular to the x-axis and y-axis, to plot points in space.

The points are described by ordered triples (x, y, z)

To plot point
E (−5, −2, 4)

x-coordinate / z-coordinate
    y-coordinate

first plot the point
B (−5, −2) in the xy-plane
then move the point to
the 4 position on the
z-axis.

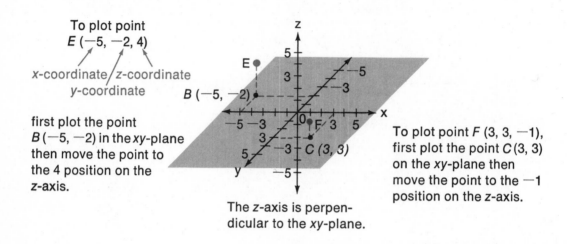

The z-axis is perpen-
dicular to the xy-plane.

To plot point F (3, 3, −1),
first plot the point C (3, 3)
on the xy-plane then
move the point to the −1
position on the z-axis.

Plot (−5, −1) in xy-plane
then move point to 2
position on z-axis.

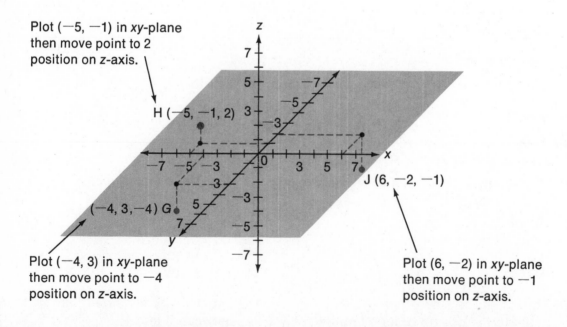

Plot (−4, 3) in xy-plane
then move point to −4
position on z-axis.

Plot (6, −2) in xy-plane
then move point to −1
position on z-axis.

What does the graph of the equation $z = 4$ look like?

Graph $\{ (x, y, z) \mid z = 4 \}$.

the set of all   such $z = 4$
ordered triples   that

All points in space which have z-coordinate 4 lie in a plane parallel to the xy-plane and 4 units above it.

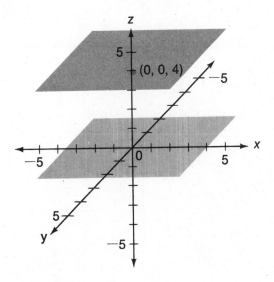

Similarly, the graph of $\{(x, y, z) \mid y = 2\}$ is a plane parallel to the xz-plane and perpendicular to xy-plane.

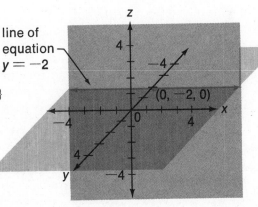

line of
equation
$y = -2$

What do you think the graph of $\{(x, y, z) \mid x = -3\}$ looks like?
Draw a three-dimension system and graph $x = -3$.

Tables of Trigonometric Ratios

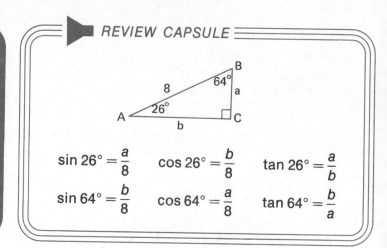

REVIEW CAPSULE

$$\sin 26° = \frac{a}{8} \qquad \cos 26° = \frac{b}{8} \qquad \tan 26° = \frac{a}{b}$$

$$\sin 64° = \frac{b}{8} \qquad \cos 64° = \frac{a}{8} \qquad \tan 64° = \frac{b}{a}$$

The table gives decimal approximations. ⟶ The table on page 479 gives the values of sine, cosine, and tangent for angles from 0° to 90°.

Part of the table ⟶

Angle Measure	Sin	Cos	Tan	Angle Measure	Sin	Cos	Tan
10°	.1736	.9848	.1763	56°	.8290	.5592	1.483
11°	.1908	.9816	.1944	57°	.8387	.5446	1.540
12°	.2079	.9781	.2126	58°	.8480	.5299	1.600
13°	.2250	.9744	.2309	59°	.8572	.5150	1.664
14°	.2419	.9703	.2493	60°	.8660	.5000	1.732
15°	.2588	.9659	.2679	61°	.8746	.4848	1.804
16°	.2756	.9613	.2867	62°	.8829	.4695	1.881
17°	.2924	.9563	.3057	63°	.8910	.4540	1.963

EXAMPLE 1   Use the table to find sin 61°, cos 61°, and tan 61°.

Find 61° in the angle column. ⟶ sin 61° = .8746   cos 61° = .4848   tan 61° = 1.804

EXAMPLE 2   Find m ∠ A if tan A = .3249.

Find .3249 in the tan column. ⟶
$$\tan 18° = .3249$$
Thus, m ∠ A = 18.

EXAMPLE 3   Find m ∠ B to the nearest degree, if cos B = .5392.

Find the closest value to .5392 in the cos column. ⟶
$$\cos 57° = .5446$$
Thus, m ∠ B = 57, to the nearest degree.

ORAL EXERCISES

Use the table on page 479 to find each value.

1. sin 5°   **2.** tan 21°   **3.** cos 78°   **4.** tan 36°   **5.** sin 59°
6. cos 48°   **7.** cos 8°   **8.** tan 12°   **9.** sin 86°   **10.** tan 53°
11. sin 74°   **12.** cos 81°   **13.** sin 26°   **14.** cos 30°   **15.** tan 89°
16. cos 18°   **17.** tan 65°   **18.** sin 42°   **19.** sin 15°   **20.** cos 61°

Use the table on page 479 to find $m \angle A$.

21. cos A = .3256   **22.** sin A = .9781   **23.** tan A = .6494
24. sin A = .2250   **25.** tan A = 1.428   **26.** sin A = .6428
27. cos A = .9998   **28.** tan A = 28.64   **29.** cos A = .7193
30. tan A = .1763   **31.** cos A = .8910   **32.** sin A = .7547

EXERCISES

PART A

Find $m \angle B$, to the nearest degree. Use the table on page 479.

1. tan B = .1398   **2.** cos B = .7452   **3.** sin B = .3915
4. cos B = .9281   **5.** tan B = .6637   **6.** cos B = .5099
7. sin B = .7583   **8.** tan B = 1.396   **9.** sin B = .9725
10. tan B = 1.126   **11.** cos B = .1186   **12.** sin B = .0716

PART B

True or false? Use the figure at the right.

13. $\tan A = \dfrac{b}{a}$ **14.** $\sin B = \dfrac{b}{c}$ **15.** $\cos A = \dfrac{b}{c}$

16. $\tan A = \tan B$ **17.** $\sin A = \cos B$ **18.** $\tan A = \dfrac{1}{\tan A}$

19. $\sin B = \cos B$ **20.** $a^2 + b^2 = c^2$ **21.** $a + b = c$

22. $\angle A$ and $\angle B$ are complementary.
23. $\angle A$ and $\angle B$ are acute.
24. If $m \angle A > m \angle B$, then sin A > sin B.
25. If $m \angle A > m \angle B$, then cos A > cos B.
26. If tan A < tan B, then $m \angle A > m \angle B$.
27. $(\sin A)^2 + (\cos A)^2 = 1$
28. sin 45° = cos 45°
29. $(\cos A)^2 = 1 - (\sin A)^2$

PART C

Suppose $m \angle A$ increases from 0° to 90°.

30. What happens to sin A? Why?

31. What happens to cos A? Why?

32. What happens to tan A? Why?

Solving Right Triangles

▶ REVIEW CAPSULE

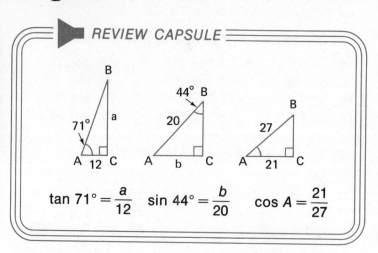

$$\tan 71° = \frac{a}{12} \qquad \sin 44° = \frac{b}{20} \qquad \cos A = \frac{21}{27}$$

EXAMPLE 1   If $m\angle A = 65$ and $c = 15$, find a, to the nearest tenth.

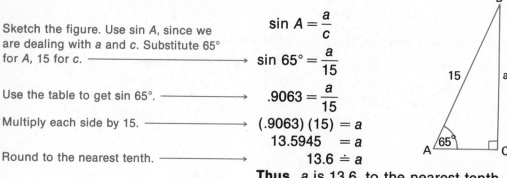

Sketch the figure. Use sin A, since we are dealing with a and c. Substitute 65° for A, 15 for c. ⟶

$$\sin A = \frac{a}{c}$$

$$\sin 65° = \frac{a}{15}$$

Use the table to get sin 65°. ⟶

$$.9063 = \frac{a}{15}$$

Multiply each side by 15. ⟶

$$(.9063)(15) = a$$
$$13.5945 \quad = a$$

Round to the nearest tenth. ⟶

$$13.6 \doteq a$$

Thus, a is 13.6, to the nearest tenth.

EXAMPLE 2   If $m\angle B = 51$ and $a = 10$, find c, to the nearest tenth.

$$\cos B = \frac{a}{c}$$

Substitute 51° for B, 10 for a. ⟶

$$\cos 51° = \frac{10}{c}$$

Use the table. ⟶

$$.6293 = \frac{10}{c}$$

Multiply each side by c. ⟶

$$.6293c = 10$$

Divide each side by .6293. ⟶

$$c = \frac{10}{.6293}$$

$$c \doteq 15.9$$

Thus c is 15.9, to the nearest tenth.

EXAMPLE 3 If $m\angle A = 27$ and $a = 18$, find b, to the nearest tenth.

Sketch the figure. ⟶

B

27°

18

A _____ C
     b

	First way	**Second way**

First way

$$\tan A = \frac{a}{b}$$

$$\tan 27° = \frac{18}{b}$$

$$.5095 = \frac{18}{b}$$

$$.5095b = 18$$

$$b = \frac{18}{.5095}$$

$$b \doteq 35.3$$

We can use tan A or tan B. ⟶

$$\tan A = \frac{18}{b}$$

$$\tan B = \frac{b}{18}$$

Second way

$$m\angle B = 90 - 27 = 63$$

$$\tan B = \frac{b}{a}$$

$$\tan 63° = \frac{b}{18}$$

$$1.963 = \frac{b}{18}$$

$$(1.963)(18) = b$$

$$35.334 = b$$

$$35.3 \doteq b$$

Note: In the second way, we multiply rather than divide.

Thus, b is 35.3, to the nearest tenth.

EXAMPLE 4 If $a = 16$ and $b = 10$, find $m\angle A$, to the nearest tenth.

$$\tan A = \frac{a}{b}$$

Substitute 16 for a, 10 for b. ⟶ $\tan A = \dfrac{16}{10}$

$$\tan A = 1.600$$

Use the tan column: $\tan 58° = 1.600$. ⟶ $m\angle A \doteq 58$

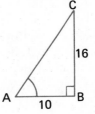

C

16

A _____ B
    10

Thus, $m\angle A$ is 58, to the nearest degree.

EXAMPLE 5 If $a = 12$ and $c = 18$, find $m\angle B$, to the nearest degree.

Note: An alternate way is to use sin A.

$$\cos B = \frac{a}{c}$$

Substitute 12 for a, 18 for c. ⟶ $\cos B = \dfrac{12}{18}$

$$\cos B = \frac{2}{3}$$

$$\cos B = .6667$$

Use the cos column: $\cos 48° = .6691$. ⟶ $m\angle B \doteq 48$

B

18   12

A _____ C

Thus, $m\angle B$ is 48, to the nearest degree.

EXERCISES

PART A

Find the indicated measure (side, to the nearest tenth or angle, to the nearest degree).

1.

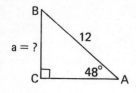

2.

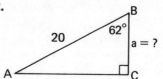

3.

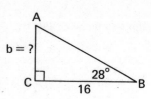

4.

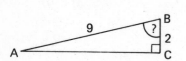

5.

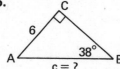

6.

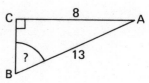

Find the indicated measure (side to the nearest tenth or angle to the nearest degree). Use the figure at the right.

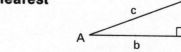

7. If $c = 7$ and $m\angle A = 42$, find a.
9. If $b = 18$ and $m\angle A = 10$, find c.
11. If $a = 2$ and $c = 4$, find $m\angle A$.
13. If $b = 18$ and $m\angle B = 35$, find a.

8. If $b = 8$ and $c = 13$, find $m\angle B$.
10. If $b = 28$ and $m\angle B = 82$, find a.
12. If $b = 16$ and $c = 20$, find $m\angle A$.
14. If $c = 30$ and $m\angle A = 27$, find a.

PART B

Find all the missing measures (sides to the nearest tenth or angles to the nearest degree).

15.

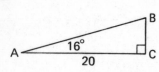

16.

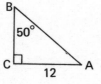

17.

18.

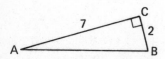

19.

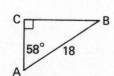

20.

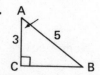

Applications of Trigonometry

<table>
<tr><td>

OBJECTIVE

■ To solve applied problems by using trigonometry

</td></tr>
</table>

Find x, to the nearest tenth.

$$\tan 36° = \frac{x}{12}$$

$$.7265 = \frac{x}{12}$$

$$(.7265)(12) = x$$

$$8.7180 = x$$

$$8.7 \doteq x$$

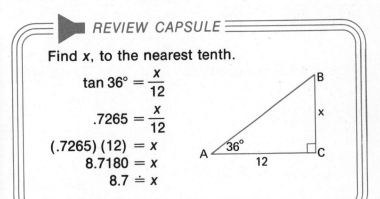

EXAMPLE 1   Find the height of the tree, to the nearest tenth of a foot.

Let x = height of tree in feet.

$\tan = \dfrac{\text{opp.}}{\text{adj.}}$ ⟶

Use tan column. ⟶

Multiply each side by 25. ⟶

$$\tan 42° = \frac{x}{25}$$

$$.9004 = \frac{x}{25}$$

$$(.9004)(25) = x$$

$$22.5100 = x$$

$$22.5 \doteq x$$

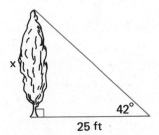

Thus, the tree is 22.5 feet tall, to the nearest tenth.

EXAMPLE 2   Find the distance across the lake from P to Q, to the nearest tenth of a meter.

Let x = PQ in meters.

$\cos = \dfrac{\text{adj.}}{\text{hyp.}}$ ⟶

Use cos column. ⟶

Multiply each side by x. ⟶

Divide each side by .3746. ⟶

$$\cos 68° = \frac{36}{x}$$

$$.3746 = \frac{36}{x}$$

$$.3746x = 36$$

$$x = \frac{36}{.3746}$$

$$x \doteq 96.1$$

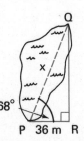

Thus, the distance from P to Q is 96.1 meters, to the nearest tenth.

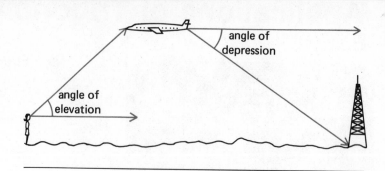

EXAMPLE 3   A power-line tower casts a 160-foot shadow when the angle of elevation of the sun measures 20°. How high is the tower?

$\tan = \dfrac{\text{opp.}}{\text{adj.}}$ ⟶

Use tan column. ⟶

Round to the nearest tenth. ⟶

$$\tan 20° = \frac{x}{160}$$

$$.3640 = \frac{x}{160}$$

$$(.3640)(160) = x$$
$$58.2400 = x$$
$$58.2 \doteq x$$

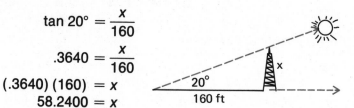

Thus, the power-line tower is about 58.2 feet high.

EXAMPLE 4   A skin diver is 10 feet away from his boat. The angle of depression from the diver to a coral formation measures 80°. The coral is directly below the boat. How far is it from the diver?

Let x = distance between diver and coral in feet; $\cos = \dfrac{\text{adj.}}{\text{hyp.}}$ ⟶

Use cos column. ⟶

Divide and round to the nearest tenth. ⟶

$$\cos 80° = \frac{10}{x}$$

$$.1736 = \frac{10}{x}$$

$$.1736x = 10$$

$$x = \frac{10}{.1736}$$

$$x \doteq 57.6$$

Thus, the coral is about 57.6 feet from the diver.

EXERCISES

PART A

Find x, to the nearest tenth.

1.
36 m

2.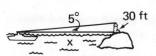
28° 42 ft

3.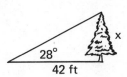
80 yd 54°

4.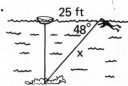
25 ft 48°

5.
5° 30 ft x

6.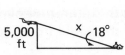
5,000 ft x 18°

7.
x 32° 55 mi

8.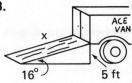
ACE VAN x 16° 5 ft

Give answers to the nearest tenth or to the nearest degree.

9. The angle of elevation from a ship to the top of a 50-foot lighthouse on the coast measures 13°. How far from the coast is the ship?

10. A kite is flying at the end of a 200-foot string (straight). The string makes an angle of 68° with the ground. How high above the ground is the kite?

11. A tree casts a 60-foot shadow when the angle of elevation of the sun measures 58°. How tall is the tree?

12. A ramp is 400 feet long. It rises a vertical distance of 32 feet. Find the measure of its angle of elevation.

13. Each step of a stairway rises 7" for a tread width of 11". What angle does the stairway make with the floor?

14. A 30-foot ladder makes an angle of 55° with the ground as it leans against a building. At what height does it touch the building?

15. A plane is flying at an altitude of 10,000 feet. The angle of elevation from an object on the ground to the plane measures 28°. How far is the object from the plane?

16. A cliff is 150 feet above the sea. From the cliff the angle of depression of a boat in the sea measures 8°. How far is the boat from the base of the cliff?

PART B

17. The leg opposite the 20° angle in a right triangle measures 6 feet. Find the area of the triangle. (Hint: $A = \frac{1}{2}bh$.)

18. A 12-foot diagonal of a rectangle makes an angle of 56° with a side of the rectangle. Find the dimensions of the rectangle.

Chapter Sixteen Review

In each case, $\triangle ABC \sim \triangle DEF$. Find x and y. $[p.\ 448]$

1.

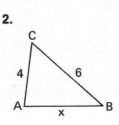

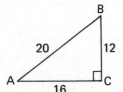

2.

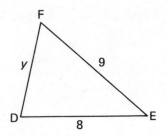

Find tan A, sin A, cos A, tan B, sin B, and cos B, to three decimal places. Then find $m \angle A$ and $m \angle B$, to the nearest degree. Use the table on page 479. $[p.\ 451,\ 456]$

3.

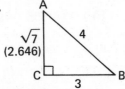

4.

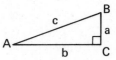

5.

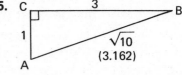

Find the indicated measure (side to the nearest tenth or angle to the nearest degree). Use the figure at the right. $[p.\ 458]$

6. If $b = 12$ and $m \angle B = 36$, find c.
7. If $a = 20$ and $m \angle B = 16$, find b.
8. If $c = 8$ and $m \angle A = 59$, find a.
9. If $b = 6$ and $c = 10$, find $m \angle A$.
10. If $c = 16$ and $m \angle B = 82$, find a.
11. If $b = 18$ and $m \angle A = 30$, find c.
12. If $a = 9$ and $b = 13$, find $m \angle B$.
13. If $a = 26$ and $m \angle A = 73$, find b.

14. An angle measures 15° less than twice its complement. Find the measure of the angle and its complement. $[p.\ 445]$

15. One acute angle of a right triangle measures 10° more than 4 times the other. Find the measures of the two acute angles. $[p.\ 445]$

16. Two angles of a triangle have the same measure. The third angle measures 4° more than the sum of the first two. Find the measures of the three angles. $[p.\ 445]$

17. Jane is 5 ft 9 in tall. She casts a shadow 10 feet long while a tree casts a shadow 13 ft 4 in long. How tall is the tree? $[p.\ 448]$

18. The angle of elevation from point A to the top of a building measures 38°. Point A is 40 meters from the base of the building. How tall is the building? $[p.\ 461]$

19. A ramp is to be constructed so that it rises 6 feet and makes an angle of 12° with the ground. How long should the ramp be? $[p.\ 461]$

Chapter Sixteen Test

In each case, △ABC ~ △DEF. Find x and y.

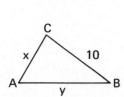

2.

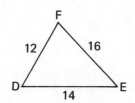

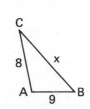

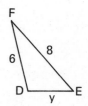

For △ABC, find the following, to three decimal places, or to the nearest degree. Use the table on page 479.

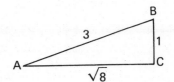

3. cos A

4. cos B

5. sin A

6. tan B

7. m∠A

8. m∠B

Find the indicated measure (side to the nearest tenth or angle to the nearest degree). Use the figure at the right.

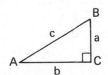

9. If c = 16 and m∠A = 38, find a.

10. If b = 22 and m∠A = 71, find c.

11. If a = 15 and m∠B = 47, find b.

12. If a = 17 and c = 22, find m∠B.

Find x, to the nearest tenth.

13.

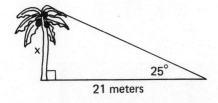

21 meters

14.

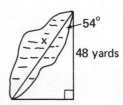

48 yards

15. The complement of an angle measures 14° less than 3 times the measure of the angle. Find the measure of the angle and its complement.

16. One angle of a triangle measures 5° more than the second. The third angle measures 25° less than twice the measure of the second. Find the measures of the three angles.

17. A 24-foot ladder makes an angle of 62° with the ground. At what height does it touch the side of the building which it leans against?

18. A building casts a 200-foot shadow when the angle of elevation of the sun measures 55°. How tall is the building?

Distance Formula

PROBLEM: Find the distance between A (3, 2) and B (7, 5).

Plot the points

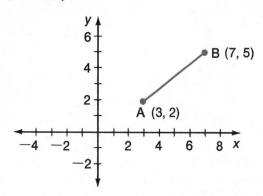

Draw a right triangle.

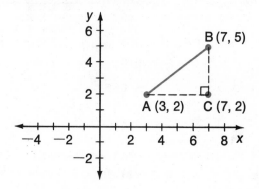

Use the Pythagorean Theorem.

$$(AB)^2 = (AC)^2 + (BC)^2$$

$$(AB)^2 = 4^2 + 3^2$$
$$AB = \sqrt{16 + 9}$$
$$AB = \sqrt{25}$$
$$AB = 5$$

Distance Formula

The distance between points A and B is

$$d = \sqrt{(x\text{-coord. } B - x\text{-coord. } A)^2 + (y\text{-coord. } B - y\text{-coord. } A)^2}$$

Use the distance formula to show that the triangles with these given vertices are isosceles

1. A (1, 0)   B (5, 0)   C (3, 4)
2. A (2, 3)   B (5, 7)   C (1, 4)

GLOSSARY

The explanations given in this glossary are intended to be brief descriptions of the terms listed. They are not necessarily definitions.

Absolute value The absolute value of a positive number or zero is the number itself. The absolute value of a negative number is the opposite of the number. We read $|x|$ as the absolute value of x.
Examples $|-3| = 3, |2| = 2, |0| = 0$

Acute An angle is an acute angle if its measure is less than $90°$.
Example $m \angle A = 72; \angle A$ is an acute angle.

Addition property for equations We can add the same number to each side of an equation. If $a = b$ is true, then $a + c = b + c$ is also true, for all numbers a, b, and c.

Addition property for inequalities We can add the same number to each side of a true inequality, and the result is another true inequality of the same order. If $a < b$, then $a + c < b + c$.

Additive identity Zero is the additive identity since adding zero to a number gives the same number.

Additive inverse The additive inverse of a number is the opposite of the number. -6 is the additive inverse of 6. 8 is the additive inverse of -8. 0 is its own additive inverse.

Adjacent side In a triangle, a side is adjacent to an angle if it is contained in the angle.

Angle An angle is a figure formed by two rays with a common endpoint.

Area of a rectangle The area of a rectangle is given by the formula $A = l \cdot w$, where l is the length and w is the width.

Associative property of addition When adding, we can change the grouping of the addends. $(a + b) + c = a + (b + c)$, for all numbers a, b, and c.

Associative property of multiplication When multiplying, we can change the grouping of the factors. $(a \cdot b) \cdot c = a \cdot (b \cdot c)$, for all numbers a, b, and c.

Base   In 3^4, the 3 is the base. $3^4 = 3 \cdot 3 \cdot 3 \cdot 3$. The base is used 4 times as a factor.

Binomial   A binomial is a polynomial with two terms.

Coefficient   A coefficient is the multiplier of a variable. In $6a - 3b + 8$, 6 is the coefficient of a, and -3 is the coefficient of b.

Combine   To combine like terms in an expression such as $5y - 9y$, we use the distributive property.
$$5y - 9y = (5 - 9)y$$
$$= -4y$$

Commutative property of addition   When adding, we can change the order of the addends. $a + b = b + a$, for all numbers a and b.

Commutative property of multiplication   When multiplying, we can change the order of the factors. $a \cdot b = b \cdot a$, for all numbers a and b.

Complement   If the sum of the measures of two angles is 90°, then each angle is the complement of the other.

Complementary angles   Two angles are complementary if the sum of their measures is 90°.

Completing the square   Completing the square is a method for finding the solution set of a quadratic equation.

Complex fraction   A complex fraction is one whose numerator or denominator or both contain a fraction. $\frac{\frac{3}{4}}{\frac{1}{3}}$ is a complex fraction.

Consecutive even integers   Consecutive even integers have a factor of 2 and follow each other from smallest to largest. 6, 8, and 10 are consecutive even integers.

Consecutive integers   Consecutive integers follow each other from smallest to largest.
Examples   4, 5, 6; $-23, -22, -21, -20$

Consecutive odd integers   Consecutive odd integers do not have a factor of 2, and they follow each other from smallest to largest. 7, 9, and 11 are consecutive odd integers.

Constant function   A constant function is a function whose graph is a horizontal line or a subset of a horizontal line.

Constant of variation   For a direct variation $\frac{y}{x} = k$, k is the constant of variation, or constant of proportionality. For an inverse variation $xy = k$, k is the constant of variation.

Convenient form   A polynomial is in convenient form if its terms are in descending order of exponents, and the coefficient of the first term is positive. $6x - 2x^2 + 3$ is in convenient form when it is expressed as $-1(2x^2 - 6x - 3)$.

Converse   The converse of an if–then statement is formed by reversing the if and the then parts.

Converse of the Pythagorean theorem   If the sum of the squares of the lengths of two sides of a triangle equals the square of the length of the third side, then the triangle is a right triangle. In a triangle, if $a^2 + b^2 = c^2$, then the triangle is a right triangle.

Coordinate(s) of a point   On a number line, the coordinate of a point is the number which corresponds to the point. In a coordinate plane, the coordinates of a point make up the ordered pair which corresponds to the point.

Coordinate plane   Two perpendicular number lines in a plane make up a coordinate plane, or a coordinate system. Each point in a coordinate plane corresponds to an ordered pair of numbers, and vice versa.

Correspond   A number corresponds to a point on a number line, and vice versa. An ordered pair corresponds to a point in a coordinate plane, and vice versa.

— "Corresponds to" means "is associated with."

Corresponding angles The corresponding angles of two similar figures are the pairs of angles which have the same measure.

Corresponding sides The pairs of corresponding sides of two similar figures are the sides which lie opposite the pairs of corresponding angles.

Cosine of an angle The cosine of an acute angle of a right triangle is the ratio of the length of the side adjacent to the angle to the length of the hypotenuse.

Decrease 12 decreased by 8 means $12 - 8$, or 4.

Denominator In the fraction $\frac{7}{8}$, 8 is the denominator.

Descending order A polynomial is in descending order of exponents if the terms are arranged so that the exponents decrease from highest to lowest. $7x^3 - 4x^2 + x - 8$ is in descending order.

Diagonal A diagonal of a figure is a line segment joining opposite corners.

Difference The difference is the result of a subtraction. In $17 - 8 = 9$, 9 is the difference.

Difference of two squares $a^2 - b^2$ represents the difference of two squares. $a^2 - b^2$ may be factored as $(a + b)(a - b)$.

Diminish 8 diminished by 5 means 8 decreased by 5, which is $8 - 5$, or 3.

Directed distance The directed distance from P to Q on a number line is equal to the coordinate of Q minus the coordinate of P. $\vec{d}(PQ) =$ coordinate of $Q -$ coordinate of P.

Direct variation A direct variation is a function in which the ratio y to x is always the same. $\frac{y}{x} = k$, or $y = kx$ is a direct variation. y varies directly as x, or y is directly proportional to x.

Distributive property of multiplication over addition Multiplication is distributive over addition. $a(b + c) = a \cdot b + a \cdot c$ and $(b + c)a = b \cdot a + c \cdot a$, for all numbers a, b, and c.

Division property for equations We can divide each side of an equation by the same nonzero number. If $a = b$ is true, then $\frac{a}{c} = \frac{b}{c}$ is also true, for all numbers a, b, and c, $[c \neq 0]$.

Division property for inequalities We can divide each side of a true inequality by the same positive number, and the result is another true inequality of the same order. If $a < b$ and $c > 0$, then $\frac{a}{c} < \frac{b}{c}$.

We can divide each side of a true inequality by the same negative number, and the result is another true inequality of the reverse order. If $a < b$ and $c < 0$, then $\frac{a}{c} > \frac{b}{c}$.

Domain of a relation The domain of a relation is the set of all first elements of the ordered pairs in the relation. For the relation $\{(0, 1), (2, -5), (4, 3)\}$, the domain is $\{0, 2, 4\}$.

Elements The objects which belong to a set are the elements, or members of the set.

Empty set The empty set is the set containing no elements. The symbol ϕ means the empty set.

Equal sets Two sets are equal if they have the same elements.

Equation A setence with $=$ is an equation.

Equation of a line $y = mx + b$ is an equation of a line in a coordinate plane. m is the slope of the line and b is the y-intercept.

Equivalent equations Equivalent equations are equations which have the same solution.

Evaluate To evaluate an expression means to find its value. To evaluate $7x + 4$ if $x = 3$, we replace x with 3 and compute.
Example $7x + 4$
$7(3) + 4$
$21 + 4$
25

Even integer   An even integer has a factor of 2. $\ldots, -4, -2, 0, 2, 4, 6, \ldots$ are even integers.

Exponent   In 3^4, the 4 is an exponent. $3^4 = 3 \cdot 3 \cdot 3 \cdot 3$. A positive integer tells how many times the base (3) is used as a factor.

Extraneous solution   An extraneous solution of an equation is an apparent solution that does not check.

Extremes   In the proportion $\frac{a}{b} = \frac{c}{d}$, a and d are the extremes.

Factors   Factors are numbers which are multiplied. In $5 \cdot 8 = 40$, 5 and 8 are factors.

Factor a number   To factor a number means to rename the number as a product of whole numbers. We may factor 12 as $12 \cdot 1$, $6 \cdot 2$, or $3 \cdot 4$.

Factor a trinomial   To factor a trinomial means to express it as the product of two binomials. $x^2 - 5x + 6$ can be factored as $(x - 2)(x - 3)$.

Finite set   A set is finite if it contains a definite number of elements. $\{2, 4, 6\}$ is a finite set.

Fraction   A fraction is an indicated quotient of two numbers.

Fractional equation   A fractional equation is an equation which contains one or more fractions.

Fulcrum   The fulcrum of a lever is the point where the lever balances.

Function   A function is a relation in which no two ordered pairs have the same first element.

Graph of an equation (inequality)   In a coordinate plane, the graph of an equation (inequality) is the set of all points and only those points whose coordinates satisfy the equation (inequality).

Graph of a number   On a number line, the graph of a number is the point which corresponds to the number.

Graph of an ordered pair   In a coordinate plane, the graph of an ordered pair is the point which corresponds to the ordered pair.

Graph of a set   The graph of a set is the graph of all the numbers or all the ordered pairs in the set.

Greatest common factor (GCF)   The greatest common factor of two numbers is the greatest number which is a factor of both numbers. 8 is the GCF of 16 and 24.

Horizontal line   A horizontal line in a coordinate plane is parallel to the x-axis.

Hypotenuse   The hypotenuse of a right triangle is the side opposite the right angle.

Increase   3 increased by 7 means $3 + 7$, or 10.

Inequality   An inequality is a sentence with $\neq, <, >, \leq,$ or $\geq$. $x + 3 < 7$ is an inequality.

Infinite set   A set is infinite if it contains no definite number of elements. $\{1, 2, 3, 4, \ldots\}$ is an infinite set.

Integer   The numbers $\ldots, -4, -3, -2, -1, 0, 1, 2, 3, 4, \ldots$ are integers.

Intersection of sets   The intersection of two sets A and B is the set of all elements common to both sets A and B. $\cap$ is the symbol for intersection.

Inverse of a relation   Relation B is the inverse of relation A if the first and second elements of the ordered pairs in A are interchanged to form B.

Inverse variation   An inverse variation is a function in which the product xy is always the same. $xy = k$, or $y = \frac{k}{x}$ is an inverse variation. y varies inversely as x, or y is inversely proportional to x.

Irrational number   An irrational number cannot be expressed in the form $\frac{a}{b}$, where a and b are integers and $b \neq 0$. Nonrepeating decimals are irrational numbers.

Least common denominator (LCD) The least common denominator of two or more fractions is the smallest number which has each denominator as a factor. The LCD of $\frac{1}{2}$, $\frac{2}{3}$, and $\frac{3}{4}$ is 12.

Leg The legs of a right triangle are the two sides which form the right angle.

Less than 7 less than 9 means $9 - 7$, or 2.

Like radicals Like radicals are expressions which contain the same radical. $5\sqrt{2x}$ and $-3\sqrt{2x}$ are like radicals.

Like terms Like terms contain the same variable or variables. $5xy$ and $-3xy$ are like terms. $-8b$ and $11b^2$ are unlike terms.

Linear function A linear function is a function whose graph is a line or a subset of a line which is neither vertical nor horizontal.

Means In the proportion $\frac{a}{b} = \frac{c}{d}$, b and c are the means.

Member of a set The objects which belong to a set are the members (elements) of the set. In $\{3, -1, 0\}$, the members of the set are 3, -1, and 0.

Monomial A monomial is a polynomial with one term.

More than 8 more than 5 means $5 + 8$, or 13.

Multiplication property for equations We can multiply each side of an equation by the same number. If $a = b$ is true, then $a(c) = b(c)$ is also true, for all numbers a, b, and c.

Multiplication property for inequalities We can multiply each side of a true inequality by the same *positive* number, and the result is another true inequality of the *same order*. If $a < b$ and $c > 0$, then $a \cdot c < b \cdot c$.
We can multiply each side of a true inequality by the same *negative* number, and the result is another true inequality of the *reverse order*.
If $a < b$ and $c < 0$, then $a \cdot c > b \cdot c$.

Multiplication property of -1 Multiplying any number by -1 gives the opposite of that number. $(-1)(a) = -a$ and $(a)(-1) = -a$, for each number a.

Multiplicative inverse Two numbers are multiplicative inverses (reciprocals) if their product is 1.

Negative number A number is negative if it lies to the left of zero on a number line. $-5, -1, -\frac{1}{2}$, and $-\frac{4}{3}$ are negative numbers.

Nonrepeating decimal A nonrepeating decimal has no digit or group of digits which repeats forever. The decimal .010110111011110 . . . is a nonrepeating decimal.

Nonterminating decimal A nonterminating decimal has an infinite number of digits.

Numerator In the fraction $\frac{7}{8}$, 7 is the numerator.

Odd integer An odd integer does not have a factor of 2. $. . ., -5, -3, -1, 0, 1, 3, 5, 7, . . .$ are odd integers.

Open sentence An open sentence is a sentence which contains a variable. $7y - 3 = 5$ is an open sentence because it contains the variable y.

Opposite numbers Opposite numbers are the same distance from zero on the number line. -5 is the opposite of 5. 12 is the opposite of -12. 0 is its own opposite. The symbol $-x$ is read the opposite of x.

Opposite side In a triangle, a side is opposite an angle if it is not contained in the angle.

Ordered pair $(-4, 1)$ is an ordered pair of numbers. Each ordered pair of numbers corresponds to a point in a coordinate plane, and vice versa.

Order of inequalities   Two inequalities are of the same order if both contain < or if both contain >. Two inequalities are of the reverse order if one contains > and the other contains <.

Order of operations   When both multiplications and additions occur, we agree to multiply first and then add.
Example $5 + 7 \cdot 3 = 5 + 21$
$= 26$

Origin   The origin is the point for zero on a number line. The origin is the point for $(0, 0)$ in a coordinate plane.

Parallel   Lines are parallel if they lie in the same plane and never meet.

Perfect square   A perfect square is a number whose principal square root is a whole number. 36 is a perfect square since its principal square root is 6, and 6 is a whole number. 37 is not a perfect square.

Perimeter   The perimeter of a figure is the distance around the figure. If a triangle has sides measuring 6 inches, 7 inches, and 10 inches, then its perimeter is $6 + 7 + 10$, or 23 inches.

Perpendicular lines   Two lines are perpendicular if they form right angles $(90°)$. $\perp$ means is perpendicular to.

Plane   A plane is a flat surface.

Plot   To plot a point in a coordinate plane means to mark the point which corresponds to a given ordered pair of numbers.

Polynomial   A polynomial contains one or more terms.
Examples $2x^2$, $5x + 3$, $7a^2 - 5a - 2$

Positive number   A number is positive if it lies to the right of zero on a number line. 8, 2, $\frac{1}{3}$, and $\frac{16}{5}$ are positive numbers.

Power 3^4 means the fourth power of 3. $3^4 = 3 \cdot 3 \cdot 3 \cdot 3$. 3 is used 4 times as a factor.

Power of a power   To raise a power to a power, we can multiply the exponents. $(x^m)^n = x^{m \cdot n}$.

Power of a product   To raise a product to a power, we can raise each factor in the product to that power. $(x^m \cdot y^n)^p = x^{m \cdot p} \cdot y^{n \cdot p}$.

Prime factorization   The prime factorization of 20 is $2 \cdot 2 \cdot 5$, since $2 \cdot 2 \cdot 5 = 20$, and 2 and 5 are prime numbers.

Prime number   A prime number is a whole number greater than 1 whose only factors are itself and 1. 2, 3, 5, 7, 11, . . . are prime numbers.

Principal square root   The principal square root of a number is the positive square root of the number. 6 is the principal square root of 36. We use the symbol $\sqrt{}$ to indicate the principal square root of a number.

Product   The product is the result of a multiplication. In $5 \cdot 6 = 30$, 30 is the product.

Product of powers   When multiplying two powers, if the bases are the same, we can add the exponents. $x^m \cdot x^n = x^{m+n}$.

Property of additive identity   Adding zero to a number gives the same number. $a + 0 = a$ and $0 + a = a$, for each number a.

Property of additive inverse   Adding two opposite numbers (additive inverses) gives zero. $a + (-a) = 0$, for each number a.

Property of multiplicative identity   Multiplying any number by 1 gives the same number. $(1)(a) = a$ and $(a)(1) = a$, for each number a.

Property of zero for multiplication   Multiplying any number by zero gives zero. $a \cdot 0 = 0$ and $0 \cdot a = 0$, for each number a.

Proportion   A proportion is an equation which states that two ratios are equal. $\frac{a}{b} = \frac{c}{d}$ is a proportion.

Protractor   A protractor is a tool for measuring angles.

Pythagorean theorem In any right triangle, the square of the length of the hypotenuse equals the sum of the squares of the lengths of the other two sides. If $\triangle ABC$ is a right triangle, then $a^2 + b^2 = c^2$.

Quadrant The x- and y-axes divide the coordinate plane into four quadrants.

Quadratic equation In a quadratic equation, the variable in one term is raised to the second power, but no higher. $3x^2 - 5x + 4 = 0$, $x^2 - 49 = 0$, and $6x^2 = 2$ are quadratic equations.

Quadratic formula The solutions of a quadratic equation of the form $ax^2 + bx + c = 0$ may be found by the formula $x = \dfrac{-b \pm \sqrt{b^2 - 4ac}}{2a}$. The formula is called the quadratic formula.

Quotient The quotient is the result of a division. In $54 \div 9 = 6$, 6 is the quotient.

Radical equation In a radical equation, the variable is in the radicand. $\sqrt{2x} = 6$ is a radical equation.

Range of a relation The range of a relation is the set of all second elements of the ordered pairs in the relation. For the relation $\{(0, 1), (2, -5), (4, 3)\}$, the range is $\{1, -5, 3\}$.

Ratio The ratio of a to b is the quotient $\dfrac{a}{b}$, or $a:b$. A ratio is a comparison of two numbers by division.

Rationalize the denominator To rationalize the denominator of a fraction means to write the fraction with no radical in the denominator. To rationalize the denominator of $\dfrac{\sqrt{5}}{\sqrt{3}}$, we multiply by $\dfrac{\sqrt{3}}{\sqrt{3}}$.

$$\frac{\sqrt{5}}{\sqrt{3}} \cdot \frac{\sqrt{3}}{\sqrt{3}} = \frac{\sqrt{15}}{3}.$$

Rational number A rational number is a number which can be written in the form $\dfrac{a}{b}$, where a and b are integers and $b \neq 0$. $\dfrac{3}{5}, \dfrac{-24}{7}$, 8, and .63 are rational numbers.

Real number The set of real numbers contains all the rational and all the irrational numbers. $\{\text{rationals}\} \cup \{\text{irrationals}\} = \{\text{reals}\}$.

Rearrange In an expression like $9x + 8 - 12x + 7$, we can rearrange the terms to simplify.
$$9x + 8 - 12x + 7 = (9x - 12x) + (8 + 7)$$
$$= -3x + 15$$
In an expression like $7 \cdot x \cdot 5 \cdot y$, we can rearrange the factors to simplify.
$$7 \cdot x \cdot 5 \cdot y = (7 \cdot 5) \cdot (x \cdot y)$$
$$= 35xy$$

Reciprocal Two numbers are reciprocals (multiplicative inverses) if their product is 1. 5 and $\dfrac{1}{5}$ are reciprocals since $5\left(\dfrac{1}{5}\right) = 1$.

Rectangle A rectangle is a four-sided figure with opposite sides the same length and four right angles.

Relation A relation is a set of ordered pairs. $\{(0, 1), (2, -5), (-4, 2)\}$ is a relation.

Relatively prime Two numbers are relatively prime if their only common factor is 1.

Repeating decimal A repeating decimal has a digit or a group of digits which repeats forever. The decimal .5858585858..., or $.58\overline{58}$, is a repeating decimal. The bar indicates that the digits repeat forever.

Replacement set A replacement set is the set of all numbers which may replace the variable in an open sentence or expression.

Right triangle A right triangle is a triangle with one right angle.

Root A root of an equation is a solution of the equation.

Satisfy If a variable in an equation is replaced with a number, and the result is a true statement, then the number satisfies the equation.

Sentence A mathematical sentence contains either $=$, $\neq$, $>$, $<$, $\geq$, or $\leq$. $4 + 5 = 9$ and $7 \leq x - 3$ are mathematical sentences.

Set A set is a collection of objects. We use braces { } to show a set.

Similar Two figures are similar if the corresponding angles are congruent and the lengths of the corresponding sides have the same ratio.

Simplest radical form An expression is in simplest radical form if it contains no factor which is a perfect square.

Simplify To simplify an expression means to replace it with the least complicated equivalent expression.

Sine of an angle The sine of an acute angle of a right triangle is the ratio of the length of the side opposite the angle to the length of the hypotenuse.

Slope of a line The slope of a line in a coordinate plane is the slope of any segment on the line. The slope of a horizontal line is zero. The slope of a vertical line is undefined.

Slope of a segment The slope of a segment in a coordinate plane is
$$\frac{\text{difference of } y\text{-coordinates}}{\text{difference of } x\text{-coordinates}}.$$

Solution A solution of an open sentence is a replacement of the variable which makes the sentence true. In $5x - 3 = 32$, 7 is a solution since $5(7) - 3 = 35 - 3 = 32$.

Solution set The solution set of an open sentence is the set of all members of the replacement set which are solutions of the sentence.

Solve To solve an open sentence means to find all of its solutions.

Square To square a number means to multiply it by itself.

Square of a number The square of a number is the product of the number and itself.

Square root x is a square root of n if $x \cdot x = n$. 6 is a square root of 36 since $6 \cdot 6 = 36$. Also, -6 is a square root of 36 since $(-6)(-6) = 36$.

Standard form A quadratic equation is in standard form if the coefficient of the x^2 term is positive, the polynomial is equal to zero, and the terms are arranged in descending order of exponents. $3x^2 - 6x + 1 = 0$ is in standard form. We use $ax^2 + bx + c = 0$ to represent the standard form of a quadratic equation.

Subset Set B is a subset of set A if every element of B is also in A. $B \subseteq A$ means B is a subset of A.

Substitute To substitute a value for a variable means to replace the variable with the particular value. For $8y - 9$, we can substitute the value 5 for y.
$$8y - 9$$
$$8(5) - 9$$
$$40 - 9$$
$$31$$

Subtract To subtract b from a means to add the opposite of b to a. $a - b = a + (-b)$, for all numbers a and b.

Sum The sum is the result of an addition. In $7 + 8 = 15$, 15 is the sum.

System of equations Two equations in two variables form a system of equations.
$$\begin{matrix} 2x + 3y = 6 \\ x - 4y = -3 \end{matrix} \text{ is a system.}$$

Tangent of an angle The tangent of an acute angle of a right triangle is the ratio of the length of the side opposite the angle to the length of the side adjacent to the angle.

Terminating decimal A terminating decimal has a finite number of digits.

Terms In $7x - 3y + 8$, the terms are $7x$, $-3y$, and 8. Terms are added.

Theorem A theorem is a property which can be proved.

Triangle   A triangle is a three-sided figure.

Trinomial   A trinomial is a polynomial with three terms.

Twice   Twice a number means two times the number. Twice x means $2x$.

Undefined fraction   A fraction is undefined if its denominator is zero.

Union of sets   The union of two sets A and B is the set of all elements belonging to set A or to set B or to both sets A and B. $\cup$ is the symbol for union.

Value of a function   If (x, y) is an ordered pair in function f, then the value of f at x is y. We read $f(x) = y$ as the value of f at x is y, or as f at x is y.

Variable   A variable takes the place of a number. In $5x - 3 = 7$, x is a variable.

Vertical line   A vertical line in a coordinate plane is parallel to the y-axis.

Vertical line test   A relation is a function if no vertical line crosses its graph in more than one point.

Whole number   The numbers 0, 1, 2, 3, . . . are whole numbers.

x-axis   The x-axis is the horizontal number line in a coordinate plane.

x-coordinate   The x-coordinate of an ordered pair of numbers is the first number in the pair. For $(5, -2)$, 5 is the x-coordinate.

y-axis   The y-axis is the vertical number line in a coordinate plane.

y-coordinate   The y-coordinate of an ordered pair of numbers is the second number in the pair. For $(5, -2)$, -2 is the y-coordinate.

y-intercept   The y-intercept of a line in a coordinate plane is the y-coordinate of the point of intersection of the line with the y-axis. In the equation of a line, $y = mx + b$, b is the y-intercept.

Zero   Zero (0) lies between the positive and the negative numbers on a number line. Zero is neither positive nor negative.

TABLES

Table of Roots and Powers

No.	Sq.	Sq. Root	Cube	Cu. Root	No.	Sq.	Sq. Root	Cube	Cu. Root
1	1	1.000	1	1.000	51	2,601	7.141	132,651	3.708
2	4	1.414	8	1.260	52	2,704	7.211	140,608	3.733
3	9	1.732	27	1.442	53	2,809	7.280	148,877	3.756
4	16	2.000	64	1.587	54	2,916	7.348	157,564	3.780
5	25	2.236	125	1.710	55	3,025	7.416	166,375	3.803
6	36	2.449	216	1.817	56	3,136	7.483	175,616	3.826
7	49	2.646	343	1.913	57	3,249	7.550	185,193	3.849
8	64	2.828	512	2.000	58	3,364	7.616	195,112	3.871
9	81	3.000	729	2.080	59	3,481	7.681	205,379	3.893
10	100	3.162	1,000	2.154	60	3,600	7.746	216,000	3.915
11	121	3.317	1,331	2.224	61	3,721	7.810	226,981	3.936
12	144	3.464	1,728	2.289	62	3,844	7.874	238,328	3.958
13	169	3.606	2,197	2.351	63	3,969	7.937	250,047	3.979
14	196	3.742	2,744	2.410	64	4,096	8.000	262,144	4.000
15	225	3.875	3,375	2.466	65	4,225	8.062	274,625	4.021
16	256	4.000	4,096	2.520	66	4,356	8.124	287,496	4.041
17	289	4.123	4,913	2.571	67	4,489	8.185	300,763	4.062
18	324	4.243	5,832	2.621	68	4,624	8.246	314,432	4.082
19	361	4.359	6,859	2.668	69	4,761	8.307	328,509	4.102
20	400	4.472	8,000	2.714	70	4,900	8.357	343,000	4.121
21	441	4.583	9,261	2.759	71	5,041	8.426	357,911	4.141
22	484	4.690	10,648	2.802	72	5,184	8.485	373,248	4.160
23	529	4.796	12,167	2.844	73	5,329	8.544	389,017	4.179
24	576	4.899	13,824	2.884	74	5,476	8.602	405,224	4.198
25	625	5.000	15,625	2.924	75	5,625	8.660	421,875	4.217
26	676	5.099	17,576	2.962	76	5,776	8.718	438,976	4.236
27	729	5.196	19,683	3.000	77	5,929	8.775	456,533	4.254
28	784	5.292	21,952	3.037	78	6,084	8.832	474,552	4.273
29	841	5.385	24,389	3.072	79	6,241	8.888	493,039	4.291
30	900	5.477	27,000	3.107	80	6,400	8.944	512,000	4.309
31	961	5.568	29,791	3.141	81	6,561	9.000	531,441	4.327
32	1,024	5.657	32,768	3.175	82	6,724	9.055	551,368	4.344
33	1,089	5.745	35,937	3.208	83	6,889	9.110	571,787	4.362
34	1,156	5.831	39,304	3.240	84	7,056	9.165	592,704	4.380
35	1,225	5.916	42,875	3.271	85	7,225	9.220	614,125	4.397
36	1,296	6.000	46,656	3.302	86	7,396	9.274	636,056	4.414
37	1,369	6.083	50,653	3.332	87	7,569	9.327	658,503	4.431
38	1,444	6.164	54,872	3.362	88	7,744	9.381	681,472	4.448
39	1,521	6.245	59,319	3.391	89	7,921	9.434	704,969	4.465
40	1,600	6.325	64,000	3.420	90	8,100	9.487	729,000	4.481
41	1,681	6.403	68,921	3.448	91	8,281	9.539	753,571	4.498
42	1,764	6.481	74,088	3.476	92	8,464	9.592	778,688	4.514
43	1,849	6.557	79,507	3.503	93	8,649	9.644	804,357	4.531
44	1,936	6.633	85,184	3.530	94	8,836	9.695	830,584	4.547
45	2,025	6.708	91,125	3.557	95	9,025	9.747	857,375	4.563
46	2,116	6.782	97,336	3.583	96	9,216	9.798	884,736	4.579
47	2,209	6.856	103,823	3.609	97	9,409	9.849	912,673	4.595
48	2,304	6.928	110,592	3.634	98	9,604	9.899	941,192	4.610
49	2,401	7.000	117,649	3.659	99	9,801	9.950	970,299	4.626
50	2,500	7.071	125,000	3.684	100	10,000	10.000	1,000,000	4.642

Trigonometric Ratios

Angle Measure	Sin	Cos	Tan	Angle Measure	Sin	Cos	Tan
0°	0.000	1.000	0.000	46°	.7193	.6947	1.036
1°	.0175	.9998	.0175	47°	.7314	.6820	1.072
2°	.0349	.9994	.0349	48°	.7431	.6691	1.111
3°	.0523	.9986	.0524	49°	.7547	.6561	1.150
4°	.0698	.9976	.0699	50°	.7660	.6428	1.192
5°	.0872	.9962	.0875	51°	.7771	.6293	1.235
6°	.1045	.9945	.1051	52°	.7880	.6157	1.280
7°	.1219	.9925	.1228	53°	.7986	.6018	1.327
8°	.1392	.9903	.1405	54°	.8090	.5878	1.376
9°	.1564	.9877	.1584	55°	.8192	.5736	1.428
10°	.1736	.9848	.1763	56°	.8290	.5592	1.483
11°	.1908	.9816	.1944	57°	.8387	.5446	1.540
12°	.2079	.9781	.2126	58°	.8480	.5299	1.600
13°	.2250	.9744	.2309	59°	.8572	.5150	1.664
14°	.2419	.9703	.2493	60°	.8660	.5000	1.732
15°	.2588	.9659	.2679	61°	.8746	.4848	1.804
16°	.2756	.9613	.2867	62°	.8829	.4695	1.881
17°	.2924	.9563	.3057	63°	.8910	.4540	1.963
18°	.3090	.9511	.3249	64°	.8988	.4384	2.050
19°	.3256	.9455	.3443	65°	.9063	.4226	2.145
20°	.3420	.9397	.3640	66°	.9135	.4067	2.246
21°	.3584	.9336	.3839	67°	.9205	.3907	2.356
22°	.3746	.9272	.4040	68°	.9272	.3746	2.475
23°	.3907	.9205	.4245	69°	.9336	.3584	2.605
24°	.4067	.9135	.4452	70°	.9397	.3420	2.747
25°	.4226	.9063	.4663	71°	.9455	.3256	2.904
26°	.4384	.8988	.4877	72°	.9511	.3090	3.077
27°	.4540	.8910	.5095	73°	.9563	.2924	3.270
28°	.4695	.8829	.5317	74°	.9613	.2756	3.487
29°	.4848	.8746	.5543	75°	.9659	.2588	3.732
30°	.5000	.8660	.5774	76°	.9703	.2419	4.010
31°	.5150	.8572	.6009	77°	.9744	.2250	4.331
32°	.5299	.8480	.6249	78°	.9781	.2079	4.704
33°	.5446	.8387	.6494	79°	.9816	.1908	5.145
34°	.5592	.8290	.6745	80°	.9848	.1736	5.671
35°	.5736	.8192	.7002	81°	.9877	.1564	6.314
36°	.5878	.8090	.7265	82°	.9903	.1392	7.115
37°	.6018	.7986	.7536	83°	.9925	.1219	8.144
38°	.6157	.7880	.7813	84°	.9945	.1045	9.514
39°	.6293	.7771	.8098	85°	.9962	.0872	11.43
40°	.6428	.7660	.8391	86°	.9976	.0698	14.30
41°	.6561	.7547	.8693	87°	.9986	.0523	19.08
42°	.6691	.7431	.9004	88°	.9994	.0349	28.64
43°	.6820	.7314	.9325	89°	.9998	.0175	57.29
44°	.6947	.7193	.9657	90°	1.000	0.000	
45°	.7071	.7071	1.000				

INDEX

INDEX

Absolute value, 231–233
Addition
  associative property of, 6–8, 24–26
  commutative property of, 6–8, 24–26
  distributive property of multiplication over, 9–11, 14–17, 30
  of fractions, 203–205, 210–220
  of integers, 21–26
  of polynomials, 128–130
  omitting plus signs in, 37
  properties of for integers, 24–26
  solving systems of equations by, 291–298
  subtraction interpreted as, 38
Addition property for equations, 59–62
Addition property for inequalities, 99–101
Additive indentity, 24–26
Additive inverse, 24–26
Algebraic expressions
  evaluating, 4–5, 40–41
  simplifying, 14–15, 42–43
Angle(s), 445–447
  acute, 446
  complementary, 445
  congruent, 448
  corresponding, 448–450
Associative property
  of addition, 6–8, 24–26
  of multiplication, 6–8, 30

Base (exponential), 119–120
Between, 91
Binomial, 124, 145–147

Chapter reviews, 18, 52, 88, 116, 138, 172, 200, 228, 258, 282, 314, 338, 378, 414, 442, 464

Chapter tests, 19, 53, 89, 117, 139, 173, 201, 229, 259, 283, 315, 339, 379, 415, 443, 465
Coefficient(s), 4–5
  adding, 42
Commutative property
  of addition, 6–8, 24–26
  of multiplication, 6–8, 29–30
Completing the square, 423–426
Consistent system of equations, 287
Converse, 400
Coordinate of a point, 236
Cosine, 451–453

Decimals, 358–360
  nonrepeating, 382–383
  repeating, 361–363
  terminating, 361–363
Denominator(s), 175
  rationalizing, 408–410
Directed distances, 236–238
  horizontal, 249
  on lines parallel to one of the axes, 248–250
  vertical, 249
Direct variation, 330–333
Distributive property of multiplication over addition, 9–11, 14–17, 30
Division
  comparison of two numbers by, as ratio, 261
  distributive property of multiplication over, 11
  of fractions, 198–199
  of integers, 31–33
  of radicals, 408–410
  related to multiplication, 31
  see also Quotient
Division property for equations, 60–62
Division property for inequalities, 100–101

Domain
of a function, 323–324
of a relation, 317–319
Dry mixtures, 300–305

Empty set, 92, 105
English phrases to algebra, 70–71
Equation(s)
absolute value in, 234–235
as proportion, 261–262
equivalent, 341
fractional, 341–344, 346–349
graphs of, *see* graph(s)
of a line, 265–275
parentheses in, 68–69
properties of, 59–62
quadratic, 423–429, 434–437
radical, 417–422
solving, 59–62
system of, 285–287, 290–298
with decimals, 358–360
with variable on both sides, 64–66
Exponent(s), 119–123
evaluating, 119–120
even, 394–395
in simplifying radicals, 394–397
odd, 396–397
positive integers as, 119–120
properties of, 121–123
Expressions, *see* Algebraic expressions
Extraneous solution, 349
Extremes of a proportion, 262–264

Factor(s), 132–134
common monomial of fractions, 191–193
Factoring, 132–137
combined types of, 153–155
difference of two squares, 150–152
of polynomials in two variables, 156–157
of quadratic equations, 158–164
of trinomials, 145–148
out a common monomial, 135–137

Formula(s), 374–376
area of a rectangle, 385
area of a square, 385
perimeter, 374
Fractional equations, 341–344, 346–349
Fractional radicand, 411–412
Fractions, 175–199
addition of, 203–205, 210–220
common monomial factors of, 191–193
complex, 368–373
division of, 198–199
least common denominators of, 211
multiplication of, 180–183
reciprocal of, 175–176
rewriting in simplest form, 184–186
simplifying products, 194–196
simplifying using the negative one technique, 188–190, 224–226
subtraction of, 221–223
undefined, 176
Function(s), 317–324
constant, 320–322
domain of, 323–324
linear, 320–322
range of, 323–324

Graph(s)
of a function, 320–322
of a line, 272–278
of a relation, 317–319
of a vertical line, 279–280
of equations, 92–93
of inequalities, 94–96
of inequaltiies in two variables, 326–329
of intersection of two sets, 112–114
of solution sets involving absolute value, 233
of solution sets of inequalities, 94–96, 102–104
of systems of equations, 285–287
on the number line, 92–93

Greatest common factor, 135

Hypotenuse, 399

Identity
  additive, 24-26
  multiplicative, 44-45
Inconsistent system of equations, 287
Inequalities, 94-104
  graphing, 94-96
  graphs of solution sets, *see* graph(s)
  in two variables, 326-329
  properties for, 98-101
  solution sets of, 94-96, 102-104
Integers, 21
  addition of, 21-26, 36-38
  addition properties of, 24-26
  consecutive, 165-170
  consecutive even, 165
  consecutive odd, 166
  division of, 31-33
  multiplication of, 28-30
  multiplicative properties of, 28-30
  negative, 21
  omitting plus signs in addition of, 37
  on the number line, 21
  positive, 21
  subtraction of, 50-51
Inverse of a relation, 319
Inverse variation, 334-337
Irrational numbers, 382-383, 390

Least common denominator, 211,
  341-344, 346-349
Line(s)
  equations of, 265-275
  graphs of, 272-278
  parallel to the axes, 246-247
  perpendicular, 240
  slant of, 255-257

  vertical, 279-280
Line segment(s)
  slope of, 251-254, 255-257, 272-
  275

Means of a proportion, 262-264
Monomial, 124, 135-137
Multiplication
  associative property of, 6-8, 30
  commutative property of, 6-8, 29-
  30
  distributive property of over addi-
    tion, 9-11, 14-17, 30
  identity property of, 44-45
  of fractions, 180-182
  of integers, 28-30
  of polynomials, 141-143
  see also Product(s)
  property of negative one, 44-45, 48-
  49
  property of zero for, 28-30
  related to division, 31
Multiplication property for equations,
  60-62
Multiplication property for inequalities,
  99-101
Multiplicative inverse(s), 177

Number(s)
  absolute value of, 231-233
  corresponding to a point on the num-
    ber line, 21
  decimals, 358-360
  directed, 236-238
  even, 165
  integers, 21
  irrational, 382-383, 390
  odd, 165
  opposite, 24-25, 50-51
  prime, 132
  rational, 176, 361-363
  real, 382-383
  relatively prime, 184
  square root of, 384-386, 388-390
Number line
  absolute value and, 231
  addition of integers on, 21-22
  directed distance on, 236-238
  fractions on, 175
  integers on, 21
  origin of, 21
Numerator, 175

Operation(s)
   order of, 1–2
   related, 31
Opposite
   of a number, 24–25, 50–51
Ordered pair, 240
Order, of operations, 1–2
Origin, of a number line, 21
Origin, of a plane, 241

Parabola, 322
Parentheses, 1
   equations with, 68–69
   inner, 17
   removing, 46–47
Perfect square(s), 385–386
Perfect square trinomial, 423–426
Perimeter, 84–86, 374
Plane
   points in, 240–244
Point(s)
   coordinate of, 236
   corresponding to a number, 21
   locating in a plane, 240–241
   plotting in a plane, 242–244
Polynomial(s), 124–125, 128–130
   addition of, 128–130
   as denominators, 214–216
   classifying, 124–125
   convenient form of, 188
   factoring, 132–164
   factoring in two variables, 156–157
   multiplication of, 141–143
   simplifying, 124–125, 128–130
   subtraction of, 128–130
Power(s)
   of a number, 119–120
   of a power, 122–123
   of a product, 122–123
   product of, 121–123
Prime factorization, 132–133
Prime number, 132
Problems
   amounts of work, 350–357
   area, 437–439
   coin, 80–82
   consecutive integers, 168–170

dry mixtures, 300–305
   equations, 72–79
   fractional equations, 350–357
   number, 72–79
   number relations, 310–313
   perimeter, 84–86, 313
   quadratic equations, 437–439
   similar triangles, 448–450
   systems of equations, 302–305, 310–313
   translating English phrases to algebra, 70–71
   trigonometry, 461–463
Product(s)
   of extremes, 262–264
   of fractions, 175–176
   of means, 262–264
   of powers, 121–123
   of radicals, 404–406
   of two numbers with like signs, 28–30; with unlike signs, 28–30
   simplifying for fractions, 194–196
Proportion, 261–264
   extremes in, 262–264
   means in, 262–264
Protractor, 445
Pythagoras, 399
Pythagorean theorem, 399–401

Quadrant, 241
Quadratic equations, 158–164
   standard form of, 162–164
Quadratic formula, 427–429, 434–436
Quotient
   of two numbers with like signs, 31–33
   of two numbers with unlike signs, 32–33

Radical(s), 391–397
   combining, 402–403
   division of, 408–410
   even exponents, 394–395
   odd exponents, 396–397
   products of, 404–406
Radical equations, 417–422
Radicand, 392
   fractional, 411–412

Range
of a funtion, 323–324
of a relation, 317–319
Ratio(s), 261–264
trigonometric, 451–453, 456–457
Rationalization of denominators, 408–410
Rational numbers, 176, 361–363
Real number(s), 382–383
Reciprocal
of a fraction, 175–177
Rectangle
vertices of, 244
Relations(s), 317–319
domain of, 317–319
inverse of, 319
range of, 317–319
Relatively prime numbers, 184
Replacement set, 57

Sentences
false, 56
open, 56–58
true, 56
Set(s), 91–93
as subset of itself, 105
element of, 91
empty, 92
empty set as subset of every set, 105
equal, 91
finite, 91
infinite, 91
intersection of, 106–107, 112–114
member of, 91
replacement, 92
solution, *see* Solution Set(s)
subset of, 105–107
union of, 106–107, 112–114
Set notation, 91–92
Sine, 451–453
Slant of a line, 255–257
Slope
of a line, 272–275
of line segments, 251–254
Solution, 57
extraneous, 349

Solution set(s), 92
absolute value and, 232–233
graphing, *see* graph(s).
of fractional equations, 341–344, 346–349
of inequalities, 94–97, 102–104
of quadratic equations, 423–429, 434–437
of radical equations, 420–422
of systems of equations, 285–287
Square root(s), 384–386, 388–390
approximating, 388–390
negative, 384
of a negative number, 394
principal, 384
Substitution, solving systems of equations by, 290–292
Subtraction
distributive property of multiplication over, 11
interpreted as addition problems, 38
of fractions, 221–223
of integers, 50–51
of polynomials, 128–130
Symbols
braces, 91
brackets, 17
for a set, 91–92
for empty set, 92
infinite set, 91
inner parentheses, 17
is approximately equal to, 385
is a subset of, 105
is congruent to, 448
is equal to, 94
is greater than, 94
is less than, 94
is not equal to, 94
is perpendicular to, 240
negative integer, 21
parentheses, 1
positive integer, 21
radical sign, 392
raised dot, 1
square root of, 384
times sign, 1
union of, 106

Systems of equations, 285–287, 290–298

Tangent, 451–453
Terms, 4–5
   combining, 14–15
   combining like, 42–43
   like, 14–15
   of a polynomial, 124–125
   unlike, 14–15
Theorem, 399
Triangle(s), 445–450
   equilateral, 330
   right, 399–401, 451–453, 458–460
   similar, 448–450
Trigonometric ratios, 451–453, 456–457
   tables of, 456–457
Trigonometry, 451, 461–463
Trinomial, 124, 145–147, 423–426

Variable, 4–5
Vertex (of a rectangle), 244
Vertical lines, 279–280
Vertical line test, 320–322

x-axis, 241
x-coordinate, 240

y-axis, 241
y-coordinate, 240
y-intercept, 272–275

Zero
   as additive identity, 24–26
   as neither positive nor negative, 21
   in the denominator, 256
   property of for multiplication, 28

SELECTED ANSWERS

PAGE 2

1. 25 **4.** 47 **7.** 35 **10.** 6 **13.** 40 **16.** 24
19. 26 **22.** 54 **25.** 0 **28.** 32 **31.** 71 **34.** 19
36. 79 **38.** 46 **40.** 73 **42.** 53 **44.** 61
46. 57 **48.** 220 **50.** 262

PAGE 5

1. 13 **4.** 17 **7.** 18 **10.** 22 **12.** 39 **14.** 70
16. 51 **18.** 45 **21.** 95 **24.** 265 **25.** 222

PAGE 8

1. 77 **4.** 127 **7.** 80 **10.** 600 **13.** 1,700
16. 3,900 **19.** 56,000 **22.** Comm. Prop. Add.
25. Comm. Prop. Mult. **28.** Comm. Prop. Add.
31. Assoc. Prop. Mult. **34.** no **36.** no

PAGE 11

1. 32 **4.** 16 **7.** 98 **10.** $6(3) + 6(5)$
13. $8 \cdot 5 + 1 \cdot 5 + 9 \cdot 5$ **16.** $7(5) + 7(1) +$
$7(9) + 7(2)$ **19.** $3 \cdot 2 + 3 \cdot 6 + 3 \cdot 4 + 3 \cdot 8$
22. $4(8) + 4(1) + 4(3) + 4(5) + 4(9)$ **25.** $4(6 + 2)$
27. $(5 + 9)6$ **29.** $8(3 + 7)$ **31.** $5(4 + 2 + 7)$
33. $(6 + 4 + 7)8$ **35.** $4(3 + 7 + 1)$
37. $7(8 + 4 + 2)$ **39.** $6(3 + 4 + 1 + 2)$ **41.** yes
43. no

PAGE 15

1. $10x + 3$ **4.** $8m + 2$ **7.** $6z + 12$ **10.** $6x +$
11 **13.** $5y + 1$ **16.** $5m + 9$ **19.** $8z + 13$ **22.** $8a$
$+ 15b$ **25.** $11x + 8y + 1$ **28.** $10a + 4b + 9c$
31. 25 **33.** 64 **35.** 54 **37.** 86

PAGE 17

1. $43y + 7$ **3.** $29m + 36$ **5.** $36c + 14$ **7.** $29x +$
12 **9.** $42r + 56$ **11.** $27y + 30$ **13.** $39c + 5$
15. $8x + 11$ **17.** $13x + 24$ **19.** $18c + 11$
21. $14x + 26$ **23.** $22r + 29$ **25.** $38e + 38$
27. $170c + 70$ **29.** $87x + 120$

PAGE 18

1. 22 **3.** 4 **5.** 14 **7.** 25 **9.** 13 **11.** 65
13. 44 **15.** 85 **17.** $5, 9x; x; 9$ **20.** 87 **22.** 525
24. 97,000 **26.** Comm. Prop. Add. **28.** Assoc.
Prop. Add. **30.** $7(4) + 7(9)$ **32.** $5(9) + 2(9) + 6(9)$
34. $5(6 + 3)$ **36.** $7(6 + 1 + 6)$ **38.** $10x + 8$
40. $8t + 16$ **42.** $23r + 6$ **44.** $49p + 18$ **46.** $20x$
$+ 27$ **48.** $60x + 62$ **50.** 89 **52.** 30

PAGE 23

1. $+10$ **5.** -10 **9.** $+5$ **13.** -1 **17.** -16
21. -10 **25.** -3 **29.** -13 **33.** $+5$ **37.** -23
41. $+9$ **45.** $+5$ **49.** $+6$ **53.** -4 **57.** -2
61. 0 **65.** 0 **69.** -22 **73.** $+67$ **77.** $+8$
81. -131 **85.** $+189$ **89.** $+22$ **93.** -132
97. Drop the signs; add the numbers; give a
positive sign to the result. **99.** Drop the signs;
subtract the smaller number from the larger; give
the result the same sign as the larger number.

PAGE 25

1. $+1$ **3.** $+5$ **5.** -13 **7.** -8 **9.** Comm.
11. Add. Iden. **13.** Add. Inden. **15.** Comm.
17. Assoc. **19.** Add. Inv. **21.** Comm. **23.** -3
26. -8 **29.** The opposite of a negative number is a
positive number. **30.** Same as 29.
31.

Expression	Reason
$(-9 + +4) + -8$	Given
$(+4 + -9) + -8$	Comm.
$+4 + (-8 + -9)$	Comm.
$(+4 + -8) + -9$	Assoc.
$(-8 + +4) + -9$	Comm.

33.

Expression	Reason
$(-3 + +5) + +3$	Given
$(+5 + -3) + +3$	Comm.
$+5 + (-3 + +3)$	Assoc.
$+5 + 0$	Add. Inv.
$+5$	Add. Iden.

35.

Expression	Reason
$(x + y) + z$	Given
$(y + x) + z$	Comm.
$y + (x + z)$	Assoc.
$y + (z + x)$	Comm.
$(y + z) + x$	Assoc.
$(z + y) + x$	Comm.

PAGE 30

1. $+21$ **5.** -45 **9.** -7 **13.** $+27$ **17.** -8
21. $+72$ **25.** 0 **29.** 0 **33.** -39 **37.** -32
41. $+250$ **45.** -720 **49.** $+900$ **53.** $+90$
55. $+144$ **57.** $+1,512$ **59.** $-5,040$
61. $(-4)(+2) = (+2)(-4); (-6)(-5) = (-5)(-6)$

1. +2 7. +9 13. +6 19. −3 25. −42
31. −9 35. +15 39. −20 43. +6 47. Any
(nonzero) number divided by +1 is equal to that
number. 48. +1 52. Any number divided by itself is equal to +1. 53. +9 55. +1 57. −3
59. −5 61. −2

1. −6 5. 0 9. 12 13. 19 17. 17 21. 5
25. −126 28. −17 31. −102 34. −5

1. 14 3. −2 5. 11 7. 12 9. 63 11. 3
12. −85 13. 94 14. −32 15. 40 16. 25
17. −68 18. 95 19. −74 20. 80 21. −132
23. 14 25. −36 27. −117 29. −26 31. −38

1. $5y$ 4. $-11x$ 7. $-5r$ 10. $2x-5$ 13. $-5y$
$+6$ 16. $-2q-9$ 19. $7a-7$ 22. $2t+16$
25. $2x+6y+3$ 27. $4r-6s-6$ 29. $-14x+$
$4y+8$ 31. $-5r-14s+6$ 33. $-10x+3y-4$
35. $13a-4c-16$ 37. $-4r-2t-3$ 39. $-6a+$
$3b+1$ 41. -25 43. -56 45. -2 47. -11

1. 0 3. $3b$ 5. $12r$ 7. $-a+2$ 9. $c-1$
11. $-e-3$ 13. $-9g+15$ 15. $2p-7$ 17. $13x$
-1 19. $-5d-10$ 21. $-3a+2$ 23. $9x+4$
25. $-7z+16$ 27. $-g+3$ 29. $14b-14$
31. −36 33. −4 35. −28 37. −47 39. 16
41. −37

1. $29x-16$ 3. $14y-14$ 5. $-8a+38$
7. $2x-27$ 9. $-39a-63$ 11. $-22y+63$
13. $-29a-21$ 15. $-6x-11$ 17. $25c-27$
19. $17x$ 21. $21c-29$ 23. $-38y-74$ 25. 104
27. 142 29 −97 31. 67 33. 13 35. 16
37. $-33x+14$ 39. $-29y+33$ 41. $87z+19$
43. $-20a-22$ 45. $-20x-48$ 47. $-46y-26$

1. $-11y-2$ 3. $-5z-12$ 5. $-2c+8$ 7. $3f-$
8 9. $9y-9$ 11. $8y-17$ 13. $-6e-13$
15. $-6d-1$ 17. $4y-4$ 19. $-11z+6$
21. $-19b-10$ 23. -12 25. -23 27. 39
29. −7 31. −7 33. $-23y+33$ 35. $-4z-2$
37. $9r-2$ 39. $-8x+10$

1. 3 4. −13 7. 9 10. −11 13. 18 16. 33
19. $2x-1$ 21. $5y+8$ 23. $3x+9$ 25. $8x+$
17 27. $-12a+3$ 29. $20y+3$ 31. $4x-4$
33. $3a+3$ 35. $a-b=a+-b$ (meaning of $a-b$)
$=a+(-1)b$ (Mult. Prop. −1)

1. +10 4. −5 7. +16 10. −5 13. −23
16. −63 19. +105 22. +7 25. +13 28. 57
30. 49 31. $17y$ 33. $4d-2$ 35. $-10c-3$
37. $16y-6$ 39. $-27x+8$ 41. 73 43. −81
45. −13 48. $4x+12$ 50. Comm. Prop.

1. 5 3. 9 5. 5 7. 9 9. 7 11. 4 13. 5
15. 7 17. 4 19. 3 21. 4 23. 2 25. 6
27. 3 29. 0 31. $\frac{1}{4}$ 33. −3 35. none 37. $\frac{1}{2}$

1. 4 4. 9 7. −3 10. 4 13. −1 16. 2
19. 1 22. 5 25. 10 28. 11 31. $\frac{1}{5}$ 34. $\frac{1}{3}$
37. $\frac{2}{5}$ 40. $\frac{5}{6}$ 43. $\frac{8}{3}$ 46. $\frac{5}{8}$

1. 3 4. 4 7. 15 10. 5 13. −11 16. 5
19. 4 22. 4 25. 6 28. 9 31. 1 34. −6
37. −3 40. $-\frac{2}{3}$ 43. $\frac{5}{6}$ 46. $\frac{9}{5}$ 52. $-\frac{7}{3}$

1. 7 3. −7 5. 8 7. −6 9. 20 11. −8
13. 9 15. −1 17. 10 19. 5 21. −3
23. −4 25. 2 27. 2 29. −1 31. 1 33. 11
35. 3 37. −2 39. 1 41. $\frac{16}{5}$ 43. $\frac{1}{13}$ 45. $-\frac{1}{6}$
47. $-\frac{3}{19}$ 49. 2 51. 9 53. $\frac{42}{11}$ 55. $-\frac{3}{8}$
57. $-\frac{4}{9}$

1. $8-5$ 3. $12-6$ 5. $23+2$ 7. $y+4$
9. $n-8$ 11. $5y+3$ 13. $3n-6$ 15. $25-4n$
17. $4x+8$ 19. $14+2n$ 21. $9n-7$ 23. $x+y$
25. $7x-2y$ 27. $xy+9$ 29. $y-5x$ 31. $5+7y$
$+8$, or $7y+13$ 33. $5n-2+9$, or $5n+7$

PAGE 74
1. 4 **3.** 3 **5.** 1 **7.** 3 **9.** −2 **11.** −3
13. 1 **15.** −36 **17.** 5 **19.** 7 **21.** −8
23. −10 **25.** 7 **27.** −9 **29.** 1 **31.** −3

PAGE 78
1. 7, 35 **3.** 39, 11 **5.** 37, 46 **7.** 7, 16 **9.** 51,
17 **11.** $31, $58 **13.** 8, 11, 15 **15.** 9, 12, 17,
26, 13 **19.** 14, 17

PAGE 82
1. 12 nickles, 3 dimes **3.** 2 quarters **5.** 18-$1
bills, 24-$5 bills **7.** 7 dimes, 4 quarters **9.** 16
quarters, 23 nickels **11.** 502 $1 tickets **13.** 3
nickels, 18 dimes, 20 pennies **15.** 17 pennies, 22
nickels, 44 dimes, 46 quarters

PAGE 86
1. 13 ft, 7 ft **3.** 19 ft, 8 ft **5.** 15 ft, 13 ft, 21 ft
7. 9 in., 12 in., 17 in. **9.** 11 in., 11 in. **11.** 16 ft
13. 18 cm, 9 cm **15.** 9 in., 6 in.

PAGE 88
1. 1.7 **3.** 3 **5.** none **7.** −11 **9.** $-\dfrac{8}{5}$

11. 5 **13.** 1 **15.** $\dfrac{23}{2}$ **17.** 3 **19.** 22 **21.** −4

23. −13 **25.** −5 **27.** −3 **29.** 8 **31.** −2
33. $6 + x$ **35.** $n - 3$ **37.** $2y - 5$ **39.** 4
41. 5, 22 **43.** 26 ft, 8 ft

PAGE 93
1–6. {1, 6, 3, 5}, {6, 3, 1, 5}, {1, 1 + 2, 1 + 4,
1 + 5} **7.** finite; the set of all integers between
−1 and 5 **10.** finite; the set of all negative integers
between 0 and −5 **13.** finite; the set of all integers
between −3 and 3 **16.** {5, 4, 3, 2, 1}
20. ∅ **22.** {7} **25.** {−3} **28.** ∅ **31.** {−6}
37. ∅ **40.** {all numbers}

PAGE 96
1. all points to the left of 3 **5.** −2 and all
points to the left **9.** 0 and all points to the
right **13.** the point −2 **17.** all points to the
right of 4 **21.** 1 and all points to the left
25. all points to the left of −3 **29.** the point
−3 **33.** −1 and all points to the right **37.** all
points to the right of −2 **41.** the point 1
45. all points to the right of −3

PAGE 101
1. 10 > 9 **3.** −24 < 4 **5.** −4 < −1 **7.** −21 <
14 **9.** 0 > −15 **11.** −8 < 4 **13.** −42 < 6
17. 2 > −2 **19.** 3 ⩾ −10 **21.** 0 ⩽ 15
23. 7 ⩽ 11 **25.** 6 > 5 **27.** Add −3.
31. Add 5. **33.** Divide by −3.

PAGE 104
1. $\{x \mid x > -2\}$ **3.** $\{y \mid y > -1\}$ **5.** $\{x \mid x > 7\}$
7. $\{a \mid a \leqslant 8\}$ **9.** $\{x \mid x \geqslant 5\}$ **11.** $\{d \mid d < -3\}$
13. $\{r \mid r \geqslant 4\}$ **15.** $\{x \mid x \leqslant 3\}$ **17.** $\{x \mid x < 4\}$
19. $\{y \mid y \leqslant 3\}$ **21.** $\{x \mid x \leqslant 6\}$ **23.** $\{y \mid y > 3\}$
25. $\{x \mid x \geqslant 8\}$ **27.** $\{x \mid x \leqslant -4\}$ **29.** $\{y \mid y > 9\}$

PAGE 107
1. $A \nsubseteq B$; $B \subseteq A$ **3.** $A \subseteq B$; $B \nsubseteq A$ **5.** $A \subseteq B$;
$B \nsubseteq A$ **7.** $A \subseteq B$; $B \nsubseteq A$ **9.** $A \subseteq B$; $B \subseteq A$
11. $A \nsubseteq B$; $B \nsubseteq A$ **13.** $A \nsubseteq B$; $B \subseteq A$ **15.** $A \subseteq B$;
$B \nsubseteq A$ **17.** {1, 2}, {1}, {2}, ∅; 4 **20.** ∅; 1
23. {3, 5}; {1, 3, 5} **25.** ∅; {4, 5, 6, 7} **27.** ∅;
{0, 2, 4} **29.** ∅; {−3, −2, −1, 1, 2, 3}
33. {6}; {2, 4, 6, 8, 10} **35.** {2, 5,
8, 9}; {2, 5, 8, 9} **37.** ∅; {0, 1, 2, 3, . . . }
41. {0}; {integers} **43.** {positive integers};
{whole numbers} **45.** {0, 1, 2, 3, 4, 5, 6} **48.** ∅

PAGE 114
1. $\{x \mid x > -2 \text{ and } x < 5\}$; {all numbers }
3. $\{x \mid x \geqslant -4 \text{ and } x < 2\}$; {all numbers }
7. $\{x \mid x \geqslant -1 \text{ and } x \leqslant 3\}$, {all numbers }
9. $\{x \mid x < 0\}$; $\{x \mid x < 4\}$ **11.** {1}; {all numbers }
13. $\{x \mid x > -4\}$; $\{x \mid x > -5\}$
15. $\{x \mid x \leqslant 2 \text{ and } x > -1\}$; {all numbers }
17. $\{x \mid x > 3\}$; $\{x \mid x \geqslant 3\}$ **21.** ∅; $\{x \mid x \geqslant 5\}$
23. $\{x \mid x \geqslant -3 \text{ and } x \leqslant 3\}$; {all numbers }
25. {−3}; $\{x \mid x \leqslant -3\}$ **27.** $\{x \mid x > 3 \text{ and } x \leqslant 4\}$;
{all numbers} **31.** $\{x \mid x \geqslant 1 \text{ and } x \leqslant 4\}$
35. $\{x \mid x \leqslant -2 \text{ or } x \geqslant 0\}$ **39.** \ segment with
endpoints 0 and 5

PAGE 116
1–4. {8, 9, 5, 2}, {2, 2 + 3, 2 + 6, 2 + 7}
5. infinite; the set of all positive odd integers
8. {−4, −3, −2, −1} **10.** ∅ **13.** 0 **16.** all
points to the right of −2 **20.** all points to the
left of −1 **24.** 1 ⩾ −3 **26.** 1 > −6
30. $\{z \mid z > 5\}$ **32.** $\{x \mid x > \dfrac{12}{13}\}$ **34.** $A \subseteq B$;
$B \nsubseteq A$ **37.** {3}, ∅; 2 **40.** {5, 9}; {4, 5, 9}

1. -27 4. -18 7. 64 10. -32 13. -27
16. -64

1. $12a^8$ 5. $28x^{12}$ 9. $4a^5$ 13. $-8a^8$ 17. $8a^4$
21. $12a^5b^6$ 24. $-8a^3b^8$ 27. a^6 33. r^{30}
39. $16x^8$ 44. $16a^6m^4$ 49. -64^9m^{12}
54. $x^9y^6z^{12}$ 57. $27a^9b^6$ 60. x^{4a} 63. x^{6a}

1. $3x^2 - 3x - 8$ 3. $9x^2 + 4x + 5$ 5. $5x^2 -$
$11x + 3$ 7. $m^2 - 9$ 9. $7x^3 - 9x^2 + 9x$
11. $-m^3 + 5m$ 13. $8a^4 + 2a^2$ 15. $2a^2 + a -$
1 17. $7b^3 - 2b^2 - b + 8$ 19. $10a^3 + 2a^2 - 12a -$
4 21. $3a^4 - 7a^3 + 2a^2 + a - 6$ 22. $-9b^4 -$
$b^3 + 9b^2 - 6b - 3$ 23. $-22m^9 - m^6 - 3$
24. $-7b^7 + 4b^5 + 4b^4 - 2b^2$ 25. $a^4 + 4a^3 -$
$10a^2 + 13a - 19$

1. $6f^4 - 10f^3 + 8f^2$ 4. $15b^3 - 20b^2 + 15b$
7. $24b^3 - 30b^2$ 10. $-2b^2 + 5b$ 13. $-2x^2 -$
$5x + 7$ 16. $x^2 + x + 2$ 19. $9a^3 + 15a^2 - 6a$
22. $-2a^3 + a^2 + 3a$ 25. $x^3 + 8x^2 - 12x +$
9 27. $2x^3 + x - 9$ 29. $x^5 + x^3 - 8x + 7$
31. $3a^2 - 2a - 7$ 33. $4x^2 - 9x + 17$
35. $6a^2 - 11a$ 37. $5x^4 - 2x^3 + 4x^2 -$
3 39. $x^4 + x^3 + 3x^2 - 3x + 3$ 41. $2m^5n^2 -$
$3m^4n^3 + m^3n^4$ 43. $2a^3b - 6a^2b^2 + 10ab^3$
45. $-2x^3y^2 + x^2y^3 - xy^4$ 47. $-2a^4c +$
$2a^3c^2 - 2a^2c^3 + 2ac^4$ 49. $3m^5n^2 - 5m^4n^3 +$
$4m^3n^4$ 50. $-7a^3b + 15a^2b^2 + 37ab^3$
51. $-2x^3y^2 + x^2y^3 - 6xy^4$

1. $2 \cdot 2 \cdot 3$ 5. $3 \cdot 3 \cdot 5$ 9. $5 \cdot 5 \cdot 2$
17. $7x^2$ 19. $6m^3$ 21. $-9x^2$ 23. $7x^5$
25. $-10x^4$ 27. b^5 29. $-2b$ 31. $9a^3b$
33. $8a^2m^2$ 35. $-ab$ 37. $-x^2y^4$ 39. x

1. $3(x^2 + 9x + 3)$ 5. $7(a^2 - 3a + 7)$
9. $a(2a^2 - a + 1)$ 13. $4a^2(a + 2)$ 17. $4a(a^2 - 3a + 2)$ 21. $4(m^2 - 5)$ 25. $7a^3(a^2 - 5a + 3)$

27. $3(a^2 + 4ab + 12b^2)$ 29. $9m(2m^3 - 3m^2 - 5m + 4)$

1. -8 4. -128 7. 64 10. x^{10} 13. $15b^3$
16. $-14a^6$ 19. $27a^6$ 22. binomial
28. $2x^2 + 10x + 5$ 30. $3m^2 - 11$
34. $a^5 + a^4$ 36. $12a^5 - 18a^4$ 38. $a^3 - 2a^2 + 3a$
40. $a^2 + a + 1$ 42. $3x^5 - 2x^4 + 6x^3 - 3x^2 + 5$
44. $3a^3b - 15a^2b^2 + 12ab^3$
48. $2x^3 - 6x^2 + 8x - 2$ 50. a^5 53. $5a$
56. $2(2a^2 - 4a + 3)$ 59. $a(a^2 - 7a + 3)$

1. $6x^2 + 25x + 14$ 4. $6x^2 - x - 1$
7. $m^2 - 25$ 10. $3x^2 + 5x - 2$
13. $2y^2 + 3y - 20$ 16. $4d^2 + 7d - 2$
19. $9y^2 - 1$ 22. $3a^2 - 23ab + 40b^2$
25. $9y^2 - 30y + 25$ 29. $6x^3 + 10x^2 + 5x - 3$
32. $x^3 - 12x^2 + 36x - 5$
35. $x^2 - 14x + 49$

1. $(2x + 5)(x + 1)$ 4. $(4x - 3)(2x - 1)$
7. $(x + 3)(x - 2)$ 10. $(2a + 1)(a - 4)$
13. $(x + 5)(x + 2)$ 16. $(y - 8)(y - 2)$
19. $(a - 5)(a + 4)$ 22. $(x + 1)(x + 1)$
25. $(2a - 3)(a - 2)$ 28. $(2m - 1)(m + 5)$
31. $(3x - 5)(x + 5)$ 34. $(3a - 1)(2a + 1)$
37. $(2b + 5)(b + 6)$ 40. $(3x - 2)(x + 5)$
43. $(2x + 5)(x - 8)$ 46. $(2a - 5)(a - 10)$
49. $(3m + 5)(m + 8)$ 52. $(5d - 3)(3d - 2)$
55. $(2a - 5)(2a - 5)$ 58. $(5x - 3)(3x - 4)$

1. $(x - 4)(x + 4)$ 4. $(a - 9)(a + 9)$
7. $(m - 8)(m + 8)$ 10. $(3a + 5)(3a - 5)$
13. $(7y - 2)(7y + 2)$ 16. $(6a - 5)(6a + 5)$
19. $(5 - x)(5 + x)$ 22. $(6 - a)(6 + a)$
25. $(1 - y)(1 + y)$ 28. $(1 - 3x)(1 + 3x)$
31. $(12a - 9)(12a + 9)$ 34. $(2m + 13)(2m - 13)$
37. $(13p + 4)(13p - 4)$ 40. $(11 - 4b)(11 + 4b)$
43. $(15a - 13)(15a + 13)$

PAGE 155

1. $2(a-4)(a-1)$
4. $m(2m-3)(m-1)$
7. $2x(x+1)(x-1)$
10. $2x(x-3)(x-4)$
13. $4a(a-5)(a+2)$
16. $4(a-5)(a-1)$
19. $(2a-1)(a+7)$
22. $2(3x-7)(3x+7)$
25. $y^2(3y+5)(y-4)$
28. $3(5a-9)(a-2)$
31. $(x-a)(m+n)$
33. $(r+t)(p-2)$
35. $(y+1)(p+5)(p-5)$

PAGE 157

1. $(a+b)(a+3b)$
4. $4(a+3b)(a-3b)$
7. $(2m-5b)(m+2b)$
10. $(a-7b)(a+6b)$
13. $2(a+7b)(a+3b)$
16. $2(m-5n)(m+4n)$
19. $b(ab-5)(ab+5)$
22. $(7x-2y)(x+3y)$
25. $2(2k-5r)(k-8r)$
28. $5(2m+3n)(2m+3n)$
31. $(5x+3y)(2x+3y)$

PAGE 160

1. $2, 3$
4. $0, 6$
7. $\{\frac{1}{2}, -5\}$
10. $\{\frac{1}{3}, -5\}$
13. $\{\frac{1}{3}, 7\}$
16. $\{8, -\frac{1}{2}\}$
19. $\{\frac{3}{2}, 5\}$
22. $\frac{3}{2}, -8$
25. $\frac{7}{2}, -6$
28. $\frac{4}{3}, 9$
31. $0, 3, -3$
34. $0, 2$

PAGE 164

1. $-3, -5$
4. $2, -9$
7. $0, -9$
10. $\{1, -5\}$
13. $\{0, -13\}$
16. $\{-\frac{1}{2}, -1\}$
19. $\{\frac{1}{2}, -1\}$
22. $\{\frac{1}{2}, -\frac{1}{2}\}$
25. $\{\frac{1}{2}, -6\}$
28. $-\frac{7}{4}, \frac{5}{3}$
31. $\frac{2}{3}, -\frac{5}{2}$
34. $\frac{15}{2}, -\frac{15}{2}$
37. $0, -8$
40. $-2, -4$

PAGE 167

1. $x + (x+1) + (x+2) = 27$
3. $x + (x+1) + (x+2) = -15$
5. $x(x+2) = 35$
9. $x + (x+2) + (x+4) + (x+6) = 40$
11. $2(x+1) - x = 5$
13. $2(x+2) - x = 11$
15. $3(x+2) - 2x = 48$
17. $x(x+1)(x+2) = 8[x + (x+1) + (x+2)]$

PAGE 170

1. $22, 23$
3. $29, 30, 31, 32, 33$
5. $7, 8, 9$
7. $37, 39, 41$
9. $-4, -3$ or $3, 4$
11. $4, 6$ or $-6, -4$
13. $7, 9$ or $-9, -7$
15. $-3, -2, -1,$ or $2, 3, 4$
17. $5, 6, 7$ or $-4, -3, -2$
19. $-5, -3$ or $2, 4$
21. $-2, -1, 0, 1$
23. $-7, -6, -5, -4$ or $4, 5, 6, 7$

PAGE 172

1. $x^2 + 8x + 15$
4. $3x^2 + 17x - 6$
7. $12z^2 - 11z + 2$
10. $x^3 + 2x^2 - 32x - 15$
13. $9a^2 - 30a + 25$
17. $(x-3)(x-4)$
20. $(x-3)(x-2)$
23. $(2m-5)(m+4)$
26. $2(2a-1)(a+1)$
29. $(a-2)(a+2)$
33. $3(x+3)(x+4)$
36. $3(b+5)(b-3)$
39. $6x(x-3)(x-1)$
42. $(a+3b)(a-3b)$
45. $(12x-13y)(12x+13y)$
48. $y(x+2y)(x-2y)$
51. $1, 2$
54. $2, -2$
57. $\{6, 7\}$
60. $\{\frac{7}{2}, 3\}$
63. $8, 9$ or $-9, -8$
65. $7, 8, 9$ or $-2, -1, 0$

PAGE 178

1. $\frac{5}{6}$
4. $\frac{6}{1}$
9. $\frac{4}{5}$
13. 7

PAGE 183

1. $\frac{6}{48}$
5. $\frac{10a^5}{18b^9}$
9. $-\frac{x^5}{y^{11}}$
13. $-\frac{2x^2 - x - 3}{2x^2 + 7x + 6}$
16. $\frac{3x-3}{x+5}$
19. $\frac{2x^2 - 11x - 21}{x-4}$
22. $\frac{a^{10}}{b^6}$
25. $\frac{x^2 - x - 2}{x^2 + 9x + 20}$
28. $\frac{a^2 - b^2}{x^2 + xy - 2y^2}$
31. $\frac{x^2 + xy - 2y^2}{x+y}$
34. $\frac{9a^2 + 6ab + b^2}{4a^2 + 4ab + b^2}$
37. $\frac{25a^2 - 10ab + b^2}{9a^2 - 6ab + b^2}$

PAGE 186

1. $\frac{1}{3}$
5. $\frac{a-5}{2a-1}$
9. $\frac{1}{4}$
13. $\frac{4}{b+3}$
17. $\frac{3(x+2)}{2}$
21. $\frac{3p-1}{5}$
25. $x+4$
27. $x+5$

PAGE 190

1. $-\frac{1}{x+4}$
5. $\frac{a+5}{4}$
9. -2
13. $-(a+2)$
17. $-\frac{y+6}{y+2}$
21. $-\frac{n-4}{2(n-3)}$
24. $-\frac{2x-y}{2}$
27. $-\frac{a^2 - b^2}{a}$
30. $-a$

1. $\dfrac{2m^3}{3n^2}$ 4. $-\dfrac{x(a+5)}{y^2}$ 7. $2a^3b^2(x-2)$

10. $\dfrac{y}{a+5}$ 13. $\dfrac{a+2}{n(a-1)}$ 16. $\dfrac{c+7}{ab^2}$

19. $\dfrac{y-1}{x^4}$ 22. $\dfrac{1}{a^2(x+3)}$

1. $\dfrac{2(b-4)}{b-2}$ 4. $\dfrac{1}{3}$ 7. 3

16. $\dfrac{4x}{3y^3(2a+3)}$ 19. $\dfrac{(x+5)(2x-3)}{3(x-3)(3x+2)}$

21. $\dfrac{a+2}{a+3}$ 23. $-\dfrac{1}{x+3}$ 26. $\dfrac{2(a+2)}{a-4}$

28. $\dfrac{c}{c+d}$ 30. $\dfrac{2(x+2y)}{a^2b}$ 32. $-\dfrac{3(a+3b)}{a-2b}$

34. $-\dfrac{m+2}{2m+1}$ 36. $-\dfrac{m+1}{2}$

1. 1   4. $\dfrac{m+1}{2}$ 7. $-\dfrac{x-1}{x+1}$ 10. $\dfrac{3a^2}{2}$

13. $\dfrac{b-1}{b+3}$ 15. $\dfrac{2(a+4)}{3a^3b^5}$ 17. $-\dfrac{c(x+7)}{6b(x+5)}$

1. $\dfrac{4}{5}$ 4. $\dfrac{1}{12}$ 7. 5   10. $\dfrac{6a^5}{35b^9}$ 13. $\dfrac{3}{4}$

18. -3 21. $\dfrac{1}{a^7}$ 24. $\dfrac{3}{2}$ 26. $\dfrac{1}{3}$ 28. 1

30. $-\dfrac{(k-3)(3k+2)}{8}$

1. $\dfrac{2}{3}$ 5. $\dfrac{11a}{3}$ 8. $\dfrac{1}{x-2}$ 11. $\dfrac{1}{a+4}$

17. $\dfrac{1}{2}$ 19. $\dfrac{3a+2b}{7}$ 21. $\dfrac{1}{x+5}$ 23. $\dfrac{a+3}{3a+5}$

25. $a+3$ 27. $4x+3y$

1. $\dfrac{3}{2}$ 5. $\dfrac{b}{2}$ 9. $\dfrac{19}{18m}$ 12. $\dfrac{14a+15}{6}$ 15. $\dfrac{7}{3}$

18. $\dfrac{17a+3}{6}$ 20. $\dfrac{17m+36}{54}$ 22. $\dfrac{19l}{21}$

24. $\dfrac{9x^2+7x-32}{15x}$ 26. $\dfrac{9m^2+7m-1}{28}$

1. $\dfrac{9a+23}{(a-4)(a+4)}$ 3. $\dfrac{x+2}{x}$ 5. $\dfrac{3x+22}{x(x+5)}$

7. $\dfrac{2x+11}{(x-3)(x+3)}$ 9. $\dfrac{3x+11}{(x-8)(x+2)}$

11. $\dfrac{9a+1}{(a-1)(a+1)}$ 13. $\dfrac{10a+12}{(2a-5)(a+3)}$

15. $\dfrac{k^2+3k-5}{(k-3)(k-2)}$

1. $\dfrac{2m+3}{m}$ 4. $\dfrac{11a+10}{(a-1)(a+2)}$ 7. $\dfrac{17a+4}{(a-3)(2a+5)}$

10. $\dfrac{7y^2+10y-9}{15y^3}$ 13. $\dfrac{5m^2+3m+2}{m^2}$

16. $\dfrac{19a^2+9a+3}{6a^3}$ 18. $\dfrac{-10x^3-x^2+37x+3}{10x^3}$

20. $\dfrac{a^2+3a-6}{a+5}$ 23. $\dfrac{4x^2-3x-6}{2x-1}$

26. $\dfrac{7m+6}{3mn}$

1. $\dfrac{-2}{a+b}$ 4. $\dfrac{-2x+1}{(x-2)(x+2)}$ 7. $\dfrac{10x-3}{2x}$

10. $\dfrac{4x+32}{(x+7)(x-7)}$ 13. $\dfrac{-2b+39}{(3b-1)(2b+7)}$

16. $\dfrac{1}{m-2}$ 19. $\dfrac{-2a^2-2a+7}{(a+3)(a+2)}$

25. $\dfrac{a^2-10a+22}{(2a-5)(a+4)}$ 27. $\dfrac{y^2-4y-8}{(y-4)(2y+3)}$

1. $\dfrac{-3x-14}{(x-7)(x+7)}$ 3. $\dfrac{2}{b-1}$ 5. $\dfrac{-b-5}{(b-2)(b+1)}$

7. $\dfrac{10y-6}{(y-5)(y-2)}$ 9. $\dfrac{a}{a+2}$ 11. $\dfrac{10m-3}{(m+2)(m-2)}$

13. $\dfrac{-k^2+3k+2}{(k-6)(k-2)}$ 15. $\dfrac{m}{m-5}$

19. $\dfrac{6n^2-5n+9}{(n+3)(n-3)}$

21. $\dfrac{a^2+2ab+2a+2b-3b^2+7}{(a-b)(a+b)}$

23. $\dfrac{b^2+bc+c^2}{(b+c)(b-c)}$

1. $\dfrac{1}{m-2}$ 3. $\dfrac{17b}{4}$ 5. $\dfrac{5a-37}{(a+1)(a-8)}$

7. $\dfrac{4+3y}{y(y-5)}$ 9. $\dfrac{4+3a}{a}$ 11. $\dfrac{2m+11}{m+4}$

13. $\dfrac{30a^2+8a+9}{12a^3}$ 15. $\dfrac{17x^2+10x+12}{12x^3}$

19. $\dfrac{n-3}{(n-7)(n+1)}$ 21. $\dfrac{12x+40}{x(x-9)}$

23. $\dfrac{-3b+13}{(b-5)(b-2)}$ 25. $\dfrac{-b^2+b-12}{(b+3)(b-1)}$

27. $\dfrac{5a-17}{(a-5)(a+5)}$

1. 3 4. 10 7. 18 10. 38 13. 4, −4 17. $\dfrac{18}{5}$

19. $\dfrac{8}{3}$ 21. $\{x \mid -2 < x < 2\}$ 24. $\{x \mid x < 0 \text{ or } x > 0\}$

1. −1, 7 4. 6, −1 7. 1, 13 10. $\{1, 5\}$

13. $\{-\dfrac{2}{7}, \dfrac{8}{7}\}$ 16. $\{-\dfrac{3}{2}, \dfrac{9}{2}\}$ 19. $\{-\dfrac{1}{3}, -\dfrac{7}{3}\}$

22. $\{\dfrac{13}{2}, \dfrac{15}{2}\}$ 25. 0, 6 27. 0, 5

1. 4 4. 18 7. 18 10. $\dfrac{31}{4}$ 13. 3

1. (1, 3) 4. (3, −2) 7. (−2, 2) 10. (3, −2)
13. (3, 4) 16. 3 19. 3 22. x-coord. neg.;
y-coord. pos.

1. right 6. up 6 11. right 4, down 1 16. origin
21. (2, 5)

1. x-axis 4. y-axis 7. x-axis 10. −4
12. 4 14. 3

1. −7 4. −8 7. −3 10. −3 13. −6
16. 47 19. $-\dfrac{5}{4}$ 21. $-\dfrac{13}{6}$ 23. $\dfrac{19}{15}$ 25. .8
27. $-\dfrac{23}{8}$ 29. −8a 31. −3k 33. $-\dfrac{5m}{6}$

1. $\dfrac{3}{4}$ 4. $\dfrac{6}{11}$ 7. $-\dfrac{4}{15}$ 10. $\dfrac{3k}{2b}$ 12. $\dfrac{11d}{7c}$

1. undefined; vertical 4. $-\dfrac{1}{12}$; down to the
right 7. undefined; vertical 10. no 13. yes
15. no 17. no 19. yes

1. 6 5. 7, −7 9. 9 12. (2, 2) 13. (5, 1)
14. (3, −1) 15. (1, −3) 16. (−2, −2)
21. (−2, 0) 22. right 3, up 5 26. x-axis
29. −5 31. 11 34. 4; up to the right

1. $\dfrac{10}{3}$ 4. $\dfrac{14}{3}$ 7. 4 10. 42,000 12. 10,000
14. 6, −6 18. 9, 15 20. 9, 24

1. $y = 2x - 1$ 4. $y = x - 3$ 7. $y = 4x - 2$
10. $y = -3x - 1$ 13. $y = -3x + 4$
16. $-1 = 2(-1) + 1$ 19. $y = 4x; \ 12 = 4(3)$
21. $y = 3x - 5; \ 4 = 3(3) - 5$ 23. $y = 2x + 5$

1. $y = \dfrac{3}{2}x + \dfrac{1}{2}$ 4. $y = \dfrac{1}{4}x + 5$ 7. $y = \dfrac{4}{5}x + \dfrac{8}{5}$ 10. $y = \dfrac{3}{4}x + 2$; 5 12. $y = \dfrac{2}{5}x + 1$; −1
14. (−1, 0), (0, 1), (1, 2) 17. (−2, −3), (0, −2),
(2, −1) 20. $y = 3x + 1$; (−1, −2), (0, 1), (1, 4)
23. $y = \dfrac{1}{2}x - 6$; (−2, −7), (0, 6), (2, −5)

1. $y = 2x + 4$ 4. $y = \dfrac{1}{2}x + 2$ 7. (−3, −1),
(3, 3) 10. (1, 4), (2, 7) 12. (1, 2), (2, 0)
15. (3, 8), (−3, 4) 18. (−1, −2), (1, 2)

1. $(2, \dfrac{3}{2}), (4, \dfrac{9}{2})$ 4. (−1, 0), (1, 2) 7. (−3, 2),
(3, 6) 10. (−1, 4), (1, 4) 13. (−1, 2), (1, 4)
16. (−1, 3), (1, −1)

1. $(-2, -1)$, $(-2, 0)$, $(-2, 1)$ 5. $(3, -1)$, $(3, 0)$, $(3, 1)$ 9. $(3, -1)$, $(3, 0)$, $(3, 1)$

1. extremes x, 3; means 4, 6; 8 5. extremes $2x + 1$, 4; means 5, x; $\frac{-4}{3}$ 9. 6,000

11. $y = 2x - 5$ 14. $y = \frac{1}{2}x + \frac{1}{2}$ 17. $y = 2x$; $8 = 2(4)$ 19. $y = \frac{2}{3}x - 5$ 22. $\frac{2}{3}$; -4; $(-3, -6)$, $(3, -2)$ 25. 2; 1; $(-1, -1)$, $(1, 3)$ 28. $(-1, -3)$, $(1, 1)$ 31. $(3, 0)$, $(3, 3)$ 34. $(1, 0)$, $(1, 3)$

1. $(2, -3)$ 2. $(2, 7)$ 3. $(0, 4)$ 4. $(3, 3)$ 5. $(2, 6)$ 6. $(2, 1)$ 7. $(2, 5)$ 11. $(0, 2)$ 15. inconsistent

1. $(3, 6)$ 5. $(3, 0)$ 9. $(\frac{11}{2}, -\frac{1}{2})$ 13. $(-1, -\frac{2}{5})$

1. $(6, 2)$ 5. $(2, 1)$ 9. $(3, 2)$

1. $(2, 1)$ 5. $(5, 1)$ 9. $(2, 1)$ 13. $(-2, 6)$ 17. $(3, 2)$

1. 11 lb; 10 35¢ 4. $(x + y)$ lb; $(215x + 335y)$¢ 7. $(x + y)$ lb; $(135x + my)$¢

1. $x + y = 7$; $45x + 65y = 375$ 3. $y = x + 2$; $5x + 15y = 130$ 5. $x = y - 2$; $115x + 85y = 370$ 7. 5 lb at $.25; 4 lb at $.35 9. 2 at $.15; 9 at $.35 11. 4 lb at $.80; 8 lb at $.90 15. 5 lb at $.80; 8 lb at $.40 17. 5 lb pecans; $2\frac{1}{2}$ lb almonds; $2\frac{1}{2}$ lb cashews 19. beef $1.89 lb; pork $1.69 lb

1. 10, 40 3. 6, 12 5. 4, 13 7. 5, 17 9. 8, 12 11. width 7 ft; length 14 ft 13. width 10 yd; length 68 yd

1. $(5, 3)$ 2. $(2, 6)$ 3. $(4, 4)$ 4. $(2, 8)$ 5. inconsistent 9. $(3, 1)$ 13. $(3, 6)$ 17. 3 lb at $.75; 2 lb at $.95 19. 2 sheets at $.40; 4 sheets at $.30 21. 16, 24 23. 5, 13

1. $\{(-4, -5), (-2, -3), (3, 2), (3, 4), (5, 1)\}$; $D = \{-4, -2, 3, 5\}$; $R = \{-5, -3, 2, 4, 1\}$; no 4. $D = \{0, -1, 3, -4\}$; $R = \{1, -2, 4\}$; yes 6. $D = \{2\}$; $R = \{-2, -3, -1, 0\}$; no 8. $D = \{-1, -2, 0, 1, 2\}$; $R = \{1, 2, 0, -1, -2\}$; yes 9. $D = \{-1, -2, 0, 1, 2\}$; $R = \{-1, -2, 0, 1, 2\}$; yes 10. $D = \{3, -1, 2, 0\}$; $R = \{0, 2, 4, -4, -2\}$; no 11. $D = \{0, 1, 4\}$; $R = \{0, -1, 1, -2, 2\}$; no 12. $D = \{-3, -2, -1, 0, 1, 2\}$; $R = \{1, -1\}$; yes 13. $D = \{-4, -3, -1, 0, 2, 3, 4, 5\}$; $R = \{-5, -4, -3\}$; yes 14. $\{(4, -2), (1, -1), (4, 0)\}$; yes; no 16. $\{(1, -1), (1, -2), (1, 0), (1, 1), (1, 2)\}$; yes; no 17. $\{(0, -2), (1, -1), (2, 0), (3, 1), (4, 2)\}$; yes; yes 18. $\{(0, 1), (0, -1), (2, 3), (1, 2), (-1, 3)\}$; no; no

(Two points belonging to each relation are given.)
1. $(0, 0)$, $(1, 3)$; function; linear function 4. $(0, 5)$, $(2, 5)$; function; constant function 7. $(3, 0)$, $(3, 2)$ 10. $(0, 0)$, $(4, 1)$; function; linear function 13. $(0, 0)$, $(2, 0)$; function; constant function 16. $(0, 3)$, $(1, 1)$; function; linear function 19. $(4, 0)$, $(0, 4)$; function; linear function 22. $(0, -3)$, $(2, -3)$; function; constant function 25. $(-4, 0)$, $(2, 2)$; function; linear function 28. $(0, 1)$, $(2, 5)$; function; linear function 31. $(-2, 4)$, $(0, 0)$, $(2, 4)$; function 34. $(-1, 2)$, $(0, 0)$, $(1, 2)$; function 37. $(4, 2)$, $(0, 0)$, $(4, -2)$ 40. $(-2, -1)$, $(0, 0)$, $(-2, 1)$ 43. $(-2, -8)$, $(-1, -1)$, $(0, 0)$, $(1, 1)$, $(2, 8)$; function 46. $(-2, 8)$, $(-1, 1)$, $(0, 0)$, $(1, -1)$, $(2, -8)$; function

1. -2 6. 11 11. -5 16. $R = \{-3, 1, 5\}$ 18. $R = \{-13, -17, -21\}$ 20. $R = \{10, 1, 82\}$ 22. $R = \{5, 1, -1\}$ 24. $R = \{-7, -7\frac{1}{2}, -7\frac{1}{3}\}$ 26. $R = \{1, 9, 25\}$ 28. $R = \{4\}$ 30. 10 34. 4

1. $y < -x + 3$ 5. $y > \dfrac{-3}{2}x$ 9. $y < \dfrac{5}{2}x$

13. above; (0, 3), (2, 3) 17. below; (0, 0), (1, 3) 21. below and including; (0, 5), (2, 7)
25. below and including; (0, 1), (2, 5) 29. below; (0, 1), (3, 3) 33. above; (0, 2), (2, 0) 37. above; (0, 1), (2, 1); (3, 7) 39. above; (0, −6), (2, −4); (3, 8) 41. above and including; (0, 2), (2, 4); (4, 6)
43. below and including; (0, 1), (2, 7); (3, 0)
45. below; (0, 4), (2, 4) 49. above and including; (0, −3), (2, 0) 53. above and including; (0, −2), (3, 2) 57. above and including; (0, −3), (5, 0)

1. 6 3. −4 5. −2 6. 32 7. 14 8. 5
9. −54 10. 15 cups 12. $3\frac{1}{8}$ in. 14. $333\frac{1}{3}$ ft
16. 44 lb 18. 23 ft 9 in. 20. $112
22. 108,000 sq mi 24. 1,078 ft

1. 18 4. 100 5. −1 6. 48 7. 4 8. −14
9. $6\frac{6}{11}$ ft, or approximately 6 ft $6\frac{1}{2}$ in. 11. 9 ft
13. $3\frac{3}{4}$ hr, or 3 hr 45 min 15. $750 17. 24 cm
19. $5\frac{1}{3}$ yd 21. 6 ft 23. 18 ft

1. $\{(-1, -3), (0, -1), (1, 1), (2, 3), (3, 5)\}$; $D = \{-1, 0, 1, 2, 3\}$; $R = \{-3, -1, 1, 3, 5\}$; yes 4. $D = \{-2, -1, 0\}$; $R = \{-2, -1, 0, 1, 2\}$; no 5. $D = \{-2, -1, 0, 1, 2\}$; $R = \{1\}$; yes
(Two points of the boundary line are given.)
6. (0, 0), (1, 2); function; linear function
9. (0, −1), (1, 2); function; linear function
12. 3 17. $R = \{-2, 1, -5\}$ 19. above; (2, 9) 21. direct variation; 3

1. −3 4. $\frac{3}{4}$ 7. $-\frac{10}{9}$ 10. −2 13. 1 15. 1

1. $\frac{27}{2}$ 3. −19 5. $\frac{11}{5}$ 7. $\frac{45}{2}$ 9. $\frac{15}{13}$ 11. 11
13. 1, 3 15. −1 17. 5

1. Jake, $\frac{3}{5}$; Bill, $\frac{3}{x}$ 3. Mario, $\frac{12}{x}$; Todd, $\frac{6}{x}$
5. Lester, $\frac{7}{m}$; Jim, $\frac{14}{m+1}$ 7. Mark, $\frac{3}{3m+1}$; Stuart, $\frac{3}{m-4}$ 9. Joe, $\frac{5}{7}$; Helene, $\frac{2}{7}$ 11. Eleanor, $\frac{x}{5}$; Ted, $\frac{x}{10}$ 13. Donald, $\frac{5}{x}$; Merv, $\frac{5}{3x}$

1. $1\frac{5}{7}$ hr 3. $7\frac{1}{2}$ hr 5. $1\frac{1}{3}$ hr 7. Joseph, 8 hr; Lois, 24 hr 9. $1\frac{13}{47}$ hr 11. $2\frac{2}{5}$ hr 13. 10 hr

1. $\frac{20}{3}$ 4. 35.7 7. $\frac{615}{2}$ 10. −50
13. $\frac{15}{2}$ 15. 5 17. $-296\frac{1}{3}$

1. $\frac{-1}{1}$ 8. $\frac{7}{9}$ 15. $\frac{13}{18}$ 22. $\frac{16}{99}$ 27. $\frac{41}{333}$

1. $\frac{7}{4}$ 5. $\frac{17}{10}$ 9. $\frac{40a+2}{16a+1}$ 13. $x + 1$

1. $\frac{2a-1}{6a-18}$ 4. $\frac{9a-2}{5}$ 7. 1 10. 4
13. $\frac{-3x-2}{7x-6}$ 16. $\frac{x^2-2x+2}{4x+1}$ 19. $\frac{a+b}{a-b}$

1. $x = \frac{2}{a}$ 5. $x = -3a$ 9. $x = \frac{d+c}{2}$
13. $x = \frac{8}{k+2}$ 17. $x = \frac{3b+c}{2}$ 21. $\frac{p}{4}$; 7 23. $s = \frac{p-b}{2}$; 19 25. $r = \frac{C}{2\pi}$; 226
27. $h = \frac{V}{lw}$; 4 29. $x = \frac{3c-5a}{2b}$
32. $x = \frac{3}{2}$ 35. $x = a + 2$ 38. $f = \frac{9}{5}C + 32$; 59 40. $l = \frac{T-\pi r^2}{\pi r}$; 20 42. $h = \frac{T-2\pi r^2}{2\pi r}$; 8

PAGE 378

1. -1 **3.** $-\frac{1}{3}$ **5.** $-1, -2$ **7.** $\frac{45}{4}$ hr $\frac{28}{3}$ mo;

28 mos. **11.** $\frac{700}{3}$ **14.** $\frac{-18}{1}$ **20.** $\frac{11}{7}$

23. $\frac{10a-12}{7}$ **26.** $\frac{3m+8}{b}$ **30.** $\frac{a}{mq}$; $\frac{16}{7}$

PAGE 383

1. R **5.** I **9.** I **13.** I **17.** R **21.** Answers
may vary. **23.** Answers may vary. **25.** irrational
27. Answers may vary. irrational **29.** F **31.** T
33. T

PAGE 386

1. 6.1 ft **5.** 5.5 yd, 16.5 yd **9.** 33.0 m, 6.6 m
11. 2.8 in.

PAGE 390

Irrat. nos. and approx.: **1.** 5.1 **15.** 5.7 **22.** 5.3

PAGE 393

1. $\sqrt{10}$ **6.** $\sqrt{65}$ **11.** $\sqrt{30}$ **16.** 15 **21.** $2\sqrt{3}$
26. $7\sqrt{2}$ **31.** $2\sqrt{7}$ **36.** $4\sqrt{15}$ **41.** $10\sqrt{2}$;
14.1 **46.** $15\sqrt{6}$; 36.7 **51.** $5\sqrt{22}$ **56.** $7\sqrt{17}$
61. $-14\sqrt{7}$

PAGE 395

1. x^4y^2 **4.** $5x$ **7.** $-9ab^3$ **10.** $-4x^4y^6$
13. $a^2b^3c^4$ **16.** $-2xy^4z$ **19.** $8a^2b^6c$
22. $-10xy^6z^5$ **25.** $11c^4d^3e$ **28.** $2xy^4\sqrt{5}$
31. $-4a^3b^6\sqrt{2}$ **34.** $10x^2yz^3\sqrt{2}$
37. $-7a^2b^4c^8\sqrt{2}$ **40.** $.2xy^4$
43. $\frac{1}{5}x^5yz^6$

PAGE 397

1. $x\sqrt{x}$ **5.** $2x^2\sqrt{x}$ **9.** $x^2y^3\sqrt{y}$
17. $a^2b^4\sqrt{a}$ **21.** $6x\sqrt{y}$ **25.** $x^2y^4\sqrt{19xy}$
29. $8yz^3\sqrt{11x}$ **32.** $x^2z^4\sqrt{xy}$
38. $20a^5b^4\sqrt{3b}$ **41.** xy^3 **44.** $-x^2y^3$
47. $-4ab^2\sqrt[3]{a}$ **50.** $-2b^2c^3\sqrt[3]{7ac}$ **53.** xy^3
56. $2xy$ **59.** $-2b\sqrt[5]{3a^2b^2c^3}$

PAGE 401

1. no **5.** no **9.** yes **13.** yes **17.** $c=10$
20. $c=2\sqrt{10}$ **23.** $c=7\sqrt{2}$ **26.** $a=8\sqrt{2}$
29. $b=48$ **32.** 8.5 mi **34.** 19.2 in.

PAGE 403

1. $9\sqrt{5}$ **3.** $15\sqrt{6}$ **5.** $\sqrt{10}$ **7.** $2\sqrt{6}+6\sqrt{3}$
9. $12\sqrt{5}-6\sqrt{7}$ **11.** $8\sqrt{5}-3\sqrt{2}$ **13.** $7\sqrt{2}$
15. $-5\sqrt{6}$ **17.** $2\sqrt{11}$ **19.** $9\sqrt{a}$ **21.** $7\sqrt{mn}$
23. $-3\sqrt{xy}$ **25.** $4x\sqrt{3z}-x\sqrt{5z}$
27. $-21ab\sqrt{ab}$ **29.** $4\sqrt{3x}$ **31.** cannot simplify
33. $-11\sqrt{10x}$ **35.** $8xy\sqrt{5x}$ **37.** $.6y\sqrt{x}$
39. $.22xy\sqrt{x}$ **41.** $3.56ab\sqrt{ab}$

PAGE 406

1. $40\sqrt{3}$ **4.** $42\sqrt{2}$ **7.** $108\sqrt{5}$ **10.** $2x$
13. $36x$ **16.** $6x$ **19.** $-10x^3\sqrt{2}$ **22.** $5\sqrt{2}+$
$\sqrt{6}$ **24.** $48-18\sqrt{3}$ **26.** $-9\sqrt{7}-18\sqrt{3}$
28. $\sqrt{10}+3\sqrt{2}$ **30.** $8-10\sqrt{2}$ **32.** 0
34. $3\sqrt{6}+45\sqrt{2}$ **36.** $-20\sqrt{3}-60\sqrt{2}$
38. $28+\sqrt{10}$ **40.** $-18-10\sqrt{42}$ **42.** $5+$
$2\sqrt{6}$ **44.** 2 **46.** -46 **48.** $188+24\sqrt{10}$
50. 43 **52.** $152+84\sqrt{3}$ **54.** 393 **56.** -96
58. $180-80\sqrt{5}$ **60.** $3\sqrt{x}+x$ **63.** $a-1$
66. $y-4$

PAGE 409

1. $\frac{\sqrt{2}}{2}$; .7 **6.** $\frac{\sqrt{6}}{3}$; .8 **11.** $5y\sqrt{x}$

16. $6x\sqrt{x}$ **21.** $\frac{3\sqrt{2}+5\sqrt{3}}{3}$ **25.** $\frac{4\sqrt{2}+\sqrt{3}}{2}$

29. $a+6$ **33.** $\frac{5(4-\sqrt{7})}{9}$

PAGE 412

1. $\frac{3}{4}$ **6.** $\frac{\sqrt{7}}{2}$ **11.** $\frac{\sqrt{35}}{5}$ **16.** $\frac{\sqrt{6}}{4}$

26. $\frac{3\sqrt{6xy}}{y}$ **31.** $\frac{\sqrt{6y}}{6y^2}$ **36.** $\frac{\sqrt{4x+6}}{2}$

40. $\frac{\sqrt{15-25z}}{5}$ **44.** $\frac{\sqrt{6x^2+9x}}{3x}$

1. I   5. I   9. 6.8 in.   18. 21   23. $12cd^2e^5$
28. yes   32. $c = 17$ 35. $-\sqrt{5}$ 37. $15x -$
$10\sqrt{x}$ 40. $\frac{\sqrt{3}}{3}$; .6   44. 7

1. $\{9\}$ 5. $\{\frac{1}{16}\}$ 9. $\{1\}$ 11. $\emptyset$ 13. $\{\frac{79}{3}\}$
15. $\{4\}$ 17. $\emptyset$ 19. $\{12\}$ 21. $\{12\}$ 23. $\{1\}$
25. $\{-3, -2\}$ 27. $\{5\}$ 29. 25   31. 2   33. $\{1\}$

1. $\{1, -1\}$ 4. $\emptyset$ 7. $\{3, -3\}$ 10. $\{10, -10\}$
13. $\{20, -20\}$ 16. $\{13, -13\}$ 19. $\{3, -3\}$
22. $\emptyset$ 25. $\{5, -1\}$ 28. $\{5, 1\}$ 31. $\{2, -10\}$
34. $\{10, -8\}$ 37. $\{12, 4\}$ 40. $\{1, -7\}$
43. $\{0, -16\}$ 46. $\{12, 8\}$ 49. $\{-2, -10\}$
52. $\{\sqrt{5}, -\sqrt{5}\}$ 55. $\{\sqrt{23}, -\sqrt{23}\}$
58. $\{2\sqrt{2}, -2\sqrt{2}\}$ 61. $\{3\sqrt{3}, -3\sqrt{3}\}$
64. $\{\sqrt{6}, -\sqrt{6}\}$ 67. $\{\frac{\sqrt{33}}{3}, -\frac{\sqrt{33}}{3}\}$
70. $\{\frac{2\sqrt{2}}{3}; -\frac{2\sqrt{2}}{3}\}$ 73. $\emptyset$
76. $\{-1 + \sqrt{5}, -1 - \sqrt{5}\}$
79. $\{-3 + 2\sqrt{2}, -3 - 2\sqrt{2}\}$ 82. $\emptyset$
85. $\{8 + \sqrt{7}, 8 - \sqrt{7}\}$
91. $\{-7 + \sqrt{22}, -7 - \sqrt{22}\}$

1. $\{-8, -2\}$ 4. $\{2, -4\}$
10. $\{-4 + \sqrt{13}, -4 - \sqrt{13}\}$ 13. $\{7, -11\}$
16. $\{8, -6\}$ 19. $\{13, -3\}$
25. $\{21, -1\}$ 28. $\{5, -2\}$ 31. $\{5, -10\}$
34. $\{4, 7\}$ 37. $\{3, -4\}$ 40. $\{-3, -12\}$
43. $\{7, -8\}$ 46. $\{4, 9\}$
55. $\{\frac{-7 \pm \sqrt{37}}{2}\}$ 58. $\{\frac{3 \pm 2\sqrt{3}}{3}\}$
64. $\{\frac{3 \pm \sqrt{29}}{2}\}$ 67. $\{\frac{1 \pm \sqrt{13}}{2}\}$

1. $2x^2 + 6x + 5 = 0$; $a = 2, b = 6, c = 5$
4. $2x^2 - 4x + 0 = 0$; $a = 2, b = -4, c = 0$
7. $x^2 + 0x - 5 = 0$; $a = 1. b = 0, c = -5$
10. $x^2 + 0x - 4 = 0$; $a = 1, b = 0, c = -4$
13. $x^2 - 5x + 3 = 0$; $a = 1, b = -5, c = 3$
16. $6x^2 - x + 1 = 0$; $a = 6, b = -1, c = 1$
19. $\{-3, -1\}$ 22. $\{2, -5\}$ 25. $\{5, -8\}$
28. $\{2, -3\}$ 31. $\{6, -5\}$

1. $\{-3, \frac{1}{2}\}$ 4. $\{\frac{1}{2}, 3\}$ 7. $\{-2, \frac{1}{3}\}$ 10. $\frac{5 \pm \sqrt{33}}{2}$
13. $\emptyset$ 16. $\frac{-1 \pm \sqrt{21}}{2}\}$ 19. $\emptyset$ 22. $\{5 \pm 2\sqrt{5}\}$
25. $\{-4, \frac{3}{2}\}$ 28. $\emptyset$ 31. $-2; -.5$ 34. $\emptyset$

1. $l = 8$ in.; $w = 5$ in.   3. $l = 8$ m; $w = 4$ m
5. $l = 11$ ft; $w = 4$ ft   7. $l = 5$ ft; $w = 4$ ft
9. $l = 8.4$ cm; $w = 2.4$ cm   11. $l = 7.7$ ft;
$w = 5.7$ ft   13. $l = 12$ in.; $w = 8$ in.
15. $l = 15$ km; $w = 6$ km   17. $l = 18$ mi; $w = 4$ mi

1. $\{75\}$ 4. $\{2\}$ 7. $\{10, -10\}$ 10. $\{12, -4\}$
13. 16   16. 100   19. $\{13, -1\}$ 22. $\{4, -12\}$
25. $\{-4, -2\}$ 28. $3x^2 - 5x + 4 = 0$; $a = 3$,
$b = -5, c = 4$ 31. $x^2 + 0x - 7 = 0$; $a = 1$
$b = 0, c = -7$ 34. $3x^2 - 4x - 8 = 0$; $a = 3$,
$b = -4, c = -8$ 37. $\{4, 2\}$ 40. $\{6, -1\}$
43. $\{3, -7\}$ 46. $\{6, 4\}$ 49. $\{-2, \frac{1}{3}\}$ 52. $\emptyset$
55. $\{\frac{7 \pm \sqrt{5}}{2}\}$ 58. $\{\frac{-1 \pm \sqrt{5}}{2}\}$ 61. 2.3; -1.0
63. $l = 5$ ft; $w = 4$ ft

1. $33°, 57°, 65°, 25°$ 5. $45°$ 7. $16°$
9. $15°, 75°$ 11. $70°, 75°, 35°$

1. $x = 3, y = 14$ 3. $x = 3\frac{1}{3}, y = 8\frac{2}{3}$
5. $DE = 11\frac{2}{3}, EF = 20$ 7. $CB = 13\frac{1}{3}, DF = 15$
9. 18 ft   11. 9.6 ft   13. $7\frac{1}{2}$ ft

PAGE 453

1. $\tan A = 1.333$, $\sin A = .800$, $\cos A = .600$, $\tan B = .750$, $\sin B = .600$, $\cos B = .800$
4. $\tan A = .292$, $\sin A = .280$, $\cos A = .960$, $\tan B = 3.429$, $\sin B = .960$, $\cos B = .280$

7. 1.000 **10.** $\sin A = \dfrac{a}{c}$; $\cos B = \dfrac{a}{c}$;

thus $\sin A = \cos B$ **11.** $\sin B = \dfrac{b}{c}$; $\cos A = \dfrac{b}{c}$;

thus $\sin B = \cos A$ **12.** $\tan A = \dfrac{a}{b}$; $\tan B = \dfrac{b}{a}$;

$\dfrac{1}{\tan B} = \dfrac{1}{\frac{b}{a}} = \dfrac{a}{b}$; thus $\tan A = \dfrac{1}{\tan B}$

13. $a^2 + b^2 = c^2$, $\dfrac{a^2}{c^2} + \dfrac{b^2}{c^2} + \dfrac{c^2}{c^2} = 1$. Also,

$\dfrac{a^2}{c^2} + \dfrac{b^2}{c^2} = \sin^2 A + \cos^2 A$. By substitution,

$\sin^2 A + \cos^2 A = 1$. **14.** $\tan A = .250$, $\sin A = .243$, $\cos A = .970$, $\tan B = 4.000$, $\sin B = .970$, $\cos B = .243$ **17.** Any two complementary angles may be represented as the acute angles of a right triangle ABC. $\sin A = \dfrac{a}{c}$; $\cos B = \dfrac{a}{c}$; thus, $\sin A = \cos B$, or the sine of an angle is equal to the cosine of its complement.

PAGE 457

1. 8^0 **4.** 22^0 **7.** 49^0 **10.** 48^0 **13.** F **16.** F **22.** T **24.** T **26.** F **28.** T **30.** Sin A increases from 0 to 1. The ratio of a to c approaches 1 to 1.

PAGE 460

1. $a = 8.9$ **4.** $m\angle B = 77$ **7.** $a = 4.7$ **9.** $c = 18.3$ **11.** $m\angle A = 30$ **13.** $a = 25.7$ **15.** $m\angle B = 74$, $BC = 5.7$, $AB = 20.8$ **18.** $m\angle A = 16$, $m\angle B = 74$ $AB = 7.3$

PAGE 463

1. $x = 58.5$ m **5.** $x = 342.9$ ft **9.** 216.6 ft **11.** 96.0 ft **13.** $32°$ **15.** 21,299.3 ft **17.** 49.5 sq ft

PAGE 464

1. $x = 8, y = 10$ **3.** $\tan A = .750$, $\sin A = .600$, $\cos A = .800$, $\tan B = 1.333$, $\sin B = .800$, $\cos B = .600$, $m\angle A = 37$, $m\angle B = 53$ **6.** $c = 20.4$ **8.** $a = 6.9$ **10.** $a = 2.2$ **12.** $m\angle B = 55$ **14.** $35°, 55°$ **16.** $44°, 44°, 92°$ **18.** 31.3 m